The Complete Computer Repair Textbook

Cheryl A. Schmidt
Florida Community College
at Jacksonville

Illustrations by **Donna McAfee Tucker**

Scott/Jones Inc., Publishers
P.O. Box 696, El Granada, CA 94018
Voice: (650) 726-2436
Fax: (650) 726-4693
E-mail: scotjones2@aol.com
Web site: http://www.scottjonespub.com

The Complete Computer Repair Textbook
Cheryl A. Schmidt

Illustrations by Donna McAfee Tucker
Clipart by Nova Development Corporation

V W

ISBN: 1-57676-012-X

Text Design and Composition: Cheryl A. Schmidt   *Cover Design*: Donna McAfee Tucker
Book Manufacturing: Malloy Lithographing   *Copy Editing*: Cathy Baehler

Scott/Jones Publishing Company
Sponsoring Editorial Group: Kate Kelly, Acquisitions Editor, and Lynne McCormick, Editorial
     Assistant
Production Management: Heather Bennett
Marketing & Sales: Barbara Masek, Lynne McCormick, Hazel Dunlap, and Donna Cross
Business Operations: Chuck Paetzke, Michelle Robelet, and Cathy Glenn
Publisher: Richard Jones

A Word About Trademarks
All product names identified in this book are trademarks or registered trademarks of their respective companies. We have used the names in an editorial fashion only, and to the benefit of the trademark owner, with no intention of infringing the trademark. IBM and Lotus are trademarks of International Business Machines. Intel, Pentium, Intel386, Intel486, OverDrive, and MMX are trademarks of Intel Corp. Windows, Windows 95, Windows NT, DirectX, MSD, Terminal, HyperTerminal, and Word are trademarks of Microsoft Corporation. Apple, PowerPC, and FireWire are trademarks of Apple Computer, Inc. Motorola is a trademark of Motorola, Inc. Cyrix is a trademark of Cyrix Corporation. AMD is a trademark of Advanced Micro Devices, Inc. Compaq is a trademark of Compaq Corporation. HP is a trademark of Hewlett-Packard Company. Zenith is a trademark of Zenith Electronics Corp. Epson is a trademark of Seiko Epson Corp. NEC is a trademark of NEC Corporation. Wyse is a trademark of Wyse Technology, Inc. AST is a trademark of AST Research, Inc. Tandy is a trademark of Tandy Corporation. Olivetti is a trademark of Olivetti S.p.A. SiS is a trademark of Silicon Integrated Systems Corp. OPTi is a trademark of OPTi, Inc. Award is a trademark of Award Software International, Inc. PhoenixBIOS is a trademark of Phoenix Technologies Ltd. AMI BIOS is a trademark of American Megatrends, Inc. Dell is a trademark of Dell Computer Corp. Norton Utilities is a trademark of Symantec Corp. CheckIt is a trademark of Touchstone Software Corp. Nuts & Bolts is a trademark of Helix Software Corporation. SpinRite is a trademark of Gibson Research Corp. EZ-Drive is a trademark of Western Digital Corp. Seagate is a trademark of Seagate Technology, Inc. Sound Blaster is a trademark of Creative Labs, Inc. Hayes is a trademark of Hayes Microcomputer, Inc. x2 is a trademark of 3Com Corporation. Toshiba is a trademark of Toshiba, America, Inc. Trinitron is a trademark of Sony Electronics Inc. WordPerfect is a trademark of Corel Corporation.

PREFACE

The Complete Computer Repair Textbook is intended for a variety of courses that teach computer and peripheral installation, configuration, and repair. The book is written so that it is easy to read and understand, whether the student is a novice to computers or has some knowledge because the concepts are presented in building-block fashion. The book centers on hardware, but Appendix A covers basic DOS skills and Appendix B covers basic Windows 95 skills that are needed for some of the exercises.

Some of the best features of the book include the coverage of difficult subjects in a step-by-step manner, good graphics to illustrate concepts, reinforcement questions, hands-on exercises at the end of each chapter, and practice certification review questions.

Many certifications exist for computer technicians. Many companies write exams to certify competency relating to their computer products. Many of the exams, including the A+ certification exam, Novell's CNA (Certified Novell Administrator), and Microsoft's MCP (Microsoft Certified Professional), test for a basic understanding of computer repair concepts. **The certification sections in this book are in certification test format**. If students understand computer basics and practice taking the *types* of questions presented here, they will have no problems passing the exams.

Organization of the Text

The text is organized to allow thorough coverage of all topics, but also to be a flexible teaching tool; it is not necessary to cover all the chapters, nor do the chapters have to be covered in order.

- Chapter 1 covers beginning terminology and computer part and port identification.
- Chapter 2 details components, features, and concepts related to motherboards including microprocessors, cache, expansion slots, and chipsets.
- Chapter 3 deals with configuration basics for the system and the different types of adapters installed in a system. System resources such as interrupts, I/O addresses, and DMA channels are also explained. Chapter 3 is an important chapter to cover before any other topic that could require an adapter installation such as floppy drives, hard drives, CD-ROMs, serial devices, etc.
- Chapter 4 steps the student through how to disassemble and reassemble a computer. Tools, ESD, EMI, and preventive maintenance are discussed for the first time. Subsequent chapters also include preventive maintenance topics.
- Chapter 5 deals with computer power.
- Practice certification questions are divided into three groups: those relating to Chapters 1 through 5 follow Chapter 5; those for Chapters 6 through 10 come after Chapter 10; and those relating to Chapters 11 through 13 and Appendices A and B come after Appendix B.
- Chapter 6 is a basic section covering troubleshooting skills and error codes.
- Chapter 7 covers memory concepts, installation, configuration, and troubleshooting.
- Chapter 8 involves floppy drive concepts, installation, configuration, and troubleshooting.
- Chapter 9 deals with hard drive installation, preparation, and troubleshooting.
- Chapter 10 covers CD-ROMs and sound cards.

- Chapter 11 deals with serial devices theory and configuration. An in-depth modem section includes information on digital modems, 56K modems, and troubleshooting modem problems. The chapter also looks at USB (Universal Serial Bus). Mice and keyboards have their own section in this chapter.
- Chapter 12 handles video including video memory issues.
- Chapter 13 covers dot matrix, ink jet, and laser printers including troubleshooting and preventive maintenance techniques.
- Appendix A is by no means a complete DOS text, but it does cover DOS skills essential for technicians. Topics covered include basic DOS commands, DOS file structure, the AUTOEXEC.BAT file, and the CONFIG.SYS file.
- Appendix B covers Windows 95 basics such as formatting a disk, copying a file, starting applications, using Explorer, using the Find utility, using Help, and backing up the registry. An excellent section in this appendix involves the Windows 95 boot process including troubleshooting startup problems.
- Appendix C lists Internet sites relevant to technicians, a must for any new repair person.
- Appendix D is a glossary of computer terms.

Features

Easy-to-Understand Text

Each section is written in building-block fashion beginning at the most basic level and continuing on to the more advanced. Students taught using this method understand new technologies better because of their good foundations.

End-of-Chapter Review Questions

Each chapter contains numerous review questions in various formats including true/false, multiple choice, matching, and open-ended. Also at the end of each chapter are fill-in-the-blank questions so that students get more comfortable with the computer jargon which can overwhelm the novice.

Tech Tips

Each chapter contains technical tips which are highlighted and preceded by a Sherlock Holmes picture.

Hands-on Exercises

Computer repair cannot be learned by theory and lecture alone, but is reinforced through practice and experience. The exercises at the end of the chapter help with this task.

Certification Questions

In three separate sections spread throughout the book, certification review questions are designed to help students practice for a variety of certification exams.

Objectives and Terminology

At the beginning of each chapter is a list of objectives. Following the objectives are the key terms defined and used throughout the chapter.

Instructor Support

All the pedagogical features outlined on the previous page are unique to this book in the field. They should make the instructor's job easier. In addition, an instructor's disk containing answers to the review and exercise questions and an instructor's book containing full graphics for transparencies can be obtained from the publisher.

A Note to Students

All the way through the book, I had to refrain from telling my stories, stay on track, and avoid using my mnemonics. Writing a textbook is really different from teaching class. My personality lies buried in this book. Only in a few places can you see or feel my teaching style, but I hope it comes through in subtle ways. My students are like my children except that I don't have to feed them and send them to college, so I am happy to claim any of you. I wish that I could be in each classroom as you start your computer career. How exciting!

I love what I do and what I teach. I have been repairing computers most of my life. I always tell my students that it sure beats the tobacco fields. I am not sure my father, Steve Cansler, or my brother, Jeff Cansler, would agree, though my father has been a techno-junkie all his life and my brother can fix anything he lays his hands on.

Another thing that I tell my students is that I am not an expert and to watch out for those who say or think they are. Computer repair is an ever-changing field. I've been at it a long time, but there are always products and standards being developed that I do not know very much about. Humility is a wonderful trait to keep in computer repair because if you are not humble, the industry will prove you wrong sooner or later.

To my future technicians, I offer one important piece of advice:

Consistent, high quality service boils down to two equally important things: caring and competence.
— Chip R. Bell and Ron Zemke

I can help you with the competence, but you are going to have to work on the caring part. Do not ever forget that there are people behind those machines that you love to repair. Taking care of people is as important as taking care of the computers.

A Note to Teachers

Whenever people ask me what I do, my first response is "I fix computers." In my heart, I will always be first and foremost a technician. Everything else is just a facet of that set of skills, whether it is managing a computer support department, building a new lab and networking it, or teaching microprocessors. All of these boil down to knowing technical things. Sharing what I know is as natural as walking to me, but sitting still to write down what I know is unnatural, so composing this text has been one of my greatest challenges. I managed to do it only because I needed a better textbook.

I taught computer repair classes long before I became a full-time faculty member. I was very frustrated with not having an appropriate book. During the first two terms, I taught without a textbook and my students nicknamed me "The Handout Queen." The book I have used most often is one of the best books on the subject of computer repair, but it is not a textbook. I hope this book can offer better support to teachers.

Acknowledgments

Many people have helped me along the path (and I get to be wordy in this part). Mrs. Emma Dean Trent, Mrs. Irene Paye, Ms. Barbara E. Cansler, Mrs. Rita Davis, Mr. Ronald Briggs, Mrs. Barbara Robinson, and Mrs. Dora Pratt were all teachers who have had a lot of influence in my life. These teachers came to my extracurricular activities, gave me a hug, pushed me to the limits, and showed they cared. Of course Barbara Cansler had to do these things because, besides being one of my teachers, she is my mother. My mother is a refereeing, computer teaching, web page creating, English teaching inspiration and she is a constant source of wonder and support to me and others. I constantly strive to give to my students a role model like those I learned from, expecting much and giving much in return.

A lot of people helped me in my technical career. Rick Beckstrom gave me my first management chance and kept me from failing at it. Jack Tinsley and Betty Neyer at Florida Community College supported and encouraged me to go to school. Dr. Jean Martin and Gena Casas gave me my first faculty teaching opportunity. My former boss, Joan Bearden, taught me the importance of setting goals. Even though I am a goal setter by nature, Joan taught me how to extend beyond the immediate future.

John Sumner and John Debo in the Engineering Technology Department at Florida Community College have consistently been two of my strongest supporters. Also, two of our adjuncts, Bill Sawyer and John Slevin, taught some courses so that I could work on the book instead of teaching so much. I could not have done it without their support. Ernie Friend, my co-teacher and friend, has been a great strength for me as have all of my guinea pigs, I mean students, who were in the first year of my new program. They got to suffer through all of my mistakes and my new curriculum, but they all are great technicians!

My graphic artist, Donna McAfee Tucker, is one of the most talented people I have ever met. As my students can attest, I cannot draw well, but Donna can take any concept I explain and put it into a picture or graphic. Donna's pretty funny too. She can do a lot of her own repairs and upgrades now because she has read my chapters so many times in order to get her illustration concepts right. She is a very talented lady. Another talented artistic person is Chris Nail from Florida Community College's Printing Department who gave invaluable input to this book.

Kate Kelly, my editor, held my hand throughout the writing process. I could never have written the book without her constant support and belief in the project and in me. Heather Bennett, Scott Jones' own goddess of prepress, is a wonder, and I always tell Cathy Baehler, my copy editor, that my book was good before she got hold of it, but she made it great. I would not ever want to write a book without Cathy around. Of course, Richard Jones at the top keeps us all in line and on target.

Foremost in my thoughts are my family. Karl, my husband, has had to be everything at one time or another. He has fixed supper, helped the kids with homework, held me when I was frustrated, edited my book when I was tired, written my glossary when I was behind, and loved me throughout it all. My daughters, Raina and Karalina, have been wonderful and supportive through the entire project. I can never say thank you enough to them.

Many parts of the manuscript has also been class tested at Florida Community College at Jacksonville. My colleagues and students have offered numerous valuable suggestions for improvement. Finally, the faculty members who reviewed individual chapters have my undying gratitude for their input and a special thank you to Vickie Clements at Computer Learning Network for all of her efforts. Jim McDonald at College of San Mateo also provided a great deal of insight after teaching from the text. Reviewers are listed on the following page:

Scott Beckstrand
Southern Nevada Community College

Vickie Clements
Computer Learning Network

Jackson Beebe
Lincoln Land Community College

Donald E. Coffman
Pellissippi State Technical Community College

Rick Burgess
Lewis and Clark Community College

Thomas Cress
Belleville Area College

Joseph Dvorak
Community College of Alleghany County

Dave Filer
Dabney S. Lancaster Community College

Cathy Frazier
TriCounty Technical College

Tony Gaddis
Haywood Community College

BJ Honeycutt
Clayton State College

Rod Kosmick
Kellogg Community College

Doug Minter
Heartland Community College

Stan Popovich
A:1 Computers

Greg Rasmussen
St. Paul Technical College

Edward Serwon
Erie Community College

These people made a huge impact on the book's final form, but I am responsible for any remaining errors. Please contact me with any corrections or suggestions at either of the following e-mail addresses:
CSchmidt@fccj.cc.fl.us, SchmidtC97@aol.com, or let the publisher know at ScotJones2@aol.com

TABLE OF CONTENTS

INDEX OF FIGURES & TABLES

Chapter 8: Floppy Drives

Chapter 9: Hard Drives

Chapter 10: CD-ROM Drives and Sound Cards

Chapter 11: Serial Devices, Mice, and Keyboards

Chapter 12: Video

Chapter 13: Printers

Appendix A: Introduction to DOS

Appendix B: Windows 95

Chapter 1: Introduction to Microcomputer Repair

OBJECTIVES

After completing this chapter you will
1.   Understand basic computer terms.
2.   Identify the parts of a computer.
3.   Recognize and identify external computer connectors.

KEY TERMS

adapter   modem
ARCnet   monitor
bus mouse   motherboard
cold boot   mouse
Ethernet   mouse and keyboard ports
expansion slot   parallel port
female port   port
firmware   POST
floppy drive   power supply
floppy disks   riser board
game port   ROM BIOS
hard drive   serial port
hardware   software
keyboard   TokenRing
male port   video ports
memory: RAM & ROM   warm boot
microcomputer

OVERVIEW

A computer technician must be a jack-of-all-trades: a software expert in various operating systems and applications; a hardware expert on everything ranging from microprocessors to the latest laser printer; a communicator extraordinaire to handle the occasional irate, irrational, upset, or computer-illiterate customers; a good listener to elicit computer symptoms from customers (and from the computer); an empathetic counselor to make the customers feel good about their computers and confident in the technician's skills; and lastly, a master juggler of time and priorities. All of these traits do not come overnight; not all of these traits can be taught, but a technician can constantly develop and fine-tune each.

This book covers computer repair basics — basic knowledge to get one started in the computer repair industry. Standards relating to computer repair are important and technicians must stay abreast of old, current, and emerging standards. Some computer standards allow a great deal of leeway for manufacture design that can cause a great deal of heartache for the computer technician. However, if a technician understands the basics of computer repair, the problems from manufacturer design or hardware not covered in this book can still be resolved.

There is no substitute for experience, and there is no substitute for knowing the basics of how the individual computer parts work. The basics help you understand other emerging technologies as well as proprietary devices. Once a technician has a job in the industry, hands-on time will increase his or her depth of knowledge and experience level. Use the hands-on time in the classroom wisely. The classroom is the place to learn the ropes — the basics.

Having a teacher to guide you through the basics, classmates to share information with, and a book to supplement your instruction all are important to get you started in computer repair. This book is a textbook. There are other books which are excellent reference books. Most technicians have *Upgrading and Repairing PCs* by Scott Mueller and *The Complete PC Upgrade & Maintenance Guide* by Mark Minasi on their bookshelves or in their vehicle. This book is not a reference book, but instead, it supplements your instructor as a textbook on computer repair.

The best quality a technician can possess is logic. A good technician narrows a problem to a general area, subdivides the problem into possible culprits, and eliminates the possibilities one-by-one in a timely and logical manner. A technician is like a detective, constantly looking for clues, using common sense and deductive reasoning, gathering information from the computer and the computer user, and finally solving the mystery. As one computer teacher puts it, a computer technician works smart, not hard. Because detective work is so important to a technician's job, each important technical

tip in the book is preceded by a computer detective:

Repairing computers is very rewarding, but can be frustrating if you do not understand the basics. With good reasoning ability and a good foundation in computer repair, no repair will remain unsolved. Never forget as you are going through the various technologies and exercises that if every repair was simple, no one would need technicians. Enjoy the class!

BEGINNING TERMINOLOGY

A technician must be familiar with and thoroughly understand computer terminology to (1) speak intelligently to other technical support staff, (2) explain to the user what the problem is, and (3) be proficient in a chosen field. Unfortunately, some computer technicians use the technical language of the trade around people who are not attuned to this type of lingo. Using too many technical terms around end-users serves only to confuse and irritate them.

In addition to knowing and using the correct terminology, a technician must use it appropriately, and explain computer terms with simple, everyday language and examples. This book illustrates the terminology in easy to understand terms and analogies that can be used with customers.

COMPUTER BASICS

Computer systems are composed of hardware, software, and firmware. **Hardware** is something you can touch and feel; the physical computer itself is an example of hardware. The monitor and keyboard are hardware components. **Software** is the computer applications that make the hardware work. DOS, Microsoft Word, Lotus 1-2-3, and WordPerfect are all examples of software. A computer is nothing more than a doorstop unless there is software to allow the hardware to accomplish something. **Firmware** combines hardware and software into important chips inside the microcomputer that you can touch and feel like hardware, but with software written into them. An example of firmware are ROM chips. ROM chips are electronic chips that have software inside them all of the time.

The simplest place to start learning about microcomputer repair is with the hardware components and their common names. A **microcomputer**, sometimes called a computer, is a unit that performs tasks using software applications. Microcomputers come in three basic models: (1) a desktop model that normally sits on top of a desk, (2) a tower model that sits on the floor under a desk, and (3) a laptop model which is the portable microcomputer model. The microcomputer consists of a case, a **keyboard** that allows users to communicate with the computer, a **monitor** to display information from the computer, and a **mouse** that is used to move a cursor to allow data input or select menus and options. Introduction Figure #1 shows a desktop computer's case, monitor, keyboard and mouse.

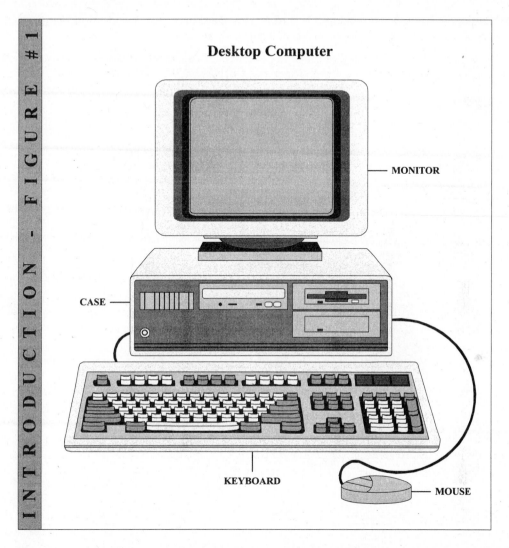

Once the case is removed from the computer, the parts inside can be identified. The easiest part to identify is the **power supply** which is the metal box normally located in the back right corner of the case. The power cord that goes from the computer to a wall outlet or surge strip plugs into the back of the power supply. The purpose of the power supply is to convert the AC voltage that comes out of the wall to DC voltage the computer can use. The power supply also supplies DC voltage to the internal parts of the computer. A fan located inside the power supply keeps the computer cool to avoid damage to the components.

A computer user must have a device to store software applications and files. Two common storage devices are the floppy drive and the hard drive. The **floppy drive** is easily identified by a slot accessible from the front of the computer. The floppy drive allows data storage to **floppy disks** (sometimes called diskettes) that can be used in other computers. Floppy disks store less information than hard drives. The **hard drive** is a rectangular box normally inside the computer's case that is sealed to keep out dust and dirt. In a desktop computer, the hard drive is normally mounted below or beside the floppy drive. Another name for hard drive is hard disk. See Introduction Figure #2 for an illustration of a power supply, a floppy drive, and a hard drive.

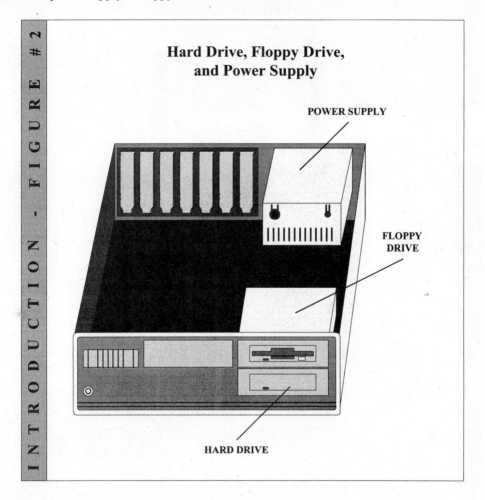

INTRODUCTION - FIGURE # 2

Hard Drive, Floppy Drive, and Power Supply

POWER SUPPLY

FLOPPY DRIVE

HARD DRIVE

The **motherboard** is the main circuit board of a microcomputer. It is normally located on the bottom of a desktop or laptop computer and mounted on the side of a tower computer. Other names for the motherboard include mainboard, planar, or systemboard. The motherboard is the largest electronic circuit board in the computer. The keyboard and mouse frequently connect directly to the motherboard in the back of the microcomputer, although some computers do have the keyboard connection in the front of the computer case.

To connect devices such as the floppy drive or the hard drive to the motherboard, adapters are used. **Adapters** are smaller electronic circuit cards that normally plug into an **expansion slot** on the motherboard. Other names for an adapter are controller, card, controller card, circuit card, circuit board, and adapter board. The number of available expansion slots on the motherboard depends on the manufacturer. See Introduction Figure #3 for an illustration of a motherboard, various expansion slots, and an adapter in an expansion slot.

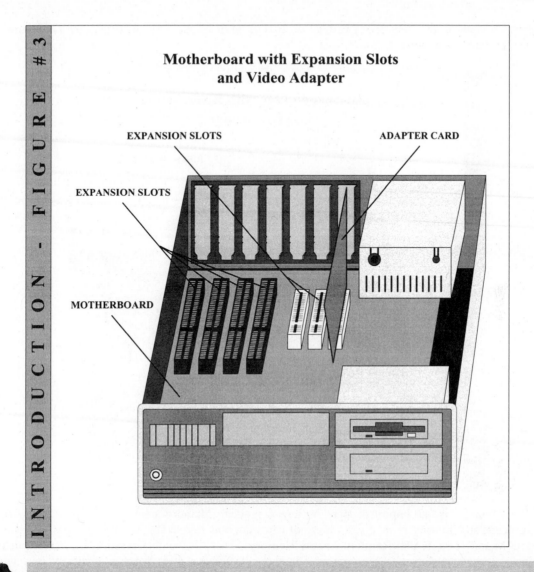

Motherboard with Expansion Slots and Video Adapter

EXPANSION SLOTS

ADAPTER CARD

EXPANSION SLOTS

MOTHERBOARD

INTRODUCTION - FIGURE #3

An adapter's function can usually be identified by tracing the cables attached to the adapter or looking at the devices connected to the adapter.

For example, the hard drive controller has one or more cables between the adapter and the hard drive. A mouse sometimes plugs into an adapter rather than the motherboard. An adapter may control multiple devices such as the hard drive, the floppy drive, and the printer. All these devices have a cable connecting to the adapter inside the computer or to a connector at the back of the computer. A printer sometimes connects to an adapter's external connector.

An alternative to an adapter which plugs into the motherboard is the use of a riser board. A **riser board** with its own expansion slots plugs into the motherboard. Adapters can plug into the expansion slots on the riser board instead of directly into the motherboard. Introduction Figure #4 shows an illustration of a riser board.

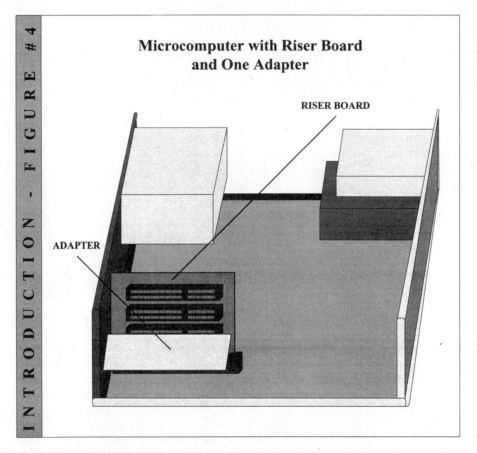

Memory is an important part of any computer. Memory chips hold applications, user documents, and information that tell a piece of hardware how to operate. Two basic types of memory are RAM and ROM. **RAM (Random Access Memory)** is volatile memory meaning the data inside the chips is lost when power to the computer is shut off. When a user types a document in a word processing software package, both the word processing application *and* the document are in RAM. If the user turns the computer off without saving the document to a disk or the hard drive, the document is lost because the information *does not* stay in RAM when power is removed.

Software inside ROM chips will remain when the power is removed. **ROM (Read-Only Memory)** is known as non-volatile memory because data stays inside the chip even when the computer is turned off. An important ROM chip on the motherboard is the ROM BIOS chip. Some of today's motherboards contain two ROM BIOS chips. The **ROM BIOS (Basic Input/Output System)** chip has start-up software that must be present with an operating system for a computer to operate. The ROM BIOS also contains important hardware parameters that determine (*to some extent*) what hardware can be installed. For example, to install a 3.5" floppy drive in an older computer, (1) the BIOS had to support the drive and (2) the operating system had to be a high enough version to support the drive. Common ROM BIOS manufacturers for today's computers include AMI (American Megatrends, Inc.),

Award, and Phoenix. Many companies such as IBM, COMPAQ and Zenith also produce their own BIOS chips.

You cannot replace the ROM BIOS chip with one from a different vendor unless the motherboard supports it. Check the motherboard's documentation to determine which ROM chip works with the motherboard.

RAM and ROM chips come in three different styles of chips — DIP (Dual In-line Package), SIMM (Single In-line Memory Module), and DIMM (Dual In-line Memory Module). RAM chips can be any of the three types, but usually are SIMM or DIMM. ROM chips are normally DIP chips. Introduction Figure #5 shows RAM and ROM chips.

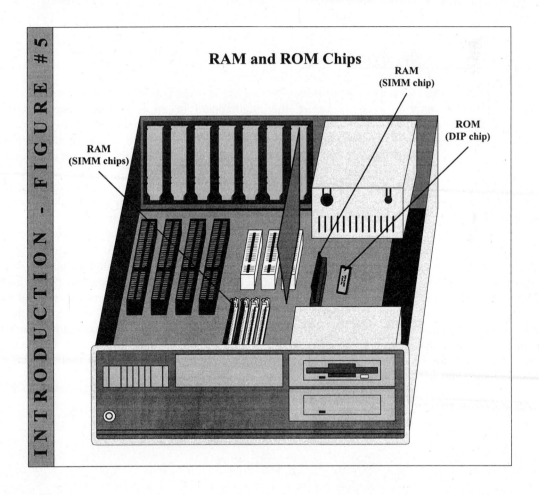

INTRODUCTION - FIGURE #5

RAM and ROM Chips

RAM
(SIMM chip)

ROM
(DIP chip)

RAM
(SIMM chips)

Part of the startup software the ROM BIOS chip contains is known as POST. **POST** or **Power On Self Test** performs a basic test of the individual hardware components such as the motherboard, RAM memory chips, keyboard, floppy drive, and the hard drive. When a computer is turned on with the power switch, the ROM BIOS chip executes POST. Numbers appearing in the upper left corner of the monitor indicate that POST is checking the RAM chips. Turning the computer on with the power switch is known as a **cold boot**. Users perform a cold boot every time they come to work and power on their computer. A technician performs a cold boot when troubleshooting a computer and needs POST executed. Only a cold boot performs POST. A computer can be restarted with a **warm boot** by holding down the CTRL key, then the ALT key, and finally the DEL key on the keyboard. A warm boot does not put as much strain on a computer. Frequently, a technician makes changes to the files that execute when powering on the computer. These files control some of the computer components. Warm booting the computer causes the new changes to take effect.

Other devices such as CD-ROMs and tape backup units can be installed in a microcomputer, but the most basic components of a computer are the monitor, keyboard, mouse, power supply, floppy drive, hard drive, motherboard, and adapters.

EXTERNAL CONNECTORS

A motherboard inside a computer sometimes has the keyboard, mouse, parallel, serial, or video ports built in. (A **port** is a connector on the motherboard or on a separate adapter). These motherboards are called integrated motherboards because the ports are included as part of the motherboard and are not on separate adapters. A technician needs to be able to readily identify these common ports so that (1) the correct cable plugs into the port, and (2) the technician can troubleshoot problems in the right area.

The connections for these ports are called male or female ports. **Male ports** have metal pins that protrude out from the connector. **Female ports** have holes in the connector and a male cable with pins inserts into these holes. A male port requires a cable with a female connector.

Most connectors on integrated motherboards are either D-shell connectors or DIN connectors. A D-shell connector has more pins or holes on top than on the bottom so a cable connected to the D-shell connector can only be inserted in one direction and not accidentally flipped upside down. Parallel, serial, and video ports are examples of D-shell connectors. A DIN connector (DIN previously stood for Deutsche Industrie Norm, now it stands for Das Ist Norm — "that is the norm") is round with small holes and is normally keyed. When a connector is keyed, it has an extra metal piece or notch that matches with an extra metal piece or notch on the cable and the cable can only be inserted into the DIN connector one way. Keyboard and mouse connectors are examples of DIN connectors. Introduction Figure #6 shows the back of a computer with an integrated motherboard. On the motherboard are various D-shell and DIN connectors.

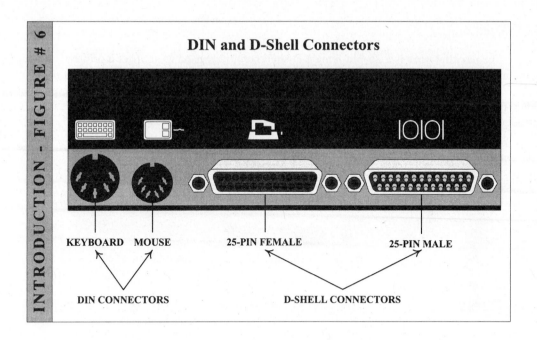

DIN and D-Shell Connectors

INTRODUCTION – FIGURE # 6

KEYBOARD   MOUSE   25-PIN FEMALE   25-PIN MALE

DIN CONNECTORS   D-SHELL CONNECTORS

VIDEO PORTS

Two different connectors are available for **video port** connections: a 9-pin female D-shell and a 15-pin female D-shell. The 9-pin connector is used with older monitors such as monochrome, CGA, and EGA monitors. The 15-pin female connector is used with today's monitors and connects to VGA, SVGA, or XGA monitors. Introduction Figure #7 has examples of video port connectors.

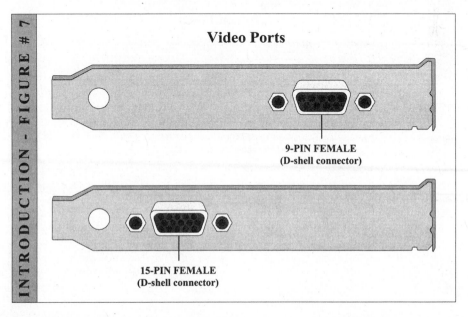

Video Ports

INTRODUCTION – FIGURE # 7

9-PIN FEMALE
(D-shell connector)

15-PIN FEMALE
(D-shell connector)

PARALLEL PORT

The **parallel port** is a 25-pin female D-shell connector used to connect a printer to a computer. Some motherboards have a small picture of a printer etched over the connector. Parallel ports transfer eight bits of data at a time to the printer or any other parallel device connected to the parallel port. Other parallel devices include tape drives, Iomega's Zip drive, and external hard drives. Look at Introduction Figure #8 for an illustration of a parallel port.

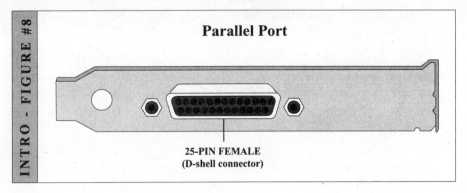

Parallel Port

INTRO - FIGURE #8

25-PIN FEMALE
(D-shell connector)

SERIAL PORTS

A **serial port** connector can be a 9-pin male D-shell connector or a 25-pin male D-shell connector. Introduction Figure #9 shows the two different serial ports.

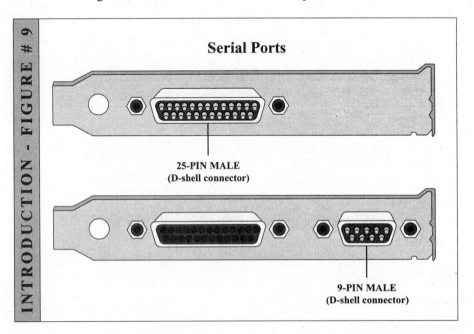

Serial Ports

INTRODUCTION - FIGURE # 9

25-PIN MALE
(D-shell connector)

9-PIN MALE
(D-shell connector)

Serial ports are used for a variety of input devices: mice, modems, digitizers, trackballs, etc. The serial port transmits one bit at a time and is much slower than the parallel port which transmits eight bits at a time. Special connectors are available to convert a 9-pin serial port to a 25-pin port or to convert a 25-pin port to a 9-pin one. This converter is needed if someone has a 25-pin serial cable and their new computer has a 9-pin serial port connector on the back. Serial ports sometimes have a small picture of two rows of square blocks tied together etched over the connector. Look back at Introduction Figure #6 for an example of the serial picture over the 25-pin male connector.

MOUSE AND KEYBOARD PORTS

The **mouse and keyboard ports** on a computer are DIN connectors. Three types of DIN connectors are the 5-pin, 6-pin, and 9-pin. The 5-pin connector is actually bigger than the 6-pin connector and is only used for a keyboard. The 6-pin keyboard or mouse connector is commonly known as a mini-DIN or a PS/2 mouse connection. The 9-pin DIN is normally on a bus mouse adapter. A **bus mouse** is used in a computer without a mouse port built in. The 9-pin DIN is not as common as the 5 or 6-pin DIN connectors.

The mouse and keyboard ports are not interchangeable even though they are of the same pin configuration. The keyboard cable must plug into the keyboard port connector. The mouse cable must plug into the mouse port connector.

Introduction Figure #10 shows a 5-pin DIN keyboard connector and the 6-pin mini-DIN connector used with a keyboard or a mouse.

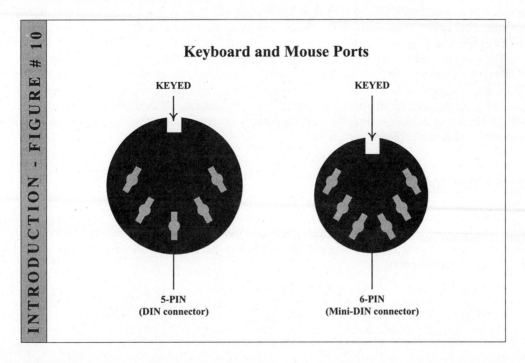

INTRODUCTION - FIGURE # 10

Keyboard and Mouse Ports

KEYED   KEYED

5-PIN
(DIN connector)

6-PIN
(Mini-DIN connector)

A common converter for technicians to have in their toolkit is a 5 to 6-pin DIN converter or a 6 to 5-pin DIN converter. Most manufacturers put a small diagram of a keyboard and of a mouse over the connectors. Look back to Introduction Figure #6 to see the diagrams over the connectors.

PROS AND CONS OF INTEGRATED MOTHERBOARDS

An integrated motherboard provides expandability because ports are built in and do not require separate adapters. For example, serial and parallel ports are commonly on the same adapter. Some video adapters may contain a parallel port as well. The space these adapters do not use is available for other adapters such as network or sound cards. The number of available expansion slots in a system depends on the manufacturer of the computer or motherboard.

Ports built into the motherboard are faster than those on an expansion board. All adapters in expansion slots run slower than the components on the motherboard. Computers with integrated motherboards are easier to set up because the manufacturer configures the ports. Systems with integrated motherboards are normally easier to troubleshoot because the components are on one board. However, one drawback is replacing the motherboard when one port goes bad is a lot more expensive than replacing a port on an adapter.

One important feature to look for on an integrated motherboard is the ability to disable a port. If a port is faulty, disable the port and add an adapter.

If the parallel port integrated into the motherboard is faulty, disabling the port and adding a $15 parallel port adapter is an inexpensive repair, but not all integrated motherboards allow this. An integrated motherboard with ports that cannot be disabled can be very costly or cause some headaches with configuring other expansion cards. Beware of integrated motherboards that do not allow the flexibility of disabling the ports!

A closely related feature to look for is the ability to change the configuration of the port. Ports have different parameters set to keep one port from interfering with another. The ability to alter the configuration is important to a technician. Of course, having good documentation on the features and abilities of an integrated motherboard is crucial for a technician. Without the documentation, you cannot disable a port or change a port's settings. Also, you cannot know the features of the individual ports or of the other motherboard components.

MORE PORT IDENTIFICATION

Other ports such as network ports, game ports, and modem ports can be on a separate adapter or built into the motherboard. A technician needs to be familiar with the more common ones in industry. A system is hard to troubleshoot if the technician cannot access the right area or know what to order as a replacement part.

NETWORK PORTS

Three different network adapters, ARCnet, Ethernet, and TokenRing are available. The ports on these adapters can be quite confusing because the connectors are sometimes the same. **ARCnet** ports have a BNC connector, a RJ-45 connector, or both, on the adapter. ARCnet adapters frequently have DIP switches used to pick a network address. A network address is a unique hexadecimal number assigned to each ARCnet adapter. Introduction Figure #11 has an example of an ARCnet adapter.

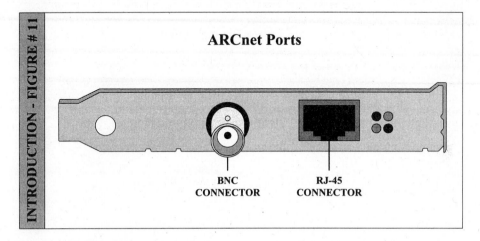

Ethernet adapters can have a BNC, a RJ-45, a 15-pin female D-shell connector, or a combination of these on the same adapter. The 15-pin female D-shell connector is confusing because this connector is also used with game ports. The RJ-45 connector looks like a phone jack, but on careful inspection you find the RJ-45 connector is larger. Introduction Figure #12 shows examples of different Ethernet adapter ports.

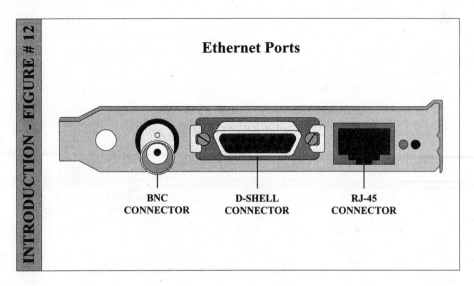

TokenRing adapters have two different connectors: RJ-45 or 9-pin female D-shell connectors. Some adapters have a little green sticker with the numbers *4/16* on it. The 4/16 indicates the two speeds, 4Mbps and 16Mbps, at which TokenRing adapters can run. The 4/16 sticker is a helpful indicator that the port is a TokenRing port. TokenRing adapters are frequently confused with monochrome, CGA, or EGA ports because these ports can also have a 9-pin female D-shell connector. Because these types of video ports are not common today, assume the adapter is a network adapter. Look at Introduction Figure #13 for the two different TokenRing ports.

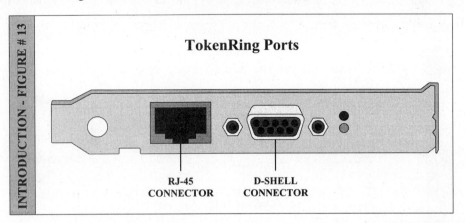

Network ports are frequently confusing because there are so many similar ports on the three different network adapters. Sometimes the only way to identify the port is to look on the adapter for the name.

GAME (JOYSTICK) PORTS

A **game port** is an input port that connects a joystick to the computer. Game ports are 15-pin female D-shell connectors. Game ports are sometimes confused with Ethernet connectors, but game ports are frequently on an adapter with serial and/or parallel ports and Ethernet ports are not. See Introduction Figure #14 for an illustration of a game port.

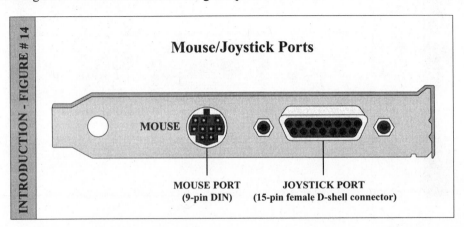

Notice in Introduction Figure #14 how the joystick port is on an adapter with a bus mouse port.

MODEM PORTS

A **modem** connects a microcomputer to a phone line. An external modem is a separate device that sits outside the computer and connects to a 9-pin or 25-pin serial port. An internal modem is on an adapter inside the computer and has one or two RJ-11 connectors. These connectors are smaller than the RJ-45 and look like the phone jacks in a home. With two connectors, a phone and a computer can connect to the phone jack. The line plug is for the modem to connect to the phone jack. The phone plug is for the phone. An internal modem with only one connector allows the modem to connect to the phone jack. Look at Introduction Figure #15 which shows an internal modem with two connection ports.

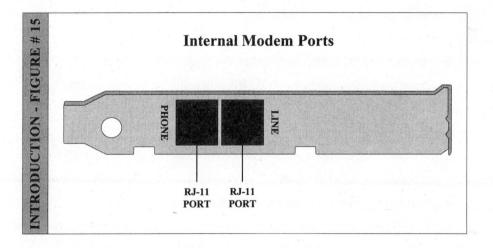

Being able to identify ports quickly and accurately is a critical skill in microcomputer repair.

Name _____

Introduction Review Questions

1.   List three qualities of a good computer technician.

2.   Describe how a computer technician must be like a detective.

3.   What is firmware?

4.   List one purpose of a power supply.

5.   Where is the hard drive normally located on a desktop computer?

6.   List three names for an adapter.

7.   How can you easily determine an adapter's function?

8.   What is the difference between RAM and ROM?

9.   List one function of the ROM BIOS contained on the motherboard.

10. T/F   One cannot randomly change the ROM BIOS to a different manufacturer.

11. List two types of RAM chips.

12. Why must technicians be able to identify common ports?

13. What is the difference in data transmission between the serial and parallel ports?

14. What are some common parallel devices?

15. List two common serial devices that connect to the serial port.

16. T/F   The keyboard and mouse cables can plug into either port on the back of a computer.

17. How can one distinguish between a keyboard port and a mouse port?

18. What are at least two advantages of an integrated motherboard?

19. Why is documentation an important issue with ports on an integrated motherboard?

20. How can you distinguish between a serial and a parallel port?

21. Which ports are often confused with Ethernet ports?

22. Which ports are often confused with TokenRing ports?

23. List at least two identification tips for distinguishing between network adapters.

24. What normally connects to a game port?

25. T/F   An internal modem with one RJ-11 jack has a phone connected to the port.

Name _____

Introduction Fill-in-the-Blank

1. An operating system is an example of _____. The floppy drive, hard drive, and monitor are examples of _____.

2. A small input device connected to the motherboard or an adapter is a _____.

3. The _____ provides DC voltage to various parts of a computer.

4. Disks used to store data insert into the _____.

5. The largest electronic circuit board in the microcomputer is the _____.

6. Adapters plug into an _____ on the motherboard.

7. A _____ plugs into the motherboard and holds adapters in some computer models.

8. Two basic types of memory found inside the microcomputer are _____ and _____.

9. The chip that contains software to start the computer is the _____.

10. _____ performs a hardware check during a cold boot.

11. Most connectors are either the _____ or the _____ type.

12. A connector with a notch or an extra metal piece that allows a cable to be inserted only one way is said to be _____.

13. The keyboard or mouse connector can be a _____ or a _____.

14. The 25-pin female D-shell connector is used for the _____ port.

15. The 9-pin or 25-pin male D-shell connector is used for the _____ port.

16. The 9-pin or 15-pin female D-shell connector is used for a _____ port.

17. The _____ network adapter sometimes has DIP switches on the outside to set the network address.

 Name _____

IDENTIFICATION OF COMPUTER PARTS PAPER EXERCISE

Objective: To correctly identify various microcomputer ports

Using Introduction Exercise Figure 1, identify each part of the microcomputer shown.

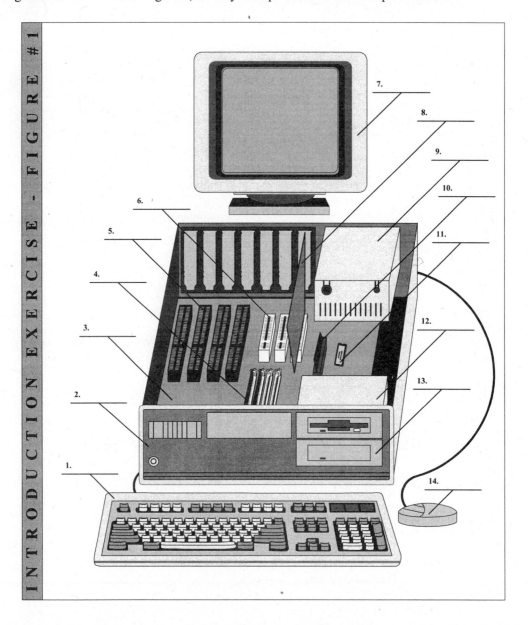

Name_____

IDENTIFICATION OF COMPUTER PORTS PAPER EXERCISE

Objective: To correctly identify various microcomputer ports

Using the drawings shown in Introduction Exercise Figures 2, 7-10 to identify the ports shown:

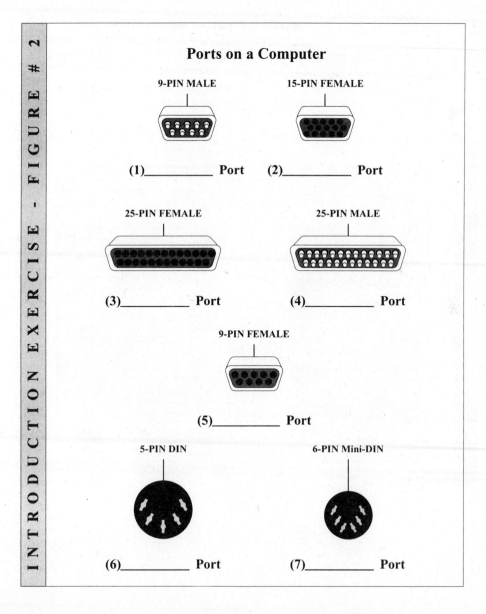

INTRODUCTION EXERCISE - FIGURE # 2

Ports on a Computer

9-PIN MALE

15-PIN FEMALE

(1)_____ Port   (2)_____ Port

25-PIN FEMALE

25-PIN MALE

(3)_____ Port   (4)_____ Port

9-PIN FEMALE

(5)_____ Port

5-PIN DIN

6-PIN Mini-DIN

(6)_____ Port   (7)_____ Port

Name_____

PORT IDENTIFICATION EXERCISE

Objective: To correctly identify various microcomputer ports

Parts: Computer ports either built into a specific computer or separate adapters

1.   Contact the instructor for either a computer on which to work or to obtain adapters.

2.   Identify the computer port(s) given to you by the instructor. Use Motherboard Exercise Table #1 and fill in the connector type, number of pins, and port type.

Connector Type (D-Shell, DIN, etc.)	Number of Pins	Port Type (Video, Parallel, Serial, etc.)
1.		
2.		
3.		
4.		
5.		
6.		
7.		
8.		
9.		
10.		

INTRODUCTION EXERCISE - TABLE # 1

Chapter 2:
On the
Motherboard

OBJECTIVES

After completing this chapter you will
1. Understand the major components on a motherboard including the microprocessor, chipset, math co-processor, and expansion slots.
2. Understand the basic operation of a microprocessor and what must be considered when upgrading a microprocessor.
3. Recognize and identify the microprocessor.
4. Understand the differences between the various architectures and local buses.
5. Recognize the different expansion slots.
6. Recognize what type of expansion slot an adapter takes.

KEY TERMS

architecture	
ATX form factor	L2 cache
bit	L3 cache
bus	local bus
bus-mastering	math co-processor
byte	MCA
cache memory	megabyte
CardBus	MegaHertz
chipset	microprocessor
clones	overdrive
COAST	PC
EISA	PC Bus
exabyte	PC Card
expansion slot	PCI
external data bus	pipeline
gigabyte	Plug and Play (PnP)
intelligent I/O	terabyte
internal data bus	VL-bus
ISA	word size
jumper	write-back cache
kilobyte	write-through cache
L1 cache	ZV port

MICROPROCESSOR OVERVIEW

At the heart of every microcomputer is a special chip normally located on the motherboard called the **microprocessor** which determines, to a great extent, the power of a computer. Each motherboard has electronic chips designed to certain specifications. The microprocessor is the central electronic chip that must work with these other components on the motherboard. Whether or not these other components can keep up with the microprocessor, depends on the individual component's specifications. The major microprocessor manufacturers today are Intel, Motorola, Cyrix, and AMD. The microprocessors designed by Motorola have been used in Apple computers for years. Intel designed the microprocessors IBM used in their first computers.

IBM is the company that put microcomputers in the workplace and the home. A lot of what happened in the computer industry was influenced by those early computers. The computers sold by companies who copied IBM's first computers were known as **clones** or IBM-compatibles. These two terms are still used in the computer industry today even though companies are not copying IBM anymore. Another name for the computer is **PC** or Personal Computer. This book focuses on IBM-compatible computers because they are the majority of what is used in businesses today. Intel microprocessors are covered extensively because they are the most common in the computer industry. Intel's line of microprocessors is known as the X86 microprocessors from the numbering scheme Intel used in designating their microprocessors.

Intel made a microprocessor called the 8086. IBM wanted a cheaper, scaled-down model of the 8086 for their first computer, the IBM PC, so Intel designed the 8088 microprocessor. This microprocessor was in the IBM PC and XT models as well as many other computers. The design of this microprocessor influenced microcomputers in the past and the ones available today.

MICROPROCESSOR BASICS

All microprocessors run on 1s and 0s. One 1 or one 0 is a **bit**. Eight bits grouped together are a **byte**. The letter *A* looks like 01000001 to the microprocessor. Each character on a keyboard appears as one byte or eight bits to the microprocessor. Approximately 1,000 bytes are a **kilobyte**. (1,024 bytes to be exact, but the computer industry rounds the number off to the nearest thousand for ease of calculations.) Ten kilobytes are shown as 10K or 10KB. Approximately one million bytes is a **megabyte**. 540 megabytes are shown as 540MB or 540M. A true megabyte is 1,048,576 bytes. Approximately one billion bytes (1,073,741,824 bytes) are a **gigabyte** and is shown as 1GB or 1G. Beyond the gigabyte is a **terabyte** which is approximately one trillion bytes. Finally, an **exabyte** is approximately one billion time one billion bytes or 2 to the 60th power.

How many bits are processed at one time is the microprocessor's **word size**. Another term some industry books and magazines use is register size. Intel's 8086 microprocessor's word size is 16 bits or two bytes. Today's microprocessors have word sizes of 32 bits. Future microprocessors will have 64-bit word sizes.

The 1s and 0s must travel from one place to another inside the microprocessor as well as outside to other electronic chips. To move the 1s and 0s around, electronic lines called a **bus** are used. The electronic lines inside the microprocessor are known as the **internal data bus**. In the 8086, the internal data bus is comprised of 16 separate lines with each line carrying one *1* or one *0*. The word size and the number of lines for the internal data bus are equal. The 8086, for example, has a 16-bit word size and 16 lines carry 16 bits on the internal data bus. In today's microprocessors, several groups of 32 internal data bus lines operate concurrently.

For the microprocessor to communicate with devices in the outside world, the 1s and 0s travel on the **external data bus**. The external data bus connects the microprocessor to the adapters, the keyboard, the mouse, the floppy drive, the hard drive, etc. The external data bus is also known as the external data path. One can see the external data lines by looking between the expansion slots on the motherboard. Some solder lines between the expansion slots are used to send data out along the external data bus to the expansion slots. The Intel 8088 had an 8-bit external data bus. Today's microprocessors have 64-bit external data paths.

To make sense of all of this, take a look at a letter typed on a computer that starts out: DEAR MOM. To the microcomputer, the letters of the alphabet are different combinations of eight 1s and 0s. For example, the letter *D* is 01000100; the letter *E* is 01000101. The 8086 microprocessor has a word size of 16-bits and an external data path of 16-bits. Therefore, the letters *D* and *E* travel together down the bus; the letters *A* and *R*, then the letters (*space*) and *M*, and finally the letters *O* and *M* travel as 1s and 0s. Each 1 or 0 travels along a single line of the data path. Intel's 80386DX microprocessor has 32-bit internal and external data buses. With the same DEAR MOM letter, the letters *D*, *E*, *A*, and *R* are processed at the same time, followed by (*space*), *M*, *O*, and *M*. One can see that the size of the bus greatly increases performance on a microcomputer. Motherboard Table #1 shows the different models of Intel microprocessors and their internal and external data paths.

MOTHERBOARD - TABLE # 1	Intel Microprocessors		
	Microprocessor	Word Size (in bits)	External Data Bus Size (in bits)
	8088	16	8
	8086	16	16
	80286	16	16
	80386DX (386)	32	32
	80386SX	32	16
	80486DX (486)	32	32
	80486SX	32	32
	Pentium	32*	64
	Pentium Overdrive	32*	32
	Pentium Pro	32*	64
	Pentium II	32*	64
	*Multiple 32-bit paths		

Notice in Motherboard Table #1 the 8088 microprocessor has a 16-bit internal data path and an 8-bit external data path; this is bad news. Imagine the DEAR MOM letter as it is processed in the computer. The microprocessor handles the letters *D* and *E* simultaneously, but when the letters go outside the microprocessor such as to the monitor, the letter *D* goes out the external data bus, then the letter *E*. An external data path with one-half the size of the internal data path considerably slows down a microcomputer. Why would a microprocessor manufacturer make such a product? The answer is simple — lower costs. In many issues relating to microcomputers, the bottom line is profit. IBM wanted to keep their costs down on their original PC to keep it affordable, so they used Intel's 8088 microprocessor in their first business and home microcomputers. Notice that Intel's 80386SX microprocessor has the same concept applied: internally the microprocessor handles 32 bits at a time; externally, only 16 bits transfer over the external data bus lines.

Motherboard Table #1 shows Intel's Pentium, Pentium Overdrive, Pentium Pro, and Pentium II microprocessors as having 32* bits for the internal data buses. These microprocessors have multiple **pipelines** which are separate internal buses that operate simultaneously. The microprocessor handles 32 bits at a time, but has separate paths which each handle 32 bits. For example, the Pentium microprocessor has two pipelines. In the DEAR MOM scenario, the letters *D*, *E*, *A*, and *R* can be in one pipeline, while (*space*), *M*, *O*, *M* can be in the other pipeline. Motherboard Figure #1 shows some of Intel's microprocessors.

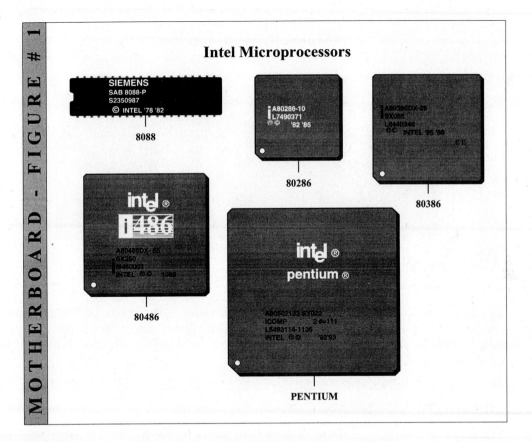

The Pentium Pro has three pipelines. The Pentium II has five execution pipelines although they only output 64 bits at a time to the external data bus. AMD's K-6 microprocessor has six execution pipelines.

Distinguishing whether the microprocessor is an 80486, a Pentium, or Pentium Pro is best done by looking at the microprocessor size. The 80486 is a 169-pin socket; the Pentium is a 273 or 296-pin socket, and the Pentium Pro is a 387-pin socket. Also the 80486 socket frequently has extra pin holes for a Pentium upgrade.

The Pentium II microprocessor looks different than the other rectangular and square microprocessors. To achieve speeds up to 300MHz, Intel redesigned the microprocessor casing for the Pentium II which uses an SEC (Single Edge Contact) cartridge to mount onto the motherboard. Motherboard Figure #2 shows the Pentium II SEC cartridge. Future Intel microprocessors will be manufactured in a similar cartridge for easy installation and upgradability.

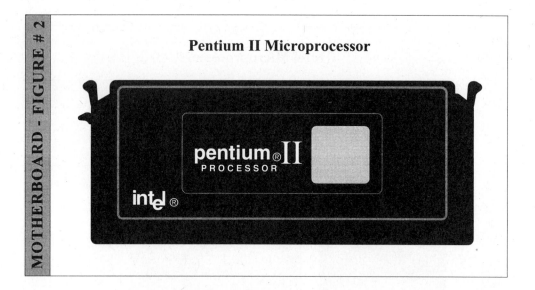

MOTHERBOARD - FIGURE # 2

Pentium II Microprocessor

The microprocessor to watch for is a joint venture between Intel and Hewlett-Packard with the code name Merced. The Merced is supposed to be a 64-bit microprocessor with a new microprocessor architecture, but still be able to run applications designed for the older X86, Pentium, Pentium II line. The clock speed of the Merced is expected to be 1,000MHz.

MMX MICROPROCESSORS

MMX is a new microprocessor technology from Intel designed for the X86 microprocessors. Intel placed 57 new commands in the MMX microprocessors that help with multimedia and communications software. Keep in mind almost all software applications now include some pictures, sounds, movies, etc. If a particular software is not specifically written using the 57 new instructions, the software application's performance can still increase 10-20 percent. On the flip side, with a particular application written to take advantage of the MMX technology, the software can still operate on non-MMX microprocessors, but the application speed will be slower.

MMX technology is not exclusive to Intel microprocessors. AMD's K-6 microprocessor also uses the MMX instructions in its command set. For future applications, and faster multimedia applications, the MMX technology is necessary.

MATH CO-PROCESSORS

The difference between the 80486SX and the 80486DX microprocessors is their ability to perform certain math capabilities. The 80486DX microprocessor had the math co-processor built right into the microprocessor; the 80486SX did not. In prior microprocessors, a separate computer chip called a **math co-processor** or a numeric processor, was added to the motherboard to perform some of the number-crunching functions. Today's microprocessors include the math co-processor. On older computers, adding a math co-processor sped up performance especially with programs such as AutoCAD, spreadsheet applications, or graphics-intensive applications. To install a math co-processor to a machine with an 80486SX microprocessor, add an 80487SX chip to the motherboard. The 80487SX is a microprocessor and math co-processor combined in one chip similar to the 80486DX. The 80487SX microprocessor takes over for the 80486SX processor. Each microprocessor without math co-processing abilities has a specific math co-processor designed to work with it. Motherboard Table #2 shows Intel's microprocessors with the associated math co-processor as well as the ones with built-in math co-processing abilities.

Intel Math Co-processors

Microprocessor	Math Co-Processor
8088	8087
8086	8087
80286	80287
80386DX	80387DX
80386SX	80387SX
80486DX	N/A
80486SX	80487SX
Pentium	N/A
Pentium Overdrive	N/A
Pentium Pro	N/A
Pentium II	N/A

MOTHERBOARD - TABLE # 2

Notice in Motherboard Table #2 how the 80486DX, Pentium, Pentium Overdrive, Pentium Pro, and Pentium II microprocessors do not have math-coprocessors. These microprocessors have the math co-processing ability built into the microprocessor.

PROCESSOR SPEEDS

Math co-processors and microprocessors come in a variety of speeds. The speed of a microprocessor and math co-processor is measured in **MegaHertz**. Hertz is a measurement of cycles per second. One MegaHertz equals one million cycles per second and is abbreviated MHz. The 8088 microprocessor runs at 4.77MHz. Today's microprocessors run at 300MHz.

In most cases, when installing a math co-processor, the speed of the math co-processor chip should equal or be greater than the microprocessor speed. For example, in a computer with a 80386DX microprocessor running at 16MHz, the math co-processor installed should be 16MHz or greater. The exception to this rule are computers using Intel's 80286 microprocessor. When installing a math co-processor in an 80286-based computer, the math co-processor speed should be two-thirds or greater than the microprocessor speed. The speed of a microprocessor and math co-processor is indicated by the numbers on top of the chip. Look for the number after the hyphen. The only problem is many microprocessors come with fans or heat sinks on top of the chip, so the numbers are often hidden. Examples of chip speeds are in Motherboard Figure #3. The Pentium microprocessor runs at 133MHz. The 80486 runs at 66MHz.

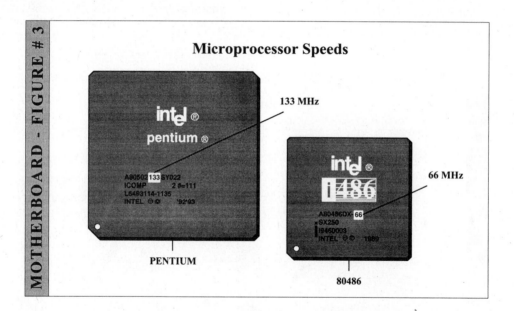

The 80486, Pentium, and Pentium II microprocessor speed is difficult to determine. These microprocessors frequently have fans or heat sinks to keep them cool. Motherboard Figure #4 shows a microprocessor with a fan and another one with a heat sink.

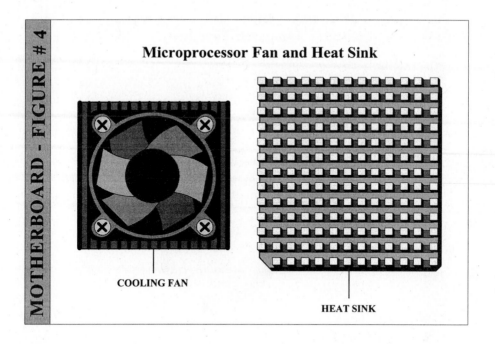

Microprocessor Fan and Heat Sink

MOTHERBOARD - FIGURE # 4

COOLING FAN

HEAT SINK

As seen in Motherboard Figure #4, a heat sink looks like metal bars protruding from the microprocessor. Any chip on the motherboard with a fan or a heat sink on top is easily recognized as the microprocessor.

Because some microprocessors need a fan or heat sink mounted on them, reading the chip speed is difficult. The documentation for the motherboard or the computer system is the best source for discovering microprocessor speed. Many motherboards accept microprocessors with different speeds. The motherboards must be configured by setting one or more jumpers. A **jumper** is a plastic cover that is either installed or removed from two metal pins on a jumper block. The pins protrude upward from the jumper block. A jumper is enabled when it is placed over two pins. When the jumper is removed, the connection between the pins is disabled. Jumper blocks are normally labeled JP1, JP2, JP3, etc. on the motherboard.

The motherboard configuration, the number of jumpers on the motherboard, the jumper labels, the use for each jumper, is determined by the motherboard manufacturer. Each jumper can have more than one setting. For example, consider a motherboard with a jumper block with three pins labeled 1, 2, and 3. The jumper can be placed over pins 1 and 2 for one setting or pins 2 and 3 for a different setting. For example, jumper pins 1 and 2 may need to be jumpered together to configure the motherboard for a 166MHz microprocessor. In that case, the jumper is placed over pins 1 and 2; pin 3 is left uncovered. Reference Motherboard Figure #5 for an illustration of JP1 pins 1 and 2 jumpered together.

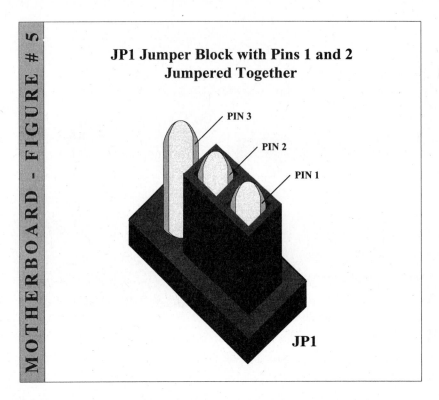

JP1 Jumper Block with Pins 1 and 2 Jumpered Together

PIN 3
PIN 2
PIN 1
JP1

MOTHERBOARD - FIGURE # 5

Motherboard Figure #5 shows an enlarged jumper; the jumper blocks and jumpers on a motherboard are much smaller.

When a jumper is not in use, instead of putting it in a desk drawer, a baggie, or in a drawer somewhere, place the jumper over a single pin in the jumper block. A jumper must connect two pins. Connecting the jumper over a single pin does not enable anything, but keeps the jumper safe and convenient for when it is needed later.

When working on a motherboard, look at it and see what jumpers are set. Then refer to the motherboard documentation to tell the microprocessor speed. Because microprocessors now have the math co-processing functions built in, knowing the microprocessor's speed is no longer an issue unless upgrading the computer to a faster microprocessor or configuring the motherboard.

The original computers used in businesses had microprocessors that ran at the same speed as the external bus, 4.77MHz and 8MHz. The external bus and the components on the motherboard cannot operate at the same speeds as the microprocessors. Microprocessor manufacturers developed a way of dealing with this dilemma by using clock doubling, tripling, and other mathematical techniques within the microprocessor. For example, the 80486DX2 microprocessor uses a clock doubling technique. An 80486DX2-50 runs at 50MHz internally and 25MHz externally. An 80486DX4-100 uses clock tripling technology running at 100MHz internally and 33MHz externally. The speed rating on the microprocessor is for *internal* microprocessor operations. The external bus connects the microprocessor to the other components and this speed cannot be changed. Be careful of this when upgrading microprocessors.

The 60 and 66MHz Pentiums run at the same speed as the motherboard. The 75, 90, and 100MHz Pentium microprocessors run at 1.5 times the speed of the motherboard; the 150 and 166MHz Pentiums run at 2.5 times the speed of the motherboard; and the 180 and 200MHz Pentiums run at triple the motherboard speed. Today's motherboards run at 100MHz.

OVERDRIVE MICROPROCESSORS

A microprocessor can be upgraded using an **overdrive** chip. Many types of overdrive upgrades are available. When upgrading a microprocessor, be sure to get the correct overdrive chip for the system. Refer to the motherboard or system documentation to determine which overdrive chip the motherboard allows. For example, when Intel produced the 80486DX2 microprocessor that runs at twice the motherboard speed, many 80486 owners wanted to upgrade their microprocessor. The original overdrive chip had 169 pins and could only be used to upgrade the 80486SX systems. Then Intel released a 168-pin overdrive chip that could be used in 80486DX or 80486SX systems.

Another upgrade chip is the Pentium Overdrive with 32K (16K more than the original Pentium) of L1 cache. However, the Pentium Overdrive chip only has one 32-bit external data path, not two like the Pentium. The original Pentium Overdrive fit in a 238-pin socket on the motherboard, but the newer 80486 motherboards have an improved 235 or 237-pin socket.

Most 80486 motherboards can be upgraded with an overdrive chip. Depending on (1) the processor currently installed and (2) the socket(s) available on the motherboard. The documentation for the motherboard or computer system *might* give upgrade details. Otherwise, Intel has a published list on the Internet at http://www.intel.com/overdrive/upgrade/index.htm.

UPGRADING MICROPROCESSORS

Two common questions asked of technicians are *can* a computer be upgraded to a higher or faster microprocessor, or *should* a computer be upgraded to a higher or faster microprocessor. Whether or not a computer *can* be upgraded to a higher or faster microprocessor depends on the capability of the motherboard. When a customer asks if a microprocessor *should* be upgraded, the technician should ask, "What operating system and applications are you using?" If the response is DOS or Windows 95 running mostly DOS and Windows 3.x applications, then the original Pentium is the optimum microprocessor. Even though Windows 95 is a 32-bit operating system, most of the code designed for the operating system is 16-bit and users are still using 16-bit applications designed for Windows 3.1.

A quick glance at the motherboard for extra pin holes around the microprocessor or an extra microprocessor socket is a good place to start to determine if the motherboard can accept a new microprocessor. Also look for the new SEC socket for a Pentium II upgrade. Read the documentation for the motherboard to determine if it can accept a faster microprocessor.

The bottom line is *do not* upgrade the microprocessor unless the documentation or the manufacturer states that the motherboard supports a newer or faster microprocessor.

Another issue to consider with microprocessor speeds is the voltage level of the microprocessor. All Intel microprocessors used in desktop or tower models up to the 80486DX use 5 volts supplied from the motherboard. The 80486SX, 80487SX, and 80486DX2 microprocessors also run on 5 volts. The 80486DX4 microprocessor runs on 3.3 volts. The Pentium line of microprocessors use varying voltages. The lower voltage microprocessors run cooler than the higher voltage ones. Newer microprocessors operate at 2.8 volts or lower. Motherboard Table #3 summarizes the voltages used with Intel microprocessors.

MOTHERBOARD - TABLE # 3

Microprocessor Voltages

Microprocessor	Voltage
80486DX, DX2, SX, 80487SX	5V
80486DX4	3.3V
Original Pentium Overdrive	5V
DX4 Overdrive (Pentium Upgrade)	3.3V
Pentium 60/66MHz & 60/66MHZ Pentium Overdrive	5V
Pentium higher than 66MHz, Pentium Overdrive higher than 66MHz, Pentium Pro, and Pentium II	3.3V or less

Some motherboards can be changed from 5 volts to 3.3 volts sent to the microprocessor as required by some microprocessor upgrades. If you accidentally insert a 3.3 volt microprocessor into the socket without changing the setting on the motherboard from 5 volts to 3.3 volts, the 5 volts going in the new microprocessor will most likely destroy it. Getting the correct microprocessor upgrade and setting the configuration jumpers on the motherboard for the correct speed and voltage are critical to a successful microprocessor upgrade.

Because the 150MHz and higher Pentiums require a lower voltage, Intel has a socket design (Socket 7 and Socket 8) specifically for these Pentiums. The Socket 7 or Socket 8 can have a Voltage Regulator Module mounted beside the socket that provides the appropriate voltage to the new microprocessor.

Upgrading things other than the microprocessor can increase speed in a microcomputer. Installing more memory or a faster hard drive sometimes improves a computer's performance more than installing a new microprocessor. All devices and electronic components must work together transferring the 1s and 0s in the most efficient and timely manner possible. The microprocessor is only one piece of the puzzle. Many people do not realize upgrading one computer component does not always make a computer faster or better.

STEPS FOR INSTALLING OR UPGRADING MICROPROCESSORS

Parts: 1.   Proper microprocessor for the motherboard (refer to motherboard documentation)
2.   Microprocessor extractor tool if necessary (normally comes with an upgrade kit)
3.   Anti-static materials

1.   Place the anti-static wrist strap around your wrist and attach the other end to a ground on the computer.
2.   Be sure power to the computer is OFF.
3.   Some old microprocessors require the use of an extractor tool included with the microprocessor upgrade. If necessary, insert the microprocessor extractor tool under one side of the microprocessor. Pry the chip up slightly. Remove the microprocessor extractor tool. Insert the microprocessor extractor tool under a side of the microprocessor adjacent to the side just lifted. Pry the side up slightly. Repeat for the remaining two sides of the microprocessor, until the microprocessor lifts from the socket. If the microprocessor is in a newer microprocessor socket, lift the retaining lever outward and upward. The microprocessor will lift gently out of the socket. Gently pull the microprocessor straight upward. Insert the old microprocessor into an anti-static bag.
4.   Insert the new microprocessor into the socket ensuring that pin 1 on the microprocessor (indicated by a dot or a notched corner) aligns with pin 1 of the motherboard socket (indicated by a dot or a notched corner).
5.   Set any jumpers or switches on the motherboard necessary for proper operation. Refer to the motherboard's documentation.

CACHE MEMORY

As the first microprocessor to include math co-processing abilities, the 80486 was the first microprocessor to include cache memory. **Cache memory** is a fast type of memory designed to increase the speed of microprocessor operations. When located inside the microprocessor, it is known as **L1 cache** or as L1 memory. The 80486 has 8K or 16K of L1 write-through cache memory built in. **Write-through cache** uses a technique in which the microprocessor writes 1s and 0s into the cache memory at the same time it writes the data to regular memory.

The type of L1 cache used in a Pentium or Pentium Pro microprocessor is different from the type used in the 80486. Instead of using a write-through cache, the Pentium and Pentium Pro microprocessors use a write-back cache. **Write-back cache** is more efficient than write-through cache. The 1s and 0s are stored and then later written to regular memory when the microprocessor is not busy.

The Pentium and Pentium Pro microprocessors come with 16K of L1 cache divided into two 8K segments. One 8K of cache handles microprocessor instructions — commands that tell the microprocessor what to do. The other 8K of cache handles data — 1s and 0s as in the DEAR MOM letter. Two separate caches and two 32-bit internal data paths speed up the microprocessor tremendously. The Pentium II microprocessor has 32K of L1 cache.

L2 cache memory is a special type of memory similar to L1 cache memory. **L2 cache** holds a small amount of data that is "guesstimated" to be the next data the microprocessor needs. It is on the motherboard for Pentium and lower microprocessors, but starting with the Pentium Pro microprocessor, the L2 cache is inside the microprocessor chip. The Pentium Pro has 256K of L2 cache built into the microprocessor; the Pentium II has 512K of L2 cache built in. The 80386, 80486, and Pentium motherboard manufacturers frequently include L2 cache sockets. The only drawback to using L2 cache is that the microprocessor must go from the microprocessor chip to the motherboard to retrieve the data in the cache. However, having L2 cache on a motherboard is still faster than not having it.

Any cache memory on a motherboard with a Pentium Pro microprocessor or higher is **L3 cache** memory. Little advantage is gained with more cache on the motherboard when the L1 and L2 cache are included in the microprocessor. The Pentium Pro is designed to handle 32-bit operating systems such as Windows 95, Windows NT, and UNIX. It can execute three instructions in one clock cycle whereas the Pentium can only execute two. The Pentium II microprocessor can handle up to five instructions in one clock cycle. It is great for the computers that control networks to execute so many instructions. Also, the Pentium II is designed to better handle high-end graphics and multimedia applications that typically run on RISC (Reduced Instruction Set Computer) machines, which are typically UNIX-based or Apple computers.

Cache chips can be DIP (Dual In-line Processor) chips, or **COAST (Cache On A STick)** chips. COAST memory modules resemble a small SIMM (Single In-line Memory Module). A DIP chip has a row of legs down each side. A SIMM or COAST is a memory module that is easier to install than a DIP chip. Older motherboards use DIP chips to upgrade cache because the older ones do not contain as much cache as the later motherboards. SIMMs hold more information than DIP chips. Newer motherboards such as those used with 80486 and higher microprocessors, use COASTs for the cache. Motherboard Figure #6 shows the two different types of cache memory chips.

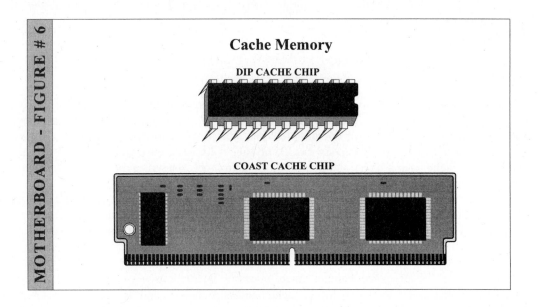

MOTHERBOARD - FIGURE # 6

Cache Memory

DIP CACHE CHIP

COAST CACHE CHIP

ARCHITECTURES

For the computer to be useful, the microprocessor must communicate with the outside world including other components on the motherboard and adapters plugged into the motherboard. An **architecture** is a set of rules that states how many bits can be transferred at one time to an adapter, what signals are sent over the adapter's gold connectors, how the adapter is set up or configured, etc. Three architectures used in PCs are ISA (Industry Standard Architecture), EISA (Extended Industry Standard Architecture), and MCA (MicroChannel Architecture). A technician must be able to distinguish between adapters designed for each architecture and configure the adapters for each architecture. The technician must also realize the abilities and limitations of each architecture when installing upgrades, replacing parts, or making recommendations to customers.

ISA (Industry Standard Architecture)

The **Industry Standard Architecture**, better known as **ISA**, is the oldest architecture used with X86 microprocessors and is still used in today's computers. ISA allows 16-bit transfers to adapters installed in ISA slots. A slot or **expansion slot** is the place to plug in an adapter. The number of expansion slots available depends on the manufacturer of the motherboard. ISA is also referred to as the AT Bus. Because computer manufacturers want customers to be able to use their old adapters in an upgraded motherboard or a new computer, ISA is still the architecture with the most adapters available on the market.

ISA operates at 8MHz although some vendors reliably achieve 10MHz throughput. Some vendors have achieved 12MHz, but the industry pronounced 10MHz as the maximum speed for ISA. With today's microprocessor speeds in the 200MHz range and greater, one can see how the ISA architecture can be a detriment. Adapters requiring high speed transfers such as network, memory, and video adapters are hampered by the slowness of the ISA standard. Many people still do not realize that some devices controlled by an ISA adapter are severely handicapped.

A memory expansion card should *never* be placed in a 386 or higher's ISA expansion slot. All the computer's memory runs at the speed of the ISA expansion slot — 10MHz. This is true even with 200MHz microprocessors.

ISA was designed to be backward-compatible with IBM's first two computer models, the PC and the XT. The PC and XT had an 8-bit external data bus. The only adapters that worked in the PC and the XT computers were 8-bit adapters. The ISA architecture allows an 8-bit adapter to fit and operate in the 16-bit ISA slot. Reference Motherboard Figure #7 for an example of the difference between an 8-bit ISA adapter and a 16-bit ISA slot.

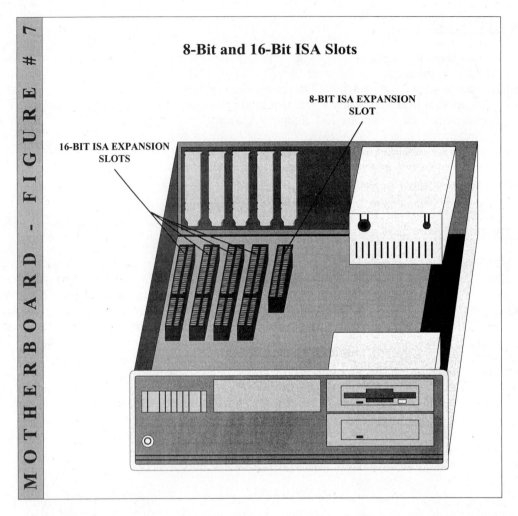

8-Bit and 16-Bit ISA Slots

8-BIT ISA EXPANSION
SLOT

16-BIT ISA EXPANSION
SLOTS

Motherboards today normally come with only 16-bit ISA slots because an 8-bit ISA adapter fits perfectly in a 16-bit slot. The extension connector on the 16-bit slot remains empty. Some books, advertisements, and vendors call 8-bit adapters ISA cards, but a true ISA adapter is a 16-bit card. The original architecture for computers that used the 8088 microprocessor was the **PC Bus**. Nevertheless, because some of the rules from the PC Bus were incorporated into the ISA standard, most people call 8-bit adapters ISA adapters.

ISA adapters are frequently configured through switches and jumpers. This is time-consuming for a technician because most computer owners do not have the documentation for the ISA adapters installed in their systems. The documentation is frequently lost or destroyed. Most companies have adapter documentation on their web site. However, some adapters do not have identifiers on them so a technician cannot tell what manufacturer produced the adapter. ISA adapters can also be configured through software which is much easier than setting jumpers or switches.

MCA (MICROCHANNEL ARCHITECTURE)

When IBM computers became cloned and IBM started losing their share of the microcomputer market, IBM decided to develop its own architecture called **MicroChannel Architecture** or **MCA** for short. The MicroChannel Architecture is *incompatible* with ISA. MCA adapters will *not* fit in ISA expansion slots, nor will ISA adapters fit in MCA expansion slots.

The MicroChannel Architecture is a 32-bit bus although most MCA adapters are 8 or 16-bit adapters. Some MCA cards are able to do 64-bit transfers using a technique called streaming. Any vendor who designs a MCA adapter pays IBM a fee. IBM maintained strict controls on their architecture so it could not be cloned like IBM's earlier computers.

MCA adapters are much easier to configure than ISA adapters because the adapters are set up through software. When a MCA adapter is sold, a disk ships with the adapter which allows the MCA computer to recognize the adapter, and any changes in the adapter's configuration. The drawback to this method is the computer users frequently lose the adapter software disk. IBM no longer manufactures computers with only MCA expansion slots.

The MicroChannel Architecture introduced a feature called **bus-mastering**. This allows an adapter to take over the external data bus from the microprocessor and execute operations with another bus-mastering adapter without going through the microprocessor. The ISA standard only allowed one bus-master adapter in an ISA machine. However, ISA bus-master adapters are few and far between. Bus-mastering is important for network and video adapters especially because of their need for speed.

EISA (ENHANCED INDUSTRY STANDARD ARCHITECTURE)

The computer industry was upset by IBM's move to a proprietary architecture. A group of nine vendors: Compaq, Hewlett-Packard, Zenith, Epson, NEC, Wyse, AST, Tandy, and Olivetti got together to develop a new architecture to rival IBM's MicroChannel Architecture. The result was the development of the **Enhanced Industry Standard Architecture**, better known as **EISA**. EISA is a 32-bit 8MHz standard (some say 10MHz, but in any case, it is slow) that allows ISA adapters to operate in the EISA expansion slots. The ISA adapters do not have access to all the upgraded features the EISA expansion slot offers. Only an EISA adapter is able to take advantage of the upgraded features of the EISA expansion slot. An EISA expansion slot is the same physical length as an ISA expansion slot. The difference between the two is the depth of each expansion slot. The EISA expansion slot is twice as deep as the ISA expansion slot. An EISA adapter's gold connectors are twice as long as the connectors found on ISA adapters. Reference Motherboard Figure #8 for an example of a motherboard with EISA and ISA expansion slots.

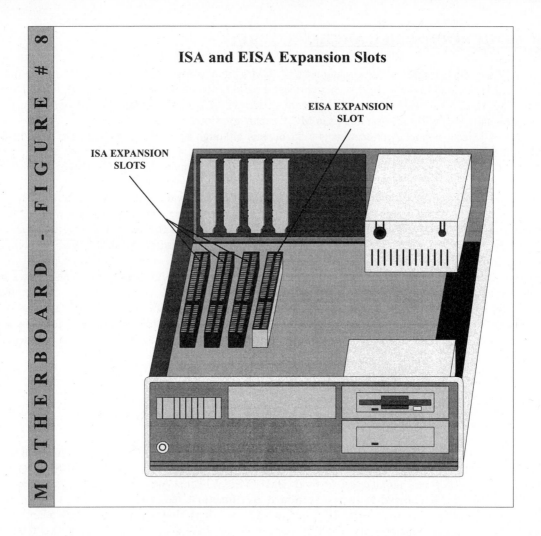

ISA and EISA Expansion Slots

EISA EXPANSION
SLOT

ISA EXPANSION
SLOTS

MOTHERBOARD - FIGURE # 8

EISA adapters, like MCA adapters are configured through software, which is simple for technicians. Also, EISA adapters can do bus-mastering like the MCA adapters. However, EISA never really caught on as much as the designers hoped. Normally in today's computer market, EISA slots are only in network server computers so older EISA adapters can still be used. (A network server is the main computer of a network.)

All three architectures, ISA, MCA, and EISA are limited by speed. EISA expansion slots are useful because ISA and EISA adapters fit and work in the expansion slots. MCA is very consistent in how all adapters are configured. MCA and EISA both support software configuration and bus-mastering which are a great improvement over ISA. Motherboard Figure #9 compares ISA, MCA, and EISA adapter connectors.

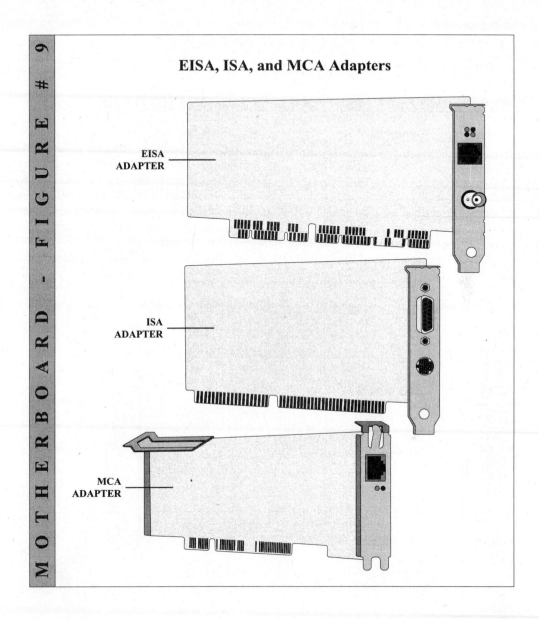

EISA, ISA, and MCA Adapters

MOTHERBOARD - FIGURE # 9

EISA ADAPTER

ISA ADAPTER

MCA ADAPTER

LOCAL BUSES

A **local bus** is a data channel that attaches differently to the microprocessor and has a different expansion slot than ISA, EISA and MCA. Because of speed and data path limitations of the three architectures (ISA, MCA, and EISA), local bus standards work in conjunction with ISA, MCA, and EISA. A local bus allows faster transfers and throughput. The two most common local buses in computers today are Peripheral Component Interconnect (PCI), and Personal Computer Memory Card Industry Association (better known as PCMCIA or PC Card). A third local bus still in the industry, but not as big an influence, is VL-BUS (Video Electronics Association Video Local Bus) or VESA. A local bus expansion slot is best suited for taking advantage of the speed and throughput of more modern microprocessors.

VL-BUS (VIDEO ELECTRONICS ASSOCIATION VIDEO LOCAL BUS)

One of the biggest industries affected by the slowness of ISA, EISA, and MCA is the video industry. Video needs a wide, fast path to transmit all the 1s and 0s to generate millions of colors, detailed pictures, and provide video motion. So, the video industry developed their own local bus standard called the **VL-bus** or VESA local bus. Other industries have taken advantage of VESA local bus such as hard drive, network, and memory adapter manufacturers. The VL-bus standard developed around the 80486 microprocessor. Because the VL-bus developed around the 80486 microprocessor, it is a 32-bit standard. In theory, the VL-bus can operate at speeds up to 66MHz (but some testing has shown that errors can occur when transmitting on the VL-bus at 66MHz).

VL-bus adapters will *not* fit in ISA, MCA, or EISA expansion slots, and require their own expansion bus. The VL-bus slot looks just like a MCA slot except for its location on the motherboard. A VL-bus expansion slot is an extra connector added to the end of an ISA, EISA, or MCA expansion slot. Motherboard Figure #10 shows a VL-bus adapter and an ISA adapter.

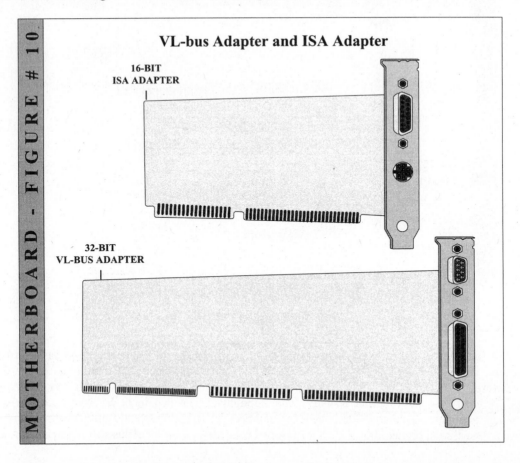

MOTHERBOARD - FIGURE # 10

VL-bus Adapter and ISA Adapter

16-BIT
ISA ADAPTER

32-BIT
VL-BUS ADAPTER

Notice in Motherboard Figure #10 how the VL-bus adapter has three different connectors on it. Two of the VL-bus connectors are just like an ISA adapter's connectors, but the third connector to the far left is what determines the adapter is a VL-bus.

VL-bus expansion cards configure through jumpers and switches. However, some VL-bus adapter manufacturers provide the capability of software configuration. More configuration issues are covered in Chapter 3.

PCI (PERIPHERAL COMPONENT INTERCONNECT)

The VL-bus rival is the **Peripheral Component Interconnect (PCI)** bus. PCI is a 64-bit 66MHz standard. PCI expansion slots are not an extension of another architecture's expansion slot like VL-bus connectors. Instead, PCI expansion slots are either a separate connector or integrated with an ISA expansion slot. If the PCI is a separate connector, the expansion slots come in four configurations based on voltage level and number of bits that transfer in or out of the slot. Motherboard Figure #11 shows the different types of individual PCI expansion slots.

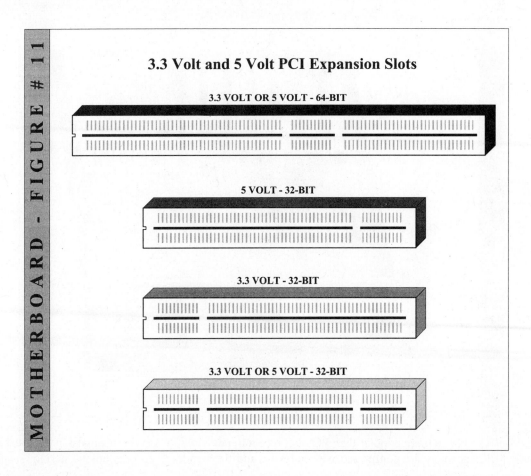

Both PCI configurations have a 32-bit and a 64-bit version. The 64-bit expansion slot adds more pins to the expansion slot. The PCI expansion slot as a separate connector has been the most popular type of PCI expansion slot until lately. The latest PCI expansion slot is a connector that combines both ISA and PCI. The expansion slot allows insertion of either one ISA adapter *or* one PCI adapter. The connector is one molded piece, but the piece contains both an ISA expansion slot and a PCI expansion slot.

PCI expansion slots are farther from the back of the computer than ISA, EISA, or MCA slots. PCI expansion slots look exactly as MCA expansion slots in that the 32-bit versions are the same dimension. The VL-bus slot is also the same dimension. Most motherboards today come with ISA and PCI slots. Reference Motherboard Figure #12 for an example of a motherboard with PCI and ISA expansion slots.

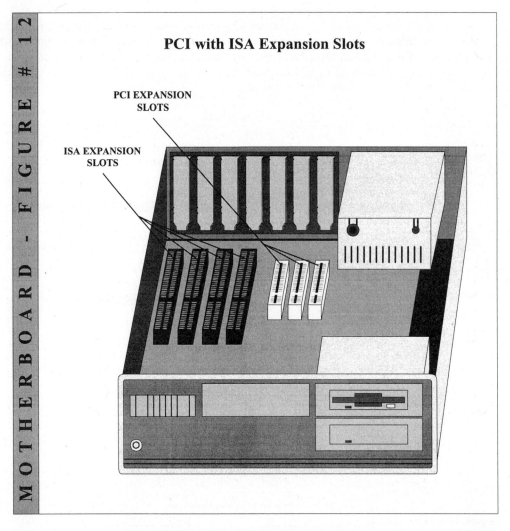

VL-bus was more popular than PCI, but recent trends show PCI as the strongest in the local bus market. PCI adapters are configured with software and the standard supports bus-mastering. A great many adapters are now available for PCI expansion slots. Unlike VL-bus, the PCI standard can be used with PCs and Apple computers. PCI expansion cards can take advantage of the speed and throughput of today's microprocessors such as Intel's Pentium, Pentium Pro, and Pentium II microprocessors.

INTELLIGENT I/O (I2O)

Intelligent I/O (I2O) is a new architecture being developed to work with the PCI architecture. The main thrust behind the Intelligent I/O architecture deals with how the microprocessor handles each interrupt (see Chapter 3 for an interrupt explanation). If the microprocessor is waiting because of slow input/output devices that create a bottleneck, the Intelligent I/O architecture will handle some of the interrupts for the processor. The Intelligent I/O architecture will have a processor that intercepts interrupt requests to the microprocessor, handles some of them that support the architecture, and passes the others to the microprocessor. The Intelligent I/O architecture is expected to be used in network server computers where input/output is a constant demand on the system.

PC CARD (FORMERLY PCMCIA)

The **PC Card** architecture, previously known as **PCMCIA (Personal Computer Memory Card International Association)** was originally designed to upgrade memory in laptop computers. However, because the standard expanded, PC Cards are now available for modems, hard drives, network adapters, etc. The PC Card's local bus can also be installed in a desktop computer, but that is not common. The original standard was a 16-bit local bus standard with 64MB of memory addressing. The new standard called **CardBus** allows 32-bit transfers at speeds up to 33MHz. CardBus was designed as a combination of the old PC Card architecture and PCI. The PC Card's CardBus also supports bus-mastering, direct memory accessing (DMA) covered in Chapter 3, and up to 4GB of memory addressing. PC Cards are about the size of a credit card, though thicker. Motherboard Figure #13 shows a PC Card.

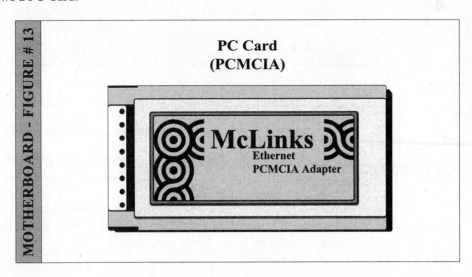

MOTHERBOARD - FIGURE # 13

PC Card
(PCMCIA)

McLinks
Ethernet
PCMCIA Adapter

The number of PC Card slots available on a computer varies between manufacturers and computer models. A PC Card inserts into the PC Card slot. However, each PC Card can control more than one PC Card slot. In theory, any PC Card can be used for any type of device. However, their use is normally denoted by the PC Card's thickness. There are three major PC Card types of different sizes known as Type I, Type II, and Type III. The Type I PC Cards are 3.3mm thick and are normally memory cards. These memory cards can be RAM or FLASH RAM with applications on the card. An application can execute from a Type I PC Card instead of the laptop's hard drive.

Upgrading memory in a 486 or higher laptop with a 16-bit PC Card is not the best solution. Because of the 16-bit transfers, a PC Card memory upgrade should be done only as a last resort. However, for some laptops, upgrading the computer's memory is the only option.

Type II PC Cards are 5mm thick and used for modem and network cards. A laptop computer with a Type II PC Card slot accepts Type II and Type I PC Cards in the slot, but only one at a time!

Type III PC Cards are 10.5mm thick are for rotating devices such as hard drives, CD-ROMs, floppy drives, etc. Type III PC Card slots also accept Type I and II PC Cards. Motherboard Table #4 lists recaps the PC Card types, sizes, and uses.

MOTHERBOARD - TABLE # 4

PC Cards

PC Card Type	Size	Useage
I	3.3mm	Memory and Applications
II	5mm	Modems and Network adapters
III	10.5mm	Storage devices such as floppy drives, hard drives, and CD-ROMs

One of the latest developments in the PC Card arena is the ZV Port. The **ZV port (zoomed video port)** allows data transfer from a PC Card to a VGA video adapter. With this new bus a notebook computer can connect to a video device such as a camera.

PC Cards ship with software called device drivers to allow the adapters to operate. After configuration, some PC Cards can be "hot swapped" meaning installed after powering on the computer.

PROPRIETARY LOCAL BUS SLOTS

Some computers have a 32-bit expansion slot built into the motherboard that is neither a VL-bus slot nor a PCI slot. These expansion slots are proprietary and the adapters that fit and work in the expansion slot must be purchased from that manufacturer (if they are still in business). Motherboard Figure #14 shows a proprietary 32-bit expansion slot on a motherboard.

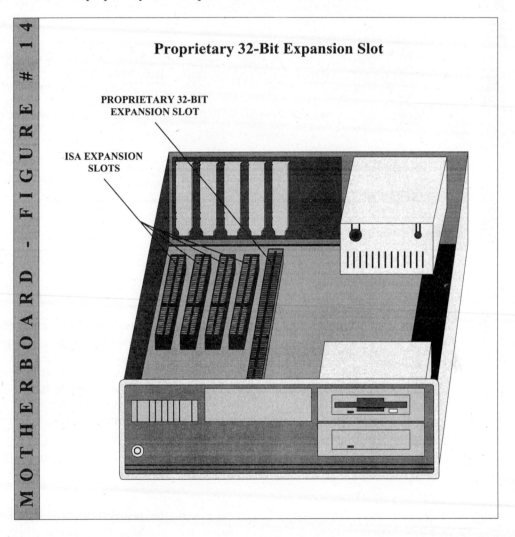

Proprietary 32-Bit Expansion Slot

PROPRIETARY 32-BIT
EXPANSION SLOT

ISA EXPANSION
SLOTS

MOTHERBOARD - FIGURE # 14

Beware of proprietary slots! Because they are proprietary, expansion cards are usually hard to obtain and the documentation for adapters used in the proprietary slots is even more rare.

The different architectures and local buses can be overwhelming. Motherboard Table #5 allows viewing the differences at a glance.

MOTHERBOARD - TABLE # 5

Architecture and Local Bus Overview

Architecture or Local Bus	Bits	Speed	Bus-Mastering
ISA	8/16	8/10MHz	Y (only 1 adapter)
MCA	16/32	10MHz	Y
EISA	32	8/10MHz	Y
VL-Bus	32	25/33MHz	Y
PCI	32/64	33/66MHz	Y
PC Card	16/32	33MHz	Y

PLUG AND PLAY

A specification called **Plug and Play (PnP)** allows automatic configuration of an adapter. A Plug and Play adapter plugs into an expansion slot without the technician having to configure the board or worry about the adapter conflicting with other adapters already installed in the system. Most computers today support Plug and Play. The ROM BIOS chip on the motherboard must be the type that supports Plug and Play. PCI supports Plug and Play and the latest revision to the VL-bus is supposed to support Plug and Play. The ISA, EISA, and MCA architectures can also be used in a Plug and Play environment. More information on configuring adapters that support Plug and Play is available in the configuration chapter (Chapter 3) and the Windows 95 chapter.

CHIPSETS

The motherboard chips that work in conjunction with the microprocessor are known as **chipsets**. These allow certain features on the computer. For example, the chipsets control the maximum amount of motherboard memory, the type of RAM chips, the motherboard's capacity for two or more microprocessors, if the motherboard supports the latest version of PCI, etc. Three common chipset manufacturers are Intel Corp., Silicon Integrated Systems Corp. (SiS), and OPTi, Inc.

A technician must keep well informed of the chipsets on the market when making recommendations for motherboard upgrades and new computer purchases.

Intel's 430HX (Triton II) chipset for the Pentium-based motherboard permits up to 512KB motherboard cache, support for two microprocessors, and support for the Universal Serial Bus, etc. Intel's 430VX chipset is for less powerful desktop computers. Just because a motherboard has a particular chipset on it does not mean that motherboard has that feature. It can possibly have the feature if the motherboard manufacturer wants it.

Usually a chipset goes with a particular microprocessor as well as determining what memory chips a motherboard can possibly have. For example, Intel's 440FX (Natoma) chipset is used with Pentium Pro microprocessors and Intel's 440LX, 440BX, and 450NX chipsets have support for the Pentium II microprocessor as well as an Accelerated Graphics Port (which is covered later in the book). Intel's 440BX and 450NX chipsets support bus speeds of 66MHz and 100MHz. Chipsets determine a lot about what a motherboard *can* allow or *can* support. When buying a motherboard, in addition to picking a proper microprocessor, pick a good chipset as well.

ATX FORM FACTOR

A new type of computer case (chassis) and motherboard design called the **ATX form factor** has hit the computer market. Prior motherboard sizes were called AT based on the size of IBM's original AT computer motherboard. Clones that used a smaller motherboard were referenced as Baby AT motherboards. The ATX form factor is similar in size to the Baby AT motherboard and case except it is rotated 90 degrees. The microprocessor no longer sits near the expansion slots on an ATX form factor motherboard. The ATX form factor provides easier installation of full-length cards, easier cabling, and more cost-effective cooling.

UPGRADING MOTHERBOARDS

Whenever upgrading a motherboard, several issues must be taken into account. The following list helps guide a technician through making the decision (or helping a customer make a decision) of whether or not to upgrade a motherboard.

1. Why is the computer being upgraded? For example, does the computer need more memory? Are more expansion slots needed? Does the computer need a bigger and faster microprocessor to run certain operating systems or applications? Sometimes, upgrading the motherboard does not help unless the other computer components are outdated. The most expensive and fastest motherboard in the world will not run applications well unless it has the proper amount of memory. Hard drives are another issue. If software access is slow, the solution might not be a new motherboard, but a faster and larger hard drive.

2.   Which type (ISA, EISA, MCA, PCI, or VL-bus) and how many adapters are needed from the old motherboard? Does the new motherboard have the required expansion slots?

3.   Are there any devices such as the hard drive or CD-ROM that currently require an adapter that could plug directly into the upgraded motherboard? This would free up expansion slots as well as speed up the devices.

4.   What type of chipsets does the new motherboard support? What features, if any, would this bring to the new motherboard? What expense is incurred if the new chipset is purchased? Will the chipset from the old motherboard operate in the new motherboard?

5.   Will the new motherboard fit in the case of the computer to be upgraded?

6.   Does the motherboard allow for future microprocessor upgrades?

7.   How much memory (RAM) does the motherboard allow? What memory chips are required on the new motherboard?

Motherboards contain the most circuitry for a microcomputer and are very important to the operation of a microcomputer. Keeping current with the options, features, microprocessors, chipsets, etc. is a responsibility required of a technician. Most technicians subscribe to computer magazines to help with this responsibility.

Name ___ _____

Motherboard Review Questions

1. What is a microprocessor?

2. List two microprocessor manufacturers.

3. What is a PC?

4. What is a bus?

5. What is the difference between the internal data bus and external data bus?

6. T/F   A computer's word size and external data path are always the same number of bits.

7. T/F   The Pentium II has a 64-bit external data path.

8. What is a microprocessor's pipeline?

9. What is the easiest way to distinguish between an 80486, Pentium, and Pentium Pro microprocessor?

10. Why did Intel use the Single Edge Connector (SEC) on the new Pentium II microprocessors?

11. What is the difference between an 80486SX microprocessor and an 80486DX microprocessor?

12. Which microprocessor speed is the fastest (10MHz, 25MHz, 100MHz, or 266MHz)?

13. List two methods for determining microprocessor speed.

14. Is the microprocessor speed the same speed as the chips on the motherboard?

15. List two advantages of a Pentium microprocessor over an 80486 microprocessor.

16. List one advantage an Intel MMX microprocessor has over a microprocessor without MMX.

17. How would you know what overdrive chip a system could handle?

18. A customer wants to upgrade their microprocessor. What questions are you going to ask them to make a recommendation?

19. How can you tell if a motherboard accepts a faster or more powerful microprocessor?

20. T/F   A 3.3 volt microprocessor automatically converts the incoming 5 volts to the lower voltage.

21. How much L1 and L2 cache does the Pentium II have?

22. What is ISA's biggest drawback?

23. Why should a memory expansion adapter never be placed in an expansion slot?

24. T/F   Computers today still use ISA.

25.   What is a computer architecture?

26.   Name three microcomputer architectures.

27.   Why must a technician be familiar with the different architectures?

28.   List two drawbacks to the MicroChannel Architecture.

29.   Why is software configuration easier than jumpers and switches on an adapter?

30.   T/F   An EISA adapter can operate in an ISA slot.

31.   What is bus-mastering?

32.   List one limitation common to microcomputer architectures.

33.   Which architectures support bus-mastering?

34.   Explain how to configure an adapter for each of the three architectures.

Match the following definitions with the most correct term.
35.   _____ VL-bus   A.   A local bus primarily used in laptop computers
36.   _____ PC Card   B.   A local bus standard developed by the video industry
37.   _____ PCI   C.   A 64-bit local bus standard

38.   T/F   PCI is a better local bus standard than VL-bus.

39.   Which local bus standards can transfer 32 bits of data at a time? (Pick all that apply)
       A.   The original PC Card standard
       B.   The new (updated) PC Card standard
       C.   VL-bus
       D.   PCI

40.   T/F   PCI is set up via jumpers and switches on the PCI adapter.

41.   Why is bus-mastering an important feature of a local bus?

42.   Can an ISA adapter be used in a Plug and Play environment?

43.   What architecture is a new one designed to work with PCI?

44.   How many bits at a time does the CardBus transfer?

45.   What are the three types of PC Cards and for what are they used?

46.   What are some features a computer chipset provides?

47.   What is the name of the latest type of computer case and motherboard design?

48.   List at least three recommendations to keep in mind when upgrading a motherboard.

Name _____

Motherboard Fill-in-the-Blank

1. The main chip found on the motherboard which executes software instructions is the _____.

2. In computer technology, a 1 or a 0 is a _____.

3. A combination of eight 1s and 0s is a _____.

4. Approximately 1,000 (one thousand) bytes are a _____.

5. Approximately 1,000,000 (one million) bytes are a _____.

6. Approximately 1,000,000,000 (one billion) bytes are a _____.

7. Approximately 1,000,000,000,000 (one trillion) bytes are a _____.

8. The number of bits that the microprocessor processes at one time is the microprocessor's _____.

9. _____ microprocessors have 57 more multimedia instructions built into them.

10. A microprocessor or math co-processor speed is measured in _____.

11. A plastic cover that enables a computer option is a _____.

12. To keep today's microprocessors cool _____ or _____ are used.

13. The type of memory that has always been found inside the microprocessor is _____.

14. The type of memory previously outside the microprocessor on the motherboard, but now inside the microprocessor chip is _____.

15. The type of cache memory written immediately to regular memory is known as _____.

16. The type of cache memory written to regular memory whenever the microprocessor is not busy is known as _____.

17. An _____ allows an adapter to be added to a motherboard or a riser board.

18. An adapter that communicates directly with another adapter without going through the microprocessor uses _____.

19. The _____ architecture is mainly for laptop computers.

20. The _____ port allows a camera to be connected to a laptop computer.

Name _____

EXPANSION SLOT IDENTIFICATION EXERCISE

1.   Using Motherboard Exercise Figure #1, label the expansion slots.

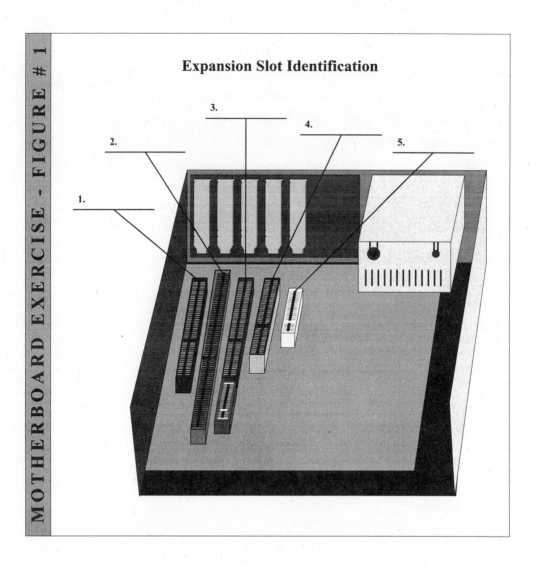

Expansion Slot Identification

MOTHERBOARD EXERCISE - FIGURE # 1

Name _____

ADAPTER AND EXPANSION SLOT IDENTIFICATION EXERCISE

Objective: To identify the adapter type and the architecture or local bus expansion slot type by looking inside a computer

Parts: Computer with adapters installed

1.   Remove the cover from a computer shown to you by your instructor.

2.   Identify all adapters installed in the microcomputer as ISA, EISA, MCA, VL-bus, PCI or PCMCIA/PC Card. Use Motherboard Exercise Table #1 to list the adapter type (video, hard drive controller, network adapter, etc.) and the architecture or local bus expansion slot used for the adapter.

Note: One can sometimes identify the adapter type by observing the cables attached to the adapter. For example, the hard drive controller has one or two cables that attach to the hard drive. Many computers have multi-function adapters able to control more than one device such as the floppy and hard drive.

	Adapter Type (Video, network, sound, floppy, hard drive, etc.)	Expansion Slot Type (ISA, EISA, MCA, VL-bus, or PC Card)
MOTHERBOARD EXERCISE - TABLE # 1	1.	
	2.	
	3.	
	4.	
	5.	
	6.	
	7.	
	8.	
	9.	
	10.	

Name_____

ADAPTER'S EXPANSION SLOT IDENTIFICATION EXERCISE

Objective: To identify the adapter type and the architecture or local bus expansion slot type by looking at an adapter

Parts: Various adapters

1.   Obtain an adapter from your instructor.

2.   By looking at the adapter, (1) determine the type of adapter (video, hard drive controller, network adapter, etc.) and (2) determine the expansion slot architecture the adapter uses. Record your results in Motherboard Exercise Table #2.

MOTHERBOARD EXERCISE - TABLE # 2

Adapter Type (Video, network, sound, floppy, hard drive, etc.)	Expansion Slot Type (ISA, EISA, MCA, VL-bus, or PC Card)
1.	
2.	
3.	
4.	
5.	
6.	
7.	
8.	
9.	
10.	

Name _____

MICROPROCESSOR UPGRADE
PAPER CONFIGURATION EXERCISE

Look at the drawing shown in Motherboard Exercise Figure #2. Using the documentation included with the figure, draw a jumper (a rectangular box) around the pins to be jumpered if installing an 80486DX-33 microprocessor on a motherboard.

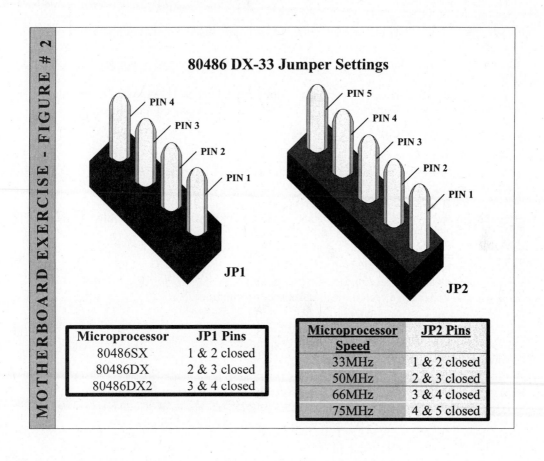

MOTHERBOARD EXERCISE - FIGURE # 2

80486 DX-33 Jumper Settings

JP1 — PIN 4, PIN 3, PIN 2, PIN 1

JP2 — PIN 5, PIN 4, PIN 3, PIN 2, PIN 1

Microprocessor	JP1 Pins
80486SX	1 & 2 closed
80486DX	2 & 3 closed
80486DX2	3 & 4 closed

Microprocessor Speed	JP2 Pins
33MHz	1 & 2 closed
50MHz	2 & 3 closed
66MHz	3 & 4 closed
75MHz	4 & 5 closed

Name _____

INTERNET DISCOVERY

***Objective*:**   To access the Internet to obtain specific information regarding a computer or its associated parts.

***Parts*:** Access to the Internet

The following scenario is provided:
    You have a customer that owns a Compaq Presario CDS 774 computer.

1.   Determine what processor the computer has by accessing the Compaq web site.
2.   Determine at what speed the microprocessor operates.
3.   If you install a 120MHz processor on this motherboard, discover what jumpers will be set on P5.
4.   If you install a 120MHz processor on this motherboard, discover what jumpers will be set on P11.
5.   After you install the new processor, you set the jumpers correctly, and you reinstall the computer cover, look on the web site for the next step that Compaq recommends.

The following information is provided:
    You have a customer who has a Toshiba Equium 5160D computer.
6.   Determine if this computer already has MMX capabilities.
7.   Find out what voltage level the microprocessor uses.
8.   See if the website helps with the type and number of expansion slots available on this model.

The following information is provided:
    A customer owns a HP Vectra 515 486 computer.
9.   See what switches are affected by a microprocessor upgrade.

The following information relates to numbers 8-10:
    A customer owns a NEC Direction SPT200 computer.
10.   Discover what chipset this computer uses.
11.   Look for the speed of the PCI slot.
12.   Determine the number of PCI slots for this model of computer.

Chapter 3:
System
Configuration

OBJECTIVES

After completing this chapter you will
1.   Understand the different ways to configure a microcomputer.
2.   Understand how to replace a battery.
3.   Understand system resources such as interrupts, DMA channels, and I/O addresses.
4.   Understand how different architectures and local bus adapters configure.
5.   Understand the effects Plug and Play and Windows 95 have on configuring adapters.
6.   Recognize what type of expansion slot an adapter requires.

KEY TERMS

card services	interrupt
cascaded interrupt	non-cascaded interrupt
CMOS	Plug and Play
device driver	point enabler
DIP switch	reference disk
DMA channel	registry
Flash BIOS	SETUP
generic enabler	socket services
I/O address	switch bank
ICM	system partition
ICU	system resources
IML	vendor-specific enabler

CONFIGURATION OVERVIEW

When assembling a computer for the first time, the technician must power up the computer and go into a SETUP program to let the computer know what hardware is installed. The **SETUP** program indicates how much RAM memory is in the computer, how many and what type of floppy drives are installed, what type of hard drive is installed, whether the computer should first boot from the hard drive, floppy drive, or CD-ROM, the current date and time, etc. A computer displays an error if the information in the SETUP program does not match the hardware.

SETUP SOFTWARE

Most computers require SETUP software to access the SETUP program that is used to configure a computer. Most often, the software is built into the ROM BIOS chip and accessed by pressing a key or a combination of keys when powering on the computer. The specific key or combination of keystrokes pressed is determined by the *manufacturer of the ROM BIOS chip*! After powering on a computer, most computers display a message stating which key(s) to press to enter the SETUP program. Configuration Table #1 shows commonly used keystroke(s) for various ROM BIOS manufacturers.

CONFIGURATION - TABLE # 1

SETUP Keystrokes

BIOS Manufacturer	Keystroke(s)
Award BIOS	CTRL+ALT+ESC or DEL
PhoenixBIOS	CTRL+ALT+S or CTRL+ALT+ESC
AMI BIOS	DEL
Zenith Computers	CTRL+ALT+INS
IBM Computers	CTRL+ALT+INS (When the cursor is in the right-hand corner of the screen), F1, or Reference Diskette
Compaq Computers	F1 or F10
Dell Computers	CTRL+ALT+ENTER or DEL
NEC Computers	F1 or F10

The ROM BIOS sometimes needs updating. Normally this requires replacing one or more chips on the motherboard. There are various reasons a computer needs an upgrade. A few reasons for a ROM BIOS upgrade include the following: support for more floppy drives or different floppy drive capacities, support for higher capacity hard drives, virus protection, password protection, problems with the current BIOS, etc.

Some older computers have a software disk that contains the SETUP program. Older Compaqs, Zeniths, IBM ATs, and some IBM PS/2 MicroChannel computers come with a SETUP program on a disk. The older IBM PS/2 SETUP disk is called a **reference disk**. Besides containing the SETUP software, the reference disk contains advanced diagnostics and special utilities for the hard drive.

Advanced diagnostics and low-level format software for the hard drive are available on the older IBM PS/2 MicroChannel reference disk by pressing the *CTRL+A* keys when the main menu appears. After accessing the SETUP program, notice the different options that appear on the menu. The directions for changing the menu options usually appear on the bottom of the screen.

CMOS MEMORY

Once the configuration is set, the information is saved into a special type of static memory on the motherboard called **CMOS (Complementary Metal Oxide Semiconductor)**. CMOS memory can run on low power for a long time. The information inside CMOS memory can be kept there for several years using a small battery. All batteries are going to die one day. When the battery dies, all configuration information in CMOS is lost and must be entered again. The SETUP information inside CMOS is the computer's *current* configuration — what the computer currently has installed.

An important record for technicians to keep in their customer files is the current settings for all the computers the technician services. If the wrong information is entered into the SETUP program and saved into CMOS, the computer will not properly operate. The correct SETUP information is crucial.

BATTERIES

Computer batteries come in various shapes and sizes. The most common battery used today is the lithium battery that looks about the size of a nickel. Look at Configuration Figure #1 for a motherboard containing a lithium battery.

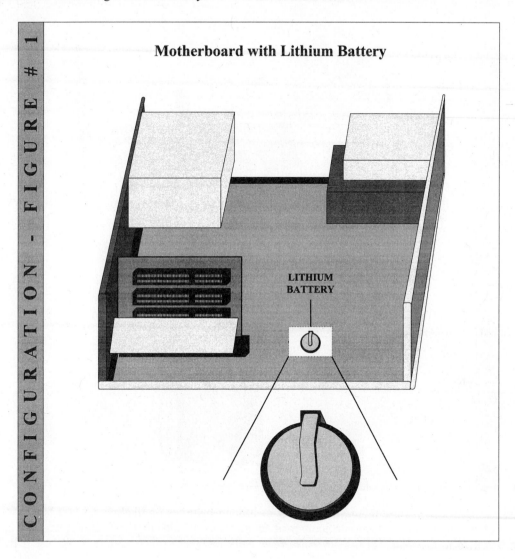

Motherboard with Lithium Battery

LITHIUM BATTERY

CONFIGURATION - FIGURE # 1

Also used in computer systems today is a 1.5 inch cylindrical battery. The battery, usually blue in color, solders onto the motherboard. Configuration Figure #2 shows this particular type of battery.

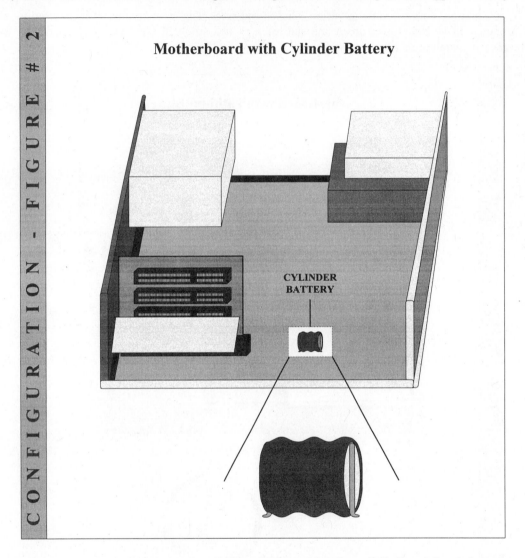

Motherboard with Cylinder Battery

CYLINDER BATTERY

CONFIGURATION - FIGURE # 2

Other computer systems use a 3.6 volt cylinder of lithium batteries or alkaline 4.5 volt batteries. AA batteries found in common electronic equipment are also used inside computers and mount in a holder held by velcro to the inside of the computer case. Still, other computer manufacturers use a battery pack.

The battery can usually be found by visual inspection of the motherboard. If the battery cannot be found on the motherboard, look for a riser board. This board extends up from the motherboard to hold expansion cards and may contain the battery.

Some computer and motherboard manufacturers use a real-time clock chip with the battery inside the chip. They are more expensive to replace than regular batteries. The real-time clock chip is commonly black, rectangular, and extends approximately 3/4 of an inch off the motherboard.

REPLACING A BATTERY

No battery lasts forever. Batteries last approximately 7 to 10 years. The newer lithium batteries last longer than their predecessors because they consume less power. Because technology allows batteries to last longer and people replace their computer in less than 7 to 10 years, batteries are not as serious an issue as before.

Before replacing a battery, check the motherboard for any evidence of battery corrosion and no battery acid has come in contact with the motherboard. If the motherboard has battery acid on it, the motherboard will probably need to be replaced. A first indication that a battery is failing is the loss of the date or time on the computer. The battery should be replaced before losing more configuration information. When batteries die, there are four options available to the technician.

Option 1:   Replace the battery with the same type if it is a battery pack or flat lithium battery obtainable from a local electronics store, computer store, or from the computer manufacturer.

Option 2:   If the battery solders onto the motherboard, look on the motherboard or in the documentation for an external battery connector usually near the existing battery. An external battery pack can be purchased at a local computer or electronics store. Many motherboards require a jumper to be set or enabled to allow the external connector to operate. Refer to the documentation for the motherboard to find this setting.

Option 3:   If the battery solders onto the motherboard and the motherboard does not allow the connection of an external battery pack, purchase a battery holder. The battery holder snaps onto the leads of the battery soldered to the motherboard. This holder permits the installation and removal of a battery while bypassing the dead battery on the motherboard. Battery holders are also sold in electronics stores.

Option 4:   If the battery solders onto the motherboard and the technician is familiar with soldering techniques, obtain a replacement battery. Disconnect the battery from the motherboard by cutting the leads to the battery and solder the new battery into place.

To replace a circular lithium battery, lift the metal tab off the battery and slide it out of the socket. Some lithium batteries are held in place by a prong that easily slides off the battery. Insert a new lithium battery into the socket or under the metal tab. Replace AA batteries in computers the same way they are replaced in a portable radio. When connecting a battery pack or battery holder, the leads that attach to the motherboard must connect properly. Refer to the motherboard documentation for the exact specifications on replacing a battery.

Always replace the battery with the proper voltage battery.

INITIAL MICROCODE LOAD (IML)

IBM uses a method called **Initial Microcode Load (IML)** which keeps the BIOS information in a hidden place on the hard drive. The machines that use IML do not have a reference disk. Instead, the same information is already pre-loaded in this special section on the hard drive. Once the information is accessed, make a backup of the configuration and the reference disk. The IML method eliminates the need for a reference disk. However, if anything ever happens to the hard drive, the only way to get back into the system is to boot from the backup reference disk. Always make a backup reference disk for an IBM computer containing the SETUP software on the hard drive.

The drawback to SETUP software on a floppy disk is if the configuration ever disappears or changes, the SETUP disk is needed to reboot. Many users lose these disks. For a technician, this is bad news, but all is not lost. The SETUP disks are frequently available from bulletin boards or across the Internet. Even for old computers, the manufacturers place the SETUP disk on their web site. Computer company Internet sites are listed in the appendix in the back of the book.

FLASH BIOS

Flash BIOS is a type of memory that computer manufacturers use as an alternative to the normal ROM BIOS chip. Systems that contain Flash BIOS on the motherboard allow updates by using a disk or downloading a file from the Internet. Flash BIOS is more expensive than the normal BIOS chip, but updates can be done quickly. Because the Flash BIOS is normally write-protected, a jumper or a switch on the motherboard sometimes must be changed to allow the update. Refer to the manual for the computer or motherboard to find the exact procedure for updating the Flash BIOS.

CONFIGURATION THROUGH SWITCHES

Some old computers such as IBM's PC and XT models do not have batteries installed; nor do they have CMOS memory or any type of SETUP program. The older computers could not keep the current date and time after powering off the computer. Instead, they use **DIP switches** to set the computer's configuration. The DIP switches are normally located on the motherboard. DIP switches are also on ISA adapters. The switches allow different configurations for the adapter. Learning how to properly set a DIP switch is important to a technician. There are two basic models of DIP switches: the slide type and the rocker type.

SLIDE TYPE DIP SWITCH

With the slide type DIP switch, a sliding tab sticks up from each switch in the bank. Each switch is normally numbered from 1 to the number of switches in the bank. Each side of the switch bank is normally labeled with either ON/OFF, 1/0, or CLOSED/OPEN. ON, 1, and CLOSED all mean the same thing; OFF, 0, and OPEN all mean the same thing. How the switch bank is labeled is up to the manufacturer of the switch bank.

To change a switch in the slide type DIP switch bank, move the tab on one switch with an ink pen or small tweaker (flat-tipped) screwdriver to one of the two positions. For example, say that a switch needs positions 5 and 8 turned ON. A technician turns the computer off, removes the computer cover, and moves the tabs in switch positions 5 and 8 to ON. Configuration Figure #3 shows an example of a slide type DIP switch with the sliding tabs in positions 5 and 8 in the ON position. Notice in Configuration Figure #3 that the switch actually has eight individual switches. The group of eight switches is sometimes called a **switch bank**.

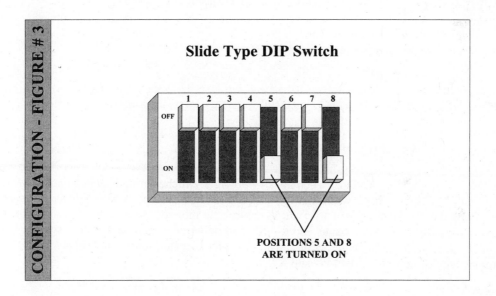

ROCKER TYPE DIP SWITCH

A rocker type DIP switch does not have a sliding tab on each switch position. Instead, each switch position has a rocker switch that presses down to either the ON position or the OFF position. To change a rocker DIP switch position, use an ink pen or small tweaker screwdriver to push *down* on one side of the rocker switch. One end of the switch will be pushed down into the switch bank and the other end will extend up from the switch bank. Whether the switch is ON or OFF, 1 or 0, or OPEN or CLOSED is determined *by the side of the rocker switch that is pushed down.* For example, Configuration Figure #4 illustrates a rocker type DIP switch with switch positions 1, 4, and 5 CLOSED (which also means ON or 1). Positions 2, 3, and 6 are OPEN (which also means OFF or 0).

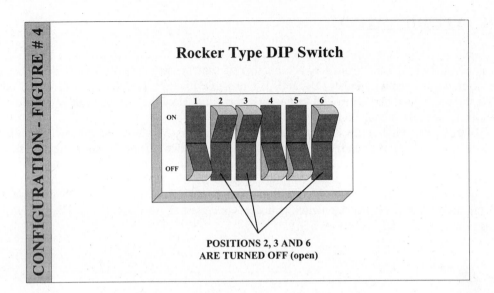

CONFIGURATION - FIGURE # 4

Rocker Type DIP Switch

POSITIONS 2, 3 AND 6
ARE TURNED OFF (open)

NEVER use a *pencil* to change a DIP switch because the pencil lead may break off into the switch. The lead is conductive. If the lead breaks off into the switch, the switch may be ruined.

PC/XT SWITCH SETTINGS

IBM's PC model has two DIP switch banks with eight switches in each switch bank. IBM's XT model has one DIP switch bank with eight switches. Different switches control different pieces of hardware. For example, switch positions 5 and 6 control the monitor attached to the computer. Even though IBM's PC had two switch banks and the XT had only one switch bank, many switches in the first switch bank control the same pieces of hardware. Reference Configuration Tables #2, #3, #4, #5, and #6 for switch settings on the IBM PC and XT.

CONFIGURATION - TABLE # 2

IBM PC & XT Floppy Drive Settings
Switch Block #1, Switch Positions 1, 7, & 8

Number of Floppy Drives Installed	Switch #1 Setting	Switch #7 Setting	Switch #8 Setting
0	ON	ON	ON
1	OFF	ON	ON
2	OFF	OFF	ON

IBM PC & XT Math Co-Processor Settings
Switch Block #1, Switch Position 2

Math Co-Processor Setting	Switch #2 Setting
Installed	OFF
Not Installed	ON

IBM PC & XT Monitor Settings
Switch Block #1, Switch Positions 5 & 6

Monitor Setting	Switch #5 Setting	Switch #6 Setting
None, EGA, or VGA	ON	ON
CGA (40 characters)	OFF	ON
CGA (80 characters)	ON	OFF
Monochrome	OFF	OFF

IBM XT Memory Settings
Switch Block #1, Switch Positions 3 & 4

Amt of Memory Installed	Switch #3 Setting	Switch #4 Setting
64K	ON	ON
128K	OFF	ON
192K	ON	OFF
256K or greater	OFF	OFF

CONFIGURATION - TABLE # 6

IBM PC Memory Settings
Switch Block #1, Switch Positions 3 & 4
Switch Block #2 Switch Positions 1, 2, 3, 4, & 5

Amt of Memory Installed	Switch Block 1		Switch Block 2				
	#3	#4	#1	#2	#3	#4	#5
16K	ON	ON	ON	ON	ON	ON	ON
32K	OFF	ON	ON	ON	ON	ON	ON
48K	ON	OFF	ON	ON	ON	ON	ON
64K	OFF	OFF	ON	ON	ON	ON	ON
96K	OFF	OFF	OFF	ON	ON	ON	ON
128K	OFF	OFF	ON	OFF	ON	ON	ON
160K	OFF	OFF	OFF	OFF	ON	ON	ON
192K	OFF	OFF	ON	ON	OFF	ON	ON
224K	OFF	OFF	OFF	ON	OFF	ON	ON
256K	OFF	OFF	ON	OFF	OFF	ON	ON
288K	OFF	OFF	OFF	OFF	OFF	ON	ON
320K	OFF	OFF	ON	ON	ON	OFF	ON
352K	OFF	OFF	OFF	ON	ON	OFF	ON
384K	OFF	OFF	ON	OFF	ON	OFF	ON
416K	OFF	OFF	OFF	OFF	ON	OFF	ON
448K	OFF	OFF	ON	ON	OFF	OFF	ON
512K	OFF	OFF	ON	OFF	OFF	OFF	ON
544K	OFF	OFF	OFF	OFF	OFF	OFF	ON
576K	OFF	OFF	ON	ON	ON	ON	OFF
608K	OFF	OFF	OFF	ON	ON	ON	OFF
640K	OFF	OFF	ON	OFF	ON	ON	OFF

(Note: Switch Block #2, Switch Positions 6, 7, & 8 are always OFF)

Many 8088-based computers have switches that use the same settings as IBM's XT computer.

· POST (Power On Self Test) runs whenever the computer cold boots. POST knows what hardware is *supposed* to be in the computer and performs a test of the installed hardware.

The wrong configuration information causes POST error codes or error messages that normally indicate a hardware problem.

Whenever working on a microcomputer with a POST error code, be certain that the user or another technician has not (1) changed the configuration SETUP or (2) removed or installed any hardware without changing the SETUP program.

ADVANCED CONFIGURATION INFORMATION

Many computers have an advanced SETUP with options such as Memory Test, Boot Sequence, Shadow RAM, Memory Speeds, NUMLOCK, Power Saver, etc. Some of the possible options list below:

Memory Test Enable/Disable: If this option is disabled, POST runs faster, but the RAM above 1MB is not tested. It is recommended to keep this option ENABLED.

Boot Sequence: This option determines if the computer first looks to the floppy drive, the hard drive, or the CD-ROM for the operating system.

Shadow RAM: This setting puts a copy of the software contained in the ROM BIOS chip into RAM. Running the ROM BIOS software out of RAM speeds up a system because accessing the information in RAM is faster than accessing it from the ROM chip. Also, some manufacturers allow the shadowing of the video adapter's ROM chip. It is recommended to shadow both ROM chips when possible.

NUMLOCK ON/OFF: Use the NUMLOCK setting to determine if the system sees the keypad keys as numbers (ON) or as cursor movement keys (OFF). The setting for this depends on the user. If the user inputs numbers frequently, set the setting to ON.

Memory Speeds: Some computer systems allow the memory speed settings changed for the RAM memory chips installed. It is recommended to leave them at their current setting.

Power Saver: The Power Saver option, when enabled, turns the system off after a certain amount of non-usage.

Power-on Password: A password required to boot the computer can be set with this option. Computer users need passwords when computer security is an issue. Some motherboards have pins that, when jumpered together, remove the power-on password. Contact the computer, motherboard, or BIOS manufacturer for the exact procedure for removing the power-on password.

The options available in SETUP and Advanced SETUP are machine-dependent due to the different ROM BIOS chips and the different chipsets installed on the motherboard. Refer to the computer or motherboard documentation for the meaning of each option!

OTHER CONFIGURATION PARAMETERS

Other possible parameters contained and set via the SETUP program are DMA (Direct Memory Access) channels, Interrupts, and I/O (Input/Output) addresses. These parameters are assigned to individual adapters and ports such as disk controllers, and the serial, parallel, and mouse ports. The same port assignments may also be configured through the individual adapter. Another parameter that can be set for an adapter is a ROM address. ROM addresses are covered in the Memory chapter. No matter how the parameters are assigned, collectively they are known as **system resources**. The system resources mentioned here are not the same term used when discussing Windows 3.x and Windows 95.

DMA (DIRECT MEMORY ACCESS) CHANNELS

A **DMA channel** is a number assigned to an adapter. The DMA assignment allows the adapter to bypass the microprocessor and directly communicate with the RAM chips. Transferring the data directly to memory speeds up data transfers. Devices that frequently take advantage of DMA are drives, tape backup units, and multimedia adapters such as sound cards. A drawback to DMA transfers is the microprocessor may be put on hold until the DMA data transfer is complete. Well-written software allows the microprocessor to function periodically during the DMA operation.

Older computers have four DMA channels labeled 0, 1, 2, and 3. DMA channel 0 is normally reserved for transfers to the RAM chips. Four DMA channels are controlled by a single DMA controller chip. Today's computers normally have two DMA controller chips, giving a total of eight DMA channels. DMA channel 4 is normally reserved for connecting the two DMA controller chips.

Due to backward compatibility issues, DMA operates at a maximum of 8MHz for an ISA slot. Any installed ISA adapter can have DMA capabilities. Even an adapter installed in a Pentium Pro-based computer completes direct transfers to memory at a maximum speed of 8MHz. A better capability than DMA is bus-mastering. A bus-mastering adapter takes control of the bus similar to how the microprocessor takes control. Bus-mastering adapters frequently have their own processor specific to the adapter's function. Bus-mastering capabilities are much more efficient than DMA. Configuration Table #7 summarizes the commonly used DMA channels.

CONFIGURATION - TABLE #7	Common DMA Channel Assignments		
	DMA	**PC/XT (8088)**	**286 and Higher**
	0	Reserved for DRAM refresh	Reserved for DRAM refresh
	1	Available	Available
	2	Floppy disk controller	Floppy disk controller
	3	Hard drive controller	Available
	4	Not available	Not available (connection to 2nd DMA controller)
	5	Not available	Available
	6	Not available	Available
	7	Not available	Available

Assign DMA channels through the SETUP program or through the adapter or the device installation process by setting jumpers/switches or running the configuration software.

 No two devices or adapters should have the same DMA channel number!

I/O (INPUT/OUTPUT) ADDRESSES

I/O addresses, otherwise known as input/output addresses, or port addresses allow the device and the microprocessor to exchange data. The I/O address is like a mailbox number. The device places data (mail) in the box for the microprocessor to pick up. The microprocessor delivers the data to the appropriate device through the same I/O address (mail box number). I/O addresses are simply addresses for the microprocessor to distinguish between the devices with which it communicates. Configuration Table #8 lists common I/O addresses used in microcomputers.

Common I/O Addresses

I/O Address	Device or Port
000-00Fh	DMA Controller (Channels 0-3)
020-021h	Interrupt Controller 1
040-043h	System timers—clocks
060h	Keyboard
070h, 071h	Real time clock/CMOS/NMI mask
081-083h & 087h	DMA Page Register (0-3)
089-08Bh & 08Fh	DMA Page Register (4-7)
0A0-0A1h	Interrupt Controller 2
0C0-0DEh	DMA Controller (Channels 4-7)
0F0-0FFh	Math Co-processor
108-12Fh	Available (may be reserved on some systems)
150-1EFh	Available (may be reserved on some systems)
170-177h	Secondary hard disk controller on some systems
1F0-1F7h	Primary hard disk controller on some systems
200-207h	Game port
20C-20Dh	Reserved
21Fh	Reserved
278-27Fh	LPT2: or LPT3:
2B0-2DFh	Alternate EGA port
2E8-2EFh	COM4:
2F8-2FFh	COM2:
370-377h	Secondary disk drive adapter
378-37Fh	LPT1: or LPT2:
3B0-3BFh	Monochrome video adapter
3BC-30Fh	1st parallel port on mono video adapter
3C0-3CFh	EGA adapter
3D0-3DFh	CGA adapter
3E8-3EFh	COM3:
3F0-3F7h	Primary disk adapter
3F8-3FFh	COM1:

CONFIGURATION - TABLE # 8

Every device *must* have a different I/O address; there are no exceptions!

I/O addresses are shown in hexadecimal format. Hexadecimal numbers are 0, 1, 2, 3, 4, 5, 6, 7, 8, and 9 just like the decimal numbers we normally use, but hexadecimal numbers include A, B, C, D, E, and F. The decimal number 10 is A in hexadecimal, 11 is B, 12 is C, 13 is D, 14 is E, and 15 is F. An example of an I/O address is 390h where the small "h" denotes hexadecimal. Configuration Table #8 uses this method. Also, notice that Configuration Table #8's left column lists a range of I/O addresses. Devices normally need more than one hexadecimal address location. The number of extra addresses depends on the individual device and what business it does with the microprocessor. In manuals or documentation for a device or adapter, a technician might see the adapter has an I/O address range instead of just one I/O address. Configuration Table #8 lists what I/O addresses *can* be used in computers. The manufacturer of the computer or an adapter can specifically set the I/O address or allow different I/O addresses to be set. I/O addresses are set for some devices and ports through the computer's SETUP program. Other added devices are configured by setting jumpers/switches or through installation software included with the device or adapter.

The important thing to remember is every device must have a separate I/O address or the microprocessor cannot distinguish between each installed device. Technicians need to document the I/O addresses used in a system before adding a new device or troubleshooting a newly installed device. I/O address conflicts are a frequent source of problems.

One problem for technicians is some documentation and SETUP programs only give the starting hexadecimal I/O address and not the ending I/O address. The range of addresses the adapter uses can conflict with another adapter or device. The only resolution is for the technician to change the I/O address on one of the two conflicting devices or adapters and try the devices again. With poor documentation, this is a hit or miss scenario.

INTERRUPT REQUEST (IRQ)

Imagine being in a room of twenty students and four students want the teacher's attention. If all four students talk at once, the teacher is overloaded and not able to respond to the four individuals' needs. Instead, a teacher needs an orderly process of acknowledging each request, prioritizing the request (which student gets to go first), and then answering each question. The same thing happens inside a microcomputer when multiple devices want the attention of the microprocessor. For example, which device gets to go first if pressing a key on the keyboard and moving the mouse simultaneously? The answer lies in what interrupt request number the keyboard and the mouse each have. Every device requests permission to do something by interrupting the microprocessor. The microprocessor must have a priority system to handle such situations.

The priority system the microprocessor uses to handle device requests is through the use of interrupts. An **interrupt** or **IRQ** (Interrupt ReQuest) is a number assigned to each expansion adapter or port so orderly communication can occur between the device or port and the microprocessor. The

IRQ number is a priority system for the microprocessor. For example, if you press a key on a keyboard and move the mouse simultaneously, which device first gets the attention of the microprocessor? The answer lies in the IRQ number assigned to each device. The keyboard, by the way, has the highest priority.

IBM's PC and XT computers had only 8 interrupts available, IRQs 0 through 7. Today's computers have 16 interrupts numbered 0 through 15. The chip that controls the interrupts is known as the interrupt controller chip. In a system with 16 interrupts, two interrupt controller chips are on the motherboard. Two methods of operation exist with the interrupt controller chips: cascaded and non-cascaded interrupts.

In a system that uses **cascaded interrupts**, the interrupt controller chip that handles IRQs 0-7 uses IRQ2 to cascade, or bridge over, to the other interrupt controller chip's IRQ9. All interrupts handled by the second interrupt controller chip go to the microprocessor through IRQ9 which bridges to IRQ2 on the first interrupt controller chip. For example, if an adapter or device has the interrupt IRQ12, the interrupt request goes to IRQ9 on the second interrupt controller chip over to IRQ2 on the first interrupt controller chip, and then on to the microprocessor. Configuration Figure #5 shows the concept of two interrupt controller chips using cascaded interrupts.

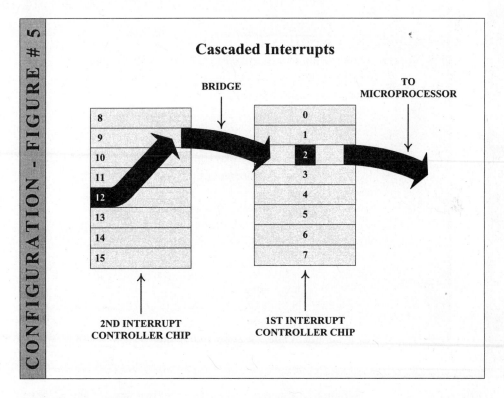

Notice in Configuration Figure #5 how IRQ12 travels across the bridge located at IRQ9 and IRQ2 to get its request to the microprocessor.

The computer's real time clock that keeps all operations running always uses IRQ0. IRQ0 has the highest priority of all interrupts. IRQ1 has the next highest priority, then IRQ2. The next highest priority depends on whether the system uses cascaded interrupts. Any interrupt handled by the second interrupt controller chip gets the priority level as if it was IRQ2. So, if an adapter has an interrupt level of 15, that adapter has a higher priority over an adapter with an interrupt level of IRQ5 to the system using cascaded interrupts. Still, on the second interrupt controller chip, a priority system exists. For example, IRQ12 has a higher priority than IRQ15.

     Non-cascaded interrupts occur when the computer has two interrupt controller chips not bridged together. Each chip handles eight interrupts that connect directly to the microprocessor. With non-cascaded interrupts, the lower a device's IRQ number, the higher its priority is to the microprocessor. Configuration Table #9 lists commonly assigned interrupts or IRQs in computers.

CONFIGURATION - TABLE # 9

Common Interrupt Assignments

IRQ	Usage
0	System timer
1	Keyboard controller
2	In 286 & higher that uses cascaded interrupts, bridges to IRQs 8-15
3	COM2: & COM4:
4	COM1: & COM3:
5	In 8088 & 8086 computers is used for hard drive controller. Sometimes used for second parallel port (LPT2:).
6	Floppy disk controller
7	First printer port (LPT1:)
8	Not available in 8088 & 8086 computers; used for real time clock in 286 and higher computers.
9	Not available in 8088 & 8086 computers; used as a link to IRQ2 in 80286 and higher computers that use cascaded interrupts.
10	Not available in 8088 & 8086 computers.
11	Not available in 8088 & 8086 computers.
12	Not available in 8088 & 8086 computers; PS/2 mouse port in 80286 and higher computers.
13	Not available in 8088 & 8086 computers; math co-processor in 80286 and higher computers.
14	Not available in 8088 & 8086 computers; hard disk controller in 80286 and higher computers.
15	Not available in 8088 & 8086 computers.

     Different interrupts are assigned to adapters and devices. No two devices should have the same interrupt. However, two serial devices can share the same interrupt *if* they have different I/O addresses. More detail is given in the Serial Devices chapter.

     Interrupts for some ports and devices can be set through the system's SETUP program. Other adapters and device interrupts are set by enabling or disabling switches or jumpers, or by running a SETUP program included with the adapter or device. A good feature to look for in an adapter is the ability to have several interrupts to choose from when installing it in a system.

DMA channels, interrupts, and I/O addresses are a source of many headaches for a technician. Documentation and utility programs are the best source of relief. Documentation for adapters is few and far between when working on a computer. Even if available, the documentation is frequently hard to read, has mislabeled settings, contains incomplete information, and is simply inadequate. Utility programs are frequently the only source of information to help with DMA, IRQ, and I/O address conflicts. However, be advised, no utility program detects all adapter and device configuration information. Always try several utility programs, documentation, and vendor technical support and ASSUME NOTHING!

UTILITIES

Some computers have their own utility programs that show the interrupt, DMA, and I/O address information. Refer to the computer's documentation for directions on accessing the program. DiagSoft's QA Info is another program available with some computers, devices, and adapters sold today. The QA Info software shows hardware configuration, IRQ, DMA, and I/O address information.

Because Microsoft DOS and Windows 3.x have a utility called MSD (Microsoft Diagnostics), many technicians rely on this utility tool. MSD allows the viewing of IRQs and some port I/O addresses. Other utilities used by technicians in resolving DMA, IRQ, and I/O address conflicts include Symantec's Norton Utilities' SYSINFO, Helix Software Corporation's Nuts & Bolts, and Touchstone Software Corporations CheckIt. Public domain software such as Steve Grant's SYSID and Snooper are also available for technicians.

CONFIGURATION ACCORDING TO ARCHITECTURE OR LOCAL BUS

ISA, EISA, and MCA adapters must be configured for the proper interrupt, I/O address, and DMA channel. The method of configuration normally depends on the system architecture. The same is true for VL-bus and PCI adapters. However, even though there are standards, the manufacturer of the adapter has the final word on configuration issues. Always refer to the adapter's documentation to find the correct configuration method.

CONFIGURATION OF ISA ADAPTERS

Some ISA adapters' interrupt, I/O addresses, or DMA channels are configured with jumpers and/or switches. Not all adapters are able to use DMA, nor do the manufacturers of the adapters allow choosing the interrupt and I/O addresses for a particular adapter. However, this is not normally the case for today's ISA adapters due to the potential conflicts this can cause. A manufacturer of an adapter for today's computers wants to have as many combinations of interrupts and I/O addresses as possible so the adapter is useable in any system.

Other ISA adapters come with configuration software on a disk. The configuration software allows different settings and saves the configuration to the adapter. This method of configuration is much easier for a technician. The only drawback is sometimes the disk is misplaced or thrown away. However, most manufacturers have the configuration software available on their web site.

Some manufacturers stencil the possible jumper or switch settings right on the adapter. Other manufacturers still rely on paper documentation that ships with the adapter. Adapter documentation is frequently available through the Internet. Technicians must become familiar with using the Internet to download documentation, support files, and software drivers needed to configure ISA adapters. An appendix of common technical sites for drivers and support files is at the back of the book.

Steps for Installing ISA adapters:

1. Use an anti-static wrist strap when handling adapters. Electrostatic Discharge, ESD, can damage electronic parts. (See the Disassembly/Reassembly chapter for more details on ESD.)
2. Gather information about the computer in which the adapter is being installed such as interrupts, I/O addresses, and the DMA channel used by the adapters previously installed.
3. If necessary, set the appropriate (non-conflicting) interrupt, I/O address, or DMA channel on the adapter being installed by referring to the adapter's documentation.
4. Be sure the computer is powered off.
5. Attach any internal device cables that connect to the adapter, if necessary.
6. Install the ISA adapter in a free expansion slot. Remove any brackets from the case or plastic covers from the rear of the computer that may prevent adapter installation.
7. Attach any cables that go to an external port on the adapter, if necessary.
8. Attach any external or internal devices to the opposite ends of the cable, if necessary.
9. Power on any external devices connected to the ISA adapter, if applicable.
10. Power on the computer.
11. If the adapter requires configuration software, refer to the adapter's documentation and load the software. Configure the adapter so it does not conflict with other installed devices.
12. Load any application software or device drivers needed for the devices attached to the ISA adapter.
13. Test the devices connected to the ISA adapter.

Configuring adapters by setting jumpers or switches is very time consuming. Reduce the time required to configure the adapter by doing the initial investigation of interrupts, I/O address, and DMA channels *before* installing the adapter!

CONFIGURATION OF MCA ADAPTERS

IBM's MicroChannel computers are configured through software. Three instances to access the configuration software are (1) an adapter or device is added or removed, (2) a re-configuration such as changing the interrupt or I/O address for a port, and (3) documentation of the current configuration. MicroChannel adapters are configured through software that ships on a disk with the adapter. The MicroChannel configuration files end in an .ADF extension. These files are text files and may be viewed with any text editor such as the MS-DOS EDIT program. The configuration file included with a MCA adapter adds to the MicroChannel computer's current configuration through configuration software. The MicroChannel computer has two methods to access the software used to configure the computer: (1) a reference disk and (2) a special partition on the hard drive called the IML (Initial Microcode Loader). Older MicroChannel computers include a reference disk that is unique for each IBM computer model. A reference disk for an IBM PS/2 Model 60 will *not* work in an IBM PS/2 Model 55. To access the configuration software, insert a backup copy of the reference disk into the A:

drive. Then, power on the computer or perform a warm boot. Once the computer boots from the reference disk, the adapter's configuration file must be added to the existing configuration software.

Always make a backup of the reference disk in case of damage or loss of the original disk. Also, if adding any adapters to the MicroChannel computer, the software that configures the adapter must be added to the reference disk. The original IBM reference disk does not allow writing to the original reference disk. The write-protect feature is permanently enabled.

Newer MicroChannel computers use the IML (Initial Microcode Load) process. The IML process loads software normally in the ROM BIOS from a special partition (section) on the hard drive or from a disk. A ROM BIOS chip is still used, but not as much information is stored there. The special section or partition on the hard drive in the newer MicroChannel computers is called the **system partition**. In addition to the IML boot record (formerly kept in the ROM BIOS), the system partition contains the system programs. The system programs include the diagnostic software, SETUP software, and software to backup the system partition. The systems programs that IBM previously shipped on the reference disk are now in the system partition.

Access the system partition by warm booting (CTRL+ALT+DEL) or cold booting the computer. A cursor appears in the upper left corner of the screen. When the cursor moves to the right corner, press the CTRL+ALT+INS keys to access the system programs software. Use this same procedure when installing MicroChannel adapters.

Steps for installing MicroChannel adapters:

1. Use an anti-static wrist strap when handling adapters.
2. Gather information about the computer in which the adapter will be installed such as interrupts, I/O addresses, and DMA channel currently used by adapters in the system. Even though the MicroChannel architecture allows the sharing of interrupts, set each adapter to a different interrupt for the best results.
3. Verify the computer is powered off.
4. Install any necessary internal cables that connect to the adapter.
5. Install the MCA adapter in an available expansion slot. Remove any brackets from the case or possible plastic covers from the rear of the computer.
6. Attach any cable that connects to the adapter's external port, if necessary.
7. Attach any external or internal devices to the other ends of the cable as necessary.
8. Power on any external devices connected to the MCA adapter, if applicable.
9. Power on the computer. A POST error code will appear. If the MCA computer is an older one that requires a reference disk, insert the disk into the floppy drive. If the MCA computer uses the IML, the computer automatically goes into the SETUP software.
10. Once the SETUP software loads, a prompt appears stating a configuration change occurred and asks if the system should be automatically configured. Choose **N** for No.
11. From the main menu, choose **Copy an Option Disk** and follow the directions given on the screen. This option copies the adapter software to the reference disk or the system partition. If using a reference disk, the reference disk and the adapter's option disk may need to be alternately inserted into the floppy drive several times until the .ADF file finally copies onto the reference disk. If using a computer with the IML, only the option disk is necessary.
12. At the main menu, choose the **Set Configuration** option.
13. From the Set Configuration menu, choose the **Run Automatic Configuration** option.
14. Press **Y** for Yes so the system will configure itself for the new adapter.

When using a MCA computer with an IML, after the option disk copies, make another backup of the system partition that contains the reference disk software!

Whenever configuring a MicroChannel computer and prompted from the SETUP software to Automatically configure the computer (Y/N)?, most users press *Y* for Yes. Pressing *Y* for Yes is a nice and easy feature, but beware of this option. In a networked environment, this option can configure a TokenRing adapter to the wrong speed. Also, conflicts between certain adapters such as external 5.25" and 3270 emulation adapters are not automatically detected. Sometimes the best option is to choose *N* for No and go into the **Change Configuration** menu and set the configuration settings manually. Verify that the settings save before exiting the configuration software.

Steps for backing up the System Partition on a MicroChannel computer:
1.   Enter the system partition programs by pressing **CTRL+ALT+DEL** on the keyboard.
2.   The cursor will move from the upper left to the upper right corner of the screen. While the cursor is on the right side, press **CTRL+ALT+INS**. The main menu appears.
3.   From the main menu, choose the **Backup/Restore System Programs** option.
4.   From the Backup/Restore System Programs menu, choose the **Backup the System Partition** option.
5.   Follow the instructions on the screen for inserting a blank disk, etc.
6.   After the backup of the system partition is made, press **ENTER**.
7.   Press **F3** to return to the main menu.
8.   Press **F3** again to exit the software and reboot the computer.

CONFIGURATION OF EISA ADAPTERS

Some EISA adapters are also configured with software like the MicroChannel adapters. However, instead of a filename extension .ADF like the MCA adapters, EISA configuration files have the filename extension .CFG. Most EISA adapters are set up through software. However, some EISA adapters still require setting jumpers or switches to configure the adapter. A technician must refer to the documentation included with the EISA adapter for configuration information.

Some EISA systems come with a configuration disk or the software used to configure the EISA computer may be pre-loaded on the hard drive. Either way, make a backup of the configuration software. When executed, it shows the current configuration held in CMOS, searches for any EISA adapters, allows new EISA adapter configuration files to be added, and writes the new configuration information to CMOS. An EISA adapter installs into a system in an EISA expansion slot using the same procedures as with any adapter. Start the EISA configuration utility software. The .CFG configuration file that ships with the adapter is added to the configuration software. The new adapter configures through the configuration software. Then, the settings save to CMOS and the computer reboots. Always refer to the EISA computer documentation as well as the adapter's documentation to find complete installation instructions.

When you configure an EISA system, the computer manufacturer sometimes recommends removing the ISA adapters from the system for initial configuration. However, this is not feasible if the ISA adapter is the video adapter.

CONFIGURATION OF VL-BUS ADAPTERS

VL-bus adapters normally configure through jumpers and switches or through software. VL-bus adapters have connectors for (1) the traditional buses: ISA, EISA, or MCA and (2) the VL-bus connector. The part of the VL connector that is the traditional connector is what establishes connection for the ISA, EISA, or MCA resources such as interrupts and DMA channels which is *not* provided by the VL-bus. Most VL-bus cards are an extension of ISA and therefore configured through jumpers and switches as traditional ISA adapters are configured. Some manufacturers have developed their own software SETUP utilities. Always refer to the VL-bus adpater's documentation for installation instructions and watch out for the same old interrupt and I/O address conflicts.

PLUG AND PLAY (PnP)

Plug and Play (PnP) is one of the latest configuration techniques on the market. Plug and Play is a software and hardware standard designed to make hardware installation easier. The system board and ROM BIOS chip must support Plug and Play to use it. Plug and Play works with existing ISA, EISA, MCA, PCMCIA (PC Card), or PCI adapters and devices. Windows 95 fully supports Plug and Play whereas Windows NT only minimally supports it — there may be extra steps in a Windows NT environment. Even if a system has Plug and Play capabilities, older adapters must still be configured manually.

A Plug and Play device or adapter has built-in registers reached through a set of three I/O port addresses so the ROM BIOS or operating system can control the configuration. In a fully compatible Plug and Play computer, both the BIOS and the operating system support Plug and Play. The ROM BIOS has the ability to control the Plug and Play adapters, determine the resources the adapter requires, and resolve conflicts between devices. Some Plug and Play computers allow choices through the SETUP program: (1) all Plug and Play adapters and devices are BIOS-configured and activated or (2) the Plug and Play adapters are checked by the BIOS, but only the adapters needed to boot the machine are activated. If SETUP does not allow a choice of these two options, assume the ROM BIOS does not configure the Plug and Play adapter unless the adapter is necessary for booting the computer. When the ROM BIOS does not configure the Plug and Play adapters, the operating system configures the adapters.

If a Plug and Play adapter boots the computer (such as the video or drive adapter), the adapter starts up in an active mode. The adapter comes online similar to conventional boards using resources assigned as power-on defaults. Because the video and hard drive adapters start the system, traditional conflicts with interrupts, I/O addresses, etc. can still be a problem even if the adapters are Plug and Play. Other Plug and Play adapters that do not activate during the boot-up process stay inactive until the operating system activates them.

Plug and Play helps with some installation problems, but vendors implement the Plug and Play features in different ways. Most manufacturers offer Plug and Play cards that can operate in a computer with a Plug and Play BIOS as well as in the old (non-Plug and Play BIOS) computers. This is usually accomplished through a software utility provided by the manufacturer. Intel has a generic Plug and Play configuration driver for the DOS/Windows environment called **ICM (Intel Configuration Manager)**. ICM detects and configures installed Plug and Play adapters. The configuration manager takes control over the BIOS and system resource assignments.

The configuration manager is only needed if the ROM BIOS *does not* support Plug and Play. Intel Configuration Manager is a TSR (memory resident program) that competes for memory space in the DOS/Windows environment. Refer to the memory chapter if memory errors occur when the ICM software loads.

Another generic utility developed by Intel for Plug and Play cards in the DOS/Windows environment is the **ICU (ISA Configuration Utility)**. ICU allows the viewing and modification of legacy (non-Plug and Play) card resources such as interrupts, I/O addresses, and DMA channels. The ISA Configuration Utility configures an ISA card instead of using jumpers or switches. Many vendors recommend the use of the ICU program and include installation steps in their adapter manual.

All devices and adapters, whether ISA, EISA, MCA, VL-Bus, PCI, or Plug and Play, require configuration of some sort. Plug and Play cannot always resolve all the system resource conflicts. Even if a BIOS and an operating system support Plug and Play, not all adapters within the system may support Plug and Play. The Plug and Play software may not determine the traditional (non-Plug and Play) adapter's resources. Ensuring all devices and adapters inside the computer are at a DMA channel, an I/O address, and an interrupt that no other device possesses has always been a challenge to technicians. Nothing beats good adapter, device, and computer documentation. However, never forget that documentation is not always accurate — it lies sometimes and cannot be trusted. Question everything and always contact the manufacturer of the device or adapter for better documentation or clarification.

CONFIGURATION OF PCI ADAPTERS

PCI adapters are the easiest adapters to configure. They do not have problems with interrupt conflicts because the PCI standard allows interrupt sharing. A PCI device configures through the ROM BIOS and system SETUP software as well as through software provided with the PCI adapter. PCI adapters have special storage registers on the adapter that store the configuration information. Furthermore, the PCI standard lends itself to Plug and Play. Most PCI adapters are Plug and Play. Keep in mind, a few of even the latest PCI cards are not Plug and Play. When installing a PCI adapter, always refer to the documentation for installation instructions.

If installing a PCI adapter in a DOS/Windows environment, normally the configuration software for the adapter is used. If installing a PCI adapter in a Windows 95 environment, the Windows 95 operating system will detect the installation of the adapter. After detection, Windows 95 adds the adapter's configuration information to the Windows 95 registry. The Windows 95 **registry** is a central database which holds hardware information and other data. All software applications access the registry for configuration information instead of going to the adapter. In a Plug and Play operating system, the system prompts for either the operating system disks or CD, or for a software disk from the PCI adapter manufacturer. Windows NT does not fully support Plug and Play, but PCI adapters still work well. Windows NT does not always automatically detect an adapter's installation. However after adding the configuration information to Windows NT's registry, applications know the adapter's resources. Like Windows 95, applications running under Windows NT access the registry instead of going to the adapter or to the BIOS. No matter which method of configuration is used, it is still simpler than traditional ISA adapter configuration.

CONFIGURATION OF ADAPTERS USING WINDOWS 95

Windows 95 supports Plug and Play and works in conjunction with a Plug and Play BIOS to automatically configure Plug and Play adapters. Windows 95 attempts to make hardware installation easier and it keeps track of the computer's configuration. When Windows 95 boots, it compares the saved configuration with what is detected during initialization. If adding or removing any hardware, Windows 95's Add New Hardware Wizard appears or is used. This wizard lets Windows 95 search for the new piece of hardware or one can specifically set the type of device or adapter.

The Add New Hardware Wizard is accessible using several methods. One way to access it is through the Control Panel option (accessed through Start menu's Settings option). The Add New Hardware icon is in the Control Panel window. Double-clicking on the icon starts the wizard. Once the Next button is clicked, the first question asked by the wizard is if Windows 95 should search for the new hardware. If the Yes option is chosen, then Windows 95 searches for the new hardware and the directions for installation appears in the windows throughout the entire process. If the No option is chosen, then a list of hardware types appears in a window. Click on the specific hardware category, click on the Next button, and follow the directions on the screen. Letting Windows 95 search for the new hardware can be a time-consuming process. If one is familiar with installing hardware, select the No option and pick the hardware category to save time. Also, selecting the No option may save some time because Windows 95 may select system resources that conflict with other devices installed in the system.

Whether or not Windows 95 searches for the new hardware, for optimum adapter performance, use the Windows 95 driver provided with the adapter. If no Windows 95 driver exists, check with the adapter manufacturer's web site to see if a Windows 95 driver exists or a new version of the driver is available. The following Windows 95 exercise shows how to examine system resources.

CONFIGURATION OF PC CARD (PCMCIA) ADAPTERS

PC Cards also support Plug and Play and can be used for a variety of purposes: network interface adapters, memory expansion, hard drive, floppy drive, CD-ROM drive access, applications, video, etc. PC Cards require different layers of software to allow them to operate. The most basic PC Card software is **socket services**. Socket services software can be a piece of software called a driver or a device driver. A **device driver** is a small piece of software that allows an operating system to access a piece of hardware. In the DOS environment, a device driver loads through the CONFIG.SYS file. In the Windows 95 environment, a device driver loads through the CONFIG.SYS file or through the VMM32.VxD file which loads any virtual device drivers referenced in the registry.

Socket services allow each PC Card type to co-exist in the same system. Socket services software is similar to the software contained in the ROM BIOS chip. In fact, some computer manufacturers place the socket services software in the ROM BIOS chip. Check the computer's documentation on the procedures for loading or enabling socket services.

The important thing to remember about socket services is the driver must match your computer system. A socket services driver from another laptop computer may not work in a different computer.

The second layer of software for PC Cards is **card services**. This software is included with operating systems such as PC DOS, MS DOS, OS/2, and Windows 95. The card services software normally loads through the CONFIG.SYS file although it can be an executable file run through a batch file. Some card services' software files are quite large in size. For this reason, many laptop computers require multiple boot options. For example, the computer can have a boot option if the computer is used with a network. Another boot option is available if the computer is used as a stand-alone computer. The pieces of software needed for each scenario will load and the other software drivers for the other scenarios do not load.

Socket services software loads before the card services software. To operate, the card services software uses the socket services software. Some computers and some PC Cards support hot swapping. Hot swapping allows the PC Card to insert into the slot when the computer is powered on. Both the computer and the PC Card must support hot swapping for automatic configuration to occur. Whether or not hot swapping is possible, each PC Card takes up system resources such as memory addresses, interrupts, etc., as other adapters do. Card services manage the allocation of system resources and keep PC Cards from interfering with one another. However, the system resources allocated to PC Cards may interfere with adapters other than PC Cards. For this reason, a third piece of software may be necessary: an enabler (sometimes called a super driver). A **generic enabler** can operate with different PC Cards and allows assignment of interrupts and I/O addresses. PC Card manufacturers can provide a vendor-specific enabler with their specific PC Card. **Vendor-specific enablers** operate with one specific PC Card and require socket services and card services software.

Problems can occur if a generic enabler and a vendor-specific enabler load in the same computer. If the PC Card can be configured by the generic enabler, do not load the vendor-specific enabler. The exception to this rule is if the PC Card is the only PC Card in the system. Contact the manufacturer of the vendor-specific enabler first if problems occur. Also, the Internet is a wonderful source of information for situations like this.

The last type of PC Card software is a point enabler. A **point enabler** is similar to the vendor-specific enabler in that the software is for a specific PC Card. A point enabler is different from the vendor-specific enabler as the point enabler software *does not* require socket services or card services software. This is good if memory management is a problem. The point enabler software ignores any loaded socket services or card services software. However, any other adapters that use socket services and card services software may not work.

Point enablers should be used only if the PC Card is the only PC Card installed in the computer.

Configuration Figure #6 illustrates how all the software pieces fit together to communicate with the PC Card. Keep in mind the illustration is an overview and not the final say for how to configure a PC Card. Always refer to the computer and PC Card documentation for instructions on how to configure and install the adapter.

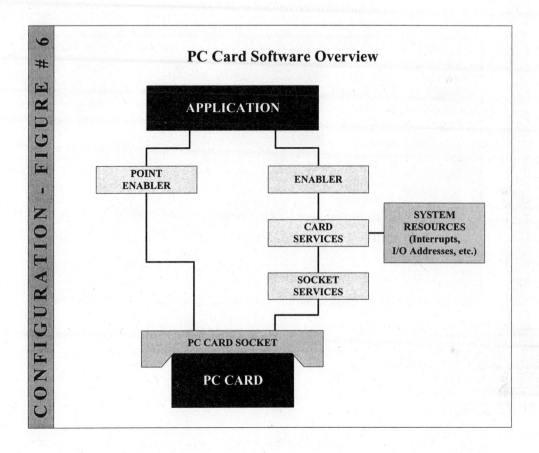

Configuration Table #10 summarizes some of the lessons learned in Chapter 2 and Chapter 3.

CONFIGURATION - TABLE # 10

Computer Standards Overview

Standard	Data Path	Bus Frequency	Bus Mastering	Plug & Play Setup Possible?
ISA	16-bit	8/10 MHz	No	Yes
MCA	16/32-bit (64-bit possible using streaming technique)	10 MHz	Yes	No
EISA	32-bit	8/10 MHz	Yes	No
VL-bus	32-bit	25/33 MHz	Yes	Yes
PCI	32/64-bit	33/66 MHz	Yes	Yes
PC Card	16/32-bit	33 MHz	Yes	Yes

Name _____

Configuration Review Questions

1. What is the purpose of a SETUP program?

2. What is the best source to find out how to enter the SETUP program?

3. What is the difference between ROM BIOS and CMOS?

4. What component keeps the information in CMOS memory even when the computer is powered off?

5. List two things to remember when replacing a battery inside a microcomputer.

6. What is one indication a battery is beginning to fail?

7. A failing battery is soldered to the motherboard. How will you handle the problem?

8. Can you replace a computer battery with one that has a higher voltage?

9. Can you replace a computer battery with one that has a lower voltage?

10. Using Configuration Exercise Figure #1, determine how the switches would be changed if positions 1, 2, and 6 are the only positions to be *enabled*.

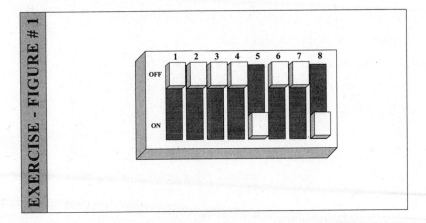

11. If a switch block like the one shown in Exercise Figure #1 had switch positions 2, 5, 6, 7 & 8 *enabled* on an 8088 motherboard, how many floppy drives are installed in the system? Use Configuration Tables 2, 3, 4, 5, and 6 to answer this question.

12.   Using Configuration Exercise Figure #2, determine which side of each switch position is pressed down if positions 1, 3, 4, & 6 are to be *disabled*?

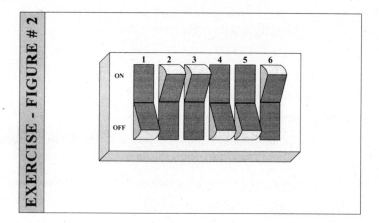

13.   If a switch block like the one shown in Exercise Figure #2 had switch positions 2, 5, 6, 7 & 8 *enabled* on an 8088 motherboard, what type of monitor is installed in the system? Use Configuration Tables #2, #3, #4, #5, and #6 to answer this question.

14.   What DMA channel is frequently used to connect to the second DMA controller?

15.   T/F   Entering the wrong SETUP information can cause a POST error.

16.   How many DMA channels do today's computers have?

17.   List one disadvantage to using a DMA channel.

18.   What is the common I/O address for the COM1: serial port?

19.   What is the common I/O address for the LPT1: parallel port?

20.   What is the decimal number 14 in hexadecimal?

21.   T/F   Every device must have a separate I/O address to communicate with the microprocessor.

22.   In a system that uses cascaded interrupts, what priority level does an adapter set to IRQ14 receive when communicating with the microprocessor?

23.   Why don't video adapters normally have an IRQ assigned to them?

24.   What interrupt is normally assigned a hard drive controller in today's computers?

25.   Why are utilities important when assigning system resources?

26.   Which of the following allow the adapter to be configured using software? (pick all that apply)
      A.   ISA
      B.   EISA
      C.   MCA
      D.   VL-bus
      E.   PCI
      F.   PC Card

27.   What makes a computer Plug and Play compatible?

28.   When would a technician need to use Intel's ICM software?

29.   Which adapters [ISA, EISA, MCA, VL-bus, PCI] are the easiest to configure?

30.   T/F   Using Plug and Play always ensures no interrupt or I/O address conflicts exist within a
      system.

31.   T/F   If a ROM BIOS chip supports Plug and Play, on boot up, the ROM BIOS chip searches
      the system for Plug and Play adapters and assigns each unique system resources.

32.   Describe the difference between ICM software and ICU software used to configure Plug and
      Play devices.

33.   T/F   ISA adapters do not support Plug and Play.

34.   What is the purpose of the Windows 95 Add New Hardware Wizard?

35.   Describe the difference between PC Card socket services and card services software.

36.   T/F   A PC Card generic enabler can be used with a variety of PC Cards rather than one
      particular PC Card.

Name _____

Configuration Fill-in-the-Blank

1.   To set the configuration for today's computers, go into the _____ program.

2.   The _____ holds the SETUP program.

3.   The configuration software for older IBM MicroChannel computers comes on a _____.

4.   A special type of memory where configuration information is saved is _____.

5.   The _____ keeps information in CMOS.

6.   An alternative to the ROM BIOS chip is _____.

7.   A _____ is used to configure older computers.

8.   A special place on a MicroChannel hard drive that contains system programs is the _____.

9.   The _____ setting copies the motherboard ROM chip contents into RAM.

10. A _____ is a number assigned to an adapter that allows bypassing the microprocessor.

11. _____ allows an adapter to take control of a bus.

12. An _____ allows communication between a microprocessor and an adapter.

13. An _____ is a number assigned to an adapter so the microprocessor can prioritize between various devices.

14. _____ use IRQ9 as a pass-through to the first interrupt controller chip.

15. MicroChannel configuration files end in a _____ extension.

16. EISA configuration files end in a _____ extension.

17. _____ is Intel's generic Plug and Play driver for DOS and Windows 3.x computers.

18. _____ allocate system resources to PC Cards.

19. The lowest level of software for a PC card is _____.

Name _____

Configuration Method Exercise and Review

Objective: To determine what configuration method a computer uses

Parts: A computer

Step   1:   Open the computer and look at the motherboard. Determine whether the computer uses (1) switches, (2) a battery to maintain CMOS information, or (3) Flash BIOS. Circle the correct method used:
A. Switches
B. CMOS Battery
C. Flash BIOS

Question 1:   What is an advantage of having a battery that keeps CMOS information instead of switches?

Question 2:   What is an advantage of Flash BIOS over a normal BIOS chip?

Question 3:   What is one of the first indications of a failing battery?

Question 4:   What determines the keystroke required to access the SETUP program?

Name _____

USING MICROSOFT DIAGNOSTICS (MSD) EXERCISE

Objective: To use Microsoft Diagnostics to evaluate a computer's resources

Parts: A computer that has Microsoft Diagnostics (MSD) loaded

Step   1:   Power on the computer and be sure the computer is at a DOS prompt such as C:\>. For DOS skills, refer to Appendix A.

Step   2:   Type **CD\WINDOWS** and press **ENTER**. The prompt changes to C:\WINDOWS>. If this does not happen, re-type the command.

Step   3:   Type **MSD** and press **ENTER**. The Microsoft Diagnostics program appears.

Step   4:   Press the letter **C** on the keyboard for COM PORTS. The COM PORTS screen appears.

Question 1:   What I/O address (port address) does COM1: use?

Step   5:   Press **ENTER** to return to the main MSD menu.

Step   6:   Press the letter **Q** on the keyboard for IRQ STATUS. The IRQ STATUS screen appears.

Question 2:   For what device or port is IRQ7 used?

Question 3:   For what device or port is IRQ3 used?

Step   7:   Press **ENTER** to return to the main MSD menu.

Step   8:   Press **F3** on the keyboard to exist MSD.

Name _____

INTERRUPT, I/O ADDRESS, & DMA CHANNEL CONFIGURATION EXERCISE (on 286 or higher computers using keystrokes to enter SETUP program)

Objective: To understand how to access a computer's resources through the SETUP program

Parts: A 286 or higher computer that uses keystrokes to enter the SETUP program

Step   1:   Power on the computer.

Step   2:   Press the appropriate key(s) to enter the SETUP program.

Step   3:   Go through the various menus or icons until you find an interrupt (IRQ) setting for a particular device or port. Write the device or port and the associated IRQ in the space below:

IRQ	Device or Port

Question 1:   Why do different devices generally not have the same interrupt?

Step   4:   Go through the various menus or icons until you find an I/O address setting for a particular device or port. Write the device or port in the space below along with the associated I/O address.

I/O Address	Device or Port

Question 2:   Why must all devices and ports have a separate and unique I/O address?

Question 3:   Who assigns I/O addresses, interrupts, and DMA channels to different adapters?

Question 4:   What is the best source for setting interrupts, I/O addresses, and DMA channels for technicians installing a new adapter into a system?

Step   5:   Exit the SETUP program.
Step   6:   Go into the MSD program and determine if the information collected in steps 3 & 4 is the same or available through the MSD program. (Reference the USING MICROSOFT DIAGNOSTICS (MSD) EXERCISE for directions to access the MSD program.)

Name _____

EXAMINING SYSTEM RESOURCES
USING WINDOWS 95 EXERCISE

Objective: To understand how to access a computer's resources using Windows 95

Parts: A computer that has Windows 95 loaded

Step 1:   Power on the computer and verify that the Windows 95 desktop appears. If Windows 95 skills are needed, refer to Appendix B.

Step 2:   Click once on the **Start** button. (Press **CTRL+ESC** if the Start button is not visible.)

Step 3:   Place the mouse pointer over the **Settings** option.

Step 4:   Click once on the **Control Panel** option.

Step 5:   Double-click on the **System** icon.

Step 6:   Click once on the **Device Manager** tab. The window shows a list of hardware devices sorted by hardware types. All the system resources seen throughout the rest of the exercise can be printed from the current window. Take note of the Print button located near the bottom of the window.

Step 7:   Double-click on the **Computer** icon.

Step 8:   The View Resources tab lists the IRQs. Use Exercise Table #1 to document the IRQs currently used.

EXERCISE - TABLE # 1	IRQ	Device	IRQ	Device
	0	System timer	8	
	1	Keyboard	9	
	2		10	
	3		11	
	4		12	
	5		13	
	6		14	
	7		15	

Step 9:   Click on the **Input/Output I/O** radio button located on the top portion of the window.
Step 10:   The I/O addresses used by the system display.

Always write down the possible I/O addresses for a new adapter and then check the I/O addresses shown on the screen to see which I/O address is available for the adapter to use.

Step 11:   Click on the **Direct memory access (DMA)** radio button located on the top portion of the window.
Step 12:   Using Exercise Table #2, write down the DMA channels used in the system.

DMA	Device	DMA	Device
0		4	
1		5	
2		6	
3		7	

EXERCISE - TABLE # 2

Step 13:   Click on the **Memory** radio button located on the top portion of the window.
Step 14:   Memory addresses that appear are used by ROM chips on the adapters and the ROM chips on the motherboard. More is covered on these addresses in the memory chapter. For now, keep in mind if an adapter has a ROM chip on it, the ROM chip must be at a different memory address than the other adapters in the system.
Step 15:   Click once in the window's close box (the X in the upper right corner).
Step 16:   Click once in the System Properties close box.
Step 17:   Click once in the Control Panel close box.

_____ Instructor's Initials

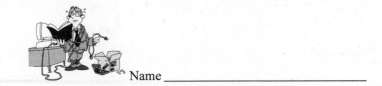

Name _____

IBM PC OR XT (8088/8086) CONFIGURATION EXERCISE

Objective: To understand how to set an 8088/8086 computer's configuration using switches
To understand the effects of changing a computer's configuration

Parts: IBM PC or XT (or compatible) computer

Step 1: Verify the computer is turned OFF. Look at the floppy disk drives on the front of the computer.

Question 1: How many floppy drives are installed in the computer?

Step 2: Remove the computer's cover and be careful of any cables that might be torn loose when removing the cover.

Question 2: Make note of the current settings for the DIP switches located on the motherboard.

Step 3: **Note:** The following steps illustrate the effects if the *wrong* configuration is set. Using a small flat-tipped screwdriver, change the configuration by setting the switches to reflect *two* floppy drives installed if the computer has only *one* floppy drive installed. If the computer has *two* floppy drives installed, change the configuration switches to show that *one* drive is installed. Reference Configuration Table #2 for the proper switch setting.

Step 4: Turn the computer ON.

Question 3: What POST error code appears?

Step 5: Turn the computer OFF.

Step 6: Set the configuration switches back to their original configuration settings. Reference the answer to Question 2 for the original settings.

Step 7: Turn the computer ON.

Question 4: Did the computer power on with any POST error codes? If so, re-check the switch settings.

_____ Instructor's Initials

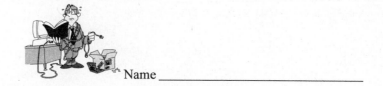

Name _____

IBM MICROCHANNEL CONFIGURATION EXERCISE

Objective: To understand how to configure a MicroChannel computer
                 To understand the effects of changing a computer's configuration

Parts: IBM MicroChannel computer
           Reference disk (if necessary)

Step   1:   Verify that the computer is turned OFF.
Step   2:   Boot the computer from the reference disk. If the computer uses an IML System Partition, when the computer displays "Starting PC DOS", press **CTRL+ALT+DEL**. When the cursor moves to the upper right corner of the screen, press **CTRL+ALT+INS**.

Question 1:   What is the advantage to using a reference disk instead of an IML System Partition?

Question 2:   What is a disadvantage of using a reference disk to set the computer's configuration?

Step   3:   From the main menu, choose **Set Configuration** by using the arrow keys to highlight that option and press **ENTER**.
Step   4:   From the Set Configuration Menu, choose the **Change Configuration** option.

Question 3:   What type of disk is installed as Disk Drive A Type? (Note: This information can be found on the Change Configuration screen under "Built In Features."

Step   5:   Using the arrow keys, highlight the **Diskette Drive A Type** option.
Step   6:   Notice at the bottom of the screen the keystrokes used to modify the configuration are displayed. All menus on the MicroChannel SETUP screens contain this information.
Step   7:   Using **F5** or **F6** on the keyboard, change the Diskette Drive A Type to a type of disk other than the one installed.

Question 4:   What disk type did you choose?

Step   8:   Save the configuration information by pressing **F10**.

Step   9:   Exit the Change Configuration screen by pressing **ESC** or **F3**, depending on the computer model. The bottom of the menu displays the appropriate keystroke.

Step 10:   Continue backing out of the configuration screens by pressing the appropriate key for **EXIT** or **QUIT** (depending on the model of MicroChannel computer) until a message appears in the bottom right corner stating the Configuration Changes have been made.

Step 11:   Press **ENTER** to restart the computer (with the reference disk installed in the floppy drive if this model requires a reference disk).

Question 5:   What happens during POST?

Step 12:   Due to the configuration error, the MicroChannel computer must be set up with the proper parameters to operate. Go back into the Change Configuration menu to set the Diskette Drive A Type back to the original drive type. Look at the answer to Question 3 for the correct type of installed disk.

Step 13:   Save the configuration information.

Step 14:   **EXIT** out of the reference disk menus. If necessary, remove the reference disk from the disk drive when the computer restarts.

Question 6:   Did the computer boot with any POST errors? If so, go back into the SETUP program and verify the setting for the disk drive.

_____ Instructor's Initials

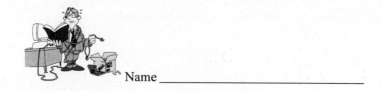

Name _____

386 AND HIGHER CONFIGURATION EXERCISE

Objective: To understand how to configure a 386 or higher computer
                 To understand the effects of changing a computer's configuration

Parts: A computer with a 386 or higher microprocessor

Note: Different BIOS manufacturers have different keystroke(s) to access the SETUP program. Refer
           to the computer manual or Configuration Table #1 for the appropriate keystroke(s).

Step   1:   Power on the computer.
Step   2:   Press the appropriate key(s) on the keyboard to access the SETUP program.

Question 1:   What key(s) did you press to access the SETUP program?

Step   3:   Using the keys shown on the menu, go to the menu screen that allows changes to the
            installed floppy drives.

Question 2:   What type of floppy drive is installed as drive A: according to the current SETUP
            information?

Step   4:   Using the appropriate keys, change the drive type for the A: drive to a type other than the
            one installed.
Step   5:   Save the configuration information by pressing the appropriate key and exit the SETUP
            program. Follow the directions shown on the screen to restart the computer.

Question 3:   Did any error codes or messages appear during POST? If so, write the code or message in the space below.

Step 6:   Go back into the SETUP program and change the type of floppy drive back to the original configuration. Refer to Question 2 for the original floppy drive type.

Step 7:   Save the configuration and exit the SETUP program by pressing the appropriate keys as displayed on the screen.

Step 8:   Reboot the computer.

Question 4:   Did the computer boot without any errors? If not, be sure that the correct floppy drive type was entered into the SETUP program.

_____ Instructor's Initials

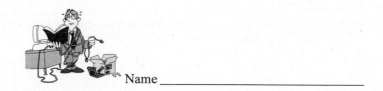

Name _____

ISA ADAPTER INSTALLATION EXERCISE

Objective: To install an ISA adapter properly setting the configuration so the adapter does not conflict with other adapters

Parts: ISA adapter and documentation (if possible)
          Software for the adapter (if applicable)
          Tools
          Anti-static materials

Note: Observe proper grounding procedures when installing an adapter.

Step   1:   Use whatever method or available software and determine what IRQs are available in the system. Use Exercise Table #3 to document the IRQs currently in use.

EXERCISE - TABLE # 3

IRQ	Device	IRQ	Device
0	System timer	8	
1	Keyboard	9	
2		10	
3		11	
4		12	
5		13	
6		14	
7		15	

Question 1:   Use the adapter's documentation and the information in Configuration Exercise Table #3 and determine what IRQs are available for the ISA adapter being installed. What are the adapter's possible IRQ settings?

Step 2: Use whatever method or software available and determine what I/O addresses are currently used by other adapters and devices in the computer.

Question 2: Using the information found in Step 2 and the adapter's documentation, what I/O addresses can the adapter use that are *not* used by any other adapter or device?

Step 3: If necessary, use whatever method or software available and determine what DMA channels are currently used and to what DMA channels the adapter can be set. Make notes if necessary.

Step 4: If the adapter configures by setting jumpers and switches, go ahead and configure the adapter for the proper interrupt, I/O address, and any other system resources needed.

Step 5: Verify that the computer is powered off.

Step 6: Remove the computer's cover.

Step 7: Find an available ISA expansion slot.

Step 8: If necessary, attach any internal device cables that connect to the adapter.

Step 9: Remove any brackets from the case or plastic covers from the rear of the computer that prevent adapter installation.

Step 10: Install the adapter in the expansion slot.

Step 11: If necessary, attach any cables that go to an external port on the adapter.

Step 12: If necessary, attach any external or internal devices to the other end of the cables.

Step 13: If applicable, power on any external devices that connect to the ISA adapter.

Step 14: Power on the computer.

Step 15: If the adapter configures through software, load the configuration software at this time following the directions included with the adapter or the README file on the software disks. Configure the adapter using the software verifying the settings chosen do not conflict with other devices. Refer to Exercise Table #3, Questions 2 and 3, and Step 3's notes when configuring the adapter.

Step 16: Load any application software or device driver needed for the ISA adapter. Always refer to the documentation for exact loading procedures.

Step 17: Test any devices that connect to the ISA adapter.

Question 3: Does the adapter (and any devices that connect to the adapter) work properly? If not, refer to the adapter's documentation and review all installation steps.

_____ Instructor's Initials

Step 18: If applicable, power off any external devices.

Step 19: Power off the computer.

Name _____

INTERNET DISCOVERY

Objective: To access the Internet to obtain specific information regarding a computer or its associated parts.

Parts: Access to the Internet

The following information is provided:
     You have a customer that owns a Compaq Presario CDS 774 computer

1.   Determine the procedure for accessing the computer's SETUP program.
2.   Determine how to remove a power-on password that has been set and the password has been forgotten.

The following information is provided:
     You have a customer who has a Toshiba Equium 5160D desktop computer.
3.   Determine what type of BIOS this computer uses.
4.   Determine whether or not this computer supports Plug and Play.

The following information is provided:
     You have a customer that owns a HP Vectra 500 Series PC Model 515

5.   Determine if this computer uses cascaded interrupts.
6.   Determine what I/O addresses the primary IDE hard disk controller uses.
7.   Determine for what DMA channel 5 is used.
8.   Determine the procedure for checking the BIOS version.
9.   Determine the latest BIOS available for this model.

The following information relates to numbers 8-10:
     A customer owns a NEC Direction SPT200 computer.
10.   Discover what key is pressed to enter SETUP.
11.   Determine what floppy drives are supported by this model's BIOS.
12.   Determine what chipset ships on the motherboard.

Chapter 4: Disassembly/ Reassembly

OBJECTIVES

After completing this chapter you will
1.   Understand how static electricity can damage a computer.
2.   Understand what type of equipment causes RFI and EMI.
3.   Know what tools a technician needs.
4.   Understand the importance of diagramming when disassembling a computer.
5.   Be able to disassemble and reassemble a computer.

KEY TERMS

anti-static wrist strap	preventive maintenance
EMI	return
ESD	RFI
head parking utility	self-parking heads
hot	solder joints
pin 1	standoffs

DISASSEMBLY OVERVIEW

Very seldom is a computer completely disassembled. However, when a technician is first learning about microcomputers, disassembly can be very informative and fun. Some technicians disassemble a computer to perform a preventive cleaning on the computer. Another example of a time to disassemble the computer is when the computer has an undetermined problem. Sometimes, the only solution is to disassemble the computer outside the case or remove components one by one to see what is causing the problem. Sometimes disassembling the computer outside the case helps with grounding problems. A **grounding** problem occurs if the motherboard or adapter is not properly installed and a trace (a metal line on the motherboard or adapter) touches the computer frame causing the adapter and possibly other components to cease working.

ELECTROSTATIC DISCHARGE (ESD)

Many precautions must be taken when disassembling a microcomputer. The electronic circuits located on the motherboard and adapters are subject to **electrostatic discharge** or **ESD**. Static electricity can be very damaging to electronic equipment without the technician feeling the static electricity. An average person requires a static charge of 3,000 volts before feeling a static charge. An electronic component can be damaged with only 30 volts of static electricity. Some electronic components may not be damaged the first time static electricity hits the component. However, the effects of static electricity can be cumulative, continually weakening or eventually destroying the electronic component.

A technician can prevent ESD using a variety of methods. The most common method is through the use of an **anti-static wrist strap** that attaches to the technician's wrist. At the other end of the wrist strap is an alligator clip that attaches to the computer. The clip attaches to a grounding post or a metal part such as the power supply. This method allows the technician and the computer to be at the same voltage potential. As long as the technician and the computer or electronic part are at the same potential, static electricity does not occur. Reference Disassembly Figure #1 for an illustration of an anti-static wrist strap.

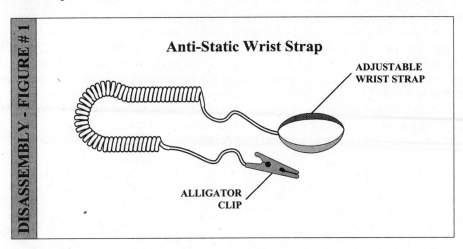

Technicians should use an ESD wrist strap whenever possible. The one time that a technician *should not* wear an ESD wrist strap is when working inside a monitor because of the high voltages inside it. When working inside a computer and wearing an anti-static wrist strap, there is a resistor inside the wrist strap to protect the technician in case something accidentally touches the ground to which the strap attaches. In the case of a monitor, the strap's resistor could not protect the technician against the voltages possible inside the monitor.

Anti-static bags are good for storing spare adapters and motherboards when the parts are not in use. Anti-static mats are available to place underneath a computer being repaired; many of the mats have a snap for connecting the anti-static wrist strap.

If an anti-static wrist strap is not available, you can still reduce the chance of ESD damage by using an alternate method. After removing the computer case, if a technician is right-handed, place the bare left arm on the power supply. Remove the computer parts one-by-one, always keeping the left elbow (or some bare part of the arm) connected to the power supply. If left-handed, place the right arm on the power supply. By using an elbow on the power supply, both hands are free to remove computer parts. This method is *not* as safe as using an anti-static wrist strap. However, it is an effective way of keeping the technician and the computer at the same voltage potential thus reducing the chance of ESD damage. Also, removing the power cable from the back of the computer is a good idea for new technicians. However, leaving the power cable plugged into the wall socket and the computer's power supply is the *best* method for ensuring a good ground.

EMI (ELECTROMAGNETIC INTERFERENCE)

EMI (ElectroMagnetic Interference or sometimes called EMR for ElectroMagnetic Radiation) is noise caused by electrical devices. Many devices can cause EMI such as the computer, a pencil sharpener, a motor, a vacuum cleaner, an air conditioner, fluorescent lighting, etc. The FCC (Federal Communications Commission) has two classes of computer specifications, Class A and Class B. The Class A specification is for computers in the design stage or devices for commercial and business use. The Class B specification covers consumer computing devices. A Class B certification is not difficult to obtain because computers do not emit much noise anyway. The electrical devices around the computer including the computer's monitors and speakers cause more problems than the computer. EMI can significantly affect a monitor. If a monitor's output is distorted, try moving the computer to a different location to see if EMI is the problem source.

A specific type of electromagnetic interference that affects computers is **RFI (Radio Frequency Interference)**. RFI is simply those noises that occur in the radio frequency range. Any time a computer has an intermittent problem, do not forget to check the surrounding devices for the source of the problem. For example, if the computer only goes down when the pencil sharpener operates or when a CD plays in the CD-player, then EMI could be the source of the problem. EMI problems are very hard to track to the source. EMI can also come through the power lines. Move the computer to a different wall outlet or to a totally different circuit to determine if the power outlet is the problem source.

DISASSEMBLY

Before a technician disassembles a computer, several steps should be performed or considered. The list below helps with these steps:

1.   If applicable, backup the CMOS SETUP configuration.
2.   If disassembling an IBM MicroChannel computer, locate the reference or adapter disks and set aside. If they are unavailable, do not disconnect the battery from the motherboard.
3.   If the computer is a 80286 microprocessor or higher, do not disconnect the battery from the motherboard if at all possible or the CMOS configuration information is lost.
4.   Use proper grounding procedures to prevent ESD damage.
5.   Keep paper and pen nearby for note taking and diagramming. Even if one has taken computers apart for years, there might be something unique or different inside the computer. Good technicians continue to diagram throughout their career.
6.   Have ample work space.
7.   When removing adapters, do not stack the adapters on one another.
8.   If possible, place removed adapters inside a special ESD protective bag.
9.   Take note of any jumper or switch settings on the motherboard or adapters before removing them from the computer. Notes are helpful if the switches or jumpers are accidentally changed.
10. Handle each adapter or motherboard on the side edges. Avoid touching the gold contacts on the bottom of adapters. Sweat, oil, and dirt cause problems.
11. Hard disk drives require careful handling. A very small jolt can cause damage to the stored data.

TOOLS

No chapter on disassembly and reassembly is complete without the mention of tools. Many technicians do not go on a repair call loaded down with a full tool case. Most repairs are accomplished with a few tools. The need for tools is divided into two categories: (1) don't leave the office without tools and (2) nice to have back in the office, home, or car tools.

Ninety-five percent of all computer repair calls are completed with a couple basic tools:

◆ medium flat-tipped screwdriver
◆ small, flat-tipped tweaker screwdriver
◆ #1 Phillips screwdriver
◆ #2 Phillips screwdriver
◆ 1/4" nut driver
◆ 3/16" nut driver
◆ pair of small diagonal cutters (dikes)
◆ pair of needlenose pliers

The screwdrivers and nut drivers take care of most disassemblies and reassemblies. Sometimes, manufacturers place tie wraps on new parts, new cables, or the cables inside the computer case. The diagonal cutters are great for removing the tie wraps without cutting cables or damaging parts. The needlenose pliers are good for getting disks or disk parts out of disk drives, straightening DIP chip legs bent from using a DIP chip inserter tool, straightening bent pins on cables or connectors, and about a million other uses that do not all come to mind right now. The small tweaker screwdriver and the needlenose pliers are irreplaceable.

Many technicians start with a basic $15 microcomputer repair kit and build from there. A specialized Swiss army knife with screwdrivers is the favorite of some technicians. Other technicians prefer the all-in-one tool carried in a pouch that connects to the belt. Individual taste and convenience sets each person's standard. However, one should be aware some tools included with the basic microcomputer repair toolkits are not useful. For example, a DIP chip inserter tool is worthless. More DIP chip legs are bent using the insertion tool than doing it by hand. Again, DIP chip legs are bent when the chip is removed because applying equal pressure while lifting straight up on the DIP chip is nearly impossible. No toolkit is complete without the anti-static wrist strap.

Tools no one thinks of as tools, but need to go on the service call with the technician every time include: a pen or pencil to take notes and fill out the repair slip, and a bootable disk containing the technician's favorite repair utilities. Usually a technician has several bootable disks for different operating systems and utilities as well as a few blank disks for saving files or testing a floppy drive. Another item is a small reference book by Sequoia Publishing, *Pocket PCRef*. It has many useful error codes, commands, and common repair items. Many 20-year technicians wish such a reference book existed when they were learning computer repair. A flashlight comes in handy when least expected. Some rooms and offices are dimly lit. Last, do not forget to bring a smile and a sense of humor.

Tools nice to have, but not used on a day-to-day or hour-to-hour basis, include:
- multimeter for checking voltages and cable continuity
- screw pick-up tool for those slippery screws that fall down into the computer and roll under the motherboard
- screwdriver extension tool for making a Phillips or flat-tipped screwdriver longer for those printers that standard screwdrivers are about an inch too short
- soldering iron, solder, and flux
- screw-starter tool
- medium-size set of diagonal cutters (dikes)
- metric nut drivers
- cable-making tools such as wire strippers and crimpers
- AC circuit tester
- right-angled, flat-tipped and Phillips screwdrivers for hard-to-reach areas
- hemostats
- pliers
- floppy disk read/write head cleaning kit
- chip removal tools for PGA (Pin Grid Array), PLCC (Plastic Leaded Chip Carrier), and PQFP (Plastic Quad Flat Pack) chips are all handy-dandy to have around, but not needed every day

One could get some nice muscle tone from carrying each of these nice to have but normally, unessential tools. Sometimes, T-10 and T-15 Torx screwdrivers are needed for some manufacturer's screws as well as a tamper-proof Torx driver. Loopback plugs help when testing some standard connectors. Not often do the ports need testing, but when they do, some utilities require such a tool for a loop-back test.

When first starting microcomputer repair, get the basics. As your personal taste, product line requirements, and your experience level grows, so will the toolkit. Nothing is worse than getting to a job site and not having the right tool. However, because there are no standards or limitations on what manufacturers can use in their product line, *always* having the tool onhand is impossible.

REASSEMBLY

Reassembling a microcomputer is easy if the technician is careful and diagrams properly during disassembly. Simple tasks, such as returning a floppy drive to the correct drive bay, become confusing after removing so many parts. Writing down reminders takes less time than troubleshooting the computer because of poor reassembly. Re-insert all components into their proper place; be careful to replace all screws and parts.

Three major reassembly components are motherboards, cables, and connectors. Motherboards frequently have plastic connectors called **standoffs** on the bottom of the motherboard. The standoffs slide into slots on the computer case. Do not remove the standoffs from the motherboard. Take the motherboard out of the case with the standoffs still attached. The first step in removing a motherboard involves removing the screws that attach the motherboard to the case. Then, the motherboard, (including the standoffs), slides to one side and lifts up. Follow the reverse procedure when re-installing the motherboard.

When re-installing the motherboard, the plastic standoffs evenly insert into the tip of the case slots. The motherboard gently slides towards the power supply until the motherboard firmly clamps into the slots. This procedure requires practice in feeling the plastic standoffs slide into the slots. After practicing this procedure several times, a technician can tell when a motherboard's standoffs do not seat properly into the slots.

CABLES AND CONNECTORS

When reassembling a microcomputer, cables that connect a device to an adapter or motherboard can be a tricky issue. Inserting a cable backward into a device or adapter can damage the device, motherboard, or adapter. Some cables are keyed so the cable only inserts into the connector one way. However, some cables or connectors are *not* keyed.

Each cable has a certain number of pins and all cables have a **pin 1**. Pin 1 on the cable connects to pin 1 on the connector.

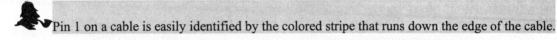
Pin 1 on a cable is easily identified by the colored stripe that runs down the edge of the cable.

In the unlikely event the cable is *not* easily identified, both ends of the cable should be labeled with either a number 1 or 2 on one side or a higher number such as 24, 25, 49, 50, etc. on the other end. Pins 1 and 2 are always on the same end of a cable. If a higher number is found, pin 1 is on the opposite end. Also, the cable connector usually has an arrow etched into its molding showing the pin 1 connection. Disassembly Figure #2 shows pin 1 on a ribbon cable.

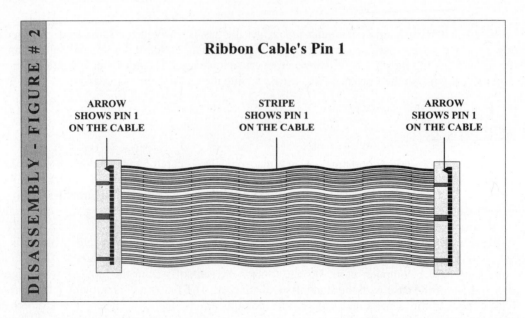

DISASSEMBLY - FIGURE # 2

Ribbon Cable's Pin 1

ARROW
SHOWS PIN 1
ON THE CABLE

STRIPE
SHOWS PIN 1
ON THE CABLE

ARROW
SHOWS PIN 1
ON THE CABLE

Just as all cables have a pin 1, all connectors on devices, adapters, or motherboards have a pin 1. Pin 1 of the cable inserts onto pin 1 on the connector. Some manufacturers stencil a number 1 or a number 2 by the connector on the motherboard or adapter. However, on a black motherboard connector, getting down to see the small number is difficult. Adapter numbers are easier to distinguish. Even if the number 2 is etched beside the adapter's connector, connect the cable's pin 1 to this side. Remember, pins 1 and 2 are always on the same side whether it is on a connector or on a cable. Disassembly Figure #3 shows an example of a stenciled marking beside the adapter's connector.

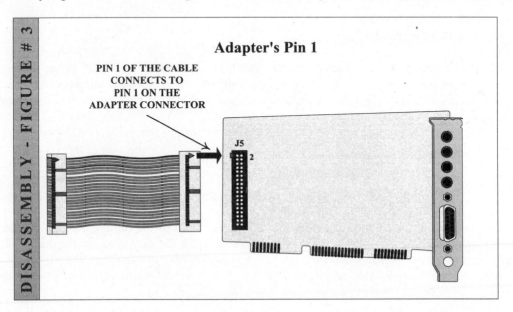

DISASSEMBLY - FIGURE # 3

Adapter's Pin 1

PIN 1 OF THE CABLE
CONNECTS TO
PIN 1 ON THE
ADAPTER CONNECTOR

J5
2

Even though Disassembly Figure #3 illustrates the number 2 etched onto the adapter, other manufacturers do just the opposite. They stencil a higher number such as 33, 34, 39, or 40 beside the opposite end of the connector.

If a higher number is stenciled beside the connector, connect pin 1 of the cable *to the opposite end of the connector*.

Still, some manufacturers make connections really tough and put no markings on the cable connector, but there is a way to determine which way to connect the cable. Remove the adapter, motherboard, or device from the computer. Look where the connector solders or connects to the motherboard or adapter. Turn the adapter over. Notice the silver blobs, known as **solder joints**, on the back of the motherboard or adapter. Solder connects electronic components to the motherboard or adapter. All chips and connectors mount onto a motherboard in the same direction — all pin 1s normally orient in the same direction. The connector's solder joints are normally all round, *except for the solder joint for pin 1*! Pin 1's solder joint is square. Look for the square solder joint on the back of the connector. If the square solder joint is not apparent on the connector needed, look for other connectors or solder joints that are square. Keep in mind if one pin 1 is found, the other connectors orient in the same direction. Insert the cable so pin 1 matches to the square solder joint of the connector. Disassembly Figure #4 shows a square solder joint for a connector on the back of an adapter.

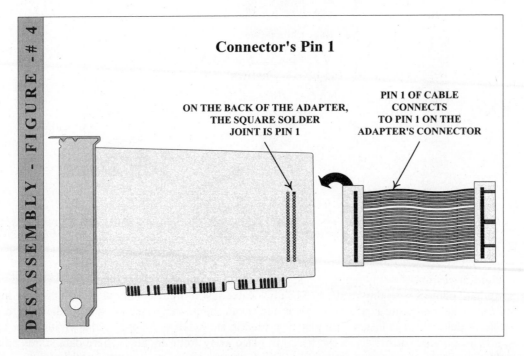

DISASSEMBLY - FIGURE - # 4

Connector's Pin 1

ON THE BACK OF THE ADAPTER, THE SQUARE SOLDER JOINT IS PIN 1

PIN 1 OF CABLE CONNECTS TO PIN 1 ON THE ADAPTER'S CONNECTOR

The power supply provides power to the different computer components. Be very careful when disconnecting various power supply connections. A very important set of cables to watch out for are the cables connecting the power supply to the motherboard. Also, be very careful if any power connectors connect from the power supply to the PC's front panel. The four wires (black, blue, white, and brown) bring AC voltage to the front panel. AC wiring has both a **hot** and a **return**. The hot and return go out to the front panel from the power supply and back into the power supply. The black wire connects the hot from the power supply to the front panel. The blue wire is the return side for the black. After pushing the front panel power switch, the black and blue wires make a connection to the power supply.

The brown wire also connects the hot from the power supply to the front panel. The white wire is the return side for the brown. After pushing the front panel power switch, the brown and white wires make a connection to the power supply. Diagramming how the wiring attaches to the front panel is very important when reassembling. If a technician reverses the cables, the computer can catch on fire. Disassembly Figure #5 shows the front panel switch wiring. However, always check the power supply's documentation and color schemes.

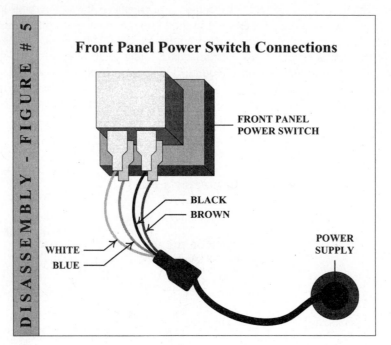

HARD DRIVES

Hard drives must be handled with care when disassembling a microcomputer. Inside the hard drives are hard platters with tiny read/write heads located just millimeters above the platters. A small jolt can make the read/write heads drop down and touch the platter possibly causing damage to the platter and/or the read/write heads. The platter is used to store data and applications. With older hard drives, a **head parking utility** locks the heads in place away from the area where data stores on the platter. Today's hard drives have **self-parking heads** that do not require software to make them pull away to a safe area. Instead, when the computer powers off, the heads pull away automatically.

Whenever disassembling a computer, if one is not sure the drive requires a head parking utility, refer to the documentation included with the hard drive or the computer. No matter which hard drive is in the computer, always be careful to neither jolt nor jar the hard drive when removing it from the computer.

The exercise at the end of the chapter contains the step-by-step directions for disassembling and reassembling a microcomputer.

PREVENTIVE MAINTENANCE

A computer should be cleaned at least once a year in a normal working environment. A computer runs longer and more efficiently if preventive measures are periodically taken. **Preventive maintenance** includes certain procedures performed to prolong the life of the computer. Some computer companies sell maintenance contracts that include a preventive maintenance program. Typical preventive measures include vacuuming the computer, cleaning the floppy drive heads, cleaning the keyboard keys, and cleaning the monitor screen. Many individual device preventive exercises are described in their respective chapters. For example, the exercise that explains how to clean the floppy drive heads is included as part of the floppy chapter. This section gives an overview of a preventive maintenance program and some general tips about cleaning solvents.

Companies frequently have a preventive maintenance kit used when going on service calls that include preventive maintenance. The kit normally includes a portable vacuum cleaner, special vacuum cleaner bags for laser printers, floppy head cleaning kit, cotton swaps, lint-free swabs, a can of compressed air, monitor wipes, lint-free cloths, general purpose cloths, general purpose cleanser, denatured alcohol, an anti-static brush, gold contact cleaner, and a CD cleaning kit.

When performing preventive maintenance, power on the computer first to be certain it operates. The worst feeling is to perform preventive maintenance on a computer, power on the computer and find it does not work. Then you always wonder if it was the cleaning that you performed or that the computer did not work from the beginning. Once the computer powers up, go into the SETUP program and copy the current settings in case the user's battery dies. Power the computer off.

Vacuuming the computer with a non-metallic attachment is a good place to begin the preventive maintenance routine. Do *not* start with compressed air or to blow the dust out of the computer because the dirt and dust simply go into the air and eventually fall back into the computer and surrounding equipment. After vacuuming as much as possible, use the compressed air to blow the dust out of hard to reach places such as inside the power supply and under the motherboard. Inform any users in the immediate area they might want to leave the area if they have allergies.

If you remove adapters from the expansion slots, replace them into the same slot. If the computer battery is on a riser board, it is best to leave the riser board connected to the motherboard so the system does not lose its SETUP configuration. The same steps covered in the chapter's disassembly portion hold true for performing preventive maintenance.

While you perform preventive maintenance is a good time to take inventory of what is installed in the computer such as the hard drive size, amount of RAM, available hard drive space, etc. During the maintenance procedure, communicate with the user. Ask them if the computer has been giving them any trouble lately or if it has been performing adequately. Computer users like to know that you care about their computing needs. Also, users frequently ask common sense questions such as if sunlight or cold weather harms the computer. Always respond with answers the user can understand. For example, computers are designed to work within a range of temperatures. Any sudden change is not good for it. If a laptop computer is in a car all night and the temperature drops, then the laptop should be returned to room temperature before you power it on. It is bad for a computer to sit in direct sunlight just as it is bad for a person to sit in the sun too long. Normally, inside the computer case it is $40°$ hotter than outside. Direct sunlight will make a computer run hotter which may exceed a particular component's temperature rating. Users appreciate it when you explain things in terms they understand and that make sense.

During the preventive maintenance call is the perfect opportunity to check the computer for viruses. Normally, the computer is cleaned first. Then, while the virus checker is running, external peripherals such as printers are cleaned. Preventive maintenance measures help limit computer problems as well as provide a chance to interact with customers and help with any problem that may seem minuscule, but could develop into a larger problem. Preventive maintenance calls are helpful for entry level technicians because they can see the different computer types and begin to familiarize themselves with the computer components.

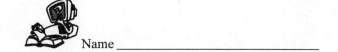

Name _____

Disassembly/Reassembly Review Questions

1. How often does a technician normally disassemble a computer?

2. If someone says that a motherboard might be *grounding*, what does that mean?

3. If you are out on a service call without an anti-static wrist strap, how can you still reduce ESD?

4. How do you solve a RFI problem?

5. Why is it important to write down the CMOS settings before disassembling a computer?

6. What tools are normally necessary to disassemble a microcomputer?

7. Why should you *not* touch an adapter's gold contacts?

8. What is the name of the board where adapter cards normally insert?

9. What does a cable being *keyed* mean?

10. How can you easily identify a ribbon cable's pin 1?

11. T/F   Pin 2 is on the same end as pin 1.

12. T/F   A square solder joint is on the opposite end from pin 1.

13. The power supply's [black, white, or brown] wire connects the power supply's hot to the front panel and returns on the blue wire.

14. The power supply's [black, blue, or white] wire is the return for the brown wire.

15. What is the most frustrating component of a microcomputer to remove?

16. What is the most frustrating component to install when reassembling the microcomputer?

17. How can the frustration listed in Question 16 be avoided?

18. What is the name of the test the computer performs to check hardware each time the computer powers on?

19. Is orienting the disk drives or controller cards' cables a difficult task? Why or why not?

20. What can be done if a screw drops and rolls under the motherboard?

21. What tool(s) should be avoided if a screw inadvertently rolls under the motherboard?

22. T/F   The first step in preventive maintenance is cleaning the computer with compressed air.

23. List three common procedures performed during a preventive maintenance call.

Name _____

Disassembly/Reassembly Fill-in-the-Blank

1.   _____ is static electricity that enters an electronic component causing damage to it.

2.   For an average person to feel static electricity, _____ volts need to be present.

3.   As little as _____ volts of static electricity can damage an electronic component.

4.   An _____ connects a technician to the computer and places both at the same potential.

5.   Random noise caused by a pencil sharpener that interferes with a computer speaker is an example of _____.

6.   All home computers should adhere to the FCC _____ specification.

7.   The plastic connectors on the bottom of the motherboard are _____.

8.   The power supply connections that connect to the front panel are called the _____ and the _____.

9.   Hard drives that do not need to execute special software before moving a computer are said to have _____.

10.   Measures taken to prolong the life of computer components are collectively known as _____.

Name _____

COMPUTER DISASSEMBLY/REASSEMBLY EXERCISE

Objective: To correctly disassemble and reassemble a microcomputer.

Parts: A computer to disassemble
         A microcomputer repair toolkit
         An anti-static wrist strap (if possible)
         Hard drive head-parking software (if necessary)

Observe proper ESD handling procedures when disassembling and reassembling a microcomputer.

PREPARATION
Step   1:   Gather the proper tools needed to disassemble the computer.
Step   2:   Clear as much workspace as possible around the computer.
Optional Step 3:   For any computer with a BIOS chip that controls configuration (which is most computers), the technician should power on the computer and write down all configuration information before disassembling the computer. Use the space below to write down the configuration information. Pay particular attention to the hard drive type.

Question 1:   Why is it important to write down the configuration information of any computer that is disassembled?

Optional Step 4:   If the computer does not have self-parking heads on the hard drive, run the appropriate hard disk head-parking software designed for the drive. Contact your instructor for the software.

Step   5:   Turn the computer and all peripherals OFF. Contact the instructor as to whether or not to remove the power cable at this point. Removing the power cable from the back of the computer is a good idea for new technicians. However, leaving the power cable plugged into the wall socket and the computer's power supply is the *best* method for ensuring a good ground.

Step   6:   Note where the monitor cable plugs into the back of the computer. Disconnect the monitor including the power cord, and move it to a safe place. Write down any notes in the space below.

EXTERNAL CABLES

Step   7:   Remove all external cables going to peripheral devices from the back of the computer. Take notes on the location of each cable. Move the peripheral devices to a safe place. Use the space below for any notes regarding external cables that connect to the computer.

Question 2:   List some ways to correctly reconnect the external cables.

COMPUTER CASE (COVER)

Step   8:   Remove the computer case. Use the space below to diagram the screw locations. Keep the cover screws separate from other screws. As a suggestion, an egg carton or a container with small compartments makes an excellent screw-holder when disassembling a microcomputer. Label each compartment and re-use the container.

ADAPTER PLACEMENT

Step   9:   Use Disassembly Exercise Figure #1 to indicate the placement of each adapter in the slots. Make any additions, deletions, or modifications to the drawing as they apply to the system being disassembled. If necessary, make a new drawing.

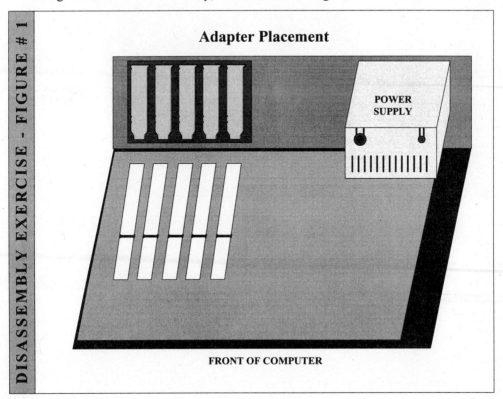

Step 10:   Use Disassembly Exercise Figure #2 to draw the internal cable connections *before* removing any adapters or cables from the computer. Make notes regarding how and where the cable connects to the adapter. Do not forget to include cables that connect to the motherboard or to the computer case. Modify the drawing as necessary or create a new one.

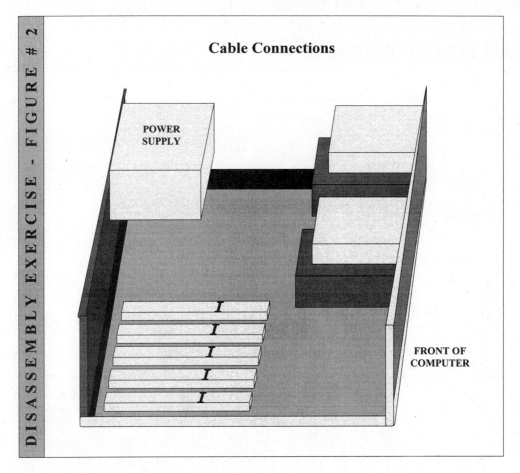

Question 3:   List some ways to determine the location of pin 1 on an adapter or cable.

INTERNAL CABLE REMOVAL

Step 11:   Remove all internal cables. Make appropriate notes below for the cable connections. Some students find labeling the cables and the associated connector make reassembly much easier. However, a few notes usually suffice.

ADAPTER REMOVAL

Step 12:   Start with the left side of the computer (facing the front of the computer) and locate the left-most adapter.

Step 13:   Write down any jumpers or switch settings for the adapter. This step may need to be performed after removing the board from the computer if the settings are inaccessible.

Step 14:   Remove the screw that holds the adapter to the case. Place the screw in a separate, secure location away from the other screws already removed. Make notes as to where the screw goes.or any other notes that will help when reassembling the computer.

Step   15:   Remove the adapter from the computer.

Question 4:   Why must one be careful not to touch the gold contacts at the bottom of each adapter?

Step 16:   Remove the remaining adapters in the system by repeating Steps 12-15. Use the space below for notes regarding screw locations, jumpers, switches, etc. for each adapter.

DRIVES

Step 17:   Remove all power connections to drives such as hard drives, floppy drives, CD-ROM drives, etc. Use Disassembly Exercise Figure #3 and the space below to note the placement of each drive and each cable, and any reminders needed for reassembly:

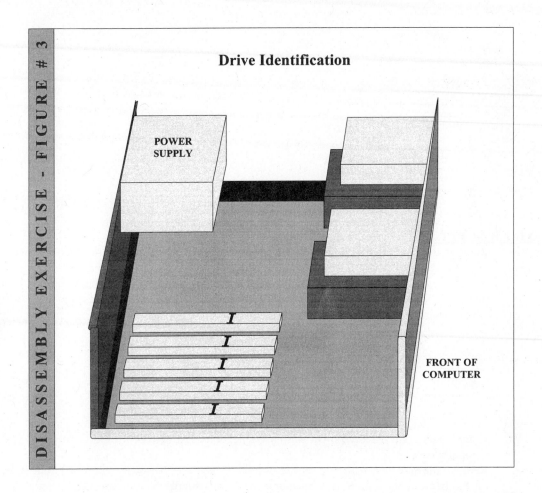

Step 18:   Remove any screws holding the disk drives in place. In the space below, make notes as to where these screws go. Keep the disk drive screws separate from earlier removed screws.

Step 19:   Remove all disk drives.

Question 5:   Why must one be careful handling any disk drive?

POWER SUPPLY

Step 20:   Remove the connectors connecting the power supply to the motherboard. Also remove the power cord going from the power supply to the AC wall outlet. Make notes here so you will be able to correctly insert the connectors into the motherboard when reassembling. If the power supply has connections to a front panel switch, make notes on the switch connections.

Step 21:   If applicable, remove any power supply connections that connect to the front panel of the computer case.

Step 22:   Remove the screws holding the power supply to the case. Normally, there are four screws on the back of the computer that attach the power supply to the case. Make notes as to where the screws attach. Place the screws in a separate location from the other screws removed from the system.

Step 23:   Remove the power supply by sliding it toward the front of the computer.

Question 6:   What is the purpose of the power supply?

MOTHERBOARD

Step 24:   Make note of any motherboard switches or jumpers and indicate if each switch position is
            on or off.

Question 7:   What is the importance of documenting the switches and jumpers on the motherboard?

Step 25:   Remove any remaining connectors *except* those that connect a battery to the motherboard.
            Use the space below to write notes.

Step 26:   Remove any screws that hold the motherboard to the case. Place these screws in a different
            location from the other screws removed from the system. Write any notes below pertaining
            to the motherboard screws.

Step 27:   Remove the motherboard. Write any notes pertaining to the motherboard removal in the
            space below. The computer case should be empty after completing this step.

_____ Instructor's Initials

REASSEMBLY

Step 28:   Reassemble the computer by reversing the steps for disassembly. Pay particular attention to cable orientation when re-installing computer cables. Refer to your notes. The first step is to install the motherboard in the computer case and reconnect all motherboard connections and screws.

Step 29:   Install the power supply by attaching all screws that hold the power supply in the case. Attach the power connectors to the motherboard. Attach any power connectors that connect to the front panel. Refer to your notes for Steps 20, 21, and 22.

Step 30:   Install all drives by attaching all screws, cables, and power connectors. Refer to your notes for Steps 17 and 18. Attach any cables that connect the drive to the motherboard. Refer to your notes from Step 10 and in Disassembly Exercise Figure #2.

Step 31:   Install all adapters beginning with the adapter closest to the power supply and work toward the outside of the case. Attach all screws and cables from the adapter to the device to which it connects. Refer to your previous notes and diagrams.

Step 32:   Connect any external connectors to the computer. Refer to previously made notes when necessary.

Step 33:   Replace the computer cover.

Step 34:   Once the computer is reassembled, power on all external peripherals and the computer.

Question 8:   Did the computer power on with POST error codes? If so, re-check all diagrams, switches, cabling, etc. Also, check a similar computer model that still works if an error was made when diagramming. A chapter regarding logical troubleshooting comes later in the book. However, for this point in the course, the most likely problem is with a cable connection or with an adapter not seated properly into the socket.

_____ Instructor's Initials

Chapter 5: Power

OBJECTIVES

After completing this chapter you will
1.   Understand the purpose of a power supply.
2.   Be able to properly connect a power supply to the front panel, motherboard, and devices.
3.   Know the voltages output by a power supply.
4.   Recognize the different power connectors.
5.   Know the different criteria for upgrading or replacing a power supply.
6.   Be able to solve power problems.
7.   Know the purpose of different power protection devices.

KEY TERMS

AC (alternating current)	picoseconds
Berg connector	phone line isolator
blackout	return
brownout	sag
clamping speed	sine wave
clamping voltage	spike
DC (direct current)	SPS
hot	square wave
joule dissipation capacity	surge
line conditioner	surge protector
modem isolator	TVS rating
Molex connector	under-voltage
MOV	UPS
nanosecods	watts
over-voltage	

POWER SUPPLY OVERVIEW

The power supply is an essential component within the computer; no other devices work without it. The power supply has an important function in the computer because it converts AC electricity to DC electricity, distributes DC power to components throughout the computer, and provides cooling through the use of a fan located inside the power supply. The power supply is sometimes a source of unusual problems. IBM did a study which showed a typical computer workstation has more than 120 power problems per month. The effects of the problems can be those not noticed by the user or those that cause the system to completely shut down.

Frequently, the power supply is overlooked by technicians when troubleshooting. For example, one new computer, when taken out of the box, would not boot. The POST error code indicated a hard drive problem. After the technician put in a new hard drive, the problem did not go away. The technician replaced the hard drive cable connected to the motherboard; the problem did not go away. The motherboard was replaced and the computer finally booted. Two days later the same problem returned. Finally, after more part swapping, the technician swapped the power supply and the problem did not recur. The ability to connect the power supply to the various components, to identify the different types of power connectors, to know what to look for when upgrading a power supply, and to troubleshoot power supply problems are all important skills to a technician.

PURPOSE OF A POWER SUPPLY

The power from a wall outlet is **AC (alternating current)**. The type of power that the computer needs to operate is **DC (direct current)**. All computer parts (the electronic chips on the motherboard and adapters, the electronics on the drives, the motors in the floppy drive, hard drive and CD-ROM drive) need DC power to operate. One purpose of the power supply is to convert AC to DC so the computer has the proper power to run the components.

Some power supplies connect the AC electricity directly to the power switch on the front panel. Be very careful of these connectors. The four wires (black, blue, white, and brown) carry the AC voltage to the front panel. AC wiring has both a **hot** and a **return**. The black wire connects the hot from the power supply to the front panel. The blue wire is the return side for the black. The brown wire also connects the hot from the power supply to the front panel. The white wire is the return side for the brown. After pushing the front panel power switch, the black, blue, brown, and white wires make a connection to the power supply.

Diagramming how the wiring attaches to the front panel is very important when reassembling. If a technician reverses the cable connections, the computer can catch on fire. Power Figure #1 shows the wiring of a front panel switch. Keep in mind each power supply manufacturer can wire the connections differently. Some power supply manufacturers place the wiring scheme on the power supply for easy reference.

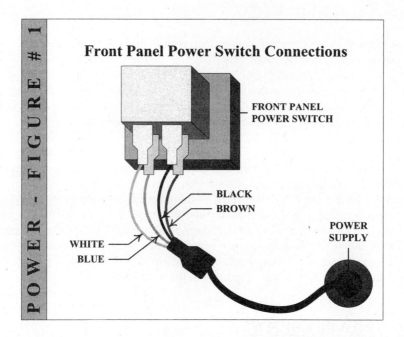

Front Panel Power Switch Connections

POWER - FIGURE # 1

FRONT PANEL
POWER SWITCH

BLACK
BROWN

WHITE
BLUE

POWER
SUPPLY

Another purpose of the power supply is to distribute the proper DC voltage to each component. Coming out of the power supply are several connectors. Two power supply connectors normally plug directly to the motherboard to provide DC power to the motherboard's components. When connecting the power supply to the motherboard, insert the connectors properly or the motherboard may be damaged when the computer powers on. Look at the power connectors that attach to the motherboard, and notice each connector has different colored wires. Also, notice both connectors have black wires.

The black wires on both connectors must be placed next to each other in the center of the P8 and P9 connectors when plugged into the motherboard.

See Power Figure #2 for an illustration of the motherboard's power connectors.

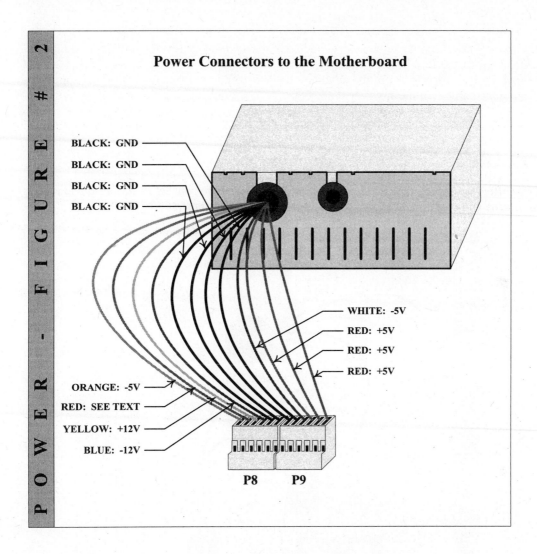

POWER - FIGURE # 2

Power Connectors to the Motherboard

BLACK: GND
BLACK: GND
BLACK: GND
BLACK: GND

WHITE: -5V
RED: +5V
RED: +5V
RED: +5V

ORANGE: -5V
RED: SEE TEXT
YELLOW: +12V
BLUE: -12V

P8   **P9**

A third purpose for the power supply is to provide cooling for the computer. The power supply's fan circulates air throughout the computer. Most computer cases have air vents on one side, both sides, or in the rear of the computer. Whether a desktop model, a tower model, or a desktop computer mounted in a stand that sits on the floor, be sure nothing blocks the air vents in the computer case!

Electronic components generate a great deal of heat, but are designed to withstand temperatures up to a certain degree. Auxiliary fans can be purchased to help cool the internal components of a computer.

Be careful when installing an auxiliary fan. Place the auxiliary fan so the outflow of air moves the same direction as the flow of air generated by the power supply. If an auxiliary fan is installed inside the case in the wrong location, the auxiliary air flow could work against the power supply air flow, defeating the purpose of the auxiliary fan.

TYPES OF POWER SUPPLY CONNECTORS

Two different connectors that extend from the power supply to connect to various devices are a **Molex connector** and a **Berg connector**. Power Figure #3 shows an illustration of each.

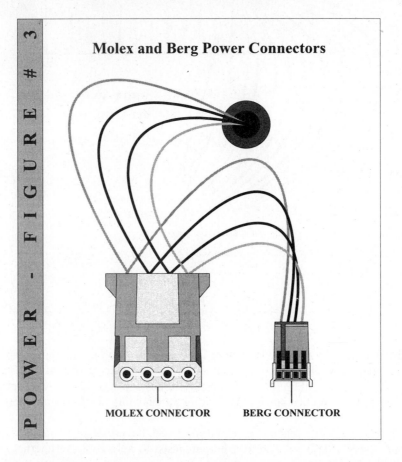

POWER - FIGURE # 3

Molex and Berg Power Connectors

MOLEX CONNECTOR   BERG CONNECTOR

Not all power supplies have the Berg connectors. If a device requires a Berg connector and the only one available is a Molex, a Molex to Berg connector converter can be purchased for just a few dollars. The Molex and Berg connectors coming from the power supply can connect to any device; there is *not* a specific connector for the hard drive, the floppy drive, etc. Also, the number of available connectors from the power supply varies between manufacturers. If there are not enough connectors from the power supply for the number of devices installed in the computer, a Y power connector can be purchased at a computer or electronics store. The Y connector adapts a single Molex connector to two Molex connectors for two devices. Verify that the power supply can output enough power to handle the extra device being installed!

A technician is well advised to carry a Molex to Berg converter and a Y power connector in the toolkit.

POWER SUPPLY VOLTAGES

The wires from the power supply carry four levels of DC voltage: +5 volts, -5 volts, +12 volts, and -12 volts. The motherboard, as well as most adapters, uses only +5 volts. Newer motherboards have some chips that run on 3.3 volts or less. A voltage regulator on the motherboard takes the 5 volts from the power supply and reduces it. Devices such as the floppy drive and hard drive use +5 volts and +12 volts. The +12 voltage is used to operate the device motors found in drives. Drives are now being made that use +5 volt motors. The negative voltages are seldom used.

A technician must occasionally check voltages in a system. There are three basic checks for power supply situations: (1) wall outlet AC voltage, (2) DC voltages going to the motherboard, and (3) DC voltages going to a device via the Molex or Berg connector.

When checking voltages, the power supply should always have a load. Be sure the connectors from the power supply connect to the motherboard and to at least one device, such as the hard drive.

A good power supply has internal circuitry that shuts down the power supply if it does not connect to something, meaning the power supply is without a load. However, some cheap power supplies can burn up if powered on without a device or the motherboard connected. Exercises at the end of the chapter familiarize the technician with voltage checks on a microcomputer. Exercise extreme caution when taking AC voltage checks; AC voltage can harm the technician! Also, be careful when checking DC voltages. Touching the meter to two different voltages simultaneously or to a DC voltage and another circuit can damage the computer!

UPGRADING A POWER SUPPLY

Power supplies are rated in **watts**. Computers in use today have power supplies with ratings ranging from 150 to 250 watts, although powerful computers such as network servers can have power supplies rated up to 600 watts. Each device inside the computer uses a certain amount of wattage and the power supply must be powerful enough to run all the devices. One example of a "not powerful enough" power supply is in a very old computer such as an 8088 or 8086 computer. Another example is a computer converted into a power machine with multiple hard drives and a variety of adapters. The amount of wattage each device or adapter requires is in the documentation for the device or adapter.

Different physical sizes of power supplies are available. So, when replacing a power supply, purchasing a power supply for a new computer, or upgrading a power supply, verify the power supply will fit in the computer case. Also verify that the power supply generates enough wattage for the installed devices and for future upgrades. Do not forget to check that the on/off switch on the new power supply is in a location that matches the computer case.

POWER PROBLEMS

Power supplies are not normally disassembled. Frequently, manufacturers rivet power supplies shut.

Even if the power supply could be disassembled, unless one has a background in electronics, the power supply should not be taken apart. Replace the entire power supply when it is faulty.

They are not expensive. Swap the power supply, make the customer happy, and be on your way! Power problems are not usually difficult to detect or troubleshoot.

The most obvious symptom of a power problem is the computer's power light being off. When suspecting a power supply problem, start by checking the computer's power light. If the light is off, check the power supply fan by placing your palm at the back of the computer near the power supply. If the fan turns, the wall outlet is providing power to the computer and the technician can assume the wall outlet is functioning. An AC circuit tester can quickly verify this assumption. Troubleshooting power problems is not difficult. The following troubleshooting questions help a technician determine the location of the power problem.

1. Has the power supply ever worked before? If not, check the 115/230 switch on the power supply and verify it is on the 115 setting.
2. Is the power supply's fan turning? If yes, go to Question 5. If not, check the wall outlet for proper AC voltages. If the wall outlet is okay, go on to Question 3.
3. Is a surge strip used? If so, check to see if the surge strip is powered on, then try a different outlet in the surge strip, or replace the surge strip.
4. Is the computer's power cord okay? Verify that the power cord plugs snugly into the outlet and into the back of the computer. Swap the power cord to verify it is functioning.
5. Are the voltages going to the motherboard at the proper level? Check the voltages to the motherboard. If they are not at the proper level, disconnect the power cable to one device and check the voltages again. Replace the power cable to the device. Remove the power cable from another device and check the motherboard voltages again. Continue doing this until the power cord for each device has been disconnected and the motherboard voltages have been checked. A single device can short out the power supply and cause the system to malfunction. Replace any device that draws the wrong voltage. If none of the devices cause the problem, replace the power supply. If replacing the power supply does not solve the problem, replace the motherboard.

Build the computer outside the computer case on an anti-static mat if possible. Start with only a power supply, motherboard, and speaker connected. Even though there normally is a POST audio error, just verify the power supply fan will turn. Most power supplies issue a click heard through the speaker before the audio POST beeps. Then, verify the voltages from the power supply. If the fan turns and the voltages are correct, power down the machine and add a video adapter and monitor to the system. If the machine does not work, put the video adapter in a different expansion slot and try again. If placing the video adapter in a different expansion slot does not work, swap out the video adapter.

If the video adapter works, continue adding devices one by one and checking the voltages. Just as any one device can cause the system to not operate properly, any one adapter can also short out the system and cause it to not operate properly. If one particular adapter causes the system to malfunction, try a different expansion slot before trying a different adapter.

If the expansion slot proves to be a problem, check the slot for foreign objects. If none are found, but the problem still occurs when using the particular expansion slot, place a note on the expansion slot so that no one will use the problem slot.

 ## SYMPTOMS OF POWER SUPPLY PROBLEMS

The following list provides several symptoms exhibited by a power supply problem.

1.   The computer's power light is off.
2.   The power supply fan does not turn when the computer is powered on.
3.   The computer sounds a continuous beep (could also be bad motherboard or stuck key on keyboard).
4.   When the computer powers on, it does not beep at all (could also be bad motherboard).
5.   When the computer powers on, it sounds repeating short beeps (could also be bad motherboard).
6.   During POST, a 02X or parity POST error code appears (where X is any number). One of the POST checks is a power good signal from the power supply. If the power supply is not working, a 021, 022, etc. indicates that the power supply did not pass the POST test.

ADVERSE POWER CONDITIONS

There are two adverse AC power conditions that can damage or affect a computer: over-voltage and under-voltage. An **over-voltage** occurs when the output voltage from the wall outlet (the AC voltage) is over the rated amount. Normally the output of a wall outlet is 110 to 130 volts AC. When the voltage rises above 130 volts, an over-voltage condition exists. The power supply takes the AC voltage and converts it to DC. An over-voltage condition is harmful to the components because too much DC voltage destroys the electronic circuits. An over-voltage condition can be a **surge** or a **spike**. A surge has a longer duration than a spike. A spike is harder to guard against than a surge because it has such short duration and intensity.

When the voltage falls below 100 volts AC, an **under-voltage** condition exists. If the voltage is too low, the power supply will not be able to provide enough power to all the computer components. Then, the power supply draws too much current causing the power supply to overheat. If the power supply overheats, the power supply components can be weakened or damaged. An under-voltage condition is known as a brownout or a sag. People sometimes refer to a **brownout** when circuits become overloaded. Sometimes the electric company intentionally causes a brownout to reduce the power drawn by consumers during their peak periods. A **sag** occurs when the voltage from the wall outlet drops momentarily. A **blackout** is a total loss of power.

ADVERSE POWER PROTECTION

Power supplies have built-in protection against adverse power conditions. However, the best protection for the computer is to unplug it during a power outage or thunderstorm. Three devices are commonly used to protect against adverse power conditions: a surge protector, a line conditioner, or an uninterruptable power supply (UPS). Each device has a specific purpose and guards against certain conditions. A technician needs to be familiar with each device to make recommendations for customers.

SURGE PROTECTORS

A **surge protector**, also known as a surge strip or surge suppressor, is commonly a 6-outlet strip with built-in protection against over-voltage. Reference Power Figure #4 for a picture of a surge protector.

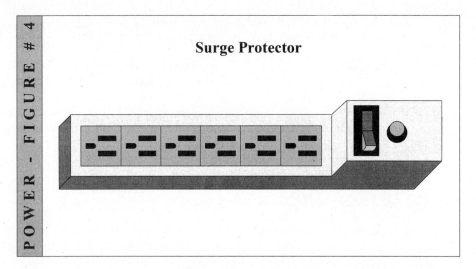

Surge protectors do not protect for the under-voltage condition. Some surge protectors have an electronic component called a **MOV (Metal Oxide Varistor)** which protects the computer or device that plugs into one of the outlets on the surge strip. The MOV, however, has some drawbacks. If a large surge occurs, the MOV will take the hit from the surge and be destroyed which is better than damaging the computer. However, with smaller over-voltages, each small surge weakens the MOV. A weakened MOV might not give the proper protection to the computer if there is a bigger surge. Also, there is no simple check for the MOV's condition. Some MOVs have indicator lamps attached, but this lamp only indicates when the MOV is destroyed, not when it is weakened. However, having an indicator lamp is better than nothing at all. Some surge protectors also have replaceable fuses and/or an indicator lamp for the fuse.

Surge protectors have two features to consider when selecting one. **Clamping voltage** is the voltage level at which the surge protector starts protecting the computer. **Clamping speed** is how much time elapses before the protection begins. Surge protectors cannot normally protect against power spikes (over-voltages of short duration) because of their rated clamping speed. Another feature to look at is the **joule dissipation capacity**. The greater the joule dissipation capacity, the more effective and durable the surge protector is. A surge protector with 630 joules of dissipation is more effective than one with 210 joules of dissipation.

Another feature to look for in a surge protector is how fast the surge protector responds to an adverse condition. Surge protectors that respond within **picoseconds** (trillionths of seconds) react faster than surge protectors that respond in **nanoseconds** (billionths of seconds). Also, for greater surge protection, choose a lower **Transient Voltage Suppressing (TVS) rating**. A 330 TVS-rated surge protector is better than a 400 TVS-rated surge protector.

Underwriters Laboratories developed the UL 1449 standard that regulates surge suppressors.

When purchasing or recommending a surge protector, be sure it conforms to the UL 1449 standard and has a MOV status lamp. Also, check to see if the vendor offers to repair or replace the equipment that will attach to the protection device.

Surge protectors are not the optimum protection for a computer system because most available provide very little protection against all adverse power conditions. Even the good ones only protect against over-voltage conditions. The ones with the UL 1449 rating and the MOV status lamp are usually more expensive. Unfortunately, people tend to put their money into their computer parts, not the protection of the parts.

LINE CONDITIONERS

An alternative for computer protection is the line conditioner. **Line conditioners**, sometimes known as power conditioners, are more expensive than surge protectors, but protect the computer from over-voltages, under-voltages, and adverse noise conditions which can occur over electrical lines. The line conditioner monitors AC electricity. If the voltage is too low, the line conditioner boosts the voltage to the proper range. If the voltage level is too high, the line conditioner clamps the voltage down and sends the proper amount to the computer.

Be careful not to plug too many devices into a line conditioner. A line conditioner is rated for a certain amount of current. Laser printers, for example, can draw a great deal of current (up to 15 amps). Some line conditioners are not rated to handle such a device. Because laser printers draw so much current, if a computer and a laser printer are on the same electrical circuit, the electrical circuit should be wired to a 20 amp circuit breaker.

UNINTERRUPTABLE POWER SUPPLY (UPS)

An **uninterruptable power supply** or **UPS** provides power to a computer or a device for a limited amount of time when there is a power outage. The UPS provides enough time to save work and bring the computer down safely. Some operating systems do not operate properly if power abruptly cuts off and the computer is not brought to a logical stopping place. A network server, the main computer for a network, is a great candidate for a UPS. Network operating systems are particularly susceptible to problems in a power outage. Some UPSs have a connection for a serial cable and special software that automatically maintains voltages to the computer, quits all applications, and powers the computer off. The UPS provides the power and the necessary time to do this.

A UPS also provides power conditioning for the devices attached to it. The AC power feeds into a battery inside the UPS. The battery inside the UPS continually recharges and supplies power to the computer. When AC power from the outlet fails, the battery inside the UPS continues to supply power to the computer. The battery inside the UPS outputs DC power and the computer expects AC power. Therefore, the DC power from the battery must be converted back to AC voltage for output to the computer. AC voltage normally looks like a **sine wave** when it is in its correct form, but cheaper UPS's produce a **square wave** that is not as effective. Some computer systems and peripherals do not process the square wave output. Reference Power Figure #5 for an illustration of a sine wave and a square wave.

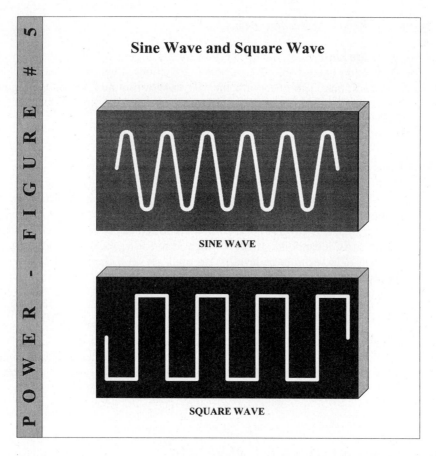

POWER - FIGURE # 5

Sine Wave and Square Wave

SINE WAVE

SQUARE WAVE

Be sure the UPS produces a proper output wave form for optimum operation. The documentation with the UPS should specify the output wave form type. The amount of time the UPS provides power to a computer or device and the number of devices that can attach to the UPS varies from model to model. Generally, the more time and the more devices the UPS handles, the more expensive it is.

UPSs are the best protection against adverse power conditions because they protect against over and under-voltage conditions and they provide power so a system can be brought down and turned off properly. When purchasing a UPS, be sure (1) the amount of battery time is sufficient to protect all devices, (2) the amount of current the UPS produces is sufficient to protect all devices, and (3) the output wave form is a sine wave.

STANDBY POWER SUPPLY (SPS)

A device similar to the UPS is the **Standby Power Supply** or **SPS**. An SPS contains a battery like the UPS, but the battery only provides power to the computer when it loses AC power, not constant power like the UPS. A SPS is not as effective as the UPS because the SPS must detect the power-out condition first then switch over to the battery to supply power to the computer. So, a feature to look for in an SPS is switching time. Any time under 5 milliseconds is normally fine for most systems.

PHONE LINE ISOLATOR

Just like AC power outlets, the phone outlet can also have power fluctuations. These enter the computer through a modem, a device used to connect a computer to a phone line. Not only can a modem be damaged by a power surge on the phone line, but other electronics inside the computer such as the motherboard can also be damaged. A **phone line isolator**, sometimes called a **modem isolator**, can be purchased at an electronics store and provides protection against phone line surges. No computer connected to a phone line through a modem should be without one. Reference Power Figure #6 for an illustration of a phone/modem isolator.

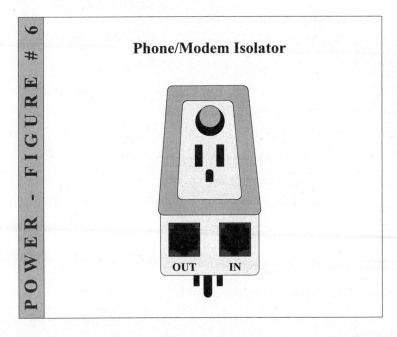

POWER - FIGURE # 6

Phone/Modem Isolator

OUT   IN

Power supplies and associated protection equipment are not very exciting to a technician, but they are very important. Power problems catch you unaware when you least expect them. Always keep power as a potential suspect in your mind when troubleshooting a computer.

Name _____

Power Review Questions

1. List three purposes of a power supply.

2. Describe how to be certain the power supply connections to the motherboard are correct.

3. List one precaution when installing an additional cooling fan inside a computer.

4. What can be done if a power supply does not have an available Berg connector for a device that requires one?

5. What can be done if a power supply does not have enough power connectors?

6. What are the four output voltages of a power supply?

7. Of the four output voltages of a power supply, which output voltage is used for electronic chips?

8. Of the four output voltages of a power supply, which output voltage is used for drive motors?

9. Why should a power supply be tested with "a load"?

10. What should you take into account when buying a power supply?

11. T/F   Power supplies are frequently disassembled for repair.

12. Describe how you can go about troubleshooting a power supply problem.

13. T/F   Most power supplies issue a single click during bootup.

14. List three power supply problem symptoms.

15. What is the difference between a surge and a spike?

16. T/F   Power supplies have their own internal protection against power problems.

17. What features should you look for in a surge protector?

18. Why is having a MOV status lamp in a surge protector important?

19. What is the optimum power protection for a computer?

20. T/F   Powerful computers that are the main component of a network should always have an UPS attached for power protection.

21. What features are important in an UPS?

22. What is the difference between an UPS and a SPS?

23. T/F   Power surges can occur over phone lines and damage internal components of a microcomputer.

Name _____

Power Fill-in-the-Blank

1.   The type of power provided by a wall outlet is known as _____.

2.   The type of power the computer uses is known as _____.

3.   For computers that connect AC to the front panel power switch, the _____ wire is the return for the black wire.

4.   For computers that connect AC to the front panel power switch, the _____ wire is the hot for the white return wire.

5.   Two power supply connectors are the _____ and the _____.

6.   All power supplies have the _____ connectors.

7.   Power supply output is rated in _____.

8.   An _____ condition is when the AC exceeds the rated amount.

9.   Two over-voltage conditions are a _____ and a _____.

10. Two under-voltage conditions are a _____ and a _____.

11. A total loss of power is also known as a _____.

12. A _____ only protects against the over-voltage condition.

13. A common component in a surge protector is the _____ which protects against power surges.

14. A surge protector's _____ is the voltage level at which protection begins.

15. A surge protector's _____ is the time it takes for the surge protector to react to an adverse over-voltage condition.

16. The _____ guards against over and under-voltages, but not for a blackout.

17. The _____ provides power from a battery to the computer during a power outage and during normal power conditions.

18. A _____ provides power to the computer from a battery only during a power outage.

19. _____ provides protection for modems.

Name_____

WALL OUTLET AND POWER CORD
AC VOLTAGE CHECK

Objective: To check the voltage from a wall outlet and through a power cord

Parts: Multimeter*
Computer power cord
*An AC wiring checker can be used instead of this procedure. Refer to the AC wiring checker documentation for proper readings.

EXERCISE EXTREME CAUTION WHEN WORKING WITH AC VOLTAGES!

Step 1:   Set the multimeter to **AC VOLTAGE** (refer to the meter's manual if unsure about this setting).
Step 2:   Power on the multimeter.
Step 3:   Insert the meter's **black** lead into the **round** (Ground) AC outlet plug.
Step 4:   Insert the meter's **red** lead into the **smaller flat** (Hot) AC outlet plug. The meter reading should be around 120 volts. Use the table below to record the reading.
Step 5:   Move the meter's **red** lead into the **larger flat** (Neutral) AC outlet plug. The meter reading should be 0 volts. Use the table below to record the reading.
Step 6:   Remove both leads from the wall outlet.
Step 7:   Insert the meter's **black** lead into the **smaller flat** (Hot) AC outlet plug.
Step 8:   Insert the meter's **red** lead into the **larger flat** (Neutral) AC outlet plug. The meter reading should be around 120 volts. Use Power Exercise Table #1 to record the reading.

POWER EXERCISE - TABLE # 1

Wall Outlet AC Checks

Connections	Expected Voltage	Actual Voltage
GND-Hot	120VAC	
GND-Neutral	0VAC	
Hot-Neutral	120VAC	

Step 9:   Plug the computer power cord into the AC wall outlet that was checked using Steps 3 through 8.

Step 10: Verify the other end of the power cord is *not* plugged into the computer.

Step 11: Perform the same checks as performed in Steps 3 through 8 except this time perform the check on the power cord end that plugs into the computer. Use Power Exercise Table #2 to record the reading.

POWER EXERCISE - TABLE # 2

Power Cord AC Checks

Connections	Expected Voltage	Actual Voltage
GND-Hot	120VAC	
GND-Neutral	0VAC	
Hot-Neutral	120VAC	

Step 12: If the voltage through the power cord is correct, power off the meter. Notify the instructor of any incorrect voltages.

Name _____

MOTHERBOARD DC VOLTAGE CHECK

Objective: To check the power supply voltages sent to the motherboard.

Parts: Multimeter
Working computer

Step 1:   Set the multimeter to **DC VOLTAGE**.
Step 2:   Power on the multimeter.
Step 3:   Power off the computer.
Step 4:   Remove the computer case.
Step 5:   Locate the power connectors that go *from* the power supply *to* the motherboard. They are normally located close to the power supply. Do *not* remove the connectors; just locate them.
Step 6:   Power on the computer.
Step 7:   Check the +5 volt DC output from the power supply by placing the meter's *black* lead on one of the ground signals* (a black wire) and the meter's *red* lead on one of the +5 volt wires (usually a red wire) on the connector to the motherboard. Reference Power Exercise Figure #1, the power supply documentation, or the motherboard documentation for the layout of the power supply connections. Power Exercise Figure #1 contains the table of acceptable voltage levels.

*Use and check all four ground connections (black wires going into the motherboard). Do not perform all the voltage checks using the same ground connection.

Write the voltage level found for each +5 volt wire in the Power Exercise Table #3.

POWER EXERCISE - TABLE # 3

Voltage Being Checked:	Voltage Found:
+5 volts	
+5 volts	
+5 volts	
+5 volts	

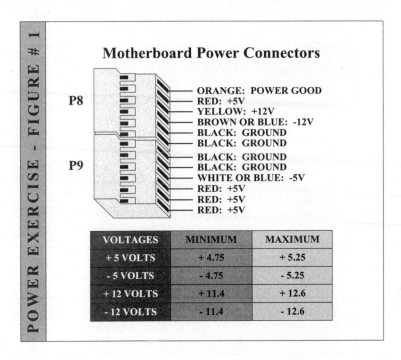

Motherboard Power Connectors

P8

ORANGE: POWER GOOD
RED: +5V
YELLOW: +12V
BROWN OR BLUE: -12V
BLACK: GROUND
BLACK: GROUND

P9

BLACK: GROUND
BLACK: GROUND
WHITE OR BLUE: -5V
RED: +5V
RED: +5V
RED: +5V

VOLTAGES	MINIMUM	MAXIMUM
+ 5 VOLTS	+ 4.75	+ 5.25
- 5 VOLTS	- 4.75	- 5.25
+ 12 VOLTS	+ 11.4	+ 12.6
- 12 VOLTS	- 11.4	- 12.6

Step 8: Check the -5 volt DC output by placing the meter's *black* lead on one of the ground signals (a black wire) and the meter's *red* lead on the -5 volt wire (normally a blue or white wire) on the connector to the motherboard (usually a white or blue wire). Reference Power Exercise Figure #1, the power supply documentation, or the motherboard documentation for the layout of the power supply connections. Power Exercise Figure #1 contains a table of acceptable voltage levels. Write the voltage level found for the -5 volt wire in Power Exercise Table #4:

Voltage Being Checked:	Voltage Found:
-5 volts	

Step 9: Check the -12 volt DC output by placing the meter's *black* lead on one of the ground signals (a black wire) and the meter's *red* lead on the -12 volt wire (normally a brown or blue wire) on the connector to the motherboard. Reference Power Exercise Figure #1, the power supply documentation, or the motherboard documentation for the layout of the power supply connections. Power Exercise Figure #1 contains a table that lists the acceptable voltage levels. Write the voltage level found for the -12 volt wire in Power Exercise Table #5:

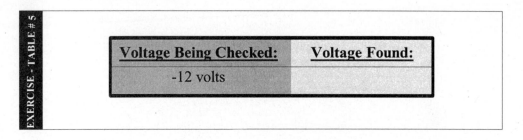

Step 10:   Check the +12 volt DC output by placing the meter's *black* lead on one of the ground
           signals (a black wire) and the meter's *red* lead on the +12 volt wire (usually a yellow wire)
           on the connector going to the motherboard. Reference Power Exercise Figure #1, the power
           supply documentation, or the motherboard documentation for the layout of the power
           supply connections. Power Exercise Figure #1 contains the table of acceptable voltage
           levels. Write the voltage level found for the +12 volt wire in Power Exercise Table #6.

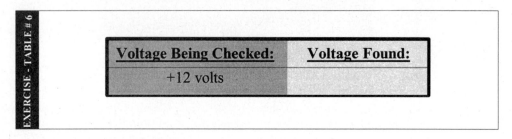

Step 11:   Notify the instructor of any voltages out of range.
Step 12:   Power off the meter.
Step 13:   Power off the computer.

Name_____

DEVICE DC VOLTAGE CHECK

Objective: To check the power supply voltages sent to various devices

Parts: Multimeter
             Working computer

Step 1:   Set the multimeter to **DC VOLTAGE** (refer to the meter's manual if unsure about the setting).
Step 2:   Power on the multimeter.
Step 3:   Power off the computer.
Step 4:   Remove the computer case.
Step 5:   Locate a Molex or Berg power connector. If one is not available, disconnect a power connector from a device.
Step 6:   Power on the computer.
Step 7:   Check the +5 volt DC output from the power supply by placing the meter's *black* lead in (if the connector is a Molex) or on (if the connector is a Berg) one of the ground signals* (a black wire). Place the meter's *red* lead on the +5 volt wire (normally a red wire) in or on the connector. Reference Power Exercise Figure #2 for the layout of the Molex and Berg power supply connections. Power Exercise Figure #2 also contains a table with the acceptable voltage levels.
         *Use and check both ground connections (black wires going into the connector); do not check all the voltages using only one ground connection.

Write the voltage level found for the +5 volt wire in Power Exercise Table #7:

Voltage Being Checked:	Voltage Found:
+5 volts	

EXERCISE - TABLE # 7

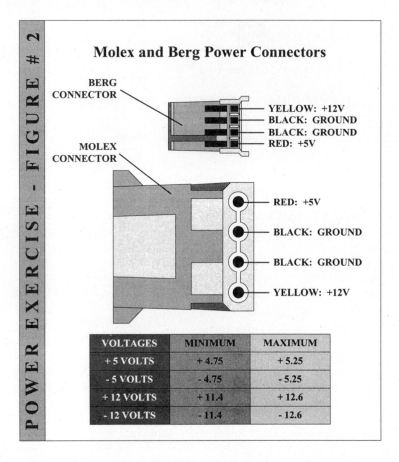

POWER EXERCISE - FIGURE # 2

Molex and Berg Power Connectors

BERG CONNECTOR

YELLOW: +12V
BLACK: GROUND
BLACK: GROUND
RED: +5V

MOLEX CONNECTOR

RED: +5V

BLACK: GROUND

BLACK: GROUND

YELLOW: +12V

VOLTAGES	MINIMUM	MAXIMUM
+ 5 VOLTS	+ 4.75	+ 5.25
- 5 VOLTS	- 4.75	- 5.25
+ 12 VOLTS	+ 11.4	+ 12.6
- 12 VOLTS	- 11.4	- 12.6

Step 8:   Check the +12 volt DC output by placing the meter's *black* lead in (if the connector is a Molex) or on (if the connector is a Berg) one of the ground signals. Place the meter's *red* lead on the +12 volts wire in or on the connector. Reference Power Exercise Figure #2 for the layout of the Molex and Berg power supply connections. Power Exercise Figure #2 also contains a table with the acceptable voltage levels. Write the voltage level found for the +12 volt wire in Power Exercise Table #8:

EXERCISE - TABLE # 8

Voltage Being Checked:	Voltage Found:
+12 volts	

Step 9:   Notify the instructor of any voltages out of range.
Step 10:   Power off the meter.
Step 11:   Power off the computer.

Name _____

1.   A 25-pin female port on the computer is a _____ port.
      A.   Video
      B.   Parallel
      C.   Serial
      D.   Network

2.   Serial ports on the computer are _____. (Pick all that apply.)
      A.   9-pin male
      B.   9-pin female
      C.   25-pin male
      D.   25-pin female

3.   T/F   Computer network ports and modem ports are the same physical ports.

4.   A 9-pin female port on the computer can be _____. (Pick all that apply.)
      A.   Monochrome video port
      B.   Modem
      C.   Serial port
      D.   TokenRing port
      E.   Parallel port

5.   The RJ11 port is for _____ .
      A.   Monitors
      B.   Networks
      C.   Printers
      D.   Modems

6.   The speed rating shown on a microprocessor is for _____ operations.
      A.   Internal
      B.   External

7.   A 15-pin female computer port is for _____ .
      A.   Video
      B.   Modems
      C.   Printers
      D.   Network adapters

C
E
R
T
I
F
I
C
A
T
I
O
N

R
E
V
I
E
W

Q
U
E
S
T
I
O
N
S

8. Which of the following describes functions of the microprocessor? (pick all that apply)
    A.   Distributes power to the adapters, devices, and motherboard
    B.   Handles communications between computer components
    C.   Stores user documents permanently
    D.   Processes software instructions

9. A 100MHz 80486DX4 microprocessor runs at _____ MHz externally.
    A.   25
    B.   33
    C.   50
    D.   75
    E.   100

10. Which of the following is *not* an Intel microprocessor?
    A.   80386DX
    B.   80486SX
    C.   80586DX
    D.   80487SX

11. A user wants to buy a computer for desktop publishing. What architecture or local bus would be best for video performance?
    A.   PC Card
    B.   ISA
    C.   EISA
    D.   MCA
    E.   PCI
    F.   VL-bus

12. T/F   All microprocessors have a separate math co-processor chip that mounts on the motherboard.

13. What architecture or local bus can provide the best performance when transferring between the Pentium II microprocessor and an adapter?
    A.   PC Card
    B.   ISA
    C.   EISA
    D.   MCA
    E.   PCI
    F.   VL-bus

14. What architecture or local bus is primarily for laptop computers?
    A.   PC Card
    B.   ISA
    C.   EISA
    D.   MCA
    E.   PCI
    F.   VL-bus

15. What math co-processor goes with the 80486SX?
    A.   80487
    B.   80487SX
    C.   80486DX
    D.   80486SX

16. If a multimeter is used to check the power supply output that goes to the hard drive, to what setting will the multimeter be set?
    A.   AC volts
    B.   DC volts
    C.   Ohms
    D.   Farads

17. If a multimeter is used to check the input to the power supply, to what setting will the multimeter be set?
    A.   AC volts
    B.   DC volts
    C.   Ohms
    D.   Farads

18. The ability to transfer information between devices without microprocessor intervention is

    _____.
    A.   Bus mastering
    B.   Direct memory access
    C.   Plug and play
    D.   High memory access

19. Motors inside the computer normally use _____ volts and electronic components normally use _____ volts.
    A.   -5 / -12
    B.   +5 / +12
    C.   +12 / +5
    D.   -12 / -5

20. When a computer is powered on, a cursor does *not* appear in the monitor's left corner. Which of the following is the LEAST suspect?
    A.   Monitor
    B.   Power supply
    C.   Hard drive
    D.   Motherboard

21. T/F   All PCI adapters are Plug and Play.

22. T/F   Maintaining polarity is important when measuring DC volts.

23. Which of the following devices ensures that power is constantly provided to the computer?
  A. Surge protector
  B. Power Conditioner
  C. Power Supply
  D. UPS

24. Which of the following items should you check when replacing a power supply? (Pick all that apply.)
  A. The correct wattage
  B. The power supply accepts AC input
  C. The size of the power supply as well as the position of the on/off switch
  D. The output voltages provided to the motherboard

25. T/F A voltage spike can affect any component even if a surge suppressor is installed.

26. In the United States, a selectable power supply should be set to the _____ setting.
  A. 110
  B. 220
  C. 5
  D. 12

27. T/F When installing a power supply, be certain the power supply is set to IRQ 1.

28. Which of the following indicate the power supply is faulty? (Pick all that apply.)
  A. The fan on the power supply does not turn
  B. The power LED on the front of the computer does not come on
  C. The power light on the monitor does not come on
  D. There is no cursor in the upper left corner of the monitor

29. Which of the following are important to consider when adding an adapter? (Pick all that apply.)
  A. Unique interrupt
  B. Expansion slot location
  C. Unique I/O address
  D. Unique ROM address

30. What is the name of the routine that is performed when a computer is powered on?
  A. Startup test routine
  B. BIOS startup
  C. System check routine
  D. Power on self test

31. T/F Windows 95 supports Plug and Play

Chapter 6: Logical Troubleshooting

OBJECTIVES

After completing this chapter you will
1.   Understand the basic procedure for troubleshooting a microcomputer
2.   Understand how the POST error codes help troubleshoot a computer
3.   Understand the importance of good communication with the
       computer user

KEY TERMS

None

TROUBLESHOOTING OVERVIEW

When a computer does not work properly, one trait must be exhibited that is essential to technicians—the will to succeed. A technician must have a good attitude and a large amount of stubbornness and drive to keep after those sometimes troublesome problems. Solving a computer problem can be easy if a troubleshooter uses logical reasoning and takes logical steps. Logical troubleshooting can be broken down into six simple steps:

1.   Re-create the problem.
2.   Divide the problem into hardware or software.
3.   Divide and conquer: divide the problem into logical areas to isolate the problem.
4.   Repair the problem.
5.   Test the solution.
6.   Provide feedback to the user.

RE-CREATE THE PROBLEM

Computer problems come in all shapes and sizes. Many problems relate to the people who operate the computers — the users. They frequently perceive the computer as the problem. The problem ends up as something the user is not doing right such as choosing the correct printer, pushing the correct key for a specific function, or issuing a correct command. Problems such as these are very frustrating to a computer technician, but must never be forgotten when arriving to help a client in response to a computer problem call.

When re-creating the situation, have the user demonstrate the problem. Because the *user* is often the most common computer problem, a great deal of time is saved with this step. Do not assume anything! Users call in their problems with a complaint such as "my hard drive does not work" when in fact, there is no power to the computer. Users often try to use computer terms they have heard or read, but cannot use them correctly or in the right syntax. By making the user re-create the problem, the technician can see it. If one cannot be in the same location as the user's computer (such as when the customer calls on the phone), the same rule applies: do not assume anything and make the user re-create the problem.

HARDWARE OR SOFTWARE

A technician determines if the computer problem is hardware or software related (or both) by using his or her senses. Watch the computer boot up and listen for beeps. Frequently a hardware problem is detected during POST (Power On Self Test) that is executed by the ROM BIOS chip during a cold boot. POST checks out the hardware in a sequential order and if it finds an error, the BIOS chip issues a beep and/or displays a numerical error code. Make note of any error codes or beeps. The number or duration of beeps and the numerical error codes that occur are different for different computers. The secret is in the manufacturer of the ROM BIOS chip. The major manufacturers of ROM BIOS chips for the motherboard include Award, AMI, IBM, and Phoenix. Logical Table #1 lists the audio beeps heard from a computer that has an AMI ROM BIOS chip installed.

LOGICAL - TABLE # 1

AMI BIOS Audio Beeps

Beeps	Description of Problem
1	DRAM refresh
2	Parity circuit
3	1st 64KB of RAM or CMOS
4	System timer
5	Microprocessor
6	Keyboard controller or A20 line
7	Virtual mode exception error
8	Display memory (read/write test)
9	ROM BIOS
10	CMOS shutdown (read/write test)
11	Cache memory
1 long, 3 short	RAM (conventional or extended)
1 long, 8 short	Display

Logical Table #2 lists the audio beeps heard from a computer with an IBM ROM BIOS chip installed.

LOGICAL - TABLE # 2

IBM POST Audio Beeps

Beeps	Description
No beeps	Power supply or system board failure
Continuous beep	Power supply or system board failure
Repeating beeps	Power supply or system board failure
1 short beep	Successful POST
2 short beeps	Initialization error on video
1 long, 1 short beep	System board failure
1 long, 2 short beeps	Video adapter failure
1 long, 3 short beeps	EGA video adapter failure

Logical Table #3 lists the audio beeps heard from a computer with a PHOENIX ROM BIOS chip installed.

LOGICAL - TABLE # 3

Phoenix Audio Beeps

Beeps	Description	Beeps	Description (cont.)
None/1-1-2	CPU register test	3-1-1	DMA register failure (slave)
1-1-3	CMOS failure (write/read test)	3-1-2	DMA register failure (master)
1-1-4	ROM BIOS failure (checksum test)	3-1-3	Interrupt mask register failure (master)
1-2-1	Programmable Interval Timer failure	3-1-4	Interrupt mask register failure (slave)
1-2-2	DMA failure (initialization test)	None/3-2-2	Interrupt vector loading in progress
1-2-3	DMA page register failure (write/read test)	3-2-4	Video failure
1-3-1	RAM refresh failed (ver. test)	None/3-3-1	CMOS RAM power bad
None/1-3-2	1st 64K of RAM test	None/3-3-2	CMOS config valid. in progress
1-3-3	1st 64K RAM chip failure (data line)	3-2-4	Keyboard controller test failed
1-3-4	1st 64K RAM failure (odd/even logic)	3-4-1	Video initialization failure
1-4-1	1st 64K RAM failure (address line)	3-4-2	Video retrace test failure
1-4-2	1st 64K RAM failure (parity)	None/3-4-3	Video ROM search in progress
1-4-3	EISA timer test in progress	None	Video scan failure
1-4-4	EISA NMI port test in progress	None	Screen is running with Video ROM
2-1-1	1st 64K RAM failure (bit 0)	None	Screen (mono) is operable
2-1-2	1st 64K RAM failure (bit 1)	None	Screen (color 40) is operable
2-1-3	1st 64K RAM failure (bit 2)	None	Screen (color 80) is operable
2-1-4	1st 64K RAM failure (bit 3)	4-2-1	Timer tick interrupt test in progress or failed
2-2-1	1st 64K RAM failure (bit 4)	4-2-2	Shutdown test in progress/failed
2-2-2	1st 64K RAM failure (bit 5)	4-2-3	Gate A20 failed test
2-2-3	1st 64K RAM failure (bit 6)	4-2-4	Unexpected interrupt in protected mode
2-2-4	1st 64K RAM failure (bit 7)	4-3-1	RAM test in progress or failure on last address line
2-3-1	1st 64K RAM failure (bit 8)	4-3-3	Interval timer test in progress or failure (Channel 2)
2-3-2	1st 64K RAM failure (bit 9)	4-3-4	Time of day clock test in progress or failure
2-3-3	1st 64K RAM failure (bit 10)	4-4-1	Serial port test in progress or failed
2-3-4	1st 64K RAM failure (bit 11)	4-4-2	Parallel port test in progress or failed
2-4-1	1st 64K RAM failure (bit 12)	4-4-3	Math Co-proc. test in progress/failed
2-4-2	1st 64K RAM failure (bit 13)	4-4-4	Cache test failed
2-4-3	1st 64K RAM failure (bit 14)	*1-1-2	System board select failed
2-4-4	1st 64K RAM failure (bit 15)	*1-1-3	Extended CMOS RAM failed

In addition to audio tones, a technician might also see numerical error codes. Just like audio clues, the numerical error codes are ROM BIOS dependent. Logical Table #4 lists IBM POST codes generally found on other systems as well.

IBM POST Error Codes

Error	Description	Error	Description
01X	Undetermined problem	115	Cache parity, ROM cksum, or DMA error
02X	Power supply	116	Port read/write error
1XX	**Motherboard Errors**	118	Parity or L2 cache error
101	Processor interrupt failed	120	Microprocessor failure
102	Timer or PS/2 real time clock failed	121	Unexpected interrupt error
103	Timer int. failed;PS/2 CMOS fail.	131-4	PS/2 DMA error
104	Protected mode failed	151	Battery or CMOS failure
105	8042 keybd cont. failed	152	PS/2 real time clock/CMOS error
106	Converting logic test failed	160	PS/2 sys bd ID not recognized
107	NMI failure	161-2	Battery; CMOS SETUP error
108	Bus test failure	163	CMOS date & time error
109	DMA failure	164	CMOS memory size error
110	PS/2 parity check failure	165	PS/2 SETUP error
111	PS/2 parity check failure	166	PS/2 adapter timeout
112	PS/2 MCA arbitration failed	167	PS/2 clock not updating
113	PS/2 MCA arbitration failed	168	CMOS math co-processor error
114	PS/2 external ROM failed	199	User indicated configuration error

LOGICAL - TABLE # 4

TABLE - 4

LOGICAL

IBM POST Error Codes (Cont.)

Error	Description	Error	Description
2XX	**Memory Errors (RAM)**	626	Disk data compare error
201	Memory failure	648	Format test failed
202	Memory address failure (0-15)	649	Incorrect media type
203	Memory address failure (ISA 16-23) (MCA 16-31)	650	Drive speed error
210	Parity error	651	Format failed
211	PS/2 1st 64K failure	652	Verify failed
3XX	**Keyboard Errors**	653	Read failed
301	Kybd reset failure/stuck key	654	Write failed
302	Keylock is enabled error	655	Adapter failed
303	Keyboard controller failure	**7XX**	**Math Co-processor Errors**
304	Keyboard or sys board failure	**9XX**	**Parallel Adapter Errors**
305	+5v error; PS/2 kybd fuse (on system board) error	**10XX**	**Alternate Parallel Port Adapter Errors**
306	Unsupported keyboard	**11XX**	**Primary Async (Serial COM1) Errors**
342	Keyboard cable error	1101	Adapter failure
366	Keyboard cable error	1107	Cable error
4XX	**Monochrome Display Errors**	1113	Transmit error
401	Mono mem., horiz. synch, or video test failure; PS/2 parallel port failure	1114	Receive error
432	Parallel port failure	1142	No IRQ4
5XX	**CGA Display Errors**	1143	No IRQ3
501	Mem., horiz. synch, vert. synch., or video test failure; CRT failure	1148	Time-out error
503	Adapter failure	1152	No DSR
6XX	**Floppy Errors**	1156	No CTS
601	Drive or controller error	**12XX**	**Alternate Async (Serial COM2, 3, 4) Errors**
602	Disk boot record error	1201	Adapter failure
603	Disk size error	1202	Internal modem failed
607	Write-protect error	1207	Cable error
610	Disk initialization error	1213	Transmit error
611	Drive time-out error	1214	Receive error
613	Adapter DMA test failure	1242	No IRQ4
621	Drive seek error	1243	No IRQ3
622	Drive CRC error	1248	Time-out error
623	Record not found error	1252	No DSR
624	Bad address mark error	1256	No CTS

IBM POST Error Codes (Cont.)

Error	Description	Error	Description
104XX	**ESDI or MicroChannel IDE Errors**	166XX	**Primary TokenRing Adapter Errors**
10450	Read/write test failure	208XX	**SCSI Device Errors**
10451	Read verify test failure	209XX	**SCSI Removable Disk Errors**
10452	Seek test failed	210XXXX	**SCSI Hard Drive Errors**
10453	Wrong drive type in CMOS	1st X after 210	SCSI ID number
10454	Controller buffer test failed	2nd X after 210	Logical Unit Number
10455	Controller failure	3rd X after 210	Host adapter slot number
10456	Controller diagnostic failure	4th X after 210	Drive capacity
10461	Drive format error	215XX	**SCSI CD ROM Errors**
10462	Controller head select problem	I99900XX	**IML Errors**
10463	Drive read/write error	I999001X	Invalid disk IML record
10464	Drive defect map problem	I999002X	Disk IML record load error
10465	Controller ECC error	I999003X	Disk IML incompatible with motherboard
10466	Controller ECC error	I999004X	Disk IML incompatible with processor
10467	Drive seek problem	I999005X	Disk IML not attempted
10468	Drive seek problem	I999006X	IML not supported on drive
10473	Read verify problem	I99900X2	Disk IML load error
10480	Drive 0 seek error	I99900X3	IML incompatible w/sys.board
10481	Drive 1 seek error	I99900X4	Disk IML incompatible with processor
10482	Controller transfer error	I99903XX	**No Bootable Device Errors**
10483	Controller reset error	I9990302	Invalid disk boot record
10484	Controller: hd select 3 error	I9990303	System partition boot failed
10485	Controller: hd select 2 error	I9990304	No bootable device found
10486	Controller: hd select 1 error	I9990305	No bootable media found
10487	Controller: hd select 0 error	I9990306	Invalid SCSI device boot record
112XX	**SCSI Adapter Errors**	I99904XX	**IML/System Mismatch Errors**
113XX	**SCSI (on sys bd) Errors**	I99906XX	**IML Errors**

LOGICAL - TABLE # 4

POST error codes only direct a technician to the right general area. Sometimes multiple POST errors occur. If this is the case, start the troubleshooting process with the first error code detected.

Because manufacturers constantly produce ROM BIOS upgrades, contact the chip manufacturer for a current list of error codes or use the Internet to download the latest copy of error codes.

Hardware errors might also occur when utilizing a particular device. For example, the monitor might suddenly go black, or the floppy drive access light does not turn on when accessing the floppy drive, or the printer constantly flashes an error code. Hardware errors are usually obvious because of POST error codes or errors that occur when accessing a particular device.

Software errors, on the other hand, occur when the computer user accesses a particular application or when the CONFIG.SYS or the AUTOEXEC.BAT files execute. If still in doubt as to whether a problem is hardware or software, run diagnostics on the hardware to prove that the problem is not hardware. Sometimes computers come with a diagnostic disk or diagnostics are part of the SETUP program. There are also third party diagnostics to test the computer such as Dominion Research Technologies, Inc.'s Check-It or DiagSoft's QA Plus.

DIVIDE AND CONQUER

Divide the problem into logical areas and continue sub-dividing the problem until it is isolated. For example, if an error appears each time the computer user saves to a floppy disk then the logical area is the floppy drive system. The floppy drive system includes the user's disk, the floppy drive, electronics that tell the floppy drive what to do, a cable that connects the floppy drive to the electronics, and the software program currently being used. Any component may be the problem. Ernie Friend, a friend of mine and technician of many years, says to divide a problem in half; then divide it in half again; divide it in half again until the problem is manageable. This way of thinking carries a technician a long way in a technical career. Always keep in mind too, that you will beat the problem at hand! The technician is smarter than the problem! Use Ernie's philosophy with the floppy problem — divide the problem in half and determine if the problem is hardware or software. To determine if the software application is causing the floppy problem, try saving a document to the floppy disk from another application. If the second application saves properly, then the problem is in the first application. If both applications have problems saving data to the disk, the problem is most likely in the disk or in the floppy hardware system. The next easiest thing to eliminate as a suspect is the disk. Try a different disk. If a different disk works, then the first disk was the problem. If both disks will not accept data, the problem is either the floppy drive, cable, or electronics. Swap parts one at a time until you locate the problem.

If a hardware problem is evident once a POST error or peripheral access/usage error occurs, consider the problem a sub-unit of the entire computer. For example, if a 601 floppy drive error occurs, the sub-unit is the floppy drive subsystem. The floppy drive subsystem consists of the floppy drive, the cable, and the controlling circuits which may be on an adapter or the motherboard.

If the problem is software, narrow the problem to a specific area. For example, determine if the problem is related to the CONFIG.SYS or AUTOEXEC.BAT files. Determine if the problem occurs only when a specific application executes.

When isolating the problem to a specific area, be practical; change or check the easy stuff first. Time is money, both to the company or person whose computer is down and to the company paying the technician's salary. If a monitor is down, swap the monitor with another before opening up the computer and swapping the video adapter. Also, check with the computer user to see if anything about the computer has changed recently. For example, ask if anyone installed or removed something from the computer or if any new software was loaded since the problem started. If the problem is hardware, diagnostics can be useful to get a problem to a sub-unit, but frequently, to isolate a problem, part-swapping is the only true test.

If one does not hear any unusual audio beeps or see any POST error codes, and a software error is suspect, reboot the computer. Press the F8 function key when the words "Starting PC DOS..." or "Starting MS-DOS..." appear to single-step through the CONFIG.SYS and AUTOEXEC.BAT files. Answer Y for YES for each command in the CONFIG.SYS and AUTOEXEC.BAT files. Note any errors in the order they occur. Sometimes errors can occur in the latter files of CONFIG.SYS or AUTOEXEC.BAT that are the result of a problem or problems in the beginning CONFIG.SYS commands.

To single-step through Windows 95's CONFIG.SYS and AUTOEXEC.BAT files, press the F8 function key when the words "Starting Windows 95" appear. From the menu shown, chose the option that refers to Step-by-Step Confirmation. For each command to be processes, press Y. To skip a command, press N.

REPAIR THE PROBLEM

Swap a part, check hardware settings, refer to documentation, etc. are all part of repairing the problem. Noting error codes or beep codes are all just part of the diagnostic routine of finding in the right area, but repairing the problem is normally the fastest step. Determining what the problem is definitely takes longer. Software problems frequently involve reloading software applications, software drivers, or getting software updates or patches from the appropriate vendor. The Internet is an excellent resource for these files. Hardware problem resolution simply involves swapping the damaged part.

TEST THE SOLUTION

Never assume the hardware component or the replaced software repairs the computer. The computer can have multiple problems, or the repair does not completely fix the problem. Test the computer *and* have the user test the computer in normal conditions to prove the problem is indeed solved.

PROVIDE FEEDBACK TO THE USER

Unfortunately, one of the biggest problems with technicians is their inability to communicate effectively with users. The best computer technicians are those with whom the customers feel at ease, the users trust, and who explain a problem in a way the customer understands. A computer repair is never finished until the user is updated with information regarding the repair. Do not use technical terms with users who are not technically competent. Do not treat a computer user as if they are not intelligent just because they are not proficient in computer technical terminology.

Each computer repair is a different scenario because of the plethora of vendors, products, and standards in the marketplace. But that is what makes the job so interesting and challenging. Break each problem down into a manageable task, isolate the problem, use all available resources including other technicians, documentation, the Internet, etc. to solve the problem, and never forget the feedback part of the repair.

The remaining chapters are dedicated to specific devices or areas of the computer. Each device or area has techniques that can be used once a problem is narrowed to that specific area. For example, if a computer problem is narrowed to a memory problem, go to the memory chapter for details of operation and troubleshooting techniques. Happy problem solving!!!

Notes Page

Name _____

LOGICAL TROUBLESHOOTING EXERCISE

Step 1: Power on a computer with a problem and perform the following steps shown in the flow chart of Logical Exercise Figure #1. Answer the questions that follow on the next page.

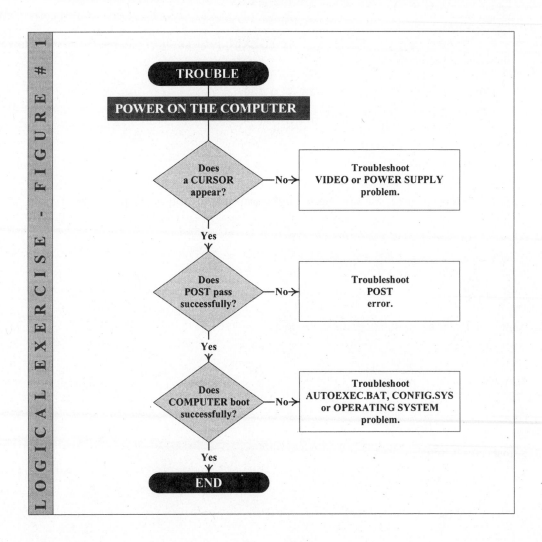

Question 1:   Are any audio clues heard? If yes, list the symptoms below:

Question 2:   Are any POST error codes seen? If yes, list the errors below in the order the errors occur:

Question 3:   Are there any CONFIG.SYS or AUTOEXEC.BAT errors? If so, list the errors below in the order the errors occur:

Question 4:   Are there any application-specific problems? If so, list the symptoms below:

Question 5:   Describe the solution to the problem.

_____ Instructor's Initials

Chapter 7:
Memory

OBJECTIVES

After completing this chapter you will
1.   Understand memory-related terminology.
2.   Be able to install and remove memory chips.
3.   Understand how memory works with different operating systems.
4.   Be able to optimize memory under different operating systems.
5.   Understand the purpose of a disk cache.
6.   Be able to troubleshoot memory problems.

KEY TERMS

access time	non-volatile memory
bank	pages
burst EDO	parity
chipset	parity chip
conventional memory	pipeline burst cache
cooperative multi-tasking	preemptive multi-tasking
data lines	RAM
DIMM	RAM drive
DIP	RDRAM
DRAM	refresh
driver	reserved area
ECC	ROM
EDO	SDRAM
expanded memory (EMS)	SGRAM
extended memory (XMS)	SIMM
FPM	SIPP
heaps	SRAM
HMA	swap file
LIM memory standard	system resources
memory map	thread
nanoseconds	upper memory blocks
nDRAM	virtual memory
non-parity	volatile memory

MEMORY OVERVIEW

Computer systems do nothing without software. For the computer to operate, the software must reside in the computer's memory. Memory is simple to upgrade, but fine-tuning memory is frequently frustrating and confusing. To thoroughly understand memory, a technician must understand the terminology, determine the optimum amount of memory for a system, install the memory, fine-tune it for the best performance, and finally, troubleshoot and solve any memory problems.

The two main types of memory are **RAM (Random Access Memory)** and **ROM (Read Only Memory)**. RAM is found on the motherboard and stores the operating system (DOS, Windows 95, or Windows NT Workstation) and the software applications (word processing, spreadsheet, database, etc.). It is also found in many adapters such as video cards. RAM is **volatile memory**; the information in RAM is lost when you power off the computer. ROM is **non-volatile memory;** the information in ROM remains stored even when the computer is powered off.

RAM is divided into two major types: **DRAM (Dynamic RAM)** and **SRAM (Static RAM)**. DRAM is less expensive than SRAM, but also slower than SRAM. With DRAM, the 1s and 0s inside the chip must be refreshed. Over time, the charge, which represents the information inside the DRAM chips, leaks out. The information, stored in 1s and 0s, is periodically rewritten to the memory chip through the **refreshing** process. The refreshing is accomplished internal to the DRAM while other processing occurs. Refreshing makes DRAM chips slower than SRAM.

Most memory on the motherboard is DRAM, but a small amount of SRAM can be found on the motherboards today. SRAM is also known as cache memory or L2 cache. Pentium motherboards frequently contain up to 512KB of cache. The cache memory holds the most frequently used data so the microprocessor does not return to the slower DRAM chips to obtain the data. Usually the more cache memory a system has, the better the system performs, but this is not always true. The system performance also depends on the efficiency of the cache controller (the chip that manages the cache memory) and the system design.

MEMORY PHYSICAL PACKAGING

Some DRAM chips are mounted on **SIMMs (Single In-line Memory Modules)**. Two types of SIMMs are available: 30-pin and 72-pin. The most current memory chip, a **DIMM (Dual In-line Memory Module),** has 168 pins and is for motherboards that use the Pentium, Pentium Pro or Pentium II microprocessor. SRAM chips are normally SIMMs or DIP chips. A **DIP (Dual In-line Package)** chip has a row of legs running down each side. Older motherboards used DIP chips for the DRAM. Memory Figure #1 shows a DIP chip, two SIMMs, and a DIMM.

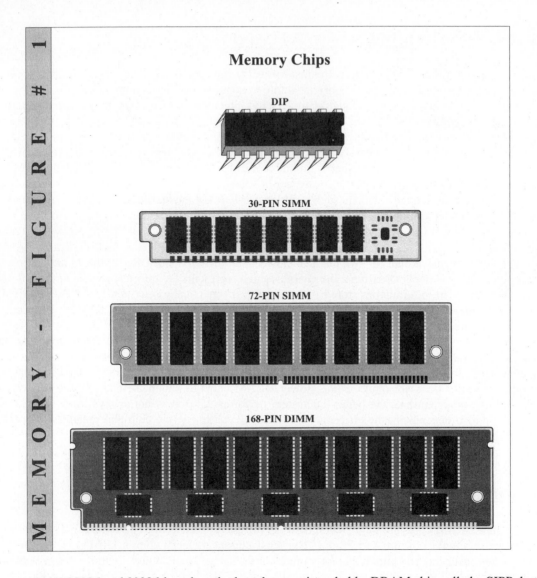

Memory Chips

DIP

30-PIN SIMM

72-PIN SIMM

168-PIN DIMM

Older 80286 and 80386-based motherboards sometimes held a DRAM chip called a SIPP, but these are few and far between. A **SIPP (Single In-line Pin Package)** is about the same size as a 30-pin SIMM. Instead of a card-edged connector, the SIPP has one row of round legs, but not two like the DIP chip. Older 8088, 8086, 80286, and even a few 80386 motherboards had DIP chips for the DRAM, but 386, 486, and Pentium computers use SIMMs for the RAM. More current Pentium, Pentium Pro, and Pentium II motherboards use DIMMs.

At the bottom of a SIMM are metal contacts that transfer the signals and data between the memory chip and the motherboard. SIMM chips have tin or gold contacts. If the computer is designed to accept tin SIMMs and you install gold SIMMs, over time, a metallic reaction occurs that damages the computer. The bottom line is, purchase the appropriate SIMM for the computer either by referring to the documentation or by examining other SIMMs already installed.

SIMMs also come in parity and non-parity versions. **Parity** is a method for checking the accuracy of data going in or out of the memory chips. For every eight bits of data, one parity bit is used. **Non-parity** memory chips are simply the chips that do not use any error-checking.

A computer system that uses parity *must* have parity memory chips installed. Computers that are non-parity systems can use either parity or non-parity SIMMs.

If the SIMM is a parity one, the parity bit is ignored by the non-parity system. However, non-parity memory chips are usually less expensive than parity memory chips. Some motherboards allow a choice of parity and non-parity memory by setting a motherboard jumper or using the SETUP program. Still other motherboards, when checking memory during POST, automatically disable the parity checking if all memory banks do not contain parity bits. All Pentium-based microcomputers with Intel's Triton-series chipset do *not* support parity.

How the parity functions depends on whether the system uses even parity or odd parity. For example, if the system uses even parity and the data bits 10000001 go into memory, the parity bit is a 0 because an even number of bits (2) are 1s. The parity changes to a 1 only when the number of bits in the data is an odd number of 1s. If the system uses even parity and the data bits 10000011 go into memory, the parity bit is a 1. There are only three 1s in the data bits. The parity bit adjusts the 1s to an even number. Sometimes the data bits will need an extra 1 to make the number even. When checking data for accuracy, the parity bit stays unchanged if no error occurs. However, if two bits are in error, the parity method of error-checking does not catch the error.

An alternative to parity checking is the ECC method. **ECC (Error Correcting Code)** uses a mathematical algorithm to verify the data's accuracy. ECC memory checking is more expensive to implement than parity. The motherboard or memory controller must have additional circuitry to process ECC bits generated and compared during each data transfer. ECC is used in computers such as network servers, database servers, or workstations running database applications. These systems need quality data for proper operation. Also, the ECC method of error-checking is used for components other than memory, such as hard drives and CD-ROMs.

SIZE (CAPACITY) OF MEMORY CHIPS

DIP memory chips normally have 64Kb, 256Kb, or 1Mb capacities. Notice these sizes are measured in *bits*, not *bytes*. A 64 Kilobit chip holds approximately 64,000 bits. To have 64 Kilobytes, eight 64Kb DIP chips work together to provide the 64KB of memory. 30-pin SIMM sizes are 256KB, 512KB, 1MB, 2MB, and 4MB, with 1MB and 4MB the most common sizes. 72-pin SIMM sizes are 4MB, 8MB, 16MB, 32MB, and 64MB capacities. 168-pin DIMM sizes are 8MB, 16MB, 32MB, 64MB, and 128MB. Notice these are Kilobyte and Megabyte capacities.

IDENTIFYING CHIP CAPACITY AND SPEED

Sometimes, you can tell the capacity of a memory chip by examining the numbers printed on the chip. For example, on a DIP chip, the numbers M41256A indicate a 256Kb chip and the numbers

MEMORY CHIP DEVELOPMENTS

New developments provide faster DRAM speeds without increasing the cost to equal the expense of the SRAM. The DRAM technologies include: Fast Page Mode (FPM) RAM, EDO (Extended Data Out) RAM, BEDO (Burst EDO) RAM, SDRAM (Synchronous DRAM), RDRAM (Rambus DRAM), and nDRAM. The motherboard must be designed to use one of these technologies or the faster memory *will not* speed up the computer unless the motherboard supports the specific memory technology.

Whether a motherboard supports faster memory chips is determined by the chipset working in conjunction with the microprocessor. A **chipset** is one to five electronic chips that control many parts of the motherboard operation. The chipset contains the circuitry to control the local bus, memory, DMA, interrupts, and cache memory. For example, the Triton II chipset by Intel supports EDO RAM and the Triton III chipset supports Burst EDO. Intel's 430VX and 440LX chipsets support the **SDRAM (synchronous DRAM)** technology. SDRAM performs very fast burst memory access similar to Burst EDO memory. New memory addresses are placed on the address bus before the prior memory address retrieval and execution completes. When SDRAM synchronizes its operation with the microprocessor's clock signal to speed up memory, it can deliver data at a rate of approximately 100MHz with the possibility of 200MHz in the future. PC100 SDRAM is for the 100MHz system bus speed motherboards. Another memory technology that can deliver data at speeds up to 100MHz is **SGRAM (Synchronous Graphic Random Access Memory)**. SGRAM memory chips are frequently used on video adapters and graphics accelerators, and have special memory techniques that speed up graphics-intensive functions.

SDRAM is a good memory technology for Pentium-based systems. However, as the microprocessors and motherboard components get faster than 200MHz, faster memory technologies evolve. **RDRAM (Rambus DRAM)**, sometimes called DRDRAM for Direct Rambus DRAM, is technology developed by Rambus, Inc. that allows data transfers up to 800MHz. Intel announced the Rambus memory technology will be used on future motherboards and most likely be the standard for memory architectures. RDRAM is already shipping on some video adapters. Intel and Rambus are working on updating RDRAM. The updated memory chips, **nDRAM**, are designed to support data transfers at speeds up to 1,600 MHz.

The **FPM (Fast Page Mode)**, **EDO (Extended Data Out)**, and **Burst EDO** technologies speed up DRAM on sequential accesses to the memory chip. For example, if you have a 50ns DRAM SIMM, a 50ns Fast Page Mode SIMM, a 50ns EDO SIMM, and a 50ns Burst EDO SIMM, each type takes 50 nanoseconds to access the memory chip the first time. But the Fast Page Mode SIMM accesses the SIMM in 40ns on the second access. The EDO SIMM is accessed in 25ns on the second access and the Burst EDO SIMM is in 15ns on the second access.

Some cache memory (L2 cache) is known as **pipeline burst cache**. Pipelining is defined as the process for microprocessors and memory to obtain computer software instructions in a timely fashion so the microprocessor is never waiting to receive an instruction. For example, when a software instruction is fetched or retrieved from memory, the microprocessor may have idle time before retrieving the next instruction. During this extra time, the next memory address goes out on the address bus before it is normally placed there. Using pipelined burst cache speeds up processing for software applications and is a nice feature to look for in a system.

Memory technology is moving quite quickly today. Chipsets also change constantly. Technicians are continually challenged to keep up with the features and abilities of the technology to make recommendations to their customers! Trade magazines and the Internet are excellent resources for updates.

HOW MUCH MEMORY?

The amount of memory that can be installed on the motherboard depends on two things: (1) the manufacturer of the motherboard and (2) the microprocessor.

RAM memory should *always* be installed on the motherboard and not on a memory expansion adapter for system memory because *the memory on the motherboard slows down to the adapter memory's speed*. The adapter memory's speed is at the speed of the adapter bus (ISA, MicroChannel, EISA, VL-bus, or PCI) which is always slower than the motherboard.

Microprocessors have a specific number of address lines connecting each memory chip with the microprocessor. Each memory chip is like a mailbox for data to be placed into it or retrieved from it. The microprocessor can connect to only a limited number of mailboxes or addresses. A mathematical relationship exists between the number of address lines and the total amount of addresses the microprocessor can recognize. A simple (but non-realistic) example is if a microprocessor has three address lines and each address line has a binary 1 or a binary 0. The different mailbox addresses the microprocessor can have are 000, 001, 010, 011, 100, 101, 110, or 111. With three address lines, eight different addresses are accessible. The mathematical relationship is 2^x where x is the number of address lines from the microprocessor. The number "2" is used because the address lines have one of two possible states, a 1 or a 0 binary digit. Memory Table #1 recaps the Intel microprocessors and the number of address lines for each along with the total amount of addresses the microprocessor can access.

MEMORY - TABLE # 1

Intel Microprocessor Address Lines

Microprocessor	Number of Address Lines	Maximum Amount of Memory Addresses
8088	20	1MB
80286	24	16MB
80386DX	32	4GB
80486DX	32	4GB
Pentium	32	4GB
Pentium Pro	36	64GB
Pentium II	36	64GB

Notice that the 8088 microprocessor can address up to approximately one million different addresses (1,048,576 addresses to be exact) and the Pentium Pro and Pentium II microprocessors can address up to 68,719,476,736 (64GB) different addresses. However, not all memory address locations are for RAM chips. The microprocessor uses the address lines for all memory chips including ROM chips on the motherboard and on various adapters installed in the computer. To look at the whole picture of the address lines' usage, a **memory map** makes things easier to see. Memory Figure #4 illustrates the memory map for the 8088 microprocessor.

address lines' usage, a **memory map** makes things easier to see. Memory Figure #4 illustrates the memory map for the 8088 microprocessor.

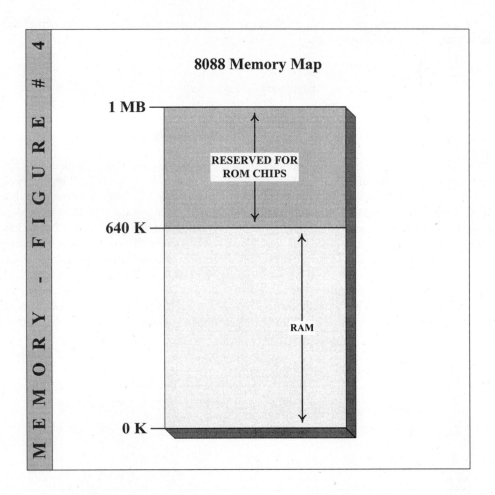

Notice the 0KB to 640KB space is for RAM chips. The upper addresses are for various ROM chips in the system and is frequently defined as the **reserved area**. On an Intel 8088 microprocessor-based computer, the maximum amount of memory on the motherboard is 640KB because that is the range possible with the 8088 microprocessor.

Today's applications and operating systems need much more than 640KB of RAM. The microprocessor allows for this increase. Memory Figure #5 shows the memory map for an 80386, 80486, or Pentium.

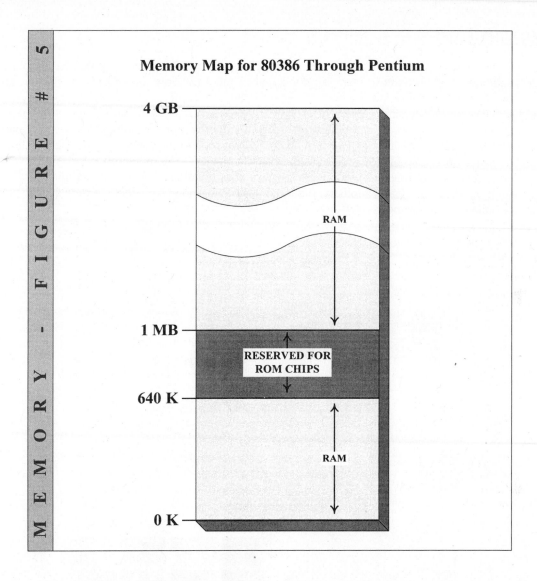

Memory Map for 80386 Through Pentium

Notice the area above 1MB in Memory Figure #5 allows for more RAM to be installed in a system. Just because the microprocessor supports the additional address lines, it does not mean a computer system has 4GB of RAM (less the 360KB reserved for ROM chips). This is where the manufacturer of the motherboard comes into the picture. The amount of RAM placed on the motherboard depends on the manufacturer. Most manufacturers of Pentium-based motherboards do not allow the full amount of RAM because most computers do not need 4GB of memory. This information is usually in the documentation that comes with the computer or motherboard.

MEMORY BANKS

When installing memory in a system, the process is called "populating the memory". To understand how to add or remove memory in a system, a few basic concepts must be explained. The best way to explain memory is to begin with how the 8088 microprocessor addressed memory and continue to the microprocessors of today.

Memory chips work together in a group called a **bank**. The number of chips in a memory bank depends on how many **data lines** extend from the microprocessor to the memory chips. Data lines are different from address lines. The address lines pick which memory chip (mailbox) to access. The data lines carry binary 1s & 0s (the mail) into the memory location (mailbox). The 8088 microprocessor has an eight-bit external data path. Memory Figure #6 illustrates how the 8088's external data path connects to the banks of memory.

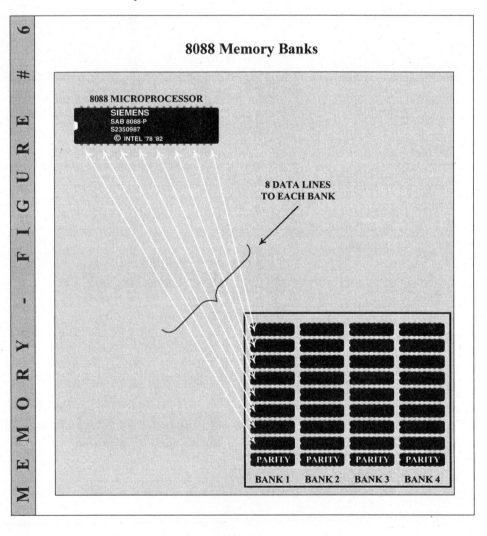

MEMORY - FIGURE # 6

8088 Memory Banks

8088 MICROPROCESSOR

SIEMENS
SAB 8088-P
S2350987
© INTEL '78 '82

**8 DATA LINES
TO EACH BANK**

PARITY   PARITY   PARITY   PARITY

BANK 1   BANK 2   BANK 3   BANK 4

Notice in Memory Figure #6 that the microprocessor outputs or accepts input of eight 1s or 0s at a time. Each data line from the microprocessor connects to one chip in the memory bank. The chips in the bank work together to transfer data to or from the microprocessor. Therefore, a bank of memory chips for an 8088 accepts eight bits of data at a time. On most 8088-based computers, a bank of memory contains *nine* DIP chips. The ninth chip is a **parity chip**. The parity chip checks the accuracy of the eight bits transferred into the bank of memory together. Look at Memory Figure #6 and notice the last chip in the bank is labeled *parity*.

Also notice in Memory Figure #6 there are four banks of memory labeled Bank 1, Bank 2, Bank 3, and Bank 4. A different manufacturer might label the banks Bank 0, Bank 1, Bank 2, and Bank 3, however the concept is the same.

When installing memory in banks, a few rules must be observed. The rules list below and then their explanation follows.

1. When you start a bank, fill a bank.
2. Use memory chips of the same capacity in the memory bank.
3. Some manufacturers require that higher capacity chips be placed in the first bank.
4. The chips in the bank should all have the same access speed, if possible.

START A BANK, FILL A BANK

When installing memory chips into a bank, whether DIPs or SIMMs, do not leave any slot or socket of the bank empty. This does not mean that all banks have to be filled. Simply, if you start putting memory chips into a bank, fill the bank you are working on with memory chips.

Memory chips in the bank work together to transfer data to and from the microprocessor and the entire bank must be completely filled with memory chips to operate correctly.

CHIPS OF THE SAME CAPACITY

Because memory chips in a bank work together, each chip in the bank must be able to hold the same amount of bits as other chips. In 8088-based computer systems, 64Kb and 256Kb chips were the most common. Bank 1, for example, would contain nine 256Kb chips, totaling 256KB of memory installed. The ninth chip, the parity chip, must be the same capacity as the memory chips to check the accuracy of data transferred into the eight memory chips. With higher microprocessor-based systems, a bank with two SIMM sockets requires two equal capacity SIMMs.

HIGHER CAPACITY CHIPS

Some manufacturers require that higher capacity memory chips be placed in the lower banks such as Bank 0 or Bank 1. The only way to be certain this is a manufacturer requirement is to check the documentation included with the motherboard or computer system.

If no documentation exists, experiment! Try the higher capacity chips in the lower banks. If that does not work, swap the memory chips and try the lower capacity chips in the lower bank numbers.

SAME ACCESS SPEEDS

Memory chips *should* have the same access speed as other chips in the bank. Mixing access speeds may work, but this simply depends on the motherboard. If you are working on a system that requires an 80ns DRAM memory chip when a DIP or a SIMM chip in the banks fails and an 80ns memory chip is not available, a faster speed chip may work as a replacement.

Never use a slower access speed chip as a replacement chip!

DETERMINE WHAT MEMORY CHIPS TO INSTALL

The best method to determine what memory chips to install in each bank is described in the following steps:

1. Determine what chip capacities can be used for the system. Look in the documentation included with the motherboard or the computer for this information.
2. Determine how much memory is needed. Ask the user what applications they are using. Refer to documentation for each application to determine the amount of RAM recommended. Plan for growth!
3. Determine what capacity chips go in each bank by drawing a diagram of the system, planning the memory population on paper, and referring to the documentation of the system or motherboard.

The 80286 has 24 address lines from the microprocessor that handle 16,777,216 different addresses (2^{16}=16,777,216). Also, the 80286 microprocessor has an external data bus of 16 bits — 16 separate lines which carry a 1 or a 0. Because 16 bits of data transmit from the microprocessor at a time, each bank of memory processes 16 bits at a time. Therefore, on an 80286 motherboard, one bank of memory normally contains 16 DIP chips, or 18 DIP chips if the motherboard uses parity. Memory Figure #7 shows memory banks on an 80286 motherboard.

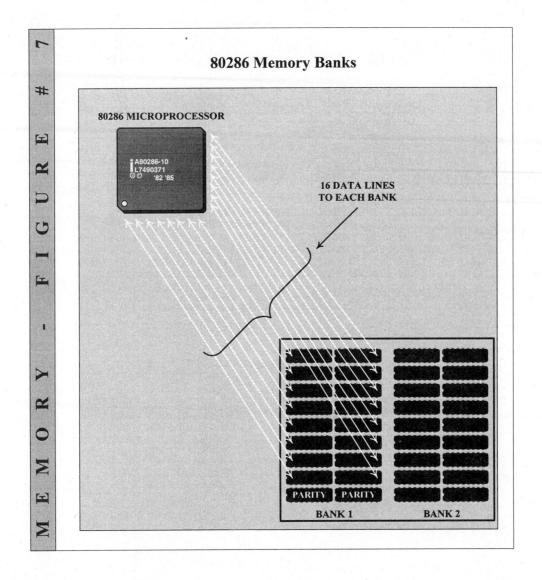

80286 Memory Banks

Notice in Memory Figure #7 how each bank of memory contains two rows of chips instead of just one row of chips as on the 8088 motherboard. Each bank contains two rows of chips because the 80286 microprocessor has 16 external data lines. Each chip connects to one data line. The 80286 microprocessor could handle more RAM on the motherboard, so memory chip manufacturers started making 1 Megabit (1Mb) DIP chips. 1Mb memory chips are two pins longer than the 64Kb and the 256Kb DIP chips. Many motherboards accepted both physical sizes of DIP chips.

When the 80386 came out with 32 address lines and 32 external data lines, manufacturers started using 30-pin SIMMs on the motherboard which accept eight bits of data at a time from the microprocessor. Therefore, one 30-pin SIMM is like one entire bank of memory in a XT. Memory Figure #8 shows this concept.

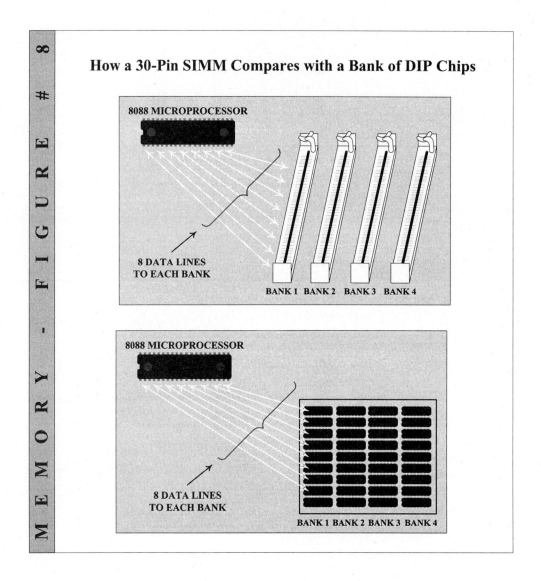

How a 30-Pin SIMM Compares with a Bank of DIP Chips

8088 MICROPROCESSOR

8 DATA LINES TO EACH BANK

BANK 1   BANK 2   BANK 3   BANK 4

8088 MICROPROCESSOR

8 DATA LINES TO EACH BANK

BANK 1 BANK 2 BANK 3 BANK 4

Notice that even though Memory Figure #8 shows a comparison of how the data lines connect to each SIMM, the 8088-based motherboards *did not* use SIMMs. Memory Figure #8 simply illustrates how the SIMM replaced eight or nine chips by placing them on a smaller, easier to install, easier to manage, and easier to troubleshoot circuit board.

Because the 80386 microprocessor has a 32-bit external data path, four 30-pin SIMMs are normally found in each bank of memory. Reference Memory Figure #9 for an 80386 motherboard with SIMM sockets instead of DIP chips.

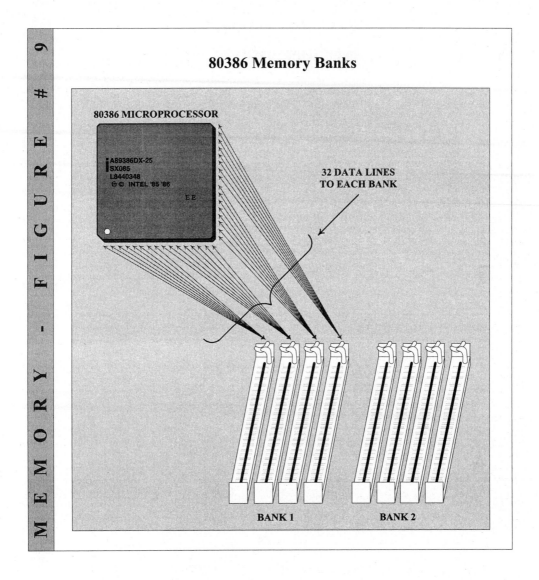

80386 Memory Banks

80386 MICROPROCESSOR

A89386DX-25
SX085
L8440348
© © INTEL '85 '86

E E

32 DATA LINES
TO EACH BANK

BANK 1   BANK 2

MEMORY - FIGURE # 9

30-pin SIMM sizes are 256KB, 512KB, 1MB, 2MB, and 4MB, although the 1MB and the 4MB are the most common. Exactly which SIMM can be used on a motherboard depends on the manufacturer of the motherboard. Memory Figure #10 illustrates an 80386 motherboard populated with 10MB of memory using 2MB and 512KB SIMM chips.

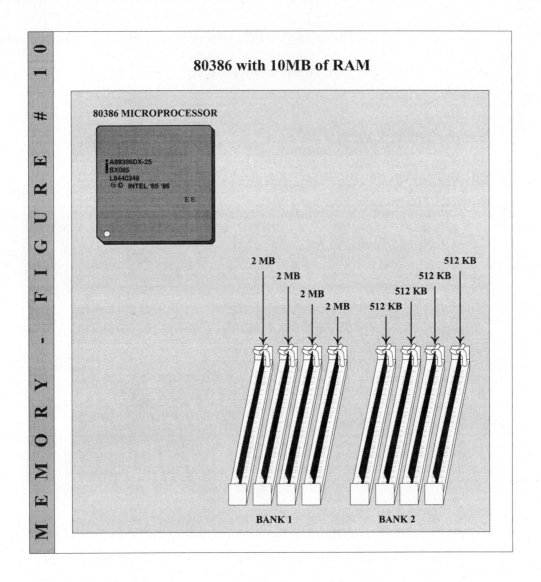

80386 with 10MB of RAM

Memory sales advertisements and technical manuals list 30-pin SIMMs in different ways. Understanding the different lists can be confusing. Memory Figure #11 shows three different memory advertisements.

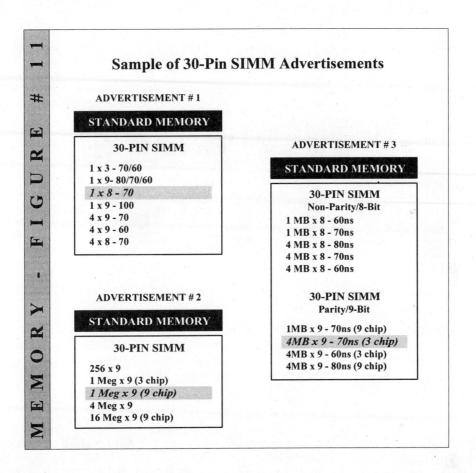

MEMORY - FIGURE # 11

Sample of 30-Pin SIMM Advertisements

ADVERTISEMENT # 1

STANDARD MEMORY

30-PIN SIMM

1 x 3 - 70/60
1 x 9- 80/70/60
1 x 8 - 70
1 x 9 - 100
4 x 9 - 70
4 x 9 - 60
4 x 8 - 70

ADVERTISEMENT # 3

STANDARD MEMORY

30-PIN SIMM
Non-Parity/8-Bit

1 MB x 8 - 60ns
1 MB x 8 - 70ns
4 MB x 8 - 80ns
4 MB x 8 - 70ns
4 MB x 8 - 60ns

30-PIN SIMM
Parity/9-Bit

1MB x 9 - 70ns (9 chip)
4MB x 9 - 70ns (3 chip)
4MB x 9 - 60ns (3 chip)
4MB x 9 - 80ns (9 chip)

ADVERTISEMENT # 2

STANDARD MEMORY

30-PIN SIMM

256 x 9
1 Meg x 9 (3 chip)
1 Meg x 9 (9 chip)
4 Meg x 9
16 Meg x 9 (9 chip)

Notice that each advertisement in Memory Figure #11 has a different SIMM chip highlighted. Ad #2 shows a 1Meg X 9 (9 chip) 30-pin SIMM. The X 9 portion of the ad means the SIMM chip uses parity. If the SIMM was a non-parity chip, the listing would say X 8 such as the one highlighted in Ad #1.

When purchasing SIMMs for a microcomputer, be sure if the computer uses parity that you buy parity SIMMs. The documentation included with the motherboard should state if the system uses parity. If a computer system does *not* use parity, SIMMs with the extra parity chip can be used in these systems. The parity chip will simply be ignored.

In Ad #3, a 4MB X 9 70ns (3 chip) line is highlighted. Some 9-bit SIMM chips have nine individual memory chips mounted on the SIMM while other 9-bit SIMM chips have only three individual memory chips mounted on the SIMM. Each of the three memory chips on the SIMM handles three bits at a time. Reference Memory Figure #12 for a comparison of a 3 chip and a 9 chip 30-pin SIMM.

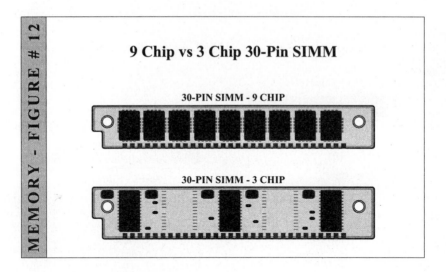

MEMORY - FIGURE # 12

9 Chip vs 3 Chip 30-Pin SIMM

30-PIN SIMM - 9 CHIP

30-PIN SIMM - 3 CHIP

Some motherboards are very particular about the type of SIMM (exactly how many chips mount on the SIMM). Systems that already have 9 chips on a 30-pin SIMM have been known to lock up when upgraded to SIMMs with only three chips mounted on the SIMM. Not all memory retailers specify in their advertisements if the SIMM is a 3 chip or a 9 chip SIMM.

When upgrading a system that uses 30-pin SIMMs, open the system and look inside at the existing memory SIMMs. Order the appropriate type of SIMM, 3 chip or 9 chip, to match what is already in the system. If installing 30-pin SIMMs on a motherboard without SIMMs, refer to the documentation included with the motherboard.

Manufacturers started using 72-pin SIMMs on the 80486-based motherboards. A 72-pin SIMM accepts 32 bits of data at a time from the microprocessor. Therefore, one 72-pin SIMM takes the place of four 30-pin SIMMs. Reference Memory Figure #13 for a comparison of banks of memory for 30-pin SIMMs and 72-pin SIMMs.

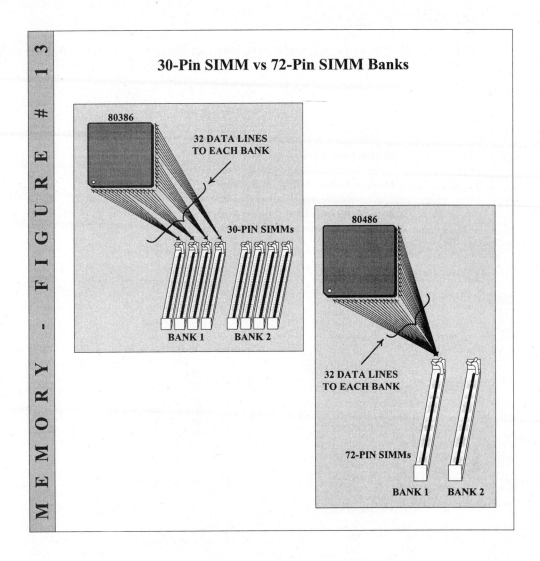

30-Pin SIMM vs 72-Pin SIMM Banks

Notice in Memory Figure #13 how a bank of four 30-pin SIMMs on an 80386-based motherboard equates to a bank of one 72-pin SIMM on an 80486-based motherboard. Some 80386-based motherboards use 72-pin SIMMs or a combination of 30-pin and 72-pin SIMMs to give consumers the choice of which to buy or the ability to use older SIMMs from another machine.

BUYING THE RIGHT 72-PIN SIMM

72-pin SIMMs are available in 1MB, 2MB, 4MB, 8MB, 16MB, 32MB, and 64MB capacities. Similar to 30-pin SIMMs, 72-pin SIMM advertisements can be very confusing. Reference Memory Figure #14 for some example advertisements for 72-pin SIMMs.

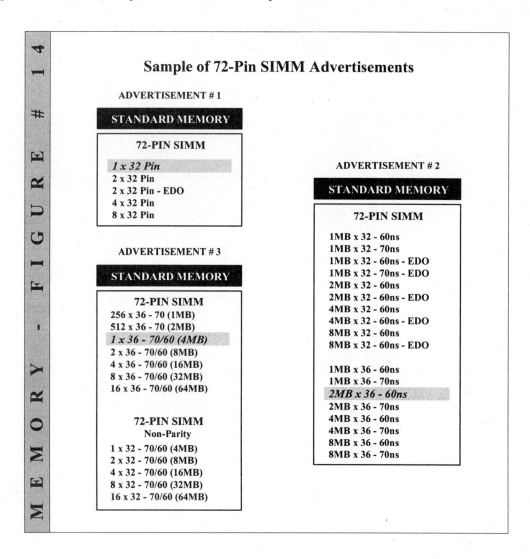

MEMORY - FIGURE # 14

Sample of 72-Pin SIMM Advertisements

ADVERTISEMENT # 1

STANDARD MEMORY

72-PIN SIMM

1 x 32 Pin
2 x 32 Pin
2 x 32 Pin - EDO
4 x 32 Pin
8 x 32 Pin

ADVERTISEMENT # 2

STANDARD MEMORY

72-PIN SIMM

1MB x 32 - 60ns
1MB x 32 - 70ns
1MB x 32 - 60ns - EDO
1MB x 32 - 70ns - EDO
2MB x 32 - 60ns
2MB x 32 - 60ns - EDO
4MB x 32 - 60ns
4MB x 32 - 60ns - EDO
8MB x 32 - 60ns
8MB x 32 - 60ns - EDO

1MB x 36 - 60ns
1MB x 36 - 70ns
2MB x 36 - 60ns
2MB x 36 - 70ns
4MB x 36 - 60ns
4MB x 36 - 70ns
8MB x 36 - 60ns
8MB x 36 - 70ns

ADVERTISEMENT # 3

STANDARD MEMORY

72-PIN SIMM
256 x 36 - 70 (1MB)
512 x 36 - 70 (2MB)
1 x 36 - 70/60 (4MB)
2 x 36 - 70/60 (8MB)
4 x 36 - 70/60 (16MB)
8 x 36 - 70/60 (32MB)
16 x 36 - 70/60 (64MB)

72-PIN SIMM
Non-Parity

1 x 32 - 70/60 (4MB)
2 x 32 - 70/60 (8MB)
4 x 32 - 70/60 (16MB)
8 x 32 - 70/60 (32MB)
16 x 32 - 70/60 (64MB)

Notice in Memory Figure #14 how Advertisement #1 highlights the 1 X 32 pin. This particular advertisement does not list the memory chip's access time which a technician needs to know when installing memory. The "1" in the 1 X 32 stands for 1 Megabit. The "32" in the 1 X 32 stands for 32 bits. The chip accepts 32 bits at one time. The total capacity for this chip is found by multiplying the 1 Megabit by 32 bits which is the same as 4 *Megabytes* (approximately 1,000,000 bits times 32 bits equals 32,000,000 bits. 32,000,000 bits divided by 8 equals the number of bytes.) So, an advertisement that lists 1 X 32 for a 72-pin SIMM has a capacity of 4MB.

An advertisement for a "X 32" is a non-parity SIMM chip. If the SIMM is a parity 72-pin SIMM, some advertisements list "X 36" instead of "X 32". Remember there is one parity bit for every eight bits. 32-bits need four additional bits for parity, one for every eight bits thus totaling 36 bits. Every chip shown in Advertisement #1 is a non-parity 72-pin SIMM.

Notice in Advertisement #2 how the memory chips are divided into non-parity SIMMs at the top of the advertisement and parity SIMMs at the bottom. Also, this particular company sells EDO memory. Another good feature of Advertisement #2 is the list of access speeds. However, just like Advertisement #1, Advertisement #2 does not list the total capacity of the SIMM. Also, the MB such as the one listed in the highlighted 2MB X 36-60ns SIMMs line of Advertisement #2 is a misnomer. The correct listing should be 2M*b* X 36-60ns SIMMs. Most manufacturers and retailers do not list the SIMMs in the correct format. A 2MB X 36-60ns SIMM has a total capacity of 8MB with four bits used for parity.

Memory Figure #14's Advertisement #3 is the best of all three ads. The retailer lists the total capacity of the chip in parentheses beside each SIMM. The access time lists to the right of each chip in the advertisement. Notice the highlighted 1 X 36-70/60 (4MB) chip. The 70/60 are the access times available for this particular model of SIMM. Lastly, this particular advertisement separates the parity and non-parity SIMMs.

POPULATING PENTIUM AND HIGHER MOTHERBOARDS

Intel's Pentium, Pentium Pro, and Pentium II microprocessors have an external data path of 64 bits. If the system uses 72-pin SIMMs, each bank of memory has two 72-pin SIMM sockets. Reference Memory Figure #15 for a layout of the 72-pin memory sockets on a Pentium-based motherboard.

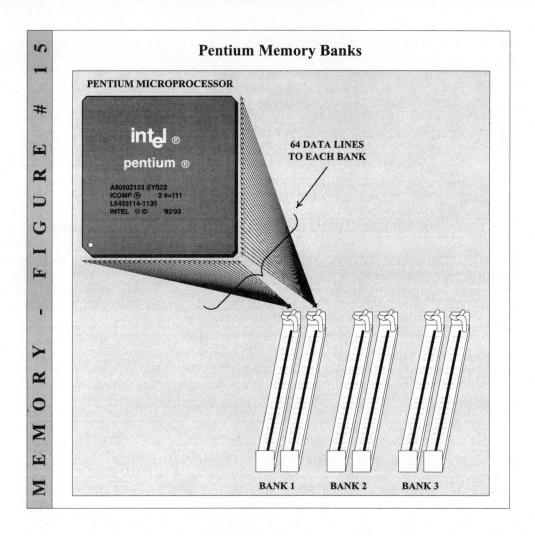

When populating memory in a machine that uses a Pentium microprocessor and SIMM sockets, insert two SIMMs into at least one bank for the computer to operate. Pentium-based motherboards also use DIMMs (Dual In-line Memory Modules). Memory Figure #16 shows a picture of a DIMM.

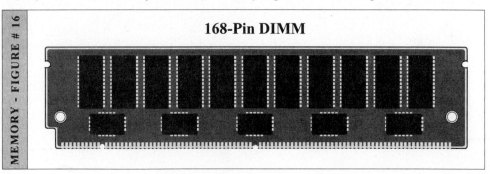

Some manufacturers produce motherboards that contain 72-pin SIMM sockets and 168-pin DIMM sockets. Memory Figure #17 shows a Pentium-Pro based motherboard that has both a DIMM socket and SIMM sockets.

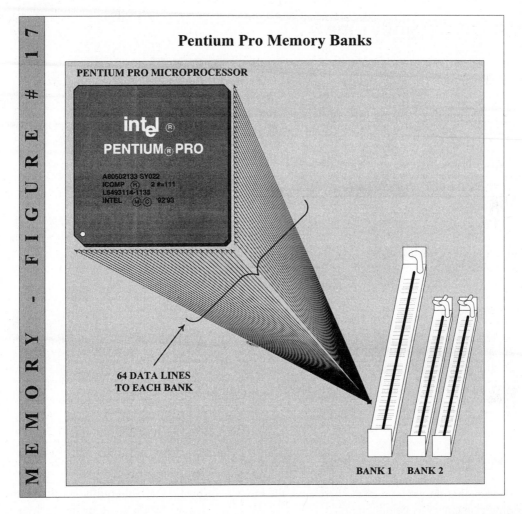

As seen in Memory Figure #17, a DIMM socket is one bank of memory for the motherboards. Some of the latest Pentium, Pentium Pro, and Pentium II motherboards ship with only DIMM sockets available.

DIMMs have capacities of 8MB, 16MB, 32MB, 64MB, and 128MB (although larger capacities are sure to come). Also, DIMMs have parity and non-parity versions. The 8MB parity DIMM lists as 1MB x 72 and the non-parity 8MB DIMM lists as 1MB x 64. The 72 on the parity DIMM is calculated by adding one parity bit for every eight bits. There are 64 bits on the DIMM, so it needs eight extra bits to handle parity checking. 64 + 8 = 72 total bits.

The exercises at the end of the chapter help you understand how to populate memory banks for the different microprocessors. Before memory chips are installed into a system, a plan of action and reference to the documentation must be made.

INSTALLING MEMORY CHIPS

Installing memory chips into a system can be broken down into three steps:

Step 1: Obtain the proper type, size, and capacity of chip(s) needed for the system.
Step 2: Remove and/or install the memory chips.
Step 3: Configure the computer for the new memory.

MEMORY TYPE, SIZE, AND CAPACITY

Step 1 involves research and planning by using the documentation included with the motherboard or the computer system to determine for the memory chip: the proper type (gold lead or tin lead; DIP, SIPP, SIMM, or DIMM); the proper size (30-pin, 72-pin or 168-pin); the proper capacity (4MB, 8MB, 16MB, 32MB, etc.); and the proper access speed (50ns, 60ns, 70ns, etc.). Many frustrations, headaches, and problems are avoidable with this first step.

If you are upgrading a computer's memory and no documentation exists, look at the memory chips already installed for clues to access speeds, type, and size. Trial and error can also be used if no documentation exists. Many vendors will allow the return or swap of memory chips if you ordered the wrong type or size. Also, Micro House's Technical Library CD has documentation for motherboards, including memory size options and jumper settings.

REMOVE/INSTALL MEMORY CHIPS

Depending on the type of motherboard, the number of banks available on the motherboard, if the computer memory is being upgraded, or if the memory is a new install, some memory chips may need to be removed to put higher capacity chips into the bank. Look at what is already installed in the system, refer to the documentation, and remove any banks of memory necessary to upgrade the memory. Use an anti-static wrist strap when removing or installing memory chips.

DIP CHIP REMOVAL

To remove a DIP chip, a small tweaker (flat-tipped) screwdriver is the best tool. Refer to Memory Figure #18.

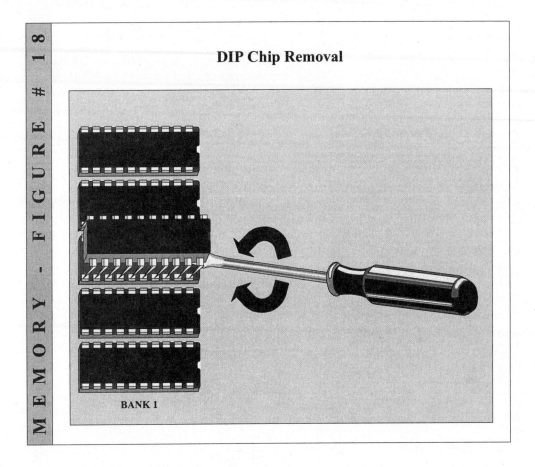

DIP Chip Removal

BANK 1

MEMORY - FIGURE # 18

Carefully insert the tweaker screwdriver under one end of the DIP chip. Rotate the screwdriver back and forth *gently* until one end of the chip slightly rises above the socket. Carefully, insert the flat-tipped screwdriver under the *opposite* end of the DIP chip. Rotate the screwdriver back and forth a few times until this end of the chip starts to rise above the socket. Keep inserting the screwdriver into alternate ends of the DIP chip until it gently lifts from the socket.

SIMM AND DIMM REMOVAL

Removing a SIMM or a DIMM is much easier than removing a DIP chip. A SIMM or a DIMM socket has two clasps, one on either side of the socket that hold the memory chip into the SIMM socket. A metal or plastic clasp is normally used with SIMM sockets. A heavy duty plastic clasp is normally used with DIMM sockets.

Be extremely careful when working with plastic clasps. If they break, they are expensive to replace and sometimes you have to purchase a new motherboard. Memory Figure #19 shows how the clasps are *gently* pulled away from the SIMM to remove the memory module from the socket.

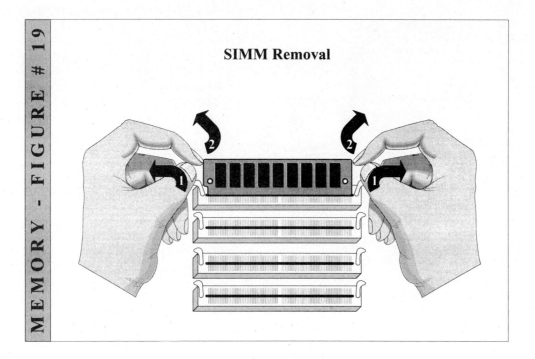

MEMORY - FIGURE # 19

SIMM Removal

Grasp the two clasps on either side of the socket with your thumbs resting on the inner side of the clasps. Gently pry the clasps out and away from the memory module. With your index finger, press the SIMM forward until it pulls away from the clasps. Removing a DIMM is very similar to a SIMM except that you push *down* on the DIMM's retaining tabs. The DIMM lifts slightly out of the DIMM socket.

DIP CHIP INSTALLATION

To insert a DIP chip, verify all legs on the DIP chip are straight and even before installing. If the legs need straightening, use a pair of needlenose pliers. Place the DIP chip over one side of the chip socket, *barely* placing each leg into the holes on one side of the socket. Reference Memory Figure #20.

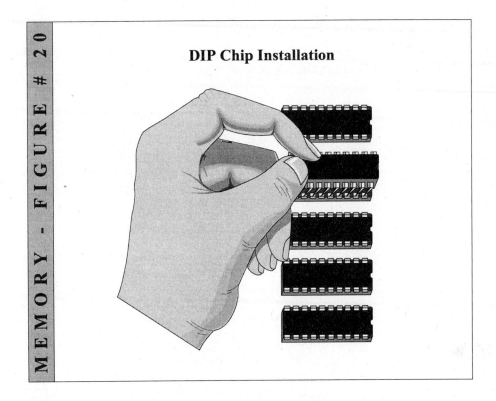

MEMORY - FIGURE # 20

DIP Chip Installation

Be sure the DIP chip orients properly in the socket. All DIP chips have a notch on the end and usually all notches of the DIP chips face in the same direction on the motherboard (or any adapter for that matter). Press gently on the DIP chip's opposite side legs. At the same time, press the chip into the socket. One advantage to using your hands rather than a chip insertion tool to install a DIP chip, is you can feel the legs going into the socket properly after practicing this technique a few times. By the same token, with practice, you can feel if a leg bends backward as it inserts into the socket.

SIMM AND DIMM INSTALLATION

A SIMM or a DIMM inserts only one way into the socket, so it cannot insert improperly (oriented the wrong way) like the DIP chip. The SIMM or DIMM has a notch on one side of the chip near the contacts. If you look carefully at the socket, you can see a plastic insert on one side. The notch on the memory module lines up with the side of the socket with the plastic insert. Reference Memory Figure #21.

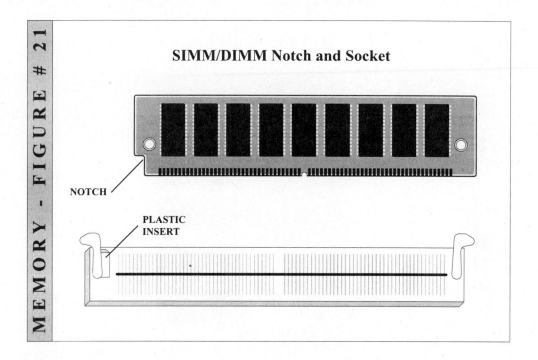

MEMORY - FIGURE # 21

SIMM/DIMM Notch and Socket

NOTCH

PLASTIC INSERT

At a tilt, position the memory module correctly over the socket. Insert the metal chip leads *firmly* into the socket. For a DIMM, make sure the side tabs are pulled out before you insert the DIMM, then close the tabs over the DIMM. For a SIMM, press the memory module backward into the socket until the two clasps clamp against the SIMM. Reference Memory Figure #22.

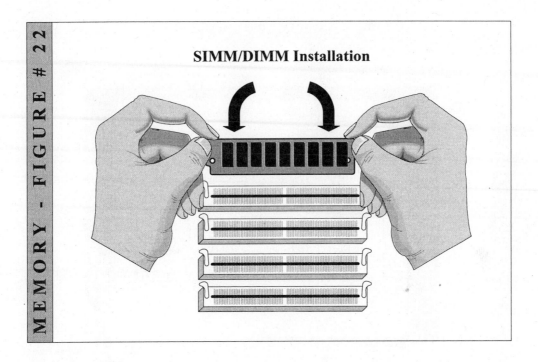

SIMM/DIMM Installation

Notice in Memory Figure #22 there is a hole on either side of the memory module. A pin on each side of the memory socket inserts into this hole when the module inserts properly into the socket.

CONFIGURE THE COMPUTER

Some motherboards require setting of jumpers or switches to denote how much memory installs on the motherboard. Refer to the motherboard or the computer system documentation for this information. Other computers require no setting except through CMOS SETUP.

Power on the computer and a POST error message appears. This is normal! The memory count in the upper left corner should count to the amount of memory installed. Reference Memory Figure #23 for an example of this screen, keeping in mind every BIOS chip is different and different messages appear depending on the BIOS chip installed. This is only a sample.

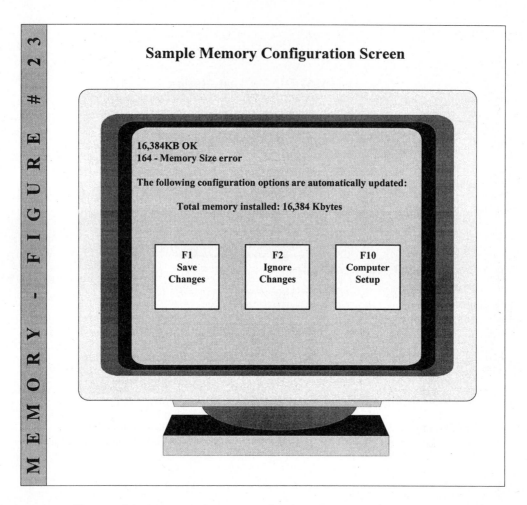

With the system illustrated in Memory Figure #23, simply press the F1 key to configure CMOS and save the changes.

MEMORY AND SOFTWARE CONSIDERATIONS

Physically installing memory in the computer is fine, but not all applications can use the available memory. Whether or not an application can use all the RAM in a system depends on the operating system/environment installed on the computer and the operating system for which the application is written. For example, an application specifically written for the DOS/Windows environment running on a system with Windows 95 behaves as if it was installed on a system with DOS. An application specifically written for Windows 95 will not run in the DOS/Windows environment. The DOS operating system has severe memory limitations.

DOS/WINDOWS 3.X AND MEMORY

To understand the memory limitations of DOS, the 8088 microprocessor is the place to start. From there we can move forward because all computers, even today's computers, are backward compatible with older microprocessors. Microprocessor designers want consumers to be able to run the software that ran on their old computers.

The 8088 microprocessor has 20 address lines for a total of 1,048,576 possible addresses. Keep in mind all memory chips, RAM and ROM alike, have different memory addresses that fit into a memory map for a specific microprocessor. Memory Figure #24 illustrates the 8088 memory map.

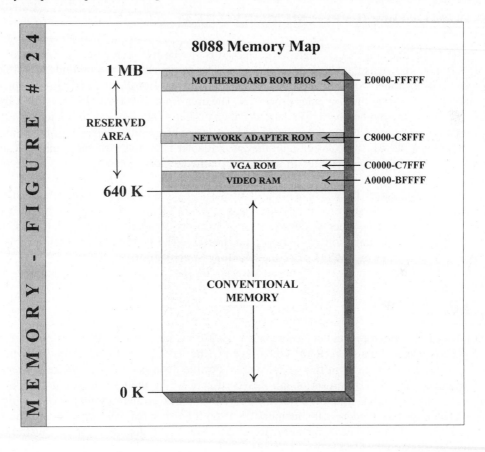

MEMORY - FIGURE # 24

8088 Memory Map

1 MB	MOTHERBOARD ROM BIOS ←	E0000-FFFFF
RESERVED AREA	NETWORK ADAPTER ROM ←	C8000-C8FFF
	VGA ROM ←	C0000-C7FFF
640 K	VIDEO RAM ←	A0000-BFFFF
	CONVENTIONAL MEMORY	
0 K		

CONVENTIONAL MEMORY

The area from 0 to 640KB is for the RAM chips installed in the 8088-based computer and is normally called **conventional memory**. All DOS applications written for the 8088 computers ran in conventional memory. The application, such as a word processor, would load into the RAM chips. Any document created within the application, such as a letter, was also kept in the RAM chips and mapped into the 0 to 640KB area of the memory map. Windows 95 also used conventional memory. Approximately 470K of conventional memory must be available before Windows 95 can load.

RESERVED MEMORY (UPPER MEMORY AREA)

The area of the memory map designated Reserved is for the ROM chips in the computer. The Reserved area is also known as the Upper Memory Area. The Reserved area is subdivided into blocks of memory that are illustrated with hexadecimal memory addresses. Hexadecimal is easier to process than the binary 1s and 0s that the computer processes. The area from E0000 to FFFFF is used by the ROM BIOS chip(s) on the motherboard. The hard drive controller in 8088-based computers has ROM chips on the adapter that normally use the memory address range of C8000 to CBFFF. If the computer has an EGA monitor installed, the ROM chip on the EGA adapter fits into the memory map at C0000-C3FFF. All ROM chips in the system must fit in a space on the memory map unoccupied by any other ROM chip.

Computer users, especially the ones who created large spreadsheets in spreadsheet software such as Lotus, frequently ran out of conventional memory due to the 0 to 640KB limitation. Lotus, Intel, and Microsoft worked together to develop a new memory standard called LIM (Lotus, Intel, Microsoft) which solves the limitation of conventional memory. The **LIM memory standard** is also known as **expanded memory** or **EMS (Expanded Memory Specification)**.

EXPANDED MEMORY

With 8088-based microprocessors, to break the 640KB memory limitation, users had to buy an expanded memory adapter with more RAM chips. For the microprocessor to communicate with this RAM, the memory chips had to fit in the memory map, but the 8088 had only 20 address lines. The EMS standard occupies a 64KB portion of the Reserved area in the memory map not used by any ROM chips (such as the 832KB to 896KB range). The 64KB block of memory map space is divided into four 16KB blocks used to address the memory chips on the expanded memory adapter. The EMS standard allows up to 32MB of EMS memory. Reference Memory Figure #25 for an illustration of how EMS memory fits into the 8088's memory map.

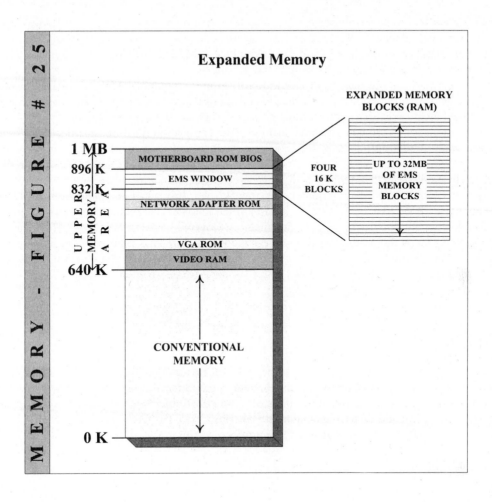

MEMORY - FIGURE # 25

Expanded Memory

The spreadsheet data or any other data using expanded memory loads into the RAM chips on the expanded memory adapter. The microprocessor accesses the data by swapping the data into the four 16KB blocks of memory in the Reserved area. If more data is needed, the original data is taken out of one of the four 16KB blocks and placed into the expanded memory block. The new data is then swapped or paged into the old data's slot in the Reserved area. Expanded Memory is also known as paged memory because it pages (swaps) the data in and out of the reserved area in four 16KB chunks at a time. Expanded memory is *very* slow because it pages in and out of the memory map.

Not all applications can use expanded memory. The application must be specifically written for it. Years ago when purchasing an expanded memory adapter, a disk containing software sometimes called a driver was included. When the software driver is loaded into the CONFIG.SYS file, a 64KB window is made available in the memory map for use as expanded memory.

Expanded memory no longer requires a separate adapter. Instead, if an application still requires expanded memory, a specified amount (up to 32MB) of the RAM on the motherboard can be specified as expanded memory and the rest is for extended memory (covered in the next section). However, even though the memory is on the motherboard, to access the RAM chips, the data is still paged in and out of the memory map through the 64KB window. A driver is still needed in the CONFIG.SYS file to access expanded memory. DOS and Windows both have an expanded memory manager for 80386 and higher microprocessors called EMM386.EXE.

EXTENDED MEMORY

A better alternative to expanded memory is extended memory and it became available with the 80286 microprocessor. **Extended memory**, also known as **XMS (Extended Memory Specification)**, is the area of the memory map above the 1MB mark. The 80286 microprocessor has 24 address lines with 16,777,216 different addresses available to the microprocessor. Reference Memory Figure #26 for an illustration of the memory map for an 80286 microprocessor.

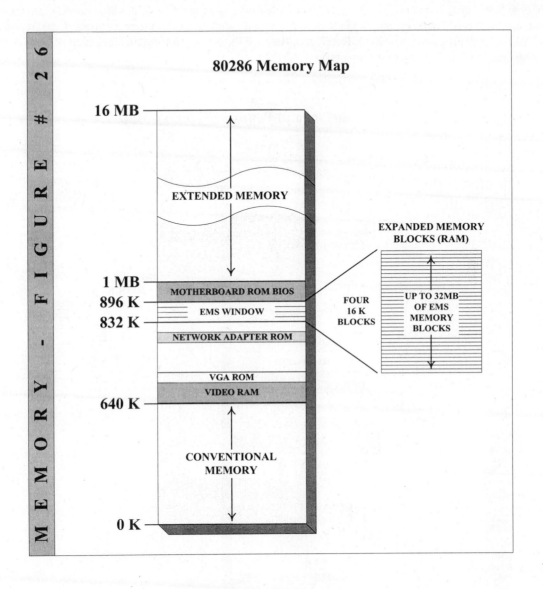

MEMORY - FIGURE # 26

80286 Memory Map

Extended memory is much faster than expanded memory. With the 80386, 80486, and Pentium-based systems the same memory map exists except the extended memory range is from 1MB to 4GB (4,294,963,296 different addresses). Reference Memory Figure #27 for the memory map of the 80386, 80486, and the Pentium microprocessors.

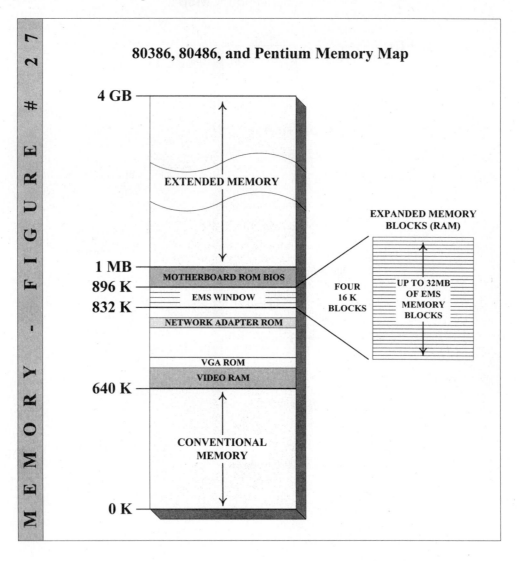

The Pentium Pro and Pentium II each have 36 address lines. The memory maps for the Pentium Pro and Pentium II look exactly like the illustration in Memory Figure #27 except the highest memory address extends beyond 4GB to 64GB.

For a system to use extended memory, a driver must be installed in the CONFIG.SYS file. The driver used to access extended memory that comes with DOS and Windows is HIMEM.SYS. Also, an application must be specifically written to use extended memory to take advantage of the extra memory. Microsoft Windows and all Windows 3.x applications are specifically written for extended memory.

FREEING MEMORY SPACE IN THE DOS/WINDOWS ENVIRONMENT

Insufficient memory errors occur frequently in the DOS/Windows environment due to conventional memory limitations. This also occurs when running DOS applications under the Windows 95 operating system. A close look at the CONFIG.SYS file is necessary to understand memory. The first line of the CONFIG.SYS file normally lists the software driver for extended memory, HIMEM.SYS. The line looks as follows:

DEVICE=C:\WINDOWS\HIMEM.SYS

The path, C:\WINDOWS, may be named C:\DOS or C:\ to indicate the correct driver location. When this line of the CONFIG.SYS executes, the area above 1MB is available to the operating system for applications able to use it. The first 64KB above the 1MB mark is the **High Memory Area (HMA)**. This area is important because the system can use it as an extended portion of conventional memory. DOS, normally one of the first pieces of software loaded into conventional memory, can load into the HMA if the following special line is in the CONFIG.SYS file: DOS=HIGH.

The BUFFERS= statement in CONFIG.SYS is for speeding up data transfer between two devices. The memory space reserved for buffers also goes into the High Memory Area with DOS if the buffers are below 42 (with DOS 6.x). Up to 47KB of conventional memory is saved by loading DOS and the buffers into the High Memory Area. Therefore, the two CONFIG.SYS lines necessary to place DOS and the buffers in the High Memory Area are as follows:

DEVICE=C:\WINDOWS\HIMEM.SYS
DOS=HIGH

Reference Memory Figure #28 for an illustration of the High Memory Area.

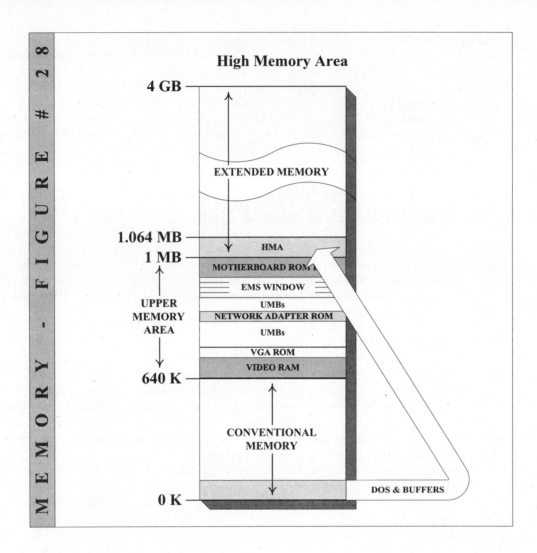

Another conventional memory saver occurs when the unused blocks of memory in the Reserved area are available for use with files normally loaded in conventional memory. The blocks of memory in the Reserved area that can be used for software other than ROM chips are also known as the **Upper Memory Blocks** or the (**UMBs**). The UMBs are part of the Upper Memory Area. To make the UMBs available to the system for use, two lines are needed in the CONFIG.SYS file:

```
DEVICE=C:\WINDOWS\EMM386.EXE
DOS=UMB
```

These two lines follow the extended memory manager CONFIG.SYS line:

```
DEVICE=C:\WINDOWS\HIMEM.SYS
DEVICE=C:\WINDOWS\EMM386.EXE
DOS=UMB
```

The DEVICE=C:\WINDOWS\EMM386.EXE line allows the system to *see* the upper memory blocks. The DOS=UMB line allows the system to *use* the upper memory blocks. A more common use of the DOS=UMB line is to combine it with the DOS=HIGH line, illustrated in this example:

```
DEVICE=C:\WINDOWS\HIMEM.SYS
DEVICE=C:\WINDOWS\EMM386.EXE
DOS=HIGH,UMB
```

After these lines are placed in the CONFIG.SYS file, any other device drivers, lines that begin DEVICE=, can load into the upper memory blocks by changing the statement to DEVICEHIGH=. Also, any lines in the AUTOEXEC.BAT file that load TSR (Terminate and Stay Resident) programs can be preceded by the LOADHIGH or LH command to load the software into the upper memory blocks, not into conventional memory. The switches available for use with the EMM386 command change the way the system accesses and/or uses the upper memory blocks. Memory Table #2 lists the proper switch to use with the EMM386 command.

MEMORY - TABLE # 2

EMM386.EXE Switches

Do You Need Expanded Memory?	Do You Need UMB Access?	EMM386 Switch
NO	NO	N/A
YES	NO	N/A
YES	YES	*XX* where *XX*=amt of mem in KB (64 to 32,768)
NO	YES	NOEMS

Most applications do *not* require expanded memory. The most frequently used EMM386 switch is NOEMS. If this switch is needed, the line in CONFIG.SYS is:

DEVICE=<path>EMM386.EXE NOEMS

The NOEMS switch is popular because expanded memory is *not* needed by most applications. The 64KB of UMB space is needed to load other software normally found in conventional memory, therefore freeing up the precious space in the 0 to 640KB range.

The MSD and the MEM programs can be used to view the Upper Memory Blocks. Exercises at the end of the chapter reinforce this concept.

All this memory management has now been automated with the latest DOS versions. Microsoft's memory management utility is MEMMAKER and IBM's memory management utility is RAMBOOST. A technician always needs to know the basics of memory management. The memory exercises at the end of the chapter help you understand memory management.

COMPUTER SPEED MEMORY ISSUES

Computer speed can be increased by several things such as adding more cache memory, adding more RAM chips, installing a disk caching program, and/or installing a RAM drive. All these items can optimize the performance of today's computers and technicians need to understand the effects of each optimization.

ADDING MORE CACHE

Most computers today have a maximum cache size of 512KB. Nevertheless, the amount of cache memory that can be installed is determined by the motherboard. Check the documentation included with the motherboard or computer to determine the correct amount of cache (SRAM).

When buying a new computer with a Pentium or lower microprocessor, buy as much SRAM as the budget allows.

ADDING MORE RAM

Adding more RAM can make a noticeable difference in computer performance (up to a point, of course). When a computer user is sitting in front of a computer waiting for a document in an application to appear, or waiting to go to a different location within a document, it might be time to install more RAM. Do not purchase a computer today if it has less than 32MB of RAM.

DISK CACHE

Another easy thing a technician can do to increase computer speed is to install a disk caching program. A disk cache will set aside a portion of memory (RAM). When applications or data are read from the disk drive (which is inherently slow), more data than requested is read and placed in RAM where the disk cache is located. Some hard drives have their own caching controllers. Caching hard drive controllers have memory installed that speed up the system by using the memory chips on the adapter rather than using the motherboard RAM.

DOS, Windows 3.x, and Windows 95 have a disk caching program called SmartDrive (SMARTDRV.EXE). This program caches data from floppy disks, CD-ROMs, hard drives, and InterLink drives. Do not use the DOS or Windows version of SmartDrive with Windows 95; Windows 95 has its own version. Also, the Windows 95 built-in caching program for CD-ROMs works better than SmartDrive. Refer to the hard drive and CD-ROM chapters for more information on Windows 95 caching programs.

The Windows 95 SETUP program sometimes hangs if the SmartDrive double-buffering is not enabled. Some hard drives require double buffering. Use the **SETUP** */C* command to prevent SmartDrive from loading during the Windows 95 installation process. If after running SETUP from Windows 3.x, the installation process hangs, try disabling 32-bit disk access from the 386 enhanced control panel before starting the SETUP program again. If that does not work, run the SETUP program from the DOS prompt.

SmartDrive uses extended memory for DOS and Windows 3.x-based machines. To install SmartDrive, add a line to the AUTOEXEC.BAT file with the path to the location of the SMARTDRV.EXE device driver. For example:

C:\DOS\SMARTDRV.EXE.

To determine if the hard drive for a particular system requires the double buffering feature in SmartDrive, put the following line in the CONFIG.SYS file:

DEVICE=C:\DOS\SMARTDRV.EXE */DOUBLE_BUFFER*

Then in the AUTOEXEC.BAT file, add the following line:

C:\DOS\SMARTDRV.EXE

Reboot the computer and run SmartDrive by typing **SMARTDRV** at the command prompt. If a YES is found anywhere in the buffering column, then the double buffering feature is needed. If buffering is not needed, remove the SMARTDRV.EXE line from the CONFIG.SYS file.

Other disk caching programs are available with programs such as Norton Utilities, PC Tools, or Mace Utilities. If SMARTDRV.EXE is used, verify it is the latest version. The version is determined by simply typing **SMARTDRV** from the DOS directory and doing the same for the Windows version.

WINDOWS 95 DISK CACHING

Windows 95 has disk caching built in to the operating system through the use of the VCACHE program. The disk cache is dynamic — it increases or decreases the cache size as needed. If the system begins to page frequently and is constantly swapping data from RAM to the hard drive, the cache size automatically shrinks. It is not necessary to change the cache size each time a new application is loaded or removed.

Remove the SMARTDRV driver from the CONFIG.SYS or the SMARTDRV.EXE line from the AUTOEXEC.BAT file so Windows 95 will use its own VCACHE program.

Windows 95 uses a temporary swap file, WIN386.SWP, that increases or decreases in size as necessary based on the amount of RAM installed in the computer and the amount of memory needed to run the application(s). A **swap file** is a certain amount of hard drive space used like RAM by applications. For optimum performance in Windows 95, have as much free hard disk space as possible to allow ample room for virtual memory and caching. **Virtual memory** is a method of simulating extra memory by using hard disk space as if it were RAM. As a default, the swap file is on the same hard drive as the Windows 95 directory. If multiple hard drives are available, a technician might want to move the swap file to a different drive. Always put the swap file on the fastest hard drive unless that hard drive lacks space. To change or adjust the virtual memory swap file: (1) open **Control Panel**; (2) select the **System** option; (3) click the **Performance** tab; (4) click the **Virtual Memory** button; (5) click the **Let me specify my own virtual memory settings** option; (6) click the **down arrow** in the area to the right of the **Hard disk:** option; (7) choose a different hard drive from the list; (8) click **OK**. The settings for the minimum and maximum size of the swap file can also be changed. However, the current settings normally work fine.

USING A RAM DRIVE

A **RAM drive** is a virtual (not real) hard disk drive created from RAM. The RAM used for a RAM drive is no longer available to the system as normal memory. A RAM drive can be created out of conventional, expanded, or extended memory, but extended memory is preferred. A RAM drive is located in memory and operates much faster than retrieving data from a hard drive. The drawback to a RAM drive is anything written to this area of memory will be erased when the computer restarts or shuts down. Therefore, permanent data should not be stored in a RAM drive. Also, the memory allocated to the RAM drive is no longer available to the system. Therefore, a RAM drive should only be created if there is RAM to spare in a system.

In older DOS versions, the RAM disk device driver was VDISK.SYS. In today's DOS, the RAM disk driver is RAMDRIVE.SYS. To create a RAMDRIVE from extended memory, insert the following line into the CONFIG.SYS file:

DEVICE=*[path]*RAMDRIVE.SYS */e [size]*

[path] is the directory where you find the RAMDRIVE.SYS file. *[size]* is the size of the RAM drive in kilobytes. The default is 64KB and the possible range is 16KB to 4,096KB.

USING WINDOWS 3.X'S 32-BIT DISK ACCESS

Windows 3.x has a feature known as FastDisk which allows Windows 3.x to talk directly to the hard drive. Normally, Windows 3.x has to go through the ROM BIOS chip to communicate with the hard drive; however, once 32-bit disk access or FastDisk is turned on, Windows 3.x communicates faster with the hard drive. To enable 32-bit disk access within Windows, several criteria must be met: (1) Windows must be running in the 386 Enhanced mode and (2) the hard drive must be Western Digital 1003 compatible. 32-bit disk access must be turned on using the 386 Enhanced icon from the Control Panel window. 32-bit access is not supported for SCSI or ESDI hard drives unless the hard disk controller manufacturer provides a 32-bit disk access driver.

The 32-bit disk access feature can be sped up by changing the statement **PageBuffers=4** to **PageBuffers=32** in the [386enh] section of **SYSTEM.INI**. The PageBuffers setting is the number of 4KB page buffers used by the 32-bit disk access. Even though this setting takes approximately 128KB not 16KB of extended memory, the payoff in increased speed is worth the extra memory. The only way this setting can be changed in the SYSTEM.INI file is to edit the SYSTEM.INI file with a text editor. Be sure a backup of the SYSTEM.INI file is made before any changes are made.

MEMORY AND WINDOWS 3.X

Microsoft Windows 3.x has two modes of operation: Standard Mode and Enhanced Mode. Windows for Workgroups only runs in Enhanced Mode. The Windows mode used depends on the microprocessor and the amount of memory installed in the computer. Many applications, including Windows 3.x have both a list of minimum requirements and preferred or recommended requirements. For best performance using any application, make sure the computer has the recommended requirements. The recommended minimum system configuration from Microsoft is shown in Memory Table #3.

Recommended Windows 3.x Requirements

	Standard Mode	Enhanced Mode
Microprocessor	80286	80386
RAM	2MB	4MB
Free Extended Memory	1408K	3456K
Free Hard Disk Space	9MB	10.5MB
Video	VGA	VGA

MEMORY - TABLE # 3

WINDOWS 3.X AND VIRTUAL MEMORY

Windows 386 Enhanced mode and Windows 95 use virtual memory to speed up Windows applications. Hard disk access is slower than RAM access, but more applications can run simultaneously than the available RAM normally allows. The amount of free hard disk space determines the possible amount of virtual memory. Applications using virtual memory access it by using virtual memory addresses mapped into physical addresses on the hard disk. When using virtual memory, part of an application is kept in RAM while other parts are kept on the hard disk in the swap file. Windows has two possible types of swap files: temporary and permanent. The permanent swap file is much better and faster than a temporary swap file in Windows 3.x because the permanent swap file exists on contiguous (adjacent) sectors on the hard drive. A temporary swap file can exist on non-contiguous (non-adjacent) sectors. Whenever using a temporary swap file, data access is slower. Nevertheless, a temporary swap file is better than no swap file at all.

Two files are created when a permanent swap file is created: (1) 386SPART.PAR, the actual swap file and (2) SPART.PAR, the file that tells Windows the size and location of the permanent swap file. The 386SPART.PAR file is located in the hard drive's root directory and is marked as a hidden and system file. The SPART.PAR file is a hidden file in the Windows directory.

A permanent swap file is created either during Windows SETUP or by clicking the 386 Enhanced icon from the Control Panel window. A permanent swap file's size is adjustable depending on the available contiguous hard disk space.

Run a hard disk compacting utility such as DEFRAG to create as much contiguous hard drive space as possible before creating a permanent swap file. Ignore the default settings for a permanent swap file. Use Memory Table #4 as a guideline for setting the permanent swap file.

MEMORY - TABLE #4

Permanent Swap File Settings

Installed RAM	Permanent Swap File Setting
8MB	1024K
16MB	2048K
32MB	4096K

Pay attention to the computer after changing the permanent swap file setting. If the hard disk drive starts thrashing (a great deal more disk activity than normal), increase the permanent swap file setting.

A temporary swap file is also created from the Windows 3.x 386 Enhanced Control Panel. A temporary swap file requires at least 1.5MB of hard disk space. The file WIN386.SWP is created on the hard disk when a temporary swap file is in use. WIN386.SWP increases or decreases in size according to what Windows requires.

OUT OF MEMORY ERRORS WITHIN WINDOWS

Whenever a Windows application gets the error "Insufficient Memory to Complete this Operation", the first thing the computer user or technician should do is *save* the work that is currently open and close all applications. Then, re-open the application running when the memory error message appeared. If the application opens properly, either the system resources (discussed below) were too low or the system truly needs more RAM. Most likely, the system resources were too low on most systems.

WINDOWS 3.X AND SYSTEM RESOURCES

Three files known as core files are the heart of Microsoft Windows. The core files are (1) KRNL286.EXE or KRNL386.EXE (depending on Windows 3.x's current operation mode), (2) GDI.EXE, and (3) USER.EXE. The kernel files, KRNL286.EXE or KRNL386.EXE, handle memory management as well as the loading and execution of Windows applications. GDI.EXE is the Graphics Device Interface that handles graphics and printing. USER.EXE handles user input, communication ports, the icons, windows, and dialog boxes. Both the GDI.EXE and the USER.EXE have memory allocated to them called memory **heaps**. When operating in Windows, every icon, every click of the mouse, every re-sizing of a window, etc., is tracked by Windows. This information is stored in the memory heaps. GDI.EXE has its own memory heap which is limited to 64KB. USER.EXE has a memory heap divided into two 64KB sections, one for menu-related tasks and the other for open file related tasks. Both memory heaps create the Windows **system resources**. Windows 3.x's system resources are not the same as the hardware system resources mentioned in Chapter 3. A computer can have 64MB of RAM and still get insufficient memory errors due to a lack of system resources.

To check how many system resources are available do the following steps. From within the Windows Program Manager, click on **Help**, then click on **About Program Manager**. At the bottom of the screen, the percentage of available system resources is shown. Also shown is the mode Windows is running in and the amount of memory available to Windows (not system resources, which is limited to the memory heaps).

If the available system resources percentage drops to 25 percent, keep the minimum number of windows open at one time. Closing windows increases the amount of system resources available. Also, closing applications not in use frees up system resources. Not all Windows applications are well written and may leave part of the program in the memory heaps after the application is closed. The only remedy for this is closing and restarting Windows.

WINDOWS 95 AND MEMORY

Windows 95 requires a minimum of 4MB of RAM, but 8MB to 16MB of memory is recommended. Windows 95 requires 417KB of *free* conventional memory to run. Windows 95 has a startup file called IO.SYS that replaces the two hidden files that MS-DOS uses, IO.SYS and MSDOS.SYS. The CONFIG.SYS and AUTOEXEC.BAT files are not required for Windows 95, but are available for use and for backward compatibility. The new IO.SYS file includes some files typically found in the AUTOEXEC.BAT and CONFIG.SYS files in the DOS environment. Memory Table #5 lists the files included with the Windows 95 IO.SYS file and the default setting for each.

MEMORY - TABLE # 5

Windows 95 Default IO.SYS Files and Values

Setting	Default Value
DOS=HIGH	N/A (IO.SYS does not load EMM386 by default)
HIMEM.SYS	N/A
IFSHLP.SYS	N/A (IFSHLP.SYS loads device drivers for the system)
SETVER.EXE	N/A
FILES=	60
LASTDRIVE=	Z
BUFFERS=	30
STACKS=	9,256
SHELL=COMMAND.COM	/P
FCBS=	4
TMP=	C:\WIN95\TEMP
TEMP=	C:\WIN95\TEMP
PROMPT=	PG
PATH=	C:\WIN95;C:\WIN95\COMMAND
COMSPEC=	C:\WIN95\COMMAND\COMMAND.COM

If a different setting is desired other than these listed in Memory Table #5 create a CONFIG.SYS file with the new value because the IO.SYS file cannot be changed. However, the FILES=, BUFFERS=, and STACKS= statement values cannot be set to a value lower than the default setting listed in Memory Table #5. The Windows 95 appendix also contains a table with default IO.SYS settings.

Even though Windows 95 uses a different memory system than DOS or Windows, it still requires approximately 420KB of conventional memory to start. Therefore, using the Upper Memory Blocks is still a good idea, even in the Windows 95 environment. Create a CONFIG.SYS file, such as the following bare-bones structure if no applications will be using expanded memory:

```
DEVICE=C:\<PATH>\HIMEM.SYS
DEVICE=C:\<PATH>\EMM386.EXE NOEMS
DOS=HIGH,UMB
```

Many hardware vendors still update the CONFIG.SYS file under Windows 95 for their product's device driver even though there is a better alternative for controlling the piece of hardware. Because Windows 95 needs as much conventional memory as possible, the CONFIG.SYS file is still frequently used.

Remove as many real-mode (old DOS) drivers and TSRs as possible and replace them with drivers and applications created for Windows 95. Some new Windows 95 commands that help create more available conventional memory are listed in Memory Table #6.

Windows 95 New CONFIG.SYS Commands

Command	Description
BUFFERSHIGH=	Memory for disk buffers; uses the memory space in the UMBs instead of convetional memory.
FCBSHIGH=	The number of file control blocks that can be open at one time for compatibility with very old software; uses the memory space in the UMBs instead of conventional memory. Note: This file is not normally needed, but is standard in Windows 95's IO.SYS
FILESHIGH=	The number of files accessible at one time; uses the memory space in the UMBs instead of conventional memory.
LASTDRIVEHIGH=	The maximum number of drives accessible; the amount of memory taken for each drive is taken from the UMBs.
STACKSHIGH=	The amount of memory reserved for hardware interrupts; uses the memory space in the UMBs instead of conventional memory.

MEMORY - TABLE # 6

Windows 95's 32-bit applications use preemptive multi-tasking. With 16-bit applications, such as those written for Windows 3.x, Windows 95 uses the cooperative multi-tasking Windows 3.x uses. With **preemptive multi-tasking**, Windows 95 controls which application receives the processor's attention. Windows NT applications also use preemptive multitasking. With **cooperative multi-tasking**, the applications themselves decide when to relinquish the microprocessor to other applications.

If a 16-bit application running under Windows 95 appears to take extra time accessing different hardware in the computer thereby slowing the system down, consider upgrading the program to a 32-bit version so the application uses preemptive multi-tasking.

WINDOWS 95 VIRTUAL MEMORY

Windows 95 uses virtual memory differently than Windows 3.x. With Windows 3.x, memory is divided into different sized segments with a 64KB limit. Windows 95 uses 32-bit demand-paged virtual memory and each process running within Windows 95 gets 4GB of address space divided into two 2GB sections. One 2GB section is shared with the rest of the system while the other 2GB section is reserved for the one application. All the memory space is divided into 4KB blocks of memory called **pages**. Windows 95 allocates as much available RAM as possible to an application. Then, Windows 95 swaps or pages it to and from the temporary swap file as needed. Windows 95 determines the optimum setting for this swap file; however, it can be changed. To change the virtual memory (swap file) setting click on the **Start button**. Select the **Settings** option and then click on **Control Panel**. In the window that appears, double-click on the **System** icon. Click on the **Performance** tab and in the Performance window, click on the **Virtual Memory** button. Click on the **Let me specify my own virtual memory settings** radio button. Be careful changing this setting. Windows 95 usually does a good job controlling the virtual memory. When a 16-bit Windows application runs under Windows 95, the old, segmented virtual memory (which has a 64KB limitation), is still used.

 MONITORING MEMORY USAGE UNDER WINDOWS 95

A utility that comes with Windows 95 is System Monitor. It evaluates different areas of performance within the computer: the file system, the IPX/SPX compatible protocol, the kernel, the memory manager, Microsoft Client for NetWare Networks and Microsoft Network Client, Microsoft Network Server, and Microsoft Network Monitor Performance Data. The areas of particular interest in regard to memory are the Kernel Monitor (the processor usage and threads settings) and the Memory Manager Monitor (the page-outs, discards, locked memory, allocated memory, and page faults settings).

The processor usage setting within the Kernel monitor provides a percentage of time the microprocessor is busy. If the Processor Usage values are high (even when the computer is not in use), check to see what particular application is using the microprocessor by pressing CTRL+ALT+DEL. The Close Program dialog box will appear containing a list of running tasks. Close a particular application and note the difference in the Processor Usage settings.

A **thread** is a unit of programming code that receives a slice of time from Windows 95 so it can run concurrently with other units of code or other threads. The Threads setting within the Kernel monitor indicates the current number of threads within the Windows 95 system. This number indicates if a particular application is starting threads and not reclaiming them. Windows 95 closes threads when exiting an application. If you can identify a thread left by a closed application that still shows as being open in the task list, the application may need to be restarted then exited again so the thread closes.

The Memory Manager's Discards setting is the number of pages of memory discarded per second. The pages of memory are not swapped to the hard disk because the information is already stored there. The Page-outs setting is the number of pages of memory swapped out of memory and written to the disk per second. If these two values are high and indicate a lot of activity, more RAM may be needed.

The Memory Manager's Locked Memory setting shows the amount of memory, including the disk cache, that cannot be paged out. To determine the exact amount of locked RAM, subtract the Disk Cache Size amount from the Locked Memory amount. The Allocated Memory setting in the Memory Manager indicates the total amount of allocated memory not stored in the swap file (Other Memory) and the number of bytes in use from the swap file (Swapable Memory). If the Locked Memory values are a large portion of the Allocated Memory value, then the system does not have enough free memory and this affects performance. Also, an application might be locking memory unnecessarily and not allowing the memory to be paged out. This comes from poorly written software or software that needs to be re-loaded.

The Memory Manager's Page Faults setting shows the number of page faults occurring each second. If this value is high, the application currently in use has memory requirements higher than what is installed in the computer. In this case, recommend to the customer to purchase more RAM for the computer.

System Monitor is a great tool and the technician should become familiar with it. Just like monitoring system resources in Windows 3.x, the system resources within Windows 95 are different, but need to be monitored as well.

 ## OPTIMIZING MEMORY USING WINDOWS 95

One of the best tips for optimizing memory speed under Windows 95 is to periodically defragment the hard disk. Fragmented hard disks dramatically slow down a Windows 95 system. To run the defragmentation program that ships with Windows 95, click on the **Start** button. Select **Programs**, **Accessories**, and then **System Tools**. Click on **Disk Defragmenter**. Use the down arrow to select the drive to be defragmented and click on the **OK** button. The defragmentation can be automated by adding the DEFRAG command to STARTUP with the following steps: (1) *right*-click the **Start** button; (2) select **Open**; (3) open the **Programs** folder; (4) open the **Startup** file; (5) *right*-click inside the window; (6) select **New**; (7) select **Shortcut**; (8) click on the **Browse** button; (9) double-click on **DEFRAG.EXE** in the Windows folder; (10) at the end of the entry in the command line box, add a **space** and the following switches: */all /u /nonprompt* (each switch is followed by a space); (11) click **OK** to save.

Because Windows 95 has its own disk caching software called VCACHE, an AUTOEXEC.BAT or CONFIG.SYS file or driver is not necessary for making disk caching available. However, the amount of cache Windows 95 allocates to the machine depends on the type of computer loaded with Windows 95: desktop, mobile, or network server.

Be sure Windows 95 has the correct type of computer set so that the proper amount of cache is allocated for the hard disk. To do this: *Right*-click on **My Computer**; choose **Properties**; click on the **Performance** tab; click on **File System**; be sure **Typical role of this machine** is set to the proper setting. If your computer has 20MB or more of RAM, try setting "Typical role of this machine" to network server even if the computer is a regular desktop computer.

The following bulleted list summarize recommendations when using the System Monitor to troubleshoot memory problems:

- ◆ If the Swap File value in System Monitor is over 5MB of swapped data, add more RAM to the computer.
- ◆ If the Cache Size value in System Monitor drops below 2MB, add more RAM to the computer.
- ◆ If the CPU Utilization value in System Monitor is 80 percent or higher consistently when running Windows 95, upgrade the microprocessor.
- ◆ When getting insufficient memory errors, try closing some programs and/or documents that are currently open.
- ◆ When Windows 95 is running out of memory, delete unused files by emptying the Recycle Bin.
- ◆ When running out of memory, be sure at least 10MB of hard disk space is available.

DOS APPLICATIONS UNDER WINDOWS 95

Most DOS applications run fine under Windows 95, but those with problems can be run in the Windows 95 MS-DOS mode. Refer to the Windows 95 appendix to troubleshoot DOS applications that execute within Windows 95.

In MS-DOS mode, Windows 95 removes almost all of itself from memory, finishes all tasks currently running, loads a real-mode copy of MS-DOS into memory, uses a customized CONFIG.SYS file and a customized AUTOEXEC.BAT file, then turns over the computer resources to the DOS application. When the DOS application finishes running, Windows 95 restarts and loads itself back into memory. DOS applications require ample available conventional memory just as a non-Windows 95 computer. Therefore, a DOS application that executes using the Windows 95 MS-DOS mode should have a customized CONFIG.SYS containing the HIMEM.SYS; DOS=HIGH,UMB; and EMM386.EXE statements. Load all possible device drivers and TSRs into the UMBs.

Another alternative is to run the DOS application after starting Windows 95 in the "Command Prompt Only" mode. To start Windows 95 in a different mode, press the F8 key when the "Starting Windows 95" message appears on the screen as the system first boots. Then, choose the "Command Prompt Only" option from the menu that appears.

 TROUBLESHOOTING OTHER MEMORY PROBLEMS

POST usually detects a problem with a memory chip and most ROM BIOS chips show a 2XX POST error code. Some computers have the CMOS option to disable extended memory checking. This is not a good idea. Endure the few seconds it takes to check the memory chips to get an early warning of a memory failure. When POST issues a memory error, turn off the computer, remove the cover and press down on any DIP memory chips. If SIMM chips are installed, reseat the chips in the memory sockets and clean out the sockets with compressed air. Reseating memory chips often corrects memory errors.

If this does not work, turn the computer on again and watch the memory count in the upper left corner of the screen. The memory count is an excellent clue for where to start troubleshooting a memory problem. For example, on a computer with 16MB of RAM installed, if the memory in the upper left corner gets to 8,378KB and a POST memory error appears, then the memory problem is on a chip somewhere after the first 8MB of RAM. If the system is a Pentium with two 8MB, 72-pin SIMMs installed, the problem is probably in the second SIMM socket. Swap the SIMM in the first socket with the SIMM in the second socket. The POST error code appears more quickly as the 186KB of memory counts on the screen. The problem is then identified as the SIMM that was in the second socket, but later moved to the first socket.

The key to good memory chip troubleshooting is to divide and conquer. Narrow the problem to a suspected bank of memory, then start swapping memory chips. Continue swapping chips until one is correctly identified as the faulty chip. Keep in mind most memory problems are not in the hardware, they are in the software, especially if operating in the DOS/Windows environment.

Most DOS memory problems are attributed to the lack of conventional memory. Run a memory management program such as RAMBOOST or MEMMAKER to optimize the memory. Also, use the MEM command to view and verify as many programs as possible load into the Upper Memory Blocks. TSRs and device drivers in the AUTOEXEC.BAT and CONFIG.SYS files can be re-ordered. Sometimes more programs can be loaded into the Upper Memory Blocks just by re-ordering the programs.

ROM address conflicts are a frequent source of problems for the technician. The ROM chips on some adapters have addresses that are selectable while others, such as the old XT hard disk controller, are pre-set and cannot be changed. All ROM chips throughout the computer system must have a separate, unique ROM address to operate within the memory map.

One of the first symptoms of a ROM address conflict is if a particular adapter will not function. Or, if a new adapter is installed in a system and now the computer will not boot off the hard drive, a ROM conflict is a likely culprit. Do not forget to consider interrupt and I/O address conflicts also.

For DOS or Windows 3.x computers, Microsoft Diagnostics is a good place to begin checking the current in-use ROM locations *before* installing any new adapters. There are other programs and utilities that perform the same function, but MSD (Microsoft Diagnostics) ships with Microsoft DOS and Windows and is therefore a frequently used program. For Windows 95 computers, the Device Manager is a great place to see the various ROM addresses.

Name _____

Memory Review Questions

1. Describe the difference between RAM and ROM.

2. What is meant by memory chip refreshing?

3. Which type of memory chips require refreshing? (Pick all that apply) [ROM, RAM, DRAM, SRAM, SDRAM, EDO, FPM, Burst EDO]

4. T/F   Most memory on the motherboard is SRAM.

5. Describe how cache increases computer speed.

6. What motherboards commonly use DIMMs? (Pick all that apply) [386, 486, Pentium, Pentium Pro, PentiumII]

7. T/F   A non-parity system can use parity memory chips.

8. Describe how to determine a memory chip's access time.

9. T/F   A 60ns memory chip is faster than a 70ns memory chip.

10. T/F   Installing faster memory chips always increases computer speed.

11. What memory developments will replace SDRAM?

12. Describe how FPM, EDO, and Burst EDO memory chips increase a memory chip's speed.

13. T/F   Any motherboard can accept Burst EDO RAM chips.

14. Which of the following are rules for populating memory? (pick all that apply)
    A.   If a bank of memory is to be used, it must be filled entirely with memory chips.
    B.   All memory chips in a bank must be the same capacity.
    C.   All banks on a motherboard must be filled with memory chips to operate properly.
    D.   Memory chips in the same bank should have the same access speed.
    E.   The memory chips in every memory bank on the motherboard must be the same capacity.

15. T/F   Pentium-based motherboards commonly use 72-pin SIMMs.

16. T/F   A 2MB X 36 72-pin SIMM has a total capacity of 8MB.

17. T/F   A 2MB X 36 72-pin SIMM does not use parity.

18. Explain how the 168-pin DIMM replaces two 72-pin SIMMs.

19. What is the best tool for removing a DIP memory chip?

20. Which is easier to install a SIMM or a DIP and why?

21.   T/F   A POST error message is normal after upgrading memory on some computers.

22.   Which area of the 80286 memory map is the area from 0 to 640KB?
       A.   Conventional
       B.   Expanded
       C.   Upper Memory Area
       D.   High Memory Area
       E.   Extended

23.   Which area of the 8088 memory map is a maximum of 32MB divided into 16KB blocks and pages in and out of a 64KB space?
       A.   Conventional
       B.   Expanded
       C.   Upper Memory Area
       D.   High Memory Area
       E.   Extended

24.   Which area of the 80386 memory map is the area from 640KB to 1MB?
       A.   Conventional
       B.   Expanded
       C.   Upper Memory Area
       D.   High Memory Area
       E.   Extended

25.   Which area of the 80486 memory map is the area from 1MB to 4GB?
       A.   Conventional
       B.   Expanded
       C.   Upper Memory Area
       D.   High Memory Area
       E.   Extended

26.   Which area of the memory map is a 64KB space that pages up to 32MB of memory in and out of the memory map, 16KB at a time?
       A.   Conventional
       B.   Expanded
       C.   Upper Memory Area
       D.   High Memory Area
       E.   Extended

27.   Which area of the Pentium memory map is the first 64KB of memory above the 1MB mark?
       A.   Conventional
       B.   Expanded
       C.   Upper Memory Area
       D.   High Memory Area
       E.   Extended

28.   Which type of memory is faster, conventional or expanded?

29.   Explain how expanded memory gets in and out of the memory map.

30.   Which of the following provides access to the Upper Memory Blocks and is the driver for expanded memory?
      A.   EMM386.EXE
      B.   HIMEM.SYS
      C.   DOS=HIGH
      D.   DOS=UMB

31.   What DOS or Windows file provides access to extended memory?
      A.   EMM386.EXE
      B.   HIMEM.SYS
      C.   DOS=HIGH
      D.   DOS=UMB

32.   Which of the following will load most of DOS into the HMA?
      A.   EMM386.EXE
      B.   HIMEM.SYS
      C.   DOS=HIGH
      D.   DOS=UMB

33.   Which of the following allows the use of the UMBs for loading device drivers and TSRs?
      A.   EMM386.EXE
      B.   HIMEM.SYS
      C.   DOS=HIGH
      D.   DOS=UMB

34.   What EMM386.EXE switch allows the use of the 64KB area of space, normally set aside for expanded memory and any other Upper Memory Blocks not being used by ROM chips, for loading TSRs and device drivers?
      A.   NOEMS
      B.   2048
      C.   No switch is needed

35.   Explain how disk caching works.

36.   What type of swap file does Windows 95 normally use?
      A.   Permanent
      B.   Temporary
      C.   Both

37.   What is a RAMDrive?

38.   What type of swap file does Windows 3.x use?
      A.   Permanent
      B.   Temporary
      C.   Both

39.   If Windows 3.x is running in enhanced mode, what are the three core files?

40.   T/F   Windows 95 requires a minimum of 16MB to operate.

41.   Which of the following files are now automatically included in the Windows 95 IO.SYS file? (Pick all that apply)
       A.   HIMEM.SYS
       B.   EMM386.EXE
       C.   DOS=HIGH
       D.   FILES=30

42.   T/F   Upper Memory Blocks are automatically available for Windows 95 usage by default.

43.   Which of the following Windows 95 commands can be used in CONFIG.SYS to make more conventional memory available? (Pick all that apply)
       A.   FILESHIGH=
       B.   LASTDRIVEHIGH=
       C.   STACKSHIGH=
       D.   DRIVERHIGH=

44.   Which of the following statements about Windows 95 are false? (pick all that apply)
       A.   Windows 95 uses preemptive multi-tasking for 32-bit applications.
       B.   Windows 95 cannot run applications which require cooperative multi-tasking.
       C.   Windows 95 virtual memory settings cannot be changed.
       D.   Windows 95 IO.SYS file cannot be changed.

45.   T/F   Each process running within Windows 95 is allowed 4GB of address space.

46.   Which of the following is a Windows 95 performance monitoring tool, useful in troubleshooting memory problems?
       A.   VCACHE
       B.   VIRTUAL
       C.   My Computer
       D.   System Monitor

47.   What cache size setting value indicates a need to add more RAM?

48.   What can you do if you get insufficient memory errors in Windows 3.x or Windows 95?

49.   What is the difference between running a DOS application using the RUN utility and running the application under Windows 95's MS-DOS mode?

Name _____

Memory Fill-in-the-Blank

1. The two main types of memory are _____ and _____.

2. _____ is non-volatile memory.

3. The major types of RAM are _____ and _____.

4. The SRAM chips on the motherboard are also known as the _____.

5. The *type* of memory chip used for RAM in today's systems are _____ with either tin or gold contact edges.

6. The type of RAM memory chips used on older motherboards and for some older cache memory are known as _____ which have one row of legs down each side of the chip.

7. _____ is a method of memory error checking in which an extra memory chip checks every 8 bits going into the bank of memory.

8. Most SIMMs have capacities measured in _____.

9. Memory access time is measured in _____.

10. Whether a system can use Fast Page Mode, EDO, or Burst EDO RAM chips depends on the _____ and the chipset used on the motherboard.

11. _____ is the process of sending constant data to the microprocessor.

12. The maximum amount of RAM that can be installed on the motherboard is determined by the number of _____ from the microprocessor.

13. The number of sockets in a bank of memory is determined by the number of bits in a microprocessor's _____.

14. The maximum amount of memory addresses on a Pentium-Pro motherboard is _____.

15. Memory chips that collectively transmit to the microprocessor are grouped into a _____.

16. _____ is also known as LIM or EMS memory.

17. _____ is located above the 1MB mark in the memory map.

18. The _____ file contains memory management drivers.

19. Windows 3.x and Windows 95's memory heaps are collectively known as _____.

20. Pressing _____ causes a task list of currently running applications to appear in Windows 95.

Name _____

PAPER MEMORY POPULATION EXERCISE FOR
8088-BASED MOTHERBOARDS

Use the drawing shown in Memory Exercise Figure #1 to populate the motherboard with 640KB of memory. The DIP memory chips to use with this motherboard are 64Kb and 256Kb.

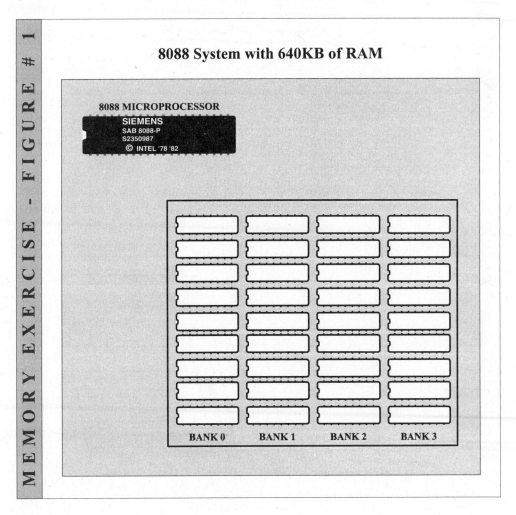

Name _____

PAPER MEMORY POPULATION EXERCISE FOR
80386-BASED MOTHERBOARDS

Use the drawing shown in Memory Exercise Figure #2 to populate the motherboard with 8MB of memory. The 30-pin SIMMs available to use with this motherboard are 1MB, 4MB, and 8MB.

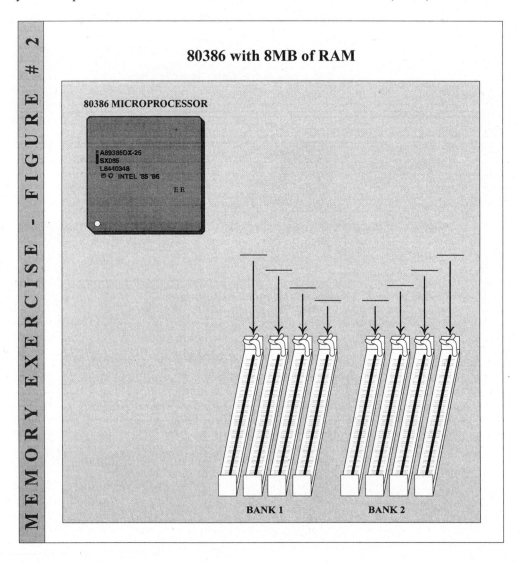

Name _____

SECOND PAPER MEMORY POPULATION EXERCISE FOR
80386-BASED MOTHERBOARDS

Use the drawing shown in Memory Exercise Figure #3 to populate the motherboard with 5MB of memory. The 30-pin SIMMs available to use with this motherboard are 256KB, 512KB, 1MB, and 4MB.

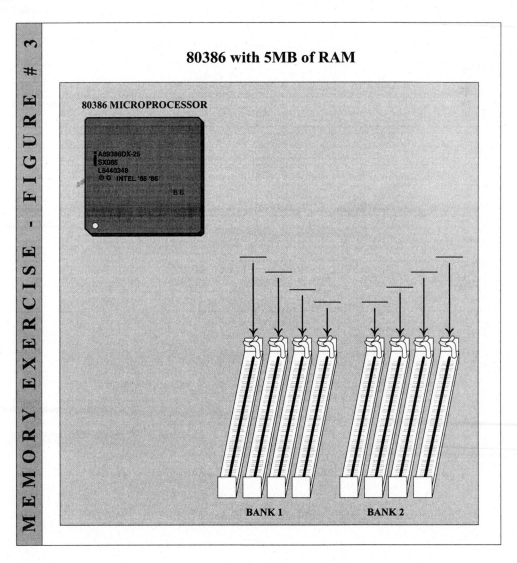

 Name _____

PAPER MEMORY POPULATION EXERCISE FOR
80486-BASED MOTHERBOARDS

Use the drawing shown in Memory Exercise Figure #4 to populate the motherboard with 8MB of memory. The 72-pin SIMMs available to use with this motherboard are 2MB, 4MB, and 8MB (these are the total capacities of the memory chips).

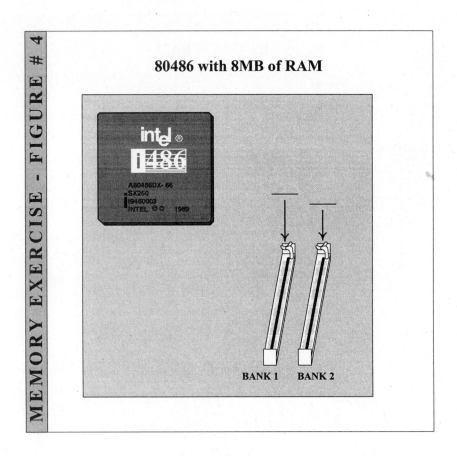

MEMORY EXERCISE – FIGURE # 4

80486 with 8MB of RAM

BANK 1   BANK 2

Name _____

SECOND PAPER MEMORY POPULATION EXERCISE FOR
80486-BASED MOTHERBOARDS

Use the drawing shown in Memory Exercise Figure #5 to populate the motherboard with 16MB of memory. The 72-pin SIMMs available to use with this motherboard are 1MB X 36, 2MB X 36, 4MB X 36, 8MB X 36, and 16MB X 36.

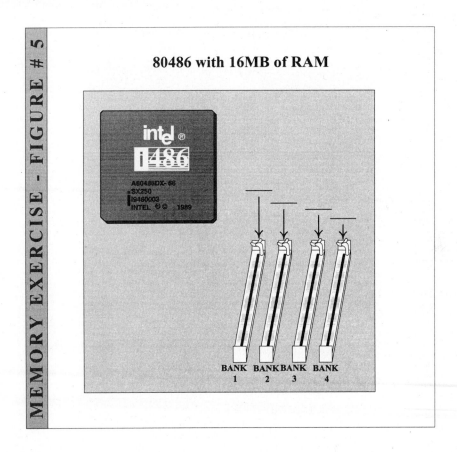

Name _____

THIRD PAPER MEMORY POPULATION EXERCISE FOR
80486-BASED MOTHERBOARDS

Use the drawing shown in Memory Exercise Figure #6 to populate the motherboard with 20MB of memory. The 72-pin SIMMs available to use with this motherboard are 1MB X 36, 2MB X 36, 4MB X 36, 8MB X 36, and 16MB X 36.

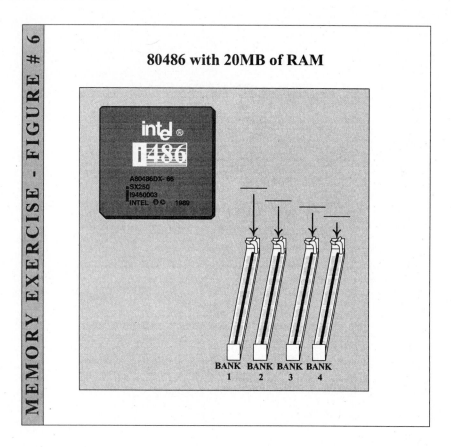

Name _____

PAPER MEMORY POPULATION EXERCISE FOR
PENTIUM-BASED MOTHERBOARDS

Use the drawing shown in Memory Exercise Figure #7 to populate the motherboard with 16MB of memory. The 72-pin SIMMs available to use with this motherboard are 1MB X 36, 2MB X 36, 4MB X 36, 8MB X 36, and 16MB X 36.

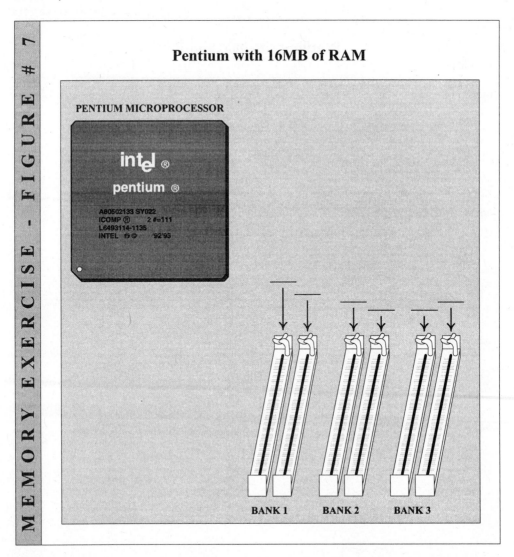

Name_____

SECOND PAPER MEMORY POPULATION EXERCISE FOR
PENTIUM-BASED MOTHERBOARDS

Use the drawing shown in Memory Exercise Figure #8 to populate the motherboard with 40MB of memory. The 72-pin SIMMs available to use with this motherboard are 1MB X 36, 2MB X 36, 4MB X 36, 8MB X 36, and 16MB X 36.

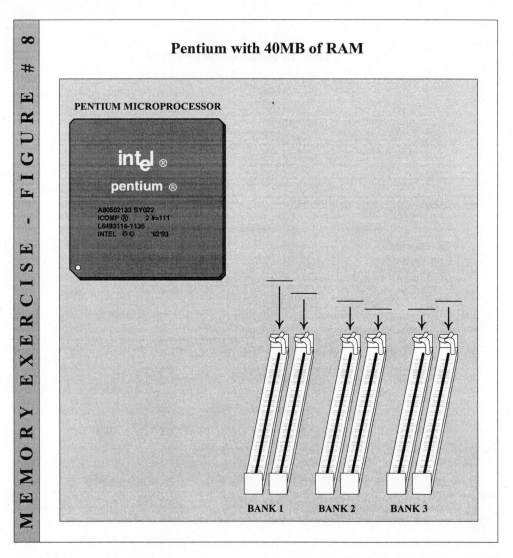

Name _____

PAPER MEMORY POPULATION EXERCISE FOR
PENTIUM-PRO AND HIGHER MOTHERBOARDS

Use the drawing shown in Memory Exercise Figure #9 to populate the motherboard with 176MB of memory. The 168-pin DIMMs available to use with this motherboard are 1MBx64, 2MBx64, 4MBx64, 8MBx64, 16MBx64.

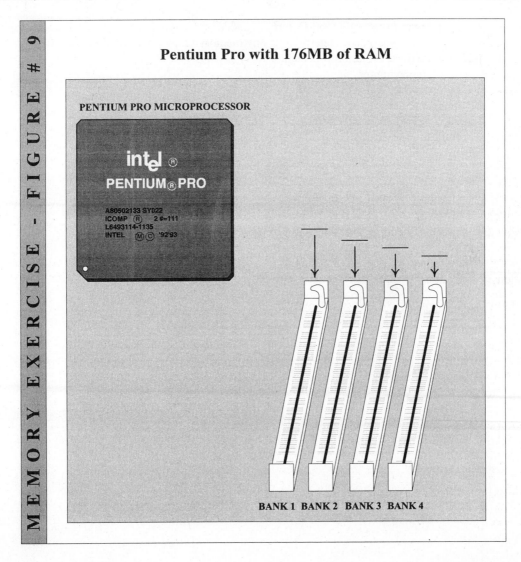

Name _____

MEMORY INSTALLATION EXERCISE

***Objective*:**   To correctly install memory into a computer

***Parts*:** Memory chips
        Anti-static strap
        Documentation for the motherboard

Step 1:   Plan the memory installation. Determine what size, type, capacity, and access speed
            memory chip(s) you need. Determine if any memory chips are to be removed. Refer to the
            motherboard documentation if possible.
Step 2:   Power off the computer.
Step 3:   Remove the cover from the computer.
Step 4:   Put on the anti-static strap and attach it to the computer.
Step 5:   Remove any memory chips necessary for the upgrade or installation if needed.
Step 6:   Install the memory chips.
Step 7:   Set any jumpers or switches necessary for a computer memory change.

Question 1:   What microprocessor is installed in the computer?

Question 2:   How many address lines does this microprocessor use?

Question 3:   What is the size (in bits) of the external data path of this microprocessor?

Step 8:   Power on the computer.
Step 9:   Configure the computer's CMOS SETUP.
Step 10:   Reboot the computer and verify that POST errors do not appear.

_____ Instructor's Initials

Name _____

SEEING THE RESULTS OF MEMORY MANAGEMENT

Objective: To see how software affects conventional memory and how to load software into the
       Upper Memory Blocks

Parts: One blank disk
       A computer with DOS 6.X loaded
       Optional software from the instructor

Step 1:   Make a bootable disk with the version of DOS currently on the computer. For DOS skills,
       refer to Appendix A.

Step 2:   Create a CONFIG.SYS file which contains the following lines:
       FILES=20
       BUFFERS=20

Step 3:   Reboot the computer from the bootable disk.
       The system is at the A:\> prompt after rebooting.

Step 4:   Go to the C: drive by typing
       C:
       The prompt changes to C:\>.

Step 5:   Type
       Prompt PG

Step 6:   Go to the DOS directory by typing
       CD\DOS
       The prompt changes to C:\DOS>

Step 7:   The MEM command allows you to view memory information on the computer. Type
       MEM

Question 1:   How many bytes of total conventional memory are available?

Question 2:   What size is the largest executable program?

Step 8:   The MEM /C command allows you to see a memory summary with details of the different
       memory classifications such as conventional and UMBs. Type
       MEM /C

Question 3:   What is the first program to load into conventional memory?

Question 4:   How much space (in bytes) does this program occupy?

Question 5:   How much conventional memory is available?

Question 6:   How much contiguous extended memory is available? (Contiguous memory is not
               broken up; it is adjacent to other memory locations).

Step   9:   No matter how much contiguous extended memory is available, none is usable without a
             memory manager such as the HIMEM.SYS program shipped with DOS, Windows 3.x, and
             Windows 95. Modify the CONFIG.SYS file and insert the HIMEM.SYS file in the first
             line. Verify the correct path statement directs the system to the HIMEM.SYS file.

Question 7:   Write your CONFIG.SYS file in the space below:

Step 10:   Create an AUTOEXEC.BAT file that contains the following files:
             PROMPT PG
             PATH=C:\DOS
Step 11:   Reboot the computer with the bootable disk inserted in the A: drive.
Step 12:   At the prompt, type
             MEM /C

Question 8:   How much conventional memory does the HIMEM.SYS file take?

Step 13:   Modify the CONFIG.SYS file on the boot disk to add the line **DOS=HIGH** after the
             DEVICE=C:\WINDOWS\HIMEM.SYS statement.
Step 14:   Reboot the computer with the bootable disk inserted into the A: drive.
Step 15:   At the prompt, type
             MEM

Question 9:   How many bytes of free conventional memory are available?

Step 16:   Modify the CONFIG.SYS file on the boot disk to include the **EMM386.EXE** expanded
             memory manager after the HIMEM.SYS statement.
Step 17:   Reboot the computer with the bootable disk inserted in the A: drive.

Question 10:   Using the MEM command, how much conventional memory does the EMM386.EXE file require?

Question 11:   Using the MEM command, how much extended memory is available for use?

Step 18:   Modify the CONFIG.SYS file to add **,UMB** to the DOS=HIGH line so that the line reads: DOS=HIGH,UMB.

Step 19:   Reboot the computer with the bootable disk inserted into the A: drive.

Question 12:   Using the MEM command, how much UMB space is now available?

Question 13:   How much extended memory is now available?

Question 14:   Why did the total amount of free extended memory reduce in size by adding ,UMB to the DOS=HIGH statement?

Step 20:   Modify the CONFIG.SYS statement on the bootable disk to include the NOEMS switch on the EMM386.EXE line.

Step 21:   Reboot the computer with the bootable disk inserted in the A: drive.

Question 15:   Using the MEM command, how much Upper Memory Block space is now available (in bytes)?

Question 16:   How much extended memory is now available?

Note: Steps 22 through 30 are optional. Check with the instructor to see if these steps are to be completed.

Step 22:   Using a device driver supplied by the instructor, load the device driver by modifying the CONFIG.SYS file on the bootable disk.

Question 17:   Write the CONFIG.SYS statements now contained on the bootable disk in the space below:

Name _____

USING MICROSOFT'S MEMMAKER (EXPRESS) EXERCISE

***Objective*:** To see how software affects conventional memory and how to load software into the Upper Memory Blocks

***Parts*:** A computer with MS-DOS 6.X loaded

Question 1: Using the MEM command, determine the amount of free conventional memory. Type **MEM** from the command prompt. For DOS skills, refer to Appendix A. Write the amount of free conventional memory in the space below:

Step 1: From the C:\> command prompt, type
MEMMAKER
For DOS skills, refer to Appendix A. The screen displays a choice of Express or Custom SETUP.

Step 2: Express SETUP is the default option. Press **ENTER** to accept the default. A screen appears asking you to specify if any programs require expanded memory.

Step 3: Because most applications today do *not* require expanded memory, the default option of **No** is the most common answer. Press **ENTER** to accept the default.

Optional Step 4: If MemMaker cannot find your Windows 3.x, MemMaker might prompt for the location of these files. If so, type in the directory where Windows 3.x is located. Contact the instructor if you are unsure.

Step 5: Later, MemMaker displays a screen stating the computer must be restarted. As the screen instructs, press **ENTER** to restart the computer. After restarting, MemMaker determines the optimum memory configuration. MemMaker determines the order for loading the device drivers and TSRs into the Upper Memory Blocks to free up the most conventional memory. This process may take a few moments depending on the complexity of the AUTOEXEC.BAT and CONFIG.SYS files.

Step 6: After determining the optimum configuration, MemMaker changes the CONFIG.SYS and AUTOEXEC.BAT files. If the computer does not respond after a long period of time, press **CTRL+ALT+DEL** to restart MemMaker, then choose the "Try again with conservative settings" option. Follow the directions on the screen. If the computer performs correctly, it still must be restarted for the changes to take effect. When prompted to do so, press **ENTER** to load MemMaker to optimize the CONFIG.SYS and AUTOEXEC.BAT files.

Step 7:   Watch carefully for any errors that appear during the restart process. MemMaker displays a question as to whether or not any errors appear. If no error messages appear, press ENTER to accept the default of YES. If errors appear or you suspect problems, press the spacebar once to change the default to NO, then press ENTER.

Step 8:   If everything boots successfully, MemMaker displays the amount of memory available before and after running MemMaker.

Question 2:   How much free conventional memory is now available?

Step 9:   Press ENTER to quit MemMaker.

_____ Instructor's Initials

Optional Step 10:   Contact the instructor to see if the configuration changes made by MemMaker are to be undone. If so, type **MEMMAKER /UNDO** at the command prompt. Press **ENTER** to restore the original AUTOEXEC.BAT and CONFIG.SYS files.

Name _____

CONFIGURING WINDOWS 3.X FOR 32-BIT DISK ACCESS
AND VIRTUAL MEMORY

Objective: To correctly configure Windows 3.x 32-bit disk access and set the virtual memory type

Parts: A computer with Windows 3.x loaded in the 386 Enhanced mode

Step 1:   Power on the computer.
Step 2:   Run a disk compacting utility such as DEFRAG.
Step 3:   Start Microsoft Windows 3.x.
Step 4:   Open the **Main** window.
Step 5:   Open the **Control Panel** window.
Step 6:   Double-click on the **386 Enhanced** icon.
Step 7:   Click in the **Virtual memory** box.
Step 8:   Click once in the **Change** box.
Step 9:   At the bottom of the window is a checkbox for 32-bit disk access *if* Windows determines the hard disk controller is WD1003-compatible. If the 32-bit disk access checkbox is available, click once inside the checkbox. If the checkbox is not available, skip to Step 12.
Step 10:   Save the settings by clicking in the **OK** box.
Step 11:   A prompt appears stating Windows must be restarted for the changes to take effect. Click in the box that says **Restart Windows**.

Question 1:   What is an advantage of using 32-bit disk access?

Step 12:   After Windows restarts, open the **Main** window.
Step 13:   Open the **Control Panel** window.
Step 14:   Double-click on the **386 Enhanced** icon.
Step 15:   Click in the **Virtual memory** box.
Step 16:   Click once in the **Change** box.
Step 17:   Click in the **Type** box **down arrow** (which either says permanent or temporary).
Step 18:   Ignore the Recommended size and set the Permanent Swap file New Size to the settings given in Memory Exercise Table #1 according to the amount of RAM installed on the motherboard.

EXERCISE - TABLE # 1

Permanent Swap File Settings

Installed RAM	Permanent Swap File Setting
8MB	1024K
16MB	2048K
32MB	4096K

Step 19:   Click on **OK**.

Step 20:   A dialog box appears asking, "Are you sure you want to make changes to the Virtual-memory settings?" Click in the **Yes** box.

Step 21:   A dialog box appears stating, "You need to quit and restart Windows so that the changes you made will take effect. Do not press CTRL+ALT+DEL to restart Windows — this will result in loss of information. Restart Windows now?" Click in the **Restart Windows** box.

Step 22:   Verify that Windows 95 starts properly after changing the virtual memory settings.

_____ Instructor's Initials

Name _____

WINDOWS 3.X MODE AND SYSTEM RESOURCES

Objective: To correctly determine Windows 3.x operation mode and what percentage of system resources are available

Parts: A computer with Windows 3.x loaded

Step   1:   Power on the computer and start Microsoft Windows.
Step   2:   From the **Program Manager**, click on **Help**.
Step   3:   Click on **About Program Manager**.

Question 1:   What percentage of system resources is available?

Question 2:   In what Windows mode is the machine running?

Question 3:   How much memory does the machine have available?

Step   4:   Click on **OK**.
Step   5:   Open up the **Accessories** Program Group window.
Step   6:   Open the Microsoft **Write** application.
Step   7:   Click in the **Program Manager** window, leaving the Write application running.
Step   8:   Click on **Help** within the Program Manager window.
Step   9:   Click on **About Program Manager**.

Question 4:   What percentage of system resources is now available?

Step 10:   Click on **OK**.
Step 11:   Return to the Microsoft **Write** application and **Exit** the program.

Question 5:   Which memory heap, USER.EXE or GDI.EXE, handles the size of the Microsoft Write application document?

Question 6:   Which memory heap, USER.EXE or GDI.EXE, handles the printing of a Microsoft Write document?

_____ Instructor's Initials

Name _____

USING MSD FOR ROM ADDRESS CONFLICTS

Objective: To use MSD to view ROM addresses

Parts: A computer with MS-DOS or Windows 3.x loaded

Step   1:   Power on the computer.
Step   2:   Change to the directory where the MSD.EXE program is located. For DOS skills, refer to
             Appendix A.
Step   3:   At the command prompt, execute the Microsoft Diagnostics by typing **MSD**.
Step   4:   From the Main Menu, press **M** for Memory.
Step   5:   Using the scroll bars on the right side of the screen, examine the memory areas from A000
             to FFFF. Look for areas that contain Fs in the blocks of memory. They are the areas of
             memory that are available. Any new adapter with a ROM chip must have the ROM address
             set to one of the available areas shown in MSD.

Question 1:   List at least two memory address ranges available for use by a new adapter.

Question 2:   If a new adapter does not have an option available for one of the ROM addresses listed
    in Microsoft Diagnostics , what could you as the technician do?

Step   6:   Exit the MSD program by pressing **ALT**, then **F**, then **X**.

_____ Instructor's Initials

Name _____

INSTALLING AND RUNNING WINDOWS 95 SYSTEM MONITOR

Objective: To install and properly use System Monitor

Parts: A computer with Windows 95 loaded

Step 1:   Power on the computer and start Microsoft Windows 95.
Step 2:   Click on the **Start** button. For Windows 95 skills, refer to Appendix B.
Step 3:   Click on the **Settings** button.
Step 4:   Double-click on the **Control Panel** option to open the Control Panel window.
Step 5:   Double-click on the **Add/Remove Programs** icon.
Step 6:   Click on the **Windows SETUP** tab.
Step 7:   In the **Components** list, be sure **Accessories** is enabled or checked. If Accessories is not checked, click on it to enable it.
Step 8:   Click on **Accessories**.
Step 9:   Click on **Details**.
Step 10:   In the **Components** list, verify **System Monitor** is enabled or checked. If System Monitor is not checked, click on it to enable it.
Step 11:   Click **OK**. The screen returns to the Windows SETUP window.
Step 12:   Click **OK**. A prompt may appear asking you to insert the Windows 95 CD-ROM disk or a Windows 95 installation disk.
Step 13:   Click **OK** after inserting the proper CD or disk into the appropriate drive.
Step 14:   Close the Control Panel window.
Step 15:   Click the **Start** button.
Step 16:   Click on the **Run** option.
Step 17:   Type **SYSMON** and press ENTER.

To Use the System Monitor Utility to Track Performance Problems:

Step 1:   Click the **Edit** menu.
Step 2:   Click on **Add Item**.
Step 3:   In the **Item List**, click on the resource(s), such as Kernel or Memory Manager, to be monitored. To select more than one resource, press and hold CTRL while clicking on the resource.
Step 4:   Click **OK**. The System Monitor window appears with the various options checked in Step 3. By opening and closing various applications, the effects on memory usage can be seen.

_____ Instructor's Initials

Name _____

ADJUSTING MEMORY FOR A MS-DOS APPLICATION
RUNNING IN THE WINDOWS 95 MS-DOS MODE

Objective: To adjust the memory configuration for a DOS application in the Windows 95 MS-DOS mode

Parts: A computer with Windows 95 loaded

Step   1:   Power on the computer and start Microsoft Windows 95.
Step   2:   Double-click on the **My Computer** icon. For Windows 95 skills, refer to Appendix B.
Step   3:   *Right*-click on the drive icon that contains the DOS application.
Step   4:   Click once on the **Explore** option.
Step   5:   Find the appropriate DOS application .EXE or .COM file which starts the application.
Step   6:   *Right*-click the DOS application's **.EXE** file.
Step   7:   Click on the **Properties** option.
Step   8:   Click on the **Memory** tab. If the DOS application is configured in the Advanced settings for MS-DOS mode, not the Suggest MS-DOS Mode as Necessary option, memory cannot be configured for the application.
Step   9:   Adjust the conventional, extended, or MS-DOS Protected Mode (DPMI) memory as needed. MS-DOS Protected Mode memory is automatically provided by Windows 95 as expanded memory if the EMM386 statement is included in the CONFIG.SYS file. Do not use the NOEMS switch if you want to use MS-DOS Protected Mode memory.

Question 1:   Because DPMI (DOS Protected Mode) memory access is provided by the EMM386 statement, where on the memory map is DPMI memory located?

Step 10:   Click **OK** when all properties are set.
Step 11:   Close the Exploring window.
Step 12:   Close the My Computer window.

_____ Instructor's Initials

Name _____

USING WINDOWS 95'S DEVICE MANAGER
FOR VIEWING VARIOUS MEMORY AREAS

Objective: To use Device Manager to help avoid memory conflicts

Parts: A computer with Windows 95 loaded

Step 1:   Power on the computer and start Microsoft Windows 95.
Step 2:   *Right*-click on the **My Computer** icon. For Windows 95 skills, refer to Appendix B. A sub-menu appears.
Step 3:   Click on the **Properties** menu option. The System Properties window appears.
Step 4:   Click on the **Device Manager** tab.
Step 5:   Verify that the Computer option is highlighted. If not, click once on the Computer option.
Step 6:   Click on the **Properties** button. The Computer Properties window appears. Currently listed is the system's interrupts or IRQ in use.
Step 7:   Click on the **Memory** radio button. The system's ROM addresses used by motherboard ROM chips or ROM chips on various adapters lists on the screen. Keep in mind that no two ROM chips can share the same memory map space.
Step 8:   Click on the **Performance** tab.

Question 1:   What is the amount of RAM installed?

Question 2:   What percentage of system resources are available?

Question 3:   What, if any, recommendations can you make for this machine in regard to memory management?

Step 9:   Click on the close box in the upper right corner.

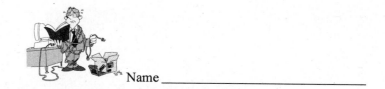

Name _____

MEMORY TROUBLESHOOTING EXERCISE

Objective: To correctly identify and solve a memory problem.

Parts: A computer with a memory problem

Step   1:   Power on a computer that has a memory problem inserted.

Question 1:   What is the first indication there is a memory problem?

Question 2:   List all troubleshooting steps taken to solve this problem.

Question 3:   Were there any CONFIG.SYS or AUTOEXEC.BAT errors? If so, list the errors in the
                     space below in the order the errors occurred:

Question 4:   Describe the solution to the problem.

_____ Instructor's Initials

Chapter 8:
Floppy Drives

OBJECTIVES

After completing this chapter you will
1.   Understand basic terms associated with floppy drives.
2.   Understand the different parts of the floppy drive system.
3.   Be able to recognize the different floppy disk capacities.
4.   Be able to clean floppy drive read/write heads.
5.   Be able to install and configure a floppy drive system.
6.   Be able to perform basic floppy drive troubleshooting techniques.

KEY TERMS

1.2MB disk	hub ring
1.44MB disk	jumper
2.88MB disk	LS-120 drive
360KB disk	read/write heads
720KB disk	sector
a:drive	straight-through cable
cluster	terminator
disk	track
drive select setting	twisted cable
floptical drive	write-protect notch
formatted (disk)	write-protect window

FLOPPY DRIVE OVERVIEW

The floppy drive sub-system consists of three main parts: (1) the electronic circuits or the controller, (2) the 34-pin ribbon cable, and (3) the floppy drive. The electronic circuits give the floppy drive instructions: "Floppy drive go to this location and read some data! Floppy drive go to this other location and write some data!" The electronic circuits can be on an adapter or built into the motherboard. For today's computers, the electronic circuits are normally built into the motherboard. A technician needs to know that the control circuits can go bad. The floppy cable connects the floppy drive to the electronic circuits. The floppy drive is the device that allows saving data to disk media. Troubleshooting and installing floppy drives involves these three main areas and the media which are the disks inserted in the floppy drive. Floppy drives are classified in two ways: by the physical size of disk used (3.5" or 5.25") and the storage capacity of disk used (360KB, 1.2MB, 720KB, 1.44MB, and 2.88MB).

FLOPPY MEDIA

The media inserted in a floppy drive is a **disk** or **floppy disk**. (The words are used interchangeably.) Though 5.25" floppy disks are not prevalent today, just in case a technician runs into one, they have two capacities: 360KB and 1.2MB. The disks have a different coating of material on their surface which is significant in determining the amount of data a disk can hold. Manufacturers label 360KB disks in various ways to identify them. The **360KB disks** are commonly known as double-sided, double-density and are labeled 2S2D, DS2D, or DSDD to indicate this. Some disks have no identifying labels and a technician should be able to tell the disk capacity by just looking at it. A 360KB disk normally has a reinforced center — a darker, thicker material, sometimes a different color. This is frequently called the **hub ring**. Floppy Figure #1 shows the two 5.25" disk capacities and the hub ring.

1.2MB disks *do not* have a hub ring. The common name for the 1.2MB disk is double-sided, high density or simply a high density disk. However, a 1.2MB floppy is labeled differently than a 360KB floppy disk. The labels you commonly see on a 1.2MB disk are DSHD, 2SHD, or HD located on the outside jacket of the disk.

5.25" disks are protected against accidental erasure by a **write-protect notch** found on the right side of the disk. Look at Floppy Figure #1 for an illustration of the write-protect notch. Cover this notch to prevent data from being written to the disk. Using the proper disk in the floppy drive is very important. A 360KB floppy disk works best when used in a 360KB floppy drive. *A 1.2MB disk only works in a 1.2MB floppy drive.*

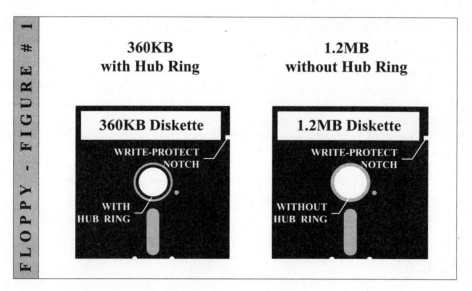

3.5" floppy disks have two major capacities: 720KB and 1.44MB. For awhile, IBM sold computers that used 2.88MB disks. **720KB disks** are double-sided, double density and are labeled DSDD, DD, 2S2D similar to 360KB disks. You can identify a 720KB disk by visual inspection. Look at the top of the disk and there is one small window in the lower left corner called the **write-protect window**. The write-protect window normally has a sliding tab that closes or opens the window. If you close the window, data can be written to the disk. If the window is open, the disk is write-protected and data cannot be written on the disk. This is true for all 3.5" disks. 720KB disks work best in 720KB drives. Floppy Figure #2 shows a 720KB disk with its write-protect window.

1.44MB disks are high density disks and are labeled by manufacturers as HD or 2HD. They are easily identified by two windows on the disk almost directly across from each other. Floppy Figure #3 shows the two-windowed high density disk.

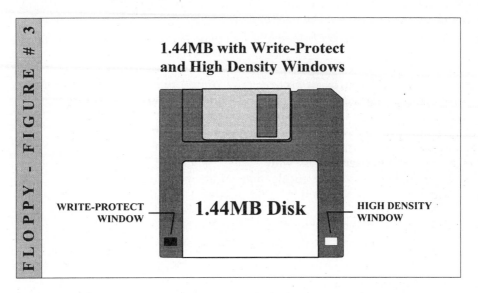

2.88MB disks are few and far between. They are known as extra-high density disks and labeled EHD or ED. These disks *only* work in 2.88MB floppy drives. 2.88MB disks are also identified by two windows with the right window across and higher up on the disk than the left window. Floppy Table #1 is a summary table to help you understand the different types of disks and floppy drives.

The extra window on the right side is used by some floppy drives to detect the disk is high density. 1.44MB disks work best in 1.44MB drives and *cannot be read by 720KB drives*.

Physical Size	Capacity	Markings	Identification Clues	Drives Used In
5.25"	360KB	DSDD, DD, 2S2D	Reinforced hub ring	360KB, 1.2MB
5.25"	1.2MB	2SHD, HD, DSHD	No hub ring	1.2MB
3.5"	720KB	DSDD, DD, 2S2D	1 left window	720KB, 1.44MB, 2.88MB
3.5"	1.44MB	2HD, HD, DSHD	2 windows across from one another	1.44MB, 2.88MB
3.5"	2.88MB	EHD, ED	2 windows; the right one is higher than the left	2.88MB

FLOPPY - TABLE # 1 — Types of Disks

FLOPPY DRIVE CONSTRUCTION

Floppy drives have two **read/write heads** responsible for placing the data, the 1s and 0s, onto the disk. The disk inserts between the two heads of the floppy drive. One read/write head mounts on the top, the other on the bottom. The disk turns inside the disk jacket and the floppy drive heads physically touch and scan the disk to read and write data.

Over time, the read/write heads become dirty. When a technician sees read/write errors occur, the first step is to clean the read/write heads.

There are two types of read/write head cleaning kits: a wet one and a dry one. The wet floppy drive cleaning kits are best for cleaning read/write heads. The cleaning kits contain a bottle of cleaning solution and a cleaning disk. Place a couple drops of the solution on the cleaning disk immediately before placing it in the drive. Always refer to the directions included with the kit. The alternative is a dry read/write cleaning kit that uses a chemically treated cloth inside the disk. The disk is placed inside the drive and used without adding any solution. Either cleaning method is better than replacing a floppy drive. An exercise at the end of the chapter explains how to use a read/write head cleaning kit.

FLOPPY DISK GEOMETRY

Before using a disk, it must be **formatted** which prepares it to accept data. Many 3.5" disks are formatted by the manufacturer. If not, the disk *must* be formatted before it can be used in a computer. To format a disk and make it bootable in a DOS/Windows-based computer, go to the command prompt and type **FORMAT A:** */S*. A prompt appears on the screen to insert a disk. Insert the disk and press **ENTER**. To format a disk and make it bootable in a Windows 95-based computer, double-click on the **My Computer** desktop icon. *Right-click* on the 3½" **(A:) icon**. Select **Format** from the drop-down menu. Click to enable the **Copy system files** option. Click the **Start** button to begin the format process.

A handy tool for any technician is a bootable system disk. There are many versions of DOS out there and a bootable disk may be your only hope in repairing certain problems.

When a disk is formatted by the manufacturer, the user, or the technician, concentric circles called **tracks** are drawn on the disk. The 360KB disk has 40 tracks. The 1.2MB, 720KB, 1.44MB, and 2.88MB disks all have 80 tracks. Floppy Figure #4 shows a disk with tracks.

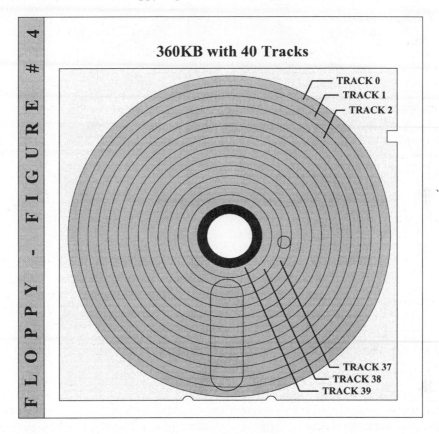

Floppy Figure #4 illustrates how the tracks are numbered. The track numbering starts at the outermost ring beginning with the number 0. The eighty tracks on a 1.44MB high density disk number from 0 to 79.

The tracks are further sub-divided into pie-shaped wedges. The section defined between a track and a intersecting line is a **sector** which holds 512 bytes of information. Each sector is identified by a track number and a sector number. Floppy Figure #5 shows various numbered sectors on a disk.

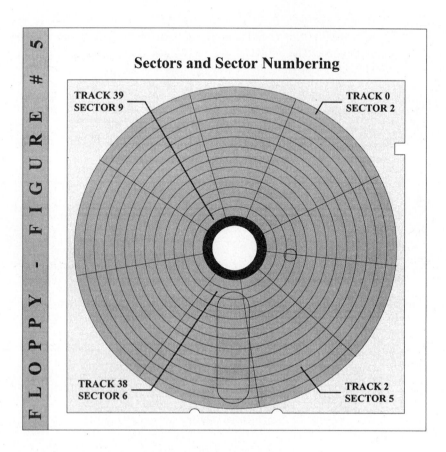

FLOPPY - FIGURE # 5

Sectors and Sector Numbering

TRACK 39
SECTOR 9

TRACK 0
SECTOR 2

TRACK 38
SECTOR 6

TRACK 2
SECTOR 5

When you save a file in DOS, the data stores in two sectors on the floppy disk. If the DOS file is larger than two sectors, two additional sectors are allocated for the file. The *minimum* amount of space one file occupies is defined as a **cluster**. On a floppy disk, a cluster is 1,024 bytes or two sectors. As a file grows in size, more clusters are used.

FLOPPY MEDIA PROBLEMS

The 360KB disk has only 40 tracks with nine sectors per track divided across the surface of the disk. The 360KB tracks are the widest of any disk mentioned in this chapter. The 360KB floppy drive heads rest in the middle of the tracks to read and write the 1s and 0s. On the other hand, the 1.2MB floppy drives have much smaller read/write heads. The 1.2MB disk has 80 tracks and 15 sectors per track allowing it to store more data. The 1.2MB disk also has a coating of a different magnetic material. The smaller 1.2MB read/write heads can read the big 1s and 0s the 360KB disk has written to it. However, when you write information to a high density disk with a 1.2MB drive, it has two tracks of data for every one track on a 360KB disk.

That is why you should *never* try to read information written by a 1.2MB drive in a 360KB floppy drive. If you write information on a 360KB disk with a 360KB drive, the 1.2MB drive is able to read the information. But, if you write to that same disk using a 1.2MB drive, the information may or may not be read by the 360KB drive.

Floppy Table #2 summarizes this information.

What Disks Work in What Drives

FLOPPY - TABLE # 2	360KB Floppy Drive		1.2MB Floppy Drive	
	Read	**Write**	**Read**	**Write**
360KB Disk	Yes	Yes	Yes	Yes, but might not be read by a 360KB drive
1.2MB Disk	No	No	Yes	Yes

3.5" drives are a different animal. All the read/write heads are the same size. The disks have a different coating and each capacity type has a different number of sectors per track: 720KB disks have 9 sectors per track, 1.44MB disks have 18 sectors per track, and 2.88MB disks have 36 sectors per track. Each time you format a disk, the operating system tries to format it to the highest capacity, unless (1) you tell DOS otherwise through the FORMAT command switches or through the Windows 95 format window, or (2) you have a floppy drive with a sensor that detects what type of disk is inserted. This is why 3.5" disks have the windows on the right side of the higher capacity disks. Some floppy drive manufacturers make floppy drives without the sensor. The disk does not get the 1s and 0s written properly causing data errors. The easiest way to determine the floppy drive capacity is to go into the computer's SETUP program and look at the configuration.

The two biggest causes of read/write errors on floppy drives are dirty read/write heads or the wrong type of disk used in a floppy drive.

FLOPPY DEVELOPMENTS

IBM tried to create a new floppy standard with their 2.88MB floppy drive, but the rest of the computer industry did not follow. Three other markets have come close to influencing the floppy drive market: (1) the CD-ROM market, (2) the floptical or laser servo technology market, and (3) the zip disk market. CD-ROM drives have made floppy drives almost obsolete because software applications are now so large, the applications require 20 or more floppy disks. CDs are preferable for the installation and running of applications, but are not suitable for storing small amounts of data. The price for CD drives that can write and read data has dropped drastically, but not down to the price range of the floppy drive. Computer buyers still include a floppy drive with their systems.

Floptical drives are floppy drives that use optical technology to move the read/write heads over the disk surface. They were the topic of many trade articles throughout the last seven years, but floptical drives never made a big impact until now. Some people in the computer industry predict the demise of the floppy drive by the year 2000. The product is called the **a:drive**. It holds 120MB of data, can read from and write to traditional 720KB and 1.44MB disks, fits in existing drive bays, and accesses data up to five times faster than the traditional drive. The a:drive (also called a **LS-120 drive** for laser servo 120MB) uses a patented laser servo technology developed by O.R. Technology, Compaq Computer Corp., Imation, and Matsushita-Kotobuki Electronics Industries Ltd. (MKE). The a:drive connects to an IDE cable on the system. (See the hard drive chapter for configuring and cabling IDE (ATAPI) devices.) The a:drive sells for around $150 and the 120MB disks sell for about $20. Windows 95 Service Release 2 and Windows NT have built-in support for the a:drive. If ever a device has the possibility of tapping into a market stagnant for years, the a:drive is one to keep an eye on.

The last product that has challenged the floppy drive market is Iomega's Zip drive. The Zip drive is not backward compatible with a floppy drive. A zip disk holds 100MB of data and the external model runs off the parallel port. An internal SCSI model is also available. (See the hard drive chapter for more information on SCSI devices.)

FLOPPY DRIVE CONFIGURATION

Before installing a floppy drive you must configure the drive. Configuring a floppy drive requires two steps: (1) setting the correct drive select jumper, and (2) terminating the floppy drive system. The **drive select setting** is a number assigned to a drive that enables the controlling circuits to distinguish between two floppy drives. Normally, a technician sets the drive select number by placing a plastic **jumper** over two pins. By doing this, the jumper assigns a drive select number to the floppy drive. Having the documentation for the drive is best at this point (but not very common). Drive select jumpers are normally found at the bottom rear or at the very back of the floppy drive. Floppy drives can have up to four drive select numbers to choose. They are normally labeled Drive Select numbers 0, 1, 2, or 3 or Drive Select numbers 1, 2, 3, or 4. The floppy drive manufacturer determines how to label the drive select numbers. Floppy Figure #6 shows two different floppy drives and the different drive select number labels.

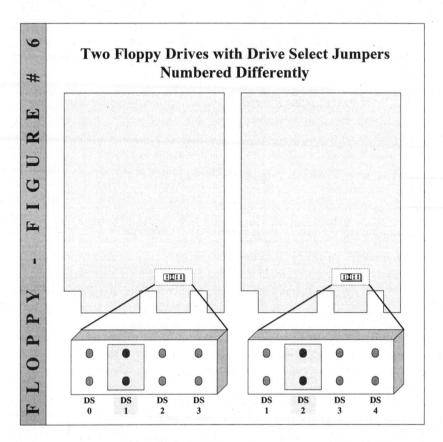

FLOPPY - FIGURE # 6

**Two Floppy Drives with Drive Select Jumpers
Numbered Differently**

| DS 0 | DS 1 | DS 2 | DS 3 | | DS 1 | DS 2 | DS 3 | DS 4 |

Each floppy drive that connects to one floppy cable must have a separate drive select number. Notice how both drives shown in Floppy Figure #6 have the jumpers over the second drive select. It does not matter how the drive select numbers are labeled. The second drive select may be numbered 1 or 2, but it is still the second drive select position. Floppy drives come from most manufacturers pre-set to the second drive select. The original cabling for floppy drives had a lot to do with why the drive select jumper is set to the second position. Floppy Figure #7 shows a common floppy drive cable.

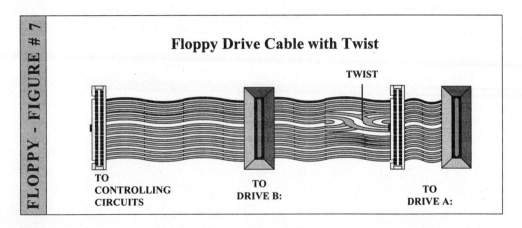

FLOPPY - FIGURE #7

Floppy Drive Cable with Twist

TWIST

TO
CONTROLLING
CIRCUITS

TO
DRIVE B:

TO
DRIVE A:

Notice in Floppy Figure #7 one end of the floppy cable is labeled "to controlling circuits." This end plugs into either an adapter or the motherboard. There are three connectors that are used to connect floppy drives: one set of connectors is labeled "to drive A:" and a separate connector is labeled "to drive B:". These are the connectors you connect to the back of the floppy drive. The connectors labeled "to drive A:" are two different connector types and only one of them connects to the A: drive. Floppy drives come with either a card-edge connector or a pin connector. In Floppy Figure #7, the last connector is a card-edge connector. The number and type of connectors available on a floppy drive cable varies between manufacturers. Also notice there is a twist in the cable just before the connector labeled "to drive A:." This twist is very important in understanding drive selects.

The **twisted cable** physically moves the drive select jumper position from the second position to the first position by crossing a few wires. Therefore, you can connect two floppy drives to this cable. The drive connected to the last connector, (the one labeled "to drive A:") is seen by the computer as drive select first position. The drive connected to the drive labeled to drive B: is seen as drive select second position. The controller can now distinguish between the drives even though they are both set to the second position drive select.

The operating system assigns drive letters to each drive detected. The drive at the end of the cable is the A: drive and is set to the second drive select number, but is seen as drive select first position due to the twist in the cable. Drive A: always connects to the last connector on the cable. The drive connected to the middle connector, also set to the second drive select number, is assigned B: by the operating system. Floppy Figure #8 shows two sample drives and their drive select jumpers set to the second drive select number.

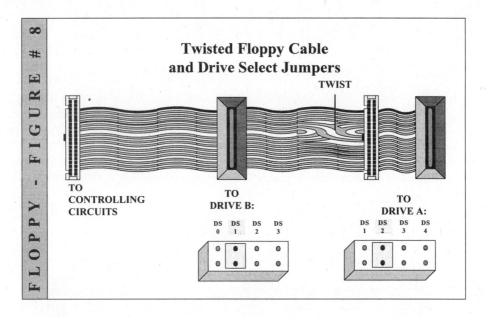

Not all manufacturers use floppy cables with a twist before the last connector. Cables without the twist are **straight-through cables**. If a system has a straight-through cable, set the A: drive to the first drive select number and the B: drive to the second drive select number and the controller can tell the difference between the drives. Floppy Figure #9 shows the drive select jumpers using a cable without a twist.

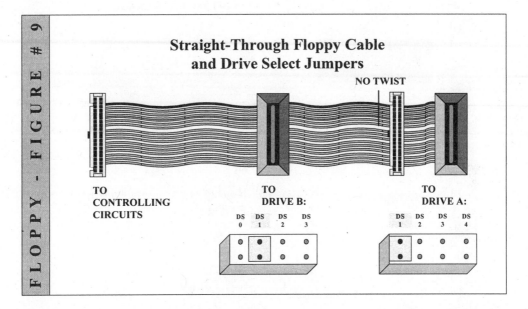

A good way to tell if you configured the drive select jumpers improperly is if both drive lights turn on at the same time or if neither drive light turns on.

TERMINATION

The second floppy configuration issue is termination. Any system with data traveling down a cable to multiple devices such as floppy drives, must have two stopping places for the data; one at each end of the floppy drive system. This will not allow the signals to bounce back up the cable wires. The signals must terminate at both ends of the system. The beginning point for a floppy drive system is the controlling card. The adapter or controlling circuits on the mother board are terminated by the manufacturer. Sometimes, you must designate the end of the floppy drive system by installing a **terminator**, sometimes called a terminating resistor, onto the floppy drive at the end of the cable. Terminators are available in several forms and colors and are on devices other than floppy drives. Terminators can be SIPs, DIPs, or a jumper set over two pins. Reference Floppy Figure #10 for the different types of terminators.

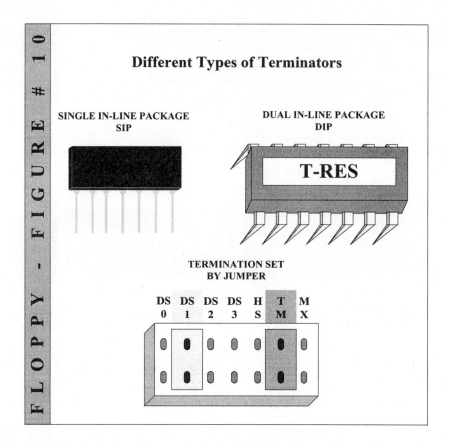

FLOPPY - FIGURE # 10

Different Types of Terminators

SINGLE IN-LINE PACKAGE
SIP

DUAL IN-LINE PACKAGE
DIP

T-RES

TERMINATION SET
BY JUMPER

| DS 0 | DS 1 | DS 2 | DS 3 | H S | T M | M X |

The terminator installs on the last drive at the end of the cable, the A: drive. Remove the terminator on the B: drive.

Another function of the terminator is to provide the correct amount of electrical resistance for the system. With terminators installed on both drives in a two drive system, too much current can flow through the floppy system. You might not detect an incorrectly terminated system by an error code or an immediate failure. Over time, this can possibly cause both drives and the controlling circuits to fail.

RELATED FLOPPY DRIVE ISSUES

Some floppy drives do not have drive select jumpers. Assume, (and you know how that goes), that the drive select jumper is set to the second position. Also, some drives do not have terminators, they are self-terminating. The drives terminate themselves if necessary and un-terminate if they are installed as the B: drive.

In summary, no matter what type of cable is used, if installing only one floppy drive, connect it to the last connector on the cable and terminate. If you are installing two drives, connect the A: drive to the connector at the end of the cable and terminate. Connect the B: drive to the middle connector on the cable and *remove* the terminator. Floppy Figure #11 shows two different floppy drive scenarios.

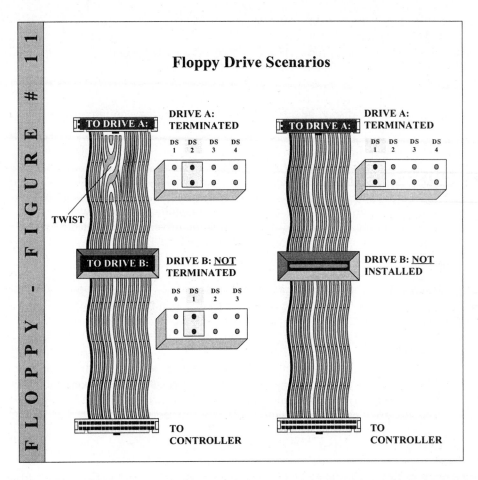

Floppy Drive Scenarios

FLOPPY - FIGURE # 11

Floppy Table #3 summarizes how to configure a floppy drive based on what cable is in the system.

Floppy Drive Configuration Summary

FLOPPY - TABLE # 3

| | Drive Select Jumper | | | |
	Cable With a Twist	Cable Without a Twist	Terminator	Cable Connector
A: Drive	2nd position	1st position	Yes	Farthest from controller
B: Drive	2nd position	2nd position	No	Middle connector

The best way to tackle any hardware device installation and configuration is to (1) have the proper documentation, (2) install or remove any jumpers and switches before the device is installed, and (3) think through the installation and configuration thoroughly.

The exercises at the end of the chapter help you understand floppy drive configurations.

FLOPPY DRIVE INSTALLATION

Installation of floppy drives is simple after doing some preliminary homework:

1. Be sure that the computer's BIOS supports the drive being installed by referring to the documentation or going into the computer's SETUP program and changing the parameters for the floppy drive to see the possible types.
2. Be sure there is a drive bay available.
3. Be sure there is a power connection available.
4. Be sure there is a floppy cable connector available, if installing a second floppy drive.
5. Be sure the floppy cable has the proper connector for the drive being installed (card-edged or pin).
6. Purchase any necessary mounting hardware for installing the drive into the case. The floppy drive attaches to the computer chassis. Normally, side brackets and screws attach to the floppy so the drive slides into the drive bay. Floppy drive brackets and screws normally are included a computer case, but are also available cheap at local computer stores.

After resolving these issues, installation is nothing more than mounting the floppy drive to the computer case and connecting the cable between the drive and motherboard or adapter. Make sure you configure the floppy's drive select setting and termination properly before you mount the drive into the case.

When connecting any cable to an adapter or a device, match pin 1 of the cable to pin 1 of the adapter or device! Devices, adapters, controlling circuits, etc., can be damaged if a cable plugs into the connector the wrong way. Some cables are keyed so they insert only one way into the connector. Most cables that connect to the floppy drive are keyed, but the other end of the cable that connects to the controlling circuits is frequently not keyed.

Pin 1 of a cable is easy to identify. There is a colored stripe down one side of the cable. This stripe connects to pin 1. If by chance, the stripe has faded or is hard to detect, look on the cable's connector end. There is normally an arrow that points to pin 1.

Pin 1 on an adapter or motherboard is not as easy to find. Some manufacturers put a small 1 or 2 by the end where the cable's pin 1 inserts. Other manufacturers put larger numbers at the opposite end. For example, if you saw the number 33 or the number 34 on the motherboard where the floppy cable inserts, pin 1 and pin 2 are on the *opposite* end of the connector.

If there are no pin number markings, look at other connections on the adapter. If you find a number 1 or 2 on a different connector, the floppy connector's pin 1 or 2 orients in the same direction. If you find a higher number (such as 39, 40, 33, 34), then pin 1 is on the opposite end. The floppy cable's pin 1 will be in the same direction as the other connector's pin 1. Also, if there are other cables plugged into the adapter, look for their colored stripe to see which way they orient; the floppy cable will orient in the same direction. If all else fails, remove the adapter from the computer and look on the back of the adapter. Most manufacturers use a square solder joint on the back of the board for the pin 1 connection and round solder joints for the other connections. If you can find one square pin 1 solder joint, then all other pin 1s orient in the same direction.

TROUBLESHOOTING FLOPPY DRIVES

Problems with the floppy drive can be narrowed down to four areas:
1. Disk
2. The floppy drive
3. The cable that connects the drive to the controlling circuits
4. The floppy controlling circuits

The most common problem for read or write errors is the disk. Disk problems can include the user using the wrong capacity disk, a bad area of a disk, and a damaged disk. Disks are affected by magnetic fields. Having a disk near a monitor, speaker, or even a kitchen magnet can damage the data contained on it. The easiest way to determine if the problem is the disk is to try a different disk in the drive or test the original disk in another floppy drive.

After eliminating the disk as the problem, the next most likely culprit is the floppy drive. Always an easy problem to fix, is if the floppy drive has dirty read/write heads. These cause errors frequently because the heads physically touch the disk surface. Drive read/write head cleaning kits are available at computer and retail stores. The exercise at the end of the chapter explains how to clean the heads.

Mechanical devices fail more frequently than electronic parts. If the read/write heads are clean and the drive still shows errors, the floppy drive is the next suspect. Any time a device has moving parts such as read/write heads or motors, these devices are more likely to fail than an electronic part, such as a controller.

The least common problem with floppy drives is the cable. Cables do not normally go bad unless they have been cut, which is not very likely. Cables are sometimes torn when replacing and removing computer cases, so be very careful during disassembly and reassembly.

POST is always a good indicator there is a problem with the floppy drive system. Floppy drive problems give a 6xx series error code for many systems. Refer to the logical troubleshooting chapter for a list of different POST error codes. Also, there are diagnostic programs that test a floppy drive, but after a technician works on computers for awhile, very few continue to use these programs. A good method for troubleshooting an intermittent floppy system problem is to execute a simple batch file that copies information from the hard drive to the floppy drive, deletes the data, and then starts over again.

Use a new floppy disk when using this method. An example of such a batch file follows:

```
Echo Floptest.bat
A:
PATH=C:\DOS
MD\TEST
CD\TEST
COPY C:\DOS\F*.*
COPY C:\DOS\A*.*
DEL F*.*
DEL A*.*
FLOPTEST
```

After running the batch file or testing the drive with diagnostics, replace the suspect component. If the batch file runs fine for awhile then starts showing floppy errors, the problem may be the floppy drive's electronics or the controlling circuits. Replacing a floppy drive is usually cheaper in today's computers because the floppy controller is built into the motherboard or built into an adapter that controls other devices as well.

Name _____

Floppy Review Questions

1. List the three parts of a floppy drive system.

2. List the two types of 5.25" floppy drives.

3. List two types of 3.5" floppy drives.

4. Why is it not a good idea to write information on a 1.2MB disk and then try to read the information on a 360KB floppy drive?

5. Why is it important to know about drive select jumpers?

6. What drive letter is assigned the first floppy drive detected in a system?

7. List one purpose of a terminator.

8. What determines whether or not you terminate a floppy drive?

9. What harm could you do if you installed both terminators on a multi-drive system?

10. If a floppy cable has two connectors and only one drive is to be connected, to which connector do you attach the drive?

11. How do you know the proper orientation to connect the cable onto the floppy controller?

12. List three considerations when adding or installing a floppy drive.

13. What is the most common part to fail in a floppy drive system?

14. What should a technician do when a computer system shows the message, "Error Reading Drive A:"?

15. What is the common POST error code series for the floppy drive system?

Name _____

Floppy Fill-in-the-Blank

1.   The circuitry that gives the floppy drive instructions can be on the _____ or on a separate adapter.

2.   A _____ is a device that allows data saving to disk media.

3.   The markings on the label of a 360KB disk can be _____, _____, or _____.

4.   The markings on the label of an 1.2MB disk can be _____, _____, or _____.

5.   The _____ is a part of a 5.25" disk that has been cut away to protect the disk from accidental erasure.

6.   A _____ floppy drive is the smallest capacity of 3.5" floppy drives.

7.   The markings on the label of a 720KB disk can be _____, _____, or _____.

8.   The markings on the label of a 1.44MB disk can be _____, _____, or _____.

9.   The _____ is a window on the left side of a 3.5" disk that, when closed, allows data to be written to the disk.

10.   One purpose of the _____ is to write 1s and 0s to the disk surface.

11.   A disk must be _____ before it is used for the first time.

12.   Concentric circles on the surface of the disk are commonly called _____.

13.   512 bytes of information are stored in a _____.

14.   The smallest amount of space DOS allocates for one file is called a _____.

15.   The _____ floppy drive has the largest read/write heads.

16.   The _____ floppy drive has read/write heads half the size of the 360KB floppy drive.

17.   A _____ floppy disk drive accepts only 5.25" double-sided, double-density disks.

18.   A _____ floppy drive can accept 3.5" high-density or double-density disks.

19.   The _____ allows the floppy controller to distinguish between two installed floppy drives.

20.   A _____ cable is installed if both floppy drives connected to the cable have their drive select jumpers set to the second position.

21.   A _____ cable is installed if the A: floppy drive has its drive select jumper set to the first position and the B: floppy drive has its drive select jumper set to the second position.

22.   The _____ is used to prevent signals from bouncing back up the cable and to provide the correct resistive load for the floppy drive system.

Name _____

PAPER CONFIGURATION OF FLOPPY DRIVES EXERCISE

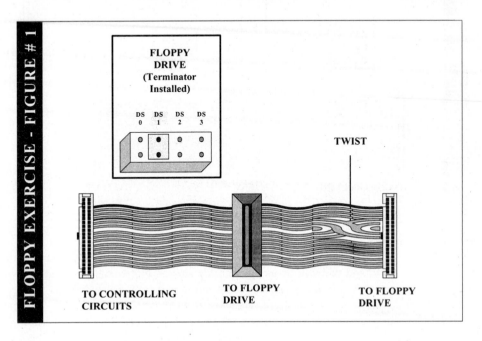

Reference Floppy Exercise Figure #1 for Questions 1-3:

Question 1:   Assume you are installing one floppy drive into a system and it is the only floppy drive in the system. The drive select jumper is set to the second position (DS1) as shown in Floppy Exercise Figure #1. Also, notice the cable has a twist at one end. To install the drive, do you move the drive select jumper to a new position or leave it set to the second position? If the drive select jumper must be moved, to which drive select number (DS0, DS1, DS2, or DS3) would you move the jumper?

Question 2:   If using the cable shown in Floppy Exercise Figure #1, to which connector on the cable will you connect the floppy drive you are installing?

Question 3:   The floppy drive has a terminator installed by the manufacturer. Will you leave it installed or remove it?

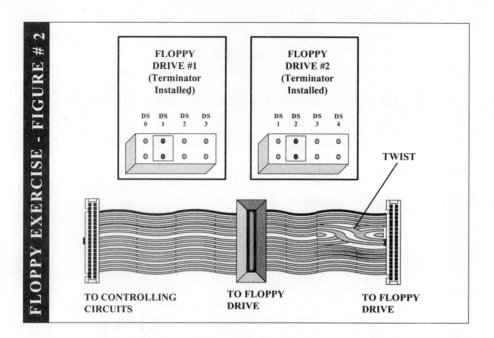

FLOPPY EXERCISE - FIGURE # 2

FLOPPY DRIVE #1 (Terminator Installed)

DS 0   DS 1   DS 2   DS 3

FLOPPY DRIVE #2 (Terminator Installed)

DS 1   DS 2   DS 3   DS 4

TWIST

TO CONTROLLING CIRCUITS

TO FLOPPY DRIVE

TO FLOPPY DRIVE

Reference Floppy Exercise Figure #2 for Questions 4-8:

Question 4:   Assume you are going to install the floppy drives shown in Floppy Exercise Figure #2 into the same system and you will be using the cable shown. Notice the cable has a twist at one end. Set up Floppy Drive #1 as the A: drive. Both drives have the drive select jumper already set to the second position. Which drive select (DS0, DS1, DS2, or DS3) will you choose for Drive #1?

Question 5:   Set up Floppy Drive #2 as the B: drive. Which drive select (DS1, DS2, DS3, or DS4) will you choose for the B: drive?

Question 6:   To which connector on the cable will you connect the A: drive?

Question 7:   To which connector on the cable will you connect the B: drive?

Question 8:   Floppy Drives #1 and #2 come with a terminator installed. What are you going to do about the terminators?
   A.   Leave both terminators installed
   B.   Remove both terminators
   C.   Install the terminator on the B: drive and remove the terminator on the A: drive
   D.   Install the terminator on the A: drive and remove the terminator on the B: drive

Name _____

CLEANING FLOPPY DRIVE HEADS EXERCISE

Objective: To clean a floppy drive's read/write heads to prevent errors

Parts: Wet floppy drive cleaning kit for 5.25" or 3.5" drive

Step   1:   Power on the computer.

Step   2:   Verify the DOS prompt is on the screen.

Step   3:   Follow the directions on the floppy cleaning kit for applying the proper number of cleaning fluid drops on the special cleaning disk.

Step   4:   Insert the moistened disk into the floppy drive.

Step   5:   Type the appropriate drive letter (A or B) followed by a colon. For example, A: and press **ENTER**.

Step   6:   Type **DIR** and press **ENTER**. A *normal* error message appears such as "Error reading Drive A: Abort (A), Retry (R), or Ignore (I)?

Step   7:   Press **R** for Retry. Do this three or four times.

Step   8:   Press **A** for Abort.

Step   9:   Remove the special cleaning disk.

Question 1:   What is an indication that the read/write heads need cleaning?

_____ Instructor's Initials

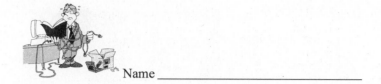

Name _____

SINGLE FLOPPY DRIVE INSTALLATION EXERCISE

Objective: Correctly install a single floppy drive in a computer

Parts: Floppy drive
          Floppy cable
          Anti-static materials
          Data disk

Observe proper grounding procedures when installing floppy drives.

Step 1:   Remove the cover from the computer. Use proper anti-static procedures.
Step 2:   Attach the 34-pin cable to the adapter or motherboard. Check to be sure the cable's pin 1 attaches to the adapter or motherboard connector's pin 1.

Question 1:   How can you determine which is pin 1 on the adapter or motherboard connector?

Step 3:   Set the drive select jumper on the floppy drive. Refer to the documentation that came with the floppy drive, if possible. If the drive's 34-pin cable has a twist in the cable immediately before the last connector on the cable, then set the drive select jumper to the second drive select position. If the drive's 34-pin cable DOES NOT have a twist in the cable immediately before the last connector on the cable, then set the drive select jumper to the first drive select position.

Question 2:   How are the drive select jumpers numbered on the drive being installed?

Question 3:   What drive select did you choose for the floppy drive?

Step 4:   If necessary, terminate the floppy drive. Refer to the documentation included with the floppy drive. Most floppy drives are terminated by the manufacturer.

Question 4: Why do you have to place a terminator on the floppy drive?

Step 5: Install any mounting hardware required on the sides of the floppy drive.

Step 6: Install the floppy drive into the computer and secure with screws.

Step 7: Connect the power cable to the drive.

Step 8: Connect the floppy cable that connects to the floppy drive. Check and be sure the cable's pin 1 connects to the floppy drive connector's pin 1. Most floppy cables are keyed to insert only one way onto the drive. **If you have a cable with two connectors on the end and the floppy is to be the A: drive, attach the cable connector that is the FARTHEST from the adapter to the floppy drive.**

Question 5: How do you determine where pin 1 is on the cable?

Step 9: If this is a PC or XT-type computer, go to Step 16.

Step 10: Power up the system. Go into the computer's SETUP program to configure the CMOS. (Frequently the keystrokes required to enter SETUP display on the screen when powering on the computer. If this is not the case, refer to the computer's documentation.) Choose the floppy drive type that matches the floppy drive you are installing (360KB, 720KB, 1.2MB, or 1.44MB). Contact your instructor if you have any questions. Entering the wrong parameters into CMOS will prohibit your drive from working properly or to it's fullest capacity and possibly cause POST errors.

Question 6: How did you get into CMOS SETUP?

Step 11: Save the SETUP information by following the directions on the screen inside the SETUP program.

Step 12: Perform a warm boot by pressing **CTRL+ALT+DEL**.

Question 7: Did the computer boot without a POST error? If not, refer to the chapter section on troubleshooting. Check all previously performed steps. Do not proceed until you solve all POST errors.

Step 13: Insert a data disk into the floppy drive you just installed.

Step 14: Verify you are at the DOS prompt. Type the following:

DIR A:

Question 8:   Did the drive perform the read operation successfully? If not, check all previously performed steps as well as the chapter section on troubleshooting.

Step 15:   Reinstall the computer cover.

_____ Instructor's Initials for 286 or higher microcomputer

The following steps are for a PC or a XT model computer:

Step 16:   Set the switches on the motherboard for the number of floppy drives installed. For one floppy drive, SW1 position 1 should be OFF, position 7 and 8 should be ON. Use an ink pen or small screwdriver to set the switches.

Question 9:   Why should you *not* use a pencil when setting switches on the motherboard?

Step 17:   Power on the computer.

Question 10:   Did the computer boot without a POST error? If not, refer to the section on troubleshooting. Check all previously performed steps. Do not proceed until all POST errors are solved.

Step 18:   Insert a data disk into the floppy drive you just installed.
Step 19:   Verify you are at the DOS prompt. Type
            DIR A:

Question 11:   Did the drive perform the read operation successfully?

Step 20:   Reinstall the computer cover.

_____ Instructor's Initials for PC or XT microcomputer

Chapter 9:
Hard Drives

OBJECTIVES

After completing this chapter you will
1.   Understand hard drive terminology.
2.   Understand the different hard drive types.
3.   Be able to set up and configure the different types of hard drives.
4.   Be able to troubleshoot hard drive problems.
5.   Understand and be able to perform common hard drive preventive maintenance routines.

KEY TERMS

32-bit disk access	file system	passive termination
active termination	fragmentation	primary partition
actuator arm	head crash	read/write head
ATA standard	high level format	read-ahead caching
ATAPI	host adapter	SCAM
cable select	IDE	SCANDISK
CHS addressing	INT13 interface	SCSI
cluster	interface	SCSI bus
cylinder	interleaving	SCSI chain
daisy chaining	layered block device driver	SCSI ID
DBR	LBA	sector
defragmentation	logical drive	sector translation
disk cache	lost clusters	S.M.A.R.T.
drive type	low-level format	ST506
ECHS	magneto-resistive heads	track
EIDE	master/slave	translating BIOS
encoding	MBR	VCACHE
ESDI	partition table	write-behind caching
extended partition	partitioning	zone bit recording
FDISK		

HARD DRIVE OVERVIEW

Hard drives are currently the most popular device for storing data. They store more data than floppy drives and process data faster than tape drives. The topic of hard drives is complicated. Hard drives are frequently upgraded in a computer, so it is important for a technician to understand all the technical issues. These issues include knowing the parts of the hard drive sub-system, how DOS and the BIOS work with a hard drive, how to configure a hard drive, and how to troubleshoot it.

The hard drive sub-system consists of four parts: (1) the electronic circuits that carry instructions to the hard drive; (2) one or two cables; (3) the hard drive; and (4) an optional adapter that connects the hard drive sub-system to the motherboard. Some hard drives connect directly to the motherboard.

HARD DRIVE GEOMETRY

Hard drives have a hard metal surface called a **platter** which holds the binary data. A hard drive has multiple platters. Each platter normally has two read/write heads, one on top and one on the bottom. The **read/write heads** read and write the 1s and 0s to and from the hard drive surface. The read/write arms hold the read/write heads and operate as one unit on an **actuator arm**. The heads move over the hard drive surface as the platters rotate. The read/write heads float on a cushion of air, without touching the platter surface. If a read/write head touches the platter, a **head crash** occurs. This can damage the hard drive surface causing corrupt data or damage to the read/write head. Reference Hard Figure #1 for an illustration of a hard drive's arms, heads, and platters.

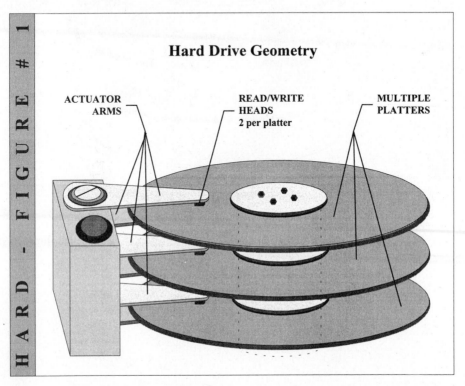

Each hard drive surface is metallic and has concentric circles called **tracks**. Tracks are numbered starting with the outermost track being track 0. One track on all surfaces of a hard drive is a **cylinder**. For example, cylinder 0 consists of all of the track 0s; all of the track 1s make cylinder 1, and so on. The number of tracks and cylinders are the same, but they are NOT the same thing. A track is a single circle on one platter. A cylinder is the same track on all platters. Hard Figure #2 shows the difference between tracks and cylinders.

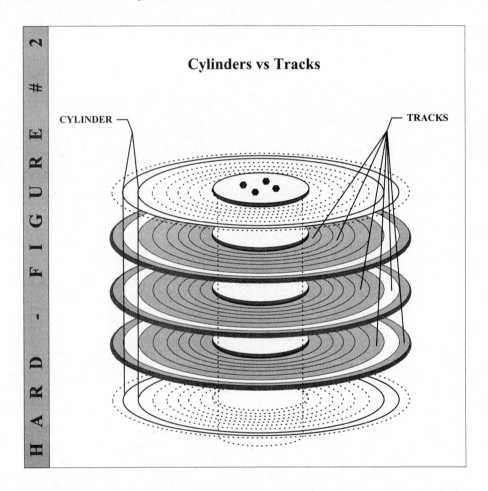

Notice in Hard Figure #2 how a concentric circle makes an individual track. A single track on all the surfaces makes an individual cylinder.

Each track is separated into **sectors** by dividing the circle into smaller pieces. 512 bytes of information store in each sector. As shown in Hard Figure #3, if 512 bytes of information can store on the smaller sectors near the center of the drive, there is wasted space on the larger, outer sectors of the older hard drives.

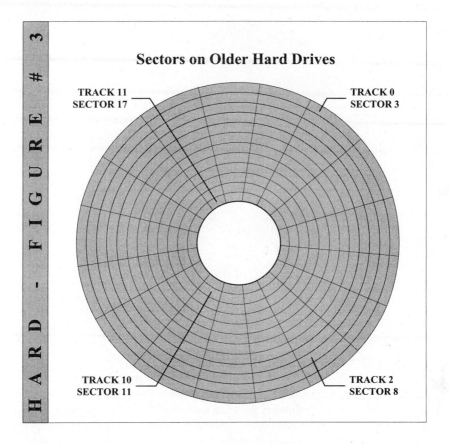

H A R D - F I G U R E   #   3

Sectors on Older Hard Drives

TRACK 11
SECTOR 17

TRACK 0
SECTOR 3

TRACK 10
SECTOR 11

TRACK 2
SECTOR 8

Keep in mind that Hard Figure #3 does not show as many tracks or sectors that an older hard drive actually has, but the concept is the same.

Today's hard drive manufacturers developed a way to use the wasted space on the outer tracks. **Zone bit recording** efficiently uses the hard drive surface by placing more sectors on the outer tracks than on the inner tracks. Instead of using pie-shaped wedges, the drives can have a different number of sectors on each track. The outer tracks of the hard drive contain more sectors than the inner tracks because each sector is the same physical size. Reference Hard Figure #4 for an illustration of today's hard drive sectors.

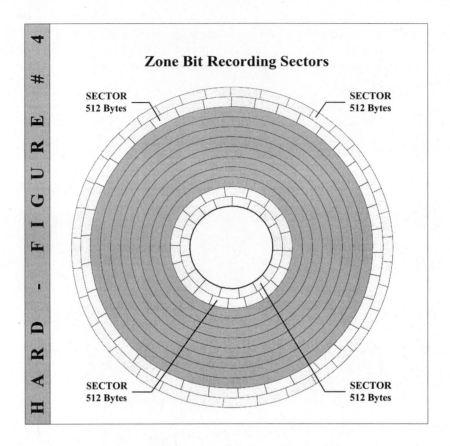

Zone Bit Recording Sectors

SECTOR
512 Bytes

SECTOR
512 Bytes

SECTOR
512 Bytes

SECTOR
512 Bytes

The basic operation of the hard drive is the read/write heads pick up data and transfer it to the controller which passes the data to the motherboard. Then, the controller asks for more data. As this occurs and the platter continues to spin, and the read/write heads are not positioned over the next sector. Therefore, the read/write heads must wait as the disk spins and the next sector is positioned under the read/write heads. A more efficient method for data transfer is to number the sectors differently.

Interleaving is a method of numbering sectors for the most efficient transfer of data between the hard drive and the controller. The numbering sequence for the sectors is the interleave factor. If a hard drive has a 1:1 (pronounced "one to one") interleave, the sectors on each track number consecutively beginning with the number 1. Older hard drives require a 2:1, 3:1, 5:1, or 6:1 interleave factor. The 1:1 interleave factor is not efficient for older drives because of their slow speeds. On older hard drives, interleaving provides the fastest means of transferring data between the hard drive and the controller without waiting for the disk to spin. Some books list interleave factors as 1:2, 1:3, 1:5, etc. The concept is the same though — the sectors do not number consecutively. Hard Figure #5 shows 3:1 interleaving.

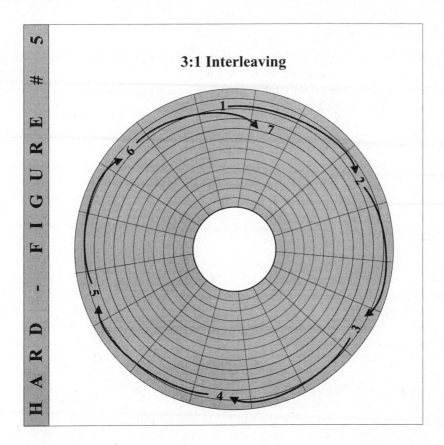

In Hard Figure #5, sector 1 is not adjacent to sector 2, it is two sectors away from sector 1. Numbering the sectors on every third sector determines the 3:1 interleave factor. Software programs such as Gibson Research's SpinRite allows the interleave factor to be changed, but it is normally set when the hard drive is first prepared for use. The procedure to set the interleave factor is covered in the Configuration and Setup portion of this chapter.

Today's hard drives normally use a 1:1 interleave. Setting the interleave factor is not an issue in today's hard drive configurations due to (1) faster hard drives, (2) caching hard drive controllers (hard drive controllers that contain memory on the adapter), and (3) faster system board buses.

HARD DRIVE INTERFACES

A hard drive system must have a set of rules to operate. These rules specify the number of heads on the drive, what commands the drive responds to, the cables used with the drive, the number of devices supported, the number of data bits transferred at one time, etc. These rules make up a standard called an **interface**. There are four hard drive interfaces:

1.   ST506
2.   ESDI
3.   IDE (ATA)
4.   SCSI

ST506 INTERFACE

The **ST506** interface is the oldest standard that evolved from the floppy drive interface. It requires two cables: one 34-pin cable for control signals, and one 20-pin cable for data. This interface is very noisy and outside interference can easily affect the hard drive signals causing a loss of data. ST506 hard drives transmit data serially (one bit at a time), at a mere 5Mbps (Megabits per second) or 7.5Mbps, depending on the encoding method.

Encoding is the way the 1s and 0s are placed on the drive. ST506 has two encoding schemes, MFM and RLL. MFM (Modified Frequency Modulation) is the oldest encoding scheme used with hard drives and limits the sectors per track to 17. RLL (Run Length Limited) is an enhanced version of encoding that requires fewer electronic pulses than MFM to write the same data; RLL allows more sectors per track because fewer pulses require less space.

Any ST506 hard drive using MFM to write the 1s and 0s onto the surface must have a MFM controller card. Any ST506 hard drive using RLL encoding must have a RLL controller. Today's more advanced hard drive interfaces, use encoding methods known as ARLL (Advanced RLL) or ERLL (Enhanced RLL).

The controlling electronics for the ST506 are placed on a separate adapter and connect to the hard drive(s) via two cable connections per drive. The electronic circuits instruct the drive to read or write information, what cylinder to go to, and what head to use. One problem with ST506 hard drives is the controlling circuitry can only tell the drive to move one cylinder at a time, another reason for the ST506 slowness. As with all interfaces, a ST506 hard drive requires a ST506 adapter.

One can see there are many limitations with the ST506 interface. Hard drive interfaces were bound to get better, faster, smarter, and more advanced. The first step in this growth path was the evolution of a hard drive interface known as ESDI (Enhanced Small Devices Interface).

ESDI (ENHANCED SMALL DEVICES INTERFACE)

The **ESDI (Enhanced Small Devices Interface)** hard drive uses the same 34-pin and 20-pin cables as the ST506. ESDI drives corrected two problems with ST506 by increasing the hard drive storage capacities and by supporting drives up to 256 heads, whereas ST506 drives had a maximum of 16 heads.

An ESDI drive holds geometry information such as number of heads, tracks, and sectors on the drive itself. This information is then sent to the controller. A ST506 drive requires extensive setup during configuration to ensure the controller knows the ST506 hard drive's geometry information.

ESDI hard drives have transfer speeds up to 24Mbps. ST506 and ESDI drives are found mostly in 8088, 8086, and 80286 computers. ESDI hard drives were never popular, and the only time you should purchase an ESDI or a ST506 hard drive is if there is already an adapter for the hard drive in the system. If the customer wants the same drive type, try to talk them out of it. Today's computer manufacturers use one of two other interfaces for hard drives: IDE (Integrated Drive Electronics) or SCSI (Small Computer System Interface).

IDE (INTEGRATED DRIVE ELECTRONICS)

The **IDE** (**Integrated Drive Electronics**) drive type has controlling circuits built directly on the drive that tell it what to do. (This is why the interface is known as integrated.) The IDE hard drive can use a separate adapter, sometimes known as a paddleboard, to connect the hard drive to the motherboard, or the IDE drive can cable directly to the motherboard. In some computers, IDE signals pass through an adapter that handles other devices as well, such as floppy drives, serial devices, or parallel devices. The adapter acts as a pass-through to allow the IDE signals to reach the motherboard.

The IDE hard drive connects to the motherboard or adapter through a single 40-pin cable. This cable allows two devices to be connected. The original standard was developed for hard drives but has since evolved to include other devices. IDE is the only interface that uses a 40-pin cable and makes IDE hard drives easy to identify.

The original IDE interface supported up to two drives and is also known as the **ATA Standard** (**AT Attachment Standard**). ATA is the set of rules, or the standard, to which an IDE drive should conform. ATA-2 is an enhanced version of ATA. The ATA-2 standard has faster transfer rates (8.3MBps, then later 16.6MBps) than the original ATA standard of 3.3MBps. The ATA-2 standard also improves drive compatibility through an Identify Drive command which allows the BIOS to better determine the drive's properties. This is essential for Plug and Play computers. ATA-3 does not provide a faster transfer rate, but includes power management features and a new technology called **S.M.A.R.T** (**Self-Monitoring Analysis & Report Technology**). S.M.A.R.T. lets the drive send messages to the user about possible failures or data loss. The ATA-4 standard includes faster transfer modes and a new product from Quantum called Ultra-ATA or Ultra DMA/33 that allows transfers up to 33MBps. This standard provides an alternative to the Ultra-SCSI Wide standard (covered later in the chapter). The Ultra DMA/33 standard targets the network server, power user, and application markets requiring fast transfers. It implements bus mastering and uses Cyclic Redundancy Checks (CRC) for data integrity and verification.

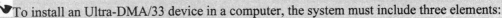

To install an Ultra-DMA/33 device in a computer, the system must include three elements:
1.   An IDE connector for the device (motherboard or adapter) must support Ultra-DMA/33.
2.   The ROM BIOS on the motherboard must be compatible with Ultra-DMA/33.
3.   An Ultra-DMA/33 device driver for the operating system.

If a motherboard contains the Intel 430TX or the 440LX chipset or higher, the system will support Ultra-DMA/33. To determine whether or not an IDE adapter supports Ultra-DMA/33, refer to the adapter's documentation or contact the adapter manufacturer. According to Intel, all future PCI chipsets and AGP chipsets will have Ultra-DMA/33 capability. If the system has the proper chipset and is running Windows 95, some Windows 95 files must be modified for an Ultra-DMA/33 device to work. Intel has a utility available through their web site that will update the Windows 95 files.

EIDE and Fast ATA are two terms frequently associated with IDE devices. **EIDE (Enhanced Integrated Drive Electronics)** is a term created at Western Digital. Many think EIDE is an IDE standard, but EIDE is a marketing program from Western Digital (and a very good one at that). EIDE has two parts: software and hardware. On the software side, the *enhanced* is the enhanced BIOS requirement — a BIOS that supports drives larger than 504MB. On the hardware side of EIDE, Western Digital specifies that the drive must conform to the ATA-2 standard and the ATAPI standard. **ATAPI** stands for **AT Attachment Packet Interface** and is designed for devices such as CD-ROMs and tape drives.

Many mistakenly think EIDE provides the ability to connect four IDE devices (two devices on one cable and two devices on a second cable). A second IDE port was included in a computer's input/output map for years, but most ROM BIOS chips did not support the second connector. With the huge growth in hard drive capacities, CD-ROM purchases, and the decline in hard drive prices, the second IDE connector became a necessity. BIOS manufacturers began to include support for the secondary IDE port in their chips. This occurred at the same time Western Digital was pushing EIDE. Computer users wanted to connect more IDE devices and Western Digital set a specification (EIDE) that stated BIOS supports two IDE connectors (four devices) and the devices must support the ATAPI standard. The term *EIDE* and the concept of four devices then became synonymous.

Fast ATA is a term Seagate Technology started using and was later endorsed by the Quantum Corporation. Fast ATA defines devices that support the ANSI PIO mode 3 standard and the multi-word DMA1 (Direct Memory Access) protocol. The PIO (Programmed Input/Output) mode is a speed standard for data transfers to and from the hard drive. The slowest PIO mode transfers data at 3.3MBps and is known as PIO Mode 0. PIO Mode 3, used with Fast ATA, transfers data at a maximum of 11.1MBps. The DMA mode allows data transfer between the hard drive and the memory chips without passing through the microprocessor. The slowest DMA mode, DMA0, transferred data at 2.1MBps. DMA1, the mode used with Fast ATA, transfers data at a maximum of 13.3MBps using multiple words. Hard Table #1 shows the PIO modes available with IDE hard drives, and Hard Table #2 shows the DMA modes.

HARD - TABLE # 1

PIO Modes for IDE Hard Drives

PIO Mode	Transfer Rate (MBps)
0	3.3
1	5.2
2	8.3
3	11.1
4	16.6
5	22.2

HARD - TABLE # 2

DMA Modes for IDE Hard Drives

DMA Mode	Transfer Rate (MBps)
DMA0 (Single word)	2.1
DMA0 (Multi-word)	4.2
DMA1 (Single word)	4.2
DMA1 (Multi-word)	13.3
DMA2 (Single word)	8.3
DMA2 (Multi-word)	16.6
DMA3 (Multi-word)	33.3

Fast ATA-2 is also a Seagate term for devices that support PIO Mode 4 and Multi-word DMA Mode 2 protocols. Fast ATA-2 has a maximum transfer rate of 16.6MBps.

Another misconception with IDE hard drives is with 32-bit transfers. Some people believe Fast ATA-2 can transfer 32 bits at a time. Currently, the IDE interface allows for a maximum of 16-bit data transfer. An adapter manufacturer who claims a 32-bit IDE data transfer is possible, actually means the adapter is a local bus adapter that can combine two 16-bit data transfers into a 32-bit stream to send these bits to the microprocessor.

IDE devices are quite common in today's computers. Two IDE connectors are contained on many motherboards and BIOS support for IDE devices is the standard, not the exception. IDE is a popular choice for computer users because of its ease of installation and low cost. IDE devices are a common upgrade request for technicians. The IDE interface's biggest competitor is the fourth hard drive interface type, SCSI.

SCSI (SMALL COMPUTER SYSTEM INTERFACE)

SCSI (Small Computer System Interface) defines many different devices such as scanners, tape drives, hard drives, optical drives, disk array subsystems (RAID), and CD-ROMs. The SCSI standard allows connection of multiple devices to the same adapter. All devices that connect to the same SCSI controller share a common data bus called the **SCSI bus**. With features such as increased speed and multiple device support, comes added cost. SCSI is more expensive than any other interface used with hard drives.

SCSI hard drives have the "intelligence" built into the drive similar to IDE and EIDE hard drives. The SCSI host adapter (that usually is a separate card) connects the SCSI device to the motherboard and coordinates the activities of the other devices connected. Three basic standards of SCSI are called SCSI-1, SCSI-2, and SCSI-3.

The original SCSI standard, SCSI-1, left a lot of room for vendor specifications on the wide range of devices that SCSI supports. What this meant to technicians is not all SCSI adapters handle all SCSI devices. SCSI-1 was primarily for hard drives because the standard included a set of software commands defined for hard drives. However, other device manufacturers such as tape drive manufacturers made do with SCSI-1 and adapted their devices as they saw fit. SCSI-1 supports up to eight devices on one SCSI 8-bit bus at a transfer rate of up to 5MBps. SCSI-2 improves on SCSI-1 by supporting more than eight devices and speeds up to 10MBps. SCSI-3 improves on data transfer rates by sending data through a 16-bit bus at speeds up to 20MBps and includes fiber optical cable standards. A newer SCSI standard is SCSI Parallel Interface 2 (SPI-2). SPI-2 allows 16-bits of data to move at the SCSI bus speed of 40 or 80MBps.

Fast SCSI is a term associated with the SCSI-2 and SCSI-3 interfaces. It transfers data at 10MBps, eight bits at a time. An improvement on the SCSI-3 interface is the SCSI-3 Fast20 Parallel Interface or simply Fast-20. This interface handles eight or 16 bits of data at a time at 20MBps. The two Fast-20 types are (1) Ultra SCSI that transfers eight bits of data at 20MBps and (2) Fast Wide SCSI that transfers 16 bits of data at 20MBps.

The new SCSI Parallel Interface-2 (SPI-2) standard has three types: (1) Wide Ultra SCSI which transfers 16 bits of data at 40MBps, (2) Ultra2 SCSI which transfers eight bits of data at 40MBps, and (3) Wide Ultra2 SCSI which transfers 16 bits of data at 80MBps. Hard Table #3 shows a breakdown of these SCSI standards.

SCSI Standards

Common Term	Interface Standard	Bus Width	Bus Speed
SCSI-1	Small Computer System Interface-1	8 bits	5MBps
Fast SCSI or Fast SCSI-2	Small Computer System Interface-2 (SCSI-2) and SCSI-3 Parallel Interface (SPI)	8 bits	10MBps
Fast Wide SCSI	SCSI-3	16 bits	20MBps
Ultra SCSI	Fast-20 Parallel Interface (Fast-20)	8 bits	20MBps
Wide Ultra SCSI	SCSI Parallel Interface-2 (SPI-2)	16 bits	40MBps
Ultra2 SCSI (Fast 40)		8 bits	40MBps
Wide Ultra2 SCSI		16 bits	80MBps

HARD - TABLE # 3

SCSI SOFTWARE STANDARDS

All SCSI devices require software to operate. Most SCSI hard drives have software built into the hard drive's BIOS chip. But, if the SCSI device needs software drivers, three types are used:

1.   ASPI (Advanced SCSI Programming Interface)
2.   CAM (Common Access Method)
3.   LADDR (Layered Device Driver Architecture)

A SCSI device can have all three software drivers written for it. The important thing to remember is if the host adapter has an ASPI driver, then any device that connects to the adapter also needs an ASPI driver. All devices along the SCSI bus (including the host adapter) should speak the same language. For example, if the host adapter has ASPI software, then all devices attached to the adapter should have ASPI software drivers. ASPI is the most common driver. CAM ships with OS/2 2.X and SCO UNIX and LADDR ships with OS/2 1.X to work with Microsoft's LAN Manager.

HARD DRIVE CONFIGURATION OVERVIEW

The configuration of a hard drive usually includes setting jumpers on the drive and sometimes on the hard drive adapter, terminating properly, and performing a few software commands. Each hard drive type has a normal configuration method. However, individual drive manufacturers may develop their own configuration steps. ALWAYS refer to the documentation included with the hard drive and the adapter or motherboard for configuration and installation information.

ST506 & ESDI HARD DRIVE CONFIGURATION

To configure a ST506 or a ESDI hard drive, three steps must be performed:
1.   Set the proper drive select jumper or switch
2.   Set or remove termination
3.   Connect the drive to the proper cable connector

ST506 and ESDI drives have drive select jumpers similar to the drive select jumpers found on floppy drives. ESDI drive systems can handle more drives, so they frequently have more drive select options than ST506 drives. Setting the drive select jumper and the terminator is the same process for ST506 and ESDI hard drives. Hard Figure #6 shows two types of drive select jumpers and two different physical placements of the terminator.

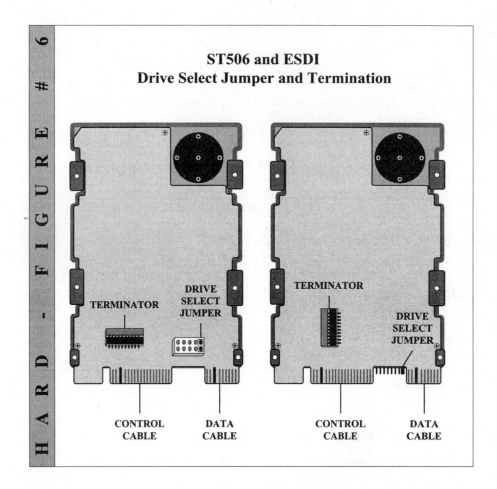

Just as with floppy drives, some hard drive manufacturers label the drive select jumpers as 0, 1, 2, and 3; and some manufacturers label the jumpers as 1, 2, 3, and 4. The correct setting for the drive select jumper or switch depends on (1) if multiple drives are connected and (2) which cable is used.

The 34-pin hard drive cable is *not* the same 34-pin cable used with floppy drives. Hard Figure #7 shows the difference between a 34-pin floppy cable and a 34-pin hard drive cable used with ST506 and ESDI hard drives.

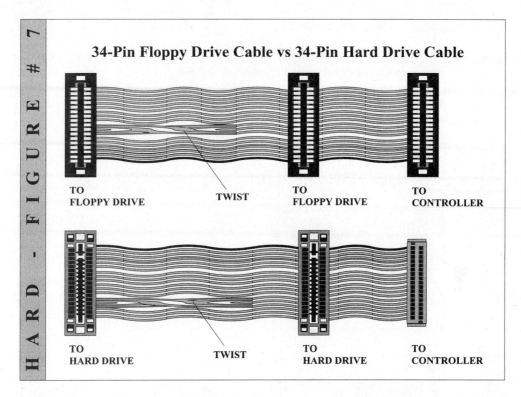

34-Pin Floppy Drive Cable vs 34-Pin Hard Drive Cable

TO FLOPPY DRIVE   TWIST   TO FLOPPY DRIVE   TO CONTROLLER

TO HARD DRIVE   TWIST   TO HARD DRIVE   TO CONTROLLER

Notice in Hard Figure #7 how the twist on the hard drive cable is farther from pin 1 than the floppy drive cable.

ONE DRIVE — ONE CABLE

If the ST506 or ESDI drive is the only drive in the system and it connects to a straight-through 34-pin control cable, then the drive select jumper is always set to the first position. You must terminate this drive because it is at the end of the cable. Hard Figure #8 shows the correct drive setting and termination.

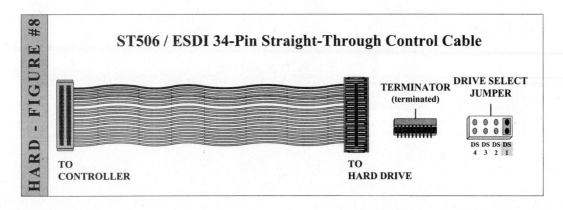

ST506 / ESDI 34-Pin Straight-Through Control Cable

TO CONTROLLER   TO HARD DRIVE   TERMINATOR (terminated)   DRIVE SELECT JUMPER

DS 4   DS 3   DS 2   DS 1

ONE DRIVE — ONE TWISTED CABLE

When you install a single hard drive into a system using a 34-pin twisted control cable, the hard drive connects to the connector farthest from the adapter. Set the drive select jumper to the second position. The twist in the cable causes the drive to appear as if it was set to the first position. Install the terminator on the drive. Reference Hard Figure #9 for an illustration of a ST506 hard drive connected to a twisted control cable.

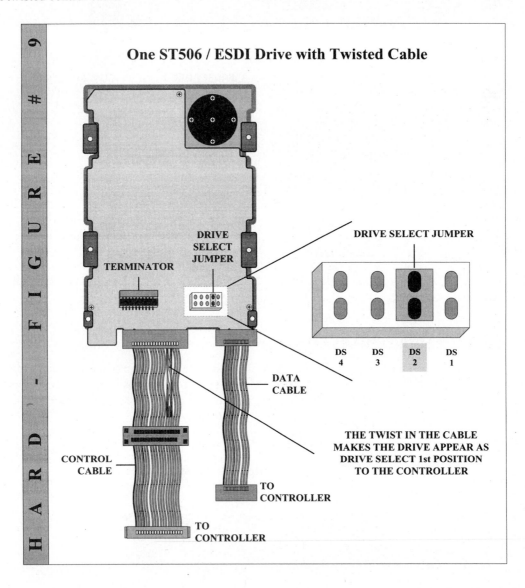

One ST506 / ESDI Drive with Twisted Cable

TWO DRIVES — ONE CABLE

If two ST506 or ESDI hard drives connect to the same adapter, use a single 34-pin cable with two drive connectors. A separate 20-pin data cable then connects to each drive. If one hard drive is connected to 34-pin cable with two connectors, use one connector and save the other connector for future expansion. Just as in a floppy drive configuration, only the drive connected at the end of the cable is terminated.

TWO DRIVES — ONE TWISTED CABLE

If two ST506 or ESDI hard drives install onto a 34-pin twisted control cable, the second drive attaches to the center connector on the cable. Set the drive select jumper to the second position and remove the terminator from the second hard drive. Hard Figure #10 shows how to set the drive select jumpers and the termination for two hard drives connected to a twisted cable.

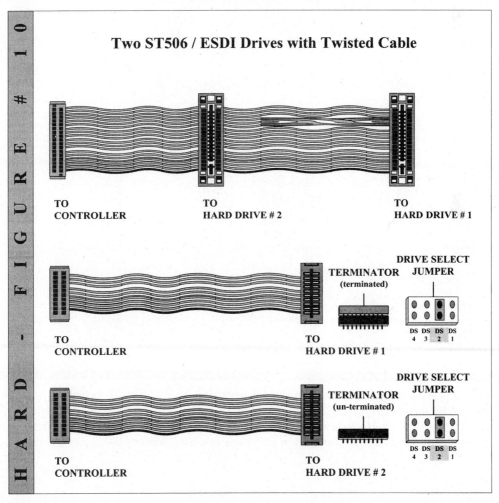

Notice in Hard Figure #10 that a separate 20-pin data cable is used for the second hard drive. Again, the twist in the control cable causes the drive to appear to the controller card as if it is set to the first position. The hard drive at the end of the cable is seen as the first hard drive in the system. The cables from the hard drive to the controller must connect to the proper adapter connectors to operate properly. Hard Figure #11 shows two different ST506 or ESDI hard drive controllers and their cable connections.

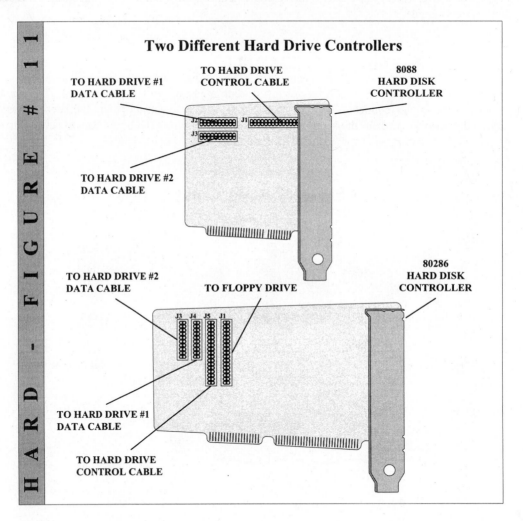

Hard drives are assigned drive letters by the operating system just like floppy drives. The first hard drive seen by the system is assigned the drive letter *C:*. The only time the first hard drive will not receive the drive letter C: is if a system supports more than two floppy drives installed in the system. However, most computers have the drive letter C: for the first hard drive installed into the system.

IDE HARD DRIVE CONFIGURATION

IDE devices (including hard drives) are the simplest to configure. IDE drives connect to a 40-pin ribbon cable and have master/slave settings, not drive select jumpers and terminators like the ST506 and ESDI drives. Termination is not an issue when configuring IDE hard drives because there are no terminators on IDE devices. If you install only one hard drive, the drive must be designated as the master, normally by setting a jumper. Hard Figure # 12 shows an illustration of an IDE hard drive configured as the master.

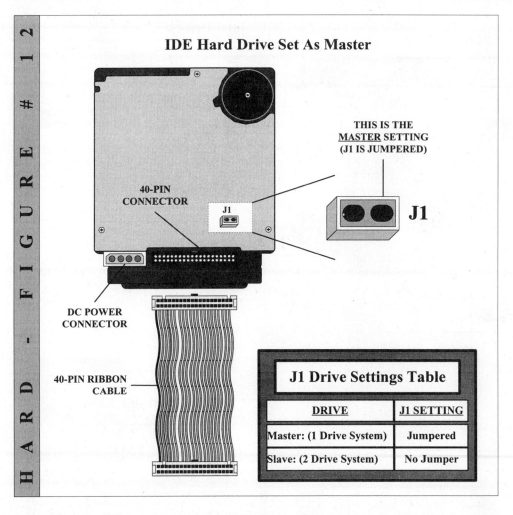

IDE Hard Drive Set As Master

THIS IS THE MASTER SETTING (J1 IS JUMPERED)

J1

40-PIN CONNECTOR

DC POWER CONNECTOR

40-PIN RIBBON CABLE

J1 Drive Settings Table

DRIVE	J1 SETTING
Master: (1 Drive System)	Jumpered
Slave: (2 Drive System)	No Jumper

Notice in Hard Figure #12 the table shows the possible configurations. A similar table is usually found either on top of the hard drive or in the documentation included with the hard drive. If only one IDE hard drive is to be installed the drive is set as the master. For the drive shown in Hard Figure #12, a jumper installs over J1 to make the drive the master.

If two IDE hard drives attach to one cable, then one drive is set as master and the other drive is set as the slave. The master device should be the faster of the two as it is the controller for both devices. A single 40-pin ribbon cable has a maximum of two connectors, one for each IDE device. When two hard drives install onto the same cable, the primary drive that boots the system is usually installed at the end of the cable. Reference Hard Figure #13 for an example of settings for two hard drives connected to the same cable. The table shown may be found imprinted on top of the hard drive or in the documentation.

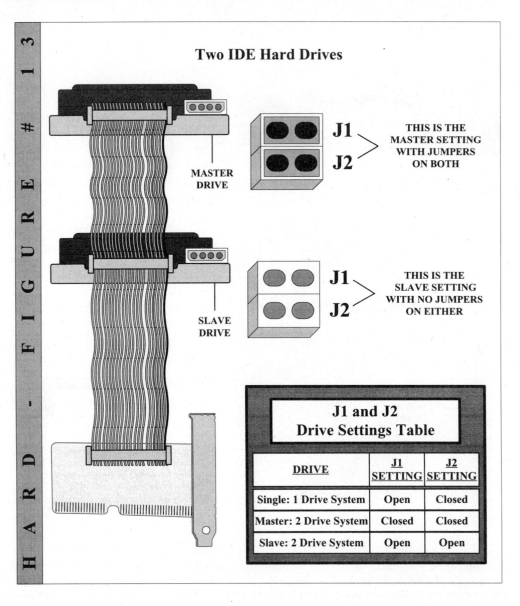

Two IDE Hard Drives

MASTER DRIVE

J1
J2
THIS IS THE MASTER SETTING WITH JUMPERS ON BOTH

SLAVE DRIVE

J1
J2
THIS IS THE SLAVE SETTING WITH NO JUMPERS ON EITHER

J1 and J2 Drive Settings Table

DRIVE	J1 SETTING	J2 SETTING
Single: 1 Drive System	Open	Closed
Master: 2 Drive System	Closed	Closed
Slave: 2 Drive System	Open	Open

HARD - FIGURE # 13

Documentation is important when setting up a hard drive. Notice in Hard Figure #13 the documentation table is different from the documentation shown in Hard Figure #12. This particular drive manufacturer lists three possible drive configurations. Single: 1 Drive System is a single drive attached to one cable. There is no slave in a single IDE drive configuration because there is only one device. Master: 2 Drive System is two IDE devices connected to one cable. If the IDE drive is to be the master of the two devices, then this setting is correct. Slave: 2 Drive System is two IDE devices connected to the same cable with the IDE device set to slave, not master. The other device on the cable is set as master for the two devices to operate. How a manufacturer uses the terms and configures the drive is up to the manufacturer. The technician must learn to adjust to poorly written and sometimes confusing documentation. Jumpers other than the master/slave jumper(s) may be present, but you must refer to the hard drive's documentation for the proper settings. If documentation is unavailable, use the Internet; most manufacturers place their jumper setting documentation online.

DASP (Drive Active/Slave Present) is a signal in the ATA interface on pin 39 of the IDE connector some manufacturers use to indicate the presence of a slave IDE device. Some older IDE devices do not support the DASP signal so they must connect to a master IDE device that recognizes them. Some manufacturers put a SP (Slave Present) jumper on the IDE device so it recognizes another device connected as a slave.

If an IDE device has a Slave Present setting, the setting is only used when installing two IDE devices on one cable where one device does not support the DASP signal. The Slave Present setting, when set on the master device, tells the slave device it is controlled by the master. The master IDE is the controller for both devices.

On some older IDE drives, the Master/Slave or Slave Present jumpers are not available. If you install a drive like this in a two-drive IDE system, one drive must be considered the master and the other drive is designated as the slave. The drive without the jumpers still may not work in a two-drive system. The only way to know is to try the older drive in a two-drive system.

Newer IDE/EIDE devices frequently have a jumper option labeled as cable select. The **cable select** option replaces the master/slave setting. To use the cable select option, a special IDE cable that has pin 28 disabled is required. Similar to the idea behind Plug and Play, cable select jumpering emerged from the idea that devices can be installed without having to change a jumper.

To use the cable select option, three criteria must be met: (1) two devices connected to the same cable must both support the option, (2) the special cable select cable must be used, and (3) the host interface must support it. When using the cable select option, the device connected to the middle connector is the master and the device connected to the last connector is the slave. If both devices are configured to use the cable select option and a regular IDE cable is used, both devices configure as the master and will not work properly.

CONFIGURATION FOR FOUR IDE DEVICES

Computers capable of connecting four IDE devices use either a paddleboard (an adapter that plugs into an expansion slot), or a motherboard with two 34-pin connections. When a motherboard or adapter has two IDE connections, it operates as two separate IDE paddleboards. Each device connected to the first connector must be set up as a master or a slave and each device connected to the second connector must also be set up as a master or a slave. Therefore, in one computer system with four IDE devices, two can be set up as a master; but one connects to the first connector through a cable, and the other connects to the second IDE connector.

The ATAPI specification for IDE connections that support CD-ROMs and tape drives states when a hard drive and a CD-ROM drive connect to the same connector, the hard drive must be set as the master. The CD-ROM drive will work (in some cases) as the master in a hard drive/CD-ROM connection, but the faster device should be the master. Hard drives are normally the fastest IDE device. Refer to the documentation included with the device for help configuring any device. Most IDE devices now have the documentation imprinted on the device. For more information on CD-ROM configuration, a chapter follows later in this book.

SCSI CABLES

SCSI cabling allows multiple devices to be connected to one SCSI **host adapter** and share the same SCSI bus; this is called **daisy-chaining**. If multiple internal SCSI devices attach to the SCSI adapter, then use a SCSI cable with multiple connectors. Most internal SCSI-1 cables are a 50-pin ribbon cable. To connect external devices, a 50-pin Centronics to 50-pin Centronics cable is used. The SCSI-1 cable is also known as the A-Cable. The SCSI-2 standard has a different cable for connecting to the first external SCSI device. This cable has a 50-pin D-shell connector which connects to the SCSI host adapter, and a Centronics connector which connects to the external device. For 16-bit SCSI devices, a second 68-pin cable, called the B-Cable, must be used in addition to the A-Cable. This B-Cable is not in the SCSI-3 specifications. SCSI-3 has a new 68-pin cable called the P-Cable for Fast Wide SCSI or Ultra SCSI devices. A cable known as the Q-Cable must be used in addition to the P-Cable for 16-bit SCSI devices. Hard Table #4 lists the SCSI cable information.

	SCSI Cables		
Cable	**Connector**		**Uses**
A-Cable	50-pin		SCSI-1 devices SCSI-2 devices (16-bit SCSI-2 devices require the **B-Cable** as well).
B-Cable	68-pin		16-bit SCSI-2 devices (These devices require the **A-Cable** as well.)
P-Cable	68-pin		SCSI-3 (16-bit SCSI-3 devices require the **Q-Cable** as well.)
Q-Cable	68-pin		SCSI-3 devices (These devices require the **P-Cable** as well.)

HARD - TABLE # 4

The most common SCSI cables found are as follows: (1) a 50-pin ribbon cable used to connect internal SCSI devices to the host adapter; (2) a Centronics-to-Centronics cable used to connect two external SCSI devices; (3) a 50-pin D-shell connector to a Centronics connector (the 50-pin mini D-shell connector connects to the host adapter's external connector and the Centronics connector connects to an external device); (4) a 25-pin D-shell connector to a Centronics connector (the 25-pin D-shell connector connects to an external SCSI port normally found on motherboards and the

Centronics connector connects to an external device). Hard Figure #14 illustrates these common SCSI cables.

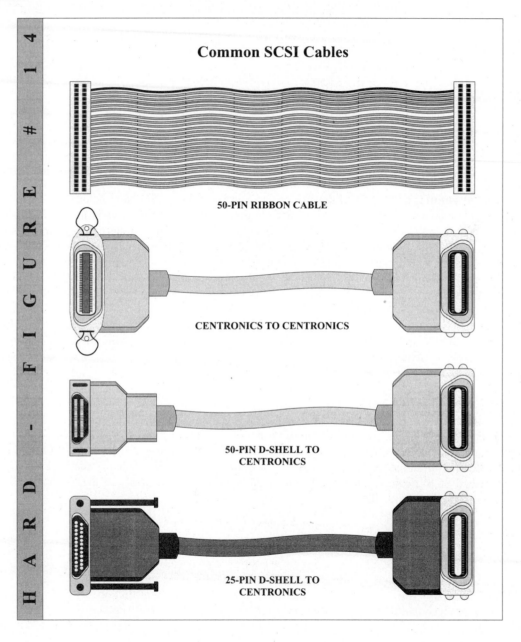

Common SCSI Cables

50-PIN RIBBON CABLE

CENTRONICS TO CENTRONICS

50-PIN D-SHELL TO CENTRONICS

25-PIN D-SHELL TO CENTRONICS

H A R D - F I G U R E # 1 4

Not all SCSI cables are created equal. Do not recommend or buy the cheaper, thinner SCSI cables available for external devices. These cheaper cables are susceptible to outside noise. The section on Configuration and Setup Procedures covers more cabling issues.

SCSI CONFIGURATION

A SCSI device is configured by
1.   setting the proper SCSI ID
2.   terminating both ends of the SCSI chain
3.   connecting the proper cable(s)

A **SCSI chain** is several SCSI devices cabled together. The SCSI chain includes SCSI devices and a single controller, sometimes called a **host adapter**. The SCSI controller is usually a separate adapter, but it may be built into the motherboard. The SCSI chain includes internal SCSI devices that connect to the SCSI host adapter and any external SCSI devices that connect to an adapter's external port. Multiple SCSI chains can exist in a system and a computer can contain multiple SCSI host adapters. Each device on a SCSI chain, including the SCSI host adapter, is assigned a **SCSI ID**. (Some SCSI hard drive manufacturers refer to this setting as the drive select ID.) The SCSI ID allows each device to share the same SCSI bus and it assigns a priority for each device. The SCSI interface allows a SCSI device to communicate directly with another SCSI device connected on the same SCSI chain. The higher the SCSI number, the higher the priority of the device on the SCSI chain. SCSI IDs are normally set using switches or jumpers.

SCSI ID CONFIGURATION

When a computer first powers on, the ROM BIOS chip on the motherboard searches the system for other adapter ROM chips that must initialize the devices they control. When the ROM BIOS chip allows the ROM chip on the SCSI host adapter to initialize, the SCSI host adapter scans the SCSI bus for any attached SCSI devices. The host adapter then determines the priority of these devices on the SCSI bus based on their SCSI ID.

Power on all external SCSI devices before powering on the computer. The host adapter detects all SCSI devices along the SCSI chain during the bootup sequence. However, if a SCSI device is not used frequently the device can be powered off. The rest of the SCSI devices operate even if a SCSI device is powered off. If two devices have the same SCSI ID, a SCSI conflict occurs and the devices will not work properly. Setting an improper SCSI ID (priority) setting results in slower performance of the SCSI device.

The SCSI host adapter is normally preset to SCSI ID 7, the highest priority and should not be changed. The host adapter is always a high priority because the adapter is the link to the rest of the computer system. Slow devices such as scanners or CD-ROMs should be assigned a higher SCSI ID number such as SCSI ID 6 or 5. By assigning the slow devices a higher SCSI ID number, the slower devices receive ample time to process data on the SCSI bus. If a hard drive is to boot the system, its setting should be SCSI ID 0. The SCSI priority system is logical. SCSI hard drives normally process data quickly. If a SCSI hard drive has a higher priority than a scanner, the scanner will not access the SCSI bus often because it must wait as the hard drive is continually accessing software. An exception to this is some IBM PS/2 computers have the hard drive preset to SCSI ID 6. The PS/2 computer will boot only if the first hard drive is set to SCSI ID 6. If you add a second hard drive, set the drive to SCSI ID 5. SCSI ID 0 is the default for most SCSI hard drives.

As long as each SCSI device has a unique SCSI ID number, the sequence of the devices cabled to the adapter is insignificant. SCSI devices do not have to be cabled in SCSI ID order. SCSI IDs are normally set using jumpers or a switch block. Technicians should always refer to the documentation included with the SCSI device or adapter for setting the SCSI ID. Many SCSI manufacturers use three jumpers or three switches and standard binary counting to set the SCSI IDs. For example, a setting of 000 is SCSI ID 0 and a setting of 010 is SCSI ID 2. Table #5 illustrates the eight possible SCSI settings with the most significant bit on the left. Be aware that a manufacturer may reverse the SCSI setting and place the most significant bit on the right.

HARD - TABLE # 5

SCSI ID Settings
(Most Significant Bit to the Left)

SCSI ID	Setting*	Setting*	Setting*
0	0	0	0
1	0	0	1
2	0	1	0
3	0	1	1
4	1	0	0
5	1	0	1
6	1	1	0
7	1	1	1

*0=OFF 1=ON

To combine this information, Hard Figure #15 shows two internal SCSI devices cabled to a SCSI host adapter. It shows the SCSI ID setting for each SCSI device and the SCSI adapter. The SCSI host adapter has a switch block for setting its SCSI ID. Switch Block 1 (S1) positions 1, 2, and 3 control the SCSI ID number. (This information is in the documentation for the adapter). The first device in the chain is the SCSI hard drive which boots the system and is set to SCSI ID 0. The hard drive uses jumpers to set its SCSI ID. Then, the last device on the chain is a SCSI CD-ROM that is set to SCSI ID 5. The CD-ROM also has jumpers that sets its SCSI ID. The documentation for both the hard drive and the CD-ROM shows how to set each SCSI ID. If the documentation is not available, the Internet is the next best place to obtain the documentation.

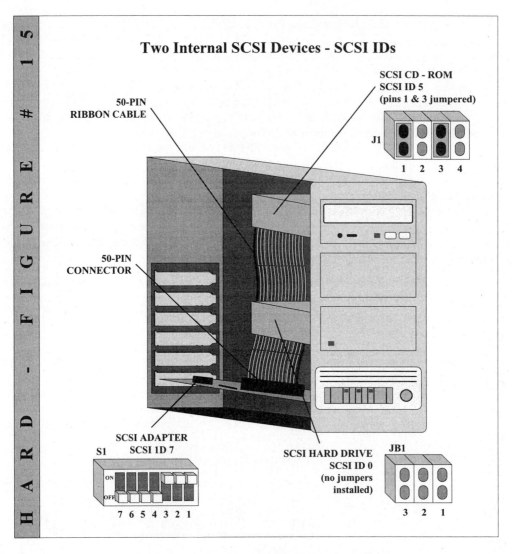

HARD - FIGURE # 15

Two Internal SCSI Devices - SCSI IDs

SCSI CD - ROM
SCSI ID 5
(pins 1 & 3 jumpered)

J1

1   2   3   4

50-PIN
RIBBON CABLE

50-PIN
CONNECTOR

SCSI ADAPTER
SCSI 1D 7

S1

ON

OFF

7 6 5 4 3 2 1

SCSI HARD DRIVE
SCSI ID 0
(no jumpers
installed)

JB1

3   2   1

All devices connected to the same SCSI host adapter make up a SCSI chain. If multiple external devices connect to the same SCSI controller, a SCSI cable daisy-chains each external device to another external SCSI device. The SCSI ID on the external device is normally set by a thumbwheel switch, jumpers, or switches located on the back of the SCSI device where the cables connect. External SCSI devices usually have two connectors on the back of the device. If the external device is in the center of the SCSI chain, the two connectors have cables that connect to other SCSI devices in the SCSI chain. For example, if a SCSI bus has two external devices such as a CD-ROM and a scanner attached, the CD-ROM has a cable that connects it to the SCSI adapter. A separate cable connects the CD-ROM drive to the scanner. Hard Figure #16 shows two SCSI devices cabled to a SCSI adapter.

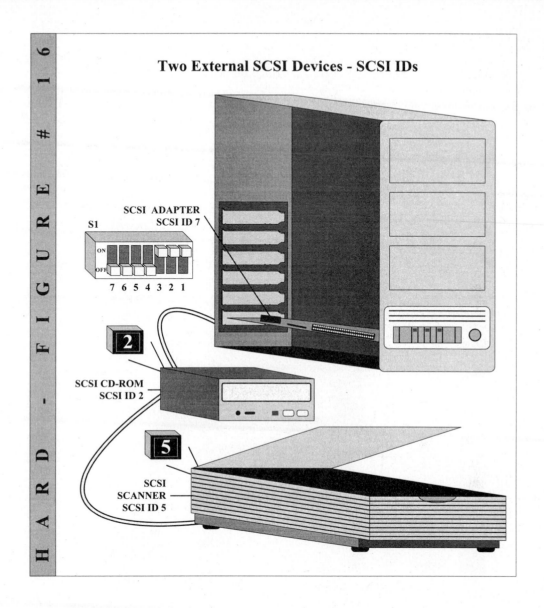

Two External SCSI Devices - SCSI IDs

A new development helpful in setting SCSI IDs is **SCAM (SCSI Configured Automatically)**. Devices and adapters that support SCAM allow automatic SCSI ID assignment. To enable the SCAM feature, check the host adapter's documentation. Using SCAM, each device connected to the SCSI adapter is assigned a unique SCSI ID during boot-up. When purchasing a SCSI adapter or device, be sure it supports SCAM for easy installation and to avoid SCSI ID conflicts.

SCSI TERMINATION

Termination of SCSI devices is very important. Proper termination of SCSI devices keeps the signals from bouncing back up the cable and provides the proper electrical current level for the SCSI chain. The SCSI bus cannot operate properly without terminating both ends of the SCSI bus. Improper termination can result in one, many, or all SCSI devices not working properly. Over time, improper termination can damage a SCSI adapter or a SCSI device. SCSI termination is performed in several ways: (1) installing a SIPP, (2) installing a jumper, (3) setting a switch, or (4) installing a terminator plug. Hard Figure #17 illustrates the four possible ways a SCSI device or a SCSI host adapter may be terminated.

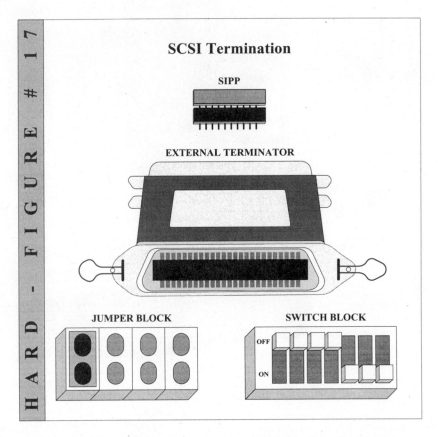

When setting or removing termination, refer to the documentation included with the adapter or device. Also, when purchasing an external SCSI device, if the terminator is not provided with the device, it must be purchased separately.

If only internal devices connect to the SCSI host adapter, terminate the adapter and the last internal device connected to the cable. Remove the termination from all other devices. Look at Hard Figure #18 to see how the SCSI chain is terminated if two internal SCSI devices connect to the same host adapter. The SCSI chain has a SCSI host adapter, an internal hard drive, and an internal CD-ROM. The two ends of the SCSI chain are the host adapter and the CD-ROM drive and each device must be terminated. The internal hard drive, which connects in the center of the SCSI chain is not terminated.

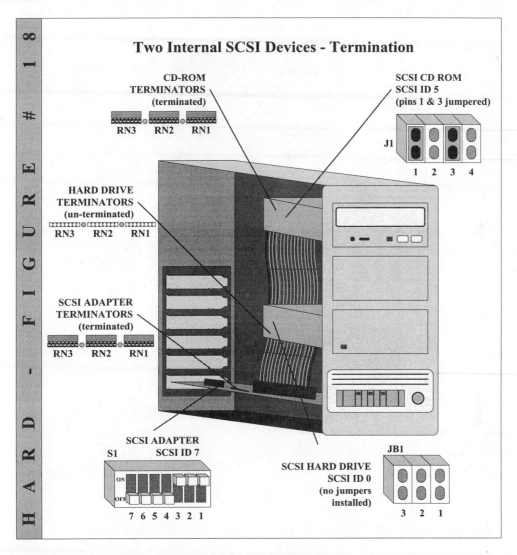

In Hard Figure #18, the SIP terminator sockets are labeled RN1, RN2, and RN3. The RN stands for resistor network. The three SIP terminators work together to provide the proper amount of current for the SCSI bus.

If connecting only external devices to the SCSI host adapter, terminate the adapter and the last external device. Remove the termination from all other external devices. See Hard Figure #19 for an illustration of termination when connecting two external SCSI devices.

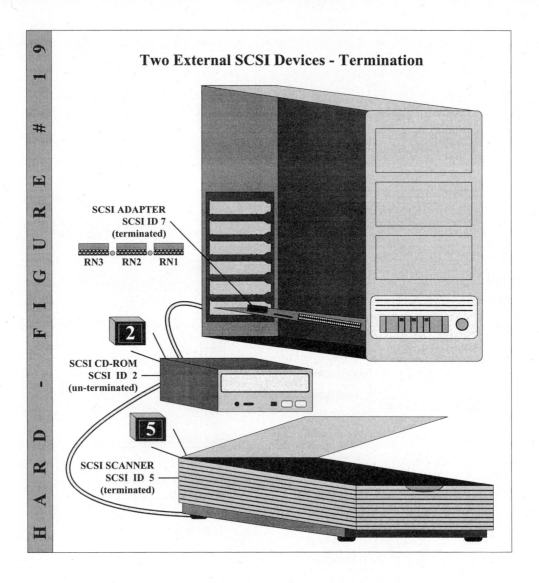

Two External SCSI Devices - Termination

SCSI ADAPTER
SCSI ID 7
(terminated)

RN3   RN2   RN1

2

SCSI CD-ROM
SCSI ID 2
(un-terminated)

5

SCSI SCANNER
SCSI ID 5
(terminated)

HARD - FIGURE # 19

In Hard Figure #19, the SCSI chain consists of the host adapter, an external CD-ROM, and an external scanner. The two devices on each end of the SCSI chain are the adapter and the scanner; therefore, these devices are terminated. The external CD-ROM is not terminated.

Notice how two cables connect to the back of the CD-ROM. One cable connects the CD-ROM to the host adapter. A separate SCSI cable connects the CD-ROM to the scanner. The scanner also has two connectors on the back. One connector, of course, contains the cable connecting the scanner to the CD-ROM. The scanner's other connector contains a terminator because the scanner is the last device on the SCSI chain.

Not all external SCSI devices have two connectors on the back. Some are pre-set to be permanently terminated. This is not a problem if only one device is designed this way because the device can be placed at the end of the SCSI chain. However, two SCSI devices with this limitation, are not usable in the same SCSI chain. For the best results and expandability, be sure that when purchasing, installing, or recommending an external SCSI device that the device can be terminated and un-terminated.

Look at Hard Figure #20 for an illustration of the SCSI IDs and termination for a SCSI chain that contains both internal and external devices.

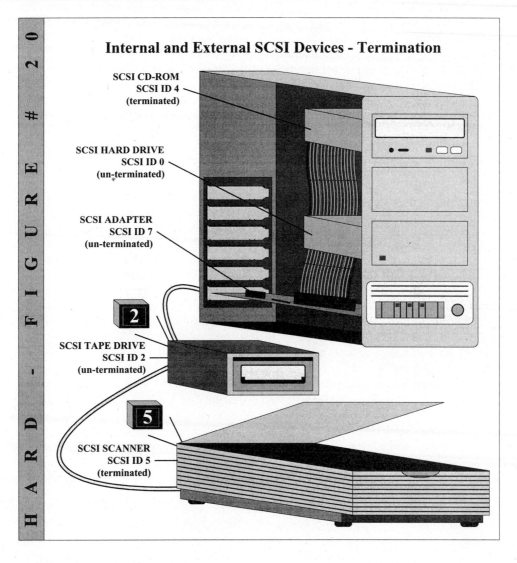

Internal and External SCSI Devices - Termination

HARD - FIGURE # 20

SCSI CD-ROM
SCSI ID 4
(terminated)

SCSI HARD DRIVE
SCSI ID 0
(un-terminated)

SCSI ADAPTER
SCSI ID 7
(un-terminated)

SCSI TAPE DRIVE
SCSI ID 2
(un-terminated)

SCSI SCANNER
SCSI ID 5
(terminated)

If both internal and external devices attach to the SCSI host adapter, the last internal device connected to the SCSI cable is terminated as well as the last external device. All other devices and the SCSI host adapter must have their terminators removed. The SCSI chain in Hard Figure #20 consists of two internal SCSI devices, (a CD-ROM and a hard drive), and two external SCSI devices, (a tape drive and a scanner). The two ends of the SCSI chain that must be terminated are the CD-ROM and the scanner and all other devices are not terminated.

Two types of SCSI termination are passive and active termination. SCSI-1 and SCSI-2 devices use **passive termination**. Passive termination is not good for long cable distances because it is susceptible to noise interference. **Active termination** was introduced with SCSI-2. It allows for longer cable distance and provides the correct voltage for SCSI signals. Active termination must be used with Fast, Wide, or Fast-Wide SCSI devices. The SCSI-2 standard recommends that active termination be used at both ends of the SCSI chain, but passive termination can be used if Fast, Wide, or Fast-Wide SCSI device is not installed. A passive terminator and an active terminator can be used on the same SCSI chain. SCSI-3 requires active termination.

A smart technician plans the configuration of the drive before installing the drive in the system. A good plan of attack is the best strategy to avoid problems during installation. Draw the configuration on a piece of paper to help get the installation straight in your mind. To help new technicians with different configurations, the exercises at the end of the chapter contain sample practice configurations.

SYSTEM CONFIGURATION FOR HARD DRIVES

The computer system is informed (in some way) of a hard drive installation. However, in a PC or XT system, no switches are set, which is the normal configuration method. This is one reason configuring hard drives in a PC or XT is the most complicated of any hard drive installation. Many steps are required to set up a drive in a PC or XT computer. On a 286 or higher system, the hard drive is configured through the SETUP program. As mentioned previously, SETUP is accessed through keystrokes, a SETUP disk from the manufacturer (IBM AT is one example), or a Reference disk (IBM's older MicroChannel computers). Once in SETUP, you must enter a Drive Type number. The **Drive Type** is a number that corresponds to a drive's geometry (the number of cylinders, heads, and sectors). The different ROM BIOS will support a variety of different hard drives. A number is entered and the drive geometry information appears to the right of the Drive Type number. In today's computers a User-Defined drive type number such as Drive Type 47 allows the hard drive geometry information to be entered. The drive type information is saved in CMOS. If the computer's battery fails, the drive type information is lost and the computer cannot boot.

For most ESDI hard drive installations, the documentation recommends setting the Drive Type to 1. The ESDI controller and drive take over from there even though that is not the parameters of the drive. The drive's geometry information is sent to the controller by the ESDI hard drive.

For SCSI hard drive installations, the most common CMOS setting for the hard drive type is type 0 or NONE. Once the system boots the SCSI controller and the SCSI ROM BIOS initializes, the SCSI hard drive takes over and drive boots the system. Even though the Drive Type number is set to 0 or None, if this step is omitted, the hard drive will not operate.

IDE hard drives are normally configured using the Auto-Detect feature included with BIOS. The Auto-Detect feature automatically determines the Drive Type for the system. Older IDE hard drive manufacturers recommend setting the CMOS drive type to 1 and using a special software package such as Ontrack's Disk Manager or Western Digital's EZ-Drive to allow the system to see the hard drive.

If the drive installed is a ST506 and is not listed in any of the drive types and no user-defined type exists, several options are available:
1.   Buy a new ROM BIOS chip that supports the drive.
2.   Choose a drive type with the drive geometry closest to the one being installed. The drawback to this option is not all drive space is available for use.
3.   Use software to get around the BIOS.

Drive manufacturers normally include documentation describing how to configure the drive in CMOS SETUP. Also, they provide software for any system that does not recognize the drive.

With an older ROM BIOS chip that does not support the hard drive, no configuration software is available, and one of the drive types available through SETUP must be chosen, certain precautions should be followed:
1.   Do NOT pick a drive type with more cylinders than the hard drive.
2.   Do NOT pick a drive type with a different write-precompensation cylinder.
3.   Do NOT pick a drive type with more heads than the hard drive.
4.   Pick the largest total capacity drive type that remains after considering precautions one through three.

BIOS LIMITATIONS

The BIOS chip on the motherboard must detect and recognize the installed hardware components, including the hard drive. The BIOS chip is the liaison between the operating system and the hard drive. However, a SCSI hard drive normally connects to an adapter containing a special ROM chip. The adapter's ROM chip takes control from the BIOS chip on the motherboard and becomes the liaison between the SCSI hard drive and the operating system.

Most system BIOS chips manufactured before 1994 do not recognize hard drives larger than 504MB. The reason for this is due to a standard many drive manufacturers use called the INT13 interface. INT13 (Interrupt 13) is the BIOS interrupt that handles reading and writing to the hard disk. BIOS sees the location of data on the hard drive at the specific cylinder, head, and sector number. The **INT13 interface** is the standard that explains how the BIOS handles locating data on the hard drive.

A hard drive has a specific number of cylinders, heads, and sectors. The BIOS talks to the hard drive based on the number of cylinders, heads, and sectors using **CHS** (cylinders, heads, sectors) **addressing**. The cylinders, heads, and sectors information is translated inside the hard drive so the BIOS recognizes the information. INT13 can only process a CHS of 1024 cylinders, 63 sectors, and 16 heads. Each sector holds 512 bytes of information; therefore, with 1024 cylinders there are 528,482,304 bytes of data (cylinders x bytes per sector x sectors x heads). The maximum amount of hard drive space the INT13 can handle is 528,482,304 bytes or 504MB. Many books and magazine articles use 528MB as the maximum. 504MB is the most accurate because 504MB equals 528,482,304 bytes.

Another way for the BIOS to handle the hard drive is **Extended CHS** or **ECHS**. A BIOS that supports Extended CHS frequently has an option for Large in the hard drive section of SETUP. Select the *Large* setting to activate Extended CHS. Normally, the hard drive translates the real number of cylinders, heads, and sectors for the BIOS. Then, the BIOS processes the interaction between the operating system and the hard drive. With Extended CHS, in addition to the hard drive translating the cylinders, heads, and sectors, the BIOS performs a second translation. However, having the cylinders, heads, and sectors translated by both the drive and the BIOS chip causes slower response than straight CHS.

A third option for the BIOS to communicate with the hard drive is **LBA** or **Logical Block Addressing**. This is a method of sector translation. Today's hard drive manufacturers put intelligence into the drive to track data in a linear fashion. Each sector is assigned a number beginning with the first cylinder, first head, and first sector of user data. The drive continues numbering the sectors until the last track, last head, and last sector are numbered. The drive must translate the cylinder, sector, head information from the BIOS into a single number the drive understands. This allows larger drives to be installed under the BIOS INT13 limitation. LBA supports hard drives up to 8GB in capacity. The 8GB limitation is inherent to the INT13 interface.

A system BIOS that supports hard drives larger than 504MB is known as a **translating BIOS**. The IDE hard drive SETUP options for the translating BIOS chips are: Normal for CHS (Cylinder, Head, Sector), Large for ECHS (Extended CHS), and LBA for Logical Block Addressing. Refer to the installation manual included with the hard drive to choose the correct option.

IBM and Microsoft have proposed an extension of the INT13 interface known as the Extended INT13 interface to support hard drives larger than 8GB. Some computers already have BIOS chips that support hard drives larger than 8GB.

If the BIOS chip installed on the motherboard is not a translating BIOS chip, then two options are available:

1.   Upgrade the BIOS chip(s) on the motherboard to a translating BIOS chip.
2.   Use a software program such as Ontrack's Disk Manager or Western Digital's EZ-Drive to allow the system to see the larger hard drive.

On-Track's Disk Manager & Western Digital's EZ-Drive programs cannot be used simultaneously on two different drives installed in the same computer system. One software program must be used on both hard drives.

HARD DRIVE PREPARATION

Once a hard drive is installed, configured properly, and the hard drive type is entered into the CMOS SETUP program (on a 286 or higher), the drive must be prepared to accept data. The three steps of hard drive preparation are as follows:

1.   Low-level format
2.   Partition
3.   High-level format

LOW-LEVEL FORMAT

The **low-level format** creates and numbers the sectors on the hard drive surface and erases all data from the hard drive. On ST506 drives, the interleave factor is chosen during the low-level format process. The drive and controller are matched in a way that the controller knows the number of tracks, sectors per track, heads, and the write pre-compensation and reduced write current cylinders. For ST506 hard drives, this step is critical in getting the controller to recognize and properly identify the hard drive to be able to instruct it.

ESDI hard drives have their geometry information built into the drive, so less information is input during the low-level format process. However, ESDI drives still require the installer to perform a low-level format. IDE and SCSI drives are low-level formatted at the factory.

The DOS DEBUG command or the use of special low-level format software such as Ontrack's Disk Manager will low-level format ST506 or ESDI hard drives. If you use DOS DEBUG, the hard drive controller must have a ROM chip that contains the software. DEBUG is just a command to access this software. The most common ROM addresses are in Hard Table #6.

HARD - TABLE # 6	Common Hard Drive ROM Addresses	
	C800:5	C800:CCC
	D800:5	D800:CCC
	C000:5	C000:CCC
	D000:5	D000:CCC

To use DOS to low-level format the hard drive, type **DEBUG** at the DOS prompt. A dash (-) appears on the screen. Type **G=** followed by the starting address of the low-level format software contained on the ROM chip. The starting address is a hexadecimal address where the low-level software begins. The software routine should appear on the screen. If nothing appears on the screen after approximately 30 seconds, reboot the computer and type **DEBUG** again. After the dash, type **G=** followed by a different address. Continue this routine until either the software routine appears or all addresses do not work. If no address works, two options remain: contact the adapter manufacturer for the starting address or special low-level format software on disk.

Once the software appears on the screen, (whether it is from the ROM chip or from a disk), the software asks for certain information. The required information depends on the software and/or the adapter's ROM chip. Some information that might be needed lists below:

1. How many cylinders does the drive have?
2. How many heads does the drive have?
3. How many sectors per track does the drive have?
4. What is the reduced write current cylinder?
5. What is the write precompensation cylinder?
6. What is the landing zone cylinder?
7. What is the model of the drive being formatted?

The number of questions and the format for the typed answer all depends on the software. The information is in the documentation included with the hard drive or on the manufacturer's Internet site.

Low-level formatting must be performed on a newly installed ST506 or ESDI hard drive. Low-level formatting is also a good idea when a ST506 or ESDI hard drive begins to have read and/or write errors. All possible data should be backed up before beginning the low-level formatting. If you install a replacement ST506 hard drive controller, the hard drive usually must be low-level formatted. Good backups are critical for all hard drives.

Never low-level format an IDE hard drive unless there is no alternative. An example of this is if an older IDE hard drive is getting numerous read errors. The data has been backed up and re-loaded, but the drive still gets read errors.

The only alternative at this point is to try the special utilities or buy a new hard drive. Some manufacturers supply formatting software with the computer. IBM provides low-level format software with their MicroChannel machines. From the main menu of the Reference Disk software, press **CTRL+A** for the Advanced Diagnostics to find the low-level format option.

PARTITIONING

The second step in preparing a hard drive for use is partitioning. **Partitioning** a hard drive divides the drive so the computer system sees the hard drive as more than one drive. DOS and Windows 95 have a software program called **FDISK** that partitions hard drives. Partitioning provides several functions which include (1) dividing a hard drive into separate sub-units which are then assigned drive letters such as C: or D: by the operating system; (2) organizing the hard drive for reasons such as separating multiple operating systems, applications, and data; (3) providing data security by placing data in a different partition to allow ease of backup as well as protection; (4) using the hard drive to its fullest capacity.

The original purpose of partitioning was to allow for loading multiple operating systems. This is still a good reason today because placing each operating system in its own partition eliminates the crashes and headaches caused by multiple operating systems and multiple applications co-existing in the same partition. An even better reason is the efficient use of drive space as hard drives keep getting larger in capacity.

The size of a hard drive's partition determines the cluster size! Remember that a **cluster** is the smallest amount of space reserved for one file. The size of the cluster is determined by the size of the hard drive's partition.

For example, if a letter was being typed,
        DEAR MOM,
and the phone rings and you quickly save the file to the hard disk. If the hard disk has a 20MB partition, then the file saves in a cluster of four sectors or 2,048 bytes (2KB) even though the file is only nine bytes long. The operating system sets aside one cluster as a minimum for every file. If the

file is on a 128MB partition, then a cluster of eight sectors, or 4KB of space, is reserved for the file. An 1GB partition sets aside 16KB of space for the same nine characters in the file. If the file grows larger than one cluster in size, additional clusters are used in sizes relational to the size of the hard drive partition. Space on the hard drive is wasted by inefficient partitioning. Hard Table #7 illustrates how the hard drive partition size affects the cluster size using the file allocation table (FAT) used with DOS and Windows 3.x.

FAT Partitions and Cluster Size

Partition Size	Number of Sectors	Cluster Size
0-15MB	8	4K
16MB-127MB	4	2K
128MB-255MB	8	4K
256MB-511MB	16	8K
512MB-1GB	32	16K
1GB-2GB	64	32K
2GB-4GB	128	64K

HARD - TABLE # 7

One can clearly see in Hard Table #7 that hard drive space is wasted by partitioning today's large drives into one partition. Most end users do not have big files. An efficiently partitioned hard drive allows more files to be saved because less of the hard drive is wasted. Computer users with CAD (Computer Aided Drafting) software would naturally have bigger files and need larger partitions.

Applications should be in a separate partition than data files. There are several good reasons for partitioning the hard drive and separating data files from application files: (1) multiple partitions on the same hard drive divide the drive into smaller sub-units which makes it easier and faster to backup the data (which should be backed up more often than applications); (2) the data is protected from operating system failures, unstable software applications, and any unusual software problems that occur between the application and the operating system; and (3) the data is in one location which makes the files easier and faster to backup, organize, and locate.

Partitions are defined as primary and extended. If there is only one hard drive installed in a system and the entire hard drive is one partition, it is the **primary partition**. The primary partition on the first detected hard drive is assigned the drive letter C:. DOS requires that the first hard drive in a system be a primary partition and must be marked as active if the drive boots the system. If the drive is divided so only part of the drive is the primary partition, the rest of the cylinders can be designated as the **extended partition**. An extended partition allows a drive to be further divided. A second operating system can reside in an extended partition.

A single hard drive can be divided into a maximum of four primary partitions, but some operating systems such as DOS, allow only one primary partition visible at one time. Look at Hard Figure #21 for an illustration of how one hard drive can be divided into partitions. The sectors are in pie-shaped wedges for easy explanation and illustration. Today's hard drives do not use sectors drawn in pie-shaped wedges; they use zone bit recording which has a different number of sectors for every track. Reference Hard Figure #4 earlier in the chapter for a refresher.

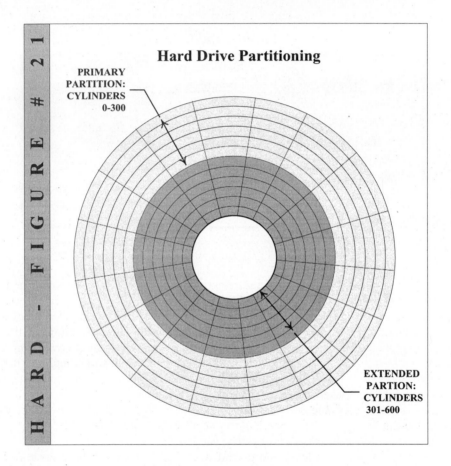

Hard Drive Partitioning

PRIMARY PARTITION: CYLINDERS 0-300

EXTENDED PARTION: CYLINDERS 301-600

HARD - FIGURE # 21

The first hard drive in a computer system must have a primary partition, but it does not require an extended partition. If the drive has an extended partition, it can be further sub-divided into **logical drives** that appear as separate hard drives to the computer system. Logical drives created in the extended partition are assigned drive letters such as D: and E:, etc. The only limit for logical drives is the number of drive letters. An extended partition can have a maximum of 23 logical drives with the drive letters D: through Z:. Hard Figure #22 shows an illustration of a hard drive divided into a primary partition and an extended partition further sub-divided into two logical drives.

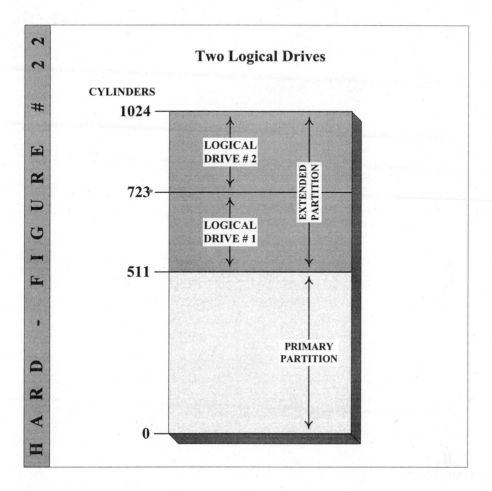

If two hard drives are installed in one computer system, the first hard drive *must* have a primary partition. The second hard drive is not required to have a primary partition and may simply have a single extended partition. If the second hard drive does have a primary partition, it can have extended partition.

When a partition is deleted, all information in the partition is lost. A partition can be re-sized by deleting the partition and re-creating it, but all information in the original partition is lost using the DOS FDISK program. The logical drives in an extended partition can be deleted and all information is lost. The other logical drives within the extended partition retain their information.

When a hard drive is first installed and partitioned, the outermost track on the platter (cylinder 0, head 0, physical sector 1) is reserved for the partition table. The **partition table** holds information about the types of partitions created and in what cylinders these partitions reside. The partition table is part of the **Master Boot Record**, commonly known as the **MBR**, which contains a program that reads the partition table, looks for the primary partition marked as active, and goes to that partition to boot the system.

HOW DOS ASSIGNS DRIVE LETTERS

DOS, or any operating system, assigns drive letters during the partitioning step. The order in which the partitions are assigned drive letters depends on three factors: (1) the number of hard drives, (2) the type of partitions on the hard drives (primary or extended), and (3) the operating system. Microsoft's MS-DOS assigns drive letters in a hierarchical fashion based on what drives (floppy, hard, or other drives), how many drives, and the order the system detects the drives. The following outline shows the order in which Microsoft's MS-DOS assigns drive letters; other DOS manufacturers or other operating systems may assign the drive letters in a different order.

1. The first floppy drive detected is assigned drive letter A:.
2. If a second floppy drive is detected, it is assigned drive letter B:. If a second floppy drive is not found, a logical drive B: is created and assigned to the first floppy drive (in addition to the drive letter A:).
3. The first hard drive primary partition detected receives drive letter C:. DOS supports up to eight different hard drives. DOS & older Windows 95 supports a maximum partition size of 2.1GB. The newer Windows 95 (Service Release 2) supports a maximum partition size of 2TB.
4. Any other primary partitions found, beginning with the second hard drive, receive the next drive letters.
5. Logical drives within any extended partitions, beginning with the first physical hard drive, are assigned the next drive letters.
6. After all logical drives are assigned drive letters, drive letters are assigned to drives such as RAM Drives or CD-ROM drives that use software drivers loaded through the CONFIG.SYS file. The order in which the drive letters are assigned depends on the order the drivers load in the CONFIG.SYS file. One exception is RAM drives are assigned drive letters before CD-ROMs no matter what order the drives load.

Example 1: A single hard drive is partitioned into one primary partition. With this scenario, DOS assigns the drive letter C: to the primary partition and this partition must be marked as active if the drive boots the system.

Example 2: A single hard drive is partitioned into one primary and one extended partition. Two logical drives are allocated in the extended partition. DOS assigns the drive letter C: to the primary partition, drive letter D: to the first logical drive in the extended partition, and drive E: to the second logical drive in the extended partition.

Example 3: Two hard drives are in the same system. Drive 1 is partitioned into one primary and one extended partition. The extended partition has one logical drive that occupies the entire partition. Physical Drive 2 also has one primary partition and one extended partition that has one logical drive. The operating system assigns drive C: to the primary partition of Hard Drive 1, drive D: to Hard Drive 2's primary partition, drive E: to Hard Drive 1's logical drive in the extended partition, and drive F: is assigned to Hard Drive 2's logical drive in the extended partition. Hard Figure #23 displays the drive letter assignments for the two hard drives in this scenario.

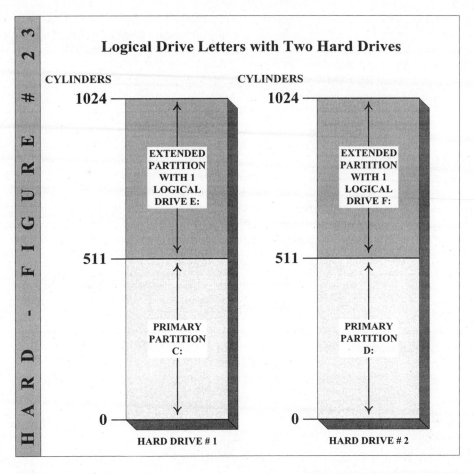

Logical Drive Letters with Two Hard Drives

HARD - FIGURE # 23

CYLINDERS

1024 —

EXTENDED
PARTITION
WITH 1
LOGICAL
DRIVE E:

511 —

PRIMARY
PARTITION
C:

0 —

HARD DRIVE # 1

CYLINDERS

1024 —

EXTENDED
PARTITION
WITH 1
LOGICAL
DRIVE F:

511 —

PRIMARY
PARTITION
D:

0 —

HARD DRIVE # 2

Partitioning can be a little confusing, but the best way to learn about partitioning is to perform the procedure. The partitioning exercises later in the chapter provide practice to reinforce the partitioning concepts and steps.

Two new products that partition the hard drive and allow re-partitioning *without any data loss* are Quarterdeck's Partition-IT and PowerQuest Corporation's Partition Magic. Both products allow the re-sizing of a hard disk without loss of data, creation of new partitions, deletion of partitions, as well as hiding partitions.

Quarterdeck's Partition-It program scans the existing partitions on the hard drive and determines the optimum cluster size depending on the type of files found. When a new partition is created with the software, the Move-It wizard allows movement of data between the partitions. The applications are automatically re-configured for the new drive letters assigned to the partition. Partition-It supports multiple operating system configurations and requires a 386DX or higher microprocessor, Windows 95 or Windows 3.1 with DOS 5 or higher, 4MB of RAM for a Windows 3.1 computer, 8MB of RAM for a Windows 95-based computer, 6MB of hard disk space, and VGA or higher monitor.

Partition Magic by PowerQuest Corporation allows partitions to be created, formatted, shrunk, expanded, or moved. Partition Magic includes IBM's Boot Manager program. This is a great utility when multiple operating systems are loaded in separate partitions. Version 3.0 supports DOS, Windows 3.1, Windows 95, Windows NT, and OS/2. Partition Magic requires a 80386SX microprocessor or greater, at least 8MB of RAM for the DOS environment, and at least 16MB of RAM for Windows 95 and NT workstation environment.

HIGH-LEVEL FORMAT

The last step in preparing a hard drive for use is high-level formatting. A **high-level format** must be performed on all primary partitions and logical drives located within extended partitions before data can be written to the hard drive. The high level format process sets up the **file system** which is how the operating system organizes and manages files. The file systems used by various operating systems list in Hard Table #8.

	File Systems	
	Operating System	**File System**
	DOS	FAT (File Allocation Table)
	OS/2	HPFS (High Performance File System)
HARD - TABLE # 8	Windows 95	VFAT (Virtual File Allocation Table) FAT32
	Windows NT Workstation	NTFS (Windows NT File System)

FAT32 is Windows 95's latest version that only comes in the Service Release 2 patch. FAT32 supports hard drive sizes up to 2TB (Terabytes). Under Windows 95's FAT32 system, partitions up to 260MB use 512 byte clusters, partition sizes from 260MB to 8GB use 4KB clusters, partition sizes of 8GB to 16GB use 8KB clusters, and partitions of 16GB to 32GB use 16KB clusters. Prior to Windows 95's Service Release 2, Windows 95's VFAT created cluster sizes proportional to the old FAT system. Hard Table #9 shows the cluster sizes used in the FAT32 file system.

HARD - TABLE # 9	Windows 95's FAT32 Cluster Size	
	Partition Size	**Cluster Size**
	0 - 260MB	512 byte
	260MB - 8GB	4 Kilobyte
	8GB - 16GB	8 Kilobyte
	16GB - 32GB	16 Kilobyte

Included with Windows 95's Service Release 2 are new FDISK, FORMAT, SCANDISK, and DEFRAG commands that can handle the FAT32 32-bit addressing. FAT32 is incompatible with some existing DOS drivers, DOS games, and DOS disk compression and defragmentation utilities. Neither Windows 3.x nor Windows NT can read the Windows 95 FAT32 hard disk volumes.

Windows NT's file system, NTFS allows support for multiple data streams and support for every character in the world. NTFS also automatically remaps bad clusters to other sections of the hard drive without any additional time or utility.

In DOS, the high-level format creates two file allocation tables (FATs) (one primary and one secondary), the root directory, and it re-numbers the sectors. The FAT keeps track of the hard disk's file locations. It is similar to a table of contents in a book as it lists where the files are located in the partition. FAT DOS partitions are recognized by DOS, Windows 95, Windows NT, and OS/2 operating systems and are limited to 2.1GB.

High-level formatting is performed using the DOS FORMAT command. A special switch, the /S switch, when used with the DOS FORMAT command, makes the partition bootable. Three files are required to make the hard disk bootable: two hidden files and COMMAND.COM. The FORMAT C: /S command copies these three files to the hard disk. This command should always be used to make the primary partition bootable.

The area of the disk containing the system files is the **DOS Boot Record** or the **DBR** and is located on the hard drive's cylinder 0 head 1 sector 1. The DOS Boot Record contains the two hidden files, IBMBIO.COM and IBMDOS.COM for IBM's PC-DOS and IO.SYS and MSDOS.SYS for Microsoft's MS-DOS, as well as the COMMAND.COM file. The FORMAT command does NOT erase all data from the hard drive, it only removes the primary FAT. If a backup of the original FAT can be restored to the hard drive or an unformat utility is performed on a logical drive that has accidentally been high-level formatted, no data is lost.

The exercises at the end of the chapter explain how to partition and high-level format a hard drive. Also, there is an exercise for using a special cable to connect two computers and transfer files between them.

LOGICALLY TROUBLESHOOTING NEWLY INSTALLED DRIVES

Most problems with new drive installation stem from improper configuration of the drive select jumpers, SCSI ID jumpers, termination, cabling or drive type configuration. The following steps assist with checking possible problems.

1.   Check the drive select or SCSI ID jumper setting(s).
2.   Check termination (if needed).
3.   Check cabling. Pin 1 of the cable should be attached to pin 1 of the adapter connector.
4.   Check drive type setting in CMOS. Refer to the documentation or contact the manufacturer of the drive for the correct setting.
5.   If the drive is a new ST506 or ESDI drive, has the drive been low-level formatted?
6.   Has the drive been partitioned?
7.   Has the drive been high-level formatted?
8.   Were the boot files copied over?
9.   Verify the mounting screw to hold the drive in the case is not too tight. Loosen the screw and power up the computer.
10. If during partitioning, the "No fixed disks present" error appears, check the hard drive cabling, power connection, configuration jumpers (drive select, master/slave, SCSI ID), termination, and CMOS configuration.
11. If the hard drive does not format to full capacity: (1) the drive parameters may be set incorrectly in SETUP, (2) the BIOS does not support large hard drives, or (3) translation is not set up for the hard drive in the SETUP program. See the section on BIOS limitations. Confirm the drive's parameters reported by FDISK with the drive's actual parameters and capacity.
12. If the error messages "No ROM Basic — System Halted" or "Disk Boot failure" appear, check if the primary partition is marked active.
13. If the error message "Non-System disk" appears, the system files are missing from the primary partition. Boot from a bootable disk and type **SYS C:**.
14. If on initial boot, the computer locks up or shows a much smaller drive capacity. Let the system try to boot for at least two minutes. Then, turn the system off, check the cable to the hard drive and to the adapter or motherboard for correct pin 1 orientation and check the configuration jumpers. Try to enter CMOS SETUP and set the drive type to auto configuration. If the system still does not respond, the computer's BIOS may not support the large hard drive.
15. If on initial boot after setting up a hard drive in CMOS SETUP, you see the message "HDD Controller Failure, Press F1 to continue". This error message occurs if the system is not partitioned or high-level formatted. Press the **F1** key and boot from a floppy disk, then partition and high-level format the hard drive. If the message still continues, check the cabling and jumper configuration(s) on the hard drive.
16. During power-on, the hard drive does not spin up or the hard drive spins down after a few seconds. Check the power connector. Check pin 1 orientation on the cable. Check the drive type in CMOS SETUP. Replace the drive.
17. Some SETUP programs try to be helpful by using drive letters to identify multiple hard drives, but inadvertently assigns the drive letters to the wrong hard drives. Do not trust the SETUP program for identifying hard drives. Instead, use the FDISK program for accurate drive lettering.
18. If the drive uses an adapter, check that the adapter seats properly in the expansion slot.
19. Run a virus checker on the system from a bootable floppy.

20. Try a warm boot (CTRL+ALT+DEL). If the drive is recognized after the warm boot, the SETUP program may be running too fast for the drive to initialize. One solution is to slow down the computer. If the computer has a turbo switch, press it to slow the computer's processor. Some computers require keystrokes to change the turbo setting. Refer to the computer or motherboard documentation for the exact procedure. Once the computer powers up properly, the system can be returned to the faster speed.

21. If the hard drive attaches to an adapter, check the IRQ, I/O address, and ROM address for conflicts with other installed adapters.

If the new hard drive is a new SCSI drive, the following are some things to check:

1. If the "Drive Not Ready" error message appears on the screen, verify the hard drive has the spin-up on power-up option enabled (usually through a jumper setting).

2. When installing a new SCSI adapter and a SCSI (non-hard drive) peripheral and an error message appears such as "No boot drives found", the BIOS on the SCSI adapter should be disabled (usually through a jumper setting).

3. An IDE hard drive and a SCSI hard drive are in the same system, but the computer does not boot off the SCSI hard drive. This is because a bootable IDE or ESDI hard drive always takes precedence over the SCSI drive. The SCSI drive cannot be the boot device when an IDE or ESDI drive is in the same system.

4. When the SCSI ASPIDISK.SYS driver loads, the error message, "Too many block devices", appears. To fix this problem, change the LAST DRIVE= statement in the CONFIG.SYS file to a higher drive letter.

5. The system hangs on boot-up after a SCSI adapter and hard drive are installed. Check for an interrupt, ROM address, I/O address, or DMA conflict. If all appears okay with each setting, disconnect the SCSI hard drive (and any other SCSI devices connected to the adapter) from the SCSI adapter. Power on the system. If the system boots properly, check for a termination problem, SCSI ID conflict, or improper cabling.

6. Verify with the drive or the SCSI host adapter manufacturer that the two devices are compatible. Not all SCSI devices work with the various SCSI adapters.

Hard drive troubleshooting can best be handled if the technician understands the boot process. With DOS, the boot procedure only works if the hard drive hardware (controller, cables, and drive) are functional and configured properly. The steps are as follows:

1. BIOS performs POST. If the computer has a Plug and Play BIOS, the Plug and Play devices are located, tested, and configured.

2. The partition table is read.

3. The boot record is read.

4. The hidden files load.

5. Depending on the opearating system, IBMBIO.COM or IO.SYS executes. The message, "Starting MS-DOS" or "Starting PC DOS" appears. IBMBIO.COM or IO.SYS reads the CONFIG.SYS file (if IBMBIO.COM or IO.SYS finds this file).

6. IBMDOS.COM or MSDOS.SYS executes.

7. COMMAND.COM loads.

8. COMMAND.COM executes the AUTOEXEC.BAT file (if COMMAND.COM finds this file).

For Windows 95, the boot procedure is a little different. The steps for Windows 95 booting are as follows:

1. BIOS performs POST. If the computer has a Plug and Play BIOS, the Plug and Play devices are located, tested, and configured.
2. The partition table is read.
3. The boot record is read.
4. IO.SYS executes.
5. Windows 95 checks the MSDOS.SYS file for boot configuration parameters.
6. The message, "Starting Windows 95", appears.
7. The SYSTEM.DAT file loads.
8. If a CONFIG.SYS file exists, the CONFIG.SYS file processes the commands.
9. If an AUTOEXEC.BAT file exists, its commands execute.
10. The WIN.COM file executes.
11. The VMM32.VxD and any other virtual device drivers referenced in the registry or the SYSTEM.INI files load.
12. The core files (Kernel, USER, and GDI) files load. If any network support is installed, it loads.
13. Any applications located in the part of the registry labeled Hkey_Local_Machine\Software\ Microsoft\Windows\CurrentVersion\RunOnce will load.

By knowing the boot process, a technician has a much better shot at locating the source of trouble. Troubleshooting begins in the section where problems start occurring.

 LOGICALLY TROUBLESHOOTING PREVIOUSLY INSTALLED DRIVES

The following are generic guidelines for hard drives that did work and are now having problems.

1. Run a virus checking program after booting from a virus-free boot disk. Many viruses are specifically designed to attack the hard drive.
2. Has someone recently added any new software or hardware? If so, be sure a device driver was not inserted into the CONFIG.SYS file that might conflict with the hard drive. Verify that there are no interrupt, I/O address, or ROM address conflicts if a new adapter was recently installed.
3. Has there been a recent cleaning of the computer or has someone recently removed the top from the computer? If so, check all cables and verify they correctly connect pin 1 to pin 1 of the adapter or motherboard. Push down firmly on all DIP chips on the hard drive adapter. Check the power connection to the hard drive.
4. Can you boot from a bootable floppy disk and see the hard drive when you type **C:** and press **ENTER**? If so, type **A:** (press **ENTER**). Make sure the floppy drive has FDISK on it. Type **FDISK** (press **ENTER**). Press 4 for Display Partition Information. Does the partition look correct for this drive? Is there a partition marked as active? If not, return to the main partition menu and make the primary partition active. If the partition information looks unusual (not the way the drive was originally set up), escape from the FDISK program back to the A: prompt. Run a virus checking program or a partition table repair utility. If you have DOS 6 or higher, type **FDISK /MBR** to fix the partition table. If you do not have DOS 6, use a hard drive utility

such as Norton Disk Doctor or PC Tools to repair the partition information. Before running FDISK /MBR, backup the partition table using a special utility or the **MIRROR /PARTN**. This command places the partition table in a file called PARTNSAV.FIL. Copy the backup copy to a floppy. Use the UNFORMAT /PARTN command to restore the partition to the hard drive. Windows 95 users do not have UNFORMAT or MIRROR commands, so the partition table can only be backed up with third party utilities.

5. If the partition table is not the problem, but you can still boot from a floppy disk and see the hard drive, then the system files are the most likely suspect. Boot from a bootable floppy of the same DOS version as the version on the hard drive. Make sure the floppy disk has SYS.COM on the disk. At the A: prompt type **SYS C:** (press **ENTER**). You will receive a message that the system files transferred. Another solution is to run a utility that repairs the DOS Boot Record. If the DOS version is lower than DOS 5, copy the COMMAND.COM file to the hard drive. Some lower DOS versions require COMMAND.COM be the first viewable file in the root directory. Sometimes on the older DOS versions, it is necessary to copy all of the files from the root directory into a temporary directory. Delete all files from the root directory, copy COMMAND.COM from the bootable floppy, and then copy the files in the temporary directory back into the root directory.

6. Place a hand on top of the drive as you turn on the computer. Does the drive spin at all? If not, the problem is probably a "sticky" drive or a bad drive. A hard drive must spin at a certain rpm before the heads move over the surface of the hard drive. To check if the drive is sticking, remove the drive and try spinning the spindle motor by hand. Otherwise, remove the drive, hold the drive in your hand, and give a quick jerk with your wrist. Another trick that works is to remove the hard drive from the case, place the drive in a plastic bag, and put in the freezer for a couple hours. Then, remove the drive and allow the drive to warm up to room temperature. Re-install the drive into the system and try it. As a *last resort*, try bopping the hard drive lightly on the top of the drive with a heavy reference book such as a dictionary as the system powers on.

7. If the hard drive flashes quickly on boot up, the controller is trying to read the partition table in the Master Boot Record. If this information is not found, various symptoms can be shown such as the error messages, "Invalid Drive Specification, 0 drives found" or "0 drives ready". Sometimes, there are no error messages if there is a problem with the partition table. To solve this problem, run FDISK /MBR or use a hard drive utility to repair the partition table. Before running FDISK /MBR, make a backup of the partition table using a special utility or type **MIRROR /PARTN.** This command places the partition table in a file called PARTNSAV.FIL. Copy the backup copy to a floppy. Use the UNFORMAT /PARTN command to restore the partition to the hard drive. Windows 95 users do not have UNFORMAT or MIRROR commands, so the partition table can only be backed up with third party utilities.

8. Beware of hard drive software that creates a small partition for its use. These partitions require a special software driver that may be missing from the CONFIG.SYS file or is a corrupt file on the hard disk and needs to be reloaded.

9. Do you receive a message such as "Disk Boot Failure", "Non-System Disk", or "Disk Error"? These errors may indicate a DOS Boot Record (DBR) problem. The solution is to boot from a bootable floppy and transfer the hidden files with the SYS command (SYS C:) or to use a hard disk utility such as Mace Utilities, Norton Utilities, or PC Tools to repair the DOS Boot Record. Also, verify the primary partition is marked as active.

10.   Do you receive the message, "Bad or Missing Command Interpreter"? If so, boot from a bootable floppy disk that is the *same* DOS version as the version on the hard drive. Copy COMMAND.COM to the hard drive.

11.   Do you receive a message such as "File Allocation Table bad, drive C:"? If so, the FAT is most likely damaged. Type **R** for Retry when the "Abort or Retry?" message appears on the screen. Use a FAT repairer such as PC Tools or Norton Utilities.

12.   If the error message "Error Reading Drive C:" appears, boot the computer from a virus-free bootable disk. Run a virus scanning program on the hard drive. Also, run the DOS SCANDISK and DEFRAG programs. Another thing to try is re-creating the master boot record. Boot off a bootable floppy that contains the FDISK command. Type **FDISK /MBR** to repair the boot record. Before running FDISK /MBR, make a backup of the partition table using a special utility or type **MIRROR /PARTN**. This command places the partition table in a file called PARTNSAV.FIL. Copy the backup copy to a floppy. Use the UNFORMAT /PARTN command to restore the partition to the hard drive. Windows 95 users do not have UNFORMAT or MIRROR commands, so the partition table can only be backed up with third party utilities.

13.   Does Windows 95 show more hard drives than it should? If so, the drive configurations or partitions have been changed more than once. One solution is to disable any changes, create a new Hardware Profile, shut the computer down, restore the changes and reboot under the new hardware profile. Another solution, which is permanent, but riskier, is to use REGEDIT and edit the Registry. Be sure to make a backup of the Registry before trying this. Go to the section HKEY_LOCAL_MACHINE\SystemCurrentControlSet\Services\Class\hdc. Delete all the keys beneath it, but do not delete the hdc key.

 ## ST506 SPECIFIC ERRORS

1.   If an error Code 80 appears during the low-level format routine, the drive select jumpers are set wrong.

2.   If an error Code 20 or 40 appears during the low-level format routine, check the cable connections. Verify that the 34-pin hard drive cable is not a floppy control cable.

3.   If on an 8088 (PC or XT) computer, the hard drive light is always on, check the cables.

4.   A 1790 post error generally indicates an unformatted hard drive.

ST506 hard drives normally give 17XX POST error codes. Refer to the Logical Troubleshooting chapter for the specifics on these error codes.

 ## ESDI SPECIFIC ERRORS

ESDI hard drives normally give 104XX POST error codes. Refer to the Logical Troubleshooting chapter for the specifics on these error codes.

IDE/EIDE SPECIFIC ERRORS

1. Has an IDE hard drive recently been installed and now the floppy drive does not work so the hard drive cannot be configured? Verify that the IDE drive is not connected to the floppy connector on the adapter or motherboard. Make sure that the IDE cable pin 1 connects to the drive pin 1 and the adapter or motherboard pin 1.
2. If the second slave IDE hard drive does not work, check if the first IDE hard drive is older. If so, check the documentation of the first IDE hard drive and be sure it can operate with a slave drive present. Some older IDE hard drives will not work in a two-drive system.
3. If you have to keep running a utility to repair the partition table on an IDE/EIDE hard drive, the CMOS SETUP is most likely set to a drive type with greater values than the drive or values the drive does not support. Backup the data and try another drive type in CMOS SETUP. The data must be reinstalled after the change.

 ## SCSI SPECIFIC ERRORS

SCSI POST error codes are quite extensive and sometimes difficult to read. Refer to the Logical Troubleshooting chapter for error code specifics, including the 210XX SCSI error codes.

1. If the BIOS on the SCSI adapter initializes, but the drive does not boot, check for an interrupt, I/O address, DMA channel conflict, or a termination problem.
2. If the SCSI adapter sees seven hard drives when only one drive is attached, check the SCSI ID on the hard drive.
3. If the computer boots up and the SCSI ROM message does not appear on a system where the SCSI adapter has the BIOS enabled, check the adapter for a memory address conflict between the adapter's ROM chip and other ROM chips in the system.
4. When the system is booting the, "No SCSI Device Found" error message appears. Check the SCSI adapter for a ROM address conflict. Set the hard drive type to None, 0, or Not Installed in the CMOS SETUP. Check the SCSI cables, SCSI IDs, and termination. Check the power connection to the SCSI device. Check the SCSI hard drive documentation to see if the parity jumper on the hard drive needs to be enabled or disabled.

 ## AUTOEXEC.BAT AND CONFIG.SYS ERRORS

Some people are frequently baffled by errors that occur during the boot process and often call technicians with the symptom that their hard drive is bad. The best way to be sure that the problem is not an AUTOEXEC.BAT or CONFIG.SYS problem is to step through the AUTOEXEC.BAT and CONFIG.SYS files one command or one driver at a time. DOS 6 allows this by pressing the F8 key when the message, "Starting PC DOS" or "Starting MS DOS" appears on the screen. On older versions of DOS, one must REM out problem lines individually to find conflicts. For Windows 95-based computers, press the F8 key when the message, "Starting Windows 95" appears on the screen. From the menu that appears, select the option for step-by-step confirmation.

WINDOWS 3.X HARD DRIVE ISSUES

Microsoft Windows 3.x has a feature called 32-bit disk access which has nothing to do with 32-bit data transfers! The **32-bit disk access** feature allows Windows to take over the ROM BIOS function of controlling the hardware and allows DOS sessions to use virtual memory. Most hard drives installed in computers today will not work with Windows 3.x's 32-bit disk access, but some hard drive manufacturers have drivers on their web site that allow Window's 32-bit access. Look in the Internet index in the appendix for the hard drive manufacturer's Internet addresses.

 ## PREVENTIVE MAINTENANCE FOR HARD DRIVES

Keeping the computer system in a clean environment as well as in a cool operating environment extends the life of a hard drive. Performing preventive maintenance on the entire computer is good for all components found inside the computer, including the hard drive subsystem.

A DOS program called CHKDSK locates clusters disassociated from data files. These disk clusters occupy disk space. When CHKDSK executes and reports there are **lost clusters**, this means the FAT cannot determine to which file or directory these clusters belong. By typing **CHKDSK /F**, lost clusters are saved and given filenames in the root directory, beginning with FILE0000.CHK. These .CHK files can sometimes, but not very often, be recovered. A better program to detect and repair lost clusters is the **SCANDISK** program included with DOS 6 and Windows 95. The exercises at the end of this chapter demonstrate the procedures for running the CHKDSK and the SCANDISK programs.

HARD DRIVE FRAGMENTATION

Over time, the files on the hard drive spread out over the surface of the drive. When the file is in clusters not adjacent to one another, the file is fragmented. **Fragmentation** occurs when files are updated over a period of time and saved at different locations. Fragmentation slows down the hard drive due to (1) the FAT keeps track of the location of all the file's clusters and (2) the hard drive read/write head assembly must move to different locations on the drive's surface for only one file. Hard Figure #24 illustrates fragmentation.

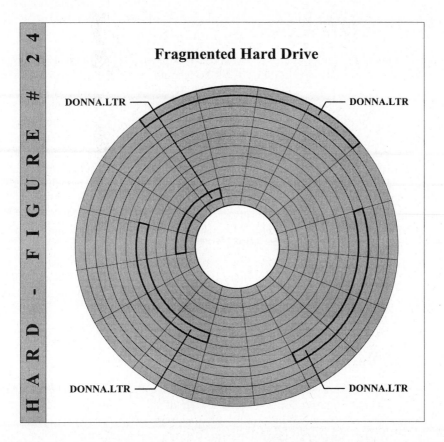

HARD - FIGURE # 24

Fragmented Hard Drive

DONNA.LTR

DONNA.LTR

DONNA.LTR

DONNA.LTR

Defragmentation is the process of placing files in contiguous sectors. Microsoft and IBM's DOS now include a DEFRAG program that defragments the hard drive. This program places the file clusters in adjacent sectors. Defragmenting the hard drive and placing files in adjacent sectors provides for faster hard disk access. These measures also extend the life of the hard drive because the drive's mechanical movements are reduced.

Defragment and re-order the files periodically on a hard drive. Users who delete files often and have large files that are constantly revised should run these utilities more often. A hard drive running DOS should be defragmented frequently depending on how often files are deleted and how much hard drive space is available. At a minimum, a hard drive should be defragmented once a month.

The defragmentation exercise is located at the end of this chapter.

DEFRAGMENTATION WITH WINDOWS 95

Even though fragmentation under Windows 95 is less of a problem than under DOS, Windows 95 comes with its own defragmentation program. DEFRAG should be run periodically on the hard drive operating Windows 95. The DEFRAG program runs the SCANDISK program by default before defragmentation is performed. Windows 95's DEFRAG program comes with some advanced options. One option is the defragmentation method with the Full Defragmentation option as the default. This option takes the longest to run and is the best choice. The Defragment Files Only option is faster than the full optimization method, but it does not consolidate the space on the hard drive. Files saved in the free space in the future, may be fragmented. This option should only be chosen when time is an issue. The Consolidate Free Space Only option locates the largest amount of free space possible on the hard drive. Then the smaller clusters of space join the largest found block. The result could be that the files on the hard disk become more fragmented. Do not choose this option.

The Check Drive for Errors checkbox (which is enabled by default) allows Windows 95 to run the SCANDISK program to check for and correct lost clusters. The last option is when to use the DEFRAG options that have been checked. Use the This Time Only option. Next time, use the Defaults Again option as the best option and it will run the advanced options that have been checked only once. The next time DEFRAG executes, full optimization and SCANDISK will be performed. An exercise at the end of the chapter explains how to execute DEFRAG under Windows 95.

HARD DRIVES AND WINDOWS 95

Windows 95 provides device support, including hard drive support, better than DOS and Windows. Windows 95 provides support for IDE drives, IDE drives that use LBA (Logical Block Addressing), and Ultra DMA/33 drives. Windows 95 also supports SCSI devices. 32-bit software drivers for SCSI controllers by Adaptec, Future Domain, etc. are included with Windows 95. It is compatible with ASPI & CAM SCSI software standards.

To manage these drives, Windows 95 uses a device driver known as a **layered block device driver** which works with groups of bytes (blocks) instead of one byte at a time. The Windows 95 drivers run in protected mode. Extensions to the INT13 disk controller support are also with the Windows 95 drivers. Windows 95 uses 32-bit disk and file access by default unless it detects a real-mode disk driver.

A new Windows 95 hard disk driver should be obtained from the hard drive manufacturer so 32-bit disk and file access can be utilized on the hard drive. To determine if the computer is using a 16-bit hard disk driver, right-click on the My Computer icon. Click on the Performance tab. At the bottom of the Performance status area is a white window that contains 16-bit drivers if any are used. For example, if the hard drive is using a 16-bit hard disk driver, the status window says "Drive C: using MS-DOS compatibility mode file system." Any device using a 16-bit driver forces the microprocessor to switch operating modes which in turn, slows the system.

DISK CACHING

An easy way to speed up the hard drive is to create a **disk cache**. This puts data into RAM where it can be retrieved much faster than if the data is still on the hard drive. When data is read from the hard drive, the next requested data is frequently located in the adjacent clusters. Disk caching reads more data from the hard drive than requested. The data is placed in a set-aside portion of RAM called the cache. Cache on a hard drive controller, sometimes called a data buffer, allows the read/write heads to read more than just one sector at a time. A hard drive can read up to an entire track of information and hold this data until needed without returning to the hard drive for each sector.

DISK CACHING USING DOS/WINDOWS

The BUFFERS statement in the CONFIG.SYS file is a very rudimentary caching program used in prior years to cache file transfers. The BUFFERS command provides a small amount of RAM for transferring files from one device to another, such as from the floppy drive to the hard drive or from memory to the floppy drive. Instead of using the BUFFERS utility, use the SmartDrive program included with both DOS and Windows 3.x. The SmartDrive program caches floppy disks, hard drives, and CD-ROMs.

If using DOS 6 or higher, the SMARTDRV command goes into the AUTOEXEC.BAT file to activate the program. When using the SMARTDRV command, the number of buffers in the BUFFERS= statement of the CONFIG.SYS file can be reduced to a number between 4 and 10.

Two types of disk caching are read-ahead caching and write-behind caching. **Read-ahead caching** tries to guess what the next requested data will be and loads the data into RAM before the data is requested from the drive. **Write-behind caching** is when data to be saved to the disk is stored in RAM until a more appropriate time is available to put the data on the drive. A drawback to write-behind caching is the data is lost if a sudden power outage occurs when the data is in RAM without being saved to the hard disk. By default, SmartDrive uses both read-ahead and write-behind caching for hard drives; but floppy disks, CDs, and drives connected via the Interlink program use only read-ahead caching. These defaults can be changed by using the switches available with SmartDrive.

DISK CACHE USING WINDOWS 95

Windows 95 uses a disk caching program called VCACHE that also uses read-ahead and write-behind caching by default for hard drives. The Windows 95 **VCACHE** program caches the hard drive and a separate cache is used for CD-ROMs. Though, instead of being a set size as in DOS and Windows, Windows 95's disk cache is dynamic. The cache grows or shrinks according to the needs of the system. The VCACHE program works with fragmented sectors on the hard drive as well as sectors that are continuous. As with any hard drive or any operating system, defragmented hard drives work faster and more efficiently.

Any settings for the SHARE or SmartDrive programs must be removed from the AUTOEXEC.BAT file. Any entries for SmartDrive that are in the CONFIG.SYS file also must be removed. Windows 95 no longer uses these programs to handle the caching for the disk drive. If a lot of disk activity is going on, the cache will shrink automatically for optimum performance. However, if the amount of disk activity is constant to the point where the system's performance is extremely slow, check if the hard disk is using a driver made for the DOS/Windows environment. If so, contact the hard drive manufacturer to obtain a Windows 95 driver.

NEW DEVELOPMENTS

A development that may eventually put hard drives out of the market is in flash memory. The SanDisk Corporation has integrated IDE hard drive technology with flash memory technology. This company created an IDE disk drive on a single chip. Currently the chip is available in only two sizes, 2MB and 4MB. The memory chips can be linked together in capacities up to 100 Megabytes. The chip performs error correction and moves (reallocates) data around bad sectors.

An area for technicians to keep an eye on is **Magneto-resistive** hard drive heads or **MR** drive heads. Hard drive manufacturers are placing more and more information on the same amount of space, using the same technology. In hard drives, the way the information gets to the drive is based on an inductive voltage produced when the hard disk platter moves past the read/write head. How much information can be stored is measured in megabits per square inch or $Mbits/in^2$. Today's hard drives store information in the 600-700 $Mbits/in^2$. Advances in the way the read/write heads are produced and designed allow the computer industry to keep up with the demands for storage capacity. However, some analysts predict that the traditional, inductive read/write head is on its way out. In its place will be the technology based on magneto-resistive (MR) read/write heads. The read and write functions are separated into two separate heads, one for reading and one for writing. Seagate Technology has worked with this technology for several years and has drives on the market using the MR read/write heads. The current MR read/write heads can sustain areal densities up to 3 $Gbits/in^2$ and increase up to 10 $Gbits/in^2$ by the year 2000.

The rest of the chapter is devoted to questions and exercises to help with all of the hard drive concepts. Good luck on them.

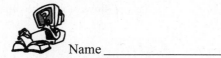

Name _____

Hard Drive Review Questions

1. What is the difference between a floppy drive and a hard drive?

2. How many surfaces are on a hard drive platter?

3. How many read/write heads are used with each hard drive platter (normally)?

4. What is the difference between a track and a cylinder?

Use Hard Exercise Figure #1 for Questions 5-9:

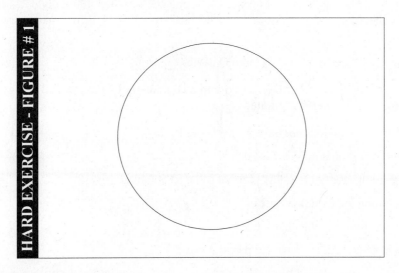

5. Draw and label Track 0.

6. Draw and label a Track 90.

7. Draw and label a Track 600.

8. Draw at least 9 sectors.

9. Shade in Track 90, Sector 3.

10. What is interleaving?

11. What interleave ratio is most common with today's hard drives?

12. List the 4 types of hard drives.

13.   Which hard drive type is the slowest and the oldest?

14.   What is encoding?

15.   Which encoding method is used with today's hard drives?

16.   Which hard drive type has the ability to daisy-chain multiple devices using the same controller?

17.   List three things to consider when adding a SCSI hard drive.

18.   List at least two reasons why you should be careful in choosing the SCSI ID for a SCSI device.

19.   List one reason why installing or removing terminators on a SCSI hard drive is important.

20.   What is the significance, if any, of an external SCSI device with only one connector on the back of the device?
      A.   No significance.
      B.   The device could be the only external device used.
      C.   The device should be taken out of the external casing and installed internally.
      D.   The device should be the last device on the chain because it is internally terminated (permanently).

21.   Describe the purpose of the SCSI A, B, P, and Q cables.

22.   What is a *hard drive type* that must be entered into a computer's CMOS SETUP program and why is it important this number is accurate?

23.   What do you do if a system does *not* have a translating BIOS?

24.   What does a low-level format do to a hard drive?

25.   What DOS command is used to low-level format some ST506 hard drives?

26.   What does partitioning the hard drive mean?

27.   Why should you partition a 1.2GB hard drive?

28.   How many logical drives can an extended partition have?

29.   List an alternative to using the DOS or Windows 95 FDISK program for partitioning the hard drive.

30.   What DOS command is used to high-level format a hard drive?

31.   What DOS command is used to partition a hard drive?

32.   If you had a friend who just bought a new computer and wanted the data from the old computer transferred to the new one, how would you recommend to go about doing this?

33.   List three things to check if a hard drive has recently been installed and it does not work properly.

34.   When powering on a computer, you notice the hard drive does not spin at all. What will you check?

35.   Upon powering up a computer system, you receive a "Drive Not Ready" error message. What are you going to do?

36.   A system with an IDE hard drive and a SCSI hard drive will not boot from the SCSI hard drive. What are you going to do?

37.   List the boot process if DOS is loaded on a bootable hard drive.

38.   List the boot process if Windows 95 is loaded on a bootable hard drive.

39.   Lists three things to check when a working hard drive quits.

40.   Upon powering up a computer system, you receive a "Bad or Missing Command Interpreter" error message. What are you going to do?

41.   What are some advances in computer technology you have read about recently?

Use Hard Exercise Figure #2 for Questions 42-45:

HARD EXERCISE - FIGURE #2

Advertisement for a computer:

Intel Pentium Pro 200MHz
64MB EDO memory
6.0GB EIDE hard drive
Fast 24x EIDE CD-ROM
Diamond Stealth 3D Graphic with 4MB
17" monitor
56K modem
MS mouse
Creative Lab SB64 sound card

42.   Which hard drive type does the above system use?

43.   If you were to buy a second hard drive just like the one listed in Figure #2, which of the three steps required to set up a hard drive would most likely be done by the manufacturer?

44.   If you were to buy a second hard drive just like the one shown in Figure #2, what two processes must you perform to set up the hard drive?

45.   If a customer has the system listed in Figure #2 and asks you as the technician whether or not they can add another hard drive, what are several things to check before answering the customer.

Name _____

Hard Drive Fill-in-the-Blank

1. The hard drive system consists of a _____, an _____ which handles telling the hard drive what to do (even though this function may be built into the motherboard), and _____ that connect the first two parts together.

2. The _____ is a part of the hard drive that holds the read/write heads.

3. One hard disk metal plate is called a _____.

4. The _____ are the part of the hard drive that actually transmit or receive the 1s and 0s to or from the hard drive.

5. One concentric circle on one surface of a hard drive platter is known as a _____.

6. One particular track on each and every platter collectively is known as a _____.

7. A _____ is the smallest division on a hard drive surface. Tracks are divided into these.

8. _____ allows more sectors on the drive by placing more sectors on the outer tracks than on the inner tracks.

9. An _____ hard drive is common in today's computers and cheaper than SCSI hard drives.

10. The ATA standard is associated with the _____ interface.

11. A _____ hard drive is used in network servers and whenever expandability (adding devices that do not necessarily have to be hard drives) is an issue.

12. The three SCSI software standards are _____, _____, and _____.

13. IDE drives are set up using the _____ setting instead of drive select jumpers.

14. A number assigned to a SCSI device which determines the device's priority on the SCSI bus is the _____.

15. Sometimes, when installing a hard drive, you must go into the computer's CMOS SETUP program and enter the _____.

16. The most common way to set an IDE drive up through CMOS SETUP is to use the _____ feature.

17. The _____ interface is named after the BIOS interrupt that handles communication with the hard drive and causes drives to have a 504MB limitation.

18.   A BIOS chip that supports hard drives larger than 504MB is known as a _____ BIOS.

19.   The step in preparing the hard drive which assigns drive letters to the hard drive is known as _____.

20.   _____ is the DOS or Windows 95 command used to partition the hard drive.

21.   A _____ is the minimum amount of space a file occupies; the number of sectors for each one is determined by the size of the partition.

22.   Only one _____ exists which is the first partition created on a hard drive.

23.   When partitioning a hard drive there can be only one primary partition and one _____, but within this section, multiple logical drives can be created.

24.   An extended partition holds _____ drives.

25.   The _____ is where the hard drive's partition information is kept.

26.   The very first sector on a hard drive is called the _____.

27.   The first detected hard drive is normally assigned the drive letter _____.

28.   The _____ process sets up the file system.

29.   The _____ is like the table of contents for a hard drive using DOS; at least two are on every hard drive.

30.   A hard drive that contains system files and is used to load software when the computer is turned on is known as a _____ hard drive.

31.   The _____ are COMMAND.COM, MSDOS.SYS, and IO.SYS on Microsoft DOS machines and COMMAND.COM, IBMBIO.COM, and IBMDOS.COM on PC DOS machines.

32.   The _____ contains the system files.

33.   To fix a partition table using DOS 6 or higher, type _____.

34.   To transfer system files from a bootable floppy to the hard drive, type _____ from the A:\> prompt.

35.   File _____ occurs when a file is located on non-consecutive clusters.

36.   The _____ program detects and repairs lost clusters.

37.   The DOS _____ program places files in contiguous (adjacent) sectors.

38.   A disk _____ speeds up hard drive data access.

39.   Windows 95's _____ program caches hard drives, but not CD-ROMs.

40.   _____ hard drive heads allow higher drive capacities.

Name _____

CONFIGURATION AND CABLING OF ST506 HARD DRIVES
PAPER EXERCISE

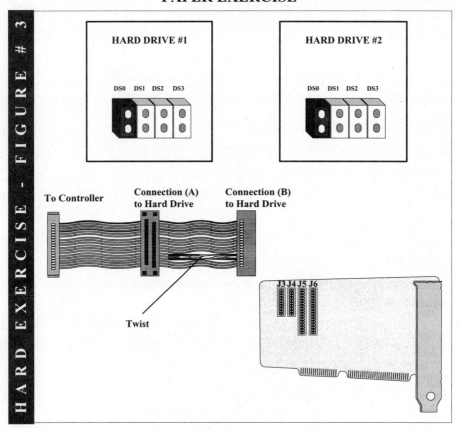

Look at Hard Exercise Figure #3 for Questions 1-9:

Question 1:   Assume the hard drives shown in Hard Exercise Figure #3 will be installed in the same computer using a twisted cable like the one shown. Hard Drive #1 is to be the C: drive. Both drives have the drive select jumper set to the first position. Which drive select (DS0, DS1, DS2, or DS3) will be chosen for Hard Drive #1?

Question 2:   Hard Drive #2 will become the D: drive. Which drive select (DS0, DS1, DS2, or DS3) will you choose for Hard Drive #2?

Question 3:   To which connector on the cable will the C: drive be connected (Connector A or Connector B)?

Question 4:   Hard Drives #1 and #2 come with a terminator installed. What will be done about the terminators?
  A.   Leave both terminators installed
  B.   Remove both terminators
  C.   Install the terminator on the drive connected to the B connection and remove the terminator on the drive connected to the A connection

Question 5:   Assuming that a controller card and cable like the ones shown in Hard Drive Exercise Figure #3 are used, which connector (J3, J4, J5, or J6) connects to the end of the cable labeled To controller?

Question 6:   What is the specific purpose of the 34-pin cable shown in Hard Drive Exercise Figure #3?

Question 7:   The ST506 hard drive normally comes with two cables: one like the one shown in Hard Exercise Figure #3 and a 20-pin cable. What is the purpose of the 20-pin cable that connects to the hard drive?

Question 8:   To which connector (J3, J4, J5, or J6) will Hard Drive #1's (the C: drive) 20-pin cable connect?

Question 9:   To which connector (J3, J4, J5, or J6) will Hard Drive #2's (the D: drive) 20-pin cable connect?

Question 10:   Which hard drive type improved on ST-506 by allowing the heads to move directly to a cylinder instead of moving one cylinder at a time?
          A.   ESDI
          B.   IDE
          C.   SCSI

Name _____

CONFIGURATION AND CABLING OF IDE HARD DRIVES
PAPER EXERCISE

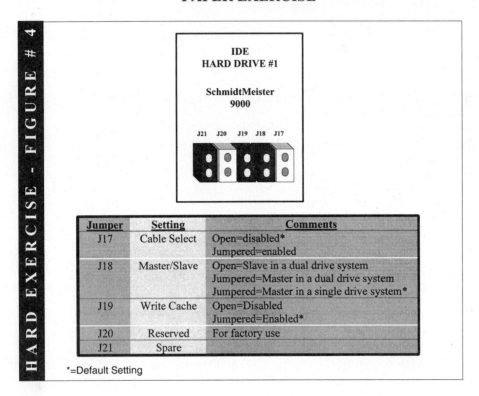

HARD EXERCISE - FIGURE # 4

IDE
HARD DRIVE #1

SchmidtMeister
9000

J21   J20   J19   J18   J17

Jumper	Setting	Comments
J17	Cable Select	Open=disabled* Jumpered=enabled
J18	Master/Slave	Open=Slave in a dual drive system Jumpered=Master in a dual drive system Jumpered=Master in a single drive system*
J19	Write Cache	Open=Disabled Jumpered=Enabled*
J20	Reserved	For factory use
J21	Spare	

*=Default Setting

See Hard Exercise Figure #4 for Question 1:

Question 1:   Using the drawing below, circle the jumpers to be enabled (set) to configure IDE Hard Drive 1 as if it is the only drive connected to an IDE port.

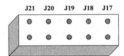

J21   J20   J19   J18   J17

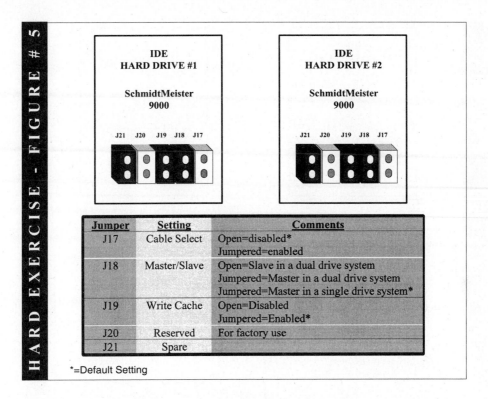

Look at Hard Exercise Figure #5 for Questions 2 and 3:

Question 2:   Using the drawing below, circle the jumpers to be enabled (set) to configure IDE Hard Drive 1 as the master drive connected to an IDE port. Keep in mind that IDE Hard Drive 2 shares the same cable with Hard Drive 1.

J21   J20   J19   J18   J17

IDE Hard Drive #1

Question 3:   Using the drawing below, circle the jumpers to be enabled (set) to configure IDE Hard Drive 2 as the slave drive. Keep in mind that IDE Hard Drive 2 shares the same cable with Hard Drive 1.

J21   J20   J19   J18   J17

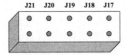

IDE Hard Drive #2

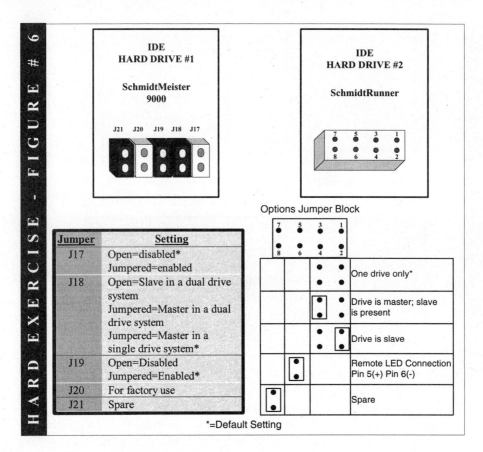

HARD EXERCISE - FIGURE # 6

IDE
HARD DRIVE #1

SchmidtMeister
9000

J21   J20   J19   J18   J17

IDE
HARD DRIVE #2

SchmidtRunner

7   5   3   1
8   6   4   2

Options Jumper Block

7   5   3   1
8   6   4   2

Jumper	Setting
J17	Open=disabled* Jumpered=enabled
J18	Open=Slave in a dual drive system Jumpered=Master in a dual drive system Jumpered=Master in a single drive system*
J19	Open=Disabled Jumpered=Enabled*
J20	For factory use
J21	Spare

One drive only*

Drive is master; slave is present

Drive is slave

Remote LED Connection Pin 5(+) Pin 6(-)

Spare

*=Default Setting

Hard Exercise Figure #6 is needed when answering Questions 4 and 5:

Question 4:   Using the drawing below, circle the jumpers to be enabled (set) to configure IDE Hard Drive 1 as the master drive connected to an IDE port. Keep in mind that IDE Hard Drive 2 shares the same cable with Hard Drive 1.

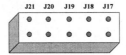

J21   J20   J19   J18   J17

IDE Hard Drive #1

Question 5:   Using the drawing below, circle the jumpers to be enabled (set) to configure IDE Hard Drive 2 as the slave drive. Keep in mind that IDE Hard Drive 2 shares the same cable with Hard Drive 1.

7   5   3   1
8   6   4   2

IDE Hard Drive #2

NOTES

Name _____

CONFIGURATION AND CABLING OF SCSI HARD DRIVES
PAPER EXERCISE

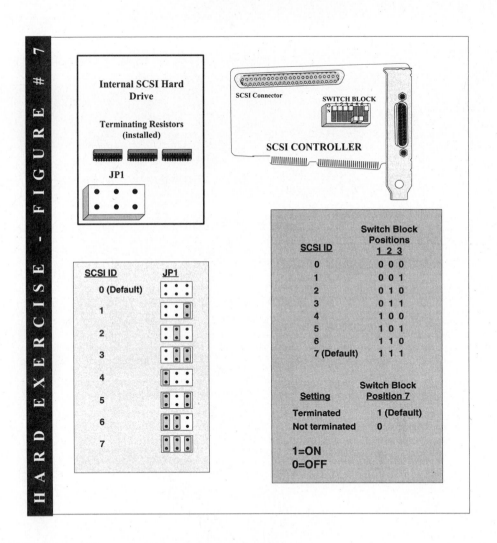

Look at Hard Exercise Figure #7 to answer Questions 1-4:

Question 1:   Hard Exercise Figure #7 shows a SCSI controller that handles internal and external SCSI devices. In this configuration, install one internal hard drive that boots the computer. To what position(s) will JP1 be set on the internal hard drive? Circle the correct jumper setting(s) for JP1.

JP1

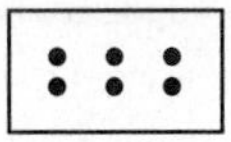

Question 2:   On the host adapter, switch block positions 1, 2, and 3 control the SCSI ID. To what position will the controller's switch block positions 1, 2, and 3 be set? Use the chart below and fill in the correct setting. Mark an X in *either* the OFF or ON column for each switch position.

SW1	OFF	ON
1		
2		
3		

Question 3:   Will the terminators be installed or removed from the internal SCSI hard drive?

Question 4:   The host adapter's switch block position 7 controls termination. To what position (ON or OFF) will switch 1 position 7 be set?

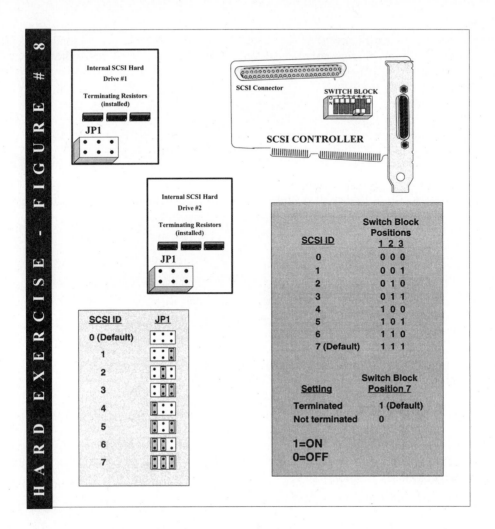

Look at Hard Exercise Figure #8 to answer Questions 5 through 10.

Question 5:   Hard Exercise Figure #8 shows the same SCSI controller used in Figure #6. In this configuration, however, two internal hard drives connect to the controller. Internal Hard Drive 1 boots the computer. What jumpers, if any, go on JP1 to configure Internal SCSI Hard Drive 1? Circle the correct jumper setting(s) for JP1 using the figure below.

JP1

Question 6:   What jumpers, if any, go on JP1 to configure SCSI Hard Drive 2? Circle the correct jumper setting(s) for JP1 using the figure below.

JP1

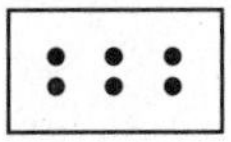

```
┌─────────────┐
│  • •  • •  • • │
└─────────────┘
```

Question 7:   On the host adapter, switch block positions 1, 2, and 3 control the SCSI ID. To what position will the controller's switch block positions 1, 2, and 3 be set? Use the chart below and fill in the correct setting. Mark an X in *either* the OFF or ON column for each switch position.

SW1	OFF	ON
1		
2		
3		

Question 8:   Will the terminators be installed or removed from internal SCSI Hard Drive 1?

Question 9:   Will the terminators be installed or removed from internal SCSI Hard Drive 2?

Question 10:   The host adapter's switch block position 7 controls termination. To what position (ON or OFF) will switch 1 position 7 be set?

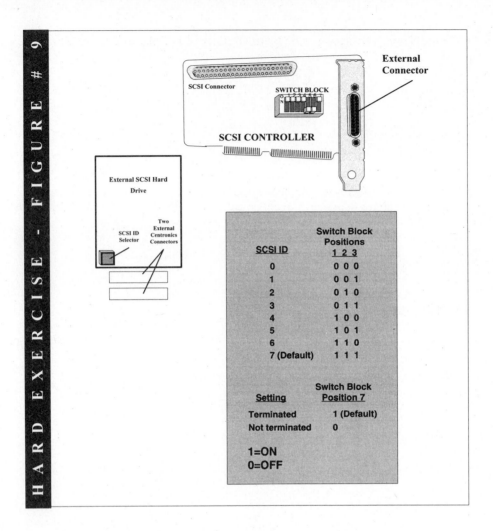

Hard Exercise Figure #9 is needed for Questions 11-14:

Question 11:   In Hard Exercise Figure #9, the same SCSI controller is used, but with one external SCSI hard drive. The external hard drive boots the computer. Switch block positions 1, 2, and 3 control the SCSI ID for the adapter. To what position will the controller's switch block positions 1, 2, and 3 be set? Use the chart below and fill in the correct setting. Mark an X in *either* the OFF or ON column for each switch position.

SW1	OFF	ON
1		
2		
3		

Question 12:   What SCSI ID will you set on the external hard drive's SCSI ID selector?

Question 13:   The host adapter's switch block position 7 controls termination. To what position (ON or OFF) will switch 1 position 7 be set?

Question 14:   Will the external SCSI Hard Drive be terminated? If so, how?

Question 15:   What is the purpose of a terminator?

Question 16:   How many devices are terminated on the SCSI chain?

Question 17:   What is the purpose of the SCSI ID?

Question 18:   T/F   The lower the SCSI ID, the higher the priority on the SCSI bus.

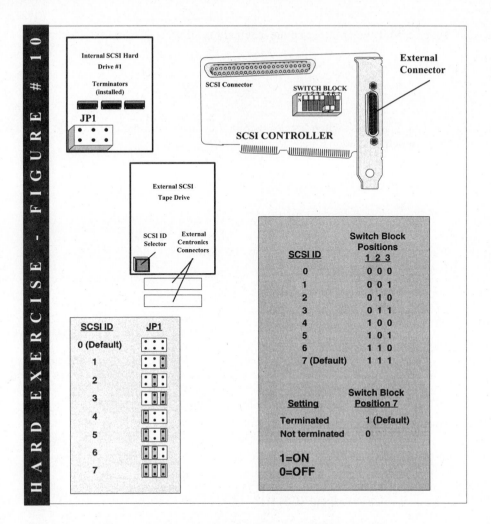

Look at Hard Exercise Figure #10 when answering Questions 19-24:

Question 19:   In Hard Exercise Figure #10, the same SCSI adapter controls an external device and an internal hard drive. The internal SCSI hard drive boots the system. Switch block positions 1, 2, and 3 control the SCSI ID for the adapter. To what position will the controller's switch block positions 1, 2, and 3 be set? Use the chart below and fill in the correct setting. Mark an X in *either* the OFF or ON column for each switch position.

SW1	OFF	ON
1		
2		
3		

Question 20:   What SCSI ID will you set on the external tape drive's SCSI ID selector?

Question 21:   To what position(s) will JP1 be set on the internal SCSI Hard Drive? Circle the correct jumper setting(s) for JP1 using the figure below.

JP1

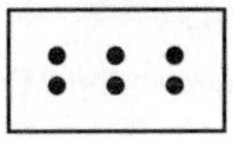

Question 22:   The host adapter's switch block position 7 controls termination. To what position (ON or OFF) will switch 1 position 7 be set?

Question 23:   Will you terminate the external SCSI Tape Drive?

Question 24:   Will the terminators be installed or removed from the internal SCSI Hard Drive?

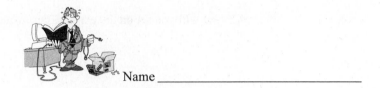

Name _____

SINGLE IDE HARD DRIVE INSTALLATION EXERCISE

Objective: To correctly install an IDE hard drive

Parts: IDE hard drive and documentation for the drive (if possible)
         IDE cable
         Tools
         Anti-static materials

Observe proper grounding procedures when installing hard drives.

Step 1:   Remove the cover from the computer. Use proper anti-static procedures.
Step 2:   Configure the hard drive for Master by referring to the documentation included with the
            hard drive or provided by the instructor. IDE hard drives are normally pre-configured to the
            Master setting.
Step 3:   Locate pin 1 on the hard drive's *connector*.

Question 1:   How was pin 1 identified on the hard drive connector?

Step 4:   Locate an available drive bay in the computer system.
Step 5:   Attach any mounting hardware needed to install the hard drive into the computer case and
            slide the hard drive into the computer case.
Step 6:   Connect the power connector to the new drive.
Step 7:   Connect the 40-pin signal cable to the hard drive verifying that the pin 1 connects to the
            hard drive connector's pin 1.
Step 8:   Locate pin 1 on the motherboard or the adapter's IDE connector.

Question 2:   How was pin 1 (in Step 8) identified?

Step 9:   Connect the other end of the 40-pin cable to the motherboard or to the adapter ensuring the cable's pin 1 connects to the adapter or motherboard's pin 1.

Step 10:   Power on the computer and go into the computer's SETUP program. Some computers will automatically go into the SETUP program when detecting a change such as the installation of a hard drive.

Step 11:   Configure the computer for the type of hard drive that is being installed. Contact the instructor if more information is needed.

Step 12:   If the hard drive is not new, the system should boot from the hard drive. Otherwise, if the drive is new, the hard drive must be partitioned and high-level formatted (which are covered later in the chapter).

Step 13:   Power off the computer and re-install the computer's cover.

Question 3:   If adding a CD-ROM to the same cable used for the hard drive, would the hard drive be left as master and the CD-ROM set to slave, or would the hard drive need to be re-configured as the slave and the CD-ROM drive set as the master device? Explain your answer.

_____ Instructor's Initials

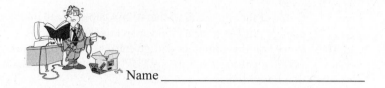

Name _____

SCSI ADAPTER AND DEVICE INSTALLATION EXERCISE

Objective: To correctly install a SCSI device

Parts: SCSI device, adapter (or motherboard with built-in SCSI), and documentation
        SCSI cable(s)
        Tools
        Anti-static materials

Observe proper grounding procedures when installing SCSI devices.

Step   1:   Remove the cover from the computer. Use proper anti-static procedures.
Step   2:   Configure the SCSI adapter's SCSI ID by referring to the documentation included with the adapter or provided by the instructor. Most SCSI adapters come pre-set to SCSI ID 7 and should be left in this position for optimum operation. Refer to the adapter's documentation for more information.
Step   3:   Install the SCSI adapter into an available slot in the computer.
Step   4:   Configure the SCSI device for the proper SCSI ID and termination by referring to the device's documentation.

Question 1:   What SCSI ID was chosen for the SCSI device?

Question 2:   Did you terminate the SCSI device? Why or why not?

Question 3:   Did you terminate the SCSI host adapter or motherboard? Why or why not?

Step   5:   Locate pin 1 on the SCSI device's connector.
Step   6:   Locate pin 1 on the SCSI adapter.

Question 4:   How is pin 1 identified on the SCSI device's connector?

Question 5:   How is pin 1 identified on the SCSI adapter?

Step   7:   If the SCSI device is internal, locate an available drive bay in the computer system.
Step   8:   If the SCSI device is internal, attach any mounting hardware needed to install the device into the computer case. Slide the device into the computer case.
Step   9:   Connect the power connector to the SCSI device.
Step 10:   Connect the SCSI cable to the device ensuring the cable's pin 1 attaches to the connector's pin 1.
Step 11:   Connect the other end of the SCSI cable to the SCSI adapter ensuring pin 1 on the cable attaches to the adapter's pin 1.
Step 12:   Power on the computer and install any SCSI software necessary for the adapter and the SCSI device.
Step 13:   If the installation process did not call for a computer reboot, warm boot the computer after the software is installed to ensure all changes take effect.
Step 14:   If a scanner, tape backup unit, etc. is being installed, the device may require additional software installation for proper operation of the SCSI device. Refer to the documentation that comes with the SCSI device for more information.

Question 6:   Does the SCSI device work? If not, refer to the chapter's section on troubleshooting.

_____ Instructor's Initials

Name _____

PARTITION THE HARD DRIVE INTO ONE PRIMARY PARTITION EXERCISE

Objective: To correctly partition a hard drive into one primary partition

Parts: A bootable DOS disk (with the same version of DOS as the hard drive) as well as the FDISK command.

Step   1:   With the bootable DOS disk (that contains the FDISK command) inserted into drive A:, power on the computer.
Step   2:   Press **ENTER** each time you are prompted for the date and time.
Step   3:   At the A:> prompt, type **FDISK** and press **ENTER**. For DOS skills, refer to Appendix A.

Question 1:   What is the purpose of the FDISK command?

Step   4:   At the menu that appears choose
            4 -Display partition information, press **ENTER**. A message appears stating that no partitions are defined. If a table appears with partition information, go to the exercise entitled Delete the Hard Drive's Partition(s) Exercise.
Step   5:   Press **ESC** to return to the FDISK Options screen.
Step   6:   At the main menu, choose
            1 -Create DOS partition, press **ENTER**.
Step   7:   At the next menu that appears choose
            1 -Create Primary DOS partition, press **ENTER**.
Step   8:   At the prompt, Do you wish to use the maximum available size for a primary DOS partition?, type **Y** (for Yes). A message appears stating that the system will restart. A prompt appears to insert a bootable DOS disk.

Question 2:   How many primary DOS partitions can be on a hard drive?

Question 3:   How many extended partitions can be on a hard drive?

Question 4:   How many logical drives can be on a hard drive?

Question 5:   List one reason why a new hard drive might need to be partitioned in today's computing environments.

Step 9:   Insert the bootable disk into Drive A: and press **ENTER** to reboot the system. Error messages may appear about drive C: at this time. Press **F** for **Fail** as many times as necessary until the A:> prompt appears. This is okay because the hard drive must be high-level formatted before information can be written on it.
Step 10:   Press **ENTER** each time you are prompted for the date and time.
Step 11:   At the A:> prompt, type **FDISK** and press ENTER.
Step 12:   From the menu, choose:
4-Display Partition size
You should see something like the example below:

Partition	MB	USAGE	
C: 1		100	100%

Show this display to the instructor.

_____Instructor's Initials

Step 13:   Press **ESC** to return to the FDISK Options screen.
Step 14:   Press **ESC** to exit FDISK.
Step 15:   A prompt appears stating to ensure that a bootable system disk is inserted into the A: drive.
Step 16:   Each partition must be high-level formatted before data can be written to the drive. Reference the High-Level Format Exercise found later in the chapter.

Name_____

PARTITION THE HARD DRIVE INTO ONE PRIMARY AND ONE EXTENDED PARTITION EXERCISE

Objective: To correctly partition a hard drive into one primary and one extended partition

Parts: A bootable DOS disk (with the same version of DOS as the hard drive) as well as the FDISK command

Step 1:   With the bootable DOS disk (that contains the FDISK command) inserted into drive A:, power on the computer.

Step 2:   Press **ENTER** each time you are prompted for the date and time.

Step 3:   At the A:> prompt, type **FDISK** and press **ENTER**. For DOS skills, refer to Appendix A.

Question 1:   What is the difference between a primary partition and an extended partition?

Step 4:   At the menu that appears choose
4 -Display partition information, press **ENTER**. A message appears stating that no partitions are defined. If a table appears with partition information, go to the exercise entitled Delete the Hard Drive's Partition(s) Exercise.

Step 5:   Press **ESC** to return to the FDISK Options screen.

Step 6:   At the menu that appears choose
1   -Create DOS partition, press **ENTER**.

Step 7:   At the next menu that appears choose
1   -Create Primary DOS Partition, press **ENTER**.

Step 8:   At the prompt, "Do you wish to use the maximum available size for a primary DOS partition?", type **N** (for No).

Step 9:   At the prompt, "Enter Partition size:", type a number that is 60 percent of your total hard drive size. For example, if the hard drive is a 30MB hard drive, then 18 is chosen. Press **ENTER** after entering the number. A message appears at the bottom of the screen indicating the Primary DOS partition was created.

Question 2:   What size (in MB) is chosen for the primary DOS partition?

Step 10: Press **ESC** to continue. You will be back at the FDISK Options screen and will receive a message at the bottom of the screen, something similar to Warning! No Partitions are set active — disk 1 is not startable unless a partition is set active.

Step 11: At the menu, choose:
2 -Set Active Partition, press **ENTER**. Enter the number of the partition you want to make active: **1**, press **ENTER**. You will receive a message that Partition 1 was made active.

Step 12: At the menu, choose:
1 -Create DOS partition, press **ENTER**.

Step 13: At the next menu, choose:
2 -Create Extended DOS partition, press ENTER.

Step 14: At the prompt, Enter Partition Size:, enter a number that is your total amount of hard drive space less the number you chose in Question 2. For example, if you have a 30MB hard drive and you entered 18 (MB) for Question 2, then you would choose 12 (MB) for this prompt (30MB-18MB=12MB). After you type your number for the extended partition, press **ENTER**. You will receive a message at the bottom of the screen indicating the extended partition was created.

Question 3: What partition size (in MegaBytes) did you choose for Step 14?

Step 15: Press **ESC** to continue. You will receive a message that states that no logical drives are defined.

Step 16: When prompted for the Logical Drive Size, enter the same number that you chose for Step 12 and press **ENTER**. You will receive a message that all available space in the extended DOS partition is assigned to the logical drives.

Step 17: Press **ESC** to continue.

Question 4: T/F All data is lost when a hard drive is re-partitioned using the DOS FDISK command.

Question 5: T/F Partitioning is a step required on all new hard drives installed into a computer system.

Question 6: T/F A logical drive is the same thing as an extended partition.

Step 18:   From the menu, choose:
           4-Display Partition size
           You should see something like the example below:

Partition	MB	USAGE
C: 1	18	60%
2	12	40%

           Show this display to the instructor.

_____   Instructor's Initials

Step 19:   When prompted, "Do you want to display logical drive info? Y/N", enter **Y** (for Yes) and press **ENTER**. You should see something like the following:

LOGICAL DRIVE	MB	USAGE
D: 1	12	100%

Question 7:   Why does the first screen that you saw in Step 16 show the second partition as 40 percent (or whatever your number is), but the logical drive of that partition shows usage as 100 percent?

Step 20:   Press **ESC** to return to the Display Partition Information screen.
Step 21:   Press **ESC** to return to the FDISK Options screen.
Step 22:   Press **ESC** to exit FDISK.
Step 23:   A prompt appears stating to ensure that a bootable system disk is inserted into the A: drive.

Question 8:   If adding a second hard drive to a computer system and the new hard drive is partitioned into just one partition, what drive letter is assigned to the logical drive in the extended partition on the first hard drive?

Step 24:   Each partition must be high-level formatted before data can be written to the drive. Reference the High-Level Format Exercise found later in the chapter.

_____   Instructor's Initials

Name _____

DELETE THE PARTITION(S) ON THE HARD DRIVE EXERCISE

Objective: To delete a hard drive partition

Parts: A bootable DOS disk (with the same version of DOS as the hard drive) as well as the FDISK command

Step   1:   With the bootable DOS disk (that contains the FDISK command) is inserted into drive A:, power on the computer.

Step   2:   Press **ENTER** each time you are prompted for the date and time.

Step   3:   At the A:> prompt, type **FDISK** and press **ENTER**. For DOS skills, refer to Appendix A.

Step   4:   At the menu that appears choose
         4   -Display partition information, press **ENTER**.

Question 1:   Does the screen displayed in Step 4 show that an *extended partition* exists?

Question 2:   If an extended partition exists on the hard drive, what logical drive letter(s) are assigned? **HINT:** If an extended partition with logical drives does exist, then a message appears on the bottom of the screen in Step 4 prompting, Do you want to display the logical drive information (Y/N)?.

Step   5:   Press **ESC** until the FDISK Options screen appears.

Step   6:   At the FDISK options menu, choose
         3   -Delete DOS Partition or Logical DOS Drive, press **ENTER**.

Step   7:   If the answer to Question #1, "Does the screen shown in Step 4 show that an extended partition exists?", is NO, move ahead to Step 18. If the answer is YES, continue to Step 8.

Step   8:   At the Delete DOS Partition or Logical DOS Drive menu, choose
         3   -Delete Logical DOS Drive (s) in the Extended DOS partition, press **ENTER**. A warning message appears at the bottom of the screen stating that all information in the logical drive will be deleted if the logical drive is deleted.

Step   9:   At the prompt, "What drive do you want to delete?", type in the drive letter of the logical drive shown on the screen. The normal choice is **D**. Press **ENTER**.

Step 10:   At the "Enter Volume Label" prompt, enter the volume label listed in the table at the top of the screen followed by **ENTER**. If there is no volume label listed, simply press **ENTER**.

Step 11:   At the "Are you sure (Y/N)?" prompt, press **Y** and press **ENTER**.

Step 12:   Repeat steps 9-11 as necessary for any remaining logical drives.

Step 13:   Press **ESC** until the **FDISK Options** menu appears again.

Step 14:   At the FDISK options menu, choose
           3 -Delete DOS Partition or Logical DOS Drive, press **ENTER**.
Step 15:   At the Delete DOS Partition or Logical DOS Drive menu, choose
           2 -Delete Extended DOS Partition, press **ENTER**. A warning message appears at the
           bottom of the screen stating that all of the information in the extended partition will be
           deleted if the extended partition is deleted.
Step 16:   At the "Do you wish to continue (Y/N)?" prompt, type **Y** and press **ENTER**. A message at
           the bottom of the screen appears stating that the Extended DOS Partition was deleted.
Step 17:   Press **ESC** to return to the FDISK Options menu.
Step 18:   At the FDISK options menu, choose
           3 -Delete DOS Partition or Logical DOS Drive, press **ENTER**.
Step 19:   At the Delete DOS Partition or Logical DOS Drive menu, choose
           1 -Delete Primary DOS Partition, press **ENTER**. A warning message appears at the
           bottom of the screen stating that all information in the primary partition will be deleted if
           the partition is deleted.
Step 20:   At the prompt, "What primary partition do you want to delete?", press the number
           corresponding to the primary partition as shown on the top of the screen. The normal
           response is 1 (and press **ENTER**).
Step 21:   At the prompt, "Are you sure (Y/N)?", press **Y** and press **ENTER**.
Step 22:   The computer must restart after deleting the partition. Follow the directions on the screen
           and remember to insert the bootable disk into drive A: when rebooting the system. In order
           to create a new partition or multiple partitions, use the exercises found earlier in the
           chapter.

_____Instructor's Initials

Name _____

HIGH-LEVEL FORMAT EXERCISE

Objective: To correctly high-level format a hard drive

Parts: A bootable DOS disk with the DOS version that you want the hard drive to boot from as well the FORMAT command on the disk.

Step   1:   With the bootable DOS disk that contains FORMAT command into drive A:, power on the computer.

Step   2:   Press **ENTER** each time you are prompted for the date and time.

Step   3:   From the A:> prompt, type **FORMAT C:/S** and press **ENTER**. For DOS skills, refer to Appendix A.

Step   4:   When asked, Proceed with format Y/N?, type **Y** (for Yes) and press **ENTER**. At the end of the FORMAT, you will be prompted to insert a system disk into the A: drive. Insert the bootable disk into the A: drive *before* pressing ENTER.

Question 1:   Why is the FORMAT command considered to be a high-level format? Exactly what is being done at this stage?

Question 2:   For what is the */S* switch used when combined with the FORMAT command?

Step   5:   After the formatting of the logical drive C: is complete, remove the bootable disk from drive A:.

Question 3:   Do you have to perform a high-level format on all logical drives? Explain.

Step   6:   Reboot the computer by pressing **CTRL+ALT+DEL**.

Question 4:   Does the computer boot to the C: drive? If not, perform the exercise again.

_____   Instructor's Initials

Optional Instructions for Formatting Other Logical Drives:

Step   7:   For each logical drive that you have created, a high-level format must be performed. Type the following command at the C:> prompt: **FORMAT D:** and press **ENTER**.

Step   8:   When asked, "Proceed with format Y/N?", type **Y** (for Yes) and press **ENTER**.

Question 5:   Why would you NOT put a /S after the command used in Step 7?

Step   9:   Perform Steps 7 and 8 for each logical drive. However, instead of typing FORMAT D:, type **FORMAT E:** or **FORMAT F:**, etc., depending on the logical drive being formatted.

_____   Instructor's Initials

If you just installed DOS version 6 onto the hard drive and you have a similar computer that you would like to copy all the files from one drive to another, go to the next exercise.

Name _____

COPYING FILES FROM ONE COMPUTER TO ANOTHER
USING A SPECIAL CABLE EXERCISE

Objective: To correctly use the Interlink program that comes with DOS

Parts: A bootable DOS disk containing the INTERLNK.EXE and INTERSVR.EXE files
           The Interlink program from DOS 6 and higher machines works on lower DOS version
               machines
           A special 3-wire serial cable, a 7-wire null-modem cable, or a bi-directional parallel
               cable (sometimes called a LapLink, Interlink, or Brooklyn Bridge cable)

When using the DOS Interlink program, the computer on which you want to copy files from is the
SERVER; the computer you want to copy files to is the *CLIENT*.

Step   1:   Insert the bootable disk into the *CLIENT* computer. Power on the computer.
Step   2:   Press **ENTER** when prompted for the date and the time.
Step   3:   From the A:> prompt, type **DIR** and press **ENTER**. For DOS skills, refer to Appendix A.
Step   4:   Look at the directory listing for a file called **CONFIG.SYS**. If there is a file called
            CONFIG.SYS, type **REN CONFIG.SYS CONFIG.BAK** and press **ENTER**.
Step   5:   Type the following command at the DOS prompt:
            COPY CON:CONFIG.SYS and press **ENTER**. *You will receive a blank screen.* The
            blank screen is normal! Nothing is going to happen, no messages, nothing.
Step   6:   At the blank screen type:
            Files=20 and press **ENTER**
            Buffers=40 and press **ENTER**
            Device=C:\INTERLNK.EXE and press **ENTER**
Step   7:   Press **F6**, then press **ENTER**. The screen displays a message that one file copied.
Step   8:   Connect the special cable between the two serial or parallel ports (depending on which
            cable you use).
Step   9:   With the bootable disk still in drive A:, reboot the computer you were just typing on by
            pressing **CTRL+ALT+DEL**. You see a message that Interlink installed. If you do not see
            this, perform Steps 5 through 9 again.
Step 10:   Press **ENTER** each time you are prompted for the date and time.
Step 11:   Go to the *SERVER* computer from which you want to copy files.
Step 12:   At the DOS prompt, type **VER** and press **ENTER**.

Question 1:   What DOS version is this machine?

Optional Step 12a: If the computer you are at is *not* DOS 6 or higher, you must complete this step. Get the disk from the *CLIENT* computer with the Interlink files. Insert the disk into the computer. Type the following command:
COPY A:\INTRSVR.* C:\DOS and press **ENTER**. Put the disk back in the *CLIENT* computer. You receive a message that one file copied.

Step 13:   Type the following commands on the *SERVER* machine (the one on which you are currently working):
C: and press **ENTER**.
CD\DOS and press **ENTER**.
INTERSVR and press **ENTER**.

Step 14:   On the CLIENT machine, be sure that the bootable floppy is inserted into the A: drive and type the following command:
INTERLNK and press **ENTER**. Notice that you are connected to the other computer and that each of the other computer's floppy and hard drive(s) are assigned a drive letter, one drive letter per device. For example, you should see something on the screen as shown below. If nothing on your screen is similar to the example below, contact your instructor.

Example of Interlink screen:
Port=LPT1

This Computer (Client)	Other Computer (Server)
E: equals	A:
F: equals	C:
G: equals	D:

Question 2:   What does your screen show? Write your drive letters and what they equal below:

_____ Instructor's Initials

Step 15:   Type the drive letter followed by a colon that equals the other computer's C: drive and press **ENTER**. For example, in the example shown in Step 14, the drive letter would be F:. You are now connected to the other computer's drives. This exercise is especially useful if you need to install software from a 3.5" disk and the computer you are working on does not have this type of disk drive or the improper size (capacity) of disk drive.

Question 3: What drive letter did you choose?

Question 4: Did you remember to put a colon after the drive letter and press **ENTER**?

Step 16: Copy any files that you want from the *SERVER* computer. If you want to copy all the files from the *SERVER*, you would simply have to type **CD\DOS** and press **ENTER**; **XCOPY F:*.* C:\ /E** and press **ENTER**. If you happen to be on a DOS version lower than DOS 5, you would have to type **CD\DOS** and press **ENTER**; **XCOPY F:*.* C:\ /E /S** and press **ENTER**. If asked "Overwrite C:\COMMAND.COM (Y/N/All)?" (or something similar), press **N** for No and then press **ENTER**.

Step 17: When you are finished, press **ALT+F4** on the *SERVER* computer to disconnect the link.

Question 5: List other ways in which you think this program could be useful to you as a technician.

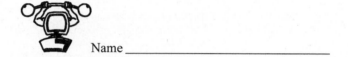

Name _____

HARD DRIVE CHKDSK EXERCISE

Objective: To use the CHKDSK program to claim lost clusters

Parts: A computer with DOS loaded. If you have the MSDOS SCANDISK program, you should use it
instead of CHKDSK.

Question 1:   Why should you use MSDOS SCANDISK instead of CHKDSK?

Step   1:   Turn the computer on and boot from the hard disk.
Step   2:   From the DOS prompt, type
            CD\DOS and press **ENTER**
            CHKDSK and press **ENTER**
            For DOS skills, refer to Appendix A. CHKDSK alerts you with a message if a file needs to
            be fixed, but does not fix the error. If CHKDSK reports only lost clusters, then it is safe,
            (and usually a good idea), to rerun CHKDSK on the same drive with the /F option. When
            CHKDSK finishes, the system returns to the DOS prompt.

Question 2:   Did CHKDSK report any lost clusters? If so, go to Step 3. If CHKDSK did not report
any problems, you may just answer the questions below, skip Step 3. If CHKDSK found problems
other than lost chains of clusters, then you need to use a disk utility software. Contact your instructor
for more information.

Optional Step 3:   From the DOS prompt, type   **CHKDSK /F**. When asked if you want to convert
            the lost chains to files, answer **Y** (for yes). After CHKDSK is through, you will find one or
            more files in the root directory with names like FILE000.CHK, FILE001.CHK, etc. You may
            view these files and then delete them if no critical information is within them. Contact your
            instructor if you cannot decide whether or not to delete the files.

Question 3:   What does the CHKDSK program do?

Question 4:   What would be an indication on the hard drive that CHKDSK needs to be run?

Question 5:   Why does the DEFRAG program require CHKDSK or SCANDISK be performed
            before it is executed?

Question 6:   What does the /F switch do when used with the CHKDSK command?

Name _____

HARD DRIVE DOS SCANDISK EXERCISE

Objective: To use the DOS SCANDISK program

Parts: A computer with MS DOS 6.X or greater loaded. SCANDISK should be performed before any
        defragmentation utility. If you run SCANDISK on a compressed drive, you are offered the
        choice of checking the physical (host) hard drive before you check the compressed drive. This
        is the best option when using a compressed drive.

Step   1:   Power on the computer.

Step   2:   From the DOS prompt, type **SCANDISK** and press **ENTER**. For DOS skills, refer to
        Appendix A. The SCANDISK utility immediately begins testing the file structure of your
        disk. A message box appears stating that the file structure testing was completed. You are
        asked if you want to perform a surface scan.

Question 1:   What does a surface scan do?

Step   3:   Press **ENTER** to accept the **YES** default when the scan is complete. If SCANDISK finds a
        problem with the hard drive, a message box appears with three options: Fix It, Don't Fix It,
        or More Info. Choose **MORE INFO** to get additional information and/or
        recommendations. Choose **FIX IT** to allow SCANDISK the opportunity to try to repair the
        problem. At the end of the SCANDISK check, a final report appears on the screen.
        Sometimes recommendations are provided. This information is also in the
        SCANDISK.LOG file that can be brought into a word processor and printed if desired. A
        good recommendation is if a hard drive has repeated problems, keep the SCANDISK.LOG
        files for documentation on the problems.

Step   5:   At the end of the scan, you can either view the log of any problems that SCANDISK found
        by pressing **ENTER** or you may press the **right arrow** once to get to the EXIT prompt and
        press **ENTER** to exit SCANDISK.

Question 2:   T/F   SCANDISK can repair any and all problems with hard drives.

Question 3:   T/F   SCANDISK is a better utility than CHKDSK.

Question 4:   T/F   SCANDISK is only available with Microsoft DOS.

Question 5:   T/F   The SCANDISK.LOG is *not* to be used as a diagnostic tool.

_____ Instructor's Initials

Name _____

HARD DRIVE DEFRAGMENTATION EXERCISE (DOS)

Objective: To correctly defragment the hard drive

Parts: A computer with IBM PC DOS 6.X or MS DOS 6.X or greater loaded

The Defragmentation Utility comes with IBM's PC DOS 6.X and MS DOS 6.X. This program should not be used until after running CHKDSK /F or SCANDISK. See the RUNNING CHKDSK or RUNNING SCANDISK exercises for more details.

Step   1:   Power on the computer.
Step   2:   From the DOS prompt, type **VER** and press **ENTER**. For DOS skills, refer to Appendix A.

Question 1:   Do you have DOS version 6 or greater? If not, please go to a computer that has DOS version 6.

Step   3:   Type at the DOS prompt **CD\DOS** and press **ENTER**.
Step   4:   Type at the DOS prompt **DEFRAG** and press **ENTER**.
Step   5:   At the prompt, "Choose the Drive You Want to Optimize", choose the default of **C:**.
Step   6:   Click on **OK** or press **TAB** to get to the OK button and press **ENTER**.
Step   7:   When you see the message, "Recommended Optimization Method", choose CONFIGURE by pressing the **right arrow** once to highlight the word CONFIGURE and press **ENTER**. The program goes to the menu at the top of the screen.
Step   8:   Choose OPTIMIZATION METHOD by pressing the **down arrow** twice, press **ENTER**.
Step   9:   Choose the default of FULL-OPTIMIZATION by pressing **ENTER**. You return to the menu.
Step 10:   At the menu, choose **BEGIN OPTIMIZATION** by pressing the **up arrow** twice and then press **ENTER**. You see the layout of the files on your hard drive and the file shuffling that occurs for defragmentation. The length of time this exercise takes varies from computer to computer. While the program is executing, go to the end of this exercise and answer the questions starting with Question 2.
Step 11:   After the defragmentation completes, a message box appears that says Finished Condensing, press **ENTER**.
Step 12:   Another message box appears stating that the optimization is complete. Press the **right arrow** twice to highlight EXIT DEFRAG, then press **ENTER**. You return to the DOS prompt.

Questions: (Use Help or the Map Legend for additional assistance)

Question 2:   What does ▐•▌ mean while DEFRAG is running?

Question 3:   What does an **X** in a block mean while DEFRAG is running?

Question 4:   What does ▮ mean while DEFRAG is running?

Question 5:   What is the difference between the Full Optimization option and the Unfragment Files
                      Only option?

Name _____

HARD DRIVE DEFRAGMENTATION EXERCISE (WINDOWS 95)

Objective: To correctly defragment the hard drive while using Windows 95

Parts: A computer with Windows 95 loaded

Step 1:   Power on the computer.
Step 2:   From the desktop, double-click on **My Computer**. For Windows 95 skills, refer to Appendix B.
Step 3:   With the *right* mouse button, click once on the icon for the hard drive that is to be defragmented.
Step 4:   Using the left mouse button, click once on the **Properties** menu item. (The Properties window appears.)
Step 5:   Click once on the **Tools** tab at the top of the Properties window.
Step 6:   Click on the **Start** button to begin defragmenting the hard drive. If more control is needed over the defragmentation process, click on the Advanced Options button instead of the Start button. For more details on the Advanced Options, refer to the chapter text.
Step 7:   When the defragmentation finishes, a dialog box appears stating that the program is complete. Click on the **Yes** button to exit the disk defragmentation program.
Step 8:   Click once in the close box of the Properties window.
Step 9:   Click once in the close box of the Control Panel window.

_____ Instructor's Initials

Chapter 10:
CD-ROM DRIVES
AND
SOUND CARDS

OBJECTIVES

After completing this chapter you will
1. Understand the various CD technologies.
2. Understand the meaning of a CD-ROM's x factor.
3. Understand how a CD-ROM drive works.
4. Know the different interfaces used with CD-ROMs and configure each interface.
5. Make recommendations regarding upgrading or purchasing CD-ROMs.
6. Understand the basic operation of a sound card.
7. Understand the software associated with CD-ROM installation.
8. Install a CD-ROM and a sound card.
9. Troubleshoot CD-ROM and sound card problems.

KEY TERMS

average access time	dye polymer
average seek time	flats
caddy	frequency response range
caddy-loaded	frequency response time
CD	ICM
CD-E	ICU
CD-R	laser lens
CD-ROM	magneto-optical
CD-ROM kit	MIDI
CD-RW	MPC
CDFS	PD
CTCM	pits
CTCU	power rating
device driver	SDX
device name	shielding
DirectX	tray loaded
DVD-RAM	UDF
DVD-ROM	WORM
DVD-WORM	

CD-ROM OVERVIEW

A **CD-ROM (Compact Disk-Read Only Memory)** is a drive that uses disks that store large amounts of information (up to 628MB). The disk for the CD-ROM drive is known as a **CD**, CD-ROM disk, or just disk. The data contained on these disks are audio files, software applications, and graphics. CD-ROMs are very important in today's business and home computers because software applications are so large. Rather than occupy valuable hard drive space with applications and graphics, CD-ROMs provide a means of running an application or storing large graphics or audio files on a compact disk rather than the hard drive. Using one CD rather than 40 disks saves time and makes the software installation or software application loading easier. In most computers today, a CD-ROM drive is standard. In fact, in 1996 alone, approximately 80 percent of the new computers included a CD-ROM drive. Technicians definitely must understand CD-ROM drives.

CD-ROM DRIVE SPEEDS

CD-ROMs come in a variety of types classified by the X factor: 1X (single speed), 2X (double speed), 3X (triple speed), 4X (quad speed), 6X, 8X, 10X, 12X, and 16X. CD-ROM Table #1 shows the transfer rates for each CD-ROM drive type.

CD-ROM Transfer Speeds

Type of CD-ROM Drive	Typical Transfer Rate (in Kilobytes per Second)
1X	150
2X	300
4X	600
8X	1200
10X	1500
12X	1800
16X	2400
24X	3600

CD-ROM - TABLE # 1

Which CD-ROM to choose for system installation depends on several factors: the microprocessor installed in the computer, how much RAM is in the system, what video card is used (PCI, ISA, VL-bus), and how much video memory is on the video card.

Take for example an 8X CD-ROM drive installed in two different computers. One computer has a 133MHz Pentium, 8MB of RAM, and an ISA video adapter with 1MB of video memory. Another 133MHz Pentium computer has 16MB of RAM and a PCI video adapter with 2MB of video memory. The CD-ROM drive in the second example can put graphics on the screen or play audio much faster than the first example. The increased amount of system RAM, increased amount of video adapter RAM, and the use of a video card that is PCI, not ISA, all contribute to the performance increase. Buying a faster CD-ROM drive does not necessarily mean the drive performs to expectations. As with all computer devices, all components in the computer must work together to provide the fastest data transfer. Many people do not realize buying the latest and greatest X factor CD-ROM drive does not provide faster access. The drawback to CD-ROM drives is they operate much slower than hard drives.

Two sometimes confusing specifications of CD-ROMs are average seek time and average access time. The **average seek time** is the amount of time the drive requires to move randomly around the disk. The **average access time** is the amount of time the drive requires to find the appropriate place on the disk and retrieve information. CD-ROM Table #2 lists average access times for different CD-ROM drives, keeping in mind that the least access time is best.

CD-ROM Access Times

Type of CD-ROM Drive	Typical Access Speed (in milliseconds — ms)
1X	400
2X	300
4X	250
6X	150
8X	130
12X	125
16X	110
24X	100

CD-ROM - TABLE # 2

CD-ROM drive access times are much slower than hard drives and CD-ROM drive manufacturers usually quote access times using only optimum test conditions. When buying or recommending a CD-ROM drive to a computer user or customer, check magazines or online data for the latest test performance results.

CD-ROM DRIVE BUFFERS

One way to increase CD-ROM data transfer is through buffer memory located on the CD-ROM drive. When requesting data, the drive looks ahead on the CD for more data than requested and places the data in the buffers. The buffer memory ensures data is constantly sent to the microprocessor instead of the microprocessor waiting for the drive's slow access time. Buffer sizes typically range from 64KB to 1MB. A drive should not be installed or purchased unless it has a minimum of 128KB buffers.

THEORY OF CD-ROM DRIVE OPERATION

A CD-ROM disk is created from a master copy. The plastic disk is coated with a reflective, metallic aluminum alloy. The aluminum alloy layer is covered by a thin layer of lacquer for protection. The aluminum alloy is the layer of the CD where data is stored. CD-ROM disks are usually single-sided. A label is normally on the *opposite side* of the data.

A CD has thousands of circular tracks in a continuous spiral from the innermost area of the disk to the outside rim. The spiral tracks are similar to the grooves in an LP record. Instead of grooves, the CD has **pits** — indentations along the track. **Flats** or lands separate the pits. The pits and lands vary in length and represent stored data on the disk.

Reading information from a CD involves using a laser diode or another laser beam producing device within the CD-ROM drive. The laser beam shines through the protective coating to the aluminum alloy layer where data is stored. To reach the aluminum alloy layer, the laser beam passes through an optical system, which is a series or combination of lenses, prisms, and mirrors. A servo motor inside the drive positions the beam on the right track through the use of the optical system. The laser beam reflects back through the optics to a photodiode detector that converts the reflected beam of light into 1s and 0s.

The light beam reflected to the photodiode detector changes in intensity when passing over the lands and the pits. The light reflected by a pit area is not as bright as the light reflected from a land area. While the disk rotates, the light beam creates a series of on and off flashes received by the photodiode. Once detected, the flashes of light convert to 1s and 0s. The transition between the lands and the pits create the variation of light intensity. CD-ROM Figure #1 shows an inside view of a CD-ROM drive.

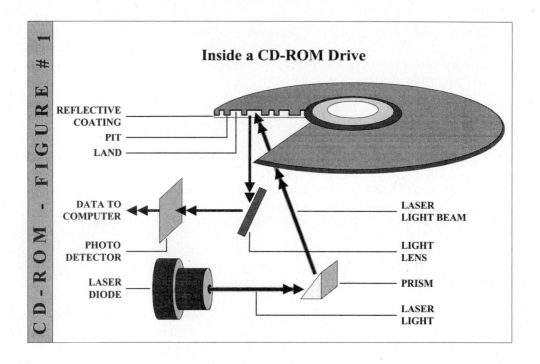

INTERNAL AND EXTERNAL CD-ROM DRIVES

A CD-ROM can be internally mounted in an available bay or it can be an external unit that sits beside the computer. If a CD-ROM uses the IDE interface, it must be an internal device because the interface does not support external devices. However, external SCSI CD-ROM drives can be purchased. A drawback to internal CD-ROM drives is the drive requires a drive bay, but internal CD-ROM drives are cheaper than external drives.

CD-ROM DISK LOADING

Two methods exist for inserting a compact disk (CD) into a CD-ROM drive: tray loaded or caddy loaded. A **tray loaded** CD-ROM drive has a tray that slides out from the CD-ROM drive, a CD disk is placed in the tray, and the tray retracts into the drive. A **caddy loaded** CD-ROM drive uses a disk **caddy** that holds the CD. After inserting the disk, close the caddy lid and insert the entire caddy into the CD-ROM drive. See CD-ROM Figure #2 for an example of a tray loaded CD-ROM drive and a CD-ROM disk caddy.

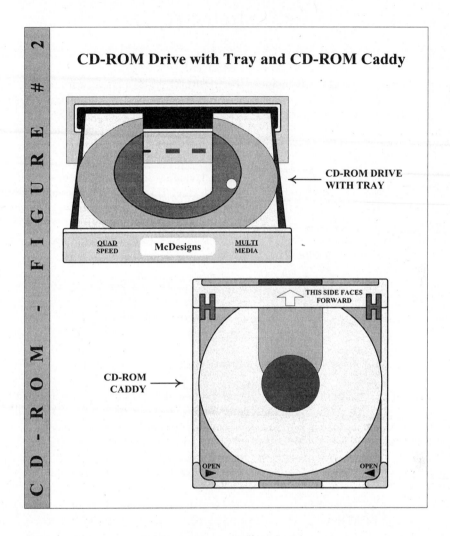

CD-ROM drives that use a caddy usually have only one caddy. Finding the one caddy when it's needed can be a hassle for some people. Using a caddy takes more time to install a disk, but it provides a more secure and clean environment for the CD disks. Tray-loaded CD-ROM drives are less expensive than the caddies, but more likely to have a worse MTBF — Mean Time Between Failure. MTBF is the average number of hours before a device is likely to fail. Another point to consider is some CD-ROM drives that use the caddy system can be vertically mounted on their side instead of the normal horizontal position. Most tray loading CD-ROM drives cannot be vertically mounted. Check the CD-ROM drive's documentation if this is an issue.

CD-ROM DRIVE INTERFACES AND CONNECTIONS

CD-ROM drives use either an IDE, a SCSI, or a proprietary (non-standard) interface. Many users want technicians to add a CD-ROM drive or a CD-ROM kit to their computer system or upgrade their existing drive. A **CD-ROM kit** includes the CD-ROM drive, a sound card, a cable that connects the audio signals to the sound card, software drivers for the drive and sound card, a set of external speakers, and sometimes extra software bundles such as entertainment or encyclopedias. The particular interface the technician recommends to the customer depends on several factors. The following questions will help customers decide what interface to use.

1.   Is the CD-ROM drive going to be an external device? If so, SCSI is the best choice.
2.   Is the CD-ROM drive going to be an internal device? If so, is price an issue? Internal CD-ROM drives can be IDE or SCSI. IDE is less expensive than SCSI, but the SCSI interface has much more expandability than IDE.
3.   Does the customer plan to add more devices such as a scanner or tape backup unit in the near future? If so, SCSI has greater expandability.

When connecting a CD-ROM to an IDE connector with a hard drive connected, verify that the CD-ROM is configured as the slave. If the CD-ROM drive connects to the IDE connector and is the sole device connected, verify that the drive is configured as the master. Some CD-ROMs do not work unless connected as the slave; check the CD-ROM drive documentation. Refer to the chapter on hard drives for more information on setting the Master/Slave setting.

The expansion capabilities of the SCSI interface make it a good choice for CD-ROM drives. However, SCSI CD-ROM drives are traditionally more expensive than IDE CD-ROMs, but the gap has recently narrowed. Microsoft's Windows 95 provides drivers for SCSI devices.

SCSI CD-ROM drives require software compatibility with the SCSI adapter such as ASPI, CAM, or LADDR. Two good universal SCSI drivers for CD-ROM drives are Corel Corporation's CorelSCSI II and Future Domain's PowerSCSI. Most SCSI CD-ROM drives today use the SCSI-2 standard.

A SCSI CD-ROM must have the SCSI ID set usually to a SCSI ID *other than* 0, 1, or 7. The terminator on the CD-ROM drive is installed or removed based on where the CD-ROM connects along the SCSI chain. If the CD-ROM is at either end of the SCSI chain, terminate the drive. Refer to the hard drive chapter's SCSI configuration section for more information on setting the SCSI ID and termination.

Proprietary CD-ROM drives come as a kit with their own interface adapter. Even though they may be cheaper than SCSI or IDE CD-ROM kits, they are best *to be avoided*. Proprietary CD-ROM drives are not usually compatible with other devices such as sound cards. When replacement or upgrading is necessary, compatible drives may be hard to find.

CD-ROM DRIVE UPGRADES

If the customer wants to upgrade a CD-ROM drive, find out why. Many times, slow access is due to the computer's other components, not the CD-ROM drive. Use the same questions listed previously for a new CD-ROM drive, but only after finding out from the customer why they want to upgrade the CD-ROM drive. If it is a 1X or a 2X drive, upgrade the drive, but be sure the other parts of the computer complement the CD-ROM drive's performance. The following questions help when upgrading CD-ROM drives.

1. Does the customer want sound (speakers)? If so, a CD-ROM kit might be necessary or if the customer is an audiophile, then special speakers may be needed.
2. What microprocessor does the customer have? The CD-ROMs available now do not perform well on a system such as a 386SX. The customer should have a 486 or higher microprocessor.
3. Is there an available slot in the computer for a sound card? Also, check if there are sound connections built into the motherboard. If so, a sound card may not be needed. Without sound connections, the user cannot have a sound adapter and may not be able to have a CD-ROM drive (if there is no other interface available).
4. Is the customer going to be using CDs that are video-intensive? If so, what type of interface is the video adapter? PCI provides the best throughput and performance for video. How much memory is on the video adapter? 2MB is the minimum amount of memory that should be on the video adapter.
5. Does the customer have enough RAM on the motherboard? At least 8MB should be installed for the DOS/Windows environment and 16MB for the Windows 95 environment.

PREVENTIVE MAINTENANCE FOR CD-ROM DRIVES

When LP records were used, handling of the records was quite a problem because fingerprints, dust, and dirt greatly affected the performance of the record. CDs are less prone to these problems because the CD has a protective coating over the aluminum alloy-based data layer. When reading information, the laser beam ignores the protective coating and shines through to the data layer. Even if the CD has some dirt on the protective coating, the laser beam can still operate because the beam is directed at the data layer rather than the disk surface. An exception to this is surface material with reflective properties. The reflection could reflect and distort the laser beam thus causing distortion or data corruption. Another exception is if the dust or dirt completely blocks the laser beam. A heavy accumulation of dust and dirt can reduce the quality of the data retrieved from the CD-ROM drive. Cleaning the CD-ROM's components is easy.

Special CD-ROM cleaning cloths are available. Using the cleaning cloth, wipe the disk from the inside (near the center hole) to the outside of the disk (*not* in a circular motion) on both sides of the disk. Also, proper handling of the CD disks aids in good CD-ROM performance. As with audio CDs used in stereos, handle the CD on the outside edge of the disk. Never touch the surface of the CD disk. Fingerprints, oil from hands, dust, and dirt on the CD disk can also cause performance problems.

A special component of the CD-ROM drive, the **laser lens** also known as the objective lens, is responsible for reading information from the CD disk. The laser lens is susceptible to dust and dirt accumulation. If the laser lens gets dust, dirt, or moisture on it, the drive may report data or read errors. Some CD-ROM drives have a self-cleaning laser lens. If the drive does not have this feature, laser lens cleaning kits are available at computer and music stores. Also, the laser lens can be cleaned with an air blower like ones used on a camera lens. Cleaning the laser lens should be a preventive maintenance routine just like cleaning the heads on a floppy disk drive. Keep the disk compartment closed to prevent dust and dirt from accumulating on the laser lens.

SOUND AND CD-ROM DRIVES

CD-ROM drives have the capability of producing sound usually through a front headphone jack. Audio CDs can be played on these drives, but the CDs do not sound as good through headphone jacks as they do through a stereo system. A better alternative is to connect the CD-ROM drive to a sound card. A cable connects from the back of the CD-ROM drive to the sound card. Look at CD-ROM Figure #3 for an illustration of an audio cable used to connect a CD-ROM drive to a sound adapter.

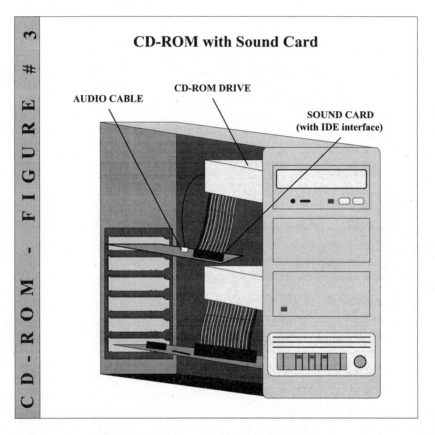

CD-ROM with Sound Card

Notice in CD-ROM Figure #3 how an audio cable goes from the back of the drive to the adapter. This cable carries the audio signals from the drive to the adapter and then out to the speakers.

Not all sound adapters will support every CD-ROM drive on the market. Also, many drives have proprietary connectors for the audio cable. For this reason, most people prefer CD-ROM drive kits.

Very few CD-ROM drives sold separately from the adapter include the interface cable, audio cable, mounting brackets, and screws. A CD-ROM kit takes some of the hassle out of the purchase.

Many sound cards have the IDE or SCSI interface and a MIDI (Musical Instrument Digital Interface) built into the adapter, and a jack for microphone input. **MIDI (Musical Instrument Digital**

Interface) is used to create synthesized music. A 15-pin female connector on the back of the sound adapter connects a joystick or a MIDI device such as a MIDI keyboard. CD-ROM Figure #4 shows a typical sound board and ports.

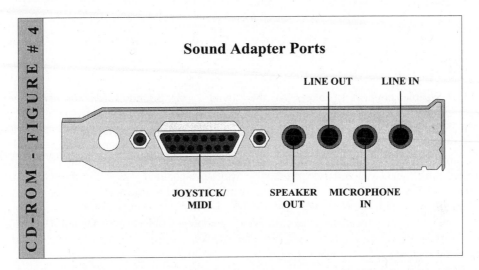

Sound Adapter Ports

LINE OUT   LINE IN

JOYSTICK/   SPEAKER   MICROPHONE
MIDI   OUT   IN

CD-ROM - FIGURE # 4

Even if a sound card has an interface connection for the drive, the CD-ROM drive does not have to connect to the sound card. Instead, the CD-ROM drive can connect to the IDE connector on the motherboard or still yet to another IDE adapter installed in the system. Just remember to connect an audio cable from the CD-ROM drive to the sound card for CD-based audio to be heard.

The sound file(s) heard from a sound card is determined by the adapter. Two major sound files are MIDI (.MID) and WAVE (.WAV) files. Most multimedia disks use WAVE files for sound, but most game CDs use MIDI files. Getting a sound adapter that can process both files is important.

Some software applications require a sound card to be *Sound Blaster-compatible*. Creative Labs' audio cards are called Sound Blasters. A card that is compatible usually indicates the sound card supports DMA channel 1, IRQ5, and I/O port 220. If purchasing a sound card separate from a CD-ROM, verify the card adheres to the MPC3 standard (see the section on MPC later in the chapter). Always make sure the card samples a minimum of 16-bits. Extras available in a sound card include the following:

1. Speaker output jacks
2. Input jack(s) for an external CD-ROM or an external audio device
3. Microphone input jack
4. 9-pin MIDI interface or 15-pin combination MIDI/joystick connector
5. Extra software
6. 3D sound
7. 4D home-theater sound
8. RAM expandability
9. DirectSound hardware accelerator

10.   Wavetable synthesis which includes the number of sampled instrument sounds
11.   Digital signal processor which provides extra functionality such as fax and voice mail
        capabilities
12.   Multiple MIDI emulations such as General MIDI (GM), Sound Blaster, and Windows Sound
        System

SPEAKERS

        Most people connect speakers to the sound card. Sound cards usually have built-in
amplification to drive the speakers. Amplification is measured in watts. Most sound cards provide up
to 4 watts of amplification which is not enough for a full-bodied sound. Many computer speakers have
built-in amplifiers to boost the audio signal for a much better and fuller sound quality. Amplification is
a good feature to look for in speakers. The speaker's **power rating** is how loud the volume can go
without distorting the sound and is expressed in watts-per-channel. Look for the RMS (root-mean-
square) power rating. 10-15 watts-per-channel is an adequate rating for most computer users.
        Another important measurement for speakers is the **frequency response range** which is the
frequency range of sounds the speaker can reproduce. People are able to hear from 20Hz to 20KHz and
the range varies for each person. Therefore, the speakers to recommend depends on the person
listening to the speakers.

The best advice to give someone regarding speakers is to listen to them without headphones,
using an audio (non-software) CD.

        Speakers usually have a magnet inside them that can cause distortion to a device such as a
monitor. These magnets can also cause damage to disks and other storage media. Because speakers
have magnets, they should be shielded. **Shielding** cancels outs the magnetic interference and keeps the
interference away from other devices. The best and fastest CD-ROM drive and sound card
combination can be downgraded by using inexpensive, poorly shielded speakers.

Extras to look for in speakers:
1.   An external volume control for when the kids or the significant other is talking to you from
        another room.
2.   Headphone jacks
3.   Headphone and microphone pass-through connectors so you do not have to dislodge the
        computer to reach the jacks.
4.   AC adapter
5.   The proper connectors for the speakers to connect to the sound card. (If the connectors are
        wrong, Radio Shack or music stores carry adapters.)

SOUND CARD THEORY OF OPERATION

Sound cards have a variety of options that can include an input from a microphone, an output to a speaker, a MIDI interface, and the ability to generate music. Take for example how to bring sound into the computer through a microphone connected to a sound card. Sound waves are shown as an analog waveform as in CD-ROM Figure #5.

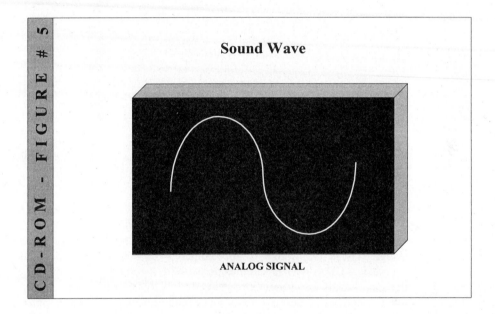

CD - ROM - FIGURE # 5

Sound Wave

ANALOG SIGNAL

Computers work with digital signals (1s and 0s) so the sound card must take the analog signal and convert it to a digital format to send the sound into the computer. Sound cards can also take the digital data from a CD and output the sound to the speakers. To convert an analog waveform to 1s and 0s, samples of the data are taken. The more samples taken, the truer the reproduction of the original signal.

The first sound cards made for the computer sampled the data using 8 bits. Eight 1s and 0s can give a total of 256 (2^8=256) different values. The analog waveform goes above and below a center value of 0. Because one of the eight bits denotes negative or positive value, the possible values lie between -127 and +127. CD-ROM Figure #6 shows an example of sampling.

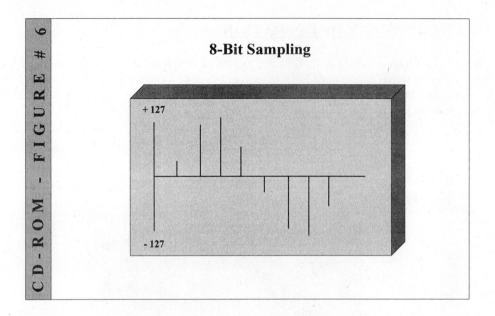

The more samples taken by the sound card, the closer the reproduction is to the original sound signal. The sound card's **frequency response** is the number of samples taken. For a good reproduction of sound, the sound wave is sampled at twice the range desired. For example, a person's hearing is in the 20Hz to 20KHz range. Twice that range is approximately 40,000 samples per second. The frequency response for a musical CD is 44,100 samples per second, a good quality sound reproduction for human ears. The first sound cards for computers used eight bits to sample the sound wave and had a frequency response of approximately 22,000 samples per second (22KHz). The sound produced from the original sound cards was better than the beeps and chirps previously heard from the computer. The sound still was grainy and better than an AM radio station, but not as good as a FM radio station or a musical CD.

16-bit sound cards arrived next for computers. The number of possible levels sampled with 16 bits is 65,536 (2^{16}=65,536). When positive and negative levels are sampled, the range is -37,768 to +37,768. The frequency response with 16-bit sound cards is 44KHz, the same resolution as stereo audio CDs. The increase in the number of sampling levels and the frequency response allows sound cards to produce quality sound equal to audio CDs. Look at CD-ROM Figure #7 for an example of 16-bit sampling and keep in mind when more samples are taken, the sound card provides a better frequency response.

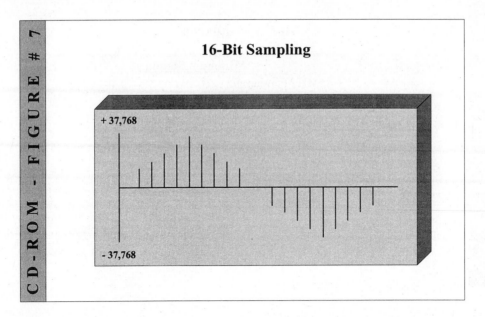

CD-ROM - FIGURE # 7

16-Bit Sampling

+ 37,768

- 37,768

Some newer cards sample sound using 64-bits. These sound cards produce fuller, richer tones needed for creating music.

Many users do not understand that the 8-bit, 16-bit, 32-bit, and 64-bit sound board descriptions are the number of possible sample levels. Many people believe that the *x*-bit number describes the board for an ISA slot, which is not the case!

When buying or recommending a sound adapter, be sure it is a 16-bit adapter which uses a minimum of 16 bits for sampling.

MPC STANDARD

The Multimedia PC Working Group is a special interest group of the Software Publishers Association (SPA) that developed the MPC standards. The **MPC** (**Multimedia Personal Computer**) specification defines multimedia standards resulting from industry-wide discussions and debates. The original MPC specification called for a minimum of a 386SX computer with 2MB of RAM, along with a 30MB hard drive, VGA monitor, 8-bit sound card, and an 1X CD-ROM.

The enhanced version is MPC2 which includes a minimum of a 25MHz 486SX microprocessor, 4MB (8MB recommended) of RAM, a 160MB hard drive, a 640 X 480 (64K colors) monitor, a 16-bit sound card, and a 2X CD-ROM drive. There are many more components to the MPC standards. Each component does not have to be installed in the computer to comply with the MPC standard. For more information, contact the Software Publishers Association or look up the standards online at www.spa.org/mpc.

CD-ROM Table #3 lists some of the specifications included in the MPC3 standard.

MPC3 Standards

CD-ROM - TABLE # 3

Component	Minimum Standard
Microprocessor	75MHz Pentium
RAM	8MB
	256KB Level 2 Cache
Hard Drive	500MB usable capacity
CD-ROM	4X (550KBps transfer rate; access time of 250ns)
Sound Card	8/16-bit samples
	stereo channels
Speakers	Frequency Response: 120Hz to 17.5KHz
	Power Rating: 3 watts-per-channel at 100Hz, 1KHz, and 10KHz; 6 watts RMS (3W+3W) into 4 ohms at 1KHz with both channels driven

The MPC standard shows technicians that the individual component (whether it be a CD-ROM, sound card, or a set of speakers) must comply with a specific set of minimum standards to market the product as MPC-compliant. When purchasing hardware that is MPC3 compliant, the individual components should be compatible with other MPC3 compliant devices. MPC2 and MPC3 both include a standard that states that if a CD-ROM drive is sold separately from a sound adapter, the drive includes a standard audio cable. Then, if a MPC2 or MPC3-compliant sound card is purchased later, the CD-ROM drive can play sound through the sound card. The only problem is many times the documentation included with the drive is not available to the technician. Users frequently misplace, lose, or never received their documentation.

CD-ROM DRIVE INSTALLATION

The steps for installing an internal CD-ROM drive are similar to installing any drive. The steps that follow are only for the CD-ROM drive installation. Software and sound card installation are later in the chapter.

1.   Install any necessary mounting brackets onto the CD-ROM drive.
2.   Check to see what interface the CD-ROM drive uses (IDE, EIDE, or SCSI). Set the appropriate master/slave, SCSI ID, or termination according to the drive interface type. Refer to the documentation included with the CD-ROM drive for the proper configuration of these settings.

Most IDE CD-ROMs are pre-configured as the slave device. Some drives will work even if it is the only device connected to the IDE connector (even though single IDE are normally set to master). Always refer to the CD-ROM's documentation for configuration issues. The manufacturers are trying to limit frustration and technical support calls by making the devices easier to install. Technicians should set the device properly because they know better!

3.	(optional) Install any interface adapter into the system. Set any interrupt, I/O address, or DMA channel as necessary. Refer to the documentation included with the adapter.
4.	Install the CD-ROM drive into the computer.
5.	Attach the power cable to the CD-ROM drive.
6.	Attach the interface cable to the CD-ROM drive and the adapter or motherboard.

Be careful when attaching the interface cable from the drive to the adapter or motherboard. Verify the cable's pin 1 attaches to the drive's pin 1. IDE CD-ROM drives can be destroyed by attaching the cable the wrong way. Pin 1 on the drive is sometimes hard to detect because the connector on the drive is frequently black in color. Look very carefully for an etched arrow on the connector on the drive. Some drive manufacturers place a drawing on top of the drive illustrating the proper orientation.

7.	(optional) Attach the audio cable from the CD-ROM drive to the sound card.

The drive is now installed, but is not operational until software drivers are installed properly.

If the drive is an IDE drive installed into a computer with an auto-detect BIOS, an indication of successful installation is if the BIOS detects the drive when the computer reboots.

CD-ROM SOFTWARE INSTALLATION (DOS/WINDOWS) OVERVIEW

There are two major steps in software installation for a CD-ROM drive. Step 1 is installing the software driver or device driver for the CD-ROM drive. A **device driver** is a small piece of software that stays in RAM to allow communication with a piece of hardware — a device. The CD-ROM driver is usually included with the CD-ROM drive and through the installation process, adds a line to the CONFIG.SYS file. Step 2 involves assigning a drive letter to the CD-ROM drive such as D:, E:, etc. After a drive letter is assigned, the drive is accessible to the system. **MSCDEX.EXE** is a program provided with DOS, Windows 3.x, and other drive manufacturers that assigns a drive letter to the CD-ROM drive. Always use the latest version of MSCDEX.EXE for the best CD-ROM drive performance.

CD-ROM SOFTWARE (DEVICE DRIVER) INSTALLATION

The software device driver for the CD-ROM drive usually goes in the CONFIG.SYS file in a statement such as the following:
DEVICE=C:\CPQIDECD.SYS /D:IDECD001
or
DEVICE=C:\SB14\SB14CD.SYS /D:IDECD001
or
DEVICE=C:\CDROMDRV.SYS /D:MSCD000

The */D:* switch is the device name used by the CD-ROM device driver. The **device name** is an eight character name unique for each CD-ROM drive. The device name is very important in later steps.

 TROUBLESHOOTING THE CD-ROM DEVICE DRIVER

Before any additional steps are taken, a technician should be sure the device driver for the CD-ROM drive loads correctly and no problems occur. No other software procedures work if the device driver does not detect a CD-ROM drive. After installing the driver for the first time, the installation software usually displays a message that states the computer must be restarted for the changes to take effect.

When the computer restarts and the message "Starting MS-DOS" or "Starting PC DOS" appears on the screen, press the F8 key and step through the CONFIG.SYS drivers one by one by replying Y for Yes to the prompt to load each driver. Look specifically for the CD-ROM driver such as DEVICE=C:\SB14\SB14CD.SYS.

If the driver loads without a problem, usually the driver prompts with a message such as "1 drive detected." Others might have quite lengthy messages, but look for an indication that a CD-ROM drive is found such as "Number of drives installed: 1". These messages are a technician's first clue that the driver is installed properly!

If the device driver message reads something like "No drive found" or "Number of installed drives: 0", then an interrupt, I/O address, or DMA conflict is very likely. Also, check the path for the correct device driver. For example, DEVICE=C:\CDROM\CDROMDRV.SYS /D:MSCD000 in the CONFIG.SYS file, indicates that the file, CDROMDRV.SYS, is in the CDROM directory on the hard drive. Verify that the directory exists and that the software driver (such as CDROMDRV.SYS), exists in the mentioned directory. Sometimes errors occur during the install process and the driver is not in the directory specified by the CONFIG.SYS statement or the driver was not placed in the directory (or anywhere) by the installation process. If the directory or file is missing, delete all directories and files created during the install process and re-install the software driver again. Do not proceed until the CD-ROM device driver loads properly and the system detects the CD-ROM drive. No other software installation steps work properly until the system sees the CD-ROM drive when the device driver loads correctly. Another problem could be with incorrect configuration and cabling of the drive. Double check all master/slave, SCSI ID, termination settings and the correct cabling between the drive and the interface connector.

INSTALLING THE MSCDEX.EXE PROGRAM

Most software installations for CD-ROM drives include adding the MSCDEX.EXE program to the AUTOEXEC.BAT file. The MSCDEX.EXE program provides access and assigns a drive letter to the CD-ROM drive in the DOS/Windows environment and Windows 95's MS-DOS mode. The MSCDEX.EXE program has some switches that provide flexibility and enhancement to the program. CD-ROM Table #4 summarizes the switches available with MSCDEX.EXE.

CD - ROM - TABLE # 4

MSCDEX.EXE Switches

Switch	Purpose
/D:*driver1*	Used to specify the specific device name
/E	Used to use expanded memory for sector buffers if expanded memory is available
/K	Used to recognize CD-ROM drive volumes encoded in Kanji
/L:*letter*	Assigns a specific drive letter to a CD-ROM drive
/M:*number*	Specifies the number of sector buffers
/S	Allows sharing of CD-ROM drives in networked environments
/V	Verbose switch used to provide more details when MSCDEX is loaded

The /D:*driver1* switch must include the exact *device name* given when the CD-ROM device driver loads in CONFIG.SYS.

For example, if the CONFIG.SYS line is DEVICE=C:\CPQIDECD.SYS */D:IDECD001*, the corresponding MSCDEX.EXE statement in the AUTOEXEC.BAT file would be C:\WINDOWS\MSCDEX.EXE */D:IDECD001*. The two device names must match in both statements to provide a drive letter to the CD-ROM drive. The MSCDEX.EXE requires the */D:driver1* to load properly.

Multiple CD-ROM drives can be controlled by the same MSCDEX.EXE line in the AUTOEXEC.BAT file. For example, if the CONFIG.SYS file contains two lines where each line controls a separate CD-ROM drive, then the two drives are assigned drive letters by the MSCDEX.EXE program. The CONFIG.SYS lines are below:

DEVICE=C:\CPQIDECD.SYS **/D:IDECD001**
DEVICE=C:\CDROM\CDROMDRV.SYS **/D:MSCD000**

The corresponding MSCDEX.EXE line in the AUTOEXEC.BAT file is below:
C:\WINDOWS\MSCDEX **/D:IDECD001 /D:MSCD000**

The drive that uses the IDECD001 device name obtains the first available drive letter. The drive that uses MSCD000 as a device name gets the next drive letter because it is the second line.

MSCDEX.EXE's */E* switch is for using expanded memory for sector buffering. If at all possible, do not use this option due to the slow nature of expanded memory. The */L:letter* option assigns a specific drive letter to the CD-ROM drive instead of letting the system assign the next available drive letter. For example, C:\WINDOWS\MSCDEX.EXE /D:MSCD000 /L:J assigns the drive the letter J:. The number of drive letters available is determined by the LASTDRIVE statement in the CONFIG.SYS file. For example, if the CONFIG.SYS file contains the statement LASTDRIVE=F

and the MSCDEX.EXE line in AUTOEXEC.BAT is C:\WINDOWS\MSCDEX /D:MSCD000 */L:G*,
then the CD-ROM drive would *not* get a drive letter because the assignment of the drive letter G: is not
allowed by the system due to the LASTDRIVE statement. If the last drive statement is a problem, one
indication is when MSCDEX.EXE loads and the message "Not enough drive letters available" appears.

Whenever the message "Not enough drive letters available" appears, check the LASTDRIVE
statement in the CONFIG.SYS file. Modify the statement to include enough drive letters for the
parameter specified in MSCDEX.EXE's */L:letter* switch.

An advantage to assigning a specific drive letter to a CD-ROM drive is for future hard drive
upgrades or new hard drive installations. For example, if a computer has one hard drive (C:) and one
CD-ROM drive (D:) and you install a second hard drive, it is assigned drive letter D: and the CD-
ROM drive changes to drive letter E:.

The problem with changing a CD-ROM's drive letter is that some applications place the drive
letter of the CD-ROM drive as the path to the location of certain software components. When the drive
letter of the CD-ROM drive changes and the software application is run, application errors occur. The
solution to this problem is to uninstall the software application with an uninstaller included with the
software application or with a product such as Quarterdeck Corp.'s Remove-IT or MicroHelp, Inc.'s
Un-Installer, and re-load the software application. You can always change the drive letter on an icon's
properties in Windows 3.x, but a small portion of an application will reside on a hard drive. Once the
application starts, it searches for the rest of the program on a specific drive letter. The drive letter is
created when the application is installed.

Assign the CD-ROM drive a drive letter such as F: or G: from the very beginning, and more
hard drives can be installed or the existing hard drive(s) can be re-partitioned into more logical drives
without reassigning the CD-ROM drive letter. The only drawback to a higher drive letter is DOS
allocates approximately 80 bytes of conventional memory for *each* drive letter up to the drive letter
specified by the *LastDrive* statement in the CONFIG.SYS file.

The */M:number* switch specifies the number of memory buffers set aside for speedier access to
the CD-ROM drive's data. Eight is the normal setting for one CD-ROM drive (with an increase of four
for each additional CD-ROM installed). Increasing the number of sector buffers decreases the amount
of conventional memory available because it is used by the MSCDEX.EXE buffers. An alternative to
the */M:number* switch used with MSCDEX.EXE is to use the SmartDrive disk caching program.

SmartDrive comes with DOS and Windows and creates a disk cache in extended memory for
floppy, hard, and CD-ROM drives. Using the SmartDrive program to cache the CD-ROM drive is a
better alternative than the MSCDEX.EXE */M:number* switch because SmartDrive uses extended
memory. Either method provides buffering in addition to the memory buffers on the CD-ROM drive.
Using a disk cache with CD-ROM drives increases CD-ROM drive performance. The CD-ROM speed
is increased for functions such as providing better video motion when reading video data from a CD.

Load the MSCDEX.EXE program before the SmartDrive program through the
AUTOEXEC.BAT file. SmartDrive cannot cache a CD-ROM drive unless the drive is assigned a drive
letter. If using the SmartDrive program, set the number of sector buffers designated with
MSCDEX.EXE's /M:*number* switch to 0 or 1.

TROUBLESHOOTING THE MSCDEX.EXE INSTALLATION

The technician must first determine by restarting the computer if the CD-ROM drive is assigned a drive letter. When the message "Starting MS-DOS" or "Starting PC DOS" appears on the screen, press the F8 key to single step through the CONFIG.SYS and AUTOEXEC.BAT files. Pay particular attention when the MSCDEX.EXE program loads. A message similar to the following appears:

MSCDEX Version 2.23
Copyright (C) Microsoft Corp. 1986-1993. All rights reserved.
   Drive D: = Driver IDECD001 Unit 0

If no drive letter is assigned to the CD-ROM drive, then verify the CD-ROM device driver in the CONFIG.SYS file loads correctly and detects a CD-ROM drive. Also, be sure the correct *device name* is in the MSCDEX.EXE command found in the AUTOEXEC.BAT file. The device name used in the CD-ROM driver /D switch (CONFIG.SYS file) *must* match the device name in MSCDEX.EXE's /D switch (AUTOEXEC.BAT file). Finally, verify the path is correct and the directory listed in the AUTOEXEC.BAT line contains the MSCDEX.EXE program.

MORE CD-ROM SOFTWARE INSTALLATION

After the CD-ROM driver and MSCDEX.EXE load, many CD-ROM drives have a CD or disk(s) that contains additional software such as programs that control the drive graphical software instead of typewritten commands. The sound drivers and software for the MIDI interface are usually loaded at this time. Usually these programs are installed through Windows similar to any Windows-based software application:

1. Insert the CD into the drive.
2. From the Program Manager menu bar, click on **File**, then click on **Run**.
3. From the Run dialog box, click on **Browse**.
4. From the Browse dialog box, click on the **down arrow** contained within the **Drives** box.
5. Click on the drive letter that corresponds to the CD-ROM. (The icon for the drive shows a CD sticking out the front of a drive.)
6. Click on the file name, usually INSTALL.EXE or SETUP.EXE, which will install the software.
7. Click on the **OK** button and follow the directions on the screen. Always refer to the documentation or the README files included with the software for exact loading procedures.

CD-ROM DRIVES (WINDOWS 95)

Windows 95 supports IDE and SCSI CD-ROM drives by default. Windows 95 supports Mitsumi, Sony, and Panasonic adapters for IDE CD-ROM drives. The drivers for these adapters are in the CONFIG.SYS file. Other adapters can be used, but the drivers must be supplied by the manufacturer. Install the software driver by clicking on the No button in the Automatic Hardware Detection dialog box. The prompts that follow allow the driver installation. Windows 95 may not recognize a CD-ROM drive that does *not* comply with the ATAPI standard.

CDFS (**CD-ROM File System**) is the Windows 95 32-bit protected mode CD-ROM file system driver. CDFS is an improvement over the older MSCDEX caching program used in the DOS/Windows environment because (1) conventional memory is not used, (2) CDFS is larger and smarter than MSCDEX, (3) multi-tasking is improved for CD-ROM access, and (4) CDFS provides a more intelligent and balanced ability to provide memory to applications and memory used to cache the CD-ROM drive. The CDFS cache is different than the one used for files from disks or networks because the CD-ROM cache can be paged to the hard disk when CD-ROM activity pauses. Applications have more room in memory to operate and this keeps the hard disk's file cache from being flushed when retrieving a large multimedia stream from the CD-ROM drive. Retrieving data from cache to a hard disk drive is still faster than accessing the information from the CD-ROM drive.

The CDFS cache is dynamic and grows or shrinks as needed. It requires no configuration or specific allocation of memory set by the user. However, an optional supplemental cache setting is available. This holds directory, file, and path table information for the CD-ROM drive. The supplemental CD-ROM cache improves CD streaming and reduces the drive's seek latency time.

An indication that the supplemental CD-ROM cache needs to be adjusted might be if the CD-ROM drive does not play files as fast as it should.

An exercise at the end of the chapter illustrates how to configure the Windows 95 CD-ROM supplemental cache size.

Some CDs designed for Windows 95 have an Autorun feature which starts an application when the CD is inserted into the drive. Some people find the Autorun feature annoying. If so, use the following steps to disable the Autorun feature:

1. Double-click on the **My Computer** icon.
2. Double-click on the **Control Panel** folder icon.
3. Double-click on the **System** icon.
4. Click on the **Device Manager** tab.
5. Click on the **CDROM** icon. A new icon with the model of CD-   ROM   installed   should   be treed below the CD-ROM icon.
6. Click once on the icon for the **CD-ROM** installed in the system.
7. Click on the **Properties** button.
8. Click on the **Settings** tab.
9. Click once to un-check the **Auto-insert notification** option.
10. Close the Properties window.
11. Close the Control Panel window.

If the *Auto-insert notification* is enabled, and an audio CD is inserted into the CD-ROM drive, the Windows 95 CD Player automatically launches. Windows 95 takes control of the CD and disables the front panel controls on the CD Player program. Even after CD Player closes, the front panel controls of the CD-ROM drive remain disabled. To fix this problem, eject the disk. Then, hold down the Shift key and reinsert the audio CD. Another fix is to press the Play button twice on the drive's front panel (if available).

Because hard drives and other devices are sometime added or removed, a CD-ROM drive is best configured for a specific drive letter in the alphabet after D:. Changing the drive letter when CD-

ROM based software applications are already installed may require re-installation of the software. An exercise at the end of the chapter delineates the steps for reassigning the CD-ROM drive letter using Windows 95.

INSTALLING SOUND CARDS

Because sound cards can include a CD-ROM interface, a MIDI interface, and audio output, they frequently require multiple resource settings. The CD-ROM drive interface port requires an interrupt, I/O address, and DMA setting separate from the audio portion, as well as the MIDI portion of the sound card. This can be quite time-consuming and frustrating to a technician when installing a CD-ROM drive and sound card into a system that contains other adapters and devices.

Before purchasing a sound card be sure the adapter supports interrupts, I/O addresses, and DMA channels that are not currently used in the system.

Some sound cards support multiple MIDI emulations. Each emulation requires its own interrupt and I/O address. Plug and Play (PnP) helps with the installation problems, but vendors implement the Plug and Play features in different ways. Most manufacturers offer PnP cards that can operate in a computer with a PnP BIOS and in the legacy (non-PnP) computers. This is usually accomplished through a software utility provided by the manufacturer. Intel has a generic Plug and Play (PnP) configuration driver for the DOS/Windows environment called **ICM** (**Intel Configuration Manager**) that detects and configures Plug and Play adapters. The configuration manager takes control from the BIOS and assigns system resource. The configuration manager is only needed if the ROM BIOS *does not* support Plug and Play. ICM is a TSR (memory resident program) that competes for memory space in the DOS/Windows environment and can cause memory problems.

Another generic utility developed by Intel for PnP cards in the DOS/Windows environment is the **ICU** (**ISA Configuration Utility**) that allows the viewing and modification of legacy (non-PnP) card's resources such as interrupts, I/O addresses, and DMA channels. ICU configures an ISA card without using jumpers or switches. Many vendors recommend the ICU program and include the installation steps in their adapter's manual. For example, Creative Labs, Inc. (manufacturer of CD-ROMs and sound cards) developed their own PnP driver and utility, **CTCM** (**CreaTive PnP Configuration Manager**) that loads through the CONFIG.SYS file. CTCM can also be run from the DOS prompt with the advantage of not staying in memory once it finishes.

Creative Lab's CTCM is for Creative Lab PnP adapters only. However, it can co-exist with other PnP configuration managers and does not *require* a PnP BIOS or ICM to operate. CTCM finds the settings for any PnP cards previously configured. But, if CTCM is needed for configuration conflicts on legacy (non-PnP) adapters, the interrupt, DMA, and I/O address resources must be entered through Creative Lab's CTCU program.

CTCU (**CreaTive PnP Configuration Utility**) is Creative Lab's configuration utility run from the DOS prompt or through the AUTOEXEC.BAT file. It executes if the computer does not have a PnP BIOS, if the system does not have ICM or ICU installed, or if the Creative Lab PnP card does not work properly with its current settings.

CreaTive PnP Configuration Manager (CTCM) executes after CTCU is used to enter all legacy resources to configure the Creative Labs PnP card so the PnP card does not conflict with the older adapters. CTCU can also be executed if the resource settings have been changed on a legacy card or if one was removed from the system. (CTCU can help free resources previously allocated to the legacy card.)

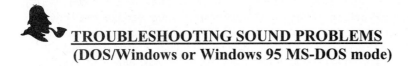

Do not use CTCU if ICM is installed as CTCU cannot access the ICM database of resource settings. Use ICU instead or disable ICM and use CTCU.

A general rule of thumb is if a computer system has a Plug and Play BIOS, a Plug and Play driver, and a configuration utility such as ICM and ICU, let the configuration driver configure the Plug and Play adapter. If possible, go into the SETUP program and disable the BIOS PnP configuration abilities. The BIOS will most likely *not* be aware of the resources used by legacy (non-PnP) adapters. Use the configuration utility to input the legacy resources and use the configuration manager to set up the PnP adapter. ALWAYS refer to the Plug and Play adapter's documentation for the vendor's recommendations.

TROUBLESHOOTING SOUND PROBLEMS
(DOS/Windows or Windows 95 MS-DOS mode)

If sound does not come out of the CD-ROM drive after the drivers and software load, the following troubleshooting tips will help.

1. Be sure an audio CD or a CD containing audio files is inserted into the CD-ROM drive.
2. Verify that the Windows 3.x [MCI] CD Audio driver loads. Find the driver by opening the **Main** program group, double-click on **Control Panel**, then double-click on **Drivers**. If the [MCI] CD Audio driver is not loaded, click on the **Install** button and insert the appropriate Windows disk as prompted on the screen.
3. Try playing an audio CD from the Windows Media Player program in the Accessories program group. After starting Media Player, click on **Device** from the menu bar. Highlight **CD Audio** from the drop-down menu. After a few seconds the buttons on the Media Player screen will darken. Click once on the left-most icon (which is a picture of a right arrow). The CD begins to play. If the CD plays within Media Player and not from the software included with the CD-ROM drive, try re-installing the vendor's software and check your steps again. Check the vendor's web site for any software patches or software installation recommendations. If the buttons on the Media Player screen never darken, check the Master/Slave, SCSI ID, termination, and software driver configurations.
4. Try playing an audio CD from a DOS CD-ROM control program. Many manufacturers include both a Windows and a DOS program for controlling the CD-ROM drive. To start the program, change into the directory that contains the software and type the command that starts the CD-ROM control program. If the CD plays from the DOS program and not from the Windows program, Windows is most likely missing the audio driver for the sound card.

5. If sound no longer comes out of the speakers, check the speaker cables. Also, a corrupted SYSTEM.INI file can cause this problem. Copy your backup of SYSTEM.INI and replace the file. If no backup exists, check for any file that starts with SYSTEM in the Windows 3.x directory. Some programs such as Norton Utilities make a backup of the SYSTEM.INI file when installed.

6. Check for an interrupt, I/O address, or DMA conflict on the audio portion of the sound card.

7. Check the proper installation of the audio cable.

8. Check that the speakers or headphones connect to the CD-ROM drive or to the sound card.

9. If using speakers, check the insertion of the cable jack on the back of the sound card. Verify the speakers have batteries installed or an AC adapter connected.

10. If using headphones, verify that the headphones work on another device before using to test the CD-ROM drive.

11. Get updated drivers from the sound card manufacturer's web site.

12. If ICM errors appear on bootup after installing a new PnP sound card, use a configuration manager provided by the manufacturer or configure the PnP card using jumpers and switches.

13. When using a configuration utility such as Creative Lab's CTCU or Intel's ICU, the settings for the PnP sound card may need to be changed several times before finding a non-conflicting combination.

14. If using ICM in a system where a Creative Labs' sound card and CTCM are installed, the CTCM statement in the CONFIG.SYS file must be placed after the ICM driver.

15. If the computer halts when the configuration manager loads, check for a memory conflict or remove the HIGHSCAN switch from the EMM386 statement in CONFIG.SYS.

16. If the monitor's image quality decreases after installing a sound card with speakers, move the speakers away from the monitor.

17. If the speakers produce a humming noise and are AC powered, move the speaker power cord to a different wall outlet. Plugging the speakers into the same circuit as the computer is best.

For more in-depth, product-specific troubleshooting, refer to the documentation or the web site of the sound card or CD-ROM drive manufacturer. Many sound card manufacturers no longer provide documentation for the DOS Windows environment or the Windows 95 MS-DOS mode.

SOUND CARDS USING WINDOWS 95

Most sound adapters are Plug and Play capable and compatible with Windows 95. When installing a PnP sound card, Windows 95 automatically determines the existing device and adapter resources. Then, Windows 95 allocates unused resources to the new PnP sound card. If the sound card is a legacy (non-PnP) card, the Add New Hardware wizard must be used.

Windows 95 does not need a configuration utility such as ICU. However, a configuration utility can be used to enter legacy card settings, even though Windows 95 has the settings. Sometimes in Windows 95, the CD-ROM drive and sound card must be set up differently for the Windows 95 operating system and the Windows 95 MS-DOS mode. This is necessary if the CD-ROM drive and the sound card functions will be used in both modes. Reference the manuals included with the CD-ROM and the sound card or contact the manufacturers when setting up the devices in both modes. Also, refer to the DOS/Windows, Windows 95 MS-DOS mode section for more information on configuring and troubleshooting CD-ROM drives and sound cards with problems only in the MS-DOS mode. Just remember a configuration utility can cause a conflict with Windows 95.

Windows 95 multimedia accessories are used to test the CD-ROM drive, sound card, microphone, etc. To test the audio section of the sound card in Windows 95, the CD audio MCI driver must be installed. To verify if the driver is enabled, perform the following steps:

1.   Go to the Control Panel by double-clicking on the **My Computer** icon, then double-click on the **Control Panel** folder icon.
2.   Double-click on the **Multimedia** icon.
3.   Click on the **Advanced** tab.
4.   Click the Plus sign next to **Media Control Devices** in the Multimedia Devices list. If CD Audio Device (Media Control) does not appear in the list, the driver is not installed. Go to the next section on how to install the driver. If CD Audio Device (Media Control) is in the list, click on it and go to Step 5.
5.   Click the **Properties** button.
6.   Click on the **Use This Media Control Device** checkbox in the Properties dialog box.
7.   Close the **Control Panel** window.

If the CD audio MCI driver is not installed, the Windows 95 Media Player cannot play audio CDs. Many technicians forget this step and begin troubleshooting the installation of the sound card or the CD-ROM drive when the problem is a software driver. To install the MCI audio driver so the Windows 95 CD Player will play audio CDs, perform the following steps:

1.   Go to the Control Panel by double-clicking on the **My Computer** icon, then double-click on the **Control Panel** folder icon.
2.   Double-click on the **Add New Hardware** option.
3.   Click on the **Next** button.
4.   Click on the **No** button when asked if you want to have Windows 95 search for your hardware. Then click on the **Next** button.
5.   Click on the **Sound, Video, and Game Controllers** option from the Hardware Types list.
6.   Click on the **Next** button.
7.   From the Manufacturers list, click on **Microsoft MCI**.
8.   From the Models list, click on the **CD Audio Device (Media Control)** option.
9.   Click the **Next** button.
10.   Click on the **Finish** button.
11.   Close the Control Panel window.

An exercise at the end of the chapter explains how to test an audio CD using the Windows 95 CD Player.

TROUBLESHOOTING WINDOWS 95 CD-ROM AND SOUND PROBLEMS

Some of the troubleshooting steps found in the DOS/Windows and the Windows 95 MS-DOS mode section, such as checking the cables, SCSI ID, master/slave jumper, etc., also apply to Windows 95. Refer to the DOS/Windows troubleshooting section of the chapter. By using the latest drivers and correcting interrupt, DMA channel, and I/O address conflicts, most installation problems are resolved.

Windows 95 also has the Troubleshooter wizard in Help. The following steps enable the Windows 95 Troubleshooter wizard.

1.   Click on the **Start** button.
2.   Choose the **Help** option.
3.   Select the **Contents** tab. The Help Topics box appears.
4.   Double-click on the **Troubleshooting** option.

The Windows 95 SETUP program checks for the existence of four device classes, of which the CD-ROM is one. If the initialization fails during hardware detection, Windows 95 creates the DETCRASH.LOG file which has information about the module that was running and the I/O port or memory resources that was accessed when the failure occurred. Sometimes a CD-ROM drive quits working because of the SETUP program's detection process. When SETUP is attempted again through another power-up, the Safe Recovery part of SETUP skips the CD-ROM device and continues through SETUP.

If Windows locks when booting and appears to be locking up on the CD-ROM drive detection, Windows 95 might not be able to find the CD-ROM drive because a hardware conflict occurred. Turn off the computer and power on again. When Windows 95 loads, run the Add New Hardware wizard found in the Control Panel to allow Windows 95 to search for, find, and configure the CD-ROM drive again.

Another problem might be that the system locks when the CD-ROM drive is found because the driver for the CD-ROM drive is a real-mode software driver and not a Windows 95 driver. If this happens, turn off the computer and try powering on again. When Windows 95 loads, use the Add New Hardware program in the Control Panel to load the Windows 95 driver for the CD-ROM drive. Another symptom might be every time the computer restarts with Windows 95, a message appears stating that "Your system configuration has changed" and Windows 95 goes into the hardware configuration program. Frequently drivers for devices such as Windows 95 do not have the proper Windows 95 drivers loaded. To get rid of the message, use the Add New Hardware program in the Control Panel. Do *not* allow Windows 95 to detect the hardware, but instead, choose No and load the proper drivers from disk.

If sound is a problem, verify the installation of the correct sound drivers. Go into the **System** Control Panel. Click on the **Device Manager** tab. Double-click on the **Sound, Video, and Game Controllers** option. Look for the specific sound driver for the sound card installed in the computer. Many sound drivers can be disabled due to a hardware conflict. Check the **General** tab in the sound driver section to determine if the driver is enabled or disabled.

The exercises at the end of the chapter help with Windows 95 CD-ROM drive and sound card installation.

OTHER CD-TYPE TECHNOLOGIES — CD-R (Compact Disk Recordable)

CD-R (Compact Disk Recordable) drives have the ability to create CDs, but they can only write once to a particular disk. The CD-R disks cannot be erased or re-used. CD-R technology is sometimes called **WORM (Write Once-Read Many)** technology. CD-R drives are used to make backups or distribute software on CDs. Disks written by CD-R drives have a temperature sensitive dye coating. To write data, the laser beam strikes the disk, changing the disk's color. This alters the disk's reflective property providing a way to distinguish between 1s and 0s. A disk written by a CD-R drive can be read by a standard CD-ROM drive. CD-R drives are no longer as expensive as in years past.

CD-R drives come in both IDE and SCSI models. The models are based on their X factor speed for reading and writing. For example, one model might be a 2x6 which is a drive that can write data at 2X speed (300 KBps) and read data at 6X (900 KBps) CD-ROM speed. Another model is a 4x4 that reads and writes at 4X CD-ROM speed (600KBps).

One problem with CD-R drives occurs when data is written to the CD-R disk. If the CD-R drive does not send data in a steady stream, a buffer underrun error occurs and the CD-R disk is ruined. To help with this problem, use a high-end computer with at least 16MB of RAM and a fast hard drive. Another problem with CD-R drives is how the drive keeps track of small data packet backups. Some CD-R drive manufacturers use a standard known as **UDF (Universal Disk Format)**; however, Windows 95 does not support UDF.

Adaptec Corporation has a driver for Windows 95 called DirectCD that overcomes the Windows 95/UDF problem. However, the CD disk created in the CD-R drive cannot be read by DOS, Windows 3.x, or Macintosh computers. Another problem is with some CD-ROM drives reading the disks created by a CD-R drive. On the problem CD-ROM drives, the laser is not calibrated to read recordable disks that have a different surface than regular CDs. An indication of this problem is if a disk created by a CD-R drive is readable by other CD-ROM drives, but not by one particular CD-ROM drive. There is no solution to this problem except to replace the drive that can read a CD-R written disk.

CD-RW (CD RE-WRITABLE) OR CD-E (CD ERASABLE)

CD-E (Compact Disk Erasable) or **CD-RW (Compact Disk Re-Writable)** can write multiple times to a disk. These disks are good for data backup, data archiving or data distribution on CDs. Originally, this technology known as **Phase-change Dual (PD)** technology used a laser to change the reflective properties of the disk. Now to read a PD disk, a PD/CD drive with a high powered, more expensive laser is used. CD-RW or CD-E drives create disks that can be read on any standard CD-ROM drive with **dye-polymer** technology which uses a laser to heat the CD. This creates a bump on the disk that reflects light differently than the flat areas on the CD.

The good thing about CD-RW drives is they are backward compatible. The reflective properties of a CD-RW disk are different (lower) than regular CD-ROM disks. Many drives that support CD-RW disks tout themselves as multi-read. Check with the individual CD-ROM drive manufacturer to determine if a particular model can read CD-RW disks. The drawback to CD-RW disk is the disks wear out after multiple writes.

MAGNETO-OPTICAL DRIVES

A similar technology used for reading and writing compact disks is **magneto-optical** (**MO**). These disks do not have the drawbacks of the dye-polymer or phase-change technologies. However, magneto-optical disks cannot be used in regular CD-ROM drives, but require a magneto-optical drive. For data backups or archiving, magneto-optical drives are great. They also use a laser beam to heat the surface of the disk, then a magnet applies a charge to the surface. They can be erased by re-heating the disk and using the magnet to erase the data. Magneto-optical disks are read using the laser similar to CD-ROM technology.

DVD-ROM

A new technology known as DVD-ROM drives may make CD-ROM drives obsolete. **DVD-ROM** (also called DVD) originally stood for Digital Video Disk, then Digital Versatile Disk, and now does not stand for anything. DVD disks provide more storage capacity than a CD-ROM disk, but can still play CDs used in regular CD-ROM drives. The disks used with DVD drives are the same diameter and thickness as traditional CDs. Like CDs, the DVD disks tolerate dust, dirt, and fingerprints. DVD disks provide high video resolution and high quality sound unmatched in the computer industry. DVD disks that contain data such as movies can transfer as fast as 4X CD-ROMs (600KBps). DVD disks can transfer regular data at 1.3MBps which is almost as fast as 10X CD-ROMs. DVD disks should satisfy the industry demand for increased storage.

DVDs are used for audio and video entertainment such as movies, video games, and interactive TV, as well as Internet access and software applications that currently require more than one CD. The DVD-ROM drives are slated for four different configurations: 4.7GB, 8.5GB, 9.4GB, and 17GB. The 4.7GB configuration has a single layer of data on one side of the disk. The 8.5GB configuration will use two layers on the same side to increase storage capacity. The 9.4GB disk will use a single layer on both sides of the disk. The 17GB disk will use dual layers on both sides of the disk. The double-sided disks will have to be manually flipped over to the second side. The data on the DVD disk has pits that are smaller and more closely spaced than CD-ROM disks.

A great deal of industry forethought went into making the standards of DVD drives. From the start, DVD-ROM drives can read single layer, dual layer, dual-sided, and dual-sided/dual-layer disks as well as the existing audio and application CDs. The DVD-ROM drives are not able to read CD-R disks. However, the new CD-R 2 disks are supposed to be compatible with CD-R drives, regular CD-ROM drives, and DVD-ROM drives.

For DVD-ROM technology to be used in computers today, the computer needs several items. Refer to the list below.

1. An 133MHz Pentium microprocessor. A Pentium Overdrive microprocessor is probably not good enough because the computer will not have the latest PCI bus. The older PCI bus is not fast enough. Some industry analysts believe a 233MHz microprocessor with MMX capabilities will be needed to realistically handle the DVD technology.
2. A DVD-ROM drive. The DVD-ROM drives will use either the SCSI or ATAPI (IDE) interface.
3. A PCI audio/video adapter that handles MPEG-2 video and AC-3 audio.
4. Windows 95 operating system.

Until Microsoft's DirectX media drivers (see the chapter section on new technologies) are available in software developer's hands, many believe the first DVD-ROM drives and software applications may have some compatibility issues. Keep this in mind when installing the first DVD-ROM drives and PCI adapters for those techno-junkie users. An indication of this problem may be the audio and video signals are not synchronized or that the software will not work at all. Microsoft's Windows 98 (code name Memphis) is supposed to contain application code to ease the transition from the traditional CD-ROM drive to the new DVD-ROM drive.

OTHER DVD TECHNOLOGIES

On the drawing board for DVD technology are drives known as **DVD Write Once** drives or **DVD-WORM (DVD Write Once-Read Many)** drives. The proposed DVD Write Once technology is supposed to record audio and video data (as well as normal data) to a disk that holds 3.9GB. Another technology down the pike is **DVD Re-writable (DVD-RAM)** which uses re-writable media that is estimated to initially hold 2.6GB. DVD-RAM drives are expected to be in the computer market in 1998.

CD STANDARDS

CDs are classified according to their standard (data format). Manufacturers of CD-ROM drives occasionally use the CD standards to state what type of disks their CD-ROM drive reads. The standards generically group into "colored books." CD-ROM Table #5 summarizes the standards for each.

CD Standards

Standard	Purpose
Red Book	Audio CD format
Yellow Book	Data CD format
Green Book	CD-i format
Orange Book	Recordable CD format (Part I is for magneto-optical. Part II is for write-once disks. The standard also includes the specification for a PhotoCD.)
White Book	Video CD format
Blue Book	CD Extra format to include data and audio
CD-ROM/XA	Bridges Yellow Book and CD-i formats (Mode 1 is standard Yellow Book sectors. Mode 2 has two forms: Mode 2 Form-1 is 2,048 data bytes with error correction. Mode 2 Form-2 is 2,324 audio/video data bytes without error correction.)
ISO 9660	File naming format
Rock Ridge	File name and symlink extensions (to be used with UNIX)
CD-RFS	Sony's incremental packet-writing file system
CD-UDF	Incremental packet-writing file system
CD-Text	Phillips audio CD standard

CD-ROM - TABLE # 5

NEW TECHNOLOGIES

Western Digital announced a new technology called SDX that could revolutionize CD-ROM drives and other removable media devices. The **SDX (Storage Data Acceleration)** technology centers around a SDX-enabled EIDE hard drive. The hard drive connects to a removable media device such as a CD-ROM through a 10-pin SDX cable and provides caching for the removable media device. The performance gain for the CD-ROM is expected to be as high as 100 percent. The SDX interface can be adapted to handle CD-R, CD-E, and DVD devices. SDX technology is already 100 percent compatible with various BIOS, software drivers, operating systems, and other hardware. How many new technologies can say that? For those who say the CD-ROM is dead, they might want to take a look at the new SDX technology.

A software development that will change the computer industry tremendously and help with the DVD technology is Microsoft's **DirectX**, the multimedia drivers, application code, and 3-D support for audio and video. DirectX takes the operating system and the audio and video functions into a new computer dimension. It incorporates support for the Universal Serial bus, 1394 bus, Accelerated Graphics Port, MPEG-1, MPEG-2, MMX extensions, and Microsoft's new Talisman graphics architecture. DirectX has a direct impact on the new DVD market because of the lack of audio and video standards needed with the new PCI audio/video adapter. DirectX has pieces of software code that software providers use so their software works with the new PCI adapters. DirectX version 5.0 will be available in Microsoft's new operating system, Windows 98 (code named Memphis), possibly with some enhanced features.

Name _____

CD-ROM Review Questions

1.   What are some other names for disks that operate in CD-ROMs?

2.   Why are CD-ROMs so important for today's computer users?

3.   What is a CD-ROM's x-factor?

4.   What factors influence what x-factor CD-ROM to install in a system?

5.   T/F   A CD-ROM that has a 400ms access speed is faster than one with a 250ms access speed.

6.   T/F   CD-ROM drives are slower than hard drives.

7.   For what are CD-ROM buffers used?

8.   T/F   CD-ROM data is normally on the same side as the disk label.

9.   Describe how a CD-ROM reads data.

10.   T/F   CD-ROMs can be external devices.

11.   What are the two ways to load a CD into a drive? Which method do you prefer, and why?

12.   What type of interface is most common for CD-ROM drives in today's computers?

13.   Why do you think the interface mentioned in Question 12 is the most common?

14.   What other interface is available for CD-ROM drives?

15.   What are some considerations when choosing a CD-ROM interface?

16.   Why is it best to avoid proprietary CD-ROMs?

Use the following scenario for Question 17:

A customer has an 80486DX computer with 4MB of RAM running DOS/Windows 3.x. The video adapter is an ISA adapter with 1MB of video memory on the adapter. The user has an EIDE hard drive installed in the computer that plugs directly into the motherboard. The customer wants to upgrade the computer by adding a CD-ROM drive and sound card.

17.   What CD-ROM interface and CD-ROM drive speed would you recommend to the customer and why?

18. What are some considerations when upgrading a CD-ROM?

19. T/F CDs have a protective coating to shield the disk and even with a small amount of dirt on it, the disk functions.

20. Describe how to use a CD cleaning cloth.

21. T/F All CD-ROM drives have a self-cleaning laser lens.

22. T/F CDs played through a drive's headphone jack is as good as a stereo.

23. T/F Some CD-ROM drives have proprietary audio cables.

24. T/F A CD-ROM connected to an IDE motherboard connector can play sound through a sound card.

25. T/F A feature to look for in a sound card is the ability to play .MID and .WAV files.

26. What does Sound Blaster-compatible mean?

27. What is the best advice to give someone who is choosing computer speakers?

28. What is shielding?

29. What are some considerations for buying a sound card?

30. Why is 40,000 samples per second a good sampling rate for a sound card?

31. What does having a 16-bit sound card mean?

32. How is the MPC standard helpful to technicians?

33. T/F IDE CD-ROMs must be set as the slave device.

34. T/F Plugging an IDE CD-ROM cable in backwards can destroy the CD-ROM.

35. What is the importance of the *device name* when installing a CD-ROM?

36. Describe how to troubleshoot the CD-ROM device driver.

37. What file normally loads the MSCDEX.EXE?

38. T/F MSCDEX.EXE's */D:* switch must have the exact device driver's name as the driver loaded through CONFIG.SYS.

39. What is an advantage or disadvantage of using MSCDEX.EXE's */L:letter* switch?

40. Which is better, increasing the number of buffers used with the */M:number* switch with the MSCDEX.EXE program or using a caching program such as SmartDrive and why?

41.   A computer has an internal CD-ROM connected to a sound card and speakers. The CD-ROM has never used an audio CD before, but any software applications run from the CD have worked fine including the audio. Using Windows 3.x's Media Player will play an audio CD. The buttons light up on Media Player's CD graphic, but no sounds are heard from the speakers. What are some things to check?

42.   T/F   The SMARTDRV line in CONFIG.SYS precedes the CD-ROM device driver to provide caching for the CD-ROM drive.

43.   T/F   Windows 95 operating system has its own CD-ROM file system.

44.   T/F   The Windows 95 CD-ROM cache must be initially set by the user or the technician for optimum performance.

45.   What is the purpose of the supplemental CD-ROM cache provided with the Windows 95 operating system?

46.   What is one indication that the CD-ROM supplemental cache might need to be adjusted?

47.   List at least three preventive maintenance items for CD-ROM drives or disks.

48.   T/F   Windows 95 supports Plug and Play sound adapters.

49.   What is an indication that the CD-ROM drive in a Windows 95-based system has a hardware conflict?

50.   What is a problem with CD-R drives?

51.   Describe the benefits and drawbacks of using DirectCD.

52.   Which of the following architectures does the DVD-ROM audio/video adapter use?
      A.   ISA
      B.   VL-bus
      C.   PC Card
      D.   PCI
      E.   MCA

53.   What is SDX?

Name _____

CD-ROM Fill-in-the-Blank

1.   A CD-ROM _____ specification is the time it takes to find specific data.

2.   On a CD, a _____ is an indentation along the spiral track.

3.   On a CD, the area that separates the pits is a _____.

4.   The CD-ROM's _____ reads data from the CD.

5.   An _____ connects a CD-ROM to a sound card.

6.   The _____ interface is used to create synthesized music.

7.   Multimedia disks normally use sound files with the _____ file extension.

8.   Most game CDs used sound files that end with the _____ file extension.

9.   A rating for how loud the volume can be without distorting sound is a speaker's _____.

10. The _____ is the range of sounds a speaker or sound card can reproduce.

11. The _____ specification defines multimedia standards.

12. The _____ DOS program assigns a drive letter to the CD-ROM.

13. A CD-ROM's _____ is an unique eight character name given to each CD-ROM drive.

14. MSCDEX.EXE's _____ switch gives more information about the installation as MSCDEX.EXE loads.

15. _____ is a DOS caching program used with CD-ROMs.

16. A _____ drive can read a CD many times, but can only write once to it.

17. The _____ standard is for CD-R drives.

18. _____ drives can write multiple times to a CD.

19. _____ drives use a laser beam to read the CD and then it writes data to the disk.

20. _____ drives combine audio and video entertainment with backward compatibility with CDs.

21. Microsoft's _____ contains multimedia software to speed up video and audio applications.

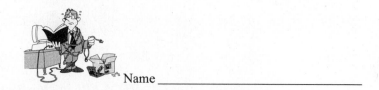

Name _____

INTERNAL CD-ROM DRIVE INSTALLATION EXERCISE

Objective: To correctly install a CD-ROM drive

Parts: CD-ROM drive and documentation for the drive (if possible)
          Adapter (if needed)
          Interface cable
          Tools
          Anti-static materials
          Available drive bay

Observe proper grounding procedures when installing a CD-ROM drive.

Step 1:   Remove the cover from the computer. Use proper anti-static procedures.
Step 2:   (optional) Install any mounting brackets necessary to install the CD-ROM drive inside the computer.
Step 3:   Check what interface the CD-ROM drive uses (IDE, EIDE, SCSI, or proprietary). Set the appropriate master/slave, SCSI ID, or termination settings depending on the drive interface type. Refer to the documentation included with the CD-ROM for the proper configuration.

Question 1:   What type of interface does the CD-ROM drive use?

Question 2:   What is an advantage of this interface (the answer to Question 1), than other interfaces available?

Step 4:   (optional) Install any interface adapter into the system. If using a sound card, an exercise later in the chapter explains how to install it. Set any interrupt, I/O address, or DMA channel as necessary ensuring these settings do not conflict with any other device or adapter installed in the system. Refer to the documentation included with the adapter. Before installing an adapter of any type inside a computer, you should know what interrupts and I/O addresses are being used by the devices and adapters already installed. If you do not know this information, go to the RUNNING MICROSOFT DIAGNOSTICS or USING WINDOWS 95'S DEVICE MANAGER exercise or use software you have available to obtain this information. Make any notes regarding installed devices and the interrupts and I/O addresses already used.

Question 3:   What would be one indication of an interrupt conflict between the CD-ROM drive and any other device in the system?

Step 5:   Install the CD-ROM drive in the computer. Keep in mind the IDE interface cable connection may be short in length.

Step 6:   Attach the power cable to the CD-ROM drive.

Step 7:   Attach one end of the interface cable to the CD-ROM drive. Verify that the cable's pin 1 on the cable attaches to the drive's pin 1. The drive's pin 1 is sometimes hard to detect because the connector is black. Look very carefully for an etched arrow on the connector on the drive. Some drive manufacturers place a drawing on top of the drive that illustrates the proper orientation for the cable.

Step 8:   Attach the other end of the interface cable to the motherboard or adapter interface connector. Verify the cable's pin 1 connects to the CD-ROM drive's pin 1.

Step 9:   Power on the computer, verifying that no POST error codes appear.

_____ Instructor's Initials

Once the CD-ROM drive is installed, software drivers are required in the DOS/Windows environment. Go to the CD-ROM SOFTWARE INSTALLATION (DOS/Windows 3.x) exercise. If using Windows 95, the operating system detects the installation of a new hardware component and configures the device or prompts for a driver disk supplied by the CD-ROM drive manufacturer.

Name _____

CD-ROM DRIVE SOFTWARE INSTALLATION
(DOS/WINDOWS 3.X) EXERCISE

Objective: To correctly install software necessary for proper CD-ROM operation

Parts: CD-ROM driver and documentation for the drive
Microsoft Windows installation disks or a disk which contains the MCI CD Audio software
A CD-based software application or files
(Optional) An audio CD

Step   1:   Install the software driver for the CD-ROM drive referring to the documentation included
with the drive for the command that starts the installation process. For DOS skills, refer to
Appendix A. Most software driver installation procedures prompt the technician to reboot
the computer for the changes to take effect. If the installation procedures do not prompt for
this, restart the computer with a warm boot.

Step   2:   When the computer restarts and the message "Starting MS-DOS" or "Starting PC DOS"
appears on the screen, press the **F8** key and step through the CONFIG.SYS drivers one by
one. Reply **Y** for Yes to the prompt to load each driver. Look specifically for the driver for
the CD-ROM drive and determine if the driver detects the installation of a CD-ROM drive.

Question 1:   Did the software driver for the CD-ROM drive load okay and detect a CD-ROM drive?
If a CD-ROM drive is detected, write the message that indicates this in the space below. If the
CD-ROM drive is not detected by the software driver, troubleshoot the CD-ROM and driver by
referring to the chapter's references on troubleshooting.

Step   3:   Using a text editor such as Microsoft's EDIT, verify that the MSCDEX.EXE program is in
the AUTOEXEC.BAT file. Most CD-ROM software driver installation programs either put
this line in the AUTOEXEC.BAT file or prompt the technician to add this line manually. In
either case, make sure you use the proper switches depending on the system and if other
caching programs such as SmartDrive are used.

Question 2:   Is the MSCDEX.EXE line in the AUTOEXEC.BAT file? If not, add the line using the
proper switches and correct device name with the program.

Question 3:   What switches are used with the MSCDEX.EXE command and what is the function of each switch?

Step 4:   Restart the computer. When the message "Starting MS-DOS" appears on the screen, press **F8** to single step through the CONFIG.SYS and AUTOEXEC.BAT files. Pay particular attention when the MSCDEX.EXE program loads. A message similar to the following should appear:
MSCDEX Version 2.23
Copyright (C) Microsoft Corp. 1986-1993. All rights reserved.
     Drive D: = Driver IDECD001 Unit 0

Question 4:   Did the MSCDEX.EXE program detect the CD-ROM drive? If not, perform troubleshooting techniques as described in the CD-ROM chapter.

Question 5:   What drive letter did the operating system assign to the CD-ROM drive?

Step   5: Install any additional software included with the CD-ROM drive and test as necessary.

Question 6:   Does the CD-ROM drive work?

Step 6:   If the CD-ROM drive is to be checked for sound through a front panel headphone connection, perform Steps 10 through 20 in the SOUND CARD INSTALLATION EXERCISE.

_____ Instructor's Initials

Optional Step 7: If performing no other work inside the computer, re-install the computer's cover.

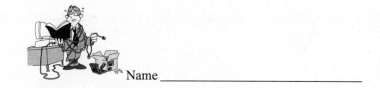

Name _____

SOUND CARD INSTALLATION EXERCISE
(DOS/WINDOWS ENVIRONMENT)

Objective: To correctly install a sound card in the DOS/Windows environment

Parts: Sound Card and documentation
         Sound Card software and drivers
         Audio cable
         Audio CD
         Tools
         Anti-static materials
         Available expansion slot

Observe proper grounding procedures when installing a sound card.

Step 1:   Unless the sound card is a Plug and Play (PnP) adapter, use the sound card documentation
           to set any jumpers or switches for the DMA channel, interrupt, and I/O address for each
           part of the sound card (MIDI, audio output, etc.). If the card is a PnP adapter, proceed to
           Step 2. Before installing an adapter of any type, you should know what interrupts and I/O
           addresses are used by the devices and adapters already installed in the computer. If you do
           not know this information, go to the RUNNING MICROSOFT DIAGNOSTICS exercise or
           use software you have available to obtain this information. Make any notes regarding
           installed devices and the interrupts and I/O addresses already used. For DOS skills, refer to
           Appendix A.
Step 2:   Remove the computer's cover.
Step 3:   Insert and secure the sound card in an available slot.
Step 4:   If the sound card has an external volume control, turn the volume to the maximum position.
Optional Step 5: If the CD-ROM drive is to use the sound card as an interface connection, attach the
           interface cable from the CD-ROM drive to the sound card. Verify that the cable's pin 1
           attaches to the adapter connector's pin 1.
Step 6:   Attach an audio cable from the CD-ROM drive to the sound card. Verify that the cable's
           pin 1 attaches to the adapter connector's pin 1.
Step 7:   Power on the computer.

Question 1:   Is the sound card a Plug and Play sound card? If yes, proceed to Step 8. If the sound
          card is not a Plug and Play card, go to Step 9.

Step 8: If the computer has a Plug and Play BIOS, the BIOS configures the Plug and Play card. The settings configured by the BIOS may conflict with legacy (non-PnP) cards. A configuration manager and configuration utility may be necessary to configure the Plug and Play sound card even though the computer has a PnP BIOS. If the computer does *not* have a Plug and Play BIOS, use the Intel Configuration Manager (ICM) and ISA Configuration Utility (ICU) or one provided by the sound card's manufacturer and configure the PnP sound card.

Step 9: Load any software drivers and any applications required for sound card operation. Refer to the sound card manual for any specific loading instructions.

Step 10: Verify the installation of Windows 3.x's MCI CD Audio software driver by double-clicking on Window's **Main** program group.

Step 11: Double-click on the **Control Panel** icon.

Step 12: Double-click on the **Drivers** icon.

Step 13: If the Windows 3.x's [MCI] CD Audio driver is not loaded, click on the **ADD** button. Choose [MCI] CD Audio driver from the list shown and insert the appropriate Windows disk as prompted on the screen.

Step 14: Once the driver loads, close all open windows.

Step 15: Double-click on the **Accessories** program group.

Step 16: Open the **Media Player** program by double-clicking on the icon.

Step 17: Insert an audio CD into the CD-ROM drive.

Step 18: Verify that speakers connect to the sound adapter (if installed), motherboard, or verify that headphones attach to the CD-ROM drive.

Step 19: Click on the **Device** option from the Media Player menu bar.

Step 20: Click once on the **CD Audio** option from the drop-down menu. After a few seconds the CD player-like buttons on the Media Player screen darken. Once the buttons darken, click once on the left-most right arrow icon. The CD begins to play if the software is properly installed.

Question 2: Does the CD-ROM drive/sound card produce sound? If not, refer to the troubleshooting section of the CD-ROM chapter and troubleshoot the CD-ROM drive and sound card software programs and the CD-ROM drive/sound card installation. Keep in mind the sound card may need to be re-configured multiple times for successful operation of all. Remember that interrupt, DMA channel, and I/O conflicts are the source of 95 percent of sound card problems.

_____ Instructor's Initials

Step 21: Turn off the computer.

Step 22: Re-install the computer's cover.

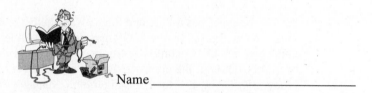

Name _____

SOUND CARD INSTALLATION EXERCISE (WINDOWS 95)

Objective: To correctly install a sound card in the Windows 95 environment

Parts: Sound Card and documentation
        Sound Card software and Windows 95 drivers
        Audio cable
        Audio CD
        Tools
        Anti-static materials
        Available expansion slot

Observe proper grounding procedures when installing a sound card.

Step   1:   Unless the sound card is a Plug and Play (PnP) adapter, use the sound card's documentation
            to set any jumpers or switches for the DMA channel, interrupt, and I/O address for each
            part of the sound card (MIDI, audio output, etc.). If the card is a PnP adapter, proceed to
            Step 2. Before installing an adapter of any type inside a computer, you should know what
            interrupts and I/O addresses are used by the devices and adapters already installed in the
            computer. If you do not know this information, go to the Chapter 3 Examining System
            Resources Using Windows 95 exercise or use the software available to obtain this
            information. Make any notes regarding installed devices and the interrupts and I/O
            addresses used.
Step   2:   Remove the computer's cover.
Step   3:   Insert and secure the sound card in an available slot.
Step   4:   If the sound card has an external volume control, turn the volume to the maximum position.
Optional Step 5: If the CD-ROM drive is to use the sound card as an interface connection, attach the
            interface cable from the CD-ROM drive to the sound card. Verify that the cable's pin 1 of
            the cable attaches to the adapter connector's pin 1.

Question 1:   Which is better, using the sound card's connector, a separate adapter, or the
            motherboard connection for the CD-ROM interface? Explain your answer.

Step 6: Attach an audio cable from the CD-ROM drive to the sound card. Verify that the cable's pin 1 of the cable attaches to the adapter connector's pin 1.

Step 7: Power on the computer.

Step 8: If Windows 95 detects the sound card, a prompt appears asking if you want to install drivers. For Windows 95 skills, refer to Appendix B. Click on the **Yes** button. Then another prompt asks for the Windows 95 installation disk, CD, or a manufacturer-provided disk. Do not use Windows 3.x drivers. Get Windows 95 drivers from the sound card manufacturer. After installing the software, the computer reboots. Proceed to Step 18. If Windows 95 does not automatically detect the sound card, Windows 95 must be forced to look for the hardware. Proceed to Step 9.

Steps 9 through 17 handle the situation that Windows 95 does not automatically detect the sound card.

Step 9: Click on the **Start** button.

Step 10: From the Start menu, select the **Settings** option.

Step 11: From the Settings menu, select the **Control Panel** option. The Control Panel window appears.

Step 12: Double-click on the **Add New Hardware** icon.

Step 13: Click on the **Next** button. A prompt asks if you want Windows 95 to search for new hardware.

Step 14: Click on the **No** button.

Step 15: Click on the **Next** button. A prompt tells you to pick from a list of hardware categories.

Step 16: Click on the **Sound, Video, and Game Controllers** option followed by a click on the **Next** button.

Step 17: Enter any IRQ, I/O address, DMA channel, etc. information requested (depending on the sound card installed).

Question 2: T/F Windows 95 is a Plug and Play operating system.

Question 3: T/F Windows 95 requires a Plug and Play BIOS to operate.

Step 18: After the system reboots, if the adapter does not work, check the cabling, use the Using Windows 95's Device Manager to Modify Hardware Resources exercise, or use this chapter's troubleshooting section. Keep in mind the sound card may need to be re-configured multiple times for successful operation of all components such as the audio output and MIDI. Remember that interrupt, DMA channel, and I/O conflicts are the source of 95 percent of sound card problems.

_____ Instructor's Initials

Step 19: Turn off the computer.

Step 20: Re-install the computer's cover.

Name _____

SETTING THE CD-ROM SUPPLEMENTAL CACHE
SIZE (IN WINDOWS 95)

Objective: To optimize the Windows 95 CD-ROM cache

Parts: A computer with Windows 95 loaded and a CD-ROM drive installed

Step   1:   Power on the computer and boot to Windows 95. Refer to Appendix B for Windows 95 skills.
Step   2:   Double-click on the **My Computer** icon.
Step   3:   Double-click on the **Control Panel** folder icon.
Step   4:   Double-click on the **System** icon.
Step   5:   Click once on the **Performance** tab.
Step   6:   Click once on the **File System** button located at the bottom of the screen in the Advanced Settings section.
Step   7:   Click on the **CD-ROM** tab.
Step   8:   Click on the down arrow in the **Optimize access pattern for:** window.
Step   9:   Select the proper speed of the CD-ROM drive installed in the system.
Step 10:   Drag the slide-bar in the **Supplemental cache size** option to the desired setting. The setting of the slide-bar changes the amount of memory allocated for the cache in the statement, "Windows will use ?? kilobytes of physical memory to perform these optimizations while data is being accessed." at the bottom of the window.
Step 11:   Click once on the **OK** button to accept the settings.
Step 12:   Close the System Properties window. A dialog box appears on the screen stating that the computer must be restarted for the changes to take effect.
Step 13:   Click once on the **Yes** button to restart the computer.

_____ Instructor's Initials

Name _____

CHANGING THE CD-ROM DRIVE LETTER EXERCISE (WINDOWS 95)

Objective: To change the CD-ROM drive letter assignment in the Windows 95 environment

Parts: A computer with Windows 95 loaded and a CD-ROM drive

Step 1:   Power on the computer and boot to Windows 95. Refer to Appendix B for Windows 95 skills.

Step 2:   Double-click on the **My Computer** icon.

Step 3:   Double-click on the **Control Panel** folder icon.

Step 4:   Double-click on the **System** icon.

Step 5:   Click on the **Device Manager** tab.

Step 6:   Double-click the **CD-ROM** sub-branch.

Step 7:   Double-click on the **CD-ROM drive**. If the CD-ROM drive is not in the tree, a DOS device driver controls the drive. To change the drive letter for a DOS-based device driver, edit the MSCDEX.EXE line in the AUTOEXEC.BAT file. See the chapter section on MSCDEX.EXE.

Step 8:   Click on the **Settings** tab.

Step 9:   Two Reserve Drive Letter fields (Start and End) are at the bottom of the dialog box. Set the drive Start range and End range to the same drive letter of your choice.

Question 1:   What drive letter did you choose for the CD-ROM drive?

Step 10:   Click on the **OK** button.

Step 11:   Close the System Properties window.

Step 12:   Close the Control Panel window.

Step 13:   Reboot Windows 95 using the Start button.

Step 14:   Verify the drive letter change using Explorer or going through the My Computer icon on the desktop.

Question 2:   How was the drive letter verified?

_____ Instructor's Initials

Name _____

PLAYING AN AUDIO CD USING WINDOWS 95'S CD PLAYER

Objective: Understand how to use Windows 95's CD Player program

Parts: A computer with Windows 95 loaded, a CD-ROM drive installed, and the MCI audio driver
         loaded. Refer to the chapter steps on how to verify (and install) the MCI audio driver.
         An Audio CD

Step 1:   Power on the computer and boot to Windows 95. Refer to Appendix B for Windows 95
           skills.
Step 2:   Insert an audio CD into the CD-ROM drive.
Step 3:   Click on the **Start** button.
Step 4:   From the Start menu, choose the **Program** option.
Step 5:   From the Program's sub-menu, choose the **Accessories** option.
Step 6:   From the Accessories menu, choose the **Multimedia** option.
Step 7:   From the Multimedia sub-menu, click on the **CD Player** option.
Step 8:   Click on the **Play** button (the right arrow) on the CD graphic.

Question 1:   Does the audio CD play? If not, verify the installation of the MCI audio driver. If the
               driver is installed, refer to the Windows 95 sound troubleshooting section of this chapter.

Step 9:   Click on the **Stop** button on the CD graphic.
Step 10:   Close and exit and **CD Player** program.

_____ Instructor's Initials

Name _____

1. Which of the following helps determine if a problem is software or hardware? (Pick all that apply.)
    A. Did POST produce any audio errors or display any error codes?
    B. Single-stepping through the AUTOEXEC.BAT and CONFIG.SYS files
    C. Determining if the problem only occurs in one software application
    D. Running diagnostics on the hardware

2. Which of the following is NOT true about memory?
    A. An access time of 50ns is faster than 60ns
    B. A bank of memory contains chips of the same capacity
    C. All memory banks must contain chips
    D. Memory POST errors usually being with a 2

3. A user has two 8MB 72-pin SIMMs in a Pentium. The user wants to upgrade to 32MB. Two SIMM sockets are available on the motherboard. What will you recommend?
    A. Remove the two 8MB SIMMs and buy one 32MB SIMM
    B. Remove the two 8MB SIMMs and buy two 16MB SIMMs
    C. Add one 16MB SIMM
    D. Add two 8MB SIMMs

4. Which of the following commands allows use of the UMBs by TSRs?
    A. DEVICE=C:\WINDOWS\HIMEM.SYS
    B. DEVICE=C:\WINDOWS\EMM386.EXE
    C. DOS=HIGH
    D. DOS=UMB

5. T/F Windows 95 needs the SmartDrive command in the AUTOEXEC.BAT file to acccess extended memory.

6. T/F Virtual memory is faster than a RAM drive.

7. Which of the following could cause out of memory errors for a Windows 3.x application? (Pick all that apply.)
    A. Not enough extended memory
    B. Not enough expanded memory
    C. Not enough heap space
    D. Not enough space for a RAM drive

8.   Which of the following provides the fastest access?
      A.   CD-ROM
      B.   DRAM
      C.   SRAM
      D.   Hard drive
      E.   Floppy drive

9.   What file is required for Windows 3.x to load?
      A.   SmartDrive
      B.   HIMEM.SYS
      C.   EMM386
      D.   VDISK

10.   A 601 error code indicates a _____ problem.
      A.   RAM
      B.   Hard drive
      C.   Floppy drive
      D.   CMOS

11.   If a SCSI device driver is causing the computer system to hang, what should be the next step?
      A.   Single-step through the CONFIG.SYS until the problem device driver is discovered
      B.   Bypass the AUTOEXEC.BAT file
      C.   Bypass the CONFIG.SYS file
      D.   Bypass both the AUTOEXEC.BAT and CONFIG.SYS files

12.   What is the *first* step when installing a new hard drive in a computer today?
      A.   Copy the system files over
      B.   Partition the new hard drive
      C.   Low-level format the new hard drive
      D.   High-level format the new hard drive
      E.   Copy the COMMAND.COM file over from a bootable floppy

13.   What is the *last* step when installing a new bootable hard drive in a computer today?
      A.   Copy the system files over
      B.   Partition the new hard drive
      C.   Low-level format the new hard drive
      D.   High-level format the new hard drive
      E.   Copy the COMMAND.COM file over from a bootable floppy

14.   SCANDISK _____
      A.   places files in non-contiguous sectors into contiguous sectors.
      B.   partitions the hard drive.
      C.   partitions the floppy disk.
      D.   checks and fixes problems in the FAT and with lost or cross-linked files.

CERTIFICATION REVIEW QUESTIONS

15. Scenario: A computer has an internal SCSI device and an external SCSI device connected to the same adapter. Which of the following is *false* concerning termination?
    A. The internal device must be terminated
    B. The external device must be terminated
    C. The adapter must be terminated

16. Which of the following commands performs disk caching?
    A. DEFRAG
    B. CACHE
    C. SMARTDRV
    D. HDCACHE

17. T/F   All new hard drives must be high level formatted before data can be stored on it.

18. What command is used to assign a logical drive a drive letter for the first time?
    A. DEBUG
    B. FORMAT
    C. ASSIGN
    D. FDISK

19. A computer boots up with the message "Bad or Missing Command Interpreter." What should be done?
    A. Change the drive type in CMOS
    B. Copy over COMMAND.COM from a bootable floppy disk
    C. Re-partition the hard drive
    D. High-level format the hard drive
    E. Use DEBUG to recover from the error

20. What is the maximum partition size for a computer with DOS 6.X or higher?
    A. 32MB
    B. 2GB
    C. 4GB
    D. 8GB

21. The two primary specifications for evaluating a CD-ROM drive are:
    A. Access speed
    B. Transfer rate
    C. Compatibility with other devices
    D. Acceleration speed
    F. Mean time between failures

22. T/F   Microsoft Windows 3.x's Media Player requires a MCI MIDI driver to play audio CDs.

C
E
R
T
I
F
I
C
A
T
I
O
N

R
E
V
I
E
W

Q
U
E
S
T
I
O
N
S

23.   To install a CD-ROM drive as a second device on the IDE connector, the CD-ROM drive must
      A.   be set to SCSI ID 1
      B.   be terminated
      C.   be set to SLAVE
      D.   be set to drive select 1

24.   T/F   For a computer to be MPC-compliant, a Creative Lab's SoundBlaster sound card must be installed.

25.   Scenario: A newly installed CD-ROM drive will not operate. Which of the following would be checked *first*?
      A.   Check the hard drive's interface cabling
      B.   Check the audio cable
      C.   Check the configuration settings such as the SCSI ID, terminators, or the Master/Slave setting
      D.   Verify that the CD-ROM drive's device driver loads
      E.   Verify that the sound card's device driver loads
      F.   Verify that the SmartDrive program loads
      G.   Verify that the MSCDEX program loads

26.   Scenario: The light on the CD-ROM lights up when the CD-ROM device driver loads in CONFIG.SYS, but the CD-ROM drive does not appear as a drive letter in Window's File Manager. Which of the following is checked *first*?
      A.   Check the interface cabling
      B.   Check the audio cable
      C.   Check the configuration settings such as the SCSI ID, terminators, or the Master/Slave setting
      D.   Verify that the CD-ROM drive's device driver loads
      E.   Verify that the sound card's device driver loads
      F.   Verify that the SmartDrive program loads
      G.   Verify that the MSCDEX program loads

27.   Which of the following is the most common problem with sound card installations:
      A.   Plug and Play configurations
      B.   Resource conflicts such as interrupts, I/O addresses, DMA channels
      C.   Audio output
      D.   Compatibility with CD-ROM drives

28.   A SCSI CD-ROM drive is to be installed in a computer. The CD-ROM must be set to
      A.   SCSI ID 0
      B.   SCSI ID 1
      C.   A SCSI ID not used by any other device or the SCSI adapter
      D.   Master
      E.   Slave

29.   T/F   A corrupted SYSTEM.INI file in Windows 3.x can cause audio output problems.

Chapter 11:
Serial Devices,
Mice, and Keyboards

OBJECTIVES

After completing this chapter you will

1. Understand the difference between serial and parallel data transfers.
2. Understand how a UART controls the serial port, the different models, how to determine which one is installed, and how to upgrade one.
3. Configure a serial port and all its associated system resources and individual settings.
4. Understand basic handshaking between a DTE and DCE.
5. Know the difference between serial cables.
6. Realize the basic problems with serial ports lies in system resource configuration and software set up.
7. Use basic tools to determine which system resources to assign to serial ports.
8. Understand basic modem concepts.
9. Understand the differences between internal and external modems.
10. Perform basic modem troubleshooting.
11. Understand the limitations of 56Kbps modems.
12. Realize that cable modems and digital modems are alternatives.
13. Recognize the potential of the Universal Serial Bus and IEEE 1394 standards.
14. Understand the different types of mice.
15. Clean mice parts.
16. Understand the different types of keyboards.
17. Clean keyboard parts.
18. Distinguish between a keyboard problem and a motherboard problem based on voltage checks.

KEY TERMS

56Kbps modem	FireWire	parity
asynchronous	flow control	phone line isolator
bps	full duplex	PS/2 mouse
breakout box	half duplex	RS232C
bus mouse	handshaking	RTS/CTS
cable modem	hub	serial mouse
capacitive keyboard	ISDN	socketed
combinational mouse	K56flex	start bit
data bits	LAPM	stop bit
data compression	loopback plug	straight-through cable
DCE	mechanical keyboard	synchronous
digital modem	mechanical mouse	trackball
DTE	MNP	UART
echo mode setting	modem	USB
error correction	modem isolator	voice/fax modem
fax modem	null modem cable	x2
FIFO setting	optical mouse	XON/XOFF

SERIAL DEVICES OVERVIEW

Serial devices can be challenging to install. Some technicians dread installing or troubleshooting serial devices, but if they are understood, technicians can conquer them easily. Serial devices can be difficult to install because (1) the serial ports may share an interrupt with another serial device, (2) serial devices may have proprietary cables, and (3) software is not always compatible with the serial device. Many serial devices support uncommon configurations. Maintaining the standards covered in Chapter 3, System Configuration avoids these types of conflicts. Reviewing Chapter 3's sections on interrupts and I/O addresses might be a good idea before trying to understand serial devices.

Common serial devices include mice, modems, digitizers, and plotters. Serial Figure #1 shows common serial devices.

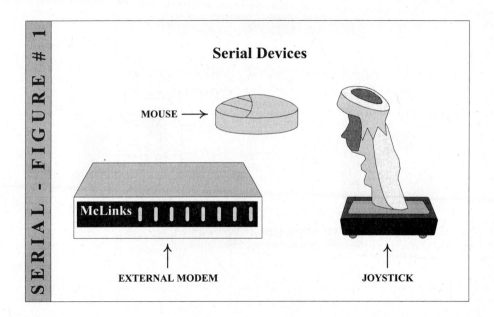

Serial devices transmit or receive information one bit at a time. In contrast, parallel devices transmit data eight bits at a time. Serial transmissions are much slower than parallel transmissions because one bit is sent at a time instead of eight. Serial Figure #2 compares serial and parallel transmissions.

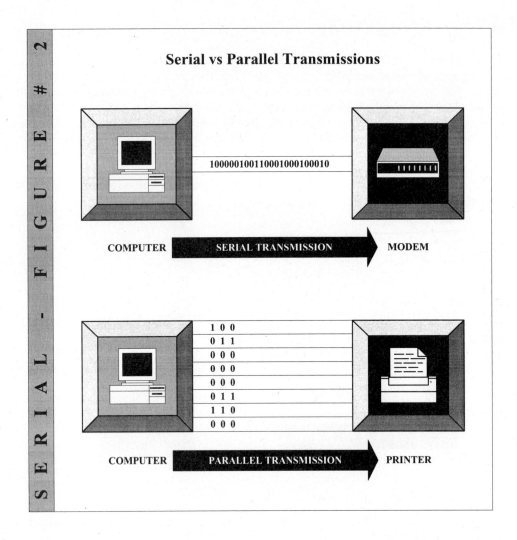

Even though serial transmissions are slower than parallel, they travel longer distances more accurately than parallel transmissions. Serial cables should be no more than 50' in length. The possibility for data loss is more likely in distances greater than 50'. Parallel cables should be no longer than 15'. Special cables exist that boost the signal for both serial and parallel devices to extend the maximum cable length. Contact any computer cabling vendor for the specifics.

Serial devices are frequently external and connect to a serial port. A device such as an internal modem may be on an adapter. Serial ports are also known as asynchronous ports, COM ports, or RS232 ports. **Asynchronous** transmissions add extra bits to the data to track when each byte starts and ends. The extra bit sent first is the **start bit** and extra bit sent last is the **stop bit**.

Another method of data transmission is **synchronous** transmissions that rely on an external clock to time the data reception or transmission. The operating system assigns the serial port a COM port number such as COM1, COM2, COM3, or COM4. Every serial device must have a different COM port number. **RS232C** is a standard serial interface approved by the EIA (Electrical Industries Association). Because serial devices on microcomputers use the 9 or 25-pin male connector specified by the RS232C standard, the devices are sometimes known as RS232 serial devices. Serial Figure #3 illustrates the two serial ports found on a motherboard or on an adapter.

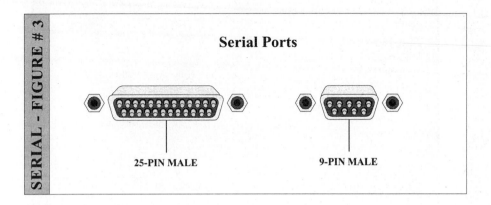

The transmission speed of serial devices is calculated in **bits per second** or **bps**. Bits per second (bps) is the number of bits the serial device receives or transmits in one second. The speed settings for serial devices include 110, 300, 1200, 2400, 4800, 9600, 19200, 38400, 57600, 115200, 230400, 460800, and 921600. Some devices can be set to different speeds. The application software must match the serial device's bits per second rate.

The chip that controls the serial device is a **UART (Universal Asynchronous Receiver/Transmitter)**. For motherboards with built-in serial ports, the UART chip is on the motherboard. Internal modems have a UART chip built into the adapter. Serial ports built into an adapter have a UART chip on the adapter. The UART chip converts a data byte into a serial data stream of single 1s and 0s for transmission. It also receives the single bit stream and stores the data in its own buffer. UARTs have buffers to allow the microprocessor to handle other tasks instead of constantly checking with the serial port. When the UART's buffer is full, the chip initiates an interrupt to the microprocessor. The microprocessor responds and transfers the data from the UART buffer into RAM. Before the 16550 UART chip, the older UARTs lost data. The received data was overwritten with new data before the microprocessor had time to transfer the first received data into RAM. Many computers and adapters still have the older UART chips to save on costs. Serial Table #1 lists the various UARTs made by the National Semiconductor Corporation.

National Semiconductor Corporation's UARTs

SERIAL - TABLE # 1

UART	Speed	Notes:
8250	up to 9600 bps	Use in PC and XT computers. There are bugs in the chip (one of which is an interrupt enable bug that is expected by the PC & XT BIOS).
8250A	up to 9600 bps	Fixes bugs in 8250 UART. Works in 286s that do *not* expect the interrupt enable bug.
8250B	up to 9600 bps	Best chip for PC/XT. OK in 286s that expect the interrupt enable bug.
16450	9600+bps	Use in 286 and higher systems. Fixed interrupt enable bug. Do not use in PC/XT systems.
16550	9600+ bps	Use in 286 and higher systems. Contains a 16-byte buffer.
16550AN	9600+ bps	Modified version of 16550; has bugs in the chip. Do not use.
16550AFN or 16550AF	9600+ bps	Corrects bugs in prior versions of 16550 UARTs.
16550D	9600+ bps	Latest UART for PCs.

Use the 16550 UART with its 16 byte buffer as a minimum because higher transmission speeds are needed with today's serial devices, microprocessors, and buses. Many operating systems such as Windows 95 and Windows NT expect the 16550A or higher UART. If a system has a 16550 series UART, then the 16550AFN or 16550AF UART is the better choice. The 16550AN has bugs (problems) in the chip that are fixed in the 16550AF or the 16550AFN UART.

National Semiconductor Corporation has a newer model of UART called the 16550D that can be placed in the FIFO (First In First Out) mode to relieve the microprocessor of excessive software overhead.

Many software utilities such as Norton Utilities, CheckIt, and Microsoft Diagnostics can identify the type of UART used on the serial device or on the serial port. Using a software utility can save time when identifying a chip. However, if a technician wants visual confirmation on the type of UART, look for the largest chip on the serial adapter or a chip close to the serial port on the motherboard. Even though National Semiconductor Corporation is the most common manufacturer of UARTs in a computer, other manufacturers produce UARTs as well.

If using MSD (Microsoft Diagnostics) to identify the type of UART, be aware that MSD incorrectly identifies a 16450 UART as an 8250 UART. A technician should always know the UART being used especially when connecting a high speed device such as a modem to a built-in serial port. The device will not operate correctly or fast unless an adequate UART is installed.

Exercises at the end of the chapter explain how to use MSD and Windows 95 to identify the UART.

UPGRADING THE UART CHIP

A **socketed** UART is one that is *not* soldered, but plugged into a chip socket. To upgrade a *socketed* 8250 or 16450, buy a newer UART for approximately $15-20 to replace the existing one. If a soldered UART chip is on a serial adapter, replace the adapter with one that has a more current UART. If the motherboard contains a soldered UART chip, see if the serial port can be disabled by a jumper, switch, or through the system's SETUP program. If the serial port can be disabled, disable it and buy a separate serial adapter that contains an upgraded UART. Look at Serial Figure #4 for a socketed UART.

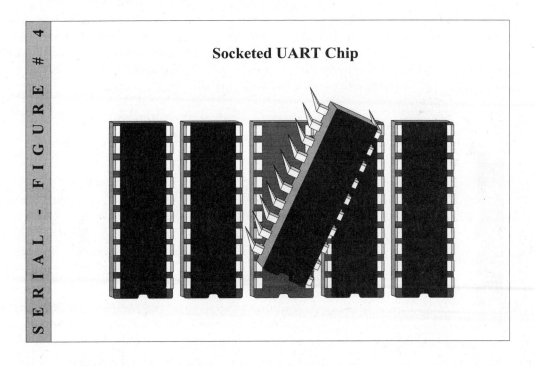

Socketed UART Chip

SERIAL - FIGURE # 4

HOW TO CONFIGURE SERIAL DEVICES

Three major issues exist when configuring serial ports or serial devices: (1) assigning an interrupt, (2) assigning an I/O address, and (3) assigning a COM port number. The original 8088 motherboard had the limitation of only eight interrupts, serial ports can share interrupts.

No two serial devices that operate simultaneously can share the same interrupt! For example, putting a mouse and a modem on the same interrupt is *not* good because most modem applications use a mouse. While using the modem, if the mouse is moved, the modem will quit working.

Serial devices are normally assigned IRQ3 or IRQ4 although some manufacturers allow other IRQ (Interrupt Request) number assignments. An IRQ is what allows each device to request the microprocessor's attention. Each serial port or device *must* be assigned a different I/O (Input/Output) address! An I/O address is a device's mailbox number so that the microprocessor can distinguish between different devices and differentiate between them. No I/O address may be shared by two devices. The assigned I/O address determines the serial port's COM port number. Every serial device or port must have a different COM port number! External serial devices inherit the COM port name assigned to the motherboard or adapter serial port to which the serial device connects.

On bootup, the BIOS looks for serial devices at I/O addresses 3F8, 2F8, 3E8, then 2E8 *in that exact order*. The serial device or port at I/O address 3F8 is assigned COM1 as the COM port number. If BIOS finds a serial device or port at I/O address 2F8, the port or device is assigned COM2. Then, for I/O addresses 3E8 followed by 2E8, the attached serial devices or ports are assigned the COM port numbers COM3 and COM4, respectively. Serial Table #2 lists the common IRQs, I/O addresses, and COM port assignments for serial devices and serial ports.

Serial Port Assignments

I/O Address	COM Port Name	IRQ
3F8	COM1	4
2F8	COM2	3
3E8	COM3	4
2E8	COM4	3

(SERIAL - TABLE # 2)

The easiest way to remember serial port interrupts is that 1 + 3 = 4; COM1 and COM3 use Interrupt 4.

Some manufacturers of serial ports or devices allow assignment of IRQs, COM names, and I/O addresses other than the ones listed in Serial Table #2. Use the assignments as they are listed in Serial Table #2 and stay out of trouble! For example, for the first serial device in the computer, assign it IRQ4 and I/O address 3F8h. The serial device becomes COM1.

Windows 95 automatically assigns COM names just as DOS does. If a serial device has a non-standard I/O address, Windows 95 can assign the device a COM name higher than COM4 such as COM5, COM6, etc. Windows 95 supports a total of 128 serial ports. However, even if Windows 95 sees the serial device and assigns it a higher COM port number, 16-bit Windows 3.x software or DOS software applications may not be able to communicate with the serial device.

Avoid settings other than those listed in Serial Table #2 if at all possible. Adhering to the standards set in Serial Table #2 will prevent conflicts! Serial ports should be configured in I/O address and COM port order. Otherwise the ROM BIOS and the operating system reassign the COM port name. The ROM BIOS COM port assignment, the serial port's COM port assignment, *and* the software's set up of the COM port must all agree for the serial device to operate. The same is true for the IRQ and I/O address settings.

If the only serial adapter in a system is set to COM2 at I/O address 2F8, the computer's BIOS detects that no serial port exists at I/O address 3F8. Then, the BIOS checks at I/O address 2F8 and detects the adapter's serial port. The operating system assigns the serial adapter to port number COM1, even though the adapter jumpers are configured to COM2. This can create a conflict. Remember, the BIOS looks for the I/O address first at 3F8, then 2F8, 3E8, and 2E8. The operating system assigns COM names to the serial ports in COM1, COM2, COM3, and COM4 based on the sequence of the I/O addresses detected no matter how the board is configured.

If a computer has two serial ports at I/O addresses 3F8 and 2F8, the operating system assigns the serial port at I/O address 3F8 to COM1 and assigns the serial port at I/O address 2F8 to COM2. Assume an internal modem is then installed. The modem is set to I/O address 2E8 and to COM4. When installing the modem, the operating system assigns the modem to COM3 (even though 2E8 is normally for COM4). Because this is so confusing, the same steps are listed below.

1.   BIOS detects I/O address 3F8.
2.   The operating system assigns the port at I/O address 3F8 the COM port name of COM1.
3.   BIOS detects I/O address 2F8.
4.   The operating system assigns the port at I/O address 2F8 the COM port name of COM2.
5.   BIOS scans for I/O address 3E8. Because no adapter or port is at this I/O address, the operating system does not assign a COM port.
6.   BIOS detects I/O address 2E8.
7.   The operating system assigns the port at I/O address 2E8 the *next* COM port name, *COM3*, not COM4.

Even with the internal modem jumpered for I/O address 2E8 and COM4, the BIOS reassigns the setting to COM3. Now, if the software has been configured to COM4, the modem will not work. This is why serial devices are so bothersome to install.

The order in which the I/O addresses are found is the order in which the serial devices and ports are assigned COM names!

Rather than use a software utility such as Microsoft Diagnostics (MSD) to determine serial port addresses, use the DEBUG command to see the serial port I/O addresses detected by the BIOS. An exercise at the end of the chapter details the steps. After documenting all currently used resources, set the new serial device settings to the next COM port name, an unused IRQ, and an unused I/O address. Never install a serial device without knowing the resources already in use.

Most software applications used with serial devices require configuration. For example, if using a communication software package with a modem, the communications software must be configured for the specific interrupt, I/O address that the modem uses. The application settings *must* match the serial device settings or the software will not operate with the serial device.

The DOS MODE command configures serial ports for the DOS environment. The Windows 3.x Ports control panel configures serial devices within the Windows 3.x environment. Windows 95 uses the System control panel. Exercises at the end of the chapter show how to view serial device resources using Windows 3.x and Windows 95. Whether using DOS/Windows, Windows 95, or Windows NT Workstation, a technician must be aware of the hardware resources used and what resources are available for serial devices.

MORE SERIAL PORT SETTINGS

A good understanding of how serial devices operate is essential to a technician's knowledge base. Before installing a serial device and configuring its associated software, a technician must be familiar with the terminology associated with serial device installation.

Data bits is a setting for how many bits make up a data word. The data bits setting is normally 8 bits per data word, but can be 7 or lower. **Parity** is a simple method of checking data accuracy. Most think of parity as even parity or odd parity. Take the example of a computer that uses even parity. If the data sent is 10101010, a total of four 1s are sent, plus a 0 for the parity bit. Four is an even number, therefore the parity bit is set to a 0 because the total number of 1s must be an even number when even parity is used. If the data sent is 10101011, a total of five 1s are sent, plus an extra 1 for the parity bit. Because five is an odd number and the system uses even parity, then the extra parity bit is set to a 1 to make the total number of 1s an even number. When parity is used, both computers must be set to the same setting. The parity system is very basic for data error checking. The choices for parity include none, odd, even, space, and mark. With a space parity setting, both computers always set the parity bit to 0. With the mark parity setting, both computers always set the parity bit to 1.

If communicating with an online service through a modem, the parity setting of the modem must match the parity setting of the online service modem. The normal setting in this case is none.

Stop bits in serial data communications are the number of bits sent to indicate the end of the data word. The number of stop bits can be 1, 1.5, or 2. One stop bit is the common choice. **FIFO settings** is an option to enable or disable the UART chip's FIFO buffer. This setting gives the microprocessor time to handle other tasks without the serial device losing data. If data is lost, it will have to be re-transmitted later when the microprocessor turns its attention back to the serial device.

The **flow control** setting in serial communications determines how two serial devices communicate. Flow control can be set using software or physical pins on the serial port (hardware). Another name for flow control is handshaking. This setting allows a serial device to tell the sending serial device, "Wait, I need a second before you send any more data." For communication to occur using hardware handshaking, things must happen in an exact sequence. **Handshaking** is the order in which things happen in order for two serial devices to communicate. Knowing this order helps with troubleshooting. Serial Table #3 delineates the hardware flow control.

SERIAL - TABLE # 3

Hardware Handshaking

Order of Execution	Explanation
Both devices (the DTE and the DCE) power on and are functional.	
The DTE sends a signal over the DTR (Data Terminal Ready) line.	The DTE says, "I'm ready."
The DCE sends a signal over the DSR (Data Set Ready) line.	The DCE says, "I'm ready, too."
The DTE sends a signal over the RTS (Request to Send) connector pin.	The DTE (such as the computer) says, "I would like some data."
The DCE sends a signal on the CTS (Clear to Send) connector pin.	The DCE (such as the modem) says, "OK, here comes some data."
Data transmits one bit at a time over a single line.	

The two common methods for flow control are XON/XOFF (software method) and RTS/CTS (hardware method). The **XON/XOFF** handshaking sends special control characters when a serial device needs more time to process data or is ready to receive more data. If one modem needs the remote modem to wait a minute, it will send a certain character (usually CTRL S). Then, when the modem is ready to accept more data, a different control character (usually CTRL Q) is sent.

RTS/CTS (hardware handshaking) uses specific wires on the serial connector to send a signal to the other device to stop or start sending data. The **CTS (Clear to Send)** and the **RTS (Request to Send)** signals indicate when it is okay to send data.

The RS232 serial communication standard was developed during a time when mainframes were the norm. A mainframe terminal known as a DTE connected to a modem known as a DCE. In today's world, **DTE (Data Terminal Equipment)** includes computers and printers. On a DTE serial connector, certain pins initiate communication with a DCE device, such as a modem. Serial Table #4 shows the common signal names as well as the common abbreviations for the signals used with DTE devices.

DTE Signal Connections

Signal Abbreviation	Signal Name
TD	Transmit Data
DTR	Data Terminal Ready
RTS	Request to Send

SERIAL - TABLE # 4

DCE (Data Circuit-terminating Equipment) includes devices such as modems, mice, and digitizers. On the DCE side, the signal names relate more to receiving data. Serial Table #5 lists the common signal names used with DCE devices.

DCE Signal Connections

Signal Abbreviation	Signal Name
RD	Receive Data
DSR	Data Set Ready
CTS	Clear to Send
CD	Carrier Detect
RI	Ring Indicator

SERIAL - TABLE # 5

SERIAL CABLES

Anyone who has been a technician for any length of time will admit that serial devices have always been difficult to configure. In addition to the problems with interrupts, I/O address, and COM ports, serial cables are also a problem. Not all serial cables are the same. Some serial device manufacturers require proprietary serial cables. Watch out for serial printers, plotters, and digitizers. Actually, watch out for all serial devices and their cables. Be certain to use the correct cable.

Because a computer serial port is either a 9 or 25-pin male connector, a 9 to 25 or 25 to 9-pin converter may be necessary when connecting a serial device. If a computer has a 9-pin serial port and the serial device has a 25-pin connector, the cable for the device may have a 25-pin connector on each end of the cable. If this is true, a simple solution is to buy a 9 to 25-pin converter as shown in Serial Figure #5.

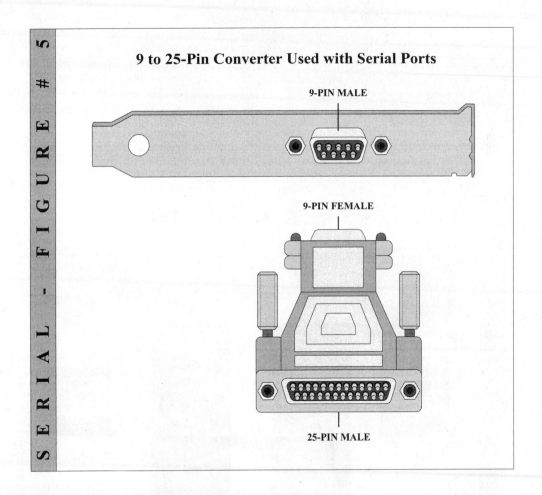

SERIAL - FIGURE # 5

9 to 25-Pin Converter Used with Serial Ports

9-PIN MALE

9-PIN FEMALE

25-PIN MALE

If an external serial modem has a 25-pin connector and it connects to the computer's 25-pin serial connector, a **straight-through serial cable** is used for the device. A **null modem cable** connects two computers without the use of a modem. Some people are confused why null modem serial cables are *not* used by modems. That is because they do not understand the null modem cable's use. A null modem connection allows (1) file transfer between computers, (2) remote control of another computer, and (3) game playing between two players on separate computers. Take for example an older computer with only a 5.25" floppy drive that needs an application loaded, but you only have 3.5" disks. You can connect the two computers with a null-modem cable and load the application from the newer computer's 3.5" floppy drive to the older computer's hard drive. DOS has a program called INTERLINK that allows this connection. The Windows 95 program is called the Direct Cable Connection or DCC. An exercise at the end of the Hard Drive chapter explains how to use INTERLINK. The Windows 95 chapter includes an exercise on setting up the DCC program. Null modem cables also connect a computer to some serial peripherals.

Be very careful with 9 to 25-pin or 25 to 9-pin null modem cables. Many pinout variations exist. The best bet is to buy a 25 to 25-pin null modem cable and use a 9 to 25-pin adapter (converter) if necessary. The only way to determine which serial cable to purchase is by reading the serial device documentation or contacting the serial device's manufacturer. However, many cables frequently come packaged in a plastic bag with no documentation. Be careful what you buy! Mark all null modem cables with a permanent marker or with colored electrical tape so the cable is distinguishable from other serial cables.

Serial Figure #6 illustrates a null modem cable.

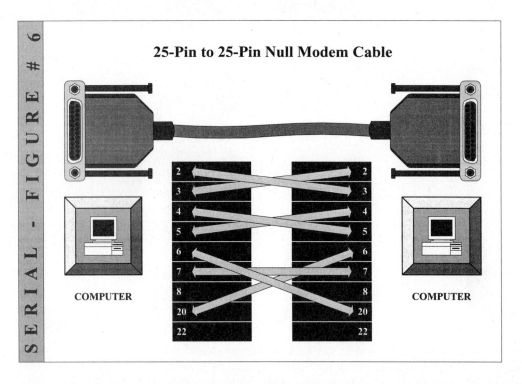

Serial Figure # 7 shows a straight-through serial cable. Notice in Serial Figures #6 through #8 you cannot tell the difference between the cables except if you had the pinouts such as the ones shown. Serial Figure #8 shows a modem connected to a computer's 25-pin port, the same cable can be used to connect a 9-pin serial device to a 25-pin computer port.

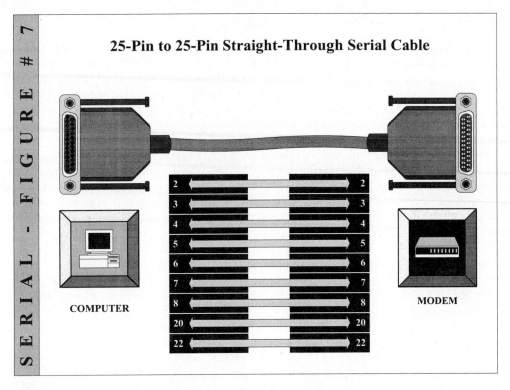

25-Pin to 25-Pin Straight-Through Serial Cable

COMPUTER

MODEM

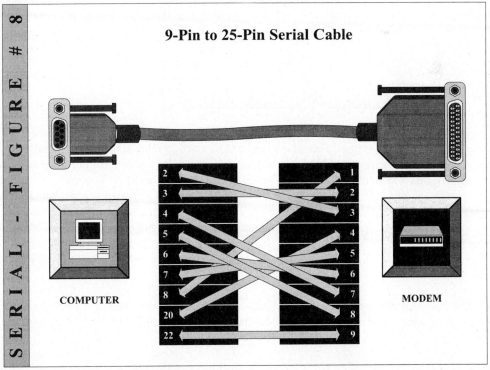

9-Pin to 25-Pin Serial Cable

COMPUTER

MODEM

SERIAL - FIGURE # 7

SERIAL - FIGURE # 8

SERIAL DEVICE INSTALLATION

Installing serial devices can be very frustrating. If ever there is an important time to know what is in the computer, it is when installing a serial device. To avoid the frustration, take inventory of what is in the system *before* installing a serial device. Write down every IRQ, I/O address, and COM port currently used in the system. Place your findings on a 3x5 card and tape it to the inside of the computer for future reference. If the serial device requires its own adapter, be sure there is an available expansion slot. If it is a non-Plug and Play adapter, set the jumpers or switches on the adapter using the adapter's documentation and the rules for configuring serial devices.

If possible, give every device a different interrupt, I/O address, and COM port. If the serial device must share an interrupt, be sure the other serial device will *not* be used simultaneously with the serial device being installed. I/O addresses and COM ports *must* be unique to each device and adapter. If possible, keep within the serial device interrupt, I/O address, and COM port standards. Refer to Serial Table #2 for those standards. Many manufacturers allow non-standard configurations of serial devices. Sometimes, the options of IRQ2, IRQ5, IRQ9, or IRQ15 are available (as well as other interrupts). Of course, IRQs 2 and 9 should be avoided. Sound cards and network cards sometimes use IRQ5. Be careful when choosing non-standard IRQs. The software package used with the serial device must be able to recognize the serial port as well.

To install a serial device that uses an expansion slot such as a modem, you frequently have to disable any built-in motherboard serial ports through the SETUP program. Even though modems are frequently able to be configured as COM3 or COM4, it is best to configure the internal modem as COM2 especially if a serial mouse takes COM1.

If the serial device is Plug and Play and the system supports Plug and Play, plug the device in and let the system configure it. Refer to the Configuration chapter for more information on Plug and Play installation and troubleshooting. After installing the serial device, load any software drivers required for operation. Also, install any software included with the serial device. Always remember to test any device installation.

 SERIAL DEVICE TROUBLESHOOTING

Most serial device problems are usually IRQ, I/O address, or COM port related. The serial device that is not working properly could be due to (1) a configuration setting conflicting with another device, (2) BIOS reassigning the COM port setting, or (3) a software's configuration setting does not match the serial device setting. Symptoms for this problem include the following: the serial device does not work, a different device quits working, the serial device works and then locks, or the computer locks during bootup. To solve this problem, go back to the discovery stage. Find out what is already installed in the computer. Try disabling unused serial ports not being used. Do not expect MSD (Microsoft Diagnostics), Check-It, Norton Utilities, or any other utility to be completely accurate. Verify every setting through documentation. Use DEBUG to see which COM ports the BIOS detects. Other problems with serial devices are below.

1.   Always check the simplest solution first. Check the cable attachment. Check for bent pins on the connector and cable. This is more common than one would think.

2.   If the device is external, check if it needs an external power source and that the external power source is working. Be sure you plugged the external device into the correct COM port and that the cable fits securely to the connector.

3.   Check if the UART is outdated. Upgrade the UART if possible. If the UART is soldered into the motherboard, consider buying an expansion card with a newer UART installed.

4.   The wrong serial cable can cause many problems. The serial device may work intermittently or not at all. If possible, swap with a known good cable. Make sure you have not used a null modem cable by mistake. Contact the device manufacturer to see if the device needs a proprietary serial cable. If the serial device manufacturer is out of business and the correct serial connections are critical, use a **breakout box**. This allows a technician to determine the required wiring between two devices such as a computer and a serial printer. Breakout boxes are most useful when a manufacturer uses a proprietary serial cabling scheme and the cable pinouts are unknown. The breakout box allows you to connect a cable on one side of the box and a cable on the other side of the box. It is then used to tie a pin from one connector to the same or different numbered pin on the connector on the other side of the box. The breakout box saves many hours on trial serial cable manufacturing. Serial cables are made either by crimping or soldering and neither way is a *fun* thing to do.

5.   Some software packages do not support the same IRQ, I/O address, or COM port as the serial device. Change the serial device settings to match the software or upgrade the software.

6.   Some software packages simply do not support the serial device attached to the computer. Check with the software manufacturer, upgrade the software, replace the software, or replace the serial device.

7.   Serial cables should not be longer than 50'; however, different grades of cable exist. Even a short, poorly made cable can be susceptible to outside interference. Cable interference is not normally a problem. If a cable is at fault or it works intermittently, do not keep the cable; throw it away! You may forget that it is bad and attempt to re-use it.

8.   If the serial port is suspect, install a loopback plug and run a diagnostic that checks the port. A **loopback plug** is a 9 or 25-pin connector that plugs into the serial port. Once diagnostics execute, signals are sent out the serial port and looped back into the port. The loopback plug tests the receive and the transmit pins. Some diagnostic programs come packaged with the loopback plug. Remember that ports do not normally go bad, but lightning storms can damage an external modem's serial port.

9.   Never forget that serial device drivers and other drivers or TSRs can conflict. Refer to the memory chapter for more help in this area.

10.   Check the system's SETUP and verify the COM port used by an external serial device is not disabled in SETUP, or does not conflict with an internal serial device.

MODEMS OVERVIEW

A very common serial device is a modem. A **modem (modulator/demodulator)** connects the computer with the outside world through a phone line. A modem converts a signal transmitted over the phone line to digital 1s and 0s read by the computer. A modem also converts the digital 1s and 0s from the computer and modulates them onto the phone line's carrier signal for transmission. Modems normally connect to a remote modem through the phone line. Modem communication normally uses hardware flow control (RTS/CTS) instead of software. Even though modems can be internal or external peripheral devices, Serial Figure #9 shows two modems connecting two computers.

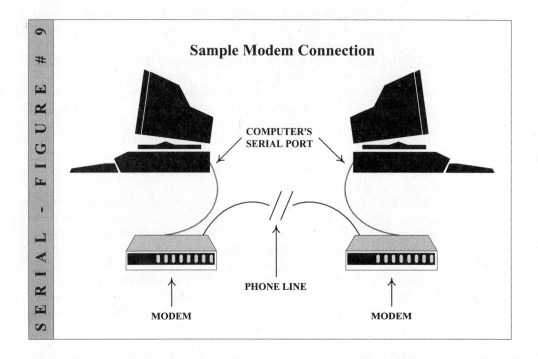

When connecting a modem to a phone line, be very careful when connecting the cable. Some modems have two jacks on the back of the modem. The modem jack labeling varies, but one is usually labeled PHONE and the other labeled LINE. The LINE jack is for the cable that goes from the modem to the phone wall jack. The modem's PHONE jack is an optional jack to connect a telephone to the modem. Some people do not want to give up the wall jack for only the computer modem.

At a medium or large organization, it may be worthwhile to standardize modem settings such as COM2, IRQ3, I/O address 2F8. This will simplify setup, troubleshooting, and helpdesk calls, eliminating the need to spend time determining how an individual computer is set and checking for conflicts. All company technicians will know where to begin resolving problems that are *not* conflict-related which are the most time consuming.

PROS AND CONS OF INTERNAL AND EXTERNAL MODEMS

The pros and cons of external modems are numerous. Internal modems require less space than an external modem, but they do require an expansion slot, generate more heat, and place a larger load on the computer's power supply. External modems connect to an existing serial port. Internal modems are cheaper than external modems. Internal modems come with their own UART so a technician does not have to wonder if the UART can keep up with the speed of the modem. External modems can easily connect to a different computer without taking the computer apart. External modems have lights on the outside that are great for troubleshooting. However, now many shareware programs exist as well as software included with the internal modems that allow a simulation of the external modem lights that can be used when troubleshooting.

Choosing between an internal modem and an external modem narrows down to the following questions: (1) Is there an existing expansion slot for an internal modem? (2) Is there an existing serial port available for an external modem? (3) Is there an available COM port that will not conflict with other devices? Some software programs do not support non-standard IRQ assignments. (4) Is money an issue? If so, get an internal modem. (5) Is desk space an issue? If so, get an internal modem. (6) Is the UART chip an issue? If so, upgrade it or get an internal modem. When installing an internal modem, follow all guidelines for any Plug and Play or ISA adapter installation. When installing an external modem, connect it to an existing serial port and configure the port accordingly.

MODEM SPEEDS AND STANDARDS

Modems transmit and receive at different speeds. A faster modem means less time on the phone line and less time for microprocessor interaction. However, because modems connect to other modems, they both must communicate at the same speed. The slowest modem determines the fastest connection speed. A slow modem can only operate at the speed it was designed. Merely connecting to a faster modem will not make the slower modem operate any faster. Fortunately, speedy modems can transmit at lower speeds. Also, communication mode standards developed by CCITT help with modem compatibility. For two modems to communicate with one another, they must adhere to the same protocol or set of rules. The CCITT (Comité Consultantif Internationale de Téléphonie et de Télégraphie) V standards regulate modem speeds and compatibility. CCITT V.10 through V.34 are standards for interfaces and voice-band modems. CCITT V.35 through V.37 standards deal with wideband modems. CCITT standards V.40 through V.42 deal with error control.

Modem **error correction** ensures the data is correct at the modem level rather than have the computer's microprocessor handle or oversee it. A modem with error correction capabilities provides for overall faster computer performance. Microcom, Inc. has their own standards for error correction as well as CCITT. The **MNP (Microcom Network Protocol)** Levels 1 through 4 determine standards for error correction. Some of the CCITT standards include the MNP data compression standard levels as well.

Like error correction, data compression is also a part of some of the modem standards. **Data compression** converts data into smaller sizes before transmitting it. Compressing the data allows faster transmissions (less data to be transmitted). A drawback to modems using some types of data compression occurs with files such as .ZIP, .GIF, or .JPG. These files have already been compressed. The modem tries to uncompress the files, then re-compress them for transmission. This process may actually slow down the computer's overall performance. Some of the CCITT standards concern data compression. MNP Level 5 is the data compression standard from Microcom.

Serial Table #6 lists some of the modem standards and their features.

Communication Standards

Standard	Comments
V.17	14.4Kbps and lower fax CCITT (ITU) standard.
V.22	1200 bps modem CCITT (ITU) standard.
V.22bis	2400 bps modem CCITT (ITU) standard.
V.29	9600 bps and lower fax CCITT (ITU) standard.
V.32	9600bps and lower modem CCITT (ITU) standard.
V.32bis	14.4Kbps and lower modem CCITT (ITU) standard.
V.32turbo	Non-CCITT standard for 12Kbps data transfer.
V.FAST	Non-CCITT standard for 28.8 Kbps data transfer. The *working name* for the V.34 standard until the standard became a reality.
V.FC	(Also known as V.Fast Class) Rockwell 28.8Kbps standard with data compression and error correction. Does not support speeds less than 14.4Kbps. May not be able to connect with other V.34/28.8Kbps modems.
V.34	28.8Kbps modem CCITT (ITU) standard. In October of 1996, the standard changed to allow faster (33.6) Kbps transfers. Automatically adjusts to lower speeds when line problems occur.
V.34bis	CCITT (ITU) data compression standard.
V.42	CCITT (ITU) error correction standard. Covers Microcom's Levels 1 through 4 for error correction as well. Also known as **LAPM (Link Access Procedure for Modems)**.
MNP-4	Microcom error correction standard.
V.42bis	CCITT (ITU) data compression standard.
MNP-5	Microcom data compression standard.

SERIAL - TABLE # 6

When recommending a modem, nothing less than a V.34 modem is satisfactory in today's computing environments. Be sure the modem supports V.42 error correction as well as MNP Level 4 error correction. If the modem is an external unit, verify that it connects to an adapter or motherboard port with a 16550 or higher UART chip. If V.42bis is not available on a modem and Microcom's MNP Level 5 data compression standard is available, disable the MNP-5 data compression when transferring pre-compressed (.ZIP, .JPG, .GIF, etc.) files. MNP-5 does not detect if the file is already compressed. MNP-5 tries to uncompress the file and then re-compress it thereby taking longer. V.42bis recognizes a compressed file and does not try to uncompress it.

CCITT standards are sometimes listed in articles or textbooks as ITU (International Telecommunications Union) standards. For all communication standards check the TIA (Telecommunications Industry Association) and ITU web sites.

As a general rule of thumb, the modem's speed setting should be set to its maximum throughput. If the modem supports data compression, higher speeds are possible. Serial Table #7 lists the maximum modem speeds based on the type of modem and the type of data compression used. Check the modem's documentation for the maximum speed setting.

SERIAL - TABLE # 7

General Guidelines for Maximum Modem Speeds

Modem Type	Type of Data Compression	Speed Setting (in bps)
V.22bis	MNP-5	4800
V.22bis	V.42bis	9600
V.32	MNP-5	19200
V.32	V.42bis	38400
V.32bis	V.42bis	38400 or 57,600

MODEM PREVENTIVE MAINTENANCE

The old adage, "An ounce of prevention is worth a pound of cure" is never more true than with modems. A power surge can come across a phone line just as it can through an electrical outlet. Most people think and worry about the computer problems that could be a result of power surges, but they do not stop to think about surges through the phone line. To provide protection for the modem and the computer, purchase a special protection device called a **phone line isolator** or a **modem isolator** at any computer or phone store. A power surge through the phone line can take out many components inside the computer, including the motherboard. Serial Figure #10 shows an illustration of a phone line isolator.

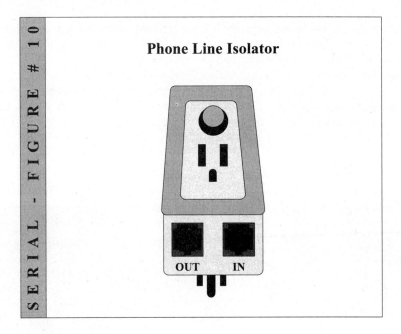

Some surge protectors also have modem protection. A phone cable from the computer plugs into the surge protector. A separate phone cable connects to another jack on the surge protector and the other end plugs into the phone wall jack. The surge protector must, of course, be plugged into a grounded outlet.

 ## TROUBLESHOOTING MODEMS

All the previously mentioned troubleshooting tips for serial ports also apply to modems. However, some additional tips listed below apply to modems.

1. If the modem is an external unit, turn the modem's power off and back on, then try the modem again. If the modem is internal, try rebooting the computer and trying the steps again.
2. If the modem does not dial the number, does not output a dial tone, or a message appears stating that the modem is not responding, check that the phone cord connects to the correct jack on the modem and to the wall phone jack. Also, be sure the correct serial cable is used, the cable secures properly to the modem and the computer, and the COM port setting is correct. Check the flow control setting or check if the phone line requires a special number such as a 9 to dial an outside line. Remove the cable from the phone outlet to the modem and plug it into a phone. The phone outlet should have a dial tone and work correctly.
3. If the modem starts to dial, but then hangs up, check if the phone cable from the wall jack to the modem inserts into the correct modem jack. This symptom also occurs if the "No dial tone" message appears.

4. If the modem hangs up after some time, other equipment (such as fax machines, answering machines, and portable phones) can cause the problem. Also, other people picking up the phone line and disconnecting the modem's connection is a common occurrence. To verify if other equipment causes the problem, disconnect the other devices on the phone line and see if the problem goes away. Also, check the UART chip to see if it is fast enough. Another problem can be the Call Waiting feature. Is Call Waiting enabled on the same phone line the modem uses? If so, disable Call Waiting or place a *70, (or whatever number disables Call Waiting for your phone) before the phone number to be dialed. Check with the modem at the other end to see if it is having problems. Lower the speed of the modem and try to connect. Turn off data compression or error checking to see if one of these settings is causing the problem.

5. Phone line problems can cause a modem to transmit at a lower speed. Some modems try to correct or compensate for phone line noise. This is a very common occurrence. Have the phone company check the line. Special modem lines provide a cleaner line and are available for home users. Check with the local phone company for details.

6. If the modem is an external unit and constantly transmits and receives at a lower speed, check the UART chip to see if it is fast enough for the modem.

7. If garbage (random characters) appear on the screen, check the handshaking, parity, stop bit, and baud rate settings. Most BBS or dial-up services require some type of emulation settings, such as VT-100 or ANSI. Check with the system provider or operator for the proper settings (or try each setting until one works).

8. Verify that the modem works by using the Windows 3.x Terminal program. After setting the modem's parameters, type **ATE1M1V1** (using all caps). Some modems are case sensitive when using modem commands. Press **ENTER**. The modem should reply with an OK on the screen. If not, the modem may not be a Hayes-compatible modem. The ATE1M1V1 is from the U.S. Robotics and Hayes modem command set. *AT* in ATE1M1V1 means Attention and must precede all other commands. *E1* tells the modem to echo whatever is sent out. *M1* turns on the modem's speaker. *V1* places the modem in verbal mode. Check the modem's documentation to be sure it understands the ATE1M1V1 command. If that is not the problem, the modem may be set up on the wrong COM port in the Terminal settings. Go back and reconfigure the settings for a different COM port. The Hayes modem command ATZ resets the modem. Each modem normally comes with a manual that lists each command it understands.

9. Verify the modem works by using the Windows 3.x Terminal program. After setting the modem's parameters, type **ATDT** and press **ENTER**. The *DT* in this command tells the modem to use touch-tone dialing. A dial tone should emit from the modem speaker. If not, the modem may not be a Hayes-compatible modem and it may not understand the command ATDT. Check the modem documentation to be sure it understands the command. Then, check the modem's connection to the wall jack and the modem's speaker volume level. Refer to the modem manual. If the phone line requires a special number to connect to an outside phone line, place that number immediately after the ATDT command.

10. If a modem is having trouble connecting, disable the error control feature.

11. Check with the other modem site to determine if the other modem is operational and the other modem settings.

12.   If a letter appears twice on the screen for every letter typed, check the echo mode setting in the communications software package. The **echo mode setting** is sometimes called the local echo setting and when enabled, sends typed commands through the modem to the screen. The setting needs to have the local echo turned *off*. If nothing appears on the screen when you type, turn the local echo setting *on*. Some software settings refer to turning the local echo *off* as the full duplex mode and turning the local echo *on* as the half duplex mode. **Full duplex** means that two devices can send each other data simultaneously. **Half duplex** means that two devices can send each other data, but only one device can transmit at a time.

13.   If the modem dials, but the high pitched, screeching noise that indicates connection to another modem or fax does not sound, check the phone number. The phone number dialed may be incorrect or the prefix such as a 1 for long distance may be inadvertently omitted. Another possibility is the modem is dialing too fast for the phone line. Consult the modem's manual for slowing down the dialing.

14.   If you have modem problems in Windows 3.x, verify that the COMM.DRV communication driver is in the WINDOWS\SYSTEM directory. Also, look for the same driver in the SYSTEM.INI's [boot] section. If any other driver lists in the [boot] section, place a semicolon before that line so Windows will ignore the line. Then, type a new line: COMM.DRV=COMM.DRV. Last, check the port settings in the Ports control panel. Verify that the port settings are correct for the service, bulletin board, etc. to which is being connected.

15.   Use an external modem's lights to troubleshoot the problem. Manufacturers label the external lights differently, but the concept is the same. Most modems use hardware handshaking, so watching the lights and listening for the dial tone and the high pitched noises are good troubleshooting hints. Look back at Serial Table #5 for the order in which the lights appear. Internal modems frequently have software to show a pictorial status of the internal modem as if the modem was external. Table #8 shows the common external modem status lights.

SERIAL - TABLE # 8

Common External Modem Lights

Abbreviation	Purpose
CD	Carrier Detect
MR	Modem Ready
RD	Receive Data
SD	Send Data
TR	Terminal Ready

16.   If the modem is Hayes-compatible, type **AT&F** to restore the factory settings and often solve obscure problems.

WINDOWS 95 MODEM INSTALLATION AND TROUBLESHOOTING

Follow the same basic serial port rules when using Windows 95 as when in the DOS/Windows environment. However, Windows 95 supports Plug and Play and many modems are Plug and Play. In theory, the installation should go much smoother, but that is not always the case. Modems, more than any other device, seem to cause the most trouble when using Windows 95.

Windows 95 has an Install New Modem wizard that automates the modem installation process. Many times conflicts arise and other devices stop working or the modem does not work after using this wizard. Many technicians avoid using the Windows 95 Install New Modem wizard to automatically detect the modem. Instead, manually select from a list of manufacturers and models or use the disk from the modem manufacturer. This is the best choice. If the Windows 95 Install New Modem wizard selects the modem type, it might only pick a compatible model. This frequently causes the conflict and the modem does not work, or does not have all of its capabilities. Some Plug and Play modems require specific settings on power up. The settings can be manually input through the Windows 95 Device Manager.

If installing an internal non-Plug and Play modem, use the Add New Hardware wizard before using the Install New Modem wizard. Access the Install New Modem wizard through the Modem control panel or through *Modem, setting up* in Windows 95's Help.

In Windows 95, if the modem is not dialing at all, check the port setting by using the Modem control panel. On the **General** tab, select the correct modem. Then, click on the **Properties** button to see the port listing. Check the port settings by clicking on the **Connection** tab.

Windows 95 has a Modem Diagnostic Tool available through the Diagnostic tab in the Modem control panel. If a Windows 3.x modem application does not work properly under Windows 95, check that the COMM.DRV is the communication driver by using the Windows 95 **Device Manager**. Click on the **plus** sign by the **Ports** section. Click on the communications port in question. Click on the **Properties** button. Click on the **Driver** tab. Also, try disabling the error control or changing the flow control setting by using the Windows 95 **Device Manager**. Click on the **plus** symbol by the Modem icon. Click on the modem installed in the computer. Click on the **Properties** tab and then the **Connection** tab. Select the **Advanced** button. Control the error control and flow control by clicking in the checkboxes beside each option.

Sometimes Windows 95 disables a modem. To verify the modem is enabled, use the System control panel. Select the **Device Manager** tab. Click once on the **plus sign** (+) beside the modem category. Select the modem from the sub-list. Then, click on the **Properties** button. Verify the Device Usage checkbox next to the modem configuration. Click on the **Resources** tab to determine if Windows 95 detects a resource conflict with any other installed device. Resolve resource conflicts as any other I/O address, IRQ, or memory address conflict is resolved. Refer to the Configuration chapter for more Windows 95 resource conflict information.

If the modem keeps losing connection in Windows 95, use the prior troubleshooting tips and try placing the modem at a lower speed. Use the Modem control panel to set the lower speed. If the modem works using the Windows 95 HyperTerminal program, but will not work with a different 32-bit communication application, try re-installing the communication program.

Exercises at the end of the chapter help with installing external serial devices. Internal serial adapters or internal modems install as any other adapter. Also, there are exercises for using the Windows 3.x's Terminal and Windows 95's HyperTerminal programs. These two programs are great for troubleshooting modem software problems. If either program works with the modem, the modem is operational and the problem is in the communication package.

FAX MODEMS & VOICE/FAX MODEMS

A **fax modem** allows a modem to use the computer and printer as a fax machine. The modem portion brings the data to the computer. The facsimile (fax) software allows viewing, printing, replying to, or sending a fax. The way that a regular modem sends data is different from the way a fax machine sends data, so a modem can do faxes only if it is a fax modem. Not all computer-based fax machines can handle modem data transfers, but a fax modem does both modem and fax transfers.

Fax standards handled by CCITT (ITU now) are in groups. Group I through Group IV concern fax machines. Group I and Group II are slow. The Group III standard is used by most computers today and has two subclasses, Class 1 and Class 2. Class 1 Group III fax machines can send and receive faxes. Class 2 fax machines handle more of the low-level communication details, (the protocol work), and the software manages the communication session as well as the fax image. The Class 2 standard took a long time to be approved. Some Class 2 modems adhered to the specification *draft* version rather than the approved version. An industry practice is that a fax machine that adheres to the final Class 2 standard is marked as a Class 2.0 standard instead of being listed as a Class 2. A Group III bis fax modem transfers data up to 14,400bps. Group IV fax modems transmit over a digital ISDN line at speeds up to 64Kbps. ISDN technology is discussed later in the chapter.

A **voice/fax modem** combines features of a voice mailbox system into the modem. The software handles message for multiple people similar to multiple answering machines or a business voice system. A drawback to a voice/fax modem in a computer is that the computer stays on all of the time. This is not a good situation unless the computer and modem are properly protected. Another drawback is some people have automated virus software dialing random numbers looking for a system with a voice/fax modem system. Once connected to the system, a virus will download to the system.

Some computer users want to connect their computer-based fax machine to their phone line and have the computer distinguish between an incoming fax and a phone call. A fax switch is available from computer and phone stores that distinguish between a voice and another fax machine. Another option is a service available from some telephone service providers that provides two phone numbers associated with the same phone line — one for the fax machine and one for voice. The service is known by different names such as Distinctive Ring, Ident-a-Ring, or SmartRing.

56KBPS MODEMS

The phone line limit was once thought to be 28.8Kbps, then 33.6Kbps. Now modem manufacturers push even that limit. However, always keep in mind many areas of the country cannot go above 28.8Kbps because some phone companies will not guarantee their phone lines above a certain speed. Check with the phone company for this figure. Nevertheless, the 56Kbps data transfer rate is only possible if the transmitted (analog) signal converts to digital once during the data transmission. Digital phone lines are *quieter* than their analog counterparts, have less noise on the line, and allow faster data transmissions. Take the example of a person dialing into the computer network at their office from their home. Serial Figure #11 illustrates this example.

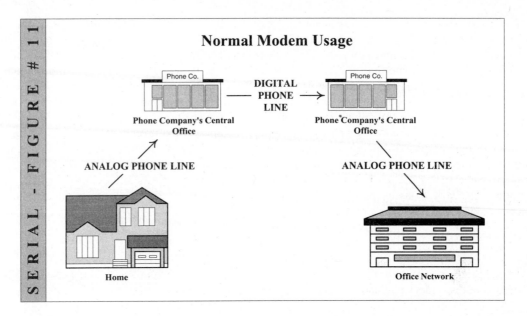

Normal Modem Usage

Notice in Serial Figure #11 how the signal converts twice. The first time the signal coverts is when the analog signal enters the phone company's central office. Between central offices, the signal stays digital. Then, when the signal leaves the central office to travel to the work building, the signal converts from a digital signal to an analog signal. 56Kbps transmission speeds do not support two conversions.

If the workplace has a digital line from the phone company or if a person dials into an Internet provider that has a digital phone connection, a 56Kbps modem is practical. Serial Figure #12 shows the difference.

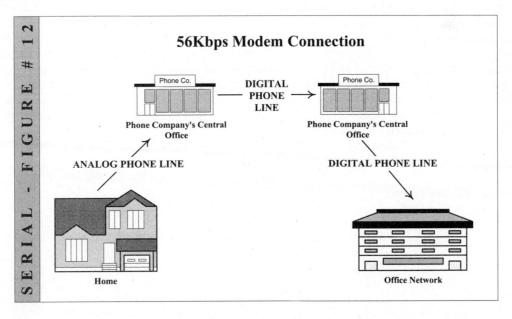

56Kbps Modem Connection

In Serial Figure #12, only one analog to digital conversion exists — the one between the home and the first central office. 56Kbps speeds, in theory, can exist when only one conversion exists. However, if the modem cannot run at 56Kbps, the modem supports lower speeds such as 33.6Kbps and 28.8Kbps. Studies estimate that 56Kbps will run at 56Kbps 10 to 20 percent of the time, about the same estimated percentage of time 33.6Kbps and 28.8bps modems run at their top speed. The problem is lack of standards. As with all new technologies, standards allow individual devices to communicate with other devices inside the computer and outside. Until a 56Kbps standard is established, 56Kbps from different manufacturers may have trouble communicating with one another.

The two proposed 56Kbps modem standards are known as K56flex and x2. The **K56flex** proposal comes from Lucent Technologies and Rockwell, International. 3Com supports the **x2** proposal. Such strong proposal contenders slow down the arrival of a solid 56Kbps standard. In the meantime, 56Kbps modems build to K56flex proposed standards will not communicate with the 56Kbps modems built to the x2 proposed standards.

If purchasing or recommending a 56Kbps modem, determine what standard the other end (such as the Internet provider) supports.

CABLE MODEMS

One of the hottest items lately in the modem industry are **cable modems** which connect a computer to a network using the same coax cable as the cable TV (CATV) network. The CATV coax cable allows a higher bandwidth which allows speeds faster than the phone cable. The cable modem takes the digital signal from the computer, modulates it onto the CATV cable, and demodulates the analog signal from the CATV cable for PC input. Data transfer rates from the computer to a remote location using a cable modem range from 512Kbps to 10Mbps. Conversely, data transfer rates from a remote location to the computer range from 6 to 30Mbps. The number of users on the cable line directly affects a cable modem's transfer speed. Many people in the computer industry are predicting connectivity problems similar to what has happened with regular modems and Internet connectivity. Nevertheless, regular analog phone modems cannot compete with cable modems for data transmission speeds. Cable modem technology provides more job opportunities for computer technicians. Just as computer sound and video fields merged with home entertainment, computer modems are now joining in the home CATV market.

Serial Figure #13 shows a cable modem connection.

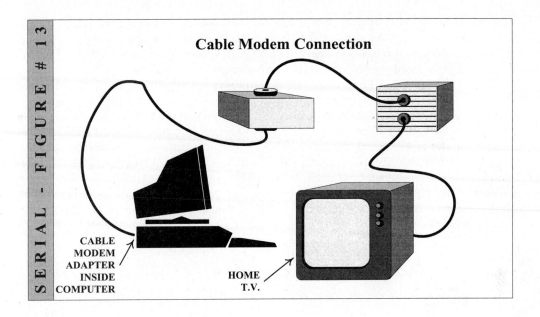

Cable Modem Connection

SERIAL - FIGURE # 13

CABLE
MODEM
ADAPTER
INSIDE
COMPUTER

HOME
T.V.

DIGITAL MODEMS & ISDN

Digital modems connect the computer directly to a digital phone line rather than a traditional analog phone line. One type of digital phone line available from the phone company is an ISDN line. An **ISDN (Integrated Services Digital Network)** line has three separate channels, two B channels and a D channel. The B channels handle data at 64Kbps transmission speeds. The D channel is for network routing information and transmits at a lower 16Kbps. The two B channels can combine into a single channel for video conferencing, thus allowing speeds up to 128Kbps. ISDN modems are increasingly evaluated by today's corporate world. They are available in large metropolitan areas for reasonable rates, making it an affordable option for home office use.

UNIVERSAL SERIAL BUS

A development called USB makes configuring serial devices easier. The **USB (Universal Serial Bus)** allows connection of up to 127 external devices without degradation of speed with each device added. The computer does not have to be restarted to recognize the USB device. In theory, there is no more worrying about interrupts, I/O addresses, DMA channels, or ROM memory address configurations. However, Phoenix Technologies is already working on a diagnostic program that helps with USB interrupt, port, and configuration conflicts.

The Universal Serial Bus devices are Plug and Play devices. The bus is controlled by a USB Host controller built into the motherboard. The host controller handles all traffic on the Universal Serial Bus. The host controller and the system software manage bus bandwidth and bus control. If the system is older without a USB host controller, a PCI adapter with two USB connectors can be purchased.

The Universal Serial Bus transfers data at two different speeds: 12Mbps and 1.5Mbps. The 12Mbps rate is for devices such as modems, CD-ROMs, printers, scanners, monitors, digital cameras, etc. The higher bandwidth can also easily connect to high speed interfaces such as ISDN or T1 phone lines. A T1 line is a high speed, leased phone line for voice and data transmission that allows for speeds up to 1.544Mbps. The 1.5Mbps USB rate is for lower speed devices such as mice and keyboards.

For USB capability, the computer must have a Pentium or higher microprocessor, an operating system that supports USB such as Windows 95 Service Release 2 or Windows NT, and a chipset that acts as the host controller and supports the Universal Serial Bus. Sometimes the USB port must be enabled through the SETUP program to operate. Intel's 430HX, 430VX, and 440FX chipsets support USB. Each Intel chipset includes two USB ports that directly connect to two USB connectors on the computer's chassis. The USB connector and socket are standardized. There are not fifty zillion different connections, terminators, or jumpers that technicians had to cope with in the past. Serial Figure #14 shows an example of the Universal Serial Bus connector.

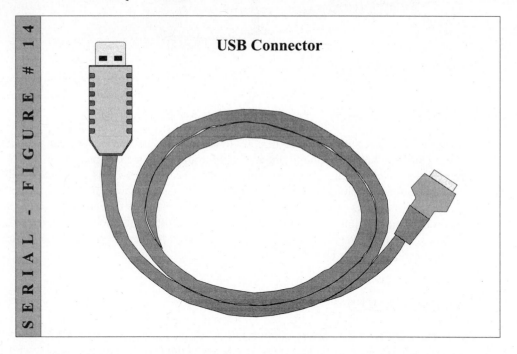

SERIAL - FIGURE # 14

USB Connector

To connect several devices along the Universal Serial Bus, a device called a hub is used. A **hub** is a separate box that connects multiple USB devices, or a hub is a USB device such as a monitor with built-in expansion capabilities. A USB hub allows immediate detection of USB devices that attach or detach from the Universal Serial Bus. Once a new device attaches to a hub and the hub informs the host controller, the Universal Serial Bus system software communicates with the device and configures it. The system software also loads a device driver if needed. This way, all applications are immediately able to use the new USB device.

Serial Figure #15 shows USB configuration using a USB hub.

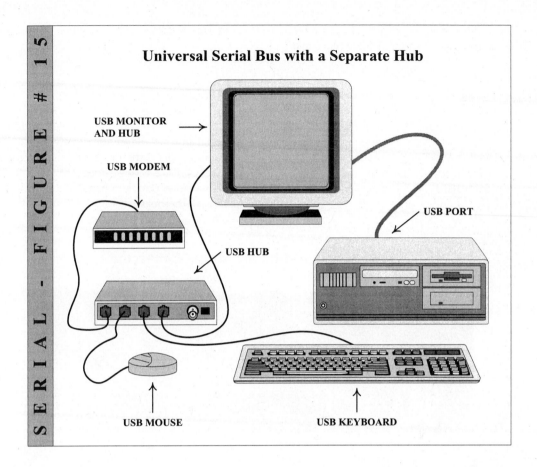

Universal Serial Bus with a Separate Hub

USB MONITOR
AND HUB

USB MODEM

USB PORT

USB HUB

USB MOUSE

USB KEYBOARD

S E R I A L — F I G U R E # 1 5

IEEE 1394 (FIREWIRE)

The IEEE 1394 serial bus standard, developed by Texas Instruments and Apple Computer, Inc. supports speeds of 100Mbps, 200Mbps, or 400Mbps. All three speeds can exist in the same topology, but a different chipset is required for each speed. (Topology is the way a network is physically connected whether it be a bus, star, or ring.) A proposal to the existing standard expands the bandwidth to 800Mbps or 1.2Gbps. The IEEE 1394 bus allows automatic installation and configuration of up to 63 devices such as a modem, keyboard, mouse, monitor, scanner, hard drive, CD-ROM, printer, and an audio/video device. Apple calls the standard **FireWire**.

The IEEE 1394 bus is independent of the platform — an Apple PowerPC, an Intel-based microcomputer, DOS, Windows 95, Windows NT, etc. The standard does not even require a computer. Two devices can connect and transfer data. Bridging the audio/visual industry and the computer industry has always presented a challenge. For anyone who ever digitized video or worked with motion video on a PC will appreciate the need for a different bus. Computer technicians are happy to hear about its Plug and Play and hot swap capabilities. The bus provides 1.5 amps of power to keep remote devices such as monitors *alive* if they are in their sleep mode or to help any low-power devices. IEEE 1394 and the Universal Serial Bus provide upgrade paths not previously available or difficult for technicians due to the expansion slot requirements, lack of standards, and the need for connecting audio/visual devices to a computing environment.

THE MOUSE

A common input device that can be a serial device is a mouse. A **serial mouse** connects to a 9 or 25-pin male port on the computer. All rules for setting serial port configurations apply to a serial mouse as well. Some motherboard manufacturers place a mouse connector on the motherboard. A mouse that connects to this port is known as a **PS/2 mouse**. A PS/2 mouse does not have to be purchased from IBM, but because IBM PS/2 computers first used this port, the name stuck with this type of mouse. Serial Figure #16 shows a PS/2 connector on the motherboard.

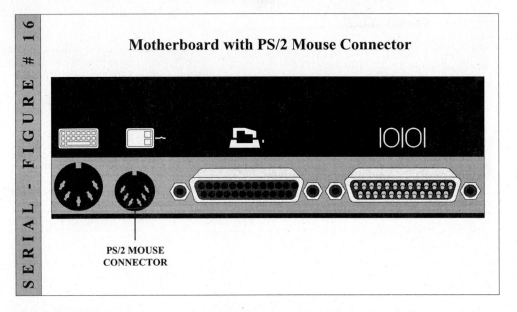

SERIAL - FIGURE # 16

Motherboard with PS/2 Mouse Connector

PS/2 MOUSE
CONNECTOR

Buying a motherboard with a built-in mouse port saves on a COM port. The built-in mouse port normally uses IRQ12, not IRQ3 or IRQ4 like a serial mouse.

A popular model of mouse is a combinational mouse. The **combinational mouse** plugs into a motherboard PS/2 mouse port or into a serial port. The mouse has a mini-DIN connector like the PS/2 mouse connector and a cable that adapts the mini-DIN connector to a 9 or 25-pin serial port connector. This adapter cable will not work on a mouse that does not have the capability to plug into both port types. A regular serial mouse can only plug into serial ports. A regular PS/2 mouse only plugs into a motherboard mouse port. Only a combinational mouse plugs into both.

A **bus mouse** connects to its own adapter and is normally used when no serial ports are available. A bus mouse is not that common and should be used only when necessary. Taking up an expansion slot for a mouse is not necessary unless too many other serial devices are in the computer. Look at Serial Figure #17 for a bus mouse adapter.

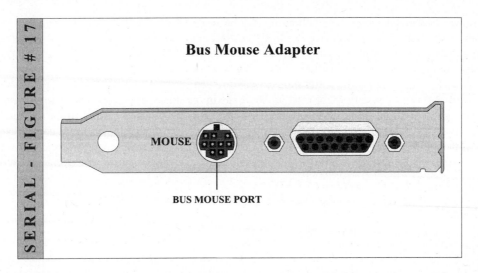

Bus Mouse Adapter

MOUSE

BUS MOUSE PORT

SERIAL - FIGURE # 17

A mouse normally requires a software driver for Windows 3.x and Windows 95. If a mouse software driver is suspect, download a new driver from the manufacturer's web site, reload the driver, or use a generic mouse driver. Most mouse problems, however, are resource conflict related or dirt related. Conflicts also occur when installing a system for the first time or adding a new piece of hardware such as a modem that conflicts with the mouse's interrupt or I/O address.

Dirt is one of a mouse's worst enemies. Using a mouse frequently causes its internal parts to become dirty. Before explaining how to clean a mouse, understanding the basic internal mouse workings is important because the two topics interrelate. There are two basic types of a mouse: a mechanical mouse and an optical mouse. A **mechanical mouse** uses a rubber ball inserted into the bottom of the mouse. The rubber ball turns small metal, rubber, or plastic rollers mounted on the side. The rollers relay the mouse movement to the computer. An **optical mouse** on the other hand, has optical sensors to detect the direction the mouse ball moves. It does not have a rubber ball at all, but uses reflections from LEDs using a grid pattern mouse pad to detect mouse location. A mechanical mouse is more common than an optical mouse.

MOUSE PREVENTIVE MAINTENANCE

Mouse cleaning kits are available in computer stores, but normal household supplies also suffice. For the mouse with a rubber ball, the ball gets dirty and gunked up with lint and dirt. Turn the mouse over and rotate the ball's retainer ring or access cover counter clockwise. Remove the mouse ball's retainer ring or access cover. A mouse sometimes has screws that secure the ball's access cover.

After removing the cover, turn the mouse over, cupping your hand over the mouse ball. Catch the mouse ball as it falls into your hand. To clean the mouse ball, use a mild detergent, soapy water, contact cleaner, or alcohol. Rinse the mouse ball and dry completely with a lint-free cloth. With compressed air or your breath, blow out where the rubber ball sits in the mouse.

With a mechanical mouse, the rollers inside the mouse ball also get dirt on them that causes erratic mouse behavior. Use a cotton swab or lint-free cloth with rubbing alcohol to clean the rollers. If you are at a customer site with no supplies, use water to clean the mouse ball. Use a fingernail or tweaker screwdriver to scrape the rollers. Occassionally, threads or hair gets wrapped around the rollers. Unwrap the obstructions for better mouse performance.

A **trackball** is a replacement for the mouse. It sits in one location and does not move around on a mouse pad or on the desk. Instead, the trackball's ball sits on top and a person uses their palm to move the mouse pointer. A trackball's rollers are similar to a mouse ball's rollers and can be cleaned the same way. With an optical mouse, use a lint-free cloth or compressed air to clean the optical sensors. Any small piece of dirt or lint blocking the sensors causes poor mouse behavior and reaction.

KEYBOARDS

Keyboards are not devices that connect to the serial ports, they are input devices. There are two main types of keyboards, capacitive and mechanical. **Mechanical keyboards** use a switch for each key. When the switch gets dirty, it sticks. Mechanical keyboards require more cleaning and are more error-prone than their capacitive counterparts. A **capacitive keyboard** is more reliable than mechanical keyboards and more expensive because of the electronics involved in the design. IBM computers use capacitive keyboards.

Keyboards have two main types of connectors, a larger 5-pin DIN and a 6-pin mini-DIN, also known as a PS/2 connector similar to the mouse PS/2 connector. See Serial Figure #18 for the 5 and 6-pin keyboard DIN connectors.

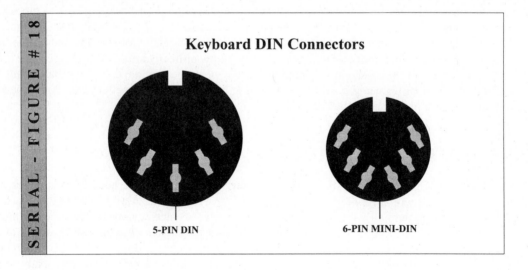

KEYBOARD PREVENTIVE MAINTENANCE

Keyboards also need periodic cleaning, especially because most are some type of mechanical keyboard. Keyboard cleaning kits and wipes are available at computer stores. Simply turn the keyboard upside down and shake it to get out the paper bits and paper clips. Compressed air also helps with keyboard cleaning. If the keys are dirty from finger oils, turn the computer off before cleaning the keys. Then, using keyboard cleaning wipes or an all purpose cleaner and an old cloth, wipe the keyboard keys. A cotton swab can get between the keys and a lint-free swab is best. Make sure the keyboard is completely dry before re-energizing.

KEYBOARD TROUBLESHOOTING

If a particular key is not working properly, remove the key cap. The chip removal tool included with PC tool kits is great for this. They are not great for removing chips, but they are good for removing key caps. A tweaker (small, flat-tipped) screwdriver also does a good job. After removing the key cap, use compressed air around the sticky or malfunctioning key.

Keyboards and mice are normally considered *throw-away* technology. The customer's cost to pay a technician to keep cleaning a keyboard over and over again would pay for many new capacitive keyboards. Keep this in mind when troubleshooting the cheaper devices. If coffee or a soft drink spills into the keyboard, all is not lost. Many people have soaked a keyboard in a bathtub, a flat pan of water, or the dishwasher's top rack. If you use a dishwasher, do not use detergent and run it through only one rinse cycle. Distilled or boiled water cooled down to room temperature is best. The keyboard can later be disassembled and/or scrubbed with lint-free swabs or cloths. Remember, though, keyboards are inexpensive and easily replaced!

To quickly determine if a problem is in the keyboard or the motherboard's keyboard circuitry, power off the computer and remove the keyboard connector from the motherboard. Power the computer on. Referring to Serial Figure #19, use a meter to check the voltages on the motherboard's keyboard connector. If the voltages are out of range, the problem is most likely in the motherboard's keyboard circuitry. If the voltages are within range, the problem is probably in the keyboard. Serial Figure #19 shows the pinouts and expected voltage levels for the 5-pin DIN and the 6-pin mini-DIN.

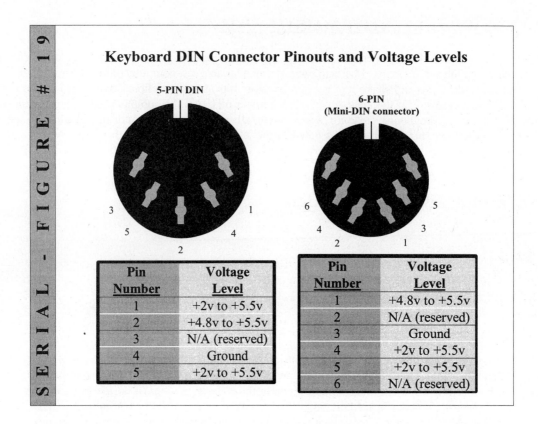

Keyboard DIN Connector Pinouts and Voltage Levels

5-PIN DIN

6-PIN
(Mini-DIN connector)

Pin Number	Voltage Level
1	+2v to +5.5v
2	+4.8v to +5.5v
3	N/A (reserved)
4	Ground
5	+2v to +5.5v

Pin Number	Voltage Level
1	+4.8v to +5.5v
2	N/A (reserved)
3	Ground
4	+2v to +5.5v
5	+2v to +5.5v
6	N/A (reserved)

Name _____

Serial Devices, Mice, and Keyboards Review Questions

1. Which device transmissions travel farther, serial or parallel?

2. Which device transmissions travel faster, serial or parallel?

3. T/F   Serial devices transmit seven bits at a time.

4. Explain the difference between serial and parallel transmissions.

5. List three serial devices.

6. Why are serial devices sometimes difficult to install?

7. Which of the following are names for a microcomputer's serial port? (pick all that apply)
    A.   COM port
    B.   Asynchronous port
    C.   Synchronous port
    D.   LPT port
    E.   RS232 port

8. Give three examples of a COM port number.

9. Describe the two common types of serial ports found on the back of a computer.

10. Which of the following controls the computer's serial port?

    A.   UART
    B.   ROM BIOS
    C.   CMOS
    D.   CPU

11. Where can a UART chip be located? (pick all that apply)
    A.   On the motherboard
    B.   On an adapter
    C.   In an external modem
    D.   On an internal modem

12. Match the description on the right to the UART on the left.
    _____ 8250B   A. Minimum UART for 9600 bps or greater
    _____ 16450   B. UART required for Windows 95
    _____ 16550A   C. Best UART for PC/XT computer

13. What are the UART buffers for?

14. How can you determine what UART is being used?

15. What is the difference between a socketed and a soldered UART?

16.   List three major issues for configuring serial ports.

17.   T/F   Serial devices can share an interrupt as long as they operate simultaneously.

18.   Which of the following must be unique for each serial port? (pick all that apply)
       A.   COM port number
       B.   Interrupt
       C.   I/O address
       D.   DMA channel
       E.   Bus-mastering address

19.   Which of the following is the correct order for I/O addresses which BIOS assigns COM port numbers?
       A.   2E8, 2F8, 3E8, 3F8
       B.   2E8, 3E8, 2F8, 3F8
       C.   3F8, 2F8, 3E8, 2E8
       D.   3F8, 3E8, 2F8, 2E8

20.   T/F   Serial ports always receive COM port numbers in I/O address order.

21.   Which COM ports are normally assigned to IRQ4? [COM1, COM2, COM3, or COM4] — pick all that apply

22.   Which COM ports are normally assigned to IRQ3? [COM1, COM2, COM3, or COM4] — pick all that apply

23.   Explain why assigning a COM port out of order can give the COM port a different number.

24.   The Windows 3.x [Ports, Serial Device, Device Manager, or System] control panel is used to configure serial devices.

25.   The Windows 95 [Serial Device, Ports, System, or Multimedia] is used to configure serial devices.

26.   List five common bps settings.

27.   Why do modems not normally use parity checking?

28.   What setting determines how two serial devices establish communication? [data bits, stop bits, parity, or flow control]

29.   What are two common flow control methods?

30.   What does CTS stand for?

31.   What does RTS stand for?

32.   Explain the difference between a DCE and a DTE.

33.   Define handshaking.

34.   Explain what happens when hardware handshaking is used.

35.   T/F   All serial cables are either 9 to 25-pin or 25 to 25-pin.

36. Scenario: An external modem has a 25 to 25-pin cable. The computer to which the modem attaches has two 9-pin serial ports. What is the most inexpensive way to connect the modem to the computer?
    A. Buy a 9 to 25-pin null modem cable
    B. Buy a 9 to 25-pin straight through cable
    C. Buy a 9 to 25-pin converter
    D. Buy a new modem

37. Why should a technician be careful when buying a 9 to 25-pin null modem cable?

38. List three recommendations to remember when installing a serial device.

39. List five troubleshooting tips for serial ports.

40. What are the majority of serial problems and why is this an issue?

41. What is the best DOS program to see the I/O addresses BIOS picks up for serial devices?

42. T/F Having an outdated UART can cause the modem not to work.

43. If a modem has only one RJ-11 port, what plugs into the port?
    A. A cable that connects to another modem
    B. A cable that plugs into a phone
    C. A cable that plugs into a phone outlet
    D. A cable that connects to another computer

44. Describe two advantages to external modems.

45. Describe two advantages to internal modems.

46. Describe how modem software can be an issue.

47. What CCITT (ITU) standards deal with modem data compression?

48. What CCITT (ITU) standards deal with fax modems?

49. What is a drawback to modem data compression?

50. T/F A modem should be set to its maximum speed.

51. What is a phone line isolator?

52. List 5 different troubleshooting tips for modems.

53. What happens if Call Waiting is enabled on a phone line with a modem attached?

54. List at least two things that can cause a modem to transmit at a lower than maximum speed.

55. If a modem does not sound a dial tone, what is the most likely conflict if the modem worked before?

56. If a Windows 95 computer uses a modem communication package written for Windows 3.x, what communication driver does Windows 95 use?

57.   What does a TR modem light indicate?
       A.   Terminal Ready
       B.   Transmit/Receive
       C.   Transmit Ready
       D.   Transmit Reset

58.   Explain whether Plug and Play technology makes serial device configuration harder, easier, or
       neither.

59.   Why does the Windows 95 installation wizard sometimes cause problems?

60.   Where do you go to start the Windows 95 modem diagnostic utility?

61.   How can you verify that Windows 95 has *not* disabled a modem?

62.   What CCITT Fax Group standard is used by most computers?

63.   If a customer wants to be able to receive and send faxes through their modem, what Group III,
       CCITT class is necessary?
       A.   Class 1
       B.   Class 2
       C.   Class 3
       D.   Class 4

64.   What is the biggest limitation to a 56Kbps modem transmitting at 56Kbps?

65.   T/F   A 56Kbps modem is a good investment for a home modem. Explain your answer.

66.   What are the two 56Kbps modem standards?

67.   T/F   A cable modem is a good investment for a home modem. Explain your answer.

68.   T/F   Digital modems require a digital phone line.

69.   Describe how the Universal Serial Bus can make configuring serial devices easier.

70.   List three USB devices.

71.   Describe what a computer needs to use a USB device.

72.   Describe the difference between how a mechanical and an optical mouse works?

73.   T/F   An optical mouse is more common than a mechanical mouse.

74.   Which type of keyboard is more reliable?

75.   How often should a keyboard and mouse be cleaned? Explain your answer.

76.   What does the term throw-away technology mean?

77.   T/F   Keyboards are considered to be throw-away technology.

Name _____

Serial Devices, Mice, and Keyboards Fill-in-the-Blank

1. _____ transmissions require a clock to send or receive data.

2. The _____ bit is used with asynchronous transmissions and signals the beginning of transmission.

3. The _____ bit is used with asynchronous transmissions and signals the end of transmission.

4. A(n) _____ converts a data byte into single transmission bits.

5. Serial devices are normally assigned the interrupts _____ or _____.

6. The normal data bits per data word is _____ bits per word.

7. The normal parity setting for a modem is _____.

8. The _____ modem setting enables the UART's buffer.

9. The _____ flow control method uses specific wires to signal data transmission.

10. The _____ flow control method uses control characters to signal data transmission.

11. Modems use a _____ cable.

12. To connect two computers and transfer data between them without a modem, a _____ cable is used.

13. A device used to help with serial pinouts is a _____.

14. A device that allows a computer to connect to a phone line is a _____.

15. _____ takes a signal from the phone line and converts it to digital format for input into the computer.

16. A modem that has _____ keeps the microprocessor from having to verify the accuracy of the data.

17. A modem that has _____ must transmit less data than one that does not have this ability.

18. The Hayes modem command _____ causes a Hayes-compatible modem to perform as if picking up a phone — it issues a dial tone.

19. The Hayes modem command _____ resets a Hayes-compatible modem.

20. The Windows 95 _____ wizard handles a modem installation.

21.   A type of digital phone line that has three channels is _____.

22.   A _____ connects multiple USB devices as well as expands the bus.

23.   A _____ mouse connects to a serial computer port.

24.   A _____ mouse connects to a 9-pin DIN connector.

25.   A _____ is an input device that works like a mouse except that it does not move on a mouse pad or desk, it stays stationary and a ball moves the tracking object.

26.   A serial device transmission speed is measured in _____.

Name _____

MSD UART IDENTIFICATION EXERCISE

Objective: Use MSD to identify the UART

Parts: Working computer with Microsoft Diagnostics (MSD) loaded

Step 1:   Power on the computer and go to the command prompt.
Step 2:   Change into the directory (DOS or WINDOWS) that contains the Microsoft Diagnostics (MSD.EXE) program. Refer to Appendix A for DOS skills.
Step 3:   Start the Microsoft Diagnostics program by typing **MSD** at the prompt.
Step 4:   Press **C** on the keyboard to access the COM Ports... option.
Step 5:   Look at the COM Ports information window. The headings across the top are COM1, COM2, COM3, and COM4. For each COM port, different criteria lists below it. Look for the last piece of information in the column which is the UART chip used criteria.

Question 1:   What UART does COM1 use?

Question 2:   Does the system being tested have a COM2 port?

Question 3:   If the system has a COM2 port, what UART does COM2 use?

Step 6:   Press **ENTER** to return to the first screen of the MSD program.
Step 7:   Press **F3** to quit MSD.

 Name _____

DETERMINING THE UART USING WINDOWS 95 EXERCISE

Objective: Use Windows 95 to identify the UART

Parts: Working computer with Windows 95 loaded

Step 1:   Power on the computer and verify that Windows 95 loads. Refer to Appendix B for Windows 95 skills.

Step 2:   Double-click on the **My Computer** icon.

Step 3:   Double-click on the **Control Panel** folder icon.

Step 4:   Use the scroll bars to locate the **System** icon.

Step 5:   Double-click on the **System** icon.

Step 6:   Click once on the **Device Manager** tab.

Step 7:   In the displayed list, click once on the **plus** (+) symbol beside the **Ports** option.

Step 8:   Double-click on the **Communications Port** sub-item under Ports.

Step 9:   Click once on the **Port Settings** tab.

Step 10:   Click on the **Advanced** button.

Step 11:   If the **Use FIFO buffers (requires 16550 compatible UART)** checkbox is checked, then the computer has a 16550 or higher UART. To determine the exact UART, remove the cover from the computer, find the UART, and look at the number on the chip.

Question 1:   Does Windows 95 detect a 16550 or higher UART in the computer?

Step 12:   Click on the **Cancel** button.

Step 13:   Click on the **Cancel** button in the Communications Properties window.

Step 14:   Click on the **Cancel** button in the System Properties window.

Optional Alternate Method is in Steps 15 through 19:

Step 15:   From the Control Panel window, double-click on the **Modems** icon. (Use the scroll bars to locate the icon if necessary.)

Step 16:   Click on the **Diagnostics** tab.

Step 17:   Click once on **COM1** to select the port.

Step 18:   Click on the **More Info** button. The port information is at the top of the window.

Question 2:   What UART does the port use?

Step 19:   Click on the **OK** button.

Step 20:   Close all windows on the desktop.

_____ Instructor's Initials

Name _____

DETECTING I/O ADDRESSES WITH THE DOS DEBUG PROGRAM EXERCISE

Objective: Use DEBUG to identify I/O addresses

Parts: Working computer with the DEBUG command available (DOS or Windows 95-based computer)

Step 1: Power on the computer and go to the command prompt. Refer to Appendix A for DOS skills.

Step 2: At the command prompt, type **DEBUG**. A dash appears on the line following the DEBUG command.

Step 3: At the dash on the screen, type **D40:0** and press **ENTER**. Hexadecimal values display on the screen.

The *D* in the *D40:0* command is the *dump* command meaning that the system is *dumping* the contents of a range of memory addresses. The *40:0* is the memory address where the I/O address information begins. The hexadecimal values of the active serial ports display first followed by the parallel ports. Deciphering the hexadecimal numbers is tricky, but Serial Exercise Figure #1 helps explain the values. *The first line of the output is all that matters!*

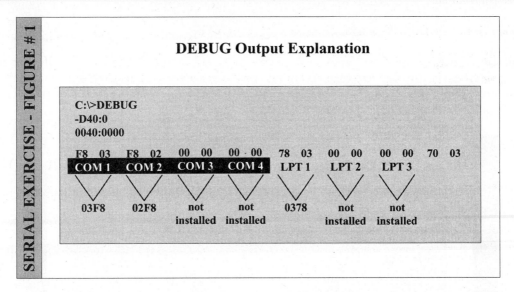

Notice in Serial Exercise Figure #1 how four different values are associated with COM1, COM2, COM3, and COM4. The four values represent the I/O address for the associated COM port. However, the address displays backward and this confuses most people. For example, COM1 lists as *F8 03*, but in reality, the values represent I/O address of *03F8*. A port address of 00 00 is an unused (or undetected) port.

Question 1:   Using Serial Exercise Table #1, write the COM port assignments and associated I/O addresses found in the computer. Once finished, have a classmate verify the COM port assignments.

	COM Port Name	I/O Address
SERIAL EXERCISE - TABLE # 1	COM1:	
	COM2:	
	COM3:	
	COM4:	

Classmate's printed name: _____

Classmate's initials: _____

Step 4: To exit the DEBUG program, type **Q** and press **ENTER**.

Question 2:   Determine if a serial device connects to the serial ports detected by the BIOS or if the serial device is a separate adapter. For the serial ports being used, use Serial Exercise Table #2 to log this information. For example, if an internal modem is using COM1, then write modem in the first space available in the Device column.

	Port	Device
SERIAL EXERCISE - TABLE # 2	COM1:	
	COM2:	
	COM3:	
	COM4:	

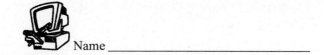
Name _____

WINDOWS 3.X COMMUNICATION PORT SETTINGS EXERCISE

Objective: Use Windows 3.x to identify serial port settings

Parts: Working computer with Windows 3.x loaded and at least one serial port installed

Step 1:   Power on the computer and verify that Windows 3.x loads.
Step 2:   Double-click on the **Main** group icon.
Step 3:   Double-click on the **Control Panel** icon.
Step 4:   Double-click on the **Ports** icon.
Step 5:   Double-click on the **COM1:** icon. The Settings for COM1: window appears.

Question 1:   What is the baud rate for COM1:?

Question 2:   What is the number of data bits for COM1:?

Question 3:   What is the flow control method used?

Question 4:   What is the difference between XON/XOFF and hardware flow control?

Step 6:   Click on the **Advanced** button.

Question 5:   What I/O address does COM1: have?

Question 6:   What IRQ does COM1: have?

Question 7:   Do the I/O address and IRQ assignments adhere to the standard for configuring serial
               devices? Refer to Serial Table #2.

Step   7:   Click on the **down arrow** in the **IRQ** setting section.

Question 8:   What interrupts are available as standard interrupts using Windows 3.x?

Question 9:   Why are IRQs 0 and 1 not available?

Step   8:   Click on the **Cancel** button.
Step   9:   From within the Settings for COM1: window, click on the **down arrow** in the **Flow
             Control** section.

Question 10:   What other flow control options are available?

Step 10:   Click on the **Cancel** button within the Settings for COM1: window.
Step 11:   Click on the **Cancel** button within the Ports window.
Step 12:   Close the **Control Panel** window.
Step 13:   Close the **Main** window.

_____ Instructor's Initials

 Name _____

WINDOWS 95 COMMUNICATION PORT SETTINGS EXERCISE

Objective: Use Windows 95 to identify serial port settings

Parts: Working computer with Windows 95 loaded

Step 1:   Power on the computer and verify that Windows 95 loads. Refer to Appendix B for
           Windows 95 skills.
Step 2:   Double-click on the **My Computer** icon.
Step 3:   Double-click on the **Control Panel** folder icon.
Step 4:   Use the scroll bars to locate the **System** icon.
Step 5:   Double-click on the **System** icon.
Step 6:   Click once on the **Device Manager** tab.
Step 7:   In the displayed list, click once on the **plus (+)** symbol beside the **Ports** option.
Step 8:   Double-click on the **Communications Port** sub-item under Ports.
Step 9:   Click once on the **Port Settings** tab.

Question 1:   What is the bits per second rate for COM1:?

Question 2:   What is the number of data bits for COM1:?

Question 3:   What is the flow control method used?

Question 4:   What is the current parity setting?

Step 10:   Click once on the **down arrow** in the **Parity** section.

Question 5:   What parity options are available?

Step 11:   Verify that the parity setting is set to the original setting. Refer to the answer given for
            Question 4.
Step 12:   Click on the **Resources** tab.

Question 6:   What I/O address does COM1: have?

Question 7:   What IRQ does COM1: have?

Question 8:   Do the I/O address and IRQ assignments adhere to the standard for configuring serial devices?

Question 9:   To what setting is the *Settings based on:* selection set?

Step 13:   Click once in the **Use automatic settings** checkbox to deselect it.
Step 14:   To change the setting, click on the **down arrow** in the **Setting based on:** section. A list of configurations appears.
Step 15:   Click once on a configuration selection different than the one specified in Question 9.

Question 10:   What happened to the I/O range and the IRQ settings? What are they set to now?

Question 11:   Does the chosen setting adhere to the standard for configuring serial devices? Refer to the chapter's Serial Table #2.

Step 16:   Set the **Setting based on:** selection back to the original configuration. Look back to the answer given for Question 9.
Step 17:   Click on the **Cancel** button.
Step 18:   Click on the **Cancel** button from within the System Properties window.
Step 19:   Close all open windows on the desktop.

_____ Instructor's Initials

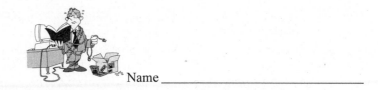

Name _____

EXTERNAL SERIAL DEVICE INSTALLATION EXERCISE
(DOS/WINDOWS ENVIRONMENT)

Objective: Connect an external serial device to a computer that uses DOS and/or Windows 3.x and configure the serial port for proper operation

Parts: Computer with DOS or Windows installed and an available serial port
Serial device
Appropriate serial cable
Tools

Observe proper grounding procedures when installing an external serial device.

Step   1:   Power on the computer.

Step   2:   Examine the back of the computer for serial ports.

Question 1:   How many total serial ports does the computer have?

Question 2:   Is there a serial port available (not being used by another serial device)? If not, install a serial adapter before continuing with this exercise.

Step   3:   Using the computer's SETUP program, MSD (Microsoft Diagnostics), DEBUG, or any other similar program, determine the COM ports, IRQs, and I/O address assignment for the computer's serial ports and any internal serial device, such as a modem. Also, list any serial devices connected to the serial ports or any internal serial devices. Use Serial Exercise Table #3 to document the results. Leave any spaces blank if no device is found or if the COM port is not available.

COM Port	IRQ	I/O Address	Device Connected
COM1			
COM2			
COM3			
COM4			
COM__			
COM__			

SERIAL EXERCISE - TABLE # 3

Step   4:   Use software such as MSD or a visual inspection around the port to determine the type of UART installed.

Question 3:   What UART is installed?

Question 4:   Is the UART fast enough for the device being installed? If not, contact the instructor.

Step   5:   Locate the serial port to which the external serial device will attach.

Question 5:   Based on the findings in Step 3, what interrupt, I/O address, and COM port assignments will be used by the external serial device being installed?

Step   6:   Power off the computer.
Step   7:   Attach the serial cable to the serial device.
Step   8:   Attach the serial cable to the computer's serial port.
Step   9:   Power on the external serial device.
Step 10:   Power on the computer.
Step 11:   Load any software drivers necessary for the external device. Refer to the serial device manual.
Step 12:   If the external device is a modem, use Windows 3.x's Terminal program to test the modem. See the chapter exercise on using Windows Terminal program if unfamiliar with it.
Step 13:   Install any software applications that come with the external serial device. If the application requires configuration parameters, refer to Question 5 for that information.

Question 6:   Does the external serial device work? If not, refer to the chapter's troubleshooting sections and repair the problem.

Question 7:   Do all other serial devices in the computer still operate? Verify this to be sure. If not, refer to the chapter's troubleshooting sections and repair the problem.

_____ Instructor's Initials

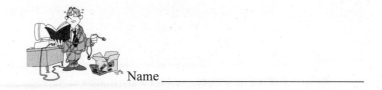

Name _____

EXTERNAL SERIAL DEVICE INSTALLATION EXERCISE
(WINDOWS 95 ENVIRONMENT)

Objective: Connect an external serial device to a computer that uses Windows 95 and configure the serial port for proper operation.

Parts: Computer with Windows 95 installed and an available serial port
        Serial device
        Appropriate serial cable
        Tools

Observe proper grounding procedures when installing an external serial device.

Step 1:   Power on the computer and verify that Windows 95 loads. Refer to Appendix B for Windows 95 skills.
Step 2:   Examine the back of the computer for serial ports.

Question 1:   How many total serial ports does the computer have?

Question 2:   Is there a serial port available (not being used by another serial device)? If not, install a serial adapter before continuing with this exercise.

Step 3:   Double-click on the **My Computer** icon.
Step 4:   Double-click on the **Control Panel** folder icon.
Step 5:   Use the scroll bars to locate the **System** icon.
Step 6:   Double-click on the **System** icon.
Step 7:   Click once on the **Device Manager** tab.
Step 8:   In the displayed list, click once on the **plus** (+) symbol beside the **Ports** option.
Step 9:   Double-click on the **Communications Port** sub-item under Ports.
Step 10:   Click once on the **Port Settings** tab.
Step 11:   Click on the **Resources** tab.

Step 12:   Using the information displayed on the screen, complete Serial Exercise Table #4. Leave any applicable spaces blank if no device is found or if the COM port is not available.

COM Port	IRQ	I/O Address	Device Connected
COM1			
COM2			
COM3			
COM4			
COM__			
COM__			

SERIAL EXERCISE - TABLE # 4

Step 13:   Click on the **Cancel** button.
Step 14:   Click on the **Cancel** button from within the System Properties window.
Step 15:   Close all open windows on the desktop.
Step 16:   Use software or a visual inspection of the port (the one to which the serial device will attach) to determine the type of UART installed.

Question 3:   What UART is installed in the computer?

Question 4:   Is the UART fast enough for the device being installed? If not, contact the instructor.

Step 17:   Locate the serial port to which the external serial device will attach.

Question 5:   Based on the findings in Step 12, what interrupt, I/O address, and COM port assignments will be used by the external serial device being installed?

Step 18:   Power off the computer.
Step 19:   Attach the serial cable to the serial device.
Step 20:   Attach the serial cable to the computer's serial port.
Step 21:   Power on the external serial device.
Step 22:   Power on the computer.
Step 23:   Load any software drivers necessary for the external device. Refer to the serial device manual.
Step 24:   If the external device is a modem, use Windows 95's HyperTerminal program to test the modem. (See the chapter exercise on using the Windows 95 HyperTerminal program if you are unfamiliar with it.)
Step 25:   Install any software applications included with the external serial device. If the application requires configuration parameters, refer to Question 5 for that information.

Question 6:   Does the external serial device work? If not, refer to the chapter's troubleshooting sections and repair the problem.

Question 7:   Do all other serial devices in the computer still operate? Verify this to be sure. If not, refer to the chapter's troubleshooting sections and repair the problem.

_____ Instructor's Initials

Name _____

USING THE WINDOWS 3.X TERMINAL PROGRAM EXERCISE

Objective: Use the Windows 3.x Terminal program to test a modem

Parts: A computer with a Hayes-compatible modem and Windows 3.x loaded

Question 1:   Before beginning this exercise, gather information about the modem's serial port. Use Serial Exercise Table #5 to record this information.

EXERCISE - TABLE # 5		
Modem (internal or external)?		
IRQ		
I/O address		
COM Port		
Maximum bps (speed)		

Step 1:   Turn the computer on and start Windows 3.x.
Step 2:   Double-click the **Terminal** icon from Program Manager's Accessories group.
Step 3:   From the menu bar, click once on **Settings**.
Step 4:   From the drop down menu, select the **Communications** option.
Step 5:   Contact the instructor for a local bulletin board number (and the proper settings, if possible).

Question 2:   What local bulletin board number did the instructor give you?

Step 6:   Select the proper speed setting for the modem in the **Baud Rate** section by clicking on the appropriate radio button. Reference Serial Exercise Table #5 for the proper speed setting.
Step 7:   Select the proper number of **data bits** by clicking on the appropriate radio button. If unknown, select 8.
Step 8:   Select the proper number of **stop bits** by clicking on the appropriate radio button. If unknown, select 1.
Step 9:   Select the proper **parity** setting by clicking on the appropriate radio button. If the parity setting is unknown, select none.

Step 10:   Select the proper **Flow Control** setting by clicking on the appropriate radio button. If unknown, select Hardware.

Question 3:   What is parity?

Step 11:   Select the proper COM port **Connector**. Refer back to Serial Exercise Table #5 if unsure about the COM port.

Step 12:   After determining all settings, click on the **OK** button.

Step 13:   To verify the modem works, type **ATE1M1V1** (in all caps) and press **ENTER**. The modem replies with an OK on the screen. If not, perform troubleshooting steps. Refer to the chapter's sections on troubleshooting serial ports and modems.

Typing the commands in capital letters is important because some modems will not recognize lowercase letters. Get in the habit of using capitalized modem commands.

Question 4:   Check with the instructor to see if the phone line you are using requires a special number to access an outside line. *If so, place that number before all phone numbers used in this exercise.*

Step 14:   To test if the modem is connecting to an outside phone line, type **ATDT** and press **ENTER**. A dial tone sounds from the modem speaker. If not, check the modem's connection to the wall jack and the modem's speaker volume level. Refer to the modem's manual. If the phone line requires a special number such as 9 to connect to an outside phone line, place that number immediately after the ATDT command.

Question 5:   Does the dial tone sound through the modem? If not, refer to the chapter troubleshooting sections. Do not proceed until Step 14 works properly.

Step 15:   Click once on the menu bar's **Phone** option.

Step 16:   Choose the **Hangup** option.

Step 17:   From the menu bar, click once on **Settings**.

Step 18:   From the drop down menu, choose **Phone Number**. The Phone Number dialog box appears.

Step 19:   Type the phone number (given by the instructor in Step 5 and written down as the answer in Question 2) into the **Dial:** field. Do not forget to preface the number with the number required to access an outside telephone line. Reference the answer to Question 4.

Step 20:   Click on the **OK** button when finished entering the phone number.

Step 21:   Click on **Phone** from the menu bar.

Step 22:   Click on the **Dial** option. The dial tone sounds as the modem dialing outputs screeching noises to the speaker. After that, the modem connects to the dialed service. If this works, the modem is working fine. If other software applications do not access the modem properly, troubleshoot the software application's specific settings. If the modem does not connect to the other modem, re-check the modems IRQ, I/O address, COM port, speed setting, parity setting, stop bits setting, data bits setting, etc.

Question 6:   Does the modem work properly? If not, refer to the chapter troubleshooting sections and resolve the problem.

_____ Instructor's Initials

Step 23:   After accessing the bulletin board, click once on the menu bar's **Phone** option.
Step 24:   Choose the **Hangup** option.
Step 25:   Close the Terminal window by double-clicking the close box in the window's upper left corner. A dialog box appears asking if the settings are to be saved.
Step 26:   Click once on the **NO** button.
Step 27:   Close all open windows on the desktop.

Name _____

USING THE WINDOWS 95 HYPERTERMINAL EXERCISE

Objective: Use the Windows 95 HyperTerminal program to test a modem

Parts: A computer with a modem and Windows 95 loaded

Question 1:   Before beginning this exercise, gather information about the modem's serial port. Use
Serial Exercise Table #6 to record the information.

EXERCISE - TABLE # 6		
Modem (internal or external)?		
IRQ		
I/O address		
COM Port		
Maximum bps (speed)		

Step 1:   Power on the computer and verify Windows 95 loads. Refer to Appendix B for Windows
95 skills.
Step 2:   Click on the **Start** button in the desktop's bottom left corner.
Step 3:   Select **Programs** from the Start menu.
Step 4:   Select **Accessories** from the menu.
Step 5:   Click once on **HyperTerminal** from the next menu. The HyperTerminal window appears.
Step 6:   Double-click on the **Hypertm.exe** icon. The Connection Description window appears.
Step 7:   In the Connection Description window, type **COMPUSERVE TEST** in the **Name:** field.
Step 8:   Using the slide bar, click once on the icon of your choice.
Step 9:   Click on the **OK** button. The phone number window appears. The cursor blinks in the
phone number field.
Step 10:   Type **346-3247** in the **Phone number:** field.
Step 11:   Verify the **Connect using** field. Verify the correct modem is selected or the modem's
correct COM port setting is selected. Click on the down arrow to change if necessary.
Step 12:   Click on the **OK** button.
Step 13:   Click on the **Dialing Properties** button.

Question 2:   Check with the instructor to see if the phone line requires a special number to access an outside line. If so, what is that number?

Step 14:   If a special number is needed to connect to an outside telephone line (reference Question 2), click once in the **To access an outside line, first dial:** text box. Type in the special number needed to access an outside phone line.

Step 15:   If Call Waiting is available on the phone line, verify that the **This location has call waiting** checkbox is checked. Then, click on the **down arrow** to select the numbers to disable it. If you are unsure of the numbers to disable Call Waiting, contact the instructor.

Step 16:   Click on the **OK** button.

Step 17:   In the Connect window, click on the **Modify** button.

Step 18:   In the **Area Code:** text field, click once after the last number shown.

Step 19:   Press the **backspace** key **three** times until the area code numbers disappear.

Step 20:   Type **800** in the **Area Code:** field.

Step 21:   Click on the **Configure** button.

Step 22:   Verify the COM port name is correct, the speaker volume is turned up, and the maximum modem speed settings are correct. Refer to Serial Exercise Table #6 at the beginning of this exercise for the correct COM port name. Modify the settings as necessary.

Step 23:   Click on the **Connection** tab.

Step 24:   Verify that the **Data bits** setting is **8**. Verify that the **Parity** setting is **None**. Verify that the **Stop bits** setting is **1**.

Question 3:   Were all settings for Step 24 set correctly? If not, what settings had to be changed?

Step 25:   Click on the **Advanced** button.

Step 26:   Verify the **Use error control** checkbox is checked.

Question 4:   Was the *Use error control* checkbox checked?

Step 27:   Verify the **Use flow control** checkbox is checked.

Question 5:   Was the *Use flow control* checkbox checked?

Step 28:   Verify the **Hardware (RTS/CTS)** radio button is selected.

Step 29:   Click on the **OK** button.

Step 30:   Click the **OK** button in the Properties window.

Step 31:   Click the **OK** button in the CompuServe Test Properties window. The *Connect* window is on the desktop.

Step 32:   Verify the telephone number shown is 1 800 346-3247. If the phone number is incorrect, redo Steps 17 through 31.

Step 33: Click **Dial** in the **Connect** window. The dial tone sounds as the modem dialing outputs screeching noises to the speaker. After that, the modem connects to the dialed service, the Connect window disappears, and a blinking cursor is on the Terminal screen. If this works, the modem is working fine. If other software applications do not access the modem properly, troubleshoot the software application's specific settings. If the modem does not connect to the other modem, re-check the modems IRQ, I/O address, COM port, speed setting, parity setting, stop bits setting, data bits setting, etc.

Question 6: Does the modem work? If not, troubleshoot the modem. Refer to the chapter troubleshooting sections for more assistance.

_____ Instructor's Initials

Step 34: Press **ENTER** after the modem connects to CompuServe. The Host Name: prompt appears.
Step 35: At the **Host Name:** prompt, type **PHONES** and press **ENTER**.
Step 36: After reading the screen, press **ENTER**.
Step 37: Press **1** and **ENTER** to Find U.S. access numbers.
Step 38: After reading the screen, press **ENTER**.
Step 39: Select the correct number for the speed of the modem being used and press **ENTER**.
Step 40: Enter the **school's phone number** or **your home phone number** as shown in the example on the screen. Then, press **ENTER**. The local CompuServe phone numbers display on the screen.
Step 41: Click on the close box in the upper right corner of the window. A dialog box appears stating that you connected.
Step 42: Click on the **Yes** button to close the session.
Step 43: At the **Do you want to save session CompuServe Test** dialog box, click on the **No** button.
Step 44: Close all windows on the desktop.

NOTES

Chapter 12: Video

OBJECTIVES

After completing this chapter you will
1.   Know the components of the video subsystem.
2.   Know the different types of monitors.
3.   Understand basic monitor theory and terminology.
4.   Recommend a resolution for a particular monitor size.
5.   Know the different types of video memory.
6.   Perform basic video troubleshooting techniques.
7.   Understand how FireWire, USB, MMX, and AGP influence video trends.

KEY TERMS

AGP	MDRAM
analog monitor	MMX
aperture grille	monochrome monitor
CGA	multi-scan monitor
color monitor	picture cell
CRT	pixel
DDC	raster
degausser	refresh rate
digital monitor	resolution
dot pitch	screen saver
dot triad	SGRAM
DPMS	shadow mask
drivers	single-ported
dual-ported	SVGA
EGA	UVGA
flyback transformer	vertical scan rate
grayscale monitor	VGA
green monitor	video processor
horizontal scanning frequency	VIS
interlacing	VRAM
MDA	WRAM

VIDEO OVERVIEW

Video quality is very important to the computer user because the monitor displays all the data and software programs, and is one of the most expensive computer components. Users usually get the most gratification from their monitor, though sound quality is now becoming as important. Technicians must look at video as a subsystem that consists of the monitor, the electronic circuits that send the monitor instructions, and a cable that connects them. The electronic video circuits are on a separate video adapter or built into the motherboard. Video Figure #1 illustrates a computer's video subsystem.

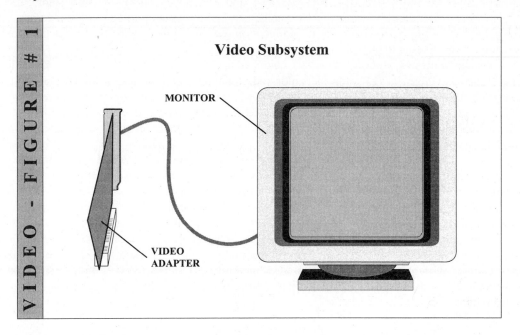

TYPES OF MONITORS

Monitors can be classified several ways: color or non-color monitors, if analog or digital signals are used to produce colors, and the video adapter used. Understanding all three classifications gives you a good perspective about monitors.

The first computer monitors manufactured were monochrome. **Monochrome monitors** project a single color (white, amber, or green) on a black background. Computer systems that run an air conditioning system, a telephone exchange, or print servers (computers that handle a printer in a network environment) all use a monochrome monitor because the output is text only, no graphics. **Color monitors** display many colors for text and graphics. **Grayscale monitors** display various shades of gray. Grayscale monitors are used by artists who do not work in colors, but black, white, and shades of gray and design engineers who work in the CAD (computer-aided design) environment.

The first monochrome monitors and the first two types of color monitors were **digital monitors** that accept digital signals from the video adapter. The drawback to digital monitors is they do not display many colors.

Digital electronics use voltage levels to represent the binary data where the 1s and 0s turn something on or off. There are no varying levels. Color monitors project different colors using red, green, and blue guns inside the monitor (one gun per color). A digital 1 or 0 goes from the video adapter to turn the specific color gun on or off. The number of colors visible on a monitor is determined by the number of bits used. A mathematical relationship exists between the number of bits used and the number of possible colors — 2^x=number of colors (where x is the number of color bits). For example, if three pins on the video adapter controls color, then eight different colors are possible. (The different combinations of the 1s and 0s determine the different colors. With three pins, the eight combinations are 000, 001, 010, 011, 100, 101, 110, and 111. So, if four bits control colors, then 16 different colors are available because 2^4=16. The human eye discerns up to 16.7 million colors which requires 24 pins on the video connector not to mention the other pins needed to control the monitor. So, analog monitors came to the rescue.

Analog monitors produce numerous colors more easily than digital monitors. Consider an analog signal waveform ⌐⌐ for the color red. Imagine different places along the waveform representing different shades of red. Now combine the red waveform with a similar green and blue waveform and you can see how monitors produce millions of colors. The color differences are limitless! Analog monitors have digital circuits inside them, but analog monitors accept analog signals not digital signals to display colors.

The first type of video adapter used with computers was the **MDA (Monochrome Display Adapter)**. The first color adapter was the **CGA (Color Graphics Adapter)**, then the **EGA (Enhanced Graphics Adapter)** arrived. All the earlier monitors, monochrome, CGA, or EGA, were digital monitors and connected to a 9-pin female D-shell connector. IBM then produced the **VGA (Video Graphics Array)** monitors. They were the first analog monitors used in mass quantities and IBM established the VGA standard. Other types of monitors advertised include **SVGA (Super VGA)** and **UVGA (Ultra VGA)**, but these two terms do not refer to video standards. SVGA and UVGA are simply monitors with more capabilities than VGA monitors. The VGA, SVGA, and UVGA monitors all connect to a 15-pin, three row, D-shell connector. Look back to Chapter 1's Introduction Figure #7 for a refresher on the video connectors.

One of the most important things to remember with video is the video adapter must match the type of monitor.

MONITOR TERMINOLOGY AND THEORY

Monitors are manufactured in different sizes. The most common sizes are 15", 17", and 21." The video industry has traditionally defined the monitor size as the diagonal length of the picture tube, but there is no industry standard that defines a specific *monitor size* measurement. The monitor case encloses the **CRT (Cathode Ray Tube)**, the main part of a monitor, and covers part of it. The size of the CRT, also called the picture tube, may not be what the computer user sees. Many manufacturers now list the *viewable area* or the **VIS (Viewable Image Size)** of the CRT to clarify the monitor size. Because Windows 95 and Windows NT allow so many windows to be open on the screen, a 17" or larger monitor is recommended to allow more working room.

Monitors have three electron guns, one each for the colors red, green, and blue while other monitors have only one electron gun that directs the three color beams. The guns shoot a beam of electrons aimed at a phosphorous dot on the back of the monitor tube. When the electron beam hits the phosphor, the dot glows and appears on the front of the screen. All figures, icons, and letters on the screen are nothing more than closely spaced dots glowing at different intensities.

A monitor has three phosphorous dots called a **dot triad** (or dot trio) grouped together at each location on the screen. The dot triad consists of a dot for red, green, and blue. When the beam of electrons hit a phosphor dot, the dot begins to glow. The beam intensity varies to create different color intensities. Because the electron beam guns hit the phosphorous dots from different angles, a **shadow mask** which is a metal plate with holes, keeps the beam directed at the proper dot. See Video Figure #2 for an illustration of how the three guns direct electron beams through the shadow mask to cause the phosphorous dots to glow.

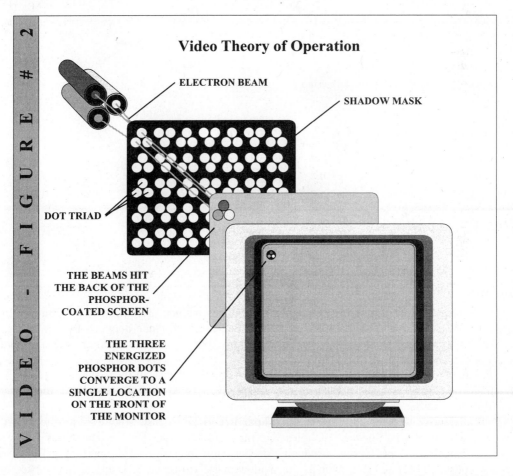

Keep in mind that Video Figure #2 shows the shadow mask holes quite large, but in reality they are the size of pin holes.

A variation of the shadow mask is a Phillips Magnavox creation, the Invar shadow mask. This reduces the heat problem of the traditional shadow mask. Another shadow mask used in NEC's Chromaclear monitors has elliptical slots instead of holes.

The phosphorous dot triad converges to make one dot on the screen called a **pixel**, short for picture element. Some view a pixel as one dot on the screen, but it takes the three different colored phosphorous dots to create the single image called a **picture cell**. Perhaps a better definition for a pixel is the smallest displayable unit on the screen.

The monitor's **dot pitch** is the distance between like-colored phosphorous dots on adjacent dot triads. Video Figure #3 illustrates dot pitch.

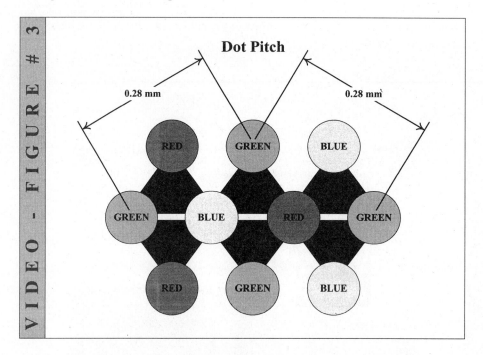

Dot pitch is measured in millimeters. Common dot pitches include .39mm, .35mm, .28mm, .26mm, .25mm, etc. The lower the monitor's dot pitch, the smaller the distance between the dot triads. The lower the dot pitch number, the better the picture quality. For example, a monitor with a .28mm dot pitch is better than one with a .35mm dot pitch.

For any monitor that uses a shadow mask (including those with an Invar shadow mask), the dot pitch should be .28mm or smaller for a quality image. On any type of shadow mask, the closer the holes are to one another, the better the dot pitch.

An alternative to the shadow mask is an **aperture grille** used in Sony Trinitron monitors that has very fine vertical wires instead of holes like the shadow mask. The vertical wires allow more electrons to reach the screen thereby producing deeper color intensities. The aperture grille wires are not as susceptible to heat and distortion as the shadow mask. However, to keep the fine vertical wires from moving or vibrating, horizontal wires are needed. These extra stabilizing wires can be seen on bright images which is not acceptable in some fields of exact science such as medical or scientific research. Some users claim this technology is better than the shadow mask, but it is simply a matter of preference. For monitors that use an aperture grille, dot pitch is relevant in a horizontal direction only.

The phosphor used to create a dot on the screen is coated in vertical strips rather than in dots. Some very high quality CRTs that use an aperture grille have dot pitches as small as .22mm, or smaller. Video Figure #4 illustrates how an aperture grille creates a pixel.

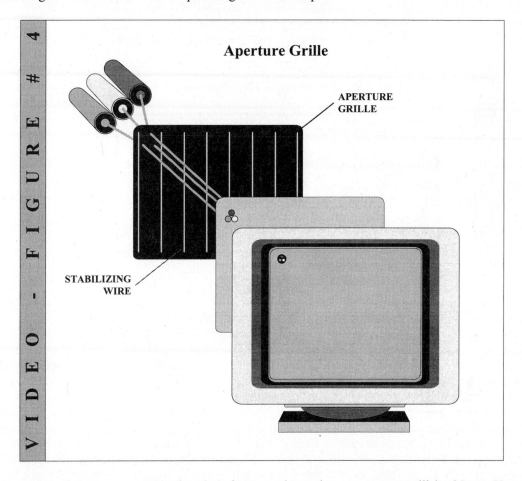

The minimum acceptable dot pitch for a monitor using an aperture grill is .25mm. However, manufacturers use different terminology to describe dot pitch when the monitor uses the aperture grille technology. Possible dot pitch descriptions include *grill pitch*, *horizontal mask pitch*, and *mask pitch*. Some Sony monitors use a variable aperture grille technology. On these monitors, two dot pitches are given, one for the center and one for the edges. Proper dot pitch is a user preference. The user must stare at the monitor all day long and needs a dot pitch suitable for his or her eyes.

Dot pitch is an important feature in choosing a monitor's **resolution** which is the maximum number of pixels on the monitor. Two numbers separated by an *x* meaning *by* describe a monitor's resolution, such as 640x480. The first number, 640, is the number of pixels that fit horizontally across the screen. The second number, 480, describes the number of pixels that fit vertically on the screen. The possible monitor resolutions depend on the monitor and the video adapter.

Some describe SVGA as a monitor that displays an 800x600 resolution and an UVGA monitor as one that displays an 1024x768 resolution. Again, these are just industry's acceptance.

The higher the monitor's resolution, the smaller the pixel appears on the screen. Picking a higher resolution will make the icons in Windows appear smaller. Many users do not know or understand this concept and set their resolution too high relative to their monitor size.

Video Table #1 lists common monitor sizes with some recommended resolutions.

VIDEO - TABLE # 1

Recommended Resolutions

Monitor Size	Resolution
14"	640 x 480
15"	640 x 480 or 800 x 600
17"	800 x 600 or 1024 x 768
19"	1024 x 768 or 1280 x 1024
20" or 21"	1024 x 768, 1280 x 1024, or 1600 x 1200

Another monitor feature that determines how sharp an image appears on the screen is its **refresh rate**. This is the maximum times a screen is scanned in one second, measured in Hz. The pixels on the screen do not stay excited very long and must be refreshed occasionally to stay lit. The electron beams start at the top left corner of the screen and cross to the right. Once the beam reaches the right side, it turns off momentarily as it returns to the left. Then, the electron beam refreshes the pixels in the row beneath the first horizontal row. The electron beam continuously sweeps left to right, scanning every row of pixels. The video card directs the electron beam and tells the beam which pixels need to be energized. The frequency the beam traverses the screen is the **horizontal scanning frequency**. This frequency is calculated by taking the inverse of the amount of time to go from the beginning of one line to the beginning of the next line. Horizontal scanning frequencies are measured in kilohertz (kHz) determined by the video adapter. VGA adapters normally have a horizontal scanning frequency of 31.5kHz. SVGA adapters have horizontal scanning frequencies ranging from 35 to 48kHz. The **vertical scan rate** is the number of times the electron beam draws from the top left corner, to the bottom right corner, and back to the top left. The horizontal scanning frequency is the rate for one line to be drawn whereas the vertical scan rate deals with drawing the entire screen. A slow vertical scan rate can cause a monitor to appear to flicker because the phosphors lose their intensity unless they are refreshed frequently.

A refresh rate greater than 60Hz is the bare minimum for a 14" or 15" monitor's refresh rate. A 72Hz, 75Hz, or 85Hz refresh rate is better especially if purchasing a 17" or 20" monitor.

With a 72Hz refresh rate the entire video screen redraws 72 times per second. The refresh rate includes the time it takes the electron beam to return from the bottom right corner to the top left corner of the screen. The monitor's refresh rate is for a specific resolution. If the electron beam has to handle more pixels, it will naturally take longer. Therefore, before purchasing or recommending a monitor to customers, be sure you know the resolution they need. Then, look at the refresh rate for that particular resolution. For the video card to control the electron beam, the video adapter's specifications *must* match the monitor's refresh specifications. Video card capabilities are the main factor in determining what refresh rate the monitor uses, provided the monitor can perform it.

A monitor that can lock onto different vertical and horizontal scanning frequencies is a **multi-scan** or a multi-synch monitor. Many users like these monitors due to their flexibility of connecting to a variety of adapters giving the user an upgrade path. Multi-scan monitors are more expensive than common monitors.

A monitor that uses **interlacing** cheats on the horizontal scanning as the electron beam scans only the odd numbered pixel rows. Then, the electron beam returns and scans the even numbered pixel rows. Interlacing causes a flickering on the screen, but is cheaper than scanning every horizontal pixel row. Some manufacturers use non-interlacing techniques up to a specific resolution. At higher resolutions, the monitor reverts to interlaced mode. Check the monitor's refresh rate specifications for the resolution at which the monitor will be operated most often. Be sure the monitor uses the non-interlaced mode of operation for that resolution.

MONITOR PREVENTIVE MAINTENANCE

A monitor is a simple device on which to perform preventive maintenance. Static builds up on the face of the monitor and the screen attracts dust and dirt like any television. Anti-static cleaning wipes are available at computer and office supply stores. A monitor can also be cleaned with a soft dampened cloth and mild household detergent, glass cleaner, or isopropyl alcohol. Do not allow any liquid to get near the edge of the CRT. The liquid can seep inside the monitor case and cause damage. If using a CRT cleaning spray or glass cleaner, spray the cleaner on the cloth, not on the monitor. If the monitor has a non-glare screen or any type of special coating, see the manufacturer's instructions for cleaning it.

Unless specifically trained for monitor repair, never remove the monitor case. The monitor holds 20,000 or more volts (depending on the monitor size and components). Voltage can still be present after turning off the power. Most technicians who work on monitors have special training working on high voltage equipment. If you must remove the monitor case to work inside a monitor, a few safety rules include: do not wear the anti-static grounding strap, unplug the AC cord from the monitor or wall outlet, do not work alone, discharge the capacitors located inside the monitor, and do not use regular test equipment to measure the monitor's high voltages.

MONITOR ENERGY EFFICIENCY

A monitor's life span is normally 20,000 to 60,000 hours. The heat generated inside a monitor can reduce the life span of the monitor's components. Some monitors called **green monitors** have energy conservation capabilities. These monitors have software that reduces the power leaving only enough to allow the monitor to be quickly reactivated to a useable state. The Environmental Protection Agency produced Energy Star guidelines to which many monitor manufacturers adhere. Many BIOS chips now support and have settings in the CMOS for energy efficient monitors.

VESA produced a **DPMS (Display Power Management Signaling)** standard that defines the signals used to tell the monitor to reduce power. If a video adapter is not DPMS-compatible, some adapters use a software program as an alternative. Windows 95 allows setting the display properties for monitors that support the DPMS specification.

Only use the energy efficiency CMOS settings, energy efficiency software, or Windows 95's energy efficiency settings if the monitor supports it. A non-green monitor can be damaged if you enable these settings when the monitor does not support energy efficiency modes of operation. Check the monitor's documentation to determine if it supports energy efficiency modes.

SCREEN SAVERS

In the olden days when monitors did not have fast refresh rates, screen savers were very important. A **screen saver** changes the image on the monitor constantly to keep any particular image from *burning* into the screen. With old monitors, if an image stayed on the screen for an extended period of time, an imprint of the image was left on the screen permanently. Today's monitors have high enough refresh rates so screen savers are not necessary, but are now an entertainment art form. Also, screen savers can provide password protection that may be important to some users.

VIDEO ADAPTERS

Using millions of colors, motion, sound and video combined, the computer's video subsystem has made dramatic technological advances. The video adapter controls most of the monitor's output. Video adapters use either the ISA, EISA, VL-bus, MCA, or PCI interface. The bus connects the video card to the microprocessor. The microprocessor accepts data in either 16, 32, or 64-bit chunks determined by the microprocessor and the bus interface. (Reference Chapter 2 for more information on the different microprocessors and bus interfaces.) One of the challenges of interfacing video is finding a good video adapter that uses a good system architecture such as PCI.

On the motherboard, the microprocessor and the chipset are responsible for how quickly data travels to and from the video adapter. Such things as upgrading the chipset, the microprocessor, or the video adapter to a faster interface, speeds up video transfer to the monitor. However, special features on the video adapter can also speed up video transfer.

Some video adapters have their own processor. The **video processor**, (sometimes known as a video co-processor or video accelerator), assists in video communication between the video adapter and the system's microprocessor. Some video processors are 64 or 128-bit processors. Many users (and technicians) have a hard time understanding how a 128-bit video processor works in a 32-bit PCI slot. The 64 or 128 bits refers to the number of bits the video adapter's accelerator chip accepts at one time. The 64 bits (or higher) video processor controls many video functions on the video adapter otherwise handled by the microprocessor. Any time information is processed on the adapter rather than the microprocessor there is faster performance. When signals pass to the microprocessor through an expansion slot, performance slows. Most video cards today contain a video processor because video is one of the biggest bottlenecks in a computer system.

One way of speeding up a video adapter's performance is to *shadow* the video adapter's ROM chip through the computer system's SETUP program. Shadowing the video ROM chip means the software inside the ROM chip is copied into the RAM chips. Accessing instructions from RAM is faster than from a ROM chip, especially a ROM chip on an adapter.

VIDEO MEMORY

One of the most important functions of the video processor is to transfer data to and from the video adapter's memory. Memory chips on the video adapter can be regular DRAM chips (including FPM and EDO memory chips — see the Memory chapter for more information on chip technologies), VRAM chips, or WRAM chips. **VRAM (Video RAM)** and **WRAM (Window RAM)** chips are **dual-ported**; they have separate read and write data paths and can be written to and read from simultaneously. DRAM chips are **single-ported**; they are read from or written to, but not simultaneously. The single-ported memory chips have a single data path in and out of the chips. Video adapters that use dual-ported memory have greater performance at resolutions greater than 800x600 and at higher color levels. The difference between the two is WRAM is cheaper than VRAM. The type of video memory can make a big difference in video performance. Reference the video adapter documentation on the type of video memory chips to use.

Advances in single-port memory chips include SGRAM and MDRAM. **SGRAM (Synchronous Graphics RAM)** chips allow the video data to clock up to four times quicker than traditional DRAM technologies. **MDRAM (Multi-bank Dynamic RAM)** chips act like multiple independent memory chips with a 32-bit path. MDRAM refreshes the monitor more efficiently than VRAM or WRAM. The objective is to get the data in and out of the video card's memory chips as fast as possible for a reasonable cost. The adapter must handle a large amount of data due to the increasing number of pixels and colors displayed. Ample and fast memory on the video card allows higher resolutions and more colors to appear on the screen in a timely fashion without the screen appearing to flicker. Dual-ported memory allows for better data flow in and out of the memory chips, and advances in single-ported memory chips allow faster throughputs while keeping the cost low.

All parts of the video subsystem must work together to get a clear picture on the screen. A very expensive video adapter with 16 trillion megabytes of memory connected to a monitor with a poor dot pitch will display a distorted picture on the screen. An expensive monitor connected to an ISA video adapter with only 256KB of memory will not provide the faster refresh rates. The monitor appears to flicker as a result. The video adapter needs to match the monitor's capabilities and be an architecture such as VL-bus or PCI bus. Furthermore, the adapter needs to contain enough memory to sustain the number of colors at the specific resolution the user must work. A technician cannot perform magic on poorly matched video components. The only solution is to upgrade the weak link.

Memory on the video card stores screen information as a snapshot of what appears on the screen. Common memory chip capacities include 256KB, 512KB, 1MB, 2MB, 4MB, and 8MB. The amount of memory on a video adapter is determined by the manufacturer. Some manufacturers make video adapters that are not upgradable. Check the adapter's documentation before making a purchase or recommendation. Video card memory upgradability is important to computer users.

The amount of video adapter memory will determine the number of colors available at a specific resolution.

To determine the amount of video memory an adapter needs, multiply the total number of pixels (the resolution) by the number of bits needed to produce a specific number of colors. Different combinations of 16 1s and 0s create 65,536 (64K) possible combinations as 2^{16}=65,536. For example, take a system that needs 65,536 colors at the resolution of 1024x768. To determine the minimum video memory necessary, multiply 16 (number of bits needed for 64K of colors) times 1024 times 768 (the resolution). The 12,582,912 result is the number of bits needed to handle the combination of 65K colors at 1024x768. Divide the bits by eight for the number of *bytes* needed. This is the minimum amount of memory needed on the video card: 12,582,912 divided by 8 = 1,572,864 or 1.5MB. The user needs more video memory if more colors, a higher resolution, or video motion is desired.

What if a user wanted 256K colors at a 800x600 resolution? What is the minimum amount of video memory needed for the system? Different combinations of 18 1s and 0s produce 256K colors (2^{18}=262,144). 18 times 800 times 600 equals 8,640,000 bits. 8,640,000 divided by 8 equals 1,080,000 bytes. The user would need at least 1MB of video RAM.

Video Table #2 lists the number of bits required for different color options.

VIDEO - TABLE # 2	Bits Required for Colors	
	Number of Bits	**Number of Colors**
	4	16
	8	256
	15	32,768 (32K)
	16	65,536 (64K)
	18	262,144 (256K)
	20	1,048,576 (1M)
	24	16,777,216 (16M)

If determining the amount of video memory seems confusing, an exercise is at the end of the chapter to help you practice configuring different scenarios.

A video adapter usually has a set of **drivers** or software to enable the adapter to work to its full potential. Any adapter that connects to a SVGA or higher monitor usually needs a driver for optimum performance. Because there are no real video standards after VGA, individual software drivers from the manufacturer provide system compatibility and performance boosts. The Internet provides a wonderful way for technicians to obtain current video drivers from adapter manufacturers. Today's adapters normally have a video driver for the Windows 3.x environment, Windows 95, and Windows NT. Be sure to use the proper video driver for the operating system.

TROUBLESHOOTING VIDEO

When troubleshooting a video problem, check the simple solutions first. Verify the monitor's power light is on. If not, check the power cable connectors and the wall outlet. Verify that no one changed the brightness and contrast settings. Do not assume anything! Double check the monitor cable connected to the video port. Ask the user if any new software or hardware has been recently installed or upgraded.

In the video subsystem, if a piece of hardware is defective, then it is either the monitor, adapter, or cable. If replacement is necessary, always do the easiest solution first. Swap the monitor with a working one. If monitor replacement is not practical, check for a conflict with non-energy efficient monitors. Disconnect the monitor from the adapter then power on the monitor and turn the brightness control to its highest position. Is there a raster? A **raster** is the monitor's brightness pattern — a bright white screen. If the raster appears, the problem is likely the video adapter. When disconnecting energy efficient monitors from the video adapter, the monitors go into their low power mode. This check does not work on monitors in the low power mode.

Most video problems are *not* hardware-related; most are software-related. There are many symptoms of a software driver problem. Anything wrong on the display can be a result of a bad driver, an incompatible driver, or an incorrect driver. The best way to be sure is to download the exact driver for the monitor or the display adapter from the Internet or obtain it from the manufacturer and load it. Some troubleshooting tips relating to video are listed below. Remember, these are only suggestions. Contact the monitor manufacturer or the video adapter manufacturer for specific instructions on troubleshooting their equipment.

1. If the monitor screen is completely black, check the monitor power light. If it is off, check the power connection at the monitor and the wall outlet. Verify that the wall outlet has power. If the monitor power light is on, check the brightness and contrast settings. Try disconnecting the monitor from the adapter to determine if there is a raster.

2. Carefully examine the monitor's cable ends. The pins can easily bend and not fit properly into the connector, yet the cable appears to plug correctly into the connector. If you find one or more bent pins, carefully use needlenose pliers to gently straighten the pins.

3. If the computer is running in the DOS or Windows 3.x environment, press the F5 key to bypass the AUTOEXEC.BAT and CONFIG.SYS files to see if there is a driver or memory conflict. See the Memory chapter for troubleshooting memory conflicts.

4. If the CRT goes bad, it is probably more cost effective to replace the entire monitor. Most monitors cost more to repair than to replace. One monitor component that frequently goes bad is the **flyback transformer** that boosts the voltage to the high levels the CRT requires. The cost of flyback transformers varies from model to model. Get a price quote before replacing.

5. If you suspect a video driver problem, change the video driver to a standard (generic) driver to see if the problem goes away and to prove that it is a software driver problem.

6. If the screen appears distorted around the edges of the monitor or the color appears distorted, check for any other equipment such as other monitors, speakers, magnets, and fluorescent lighting that might cause interference with the monitor. Move the monitor from its current location to see if the situation improves or move the computer to another location to see if the problem goes away.

7.   Another possible problem with color distortion is CRT magnetization from an outside source. Degaussing circuits neutralize a magnetic field. Some monitors have degaussing controls built into them, so try letting the monitor's internal degaussing circuits fix the problem. Turn the monitor and computer on for one minute. Then, turn off the monitor. Leave the monitor off for 30 minutes. Then, turn the monitor on again for one minute followed by turning it off and leaving it off for 30 minutes. Continue to do this for several cycles. If this does not solve the problem, try manually degaussing the CRT. A **degausser** or degaussing coil is available from electronic stores and can be used to remove the CRT magnetization. Also, a local television repair shop might perform this procedure inexpensively.

Before turning on the degausser, remove all magnetic media such as floppy disks, from the immediate area. Remove your wrist watch. Do not turn on the degausser near the rear of the monitor. Power on the monitor. This procedure sometimes causes anxiety as the colors on the screen go through all sorts of geometric distortions. Do not panic! This is only temporary. Turn on the degausser and bring the coil within a couple of inches to the center of the screen. Take the coil VERY slowly toward the monitor's top corner edge. VERY slowly, trace around the outside edges of the monitor screen, returning to the original starting position in the center of the screen. Hold the degausser pointed toward the center of the screen and back SLOWLY away from the monitor. Turn the degausser off when you are approximately four or five feet away from the monitor.

8.   If the screen has intermittent problems, check the video adapter's documentation to see how to lower the refresh rate. The monitor and the adapter's refresh rates must match. Check the monitor's documentation for its refresh settings.

9.   If a cursor appears momentarily before the computer boots, then nothing displays or a distorted display appears, check for a video driver problem.

10. A color monitor displaying in monochrome (black and white) most likely has a video driver, a memory conflict, or a software utility problem.

11. Over time, a monitor may need a focus or brightness adjustment. Even though some monitors have external adjustments for this, some monitors place the adjustments inside the monitor case. Even monitors with external adjustment knobs can be adjusted further by adjustments located inside the monitor case. When performing the internal adjustments, follow all previously-mentioned safety procedures when working inside the monitor.

 ## WINDOWS 3.X VIDEO PROBLEMS

Windows 3.x often has problems due to video drivers. Windows 3.x requires a video driver change for each resolution setting which means Windows 3.x must restart for each video driver change to take effect. The exercise at the end of the chapter describes the procedure for changing the video driver, the resolution, and the number of colors with the Windows 3.x SETUP program. If Windows is operational, access the video driver through the SETUP program through the MAIN group. If Windows is not operational, access Windows' SETUP program by typing **SETUP** from the Windows directory. SYSTEM.INI's [boot] section contains the chosen Windows video driver.

1.   If Windows 3.x boots improperly, a common problem is the video driver causing a memory conflict. To determine if the video driver is a problem, start Windows 3.x with the *WIN /D:X* switch. If Windows boots properly, there is a memory conflict. Refer to the Memory chapter for more discussion on resolving memory conflicts.

2.   If the icons in Windows 3.x are black or missing, switch to a lower resolution or a lower number of colors, or both. The Program Manager or a group window has a limitation of 64KB of memory for icons, working directory paths, executable commands, etc. Each icon requires more memory at the higher resolutions (more pixels for each icon) and fills the memory space very quickly when using a large number of icons.

3.   Set passwords in Windows 3.x by using a Windows screen saver. Once a screen saver activates, configure the password using the following procedure:
     From Program Manager, open the **Control Panel** window. Double-click on the **Desktop** icon. From the Screen Saver section, click on the **Setup** button. Click once in the **Password Protected** checkbox within the Password Options section. Click on the **Set Password** button within the Password Options section. Type in a password in the **New Password** field. Press the **TAB** key on the keyboard. Type in the same password in the **Retype New Password** field. Press **ENTER** on the keyboard or click **OK**. Click on the **OK** button in the Screen Saver Setup window. Click on the **OK** button in the Desktop window.

4.   To erase a forgotten screen saver password, edit the CONTROL.INI file. Windows System Editor utility does not open the CONTROL.INI, so use a text editor such as Notepad, or MS-DOS' EDIT. Find the [ScreenSaver] section of CONTROL.INI file. Look for a password= statement within the [ScreenSaver] section. Delete the encoded (unusual-looking) characters after the password= statement. Save the changes and restart the Windows program for the changes to take effect.

5.   During the initial load, if the Windows 3.x logo appears followed by a blank screen, check the adapter documentation. Determine how to turn off the NMI (Non-Maskable Interrupt) on the adapter.

6.   If the Windows 3.x SETUP program selects the wrong video driver, start SETUP from the Windows directory. If Windows is being installed for the first time, type SETUP /I to ignore automatic hardware detection.

 ## WINDOWS 95 VIDEO PROBLEMS

Windows 95 requires a VGA or higher monitor. Windows 95 automatically detects the monitor type during the initial installation. If an exact monitor type is not available, Windows 95 configures the setting for a generic type.

To change the monitor type, use the **System** control panel **Settings** tab. Then, click on the **Change** button from the **Change Display Type** window. Pick a particular model from the list of manufacturers and models that appears or click on the **Have Disk** option to use the disk provided by a monitor manufacturer.

If Windows 95 detects a monitor that adheres to VESA's **DDC (Display Data Channel)** specification, Windows detects such things as the monitor's maximum resolution. Selecting a specific monitor type or adapter in Windows 95 does not change the adapter's refresh rate. For adapters that allow refresh rate changes, use the software provided by the adapter manufacturer.

On initial SETUP, Windows 95 configures the video adapter based on the type of adapter detected. Windows 95 includes driver support for the major graphics accelerator chips such as those by ATI Technologies, Inc., Cirrus Logic, Matrox MGA, Tseng Labs, Western Digital, and Chips & Technologies. If Windows 95 cannot detect the type of video adapter, it uses a generic video driver (Standard Display Adapter (VGA)) which does not use all the capabilities of the installed video adapter. However, the video driver can be changed later after SETUP finishes.

Before changing the video driver, check the adapter's documentation to see what accelerator chip is used. To see if the accelerator chip Windows 95 picked is the correct one, *right-click* anywhere on a blank Desktop space. Click once on the **Properties** option. Click on the **Settings** tab. Click on the **Change Display Type** button. The video adapter type lists in the top text box. To change the adapter, click on the **Change** button. The adapter can also be changed through the **System** control panel by clicking on the **Display Adapter's plus symbol** on the **Device Manager** tab. Click on the **Properties** button followed by clicking on the **Driver** tab. Select the appropriate video driver. Click once on the **Change Driver** button. To see all the Windows 95 standard drivers, click on the **Show all devices** radio button. If the video adapter manufacturer provides a driver disk, click on the **Have Disk** button.

To determine if Windows 95 uses an old Windows 3.x video driver, use a text editor to view the SYSTEM.INI file's [boot] section. If any line other than DISPLAY.DRV=PNPDRVR.DRV appears, the driver is a Windows 3.x driver. If the driver is the PNPDRVR.DRV, then Windows 95 looks to the registry for the real video driver.

Windows 95 is not supposed to hang during boot up due to video driver incompatibility, but will load a default video driver so Windows 95 can boot. If video is a problem while working in Windows 95 and using a Windows 3.x driver, obtain an updated Windows 95 driver from the video adapter manufacturer if possible. Otherwise, try using a Windows 95 generic video driver.

If a Windows 95 driver is causing problems, go to the **System** control panel **Performance** tab and use the **Advanced Graphics Settings**. The **Hardware Acceleration** slide bar allows four settings that help in troubleshooting video problems: Full, Most, Basic, and None. The *Full* setting is the default and is for full hardware acceleration; nothing is disabled. The *Most* setting is the second setting from the right which disables the video driver's handling of cursor support. Use the Most setting if the mouse pointer's appearance on the screen is a problem.

The *Basic* setting is the third setting from the right, next to the None setting. It disables memory-mapped Input/Output for S3 and S3-compatible video drivers. Windows 95 has a universal display driver that supports and controls certain screen functions and directly controls graphical screen output. If the adapter or monitor warrants it, a 32-bit mini-driver controls hardware specific instructions. The Basic setting disables some of the 32-bit mini-driver acceleration functions except for the very basic ones. Use the Basic setting if the system locks up or the screen appears irregular and the system is using an adapter with an S3 or S3-compatible video driver.

The *None* setting disables all the video card acceleration functions by disabling the 32-bit mini-driver. Use this setting if the system is randomly hanging up and is using an S3 or S3-compatible video driver. Use the None setting if the Basic setting cannot solve the video problem.

The following are more tips for troubleshooting Windows 95 video problems. Again, the best source of information is the video adapter or monitor's manufacturer. Most problems do involve the video driver similar to Windows 3.x's video problems (just not as drastic).

1. Always check the monitor settings to verify the Windows 95 monitor detection is accurate. Use the **Display** control panel's **Settings** tab. To change the display type listed, click once on the **Change Display Type** button. If the monitor manufacturer does not appear in the manufacturer's box list, click on the **Standard Monitor Types** option. In the **Models** box, click on the appropriate monitor type that matches the type of monitor connected to the computer.

2. Check to be certain the video adapter does not cause a memory conflict with another adapter. To check for an upper memory area conflict, start Windows 95 from the command prompt by typing **WIN /D:X**. This startup option tells Windows 95 to *not* use the Upper Memory Blocks for any of its programs. If Windows 95 boots properly after using the switch, a memory conflict exists.

3. To check for resource conflicts, use the Device Manager's **Display Adapter** option (**Resources** tab). Look for any detected conflicts in the Conflicting Device List.

4. If video performance appears to be slow, adjust the monitor to a lower resolution or a lower number of colors (or both). See the exercise at the end of the chapter for step-by-step instructions. Check the video adapter driver to determine if it matches the installed adapter or if it is generic. Obtain the specific adapter's latest driver from the Internet.

5. If Windows 95 has a video problem and does not default to a generic video driver, press **F8** when the message "Starting Windows 95" displays and select the **Safe mode**. Once the machine boots properly, open the **Display** control panel. Click on the **Settings** tab. Set the resolution to a 640x480 setting and the least number of colors possible. Restart Windows 95 through the Start menu.

6. If Windows 95 continues to show general protection (GP) faults in various applications, check if the video driver is a Windows 3.x driver. If so, get an updated driver from the manufacturer or use a standard Windows 95 driver.

IEEE 1394 (FIREWIRE)

The IEEE 1394 standard known as FireWire is a serial bus that supports speeds higher than traditional serial buses. The big excitement over the standard stems from its ability to handle digital audio and video devices such as VCRs, camcorders, televisions, etc. Audio and video equipment have traditionally been proprietary devices and connecting them to computers was nearly impossible. The existing computer buses could not withstand the throughput necessary for quality audio and video transfer. A 30 frames per second high quality video at a 640x480 resolution using 16.7 million colors transfers at 221Mbps, too fast for the standard computer serial bus. FireWire has the potential to dramatically affect video for microcomputers. More information is available in the Serial Devices chapter.

UNIVERSAL SERIAL BUS

The USB (Universal Serial Bus) allows the connection of numerous devices including monitors. The Universal Serial Bus has two speeds, 1.5Mbps and 12Mbps, and is much slower than the IEEE 1394 bus. Many compare the two buses or place them in competition with one another; but in the computer world, there is room and applications for both. The USB will be great for devices such as monitors, keyboards and mice. Some monitors have the ability to act as USB hubs. The speed is fast enough to handle devices without the conflict problems common with traditional serial ports and devices. The FireWire standard has much greater throughput for applications such as video conferencing. Computers now ship with the USB connections on the motherboards and the monitors that can serve as USB hubs are on the market. Computer industry standardization helps with the new emerging buses, that have one standard connector on the device. Many people say that the new technology does it all for us and makes it easier. Others believe technology is becoming more and more involved requiring more and more technical abilities to integrate it all. Whatever the case, the support staff will not be out of jobs in the near future. The new buses are a welcome relief to the speed bottleneck and the configuration problems related to outdated buses and methods. See the Serial Devices chapter for more information on USB.

INTEL'S MMX TECHNOLOGY

Intel's latest microprocessors have a new feature known as **MMX** technology with 57 more instructions for the microprocessor written specifically for multimedia operations such as video graphics and sound. Any instructions included in a microprocessor will speed up software, though existing software will not benefit much from MMX technology. Software written to take advantage of the new MMX technology can run up to 60 percent faster. The software written for MMX technology runs fine on computers that do not have MMX, but the software does not run as fast.

MMX technology allows multiple pieces of data to be compacted together (up to 64 bits) and processed by one instruction using a technology known as SIMD or Single Instruction Multiple Data. Pentium microprocessors can process two MMX instructions at a time. Pentium II microprocessors can process three MMX instructions at a time.

INTEL'S ACCELERATED GRAPHICS PORT (AGP)

Another new technology for video is Intel's **AGP (Accelerated Graphics Port)** which is an extension of the PCI bus that speeds up 3-D graphics in software applications. 3-D stands for 3-dimensional meaning the graphical objects have height, width, and depth. Microsoft provides support in Windows 95 and Windows NT that will initialize the devices plugged into the AGP slot. Both operating systems have the DirectDraw API. The video adapter driver informs the DirectDraw API that the video adapter supports the AGP standard.

The AGP is a different motherboard connector than the PCI adapter. Look at Video Figure #5 for an illustration of an AGP connector on a motherboard.

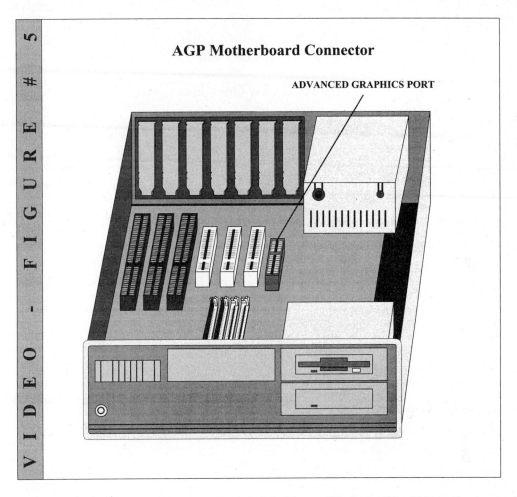

AGP Motherboard Connector

ADVANCED GRAPHICS PORT

VIDEO - FIGURE # 5

As seen in Video Figure #5, a PCI adapter does not fit in an AGP slot and an adapter that meets AGP specifications will not fit in a PCI slot.

Using AGP, the video adapter's processor directly accesses RAM without going through a bus as PCI does. Access occurs at bus speed (66MHz, 133MHz, or 266MHz depending on the motherboard and microprocessor used). 3-D graphics are resource-intensive and occupy a lot of memory. Software developers can develop better and faster 3-D graphics using AGP technology and achieve the best video performance by using the memory on the video adapter and by-passing the motherboard. However, because large amounts of memory are needed for 3-D graphics, the motherboard memory, which is larger than the amount on the video adapter, is the next best place to go. The bottleneck has always been the adapter. AGP reduces that bottleneck and allows faster throughput to the video adapter.

Exercises at the end of the chapter step through changing a monitor's resolution and the number of colors using Windows 3.x and Windows 95.

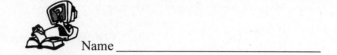

Name _____

Video Review Questions

1.   What parts make up a computer's video subsystem?

2.   What is the difference between a grayscale monitor and a monochrome monitor?

3.   What is the difference between an analog and a digital monitor?

4.   T/F   EGA monitors are the most popular monitor type for computers today.

5.   How can you tell by looking at a video adapter's port if it accepts an analog or digital monitor?

6.   T/F   The monitor type must match the video adapter.

7.   Why is a monitor's size an issue?

8.   What is the purpose of a monitor's electron gun?

9.   What component directs the electron beam to the proper location on the front of the monitor screen?

10. What is the difference between a shadow mask and an aperture grille?

11. What is dot pitch and how does it relate to resolution?

12. T/F   For monitors using an aperture grille, dot pitch is only relevant in a horizontal direction.

13. What resolution is good for a 17" monitor?

14. What determines the monitor's refresh rate?
     A.   The monitor specifications
     B.   The video adapter specifications
     C.   The video adapter and the monitor specifications
     D.   The motherboard
     E.   The ROM BIOS
     F.   The microprocessor

15. List an appropriate horizontal scanning frequency for a SVGA monitor.

16. Why is the vertical scan rate important?

17. What is a good refresh rate for a 15" monitor?

18. What term best describes when a monitor's electron beam scans the odd pixel rows and then scans the even pixel rows?
     A.   Refreshing
     B.   Interlacing
     C.   Beaming
     D.   Video Skipping

19. How do you keep a monitor static-free?

20. T/F Monitors are frequently disassembled by technicians because the parts are so inexpensive.

21. Should a monitor be left on 24 hours a day? Explain your answer.

22. What is a green monitor?

23. T/F Windows 95 supports DPMS.

24. T/F A non-green monitor can be damaged if energy efficiency software is enabled.

25. What adapter interface would you recommend for video? [ISA, EISA, MCA, VL-bus, or PCI] Explain your answer.

26. What is a video accelerator?

27. T/F Shadowing the video ROM chip provides faster video performance.

28. List three ways to increase video performance on a computer.

29. Which type of video memory chips are single-ported?

30. Why is having memory on the video adapter so important?

31. How much video memory is needed for 32K of colors at 1024x768?
    A. 1MB
    B. 2MB
    C. 4MB
    D. 512KB

32. How many colors can a 24-bit video adapter display? [16, 256, 64K, 256K, 1M, or 16M]

33. When troubleshooting a non-green monitor, you disconnect the monitor cable and the monitor has a raster. Is the problem most likely in the monitor or video adapter?

34. Why are software problems more prevalent than hardware problems in the video subsystem?

35. How do you prove the video driver is causing the problem?

36. How do you remove a screen saver password when using Windows 3.x?

37. What Windows 95 hardware acceleration setting is used if the system that uses a S3 video driver randomly hangs?

38. T/F A 16-bit video driver can cause general protection faults in any Windows 95 application.

39. Describe how the IEEE 1394 standard helps with video performance.

40. How do MMX microprocessors affect video performance?

Name _____

Video Fill-in-the-Blank

1.   _____ monitors display only one color.

2.   The two types of monitors most common today are _____ and _____.

3.   The main part of the monitor is the _____.

4.   The combination of a red dot, green dot, and blue dot is a _____.

5.   The smallest unit visible on a monitor is a _____.

6.   The distance between two dots is a monitor's _____.

7.   The total number of pixels on a monitor is the monitor's _____.

8.   The speed the horizontal beam crosses the monitor is the _____.

9.   The vertical scan rate is more commonly called a monitor's _____.

10.   A monitor that has the ability use various vertical and horizontal scan rates is a _____.

11.   _____ is the standard produced by VESA used for power saving monitors.

12.   A _____ offers password protection and entertainment for today's computer users, but on an older computer, it is used to prevent an image from burning into the screen.

13.   The _____ does processing on the video adapter normally performed by the microprocessor on the motherboard.

14.   Memory chips with separate read and write data paths are said to be _____.

15.   _____ video memory helps with the efficiency of refreshing the screen.

16.   The monitor's brightness pattern is it's _____.

17.   A _____ is used to neutralize a magnetic field around the CRT that causes color distortions.

18.   Windows 95's _____ control panel is used to change the type of monitor.

19.   The _____ Windows 95 video driver listed in the SYSTEM.INI file indicates that Windows 95 is using a 32-bit video driver.

20.   Intel's _____ port speeds up 3-D graphics.

Name _____

CHANGING THE RESOLUTION AND NUMBER OF COLORS USING WINDOWS 3.X EXERCISE

Objective: Change the video resolution and number of colors using Windows 3.x

Parts: A computer with Windows 3.x loaded

Step 1:   Power on the computer and start Windows 3.x. Verify that Windows 3.x loads.
Step 2:   From Program Manager, double-click on the **Main** group icon.
Step 3:   Double-click on the **Windows Setup** icon.

Question 1:   What video driver does the display use?

Step 4:   Click on the **Options** menu bar option.
Step 5:   Click on the **Change System Settings** option.
Step 6:   Click on the **Display** option's **down arrow**.
Step 7:   From the displayed list, locate a driver that supports the monitor, resolution, and number of colors desired. If the specific driver does not appear and you have a disk containing the video driver, select from the list the **Other display (Requires disk from OEM)** option. Follow the directions that appear on the screen.
Step 8:   Click once on the desired driver.
Step 9:   Click the **OK** button. A message appears either prompting for a driver disk or asking if Windows is to use the existing driver or replace it. If a disk is available, follow the directions that appear on the screen. Otherwise, click on the **Current** button.
Step 10:   Windows then prompts to restart for the new video driver to take effect. Click on the **Restart Windows** button.

Question 2:   Does Windows boot properly? If not, refer back to the chapter's sections on troubleshooting and fix the problem.

_____ Instructor's Initials

ON YOUR OWN:

Set the video driver back to its original configuration. Refer to Question 1's answer for the original video driver. Be sure the computer works properly after the original video driver is selected and loaded. Have a classmate verify the video driver works properly when you finish.

Classmate's printed name: _____

Classmate's initials: _____

Name _____

CHANGING THE RESOLUTION AND NUMBER OF COLORS USING WINDOWS 95 EXERCISE

Objective: Change the video resolution and number of colors using Windows 95

Parts: A computer with a color monitor and Windows 95 loaded

Step 1:   Power on the computer and verify that Windows 95 loads. Refer to Appendix B for Windows 95 skills.
Step 2:   Click on the **Start** button.
Step 3:   Select **Settings** from the Start menu.
Step 4:   Click on the **Control Panel** option.
Step 5:   Double-click the **Display** control panel.
Step 6:   Click once on the **Settings** tab.
Step 7:   Notice how the Color palette's down arrow sets the number of possible colors.

Question 1:   What part or component determines the number of Color palette settings available?

Question 2:   What is the Color palette's setting set to now?

Step 8:   Click once on the Color palette's **down arrow**.

Question 3:   How many different color choices are available?

Question 4:   What is the difference between a 16-bit and a 24-bit color palette?

Step 9:   Use the Color Palette's **down arrow** to select the *lowest* color setting (usually 16 color).
Step 10:   Locate, but do *not* change, the Desktop area's slidebar that controls the monitor resolution.

Question 5:   Looking at the Desktop area's slidebar, what is the current resolution setting?

Step 11:   While *holding* the mouse button down, move the Desktop area's slidebar back and forth to determine the different number of resolutions possible.

Question 6:   How many different resolutions are available?

Question 7:   What determines the number of resolutions possible?

Step 12:   While *holding* the mouse button down, move the Desktop area's slidebar to the left to the *lowest* resolution setting. Notice in the open window, the size of the icons showing on the monitor.

Step 13:   While *holding* the mouse button down, move the Desktop area's slidebar to the right to the *highest* resolution setting. Notice how the icons on the monitor screen get smaller in the open window.

Windows 95 does not require restarting the computer every time you choose a different resolution!

Question 8:   Why do icons get smaller at a higher resolution?

Step 14:   Using the Color Palette's down arrow select the *highest* color setting.

Step 15:   While *holding* the mouse button down, move the Desktop area's slidebar back and forth to determine the different number of resolutions possible.

Question 9:   How many different resolutions are available?

Question 10:   What is the relationship (if any) between the number of colors and the possible resolution settings?

Step 16:   Set the Color palette back to the original setting. Refer back to Question 2's answer.

Step 17:   Set the Desktop area slidebar back to the original setting. Refer back to Question 5's answer.

Step 18:   Have a classmate verify that the settings are in their original state.

Classmate's printed name: _____

Classmate's initials: _____

Step 19:   Click on the **Change Display Type** button. The Change Display Type window is where the video adapter and the monitor type can be changed if necessary. On initial SETUP, Windows 95 configures the video adapter based on the type of controller on the adapter.

Question 11:   What adapter type shows in the Change Display Type window?

Question 12:   What monitor type shows in the Change Display Type window?

Step 20:   Click on the **Cancel** button.
Step 21:   In the Display Properties window, click on the **Cancel** button.
Step 22:   Close all windows on the desktop.

Name_____

DETERMINING THE AMOUNT OF VIDEO MEMORY EXERCISE

1.   What is the minimum memory (512KB, 1MB, 2MB, 4MB, or 8MB) a video adapter needs if a
      user wants a 1024x768 resolution with 16 million colors available?

2.   What is the minimum memory (512KB, 1MB, 2MB, 4MB, or 8MB) a video adapter needs if a
      user wants a 800x600 resolution with 65,536 colors available?

3.   A video card has 1MB of memory and is a 24-bit color adapter. The user wants to display 16
      million colors at a resolution of 800x600. Is the amount of installed memory on the video
      adapter adequate? Justify your answer.

4.   A video card has 4MB of memory. The user wants a resolution of 1024x768 and 16 million
      colors. Is the amount of installed memory on the video adapter adequate? Justify your answer.

5.   What is the minimum recommended memory for a video card purchased for a brand new
      system? Explain your answer.

Chapter 13: Printers

OBJECTIVES

After completing this chapter you will
1.   Understand basic printing concepts.
2.   Know how each type of printer operates.
3.   Understand how printers require software and use it.
4.   Perform preventive maintenance on printers.
5.   Perform a printer installation.
6.   Recognize printing problems in Windows 3.x and Windows 95.
7.   Know common printer problems and solutions.

KEY TERMS

bi-directional printing	HPPCL	printwire
conditioning roller	ink jet printer	raster font
CPI	internal font	ream
CPS	laser printer	RET
density control blade	marking subsystem	scaleable font
developing cylinder	outline font	soft fonts
dot matrix printer	ozone filter	SPP
DPI	paper transport	switch box
ECP	PDL	toner puddling
EPP	pin firing	transfer corona
erase lamp	PostScript	transfer roller
felt side	primary corona	TrueType font
font	print cartridge	vector font
font cartridge	print driver	wax side
font size	print engine	wire side printer
font style	print spooler	write-black laser
fuser cleaning pad	printer emulation	write-white laser printer
fusing roller	printhead	

PRINTERS OVERVIEW

Printers are a difficult subject to cover because so many different models exist. (Of course, that can be said about any peripheral.) But, the principles are the same for the different categories of printers. The best way to begin is to look at what printers have in common. All printers have three subsystems: (1) the paper transport subsystem, (2) the marking subsystem, and (3) the print engine subsystem.

The **paper transport** subsystem pulls, pushes, rolls, etc. the paper through the printer. Printers use various methods, such as belts, tractor feeds, and rollers, to pass the paper through the printer. The **marking subsystem** or marking engine is the part of the printer responsible for placing the image on the paper. This subsystem includes ribbons, ink cartridges, toner cartridges, any part to move each of these, and anything else necessary to print the image. The **print engine** is the brains of the operation. It accepts data and commands from the computer and translates the commands into motion. The print engine subsystem also redirects feedback to the computer when necessary. Keep the three printer subsystems in mind when setting up a printer and troubleshooting it. Knowing how a specific type of printer places an image on the paper also helps when troubleshooting the printer.

PARALLEL PORTS

Printers connect to either the parallel port (transmitting eight bits at a time) or the serial port (transmitting one bit at a time). Parallel transfer is much faster than serial, the parallel cable should be no longer than 15 feet, although 25 feet has worked. Look back to Serial Figure #1 for the transmission differences between serial and parallel ports. Most printers that attach to a PC connect to the parallel port on the computer which is a 25-pin female connector. It is built into the motherboard or integrated on an adapter (sometimes, with other ports as well). Look back to Introduction Figure #8 for a picture of a parallel port.

The operating system assigns names to the parallel ports. The motherboard ROM BIOS detects any parallel ports based on their I/O addresses just as with serial ports. The parallel port names are assigned in the I/O address order found. This is not as big a conflict as serial ports because computer users do not normally want to add as many printers as they do serial devices. The parallel port names assigned include LPT1:, LPT2:, and LPT3:. The assignment of port names uses the same concept as assigning COM port names. Just as with serial ports, the DEBUG command shows the parallel ports that the ROM BIOS chip detects. Also, the Microsoft Diagnostics utility can show the parallel ports' I/O addresses. Printer Table #1 lists the common port names, interrupts, and I/O addresses assigned to each parallel port.

<table>
<tr><th colspan="3">Common Printer Port System Resource Assignments</th></tr>
<tr><th>Parallel Port</th><th>IRQ</th><th>I/O Address</th></tr>
<tr><td>LPT1:</td><td>7</td><td>378-37F</td></tr>
<tr><td>LPT2:</td><td>5</td><td>278-27F</td></tr>
<tr><td>LPT3:</td><td>7 or 5</td><td>3BC-3BF</td></tr>
</table>

PRINTER - TABLE # 1

The printer does not need to use an interrupt if printing through DOS, Windows 3.x, or Windows 95. However, other devices that connect to the parallel port may require or work faster if using an interrupt. Some print spooler programs require the use of the interrupt. A print spooler is a software program that handles print jobs. Through the print spooler software, you can delay printing, reorder the print jobs, and cancel print jobs. Refer to the print spooler's documentation for the requirements.

PRINTER SWITCH BOXES

Instead of using two ports to connect two printers to the same computer, some people prefer a **switch box** that connects two printers to one computer or connects one printer to two computers. An inexpensive switch box allows sharing a resource such as a color laser printer. Switch boxes reduce the per computer cost when a resource is shared between multiple workstations.

An automatic switch box automatically detects which computer is sending the data to the printer. A manual switch box, sometimes called an A/B switch box, requires a person to pick which printer (if multiple printers connect to a computer) or which computer (if multiple computers connect to the same printer) by turning a dial. Printer Figure #1 shows a common automatic switch box configuration.

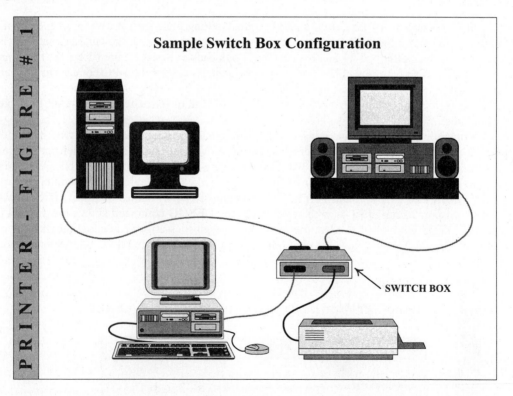

Sample Switch Box Configuration

SWITCH BOX

PRINTER - FIGURE # 1

Always use an automatic switch box if using a laser printer. A manual switch box causes problems because the voltage levels created when taking laser printers on or off line appear as noise spikes through the cables. The noise spikes or a bad switch connection can damage the parallel port or the laser printer.

CATEGORIES OF PRINTERS

Printers can be categorized according to how they put the image on the paper. The printer categories are dot matrix, ink jet, and laser. There are more, but these make up the majority of printers used in the workplace and the home. Computer users normally choose a printer based on the type of printing done. **Dot matrix printers** are good for text printing, although they can produce limited graphics. They use ribbons which keep the overall printing costs down. The cost per page for a dot matrix printer is usually less than a penny. A dot matrix printer is the only printer of the three categories that prints multi-part forms and the 132 column wide paper needed by some industries. If not for these two features, dot matrix printers would be extinct.

Most home computer users opt for **ink jet printers**. They are much quieter, weigh less, and produce higher quality graphics than dot matrix printers. The ink jet printer uses a **print cartridge** that holds the ink instead of a ribbon. A slight disadvantage to an ink jet printer is the ink is not completely waterproof like the laser printer output. Ink jet cartridges are usually $25 to $35 apiece for black ink and more for the color cartridges. The cost of the ink cartridges plus paper, makes the cost of an ink jet printer as high as 12 cents per page. Color ribbons are available for dot matrix printers, but ink jet printers are the masters of color printing. For most computer users, color output is affordable now only through ink jet technology.

Laser printers, however, produce the highest quality output at the fastest rate. With such a claim, the cost of the technology rises. Laser printers are common in the corporate network environment where users share peripherals and are used for graphical design and computer-generated art where high quality printing is a necessity. Some laser printers can produce color output like ink jet printers, but at a much higher cost. The cost for a color laser printer is prohibitive for most home computer users.

Each of the three basic printer types are discussed in greater detail in the next sections. The theory of operation for each printer type mainly concerns the marking subsystem.

DOT MATRIX PRINTERS

Dot matrix printers are called impact printers because of the way they create an image on the paper. They have a **printhead** that holds tiny wires called **printwires**. The wires individually strike a ribbon hard enough to create a dot on the paper. The dots collectively form letters or images. The speed that the printhead can place characters on the page is its **characters per second** (**cps**) specification rating. The number of printwires in the printhead determines the quality of print. The more print wires, the better the print quality. The most common print wires are 9, 18, and 24. The 24-pin printers can print Near Letter Quality (NLQ) output.

Each printwire connects to a solenoid coil. When current flows to the printwire, a magnetic field causes the wire to move away from the printhead and out a tiny hole. The print wire impacts a ribbon to create a dot on the paper. Printer Figure #2 shows a dot matrix printhead. To show the individual printwires, the casing that covers the printwires has been removed from the illustration.

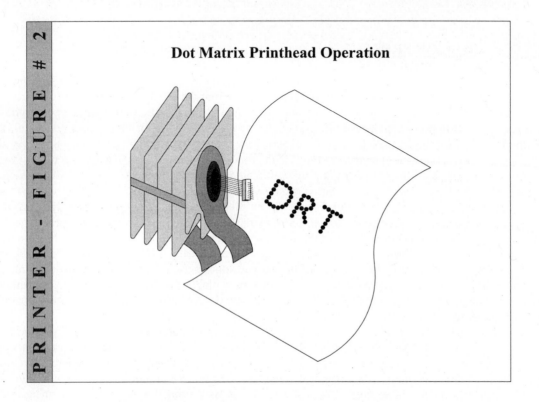

Dot Matrix Printhead Operation

PRINTER - FIGURE # 2

Each wire connects to a spring that pulls the printwire back inside the printhead. The images created are nothing more than a series of dots on the page. Dot matrix printers are impact printers because the printwire springs out of the printhead. The act of the printwire coming out of the printhead is called **pin firing**. The impact of the printer physically striking the ribbon which in turn, touches the paper causes dot matrix printers to be noisy.

Because the printwire impacts the ribbon, one of the most common point of failures with dot matrix printers is the printhead that can be expensive to frequently replace in a high-usage situation. However, refurbished printheads are available at a reduced priced, and work fine. The companies who refurbish them usually replace the wires that are not working properly and test the printhead thoroughly.

Dot matrix printers are the work horses of printers. One advantage to a dot matrix printer is it will print multiple part forms such as invoices, purchase orders, shipping documents, or wide forms. Laser and ink jet printers cannot produce multiple part forms, they can only make multiple copies of the same document. Multiple part forms print easily on dot matrix because the printer impacts the paper so hard. The maximum number of multiple copies each dot matrix printer handles depends on the printer model.

Do not stack things on top of any printer, especially a dot matrix printer. The printhead gets hot and you should not add to the heat by stacking things on top of the printer. Keep the printer in a cool environment to avoid overheating. Most dot matrix printers print bi-directionally. When the printhead gets too hot, the printer stops printing bi-directionally and prints only in the left-to-right direction. This is a normal condition and not a problem situation as some users might think. If the printer is used continuously keeping the printhead hot, consider purchasing a second printer to handle the work load.

INK JET PRINTERS

Ink jet printers are much quieter than dot matrix printers. They also have a printhead, but the ink jet's printhead does not have metal pins that fire out from the printhead. Instead, the ink jet's printhead has many tiny nozzles that squirt ink onto the paper. Each nozzle is smaller than a human hair strand.

One great thing about ink jet printers is that the printhead includes the nozzles *and* the reservoir for ink. When the ink runs out, replace the entire printhead. The ink jet printer's printhead is known as the print cartridge. Printer Figure #3 shows an ink jet printer cartridge.

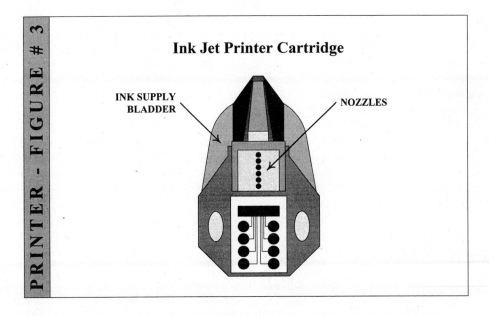

An ink jet cartridge has 50 or more nozzles instead of the 9, 18, or 24 metal pin configuration the dot matrix has. That is one reason why the ink jet quality is so much better than a dot matrix. Furthermore, every time the print cartridge is replaced, the printer gets a new printhead. Replacing the printhead, one of the most frequently used parts, keeps repair costs low.

Ink jet printers, also called bubble jet printers, use thermal (heat) technology to place the ink onto the paper. Each print nozzle attaches to a small ink chamber that attaches to a larger ink reservoir. A small amount of ink inside the chamber heats to boiling temperatures. Once the ink boils, a vapor bubble forms. As the bubble gets hotter, it expands and goes out through the print cartridge's nozzle onto the paper. The size of the ink droplet is approximately two ten-thousandths (.0002) of an inch, smaller than a human hair. As the small ink chamber cools down, suction occurs. The suction pulls more ink into the ink chamber for the production of the next ink droplet.

An alternative for producing the ink dots is to use piezo-electric technology which uses pressure, not heat, to eject the ink onto the paper. The Seiko Epson Corporation uses this technology to obtain 1440x720 dpi and higher resolutions. **DPI** is the number of **dots per inch** a printer outputs. The higher the DPI, the better the quality of ink jet or laser printer output.

Most ink jet printers have different modes of printing. The draft mode uses the least amount of ink and the near letter quality (NLQ) mode uses the most ink. The quality produced by the ink jet printer is close to a laser printer, but in most high end ink jet printers, the output is actually a higher dots per inch (DPI).

Some ink jet printers can produce color output. The color produced by an ink jet printer does not last as long as photographs. Color ink jet printers usually have a black cartridge for normal printing and a separate color cartridge for the colored ink or even separate cartridges for each color. Buying an ink jet printer that uses a single cartridge for colors is cheaper on the initial printer purchase, but more expensive in the long run. The black ink usually runs out much quicker than the colored ink. Users should buy an ink jet model with separate cartridges for black ink and colored ink.

New ink technologies enable ink jet printers to produce more vibrant colors. Epson has a new Neon ink cartridge that allows non-traditional (bright neon) color printing. There are ink jet printers that have photo-quality printing that can reproduce photographs using a special photo cartridge. Most major ink jet printer manufacturers now offer this feature. The results produce photographs with a quality near that of a photo finisher. Ink jet printers are perfect for small businesses, home computer users, and individual computer office work. They can print up to 1,000 pages per month. For higher output, the laser printer is more appropriate.

One drawback to the use of ink as a print medium is the ink sometimes smears. Different ink manufacturers vary greatly in how they respond to this problem. If the paper gets wet, some ink jet output becomes a mess. The ink also smears when touching the printed page before the ink dries. The ink can also soak into the paper and bleed down the paper. Using good quality paper helps with this particular problem. See the chapter's section or printer supplies for more information on choosing the correct paper for the different printers.

LASER PRINTERS

The term laser stands for light amplification by stimulated emission of radiation. A laser printer operates similar to a copy machine's electro-photographic process. Before describing how a laser printer works, identifying the major parts inside the laser helps understand how it works. Printer Figure #4 shows a side view of a laser printer with a toner cartridge installed.

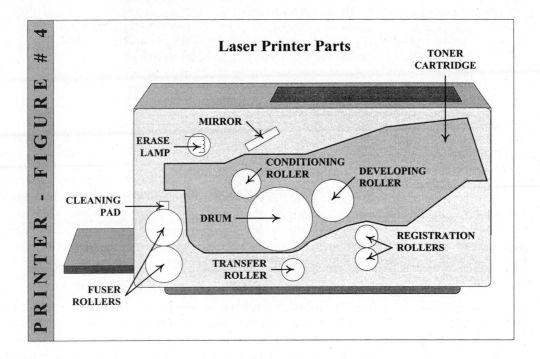

Laser Printer Parts

PRINTER - FIGURE # 4

TONER CARTRIDGE

MIRROR

ERASE LAMP

CONDITIONING ROLLER

DEVELOPING ROLLER

CLEANING PAD

DRUM

REGISTRATION ROLLERS

TRANSFER ROLLER

FUSER ROLLERS

As an overview, the computer sends 1s and 0s out the parallel port and down the parallel cable to the printer. The data transmits either through an array of LEDs or through a laser beam. The light beam strikes the photosensitive drum located inside the toner cartridge. Laser toner particles are attracted to the drum. The paper feeds through and the toner transfers to the paper. The toner is then fused or melted into the paper.

Hewlett-Packard developed steps for the laser printing process. The six steps outlined below describe what happens when a laser printer prints a page. A computer technician must be very familiar with the laser printing process for certification and for troubleshooting laser printers.

1.   **Conditioning**: Get the drum ready for use.
       Before any information goes onto the drum, the entire drum must have the same voltage level. The **primary corona**, also known as the main corona, is a thin wire located inside the toner cartridge. When the primary corona gets -600vdc applied to it, the static voltage subsequently created reaches up to -6,000 volts. The corona must generate the large amount of negative voltage to apply -600 to -1000 volts to the printer's drum surface. Some printer manufacturers use a **conditioning roller** instead of a primary corona. No matter what method the manufacturer uses, the drum receives an uniform electrical charge.

2.   **Writing:** Put the 1s and 0s on the drum's surface.
Whether the printer uses a laser beam or an LED array, the light reflects to the drum surface in the form of 1s and 0s. Every place the beam touches, the drum's surface voltage reduces to approximately -100 volts. Wherever the beam hits, the area no longer has a huge negative charge, but instead, has a reduced negative voltage. The image on the drum is nothing more than dots of electrical charges and is invisible at this point in the process.

3.   **Developing:** Get the toner on the drum. (Develop the image.)
A **developing cylinder** located inside the toner cartridge right next to the drum has a magnet that runs the length of it. When the cylinder rotates, toner is attracted to the cylinder because the toner has iron particles in it. The toner receives a negative static charge from the magnet inside the cylinder. The magnetic charge is a voltage level between -200 and -500 volts. The magnetized toner particles are attracted to the places on the drum where the light beam strikes. A **density control blade** controls the amount of toner allowed through to the drum. The blade usually connects to a toner control knob located inside the printer. The computer user can adjust the toner control knob to vary the print density. The image is no longer transparent on the drum. During this step, the image is black on the drum surface.

4.   **Transferring:** The image transfers to the paper.
A **transfer corona** or a **transfer roller** (depending on the manufacturer) is located at the bottom of the printer. The transfer corona or roller places a positive charge on the back of the paper. The positive charge is strong enough to attract the negatively charged toner particles from the drum. The toner particles leave the drum and go onto the paper. At this point, the image is on the paper; however, the particles are held only by their magnetic charge.

5.   **Fusing**: Melt the toner into the paper.
Heat and pressure make the image permanent on the paper. The paper, with the toner particles clinging to it, immediately passes through **fusing rollers** which apply pressure to the toner. The top roller applies intense heat (350° F) to the toner and paper which literally squeezes and melts the toner into the paper fibers.

Always remember to allow a laser printer to cool down completely before working in the fusing roller area.

A cleaning pad located above the top fusing roller lightly coats the roller with silicon oil to prevent the paper sticking to the roller which is often coated with Teflon. The cleaning pad also removes any residual toner from the roller.

A laser printer frequently makes an unusual noise. The noise heard is the fusing rollers turning when the printer is not in use. Otherwise, the fusing rollers would have an indentation on one side. Users not familiar with laser printers sometimes complain about this noise, but it is a normal function of the laser printer.

6. **Cleaning**: Wipe off any toner left on the drum.
   Some books list this as the first step, but the order does not matter because the process is a continuous cycle. During the cleaning stage a wiper blade or brush clears the photo-sensitive drum of any excess toner. Then an **erase lamp** neutralizes any charges left on the drum so the next printed page begins with a clean drum.

Some books, manuals, and reference materials use the six phases of the electro-photographic process instead of Hewlett-Packard's (HP) terms. The six phases are listed in Printer Table #2 with the equivalent HP terms. Keep in mind the same thing happens in each phase, only different terms are given to each phase.

PRINTER - TABLE # 2

Laser Printer Process Terms

Electro-photographic Phase and Term	Electro-photographic Process	HP Term
Phase 1: Charge	Charge the photo-conductive drum	Conditioning
Phase 2: Expose	Expose the photo-conductor	Writing
Phase 3: Develop	Develop the image	Developing
Phase 4: Transfer	Transfer the image	Transferring
Phase 5: Fuse	Fuse the image to the paper	Fusing
Phase 6: Clean	Clean the photo-conductor	Cleaning

Every laser printer that uses the six-phase process is known as a **write-black laser printer**. These laser printers produce a black dot every place the beam touches the drum. Most laser printers use the write-black technology. **Write-white laser printers** reverse the process and the toner attracts everywhere the light beam does *not* touch the drum surface. Write-black printers print finer details, but write-white laser printers can produce darker shades of black areas.

To help with the inundation of data, Printer Table #3 lists the major parts of a printer with a short description of the purpose of each part.

PRINTER - TABLE # 3

Printer Parts

Printer Part	Purpose
Cleaning blade	Wipes away excess toner from the drum before printing the next page.
Cleaning pad	Applies oil to the fusing roller to prevent sticking. It also cleans any excess toner from the roller.
Conditioning roller	Used instead of a primary corona wire to apply a uniform negative charge to the drum's surface.
Density control blade	Controls the amount of toner allowed onto the drum (usually user-adjustable).
Developing cylinder (Developing roller)	Rotates to magnetize the toner particles before they go onto the drum.
Drum (Photo-sensitive drum)	Accepts the beams of light (data) from LEDs or laser beam. Can be permanently damaged if exposed to light.
Erase lamp	Neutralizes any residual charges on the drum before printing the next page.
Fusing rollers	Applies pressure and heat to fuse the toner into the paper.
Primary corona wire (Main corona)	Applies a uniform negative charge to the drum's surface
Toner	Powder made of plastic resin particles and organic compounds bonded to iron oxide.
Toner cartridge	Holds the conditioning roller, cleaning blade, drum, developing cylinder, and toner. Always remove before shipping a laser printer.
Transfer corona wire (Transfer roller)	Applies a positive charge on the back of the paper to pull the toner from the drum onto the paper.

PAPER

The type of paper used in a printer can affect its performance and cause problems. Dot matrix printers are the most forgiving because a mechanism physically impacts the paper. Ink jet printers, on the other hand, spray ink onto the paper, so the quality of paper determines how well the ink adheres to the paper. If the paper absorbs too much of the ink, the printout appears faded. If it does not absorb enough ink, it will run down the paper. For the laser printer, how well the paper heats and absorbs the toner also affects the printed output.

A **ream** of paper contains 500 sheets. At the end of most paper reams is an arrow that points to the side on which to print. If the paper manufacturer does not have an arrow, then the printable side is usually rougher than the other side. The printable side is the **wire side**. The other side of the paper is the **felt side** or **wax side**. Paper is rated according to pounds with 20 lb. paper as the most common. An ink jet printer works best with 24-28 lb. paper. Any paper 16 lbs. or less will probably not pass through any printer easily and cause paper jams. Always refer to the printer documentation for the recommended paper poundage.

Some expensive paper has a watermark visible if you hold the paper up to a light. The paper feels rough on the watermark. Sometimes ink jet printers and laser printers do not print properly on the watermark. Erasable bond paper also does not work well in laser printers because the paper does not allow the toner to fuse properly. Every possible type of paper imaginable is available for ink jet and laser printers: transparency paper for overhead projectors, high gloss, water resistant ink jet paper, fabric paper, greeting cards, labels, recycled, etc. Recycled paper may cause printer jams and produce lower print quality.

The highest quality paper in the world does not work well if the surrounding area has too much humidity. Humidity is paper's worst enemy and it causes the paper to stick together as well as reduce the paper's strength causing feed problems. Paper affected by humidity is sometimes noticeable because of the lumpy look it gives the paper. If any damaged paper is detected, discard it immediately. For best printing results, keep paper stored in a non-humid storage area.

Another simple and useful task to do is fan the paper before you insert it into the printer's bin. Also, do not overfill a printer's paper bin. For best results, only fill a printer's paper bin three-quarters full.

REFILLING CARTRIDGES AND RE-INKING RIBBONS

Much controversy exists when it comes to re-inking dot matrix printer ribbons, refilling ink jet cartridges or buying re-manufactured laser cartridges. Many people concerned about the environment recycle their cartridges. Even if a company or an individual user decides not to purchase re-manufactured products, some send their old empty cartridges to companies that do the re-manufacturing. Refilling ink cartridges significantly lower the printing costs.

Most ink jet printer manufacturers do *not* recommend refilling the print cartridge. The companies who make the refill kits state that ink jet manufacturers simply want more money spent on their products. Who do you believe? Believe no one; test for yourself if refilling a cartridge truly works.

Testing performed in over 30 computer labs at Florida Community College at Jacksonville demonstrated that the print cartridges handled two refills without any problems. On the third refill, the cartridges were more susceptible to leakage and poor performance. On the other hand, another company using a single ink jet printer has never purchased a new ink cartridge after purchasing the printer. They always refill the same cartridge and the printer is over two years old.

If you refill the ink cartridges, add new ink before the old cartridge runs completely dry. This seems to give better results. If refilling ink cartridges, be sure the refill ink emulates the manufacturer's ink. Some ink refill companies use inferior ink that, over time, has a corrosive effect on the cartridge housing. A leaky cartridge or one that burst causing ink to get into the printer is nothing but trouble.

Some ink refill companies have an exchange system. The old ink cartridges are placed into a plastic sealed bag and returned to the company where they are re-manufactured. In return, the company ships a re-manufactured cartridge filled with ink. If the empty ink cartridge sent to the company does not fit their standards criteria, the cartridge is thrown away.

When it comes to laser cartridge re-manufacturing, the most important components are the drum and also the wiper blade that cleans the drum. Many laser cartridge re-manufacturers use the same parts over and over again. A quality refill company will disassemble the cartridge and inspect each part. When the drum and wiper blade are worn, they are replaced with new parts.

Re-inking a dot matrix printer ribbon is not a good idea. Not to mention the mess it causes, the ink is sometimes an inferior quality that causes deterioration of the printhead over time. Because dot matrix printer ribbons are so inexpensive, just replace them.

PRINTER DRIVERS

How an application outputs to a printer is determined by the operating system used. In the DOS environment, every application includes print drivers. A **print driver** is a small piece of software specifically written for a particular printer. The print driver enables the printer's specific features and allows an application to communicate with the printer. The number of print drivers included with a DOS application depends on the software manufacturer.

Every printer model needs a print driver for each DOS application. Take, for example, an IBM printer connected to a computer using the DOS operating system. The computer has both WordPerfect word processing software and Lotus spreadsheet software loaded. The print driver that comes with WordPerfect allows WordPerfect to communicate with the printer. However, WordPerfect's print driver does not work with Lotus. The Lotus software package must provide its own print driver to communicate with the printer.

One way printer manufacturers avoid this is to allow the printer to *emulate* or copy the way another printer prints. Most printers emulate an industry standard such as an IBM Proprinter, an Epson FX100 printer, a Hewlett-Packard DeskJet 500, or a Hewlett-Packard LaserJet II printer. One drawback to using a **printer emulation** is not all the printer features may be used, especially if the feature is one that the emulated printer does not have. To use all the features, use a specific print driver designed for the printer. Contact the application manufacturer or the printer manufacturer for a print driver, or check their Internet site. The procedure for setting a printer to emulate another one is in the printer's manual. Normally, one configures the printer's emulation by setting DIP switches or using the printer's front panel buttons.

DOS applications are the worst environment for printing. Back before Internet days, this meant connecting to a bulletin board system and downloading a file at 1200 or 2400 bits per second. Or worse, calling technical support and waiting a long time on hold before requesting the print driver on a disk. Now printer manufacturers charge if asked to provide a print driver disk because the drivers are so easily accessible through the Internet.

Windows 3.x and Windows 95 applications use one print driver — one written for the specific printer.

Some Windows 3.x print drivers work under Windows 95, but for optimum Windows 95 performance, obtain a Windows 95 printer driver. A Windows 95 print driver allows sharing the printer with other workstations through a Windows 95 network. Windows 95 ships with support for over 800 different printers. In most cases, using a Windows 95 print driver is better than using a Windows 3.x print driver.

Printers must accept as much data as possible from the computer, process that data, output it, communicate to the computer the need for more data, accept more data, and continue the process all over again. With Windows 3.x and Windows 95, a print spooler is used. A **print spooler** or print manager is a software program that intercepts the printer's request to print. Instead of going directly to the printer, the data goes to the hard drive. The spooler then controls the data going from the hard drive to the printer. Some printers come with their own print manager that replaces the one included with Windows 3.x or Windows 95.

The print spooler's transmission retry option is the number of seconds the print manager waits before giving up on trying to send the printer more data. With Windows 3.x, the default is 45 seconds for non-PostScript printers and 90 seconds for PostScript printers. If the document contains multiple fonts, font sizes, or graphics, the transmission retry settings may need to be changed. To change the transmission retry setting in Windows 3.x, double-click on the **Main** group icon, **Control Panel** icon, and then the **Printers** icon. Click once on the specific printer listed under the *Installed Printers* list; then click on the **Connect** button. Change the transmission retry setting in the timeout section.

For Windows 95, click on the **Start button**. From the menu, select **Settings** and then **Printers**. From within the window that appears, right-click on the specific printer needing the change. Select **Properties** from the drop-down menu. Click on the **Details** tab and change the transmission retry setting from within the *Timeout Settings* section.

FONTS

A **font** is a group of printable characters of a particular style such as Times New Roman, Script, Arial, and Courier. The **font style** refers to the appearance of the type such as bold or italic. The **font size** is in points such as 10pt. or 12pt. The larger the point size, the larger the type is on the paper. Point size is different from **Characters per Inch (CPI)**. The larger the CPI, the smaller the font size.

The most basic font is the **raster font**. Raster fonts are nothing more than dots creating an image. Dot matrix printers frequently use raster fonts. **Vector fonts** are a little more complicated and are created from a mathematical formula. All characters created using vector fonts are simply a series of lines between two points. Vector fonts are also known as **outline fonts**. The outline of each character is used to produce the printed output. The outline defines the shape of the character, but not the size. Outline fonts are **scaleable** meaning the character can be created at any size. The most advanced type of outline font is the **TrueType font** with characters that can be scaled (enlarged or shrunk) and rotated (turned on its side or upside down).

A printer can load fonts or use fonts three ways: internally, from a font cartridge, or from the hard drive. A printer's **internal fonts** are stored inside the printer on a ROM chip. Internal fonts speed up printer performance. **Font cartridges** are add-on features for printers that allow different fonts to be loaded into the printer's memory. Fonts that load from the hard drive, known as **soft fonts**, are the slowest type of font. The fonts come from the hard drive and transmit to the printer instead of all the processing done in the printer. Nevertheless, storing fonts on the hard drive keeps down printer costs.

Each printer has its own **page description language (PDL)** which is a translator between the computer and the printer. The page description language handles the overall page look and has commands that treat the entire document as a single graphic. The two most popular page description languages are Adobe Systems Inc.'s **PostScript** and **Hewlett-Packard's Printer Control Language (HPPCL)**.

If a document is created in a computer that has a PostScript printer driver loaded, and the document is taken to another computer without a PostScript printer driver, there is a good chance the printed document will not print properly.

IEEE 1284 STANDARD & SPP, EPP, ECP

The parallel port on the computer has undergone very few changes over the years. The IEEE committee established a new standard in 1984 called IEEE 1284. Before any established standards, the parallel device, (such as a printer), received data from the computer through the **Standard Parallel Port (SPP)**. The data traveled in one direction only — from the computer to the printer.

To allow status data to travel from the printer back to the computer, Intel Corp., Xircom, Inc., and Zenith Data Systems Corp., designed a standard known as **EPP (Enhanced Parallel Port)**. The IEEE 1284 standard incorporates the EPP standard as one mode of parallel communication. EPP allows bi-directional communication. With **bi-directional printing**, the printer can notify the computer that the cover is open, the printer is off-line, the paper is out, etc. Even though bi-directional printing allows two-way communication between the printer and the computer, it is only one way at a time. Either the computer is sending information to the printer or the printer is sending information to the computer. In addition to allowing bi-directional transmissions, EPP transmits data at 500 KBps to 2 MBps which is faster than SPP's 50 Bps to 150 Bps transfer rate.

Microsoft and Hewlett-Packard improved the EPP standard by creating the **Enhanced Capabilities Port (ECP)** standard. IEEE 1284 also includes ECP as a parallel communication mode that allows bi-directional communication. However with ECP, simultaneous bi-directional communication can occur over the parallel port. ECP mode allows the printer to communicate with the computer at the same time the computer is sending data to the printer. The ECP also supports data compression and DMA transfers that allow faster data exchange.

Four criteria determine whether a parallel device such as a printer and a computer can communicate using ECP.

1. The computer's parallel port must support ECP. If the port is built into the motherboard, check SETUP to determine if the port allows ECP configuration. If the parallel port is built into a separate adapter, check the adapter's documentation.
2. The printer must support ECP. Check the printer's documentation.
3. A parallel port driver that handles the ECP communication between the port and the device is needed. The operating system can contain this software. For example, Windows 95 supports ECP transfers; the DOS/Windows environment does not.
4. One also needs an ECP cable to connect the computer and the parallel device. Any cable that lists as IEEE 1284-compliant works in the ECP mode (if the other three criteria are in place). An IEEE 1284-compliant cable that connects the printer to the computer is not the same as a Laplink or Interlink cable (which are also bi-directional).

A parallel cable should be no longer than 15 feet.

The IEEE 1284 standard supports three different connectors used with the parallel port. Type A in the IEEE standard is the 25-pin female port normally found on the back of the computer. Type B in the IEEE standard is the 36-pin Centronics connector found on the printer. Type C in the IEEE standard is a new connector like the Centronics connector on the printer except smaller. The new connector is not widely used in the industry yet.

NOTICE: All the troubleshooting tips given in this chapter assume the printer connects to a parallel port. If the printer connects to a serial port, troubleshoot the serial problems as any other serial device. Refer to the book's serial chapter for more information on troubleshooting serial port problems.

PRINTER INSTALLATION

A printer is one of the easiest devices to install. Always refer to the printer documentation for exact installation and configuration specifics. The steps to install a printer are listed below:

1.   Un-box the printer and remove any shipping materials. The number one problem with new printers not working properly is all the shipping safeguards are not removed properly.
2.   Connect the printer cable from the printer to the computer. Using a cable that complies with the IEEE 1284 standard is important for today's computers.
3.   Connect the power cord from the printer to the wall outlet, surge protector, or UPS outlet.
4.   Load paper into the printer.
5.   Turn on the printer and verify the power light is on.
6.   If the printer has a self-test routine, execute it by referring to the printer documentation. The self-test ensures the printer is operational.
7.   Turn on the computer.
8.   Install the print drivers by following the manufacturer instructions for the operating system used.
9.   Perform a test print that verifies communication between the computer and printer.

The key to a successful printer installation is first reading the printer documentation, then using a good cable, loading the latest drivers from the printer manufacturer, and testing every step along the way. The step most technicians forget until a problem occurs is downloading the latest print drivers from the manufacturer's web site. Many hours of frustration for the computer user and the technician can be avoided by doing the research during the install, not after a problem occurs.

PRINTER PREVENTIVE MAINTENANCE

People sometimes forget to plug their printer into a surge protector or UPS. The printer can be damaged by electrical storms and power fluctuations just as a computer can. The laser printers' AC power module and fuser assembly are especially susceptible to power problems. Protect any printer as well as the computer, but always make sure that the UPS has the ability to handle the higher powered laser printer.

If the printer has trouble feeding the paper, always be sure you are using the correct type of paper and that printing occurs on the correct side. Refer to the chapter section on paper. One vendor quotes that 80 percent of all paper jams are due to inferior paper quality, poor paper condition such as humidity, or an operator-related problem such as the wrong paper size selected in the software program.

Dot matrix printers are very hardy and require little maintenance except for cleaning. However, dot matrix printers that use tractor-fed paper periodically require vacuuming. The chaff produced by the tractor-fed paper accumulates on the bottom of the printer and spreads throughout the printer.

Rubber rollers are normally found in the paper transport system. Over time, the rollers become slick from use. Special cleaners such as Rubber Rejuvenator are available for rubber printer rollers that have a hard time picking up the paper and sending it through the printer. Some printers have a special cleaning page for cleaning the rollers. Through software or pushing front panel buttons, print the cleaning page and run it back through the printer. Refer to the printer's manual for exact procedures. If a cleaner is unavailable, scrub the rollers with a wire brush or sandpaper to roughen them up a bit to enable them to better pick up the paper. If you do not have sandpaper or a wire brush, use the sharp edge of a paper clip to roughen up the rubber part of the roller so it can grip the paper.

Laser printers, on the other hand, do require some periodic maintenance. If any toner appears inside the printer, do *not* use the normal vacuum cleaner! The toner particles seep through the vacuum cleaner bag into the vacuum's motor (where the particles melt). Special vacuum bags are available for some vacuum cleaners.

If the laser printer has a transfer corona instead of a transfer roller, clean it when you replace the toner cartridge. Many laser printers include a small cleaning brush (usually green) to clean the corona wire. Some new toner cartridges come with a cotton swab just for the purpose of cleaning the transfer corona. The transfer corona wire is normally in the bottom of the printer protected by monofilament wires. Be extremely careful not to break the wires or the transfer corona. Insert the swab between the monofilament wires and rub the wire with the swab.

Sometimes the primary corona wire inside the toner cartridge becomes dirty too. If the wire is accessible, it can be cleaned using a cotton swab. Sometimes, if either corona wire has particles clinging to it, you can use a small amount of alcohol to dampen the swab and remove the dirt.

Ozone is a gas produced by the laser printer. The printer's **ozone filter** removes the gas as well as any toner and paper dust particles. The ozone filter needs replacing after a specific number of usage hours. Check the printer's documentation for the filter's replacement schedule. Simply vacuuming the ozone filter does not clean it. The ozone molecules are trapped and absorbed by the ozone filter. If you forget to replace the ozone filter, people in the immediate vicinity may develop headaches, nausea, irritability, and depression. Some laser printers do not have an ozone filter. With these printers, the surrounding area must be well ventilated.

The **fuser cleaning pad** (sometimes known as the fuser wand) sits above the top fusing roller and is normally replaced at the same time as the toner cartridge. However, the cleaning pad sometimes becomes dirty before it is time to replace the cartridge. If so, remove the cleaning pad. Hold the pad over a trash can. Take a small flat-tipped screwdriver and use the shaft to rub along the felt pad. Replace the cleaning pad and wipe the screwdriver with a cloth.

The fusing roller sometimes has particles that cling to it. Once the assembly cools, *gently* scrape the particles from the roller. A small amount of alcohol on a soft, lint-free cloth can help with stubborn spots.

If the laser printer uses a laser beam to write data to the photosensitive drum, the laser beam does not directly touch the drum. Instead, at least one mirror, if not more, is used to redirect the laser beam onto the drum's surface. The mirror(s) need to be cleaned periodically with a lint-free cloth.

After performing preventive maintenance on a printer, the pages may appear smudged or slightly dirty. Run a couple of print jobs through the printer to allow the dust to settle so to speak. Never do any kind of maintenance on any computer part or peripheral without testing the results of the maintenance or the repair!

Quality printer replacement parts and preventive maintenance kits are important to the technician. LaserImpact (1-800-777-4323) has numerous parts, supplies, HP Quick Reference Guides and service manuals for printers. If a printer must be sent away for repair, warranty work, etc. make sure to remove the toner cartridge, any platen knobs, and power cords before boxing the printer. Call the receiving company to see if you should send the toner cartridge in a separate box.

 ## WINDOWS 3.X PRINTER TROUBLESHOOTING

Many computer service companies specialize in the printers they service. A service manual is always helpful to a technician. If you understand the basic concepts and workings of each type of printer, many printer problems can be easily solved.

Windows 3.x uses a single printer driver for all applications running on top of the Windows environment. The best way to troubleshoot a Windows 3.x printer problem is to see if the problem occurs only within Windows or if it is a printer problem. Exit Windows completely. Redirect the AUTOEXEC.BAT file to the printer by typing **COPY AUTOEXEC.BAT LPT1**. For a PostScript laser printer, copy the TESTPS.TXT file located in the Windows' SYSTEM directory using the same method. The paper is normally fed through the printer by pushing a button on the printer. If the file does not print, check the printer's power, cabling, and do a printer self-test. The problem most likely lies within one of these three areas.

If the file prints, then look at the AUTOEXEC.BAT printout for the **SET TEMP=** line. Make sure there is such a line and the directory listed exists. Another thing to check for is 1MB of hard drive space. If 1MB of space is not available, delete some files and defragment the hard drive.

If the printer connects to a switch box, try connecting the printer directly to the computer. If the printer works this way and not through the switch box, reconnect the printer to the switch box. Then, open the **Printers** control panel. Click on the **Connect** button. Is the **Fast Printing Direct to Port** checkbox checked? If so, click once on the checkbox to disable the feature and try printing again.

Verify the correct print driver by double-clicking on the **Printers** control panel. Look in the **Installed Printers** section to verify that the driver matches the printer. The printer driver sometimes conflicts with the video driver. To see if the video driver is the problem, change the video driver to a generic one such as the VGA driver. If the problem goes away, there is a definite conflict between the video driver and the printer driver.

To see if the print driver is the problem, double-click on the **Printers** control panel. Click on the **Add** button. Click on the **Generic/Text Only** option in the **List of Printers** section. Click on the

Install button. The print driver name appears in the Installed Printers' section. Click on the **Generic/Text Only** option in the Installed Printers' section. Click on the **Set as Default Printer** button. Click the Close button. Using Windows Notepad, type a few characters and print the document. If the document prints, then the printer, cable, and port all work. Do not forget to go back into the Printers control panel and after ensuring the Generic/Text Only option is highlighted, click the **Remove** button. The problem is probably either in the print driver or the printer does not have enough memory for the print job. To reinstall the print driver, double-click on **Printers** control panel. Click on the print driver desired. Click on the **Remove** button. Click on **Yes** to remove the driver. Then add the print driver referring to the exercise instructions at the end of the chapter. Remember, if asked whether to use the existing driver or a new one, pick a new one and reload the driver from disks.

If the Notepad document does not print, check the power, cabling, and do a printer self-test. The problem most likely lies within one of these three areas.

 ## WINDOWS 95 PRINTER TROUBLESHOOTING

Windows 95 uses a single print driver for all applications just as Windows 3.x does. Windows 95 needs at least 3MB of hard drive space for the temporary environment. Insufficient free space can cause print jobs to have problems. As part of the AUTOEXEC.BAT, delete any .TMP files from the TEMP directory and any .SPL files from the print spool directory, normally located in the WINDOWS\SPOOL\PRINTERS subdirectory. Another problem may be the printer driver conflicts with the installed video driver. To determine if the video driver is the problem, change the video driver to a generic one such as the VGA driver. If the problem goes away, there is a definite conflict.

For troubleshooting printing problems, Windows 95 has a good troubleshooting wizard accessed through Help. Windows 95 also has many other Help items for printing. If none of the Help recommendations work, start Windows 95 in the Safe Mode-Command prompt only mode. (Press F8 when the "Starting Windows 95" prompt appears. Choose the Safe Mode-Command prompt only option.) At the command prompt, type **COPY C:\AUTOEXEC.BAT LPT1** or send any other text file to the printer. If the connected printer is a PostScript laser printer, then type **COPY C:\WINDOWS\SYSTEM\TESTPS.TXT LPT1** (or the path for the location for Windows 95's SYSTEM directory). Press the form feed button on the printer to eject the paper when finished.

If the printer works, then the printer, parallel port, and printer cable are all operational and the problem is in Windows 95. To see if the printer driver is the problem, use the **Add Printer** wizard to install the **Generic/Text Only** printer driver. See the exercise for more information.

The print spool setting or the bi-directional printing setting may need adjustment. Restart Windows 95. To remove the Windows 95 print spooling, use the Start menu's **Settings**, **Printers** option. Right-click on the problem printer icon. Select the **Properties** option. Click on the **Details** tab. Click on the **Spool Settings** button. Click once in the **Print directly to printer** radio button. (Disabling the print spooler slows printing performance.)

To disable bi-directional printing, in the same window click on the **Disable bi-directional support for this printer** radio button. Try printing from Windows 95 Notepad. If the printing works, try different combinations of spool settings and bi-directional support settings for optimum performance.

When copying test files directly to the printer from the command prompt, Windows 95 and the print driver are out of the loop. If this test does *not* work, remove any print-sharing devices such as a switch box. Connect the printer directly to the port and try the test again. If no print sharing devices are installed, perform a printer self-test and check the printer's power cables and connections. The problem is in the printer, port, or cable.

While using an ECP port, if there are problems printing or the output is garbled, the ECP option can usually be changed to the SPP through SETUP. To configure Windows 95 for non-ECP printing, double-click the **System** control panel. Click on the **Device Manager** tab. Click on the **Ports** branch. Double-click on the **ECP** port. On the **Driver** tab, click on the **Change Driver** button. Click on the **Show all devices** button. Click on **Standard Port Types** in the Manufacturers window. In the Models window, click **Printer Port**. Click on the **OK** button. Continue clicking on the **OK** button until you return to the System Properties window. Then, click on the Close button.

If there are problems printing to any bi-directional printer, or the Device Manager does not allow changing an ECP port to run in SPP mode, or unusual characters appear on the printout, etc., try using the alternate LPT.VXD file. The Windows 95 CD-ROM has the alternate LPT.VXD file located in the DRIVERS\PRINTER\LPT folder. The file is also available on the Internet at http://www.microsoft.com/windows.software/drivers/printer.htm. Rename the old LPT.VXD file located in Windows 95's SYSTEM subdirectory. Then copy the alternate LPT.VXD file into the SYSTEM subdirectory. Restart Windows 95 when you finish copying the file.

If you re-load the printer driver, the old printer driver must be removed first. To remove the old printer driver, click on the **Start** button. Select the **Settings** option followed by the **Printers** option. Right-click on the printer icon for the printer driver to be deleted. Click on the **Delete** option. Click on the **Yes** button when prompted if all the associated printer files are to be deleted. To re-install the printer use the **Add Printer** wizard. Refer to the steps at the end of the chapter if necessary.

 GENERAL PRINTER TROUBLESHOOTING

The printing hardware subsystem consists of the printer, cable, and communications port. If something is wrong with the hardware, it is normally one of these three areas. Always check the connections and the power between each area. The printer has the highest failure rate of the three because it is a mechanical device with motors, plastic gears, and moving parts. Printers normally have a self-test routine. Refer to the printer's documentation to determine how to run the test. On some printers, you hold down a specific front-panel button or two while applying power. Others require changing a dip switch. If a printer's self-test operates properly, the printer is operational. If the printer checks out, the problem is either the port, the cable, or software. Another problem could be that the printer is not configured for the correct parallel, serial, or network port. Check that the printer is configured for the proper port. Refer to the printer's documentation for specifics on how to configure the printer for a specific port.

If the printer is having trouble feeding paper, the first clue is to see how far the paper got along the paper path before it jammed or could not go any farther. Many paper feeding problems are due to poor paper quality or the rubber rollers that move the paper along the paper path. Refer back to this chapter's preventive maintenance section on rubber rollers.

The second highest failing part is the port. A loopback plug and diagnostics can be used to troubleshoot the port to see if it fails. A loopback plug is a special connector that attaches to the parallel port. Diagnostic routines send signals out a pin that is tied to a different pin. The test checks to see if the signal returns back into the computer. Some diagnostics include the parallel port loopback plug as part of its package.

The last part to check is the printer cable. Remember cables do not normally go bad. Just watch out for enabling the ECP mode without having a cable that handles ECP operations.

On the software side, troubleshooting involves narrowing the problem down to the print driver. Because Windows 3.x and Windows 95 use one print driver for all applications, check the printing from within several software packages. Use a simple text program such as Notepad to see if simple text will print. Printers need memory to print multiple pages of complex graphics. If the printer prints a couple pages and then stops, or prints half a page, ejects the paper and then prints the other half of the page and ejects the paper, then the printer's memory needs upgrading. If printing does not occur in all of the software packages tested, then the problem is most likely the software driver. See the earlier section for specific Windows 3.x and Windows 95 tips.

 ## DOT MATRIX PRINTER TROUBLESHOOTING

When technicians state that a printhead is not firing, one or more of the print wires are not coming out of the printhead to impact the ribbon. A printhead that is not firing is evidenced by one or more white lines that appear where the printed dots should be. On a printed page, the white line appears horizontally in the middle of a line. The most likely problem is the printhead. However be aware that the problem could be a bad driver transistor on the main circuit board or a loose cable that attaches to the printhead. But, because the printhead is a mechanical part, it is the most suspect.

If the printed page appears to have light print, adjust the printhead gap to place the printhead closer to the ribbon or replace the ribbon. If the print is light, then dark, the printer ribbon may not be advancing properly. One of the shafts that insert into each end of the ribbon may not be turning properly. Under the shaft is a set of gears that do not always mesh properly. Also, there is a motor that handles ribbon movement; the motor may need replacement. A faulty ribbon can also cause the carriage to seize up. Remove the ribbon and power up the printer. If the carriage moves when the ribbon is removed, but it will not move when the ribbon is installed, replace the ribbon. Some printers have belts that move the printhead across the page. If a belt is worn, loose, or slipping, erratic printing occurs.

If the printer prints continuously on the same line, be sure the setting for tractor-fed paper or friction-fed paper is correct. After that, a motor that controls paper movement may need replacement. If the printer moves the paper up a small bit after printing, the model may have the Auto Tear Off feature enabled. The Auto Tear Off feature is used with perforated forms used in many businesses. See the printer's documentation to disable this feature.

INK JET PRINTER TROUBLESHOOTING

Ink jet printers frequently have a built-in printhead cleaning routine. Access the routine through the printer's buttons or through software. Most manufacturers recommend cleaning the ink jet cartridge only when there is a problem such as lines or dots missing from the printed output. Otherwise, cleaning the ink jet cartridge with this method wastes ink and shortens the print cartridge's life span.

Usually ink jet manufacturers include an alignment program to align the dots more precisely. Use the alignment program when vertical lines or characters do not align properly. Always refer to the printer's documentation for troubleshooting programs such as the printhead cleaning and alignment routines.

LASER PRINTER TROUBLESHOOTING

If black streaks appear on the paper, or the print is not sharp, check the fuser cleaning pad for toner particles and use a small screwdriver to scrape off the excess particles before reinstalling. If a laser printer's output appears darker in some spots than others, remove the toner cartridge. Gently rock the toner cartridge back and forth to re-distribute the toner. If this does not fix the problem, turn down the toner's density by adjusting a dial setting. Refer to the printer's documentation for this adjustment. The dial adjustment may be necessary if the printer is using a technology known as **RET (Resolution Enhancement Technology)**. A drawback to RET is a phenomenon known as **toner puddling** where more toner dots are in some locations than in others. If the print appears light, adjust the darkness setting on the printer. Use fresh paper of the proper weight and finish. If the print appears consistently dark, adjust the darkness setting. Clean the mirrors inside the printer if necessary.

A great deal of laser problems involve the toner cartridge. That is good because the cartridge is one part people normally have on hand. Various symptoms can occur because of the toner cartridge: smearing, horizontal streaking, vertical streaking, faded print, one vertical black line, a single horizontal black line, a white streak on one side, etc. One of the easiest things to do is to remove the toner cartridge. Hold the toner cartridge in front of you with both hands, rock the cartridge away from you and then back toward you.

Sometimes, the primary corona wire or the conditioning roller inside the toner cartridge needs to be cleaned. Clean the corona wires using the provided brush or with a cotton swab. Dampen the cotton swab with alcohol, if necessary. Clean the conditioning roller with a lint-free cloth. Dampen the cloth with alcohol, if necessary.

If a horizontal line appears periodically throughout the printout, the problem is one of the rollers. Check all rollers to see if they are dirty or gouged and need replacing. The rollers in the laser printer are not all the same size, so the distance between the lines is the circumference of the roller. That is an easy way to tell which rollers are definitely not the problem or which ones are likely candidates. A printing error that occurs every 3.75 inches indicates the drum is defective.

To prove if a problem is in the toner cartridge or elsewhere in the printer, send any output to the printer. Wait until the printer is through with the writing stage and before the toner fuses to the paper, open the laser printer's cover and remove the paper. (Determining exactly when to open the cover may take a couple of tries.) If the paper is error-free, the problem is most likely in the transfer corona (or transfer roller) or fusing assembly.

Another fairly common problem occurs when the laser printer does not have enough memory. The symptoms are that when printing, the printer blinks as if it is accepting data. Then, the printer quits blinking and nothing appears or the printer prints only half the page. Some printers give an error code if there is not enough memory. For example, in a Hewlett-Packard laser printer, the 20 error code indicates not enough memory. If the printer needs more memory, upgrade it, send the print job fewer pages at a time, reduce the printer resolution such as from 1200 dpi to 600 dpi, reduce the size of the graphics, or standardize the fonts. Font standardization can be accomplished by not using as many font types, styles or font sizes. For Windows 3.x and Windows 95 computers that use a print spooler, there many not be enough free space on the hard drive. Delete old files and run SCANDISK to make more space available.

Experience is the best teacher when it comes to printers. Work on a couple of dot matrix models, a couple of ink jet printers, and a couple of laser printer models, and you will see the majority of problems. Each type of printer has very few circuit boards to replace. Normally the problems are in the moving parts. Many printer problems are software-related. The following exercises help set up printers for the Windows 3.x and Windows 95 environments. The exercises for the chapter follow the review questions. Good luck in your lives as technicians. May your life always be challenging and enjoyable — Cheryl Schmidt ☺

Name _____

Printer Review Questions

1. What do all printers have in common?

2. What major printer subsystem handles dot matrix printer ribbon movement?

3. What major printer subsystem handles moving the paper from the fuser rollers to a laser printer's output bin?

4. What major printer subsystem tells the printer how to print a particular font size?

5. What major printer subsystem sends an error message that the ink jet printer is out of paper?

6. T/F   Most printers connect to the parallel port.

7. If a customer asks for a printer recommendation, which type of printer would you recommend and why?

8. A computer user has one printer installed on the parallel port. Which of the following ports can be used to connect a second printer? (pick all that apply)
    A.   LPT1
    B.   LPT2
    C.   LPT3
    D.   LPT7
    E.   COM1
    F.   COM2

9. Of the possible answers shown in Question 8, which port would be the normal choice?

10. How does the first parallel port get the port name of LPT1?

11. Which switch box [automatic or manual] is best for a laser printer and why?

12. What type of printer is best for multi-part forms?

13. What are some common dot matrix printhead pin configurations?

14. What does a dot matrix printhead *not firing* mean?

15. A dot matrix printer that normally prints bi-directionally starts printing only left to right. What are you going to do to fix this problem?

16. Why is an ink jet cartridge better than a dot matrix printhead?

17. What is the major difference between ink jet printers and dot matrix printers?

18. T/F   Most ink jet printers use heat to make the ink squirt onto the paper.

19.   What can a user that is having problems with ink smearing on an ink jet printer's output do?

20.   What stage of the laser printing process prepares the photosensitive drum for use?

21.   Explain how data is written to the laser printer drum.

22.   T/F   The laser printer's conditioning phase precedes the writing phase.

23.   How does the toner inside a laser printer's toner cartridge get magnetically charged?

24.   T/F   The amount of toner allowed onto the laser printer's drum is normally adjustable.

25.   Explain how the toner permanently adheres to the paper from a laser printer.

26.   A customer calls to explain that their new laser printer makes this funny sound like it is printing something every 30 minutes, but nothing comes out of the printer. What is the solution to this problem?

27.   T/F   In the laser printing process, another name for the *Conditioning* phase is the *Expose* stage.

28.   What is the best preventive maintenance routine for a dot matrix printer?

29.   How do you handle printer rollers that slip and cause the paper to not feed properly through the printer?

30.   Why should you *not* use compressed air to remove toner from a laser printer?

31.   Do re-inked dot matrix printer ribbons produce the same output as a new ribbon? Explain your answer.

32.   Do refilled ink jet cartridges produce the same output as a new ink jet cartridge? Explain your answer.

33.   Explain criteria to expect when purchasing re-manufactured laser toner cartridges.

34.   What does it mean if you are running printer emulation?

35.   T/F   Windows 95 works best with a Windows 95 print driver.

36.   Give an example of a font.

37.   T/F   PostScript is a page description language every laser printer supports.

38.   What type of connector does an ECP port have on the back of the computer?
       A.   25-pin male
       B.   25-pin female
       C.   Centronics
       D.   Mini-Centronics

39.   Explain the difference between SPP, EPP, and ECP printer ports.

40.   How can you tell if a computer has an ECP port?

41.   Describe the three connectors supported by the IEEE 1284 standard.

42.   A printer that has worked before, will not print through Windows 3.x. Which of the following
       is a logical first step in troubleshooting after verifying power applies to the printer?
       A.   Exit Windows and print a file or perform a print screen
       B.   Replace the ink jet cartridge
       C.   Call an A+ Certified Technician
       D.   Perform a loopback test on the port

43.   Describe in detail what process is necessary to troubleshoot a printer problem in Windows 95.

44.   What is a loopback plug and how can it help when having a printer problem?

45.   How can you prove if the software print driver is causing a printing problem?

46.   If a white line appears across one row of dot matrix produced print, what are the possible
       suspect components?

47.   What is the most likely laser printer suspect component if a white line appears periodically
       throughout a printed page?

Name _____

Printer Fill-in-the-Blank

1.   A device that allows two printers to connect to the same parallel port is a _____.

2.   An _____ printer produces color output at a moderate price.

3.   The _____ printer produces the highest quality output at the fastest rate.

4.   The _____ printer is also called an impact printer.

5.   Dot matrix _____ houses the printwires that strike the ribbon to produce a dot on the paper.

6.   A dot matrix printer speed is measured in _____.

7.   The _____ on a dot matrix printer needs replacing at times because the pins strike a ribbon.

8.   _____ printers have tiny nozzles from which ink squirts onto the paper.

9.   The _____ holds an ink jet printer's ink and functions as the printhead.

10. Ink jet and laser printer output is commonly measured in _____. The higher this number, the better the quality of the output.

11. _____ printers operate on the same principle as a copy machine.

12. The way in which 1s and 0s write to the laser printer's surface is by using a _____ or a _____.

13. The _____ or the _____ applies an uniform negative voltage to the laser drum.

14. _____ is powder made of plastic resin particles and organic compounds bound to iron oxide.

15. The _____ controls the amount of toner allowed onto the drum.

16. The _____ or the _____ applies a positive voltage on the back of the paper in a laser printer.

17. The _____ sits on top of the fusing roller and lubricates it.

18. A _____ laser printer produces a black image every place light touches the drum.

19. The laser printer's _____ removes gas, toner, and dust produced by the printer.

20. Printing should always occur on the _____ side of the paper.

21. A _____ is a piece of software needed for printer operation.

22. _____ fonts are the most basic type.

23. _____ fonts are created from a mathematical model.

24. _____ fonts can be rotated.

25. _____ fonts are loaded from the hard drive.

26. _____ and _____ are the two most common page description languages for laser printers.

27. Any _____-compatible cable works in the ECP mode.

Name _____

ADDING OR CHANGING A PRINTER DRIVER USING
WINDOWS 3.X EXERCISE

Objective: Add or change a Windows 3.x printer driver

Parts: A computer with Windows 3.x loaded

Step 1:   Power on the computer and verify that Windows 3.x loads.
Step 2:   From Program Manager, double-click on the **Main** group icon.
Step 3:   Double-click on the **Control Panel** icon.
Step 4:   Double-click on the **Printer** icon.
Step 5:   Click on the **Add** button. A list of printers appears in a window at the bottom of the screen.
Step 6:   Use the scroll bars to find the printer model that attaches to the computer. The printers appear in alphabetical order by manufacturer.
Step 7:   Click once on the printer desired and click on the **Install** button. If the printer is not listed, a print driver disk from the printer manufacturer must be obtained. If a print driver disk is available, click on **Install Unlisted or Updated Printer** option and click on the **Install** button.
Step 8:   Follow the directions on the screen.
Step 9:   Using any simple word processor or text editor such as Windows' Notepad, perform a test by typing some sample text and printing the text on the printer.

Question 1:   Does the printer work?

Question 2:   What print driver did you load?

_____ Instructor's Initials

Name _____

ADDING WINDOWS 95'S GENERIC/TEXT ONLY
PRINTER DRIVER EXERCISE

Objective: Add or change a Windows 95 printer driver

Parts: A computer with Windows 95 installed
        Windows 95 installation disk or CD-ROM

Step 1:   Power on the computer and verify that Windows 95 loads. Refer to Appendix B for Windows 95 skills.
Step 2:   To determine if a printer driver is already selected as the default, click on the **Start** button.
Step 3:   Select **Programs**, then **Accessories**, then click on the **Notepad** option.
Step 4:   Click on the **File** menu option.
Step 5:   Click on the **Page Setup** option.
Step 6:   Click on the **Printer** button at the bottom of the window.

Question 1:   Does any printer list in the *Name* box? If so, write the printer name in the space below.

Step 7:   Click on the **Cancel** button.
Step 8:   Click on the Page Setup window's **Cancel** button.
Step 9:   Click once in the Notepad close box.
Step 10:   To install a printer driver, click on the **Start** button.
Step 11:   Select the **Settings** option, then click on the **Printers** option.
Step 12:   Double-click on the **Add Printer** icon. The Add Printer wizard starts.
Step 13:   Click on the **Next** button.
Step 14:   Use the slide bar in the Manufacturers window to locate the *Generic* option.
Step 15:   Click once on the **Generic** option. The Generic/Text Only option appears in the Printers window.
Step 16:   Click on the **Next** button. The port window appears and LPT1 is highlighted.
Step 17:   Click on the **Next** button.
Step 18:   When prompted if Windows 95 is to use the Generic/Text Only printer as the default printer, click on the **Yes** radio button.
Step 19:   Click on the **Next** button.
Step 20:   When asked whether or not to print a test page, be sure the **Yes** radio button is selected.

Step 21:   Click on the **Finish** button. When prompted for the installation disk or CD, install it into the appropriate drive.
Step 22:   If the test page prints correctly, click on the **Yes** button. If the test page does not print correctly, click on the **No** button and the Windows 95 printer troubleshooting wizard starts.

Question 2:   Did the printer print the test page correctly? If not, troubleshoot the printer using the tips presented in the chapter or using Windows 95's Help.

_____ Instructor's Initials

Step 23:   To remove the Generic/Text Only printer driver, *right-click* on the **Generic/Text Only** icon.
Step 24:   Click on the **Delete** option from the drop down menu.
Step 25:   Click the **Yes** button to confirm the driver deletion.
Step 26:   Click the **Yes** button to the prompt stating that some unnecessary files will be deleted. A prompt appears if a printer driver was present before installing the Generic/Text Only driver. Click on the **OK** button, if necessary.

Question 3:   Why would a technician need to install the Generic/Text Only driver?

_____ Instructor's Initials

Name _____

DETECTING PARALLEL PORT I/O ADDRESSES WITH THE DEBUG PROGRAM EXERCISE

Objective: Use DEBUG to determine the parallel port I/O addresses

Parts: A working computer with the DEBUG command available

Step   1:   Power on the computer and go to the command prompt. Refer to Appendix A for DOS skills.

Step   2:   At the command prompt, type **DEBUG**. A dash appears on the line following the DEBUG command.

Step   3:   At the dash on the screen, type **D40:0** and press **ENTER**. Hexadecimal values display on the screen.

The hexadecimal values of the active serial ports display first followed by the parallel ports. Deciphering the hexadecimal numbers is tricky, but Printer Exercise Figure #1 helps explain the values. The first line of the output is all that matters!

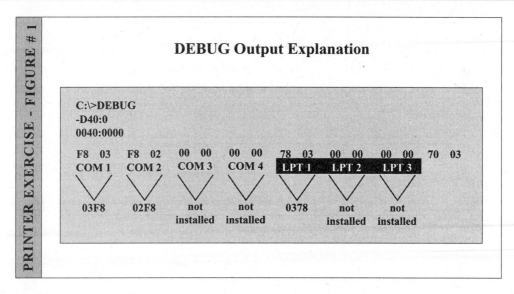

Notice in Parallel Exercise Figure #1 how three different values are associated with LPT1, LPT2, LPT3. The three values represent the I/O address for the associated LPT port (if installed). However, the addresses display backward and this confuses people. For example, LPT1 lists as 78 03, but in reality, the values represent I/O address of 0378h. A port address of 00 00 is an unused (or undetected) port.

Question 1:   How many parallel ports does BIOS detect?

Question 2:   What I/O addresses does each parallel port take? Use Printer Exercise Table #1 to place
        this information.

Port Name	I/O Address
LPT1:	
LPT2:	
LPT3:	

EXERCISE - TABLE # 1

Step   4:   To exit the DEBUG program, type **Q** and press **ENTER**.

Name _____

USING MSD FOR LPT PORT IDENTIFICATION EXERCISE

Objective: Use Microsoft Diagnostics to determine LPT ports

Parts: A working computer with Microsoft Diagnostics (MSD) loaded

Step   1:   Power on the computer and go to the command prompt. Refer to Appendix A for DOS skills.
Step   2:   Change into the directory (DOS or WINDOWS) which contains the Microsoft Diagnostics (MSD.EXE) program.
Step   3:   Start the Microsoft Diagnostics program by typing **MSD** at the prompt.
Step   4:   Press **L** to access the LPT Ports... option.
Step   5:   Look at the LPT Ports information window. The headings down the left side are LPT1, LPT2, and LPT3. For each LPT port, different criterion lists to the right of it. The second column labeled *Port Address* is the I/O address each parallel port uses.

Question 1:   What I/O address does LPT1 use?

Question 2:   Does the system being tested have a device assigned to the LPT2 port?

Step   6:   Press **ENTER** to return to the first screen of the MSD program.
Step   7:   Press **F3** to quit MSD.

NOTES

Appendix A: Introduction to DOS

OBJECTIVES

After completing this chapter you will
1. Execute and understand basic DOS commands.
2. Understand the DOS file structure and its limitations.
3. Understand the purpose of the AUTOEXEC.BAT and CONFIG.SYS files.
4. Be able to create a file using a text editor.

KEY TERMS

archive attribute	filename
ATTRIB	hidden attribute
AUTOEXEC.BAT	internal commands
batch files	MS-DOS
boot	operating system
command interpreter	path
command prompt	PC-DOS
CONFIG.SYS	pipe symbol
DELTREE	read-only attribute
device drivers	root directory
DIR ,	SmartDrive
directory	subdirectory
DOSKEY	switch
executable files	system attribute
extension	UNDELETE
external commands	wildcard

DOS OVERVIEW

Microcomputers require software to operate. An **operating system** is software that coordinates the interaction between hardware and any software applications run as well as the interaction between a user and the computer. An operating system contains commands that both the user and the computer understand. For example, if you typed the word *hop* into a computer, hop is not a command therefore the computer does not know what to do. If you type the word *DIR*, the computer recognizes the command and displays a directory or a listing of files. Operating systems also handle file and disk management. Examples of operating systems for today's microcomputers are DOS, OS/2, UNIX, Windows 95, and Windows NT Workstation. DOS has been the prevalent operating system until the last couple of years when OS/2 and Windows 95 came on strong.

Quite a few computer problems are software-related and many hardware installations have software programs that allow the hardware to work. Running diagnostic software is also something a technician performs from time to time. Even with the advent of newer and more powerful operating systems, a technician still must enter basic commands into the computer while troubleshooting. DOS skills are still very important for a technician.

DOS COMMANDS

In the past, many manufacturers created their own DOS version, but Microsoft controls the operating system market today. Microsoft's DOS is known as **MS-DOS** and IBM's DOS is **PC-DOS**. Three DOS files enable a machine to **boot** or come up to a usable point. Two of the files are hidden. Microsoft DOS hidden system files are MSDOS.SYS and IO.SYS. The third file is COMMAND.COM, also known as the **command interpreter** which is responsible for processing every command typed into the computer. These three files load from a disk or reside and load from the hard drive. IBM PC-DOS bootable files are IBMBIO.COM, IBMDOS.COM, and COMMAND.COM. Most commands with a particular manufacturer's DOS version will not work on other machines unless the other computer has the same version of DOS.

DOS has two types of commands, internal and external. **Internal commands** are not visible when viewing files on a disk or hard drive, but after you enter the commands, they will execute. Internal commands are built into the COMMAND.COM file and execute much faster than external commands. An example of an internal command is DIR. **External commands** can be seen when viewing files on a disk or a hard drive. External commands execute slower than internal commands because the external commands must retrieve data from the disk or hard drive. An example of an External command is XCOPY.

Drive letters are assigned to hardware devices when a computer boots. For example, the first floppy drive gets the drive letter A:. The colon is part of the device's drive letter. The first hard drive in a system gets the drive letter C:. The devices detected by the operating system use drive letters A: through Z:.

All communication with DOS begins at the **command prompt**, or simply a prompt. A command prompt might look like A:\> or C:\> or C:\DOS>. It can be changed to provide different information such as the drive letter, the date, or the time. The exercise that follows demonstrates how to change the command prompt. Commands are typed using a keyboard. Capitalization does not matter when using DOS, but DOS commands MUST be typed in a specific format and in a specific order. Practicing DOS commands is the best way to become proficient.

DOS FILE STRUCTURE

DOS files can be organized like chapters in a book. However, DOS files are grouped into **directories**. The starting point for all directories is the **root directory**. From the root directory, other directories can be made. The root directory has a limit as to how many files it can hold.

The floppy drive's root directory can hold a maximum of 128 files or directories. The hard drive's root directories can hold up to 512 files or directories. A hard drive will send an "out of space" error message if there are more than 512 files in the root directory. The hard drive may have many megabytes of available space and still give the error just because of a filled root directory. Creating directories is a good way for organizing files and keeping the root directory uncluttered.

The DOS file structure is called a tree because of how the directories are structured with limbs (directories) extending outward. Reference DOS Figure #1 for an example of how a hard disk's file structure might be organized.

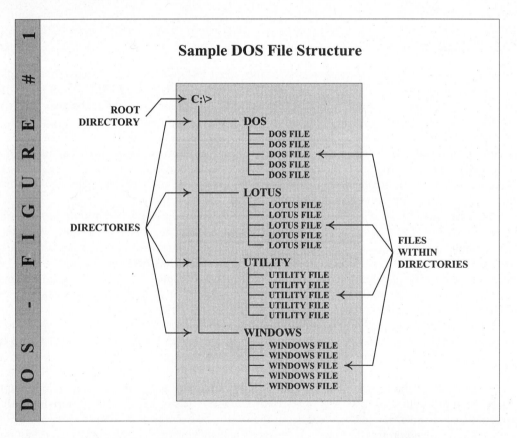

Notice in DOS Figure #1 how each directory has a unique name. An infinite number of files can exist under each directory. Each **filename** within a directory must be unique, but other directories can contain the same file. Say, for example, that the CHERYL.TXT file exists in the DOS directory. A different CHERYL.TXT file (or the same one) can exist in the WINDOWS, LOTUS, or UTILITY directory (or all three directories for that matter). However, a second CHERYL.TXT file cannot exist in the DOS directory.

The DOS tree structure allows for **subdirectory** creation underneath another directory. For example, if a DOS directory has the name BOOK, below the directory can be subdirectories titled CHAP1 and CHAP2, CHAP3, etc. Reference DOS Figure #2 for this tree structure.

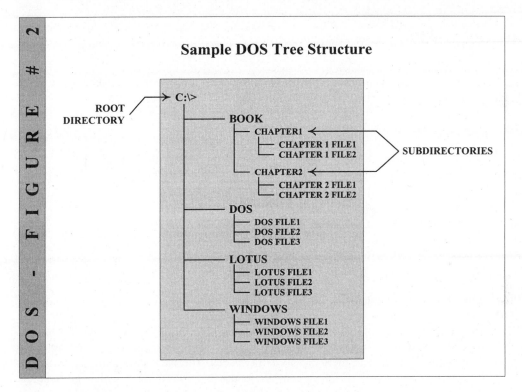

Notice in DOS Figure #2 how that the BOOK directory has more than one subdirectory. Many more subdirectories can be added to the BOOK directory as well. Each subdirectory's name must be unique; however, the same subdirectory name can be used under other directories. For example, the LOTUS directory could contain a CHAPTER1 and a CHAPTER2 subdirectory just like the book directory does.

The best way to become proficient with DOS is to use it. The following exercise illustrates some DOS basics.

Name _____

DOS INTERNAL/EXTERNAL COMMANDS & MAKING A BOOTABLE FLOPPY EXERCISE

Objective: Execute basic DOS commands and make a bootable disk

Parts: A computer with DOS loaded
          A disk with DOS files
          A blank disk

For each step requiring a typed command the *ENTER* key must be pressed to execute the DOS command. This instruction will *not* be given with each step.

Step   1:   Power on the computer on and boot from the hard disk.

Question 1:   Does the computer boot to a prompt? If the computer automatically boots to the Windows program, press and hold **ALT**. Then, press **F4** and release both keys. When a dialog box appears on the screen informing you that you are ending your Windows session, press **ENTER**. If the computer still does not boot to a prompt, and you followed every step correctly, contact your instructor.

Question 2:   Write down the prompt displayed on the computer screen.

Step   2:   From the command prompt, type
            CD\DOS
            The prompt changes to **C:\DOS>**. If a message appears stating invalid command or invalid directory, you most likely made a typing error. If you suspect an error, verify the backslash is between CD and DOS and there are no extra spaces. The backslash starts from the left side and goes to the right: \. Other commands use a forward slash which goes in the opposite direction: /. CD is the command for Change Directory which tells DOS to go to a different directory in the tree structure. \DOS immediately follows CD in the command to tell DOS to go to the DOS directory in the tree structure. The command CD\WINDOWS will take you to the WINDOWS directory.
Step   3:   At the command prompt, type
            DIR
            The files that appear on the screen are part of the DOS directory. These are the DOS external commands. When the number of files exceeds what can be shown on the screen, the files quickly scroll off the screen until all files finish displaying. The DIR command has a **switch** that controls this scrolling. A **switch** begins with a forward slash and enhances or changes the way a DOS command performs.

Step   4:   At the DOS prompt, type
              DIR /P
              After looking at the screen of data, press **ENTER** again. Continue pressing **ENTER** until
              the DOS prompt reappears. The DIR command's */P* switch tells DOS to display the files
              one page at a time.

Step   5:   At the DOS prompt, type
              DIR /W

Question 3:   What is the function of DIR's */W* switch?

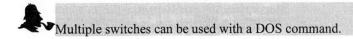
Multiple switches can be used with a DOS command.

Step   6:   At the DOS prompt, type
              DIR /W/P
              Using the DIR command */W* and */P* switches cause the DOS files to display in a wide
              format, one page at a time.

Step   7:   With the new versions of DOS, a great deal of documentation is in the online help.
              Different manufacturers have different help screens. To find out the DOS version loaded on
              the computer, at the DOS prompt, type
              VER

Question 4:   What version and manufacturer of DOS are being used on the computer?

Note: The following steps illustrate online help for Microsoft's MS-DOS version 6 and higher. If the
answer to Question 4 is lower than version 6 or if Microsoft is *not* the manufacturer, skip Steps 8-10.

Step   8:   At the DOS prompt, type
              HELP
              A list of DOS commands display on the screen.

Step   9:   If you are using a mouse, click on the **DIR** command. If you are using a keyboard, press **D**.
              Then, use the **arrow keys** to place the cursor under the **DIR** command. Finally, press
              ENTER.

Question 5:   Using HELP, find the switches available for use with the DIR command. List three DIR
              switches along with a short description of each switch.

Step 10:   Exit the HELP program by pressing **ALT** followed by **F**, then, press **X**.

Another way to receive online help about a command is to type HELP, then a space, then the name of the command. For example, HELP DIR displays information about the DIR command.

Step 11:   Type
            CD
            The CD\ command allows you to return to the root directory at any time.

Question 6:   In DOS, what is the root directory?

DOS files can have names up to eight characters long. DOS files normally have file extensions and a name. File extensions frequently give clues as to which application created the file. An **extension** is in addition to the filename and can be no more than three characters. An extension usually identifies the software package that created the file. A period (.) separates the name from the extension. The file CHERYL.DOC has a name of CHERYL and DOC is the extension. The complete filename includes the eight character name as well as the period and the extension. In the prior example, CHERYL.DOC is the filename.

Step 12:   Type
            DIR CO*.*
            The * is known as a wildcard for DOS. A **wildcard** substitutes for one or more characters. The DIR CO*.* command gives a listing of all files that begin with the letters CO. The first asterisk (*) is the wildcard for any name of a file. The second asterisk (*) is the wildcard for any extension.

Question 7:   List the files found that begin with the letter C.

Question 8:   What is the purpose of the COMMAND.COM file?

ON YOUR OWN

Write each command in the space below the instruction.
1.   Change to the DOS directory.

2.   List all DOS files that begin with the letter D, one page at a time.

3.   Look for the DIR and DISKCOPY commands in the DOS directory.

4.   Return to the root directory.

Question 9:   Why is the DISKCOPY command listed under the DOS directory and the DIR command is not? The DIR command has been used in this exercise and is a valid DOS command, yet it does not list in the DOS directory.

Step 13:   Insert a disk containing files into the first floppy drive. Then, type
           DIR A:
           Watch for the light to appear on the floppy drive.

Question 10:   What drive letter does the first bootable hard drive normally get?

Question 11:   List one filename from the disk. Do not forget to include the extension.

The following steps create a boot disk:
Step 14:   From the command prompt, type
           C:
Step 15:   From the command prompt, type
           CD\DOS
Step 16:   From the DOS prompt, type:
           FORMAT A: /S
           A message similar to the following appears on your screen:
               C:\DOS>FORMAT A: /S
               Insert a new disk for drive A:
               and press ENTER when ready ...
Step 17:   Insert a non-important disk into the floppy drive (the A: drive) then, press
           ENTER.
Step 18:   At the prompt for volume label, simply press **ENTER**.
Step 19:   At the prompt to format another, type **N**.
Step 20:   The FORMAT command */S* switch makes a disk bootable by copying over the system files. Verify that the disk is bootable. With the same disk inserted into the A: drive, press **CTRL+ALT+DEL**. Pressing CTRL+ALT+DEL is known as a warm boot. The computer reboots and the date prompt appears. Simply press **ENTER**. Then, a time prompt appears. Again, press **ENTER**. The A:\> prompt appears on the screen.

Question 12:   Did the computer boot to the A:\> prompt? If the computer *does not* boot properly to the A:\> prompt, remove the disk from the A: drive. Press **CTRL+ALT+DEL**. After the computer boots to the hard drive, re-do Steps 14 through 20.

Question 13:   Using DOS online help, determine the purpose of the FORMAT command /S switch?

_____ Instructor's Initials

A bootable floppy disk is a vital tool for a technician especially when working on hard drives.

Step 21:   Remove the bootable floppy disk from the drive.
Step 22:   Reboot the computer and go to the command prompt. Type
            CD\DOS
Step 23:   From the DOS prompt, type
            PROMPT PT

Question 14:   What happened to the command prompt on the screen?

Step 24:   From the DOS prompt, type
            PROMPT Technicians rule the world $g

Question 15:   Write down what the command prompt looks like now.

Step 25:   From the DOS prompt, type
            PROMPT $P $D $T $G
Step 26:   From the DOS prompt, type
            PROMPT $P $G
            The command prompt is in its normal format.

_____ Instructor's Initials

ON YOUR OWN

5.   Using the DOS HELP program, find at least one possible value (such as $P) for the PROMPT
        command that has NOT been used. Write the value as well as a short explanation of the value's
        purpose.

6.   Return to the root directory when finished. Write the command used to return to the root
        directory.

MORE DOS COMMANDS

In the previous exercise, the DOS CD command changes the prompt to a different directory. The CHDIR command could have been used instead. CHDIR is the full command name for change directory and the CD command is a shortcut. Be aware there are many shortcuts and different methods to issue the same DOS command. Also, when using the HELP feature within DOS, it does not show the shortcut command, it shows the full command name. Variations of DOS commands can achieve the same result. This chapter is designed as an overview of DOS and does not cover all possible ways of doing the same task. Besides, most technicians have reference books on the operating systems they support.

In the exercise, the FORMAT command is used for the first time. The DOS FORMAT command prepares a disk for use. Most disks come pre-formatted; however, there are vendors who still sell unformatted disks. You may want to completely wipe all information from the disk by using the FORMAT command. When using the FORMAT command /S switch, the system files (the two hidden files and COMMAND.COM) copy to the drive that is being formatted. A similar result can be achieved using the DOS SYS command. For example, if you type **SYS A:** from the command prompt, the two hidden files and COMMAND.COM copy over to a floppy disk (making the disk bootable). The SYS command is a valuable DOS program for technicians especially when working with hard drives and system problems.

Be aware that older DOS versions' SYS command does not work the same as today's versions. The format is the same, but with older versions of DOS, only the two hidden files copy to the disk. Also, with older versions, the COMMAND.COM file must be copied over separately to make a disk or hard drive bootable.

THE AUTOEXEC.BAT FILE

In the exercise, the PROMPT command changed the appearance of the command prompt. However, when the computer boots for the first time, the command prompt is already there. This is because of a special file called the **AUTOEXEC.BAT** file which executes every time the computer starts if it exists in the root directory. The AUTOEXEC.BAT file can execute multiple commands, one right after another. An example of an AUTOEXEC.BAT file is in DOS Figure #3.

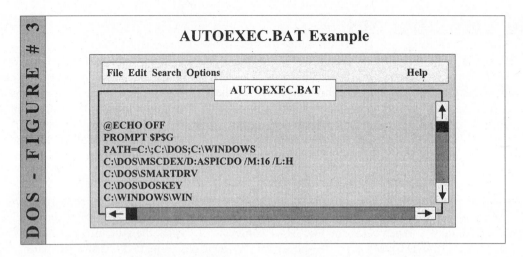

DOS - FIGURE # 3

AUTOEXEC.BAT Example

File Edit Search Options   Help

AUTOEXEC.BAT

@ECHO OFF
PROMPT PG
PATH=C:\;C:\DOS;C:\WINDOWS
C:\DOS\MSCDEX/D:ASPICD0 /M:16 /L:H
C:\DOS\SMARTDRV
C:\DOS\DOSKEY
C:\WINDOWS\WIN

The first line of the AUTOEXEC.BAT is @ECHO OFF. The **ECHO OFF** command prevents other AUTOEXEC.BAT commands from showing on the screen while the computer boots. The **@** symbol in front of ECHO OFF keeps the words ECHO OFF from also showing. The second line of the AUTOEXEC.BAT file is **PROMPT PG** which is the same command used in the exercise and it sets the command prompt's appearance.

The third line, the PATH= statement, is very important to include in the AUTOEXEC.BAT file. The PATH= command instructs DOS where to look for commands. For example, if you are at the root directory and you type HELP at the command prompt, DOS will look for the HELP.COM file in the root directory. DOS always looks in the current directory first. HELP.COM is not normally located in the root directory, so a message will appear: "Bad command or file name." However, the PATH statement tells DOS to look in the other directories listed after the equal (=) sign. A semicolon separates each directory in the PATH statement. The C:\ tells DOS to look in the root directory. The C:\DOS tells DOS to look in the DOS directory; C:\WINDOWS tells DOS to look in the WINDOWS directory for the HELP.COM file.

The PATH statement should always include (1) the root directory, (2) the DOS directory, (3) the WINDOWS directory (if Windows is used), and (4) any frequently used directory.

The fourth line of the AUTOEXEC.BAT file is C:\DOS\MSCDEX /D:ASPICD0 /M:16 /L:H. MSCDEX is an executable file located in the DOS directory and controls CD-ROM drives. The C:\DOS portion of the command defines the command's path. The **path** tells DOS in what directory to find a command. The */D:ASPICD0 /M:16 /L:H* portion is the parameters and switches used to configure the MSCDEX software program. MSCDEX.EXE is the full filename of the DOS program, yet only the name, MSCDEX, is in the line of the AUTOEXEC.BAT file.

DOS does not require the full name of a file. DOS simply looks for files that have file extensions of COM, EXE, or BAT. These files are DOS **executable files**. For ease of troubleshooting, all lines in the AUTOEXEC.BAT file should contain the file's full path (even though the file may be in one of the directories listed in the PATH statement).

The fifth line of the AUTOEXEC.BAT file is C:\DOS\SMARTDRV. The file SMARTDRV.EXE is an executable file located on the hard drive in the DOS directory. **SmartDrive** is a caching program used with hard drives and CD-ROMs. The sixth line involves the DOSKEY program. **DOSKEY** allows the use of the arrow keys to bring up previously entered DOS commands. DOSKEY is a favorite of many technicians and is used to save time while typing commands. DOS Table #1 lists the keys used with DOSKEY.

DOS - TABLE # 1

Keys Used with DOSKEY

Key	Function
Up arrow	Recalls the last typed command
Down arrow	Recalls commands
ESC	Clears current command
F7	Command history
F8	Searches command history
F9	Selects a command by number
ALT+F7	Clears command history
ALT+F10	Clears macro definitions

Even if the DOSKEY program is not used, the function keys on the keyboard allow a small amount of DOS command control. For example, the **F1 function key** displays the last DOS command one character at a time. The **F3 function key** displays all the last DOS command characters.

The last line of the AUTOEXEC.BAT, C:\WINDOWS\WIN, starts the Microsoft Windows program. The Windows program is located on the C: drive in the WINDOWS directory. Notice even though the executable file is WIN.COM, only WIN displays on the command line.

The AUTOEXEC.BAT file is a potential source of problems with computers. Because the commands do not show on the screen, one cannot easily tell if all programs and commands in the AUTOEXEC.BAT file execute. Today's DOS and Windows 95 operating systems provide an easy way to troubleshoot AUTOEXEC.BAT file problems through the use of the F8 key.

As the computer boots and the message "Starting MS-DOS" appears, press the **F8** key on the keyboard. Each line of the AUTOEXEC.BAT file executes one command at a time. If the AUTOEXEC.BAT and CONFIG.SYS files are to be bypassed, press the **F5** key when the message "Starting MS-DOS" appears. However, pressing the F5 key can cause even more problems. Some important hardware pieces such as hard drives or CD-ROMs sometimes have commands in these files that allow them to operate.

Much more information about troubleshooting specific problems with the AUTOEXEC.BAT file is included in the Memory, Hard Drive, and CD-ROM chapters.

COPYING FILES

The two DOS commands used most frequently to copy files are COPY and XCOPY. The difference between the two commands is that **COPY** is an internal DOS command and **XCOPY** is an external command residing on a disk or a hard drive. Either command is able to copy a file to a different disk, copy a file from one directory to another, copy a group of files using wildcards, or rename a file as it is being copied. XCOPY can copy multiple files and directories under other directories, but the COPY command cannot. With older versions of DOS, the COPY command replaces a file with the same name as the file being copied without any warning or prompting. However, with newer versions of DOS, a warning message appears asking if the file is to be replaced. The COPY AND XCOPY command has three parts with each part separated by a space:
1.   the command itself (COPY or XCOPY)
2.   the source (the file being copied)
3.   the destination (where the file is being copied)
The destination is optional if the file copies into the current directory. For example, if working from the A:\> command prompt and copying the DOCUMENT file from the hard drive's root directory, then the command could be COPY C:\DOCUMENT. The destination is omitted because the file will automatically copy to the current drive and directory (which is A:\)

The command requires all three parts if the destination is *not* the current drive and directory. For example, take the situation of being at the C:\> command prompt. To copy the FORMAT.COM command from the hard drive to a disk located in the A: drive, type the following command: COPY C:\DOS\FORMAT.COM A:\ Note that the COPY command is first. Then the source, the location and name of the file being copied — C:\DOS\FORMAT.COM, is next. Last is the destination, A:\, where the file is to be placed. If the current directory is the DOS directory of the hard drive (C:\DOS>), then the source path, C:\DOS, does not have to be typed. Instead the command looks like the following:

C:\DOS> COPY FORMAT.COM A:\

The backslash (\) after the A: is not necessary if the floppy drive does not have directories. The COPY command does not need the entire path in front of the command because COPY is an internal DOS command. Internal DOS commands are part of COMMAND.COM and DOS can always find internal commands no matter where in the tree structure the command executes.

Common mistakes new technicians make involve a command's correct path. The safest way when you are first learning is to type the complete path of both the source and destination locations. When using any DOS command, consider several things: (1) what command to issue; (2) where the command is located in the tree structure (3) where in the tree structure you are currently working; and (4) if copying a file or moving a file, in what directory does the file need to be placed.

THE XCOPY COMMAND

The XCOPY command is more powerful and faster than the DOS COPY command. The XCOPY command allows the copying of directories, subdirectories, and files; however, the XCOPY command does not copy over hidden or system files. The syntax or typing format for the XCOPY command includes the command, a source, and a destination just like the COPY command. If the destination is omitted, the XCOPY command copies the source files to the current directory. With DOS 6, if the destination is not a current directory and does not end with a backslash, a message appears asking if the destination is a filename or a directory. If you select directory, a new directory is created.

If you have a disk containing files in subdirectories to be copied to a different capacity disk, the XCOPY is a great command to use. There is a DISKCOPY command that copies entire disks, but DISKCOPY does not work on different capacity disks.

Name _____

COPY EXERCISE

Objective: Correctly use the COPY command

Parts: A computer with DOS loaded
            A formatted disk

For each step requiring a typed command the *ENTER* key must be pressed to execute the DOS command. This instruction will *not* be given with each step.

Step   1:   Turn the computer on and boot from the hard disk.

Question 1:   Does the computer boot to a prompt? If the computer automatically boots into the Windows program, press and hold **ALT**. Then, press **F4** and release both keys. When a dialog box appears on the screen informing you that you are ending your Windows session, press **ENTER**. If the computer still does not boot to a prompt, and you followed every step correctly, contact your instructor.

Step   2:   Type
            CD\DOS

Question 2:   What is the purpose of the CD command?

Step   3:   Type
            COPY FORMAT.COM A:
            A message appears stating that one file copied. If the message does not appear, re-do Steps 2 and 3.
Step   4:   Type
            COPY XCOPY.EXE A:
            A message appears stating that one file copied. If the message does not appear, perform Step 4 again.

Question 3:   Do a directory of the floppy disk to verify the two files copied properly. List the command used to perform this step.

Question 4:   Why did the source files, FORMAT.COM and XCOPY.EXE, *not* require the complete path of C:\DOS\FORMAT.COM and C:\DOS\XCOPY.EXE?

Question 5:   Could the backslash (\) be omitted in the command's destination (A:\)? Why or why not?

Step   5:   Type
             A:
             CD
             MD\TEST
             The A: command makes the floppy disk the default drive. The CD\ command moves to the root directory. The MD command is used to make a directory. The MD\TEST command creates a directory called TEST.

Step   6:   Type
             COPY C:\DOS\ATTRIB.EXE A:\TEST
             A message appears stating that one file copied. If a message does not appear, re-do step 6.

Question 6:   What does the command in Step 6 do?

Step   7:   To verify step 6, type
             CD\TEST
             DIR
             The command prompt should be A:\TEST>. The ATTRIB.EXE command is the only file listed in the TEST directory. If not, perform Steps 5 through 7 again.

Step   8:   Multiple files can be copied using wildcards. For example, to copy all DOS files that begin with the letter F to the TEST directory on the floppy disk, type
             COPY C:\DOS\F*.* A:\TEST
             When the copying is complete, a message appears stating how many files copied. If the message does not appear, perform the step again.

Question 7:   Why are two asterisks used in Step 8?

Question 8:   Is the A:\TEST a necessary part of Step 8's command? Why or why not?

Step   9:   The COPY command can also copy a file and rename it at the same time. For example, to copy the AUTOEXEC.BAT file to a disk and rename the file to AUTOEXEC.BAK, type the following command:
             COPY C:\AUTOEXEC.BAT A:\AUTOEXEC.BAK
             A message appears stating that one file copied. If the message does not appear, perform the step again.

Question 9:   Verify the AUTOEXEC.BAT file copies to the disk's root directory. Write the command used to verify the copying.

ON YOUR OWN

1.   Create a backup copy of the CONFIG.SYS file located in the hard drive's root directory. Name the file CONFIG.BAK and save it to the floppy drive's root directory. Complete everything using *one* DOS command. Write the command in the space below:

2.   Verify that the CONFIG.BAK file is in the floppy drive's root directory. Write *each* DOS command used to verify the file in the space below:

3.   Reboot the computer and verify that each line of the AUTOEXEC.BAT file loads properly. Refer to the chapter for instructions. Write step-by-step instructions to perform this step.

Name _____

XCOPY, ERASE, DELETE, AND DELTREE EXERCISE

Objective: Correctly use the XCOPY, ERASE, DELETE, and DELTREE commands

Parts: A computer with DOS loaded
         A formatted disk

For each step requiring a typed command the *ENTER* key must be pressed to execute the DOS command. This instruction will *not* be given with each step.

Step 1:   Power on the computer and boot from the hard disk. Be sure the computer is at the C:\DOS> prompt.
Step 2:   Insert a disk into the A: drive and type
          XCOPY F*.* A:\TEST1
          If using a higher version of DOS, a message appears asking if TEST1 is a file or a directory. Press **D** for directory. A message appears stating the number of files copied. If the message does not appear, re-do Steps 1 and 2.

Question 1:   What does the command in Step 2 do?

Step 3:   Type
          XCOPY F*.* A:\NAME
          If using a higher version of DOS, a prompt appears asking if NAME is a file or a directory. Press **D** for directory. A message appears stating the number of files copied. If the message does not appear, re-do Step 3.

Question 2:   How is the command in Step 3 different from the COPY command?

There are several ways to delete files in DOS. The ERASE, DEL (DELETE), and DELTREE are the most common commands for deleting files.

Step 4:   Type
          ERASE A:\NAME*.*
          A message appears, "All files in directory will be deleted. Are you sure (Y/N)?"
Step 5:   At the "Are you Sure (Y/N)?" prompt, press **Y** for YES.

A handy DOS command used frequently is the **UNDELETE** command which can sometimes recover deleted files. Use the UNDELETE command as soon as possible before saving any other files. A greater probability exists for files to be recovered if the UNDELETE command is used immediately after deleting the file.

Step 6: Type:
         UNDELETE A:\NAME*.*
         A message appears stating the number of deleted files and the number of files that may be recovered. Another message appears such as shown below:
         ?IND EXE 6770 9-30-93 6:20a ...A Undelete (Y/N)?
         If the message does not appear, perform the step again.
Step 7: At the prompt, press **Y** for Yes. Another message appears such as shown below:
         Please type the first character for ?IND .EXE:
Step 8: Press **F** for the filename's first letter. A message appears stating that the file was successfully undeleted. Determining the first letter of the filename is easy in this case. In Step 2, you copied only the files beginning with the letter F. However, if the filenames are not known, use your best guess for supplying the first letter of the filename.
Step 9: Messages continue to appear for each file deleted. Always press **Y** for Yes when prompted to undelete and type **F** for the first letter of the filename. Continue this procedure until all files are undeleted.
Step 10: From the DOS prompt, type
         DEL A:\NAME*.*

Question 3: Verify the deletion of all files within the NAME directory. Write the command(s) used to verify the file deletions in the area below. Return to the *hard drive's DOS* directory when you have finished.

ON YOUR OWN

1. UNDELETE *one* file from the A:\NAME directory. Write down the command you use to perform this step. How did you know what filename to use?

Another handy DOS command is the **DELTREE** command which erases entire directories and subdirectories including the directory and/or subdirectory name. Yet the ERASE and DEL commands leave the directory name intact. The **RD** or RMDIR (Remove Directory) command removes the directory name only if all the directory's files are deleted prior to issuing the RD command.

Step 11:   Verify the disk is in the first floppy drive. Type
          A:
          CD\TEST1
          MD\SUB1
          MD\SUB2
          MD\SUB3

Question 4:   Using the XCOPY command, copy all of the files located in TEST1 to each subdirectory, SUB1, SUB2, and SUB3 on the floppy disk. Verify the files copied into each subdirectory. Write the commands you used.

Question 5:   Draw a tree of the floppy disk's file structure in the area below:

_____ Instructor's Initials

Step 12:   From the C:\DOS prompt, type
          DELTREE A:\TEST1
          A message appears stating "Delete directory Test1 and all its subdirectories? [yn]." If the message does not appear, repeat the step.

Step 13:   At the prompt, press **Y** for Yes. After deletion, the command prompt reappears.

An important note to remember is the UNDELETE command does *not* work on a directory deleted using the DELTREE command.

Name _____

DOSKEY EXERCISE

Objective: Use the DOSKEY program efficiently

Parts: A computer with DOS loaded
          A formatted disk

For each step requiring a typed command the *ENTER* key must be pressed to execute the DOS command. This instruction will *not* be given with each step.

Step   1:   Power on the computer and boot from the hard disk.

Question 1:   Does the computer boot to a prompt? If the computer automatically boots into the Windows program, press and hold **ALT**. Then, press **F4** and release both keys. When a dialog box appears on the screen informing you that you are ending your Windows session, press **ENTER**. If the computer still does not boot to a prompt, and you followed every step correctly, contact your instructor.

Step   2:   From the command prompt, type
            CD\DOS
Step   3:   To install the DOSKEY program from the prompt, type
            DOSKEY
Step   4:   Insert the disk into the first floppy drive.
Step   5:   From the command prompt, type
            A:
            MD\SPECIAL
Step   6:   Verify the creation of the directory by typing
            CD\SPECIAL

Question 2:   Did the command prompt change to the A:\SPECIAL> directory? If not, re-do Steps 4 through 6.

On Your Own
1.   While in the A:\SPECIAL directory, copy all the DOS files that begin with the letter C from the hard drive to the A:\SPECIAL directory. Verify all the files copied. Write each command used. Refer to prior exercises and chapter notes if needed.

Step 7:   The DOSKEY program allows use of the arrow keys and function keys (the F1 through F12 keys on the keyboard). Press the **up arrow** once. The last typed command appears at the prompt. If the last command does not appear, then DOSKEY is not loaded properly. Perform Steps 2 through 7 again.

Step 8:   Press the **up arrow** until the MD\SPECIAL command appears at the command prompt. *Do not* press ENTER when the command appears.

Step 9:   Press the **left arrow** key 3 times until the blinking cursor is under the I in SPECIAL. *DO NOT PRESS ENTER*. The arrow keys, when used with DOSKEY, allow movement through the command line.

Step 10:   While the cursor is blinking under the letter I, type the letter **T**. *DO NOT PRESS ENTER*. The command should now read MD SPECTAL. DOSKEY is automatically in the typeover mode.

Step 11:   Press **INS** (Insert), but *DO NOT PRESS ENTER*. The cursor changes to a blinking box.

Step 12:   While the cursor is a blinking box over the letter A, type the letter **R**. The command changes to SPECTRAL because pressing the INS key causes DOSKEY to go into the insert mode.

Step 13:   Press ENTER to create a directory named SPECTRAL.

Step 14:   Press the **up arrow** key once.   The last command typed appears on the screen.

Step 15:   Press **ESC** (Escape) once. ESC erases the current command from the command prompt.

Step 16:   Press **F7** once. A list of all typed commands appears on the screen.

Step 17:   Press **F9** once. The Line Number: prompt appears. While in DOSKEY, F9 allows you to enter a specific command based on a line number (that showed when you pressed F7).

Step 18:   Type the number corresponding to the **A:** command such a 1, then press **ENTER**. The A: command appears at the command prompt.

Step 19:   Press **ESC** to clear the command.

Step 20:   Press and *hold down* **ALT**. While holding ALT down, press **F7** once, then release both keys. DOSKEY uses ALT+F7 to clear the list of commands DOSKEY tracks. Sometimes, pressing the F7 key is cumbersome to use because the command list is so long. Clearing the command list allows DOSKEY to start over tracking commands.

Step 21:   Press **F7** to verify the command list is clear.

_____ Instructor's Initials

THE ATTRIB COMMAND

The **ATTRIB** command sets, removes, or shows the attribute of a file or a directory. Attributes change how a file or directory displays on the screen or what can be done with the file or directory. Possible attributes include read-only, archive, system, and hidden. The **read-only attribute** protects files so they cannot be accidentally changed or deleted. For example, the AUTOEXEC.BAT and CONFIG.SYS files start and configure a computer. Make these two files read-only so they are not accidentally changed or deleted by a user. The **archive attribute** marks files that have changed since they were last backed up by a backup program. The RESTORE, XCOPY, and MSBACKUP commands use the archive attribute as well as any other backup software program. The **system attribute** designates a file as a system file. Files with this attribute do not show in directory listings. The **hidden attribute** allows file hiding and even directory hiding. Technicians frequently use the hidden attribute. If another person has hidden some files and the technician wants to see the files without having to change the attributes of all the files, then the **DIR ,** command displays all the files no matter what attributes the files possess.

Set each attribute using the +x switch where the +R switch adds the read-only attribute, the +S switch adds the system attribute, the +H adds the hidden attribute, and the +A adds the archive attribute. Remove each attribute using the -R, -S, -H, or -A switch with the ATTRIB command. One command can set more than one attribute on files or directories. For example, to make the CHERYL.TXT file hidden and read-only, type **ATTRIB +R +H CHERYL.TXT**.

An excellent use of the archive attribute is to copy multiple files onto a disk. Normally, if copying too many files, there is no warning that the disk cannot hold all the files until it is too late and the disk runs out of room. Traditionally, people used the BACKUP and RESTORE commands to get around this problem. However, the ATTRIB command (with the +A switch) and the XCOPY command (with the /M switch) together can copy files across multiple disks. For example, all the DOS files require more than one disk. If copying all the files to a disk, DOS copies as many files as possible, then produces an error saying the destination disk is full. To prevent this problem, use the ATTRIB command and assign all the DOS files the archive attribute. Type **ATTRIB +A C:\DOS*.*** then insert a disk into the A: drive and type **XCOPY C:\DOS*.* A: /M**. When the XCOPY command stops and displays the error message that the destination disk is full, insert a new floppy into the A: drive and repeat the command. The /M switch tells XCOPY not to copy the same files over. The /M switch only copies files that have the archive attribute set. Once the file copies, the file no longer has the archive attribute.

Most technicians have a bootable disk with their favorite utilities and commands on the disk. Different DOS versions come with different utilities. Even the two hidden files and COMMAND.COM are different between vendors and between versions of DOS.

You never know what DOS version you will encounter. Therefore, the DOS version on the bootable disk is the same version of ATTRIB that needs to be on the disk. Be careful executing DOS commands from a floppy disk if the machine did not boot from that floppy.

MOVING AROUND IN DOS

The most frequently used command for moving around in the cumbersome DOS tree structure is CD (Change Directory). Take, for example, a disk with a TEST1 directory has subdirectories called SUB1, SUB2, and SUB3 as shown in DOS Figure #4.

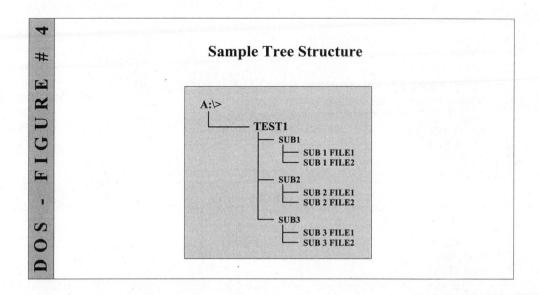

Assume the DOS prompt is at A:\>. To move to the SUB2 subdirectory, type the command **CD TEST1\SUB2**. The command prompt changes to A:\TEST1\SUB2 >. Another command that will work is CD A:\TEST1\SUB2. To move to a subdirectory that is on the same level as the SUB2 directory (such as SUB1 or SUB3), several commands are possible. The easiest and fewest keystrokes are CD SUB1. Notice there is not a backslash (\) between the CD and the SUB1. Omit the backslash only when moving along the same level in the tree structure shown in DOS Figure #4. The commands CD\SUB1, or CD A:\TEST1\SUB1, or CD TEST1\SUB1 will each take you to subdirectory SUB1. However, if the command prompt is currently located at the root directory, (A:\ >), either A:\TEST1\SUB1 or CD TEST1\SUB1 must be used. The other commands given do not operate properly because of the current location within the tree structure.

Practice is the only way to get good at moving around within DOS. The following exercise should help with these concepts.

Name _____

USING ATTRIB AND MOVING AROUND IN DOS EXERCISE

Objective: Correctly use the ATTRIB command

Parts: A computer with DOS loaded
          A formatted disk

For each step requiring a typed command the *ENTER* key must be pressed to execute the DOS command. This instruction will *not* be given with each step.

Step 1:   Power on the computer and boot from the hard disk. Be sure the computer is at the C:\DOS> prompt.

Step 2:   On the disk, make a directory called JUNK. Type
           A:
           MD JUNK

Step 3:   Under the JUNK directory make subdirectories called SUB1, SUB2, and SUB3. Type
           CD JUNK
           MD SUB1
           MD SUB2
           MD SUB3

Step 4:   Return to the floppy drive's root directory. Be sure the root directory is the default directory by looking at the command prompt after returning to the root directory.

Question 1:   What command makes the floppy drive's root directory the default directory? What does the command prompt look like?

Step 5:   Make a new directory called TRASH from the root directory of the floppy drive. Within the TRASH directory, make subdirectories called SUB1, SUB2, and SUB3. Type
           MD TRASH
           CD TRASH
           MD SUB1
           MD SUB2
           MD SUB3

Step 6:   Return to the floppy drive's root directory.

ON YOUR OWN

1. Make a new directory called GARBAGE from the floppy drive's root directory. Within the GARBAGE directory, make subdirectories called SUB1, SUB2, and SUB3. Write each command that you use.

2. Copy the AUTOEXEC.BAT and CONFIG.SYS commands from the root directory of the hard drive and place them in the GARBAGE SUB1 subdirectory on the floppy drive. Write each command that you use.

3. Copy all files that begin with the letter F from the DOS directory on the hard drive and place them in the TRASH directory SUB3 subdirectory on the floppy drive. Write each command that you use.

4. Copy all files that begin with R from the DOS directory of the hard drive and place them in the SUB2 subdirectory of the JUNK directory. Write each command that you use.

_____ Instructor's Initials

Step 7:   The DOS **TREE** command is useful for viewing the file structure of a disk or a drive. Type
TREE
A viewing of the disk structure displays on the screen. If the tree structure does not appear, perform the step again.

Step 8:   The DOS TREE command also verifies files within the tree structure when using the */F* switch. Type
A:
TREE /F
A listing of the three directories, TRASH, GARBAGE, and JUNK displays as well as the SUB1, SUB2, and SUB3 subdirectories. The */F* switch causes the files within each subdirectory to appear. The SUB2 subdirectory of JUNK holds the R DOS files. The SUB1 subdirectory of GARBAGE holds the AUTOEXEC.BAT and CONFIG.SYS files. The SUB3 subdirectory of TRASH holds the F DOS files. Repeat the On Your Own Steps 2 through 4 if these files do not appear on the screen.

Step 9:   To make the AUTOEXEC.BAT and CONFIG.SYS files read-only, use the ATTRIB command with the *+R* switch. Type
ATTRIB +R A:\GARBAGE\SUB1*.*

Step 10:   To verify the read-only attribute is set, type
           ATTRIB A:\GARBAGE*.* /S
           The */S* switch, when used with the ATTRIB command, shows the attribute of any
           subdirectory file. The SUB1 subdirectory of the GARBAGE directory should list two files
           and both have an R beside them indicating that the read-only attribute is set. If the two files
           do NOT have the read-only attribute set, perform Steps 9 and 10 again.

Step 11:   The best way to prove that the files are read-only is to try to delete them. Type
           DEL A:\GARBAGE\SUB1*.*
           A message appears on the screen stating "All files in directory will be deleted. Are you sure
           (Y/N)?"

Step 12:   From the prompt, type **Y** for Yes. A message appears on the screen stating "Access
           denied." Then, the command prompt appears. If the access denied message does not appear,
           the files were deleted which means the read-only attribute was not set. If this is the case,
           perform On Your Own Step 2, followed by Steps 9, 10, 11 and 12 of this exercise.

Step 13:   Hiding a directory is always useful to a technician. Users that constantly delete directories
           or files by mistake can sometimes be controlled by using the ATTRIB command's *+H*
           switch. Type
           ATTRIB +H A:\JUNK\SUB2
           No message appears on the screen. The command prompt appears again.

Step 14:   To verify that the directory is hidden, type
           DIR A:\JUNK*.
           Only the subdirectories under JUNK appear, not the files within the subdirectories.

If viewing only the directories or subdirectories, the DIR *. command is very handy. Notice that
the command is *not* DIR *.*, but instead uses only one asterisk.

Step 15:   The two hidden files that make a disk or a drive bootable are automatically marked as
           system files. Type
           ATTRIB C:*.*
           The two system files list similar to the example below:
               A   SHR   C:\IO.SYS
               A   SHR   C:\MSDOS.SYS
           The SHR indicates that the two hidden files have the system, hidden, and read-only
           attributes set. If a similar display does not appear, type the command in Step 15 again. If
           there are more files than will fit on one screen, type
           ATTRIB C:*.* |more
           The symbol before the word *more* is called the **pipe symbol**. For most keyboards, create the
           pipe symbol by holding down the shift key and pressing the backslash key. The symbol
           looks like two vertical dashes on the keyboard key. The pipe symbol and the word *more* are
           used with many DOS commands that do not have a switch such as */P* to display one screen
           at a time.

ON YOUR OWN (cont.)

5.   Hide the FIND command in the SUB3 subdirectory of the TRASH directory. Write the command you used.

6.   Verify that the FIND command is hidden by using the ATTRIB command. Write the command you used.

_____ Instructor's Initials

7.   Remove the hidden attribute from the FIND command in the SUB3 subdirectory of the TRASH directory. Use DOS HELP, if necessary to find the switch to remove an attribute. Write the command used in the space below:

Step 16:   Have a classmate verify that the FIND file is no longer hidden.

Classmate's printed name: _____

Classmate's initials: _____

Step 17:   Make the current drive the floppy drive's root directory. If the command prompt is not A:\>, try this step again and refer to prior notes and exercises.
Step 18:   To move around within DOS directories can be very trying when first using DOS. Move to the SUB3 subdirectory of the TRASH directory by typing
           CD TRASH\SUB3
           The command prompt changes to A:\TRASH\SUB3>.
Step 19:   To move to the SUB2 or the SUB1 directory is much simpler because the SUB1 and SUB2 directories are on the same level as SUB3. Type
           CD SUB1
           The command prompt changes to A:\TRASH\SUB1>.
Step 20:   A shortcut to move up one directory is to type **CD..** from within the SUB1 subdirectory and the prompt immediately changes to one level up (the TRASH directory). Type
           CD..
           The command prompt changes to A:\TRASH.
Step 21:   Using the CD.. command again returns one level back in the directory structure to the root directory of the floppy drive. Type
           CD..
           The command prompt changes to A:\.

ON YOUR OWN (cont.)

8.   From the root directory of the floppy drive, change to the SUB2 subdirectory of the GARBAGE directory. Write the command used in the space below:

Question 2:   How can one verify that the current directory is A:\GARBAGE\SUB2?

9.   From the A:\GARBAGE\SUB2 subdirectory, change the current directory to the *SUB3* subdirectory of the *TRASH* directory. Write the command you use.

Step 22:   Have a classmate verify that the current directory is A:\TRASH\SUB3.

Classmate's printed name: _____

Classmate's initials: _____

Step 23:   Using the **CD..** command, move from **A:\TRASH\SUB3** to **A:\TRASH**.
Step 24:   Using the **CD..** command, move from **A:\TRASH** to **A:**.

ON YOUR OWN (cont.)

10.   Using the **DELTREE** command, delete the TRASH and GARBAGE, directories including all subdirectories underneath them. Write the commands used in the space below:

11.   Using the **DEL** and the **RD** command, delete the **JUNK** directory and all subdirectories underneath. Write the commands used in the space below:

_____ Instructor's Initials

THE TYPE COMMAND

Another useful command is the **TYPE** command used to display text (.TXT) or batch (.BAT) files on the screen. Many times README.TXT or READ.ME files are included with software applications and utilities. The TYPE command allows viewing these files; however, most of the time, these files occupy more than one screen. So, using the |more parameter after the TYPE command permits viewing the file one screen at a time. For example, TYPE README.TXT|MORE allows viewing the text file one page at a time. Sometimes though, a technician needs a printout of a text file. In this case, use the redirect symbol, (the greater than sign>). For example, if the name of the file to be printed is README.TXT, then typing TYPE README.TXT >LPT1 sends the text file to the printer instead of the screen.

THE CONFIG.SYS FILE

The two files that execute automatically (if present) are AUTOEXEC.BAT and CONFIG.SYS. The **CONFIG.SYS** file customizes and configures the computer's environment. It contains parameters such as how many files can be used by a program or how many file buffers are allocated. Pieces of software called **device drivers** allow hardware devices to operate. Device drivers load through the CONFIG.SYS file.

Restart the computer for the changes made to the CONFIG.SYS or AUTOEXEC.BAT files to take effect.

An example CONFIG.SYS file is in DOS Figure #5.

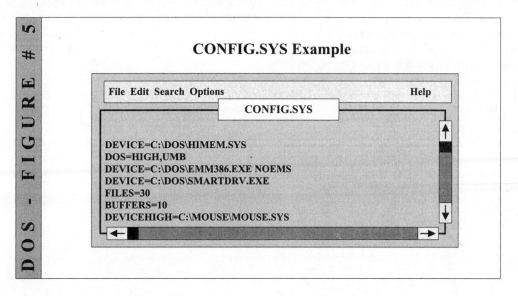

DOS - FIGURE # 5

CONFIG.SYS Example

File Edit Search Options   Help

CONFIG.SYS

```
DEVICE=C:\DOS\HIMEM.SYS
DOS=HIGH,UMB
DEVICE=C:\DOS\EMM386.EXE NOEMS
DEVICE=C:\DOS\SMARTDRV.EXE
FILES=30
BUFFERS=10
DEVICEHIGH=C:\MOUSE\MOUSE.SYS
```

The first three lines shown in DOS FIGURE #5 are for memory management. More details on these individual commands are in the memory chapter. The fourth line of the CONFIG.SYS file, DEVICE=C:\DOS\SMARTDRV.EXE is a disk caching manager. The DEVICE= statement at the beginning of the line shows that the SMARTDRV.EXE file loads as a device driver. Another device driver shown in DOS Figure #5 is on line 7, DEVICEHIGH=C:\MOUSE\MOUSE.SYS. The MOUSE.SYS is the device driver that allows the mouse to operate. When using DOS, device drivers always load via the CONFIG.SYS file. Device driver files normally have the file extension of .SYS or .EXE.

Lines 5 and 6 of the CONFIG.SYS file shown in DOS Figure #5, set various parameters for DOS programs. The FILES= statement sets how many files can be open at one time. The BUFFERS= statement sets aside a certain amount of RAM for DOS to use when transferring information to and from a disk. This number is normally lower when using a caching program such as SMARTDRV.EXE.

The order in which programs load in CONFIG.SYS is sometimes a problem. Technicians frequently need to view these files as they execute. The same technique used with the AUTOEXEC.BAT file can be used with the CONFIG.SYS file. As the computer boots and the message "Starting MS-DOS" appears, press the **F8** key and the CONFIG.SYS and AUTOEXEC.BAT files execute one line at a time. The same task can be done when using Windows 95 by pressing **Shift+F8**.

CREATING AUTOEXEC.BAT, CONFIG.SYS, OR BATCH FILES

Technicians frequently modify or create AUTOEXEC.BAT or CONFIG.SYS files. Also, a technician modifies or creates files known as **batch files** that have a .BAT file extension. AUTOEXEC.BAT is an example of a batch file. Batch files can be used to check out hardware, make user menus, or run user programs in an easier fashion. Only batch file creation is covered in this chapter, but there are some good books on the subject (although they are getting harder to find now that DOS is losing popularity).

Programs that create or modify batch programs or the CONFIG.SYS file included with DOS are **COPY CON** (all DOS versions), **E** (PC-DOS editor), or **EDIT** (MS-DOS editor). **COPY CON** (COPY CONSOLE) is the hardest to work with because once you enter a line and press ENTER, the line cannot be modified except through an editor or by creating the entire file again. The **E** and **EDIT** editors that come with IBM and Microsoft DOS are much easier to handle. The following exercises demonstrate all three editors. One should be familiar with COPY CON and EDIT as a minimum.

Name _____

COPY CON EXERCISE

Objective: Correctly use the COPY CON to create a file

Parts: A computer with DOS loaded
         A formatted disk

For each step requiring a typed command the *ENTER* key must be pressed to execute the DOS command. This instruction will *not* be given with each step.

Step   1:   Power on the computer and boot from the hard disk. Be sure the computer is at the C:\DOS> prompt.

Step   2:   From the command prompt, type
           TYPE C:\CONFIG.SYS
           The CONFIG.SYS file appears on the screen. If the CONFIG.SYS file is more than one page, type
           TYPE C:\CONFIG.SYS|MORE

Optional Step 3:   If a printer attaches to the computer, type
           TYPE C:\AUTOEXEC.BAT>LPT1
           The AUTOEXEC.BAT file prints out on the printer. If the file does not print out on the printer, perform Step 3 again or contact the instructor.

Step   4:   To create an AUTOEXEC.BAT file on the floppy disk, the disk must be bootable. Insert a disk that does not contain important data into the A: drive. Type
           FORMAT A: /Q /S
           A message appears stating "Insert new disk for drive A: and press ENTER when ready." If the message does not appear, perform Step 4 again.

Step   5:   At the prompt, press **ENTER**.
           Messages similar to the following appear on the screen:
               Checking existing disk format.
               Saving UNFORMAT information.
               Quickformatting 1.44M
               Format complete.
               System transferred

Step   6:   At the "Volume label (11 characters, ENTER for none)?" prompt, press **ENTER**.
           Disk space and serial number information appear.

Step   7:   At the "Quick Format another (y/n)?" prompt, press **N** for No then press **ENTER**.

Step   8:   To verify that the disk is bootable, reboot the computer with the disk inserted into the floppy drive. The A:\> prompt appears. If the prompt does not appear, re-do Steps 4 through 7.

Question 1:   What does making a disk or a drive *bootable* mean?

Step 9:   When ENTER is pressed after each line, NO messages appear!
           From the A:\ command prompt, type
           COPY CON:AUTOEXEC.BAT
           @ECHO OFF
           ECHO This is a fine mess you've gotten me into Ollie
           ECHO This computer is about to EXPLODE if you
           PAUSE
           ECHO press ENTER one more time.
           ECHO Haven't we completed enough DOS exercises for
           ECHO one class?????
           ECHO LATER GATOR

           Press **F6**. A caret (^) and a Z appears on the screen. Press **ENTER**. A message appears
           stating that one file copied.
Step 10:   Reboot the computer and watch for the messages created in Step 9 to appear on the screen
           as the AUTOEXEC.BAT file automatically executes.

Question 2:   Did the AUTOEXEC.BAT file run okay? If the AUTOEXEC.BAT file does not run
           correctly, perform Steps 9 and 10 again.

Step 11:   Have a classmate verify the AUTOEXEC.BAT file executes properly.

Classmate's printed name: _____

Classmate's initials: _____

Step 12:   Remove the disk from the floppy drive.
Step 13:   Re-boot the computer from the hard drive.

Name _____

PC-DOS EDITOR EXERCISE

Objective: Correctly use the IBM PC-DOS E Editor to create a file

Parts: A computer with PC-DOS loaded
          A formatted disk

For each step requiring a typed command the *ENTER* key must be pressed to execute the DOS command. This instruction will *not* be given with each step.

Step   1:   Power on the computer and boot from the hard disk. Be sure the computer is at the C:\DOS> prompt.
Step   2:   From the command prompt, type
              TYPE C:\CONFIG.SYS
              The CONFIG.SYS file appears on the screen. If the CONFIG.SYS file is more than one page, type
              TYPE C:\CONFIG.SYS|MORE
Optional Step 3:   If a printer attaches to the computer, type
              TYPE C:\AUTOEXEC.BAT>LPT1
              The AUTOEXEC.BAT file prints out on the printer. If the file does not print out on the printer, perform Step 3 again or contact the instructor.
Step   4:   To create an AUTOEXEC.BAT file on the floppy disk, the disk must be bootable. Insert a disk into the A: drive and be sure it does not contain important data. Type
              FORMAT A: /Q /S
              A message appears stating "Insert new disk for drive A: and press ENTER when ready." If the message does not appear, perform Step 4 again.
Step   5:   At the prompt, press **ENTER**.
              Messages similar to the following appear on the screen:
                   Checking existing disk format.
                   Saving UNFORMAT information.
                   Quickformatting 1.44M
                   Format complete.
                   System transferred
Step   6:   At the "Volume label (11 characters, ENTER for none)?" prompt, press **ENTER**.
              Disk space and serial number information appear.
Step   7:   At the "Quick Format another (y/n)?" prompt, press **N** for No then press **ENTER**.
Step   8:   To verify that the disk is bootable, reboot the computer with the disk inserted into the floppy drive. The **A:\>** prompt appears. If the prompt does not appear, re-do Steps 4 through 7.

Question 1:   What three files make a disk bootable?

Step 9:   Go to the DOS directory. Type
            C:
            CD\DOS
Step 10:   From the C:\DOS command prompt type
            E A:\AUTOEXEC.BAT
Step 11:   Type the following using the backspace or arrow keys to correct any mistakes. Press
            ENTER to move the cursor to the next line.
            @echo off
            Echo Sure as Schmidt we are about to get this editing down
            Echo This Schmidt woman is working our fingers to the bone.
            Pause
            Echo No one told me that we would have to type so much
            Echo Folks from Tennessee are cool! Go VOLS!
Step 12:   Press **F4** to save the file and exit the editor.
            The command prompt appears.
Step 13:   Reboot the computer and watch for the messages created in Step 11 to appear on the screen
            as the AUTOEXEC.BAT file automatically executes.

Question 2:   Did the AUTOEXEC.BAT file run okay? If the AUTOEXEC.BAT file does not run
            correctly, perform Steps 9 through 13 again.

Step 14:   Have a classmate verify the AUTOEXEC.BAT file executes properly.

Classmate's printed name: _____

Classmate's initials: _____

Step 15:   Remove the disk from the floppy drive.
Step 16:   Re-boot the computer from the hard drive.

Name_____

MS-DOS EDIT EDITOR EXERCISE

Objective: Correctly use the MS-DOS EDIT Editor to create a file

Parts: A computer with the EDIT editor loaded
        A formatted disk

For each step requiring a typed command the *ENTER* key must be pressed to execute the DOS command. This instruction will *not* be given with each step.

Step   1:   Power on the computer and boot from the hard disk. Be sure the computer is at the C:\DOS> prompt.

Step   2:   From the command prompt, type
             TYPE C:\CONFIG.SYS
             The CONFIG.SYS file appears on the screen. If the CONFIG.SYS file is more than one page, type
             TYPE C:\CONFIG.SYS|MORE

Optional Step 3:   If a printer attaches to the computer, type
             TYPE C:\AUTOEXEC.BAT>LPT1
             The AUTOEXEC.BAT file prints out on the printer. If the file does not print out on the printer, perform Step 3 again or contact the instructor.

Step   4:   To create an AUTOEXEC.BAT file on the floppy disk, the disk must be bootable. Insert a disk that does not contain important data into the A: drive. Type
             FORMAT A: /Q /S
             A message appears stating "Insert new disk for drive A: and press ENTER when ready." If the message does not appear, perform Step 4 again.

Step   5:   At the prompt, press **ENTER**.
             Messages similar to the following appear on the screen:
                  Checking existing disk format.
                  Saving UNFORMAT information.
                  Quickformatting 1.44M
                  Format complete.
                  System transferred

Step   6:   At the "Volume label (11 characters, ENTER for none)?" prompt, press **ENTER**.
             Disk space and serial number information appear.

Step   7:   At the "Quick Format another (y/n)? prompt", press **N** for No then press **ENTER**.

Step   8:   To verify that the disk is bootable, reboot the computer with the disk inserted into the floppy drive. The A:\> prompt appears. If the prompt does not appear, re-do Steps 4 through 7.

Question 1:   What three files make a disk *bootable*?

Step   9:   Go to the DOS directory. Type
              C:
              CD\DOS
Step 10:   From the C:\DOS command prompt type
              EDIT A:\AUTOEXEC.BAT
              The EDIT editor screen appears. The filename, AUTOEXEC.BAT is across the top center
              of the screen. The cursor blinks in the upper left corner.
Step 11:   Type the following using the backspace or arrow keys to correct any mistakes. Press
              ENTER to move the cursor to the next line.
              @echo off
              Echo Sure as Schmidt we are about to get this editing down
              Echo This Schmidt woman is working our fingers to the bone.
              Pause
              Echo No one told me that we would have to type so much
              Echo Folks from Tennessee are cool! Go VOLS!
Step 12:   Press **ALT**. The word File on the menu bar highlights.
Step 13:   Press **F**. The File drop-down menu appears.
Step 14:   Press **X**. A message box appears stating "Loaded file is not saved. Save it now?"
Step 15:   Press **Y** for YES. The command prompt appears.
Step 16:   Reboot the computer and watch for the messages created in Step 11 to appear on the screen
              as the AUTOEXEC.BAT file automatically executes.

Question 2:   Did the AUTOEXEC.BAT file run correctly? If not, perform Steps 9 through 16 again.

Step 17:   Have a classmate verify the AUTOEXEC.BAT file executes properly.

Classmate's printed name: _____

Classmate's initials: _____

Step 18:   Remove the disk from the floppy drive.
Step 19:   Re-boot the computer from the hard drive.

Name _____

DOS Review Questions

1.   List at least two operating systems.

2.   What does an operating system do for a microcomputer?

3.   What file is known as the command interpreter?

4.   T/F   All system files are the same between DOS versions.

5.   T/F   Internal commands are part of the command interpreter.

6.   Give an example of what the command prompt looks like in DOS.

7.   T/F   The root directory is limited in how many files can exist there.

8.   Why should directories be created on a hard disk instead of placing every file in the root directory?

9.   What is the difference between internal and external commands?

10.   What command always allows you to move to the root directory?

11.   Which of the following DOS filenames are valid?
    A.   RAINA.TXT
    B.   KARLTEXT
    C.   KARA.EXE
    D.   TROUBLE.SYS
    E.   THOMAS.BAT

12.   What is the purpose of the FORMAT command's /S switch?

13.   Which of the following commands controls how the command prompt appears? [SHOW, TREE, VIEW, PROMPT]

14.   What do the PG parameters do when used with the PROMPT command?
    A.   Displays the path and > sign
    B.   Displays the drive letter and the > sign
    C.   Keeps the prompt from showing on the screen
    D.   Tells DOS where to find commands

15.   What does the SYS command do?

16.   What is the purpose of the path statement in the AUTOEXEC.BAT file?

17.   What file extensions does DOS look for to execute? (pick all that apply)
       A.   .BAT
       B.   .TXT
       C.   .WIN
       D.   .COM
       E.   .HLP
       F.   .EXT
       G.   .EXE

18.   Which of the following keystrokes allows you to view the last executed DOS command by single characters?
       A.   F1
       B.   F3
       C.   F5
       D.   F7
       E.   F8

19.   Which of the following keystrokes brings up the last executed DOS command?
       A.   F1
       B.   F3
       C.   F5
       D.   F7
       E.   F8

20.   Which command is faster and can copy subdirectories, COPY or XCOPY?

21.   What are some common mistakes technicians make when using the COPY or XCOPY commands?

22.   T/F   The COPY command does not always require a destination.

23.   What is the difference between a directory and subdirectory?

24.   When using the DISKCOPY command to copy a 720KB disk to a 1.44MB disk, the message "Drive types or disk types not compatible" appears. What is the first step to resolving the problem?
       A.   Use a different command, because two different capacity disks cannot be used with the DISKCOPY command
       B.   Nothing, the message is normal
       C.   Reboot the computer and bypass the AUTOEXEC.BAT and CONFIG.SYS files
       D.   Boot from a bootable disk and copy over the COMMAND.COM file

25.   What program allows the use of arrow keys to bring up previously entered DOS commands?

26.   Which of the following commands can be used to delete a file? (Pick all that apply)
        A.   DELTREE
        B.   DEL
        C.   ERASE
        D.   RD

27.   T/F   The ATTRIB command cannot hide directories.

28.   When the following command executes, the message "Invalid path or file not found" appears.
        A:\> ATTRIB +R C:\DIS\FORMAT.BAT
        What causes this message?

29.   When the following command executes, the message "Bad command or file name" appears.
        A:\> ATTRIB +R C:\DOS\FORMAT.BAT
        What causes this error message?

30.   T/F   The UNDELETE command can always recover a deleted file.

31.   T/F   The UNDELETE command recovers formatted disks.

32.   T/F   Files deleted using DELTREE cannot be undeleted.

33.   T/F   Directories deleted using DELTREE cannot be undeleted.

34.   Which of the following command is for viewing text files on the screen?
        A.   VIEW
        B.   SCREEN
        C.   OUTPUT
        D.   TYPE
        E.   EDIT

35.   T/F   Every computer requires the CONFIG.SYS file.

36.   T/F   Every computer requires the AUTOEXEC.BAT file.

37.   What is the difference between the FILES= and the BUFFERS= CONFIG.SYS statements?

38.   T/F   The COPY CON command is easier to use than Microsoft's EDIT editor when editing or creating a file.

Name _____

DOS Fill-in-the-Blank

1.   A computer needs an _____ to operate.

2.   All viewable DOS commands are known as _____ commands.

3.   The first floppy drive is assigned the drive letter _____.

4.   The first hard drive partition is assigned the drive letter _____.

5.   All DOS work is done from the _____.

6.   DOS files are grouped into _____.

7.   The _____ directory is the starting place for all files and directories.

8.   DOS filenames can be up to _____ characters and have _____ letter extensions.

9.   The _____ file, if found, is a batch file that executes when the computer boots.

10.   _____ is the DOS command that keeps batch file commands from showing on the screen.

11.   The _____ DOS command is an external command used for copying files, directories, and subdirectories.

12.   The _____ command copies an entire disk's information to another disk.

13.   The _____ command shows the DOS file structure.

14.   The _____ symbol used with the word *more* is frequently used to show one screen of data at a time.

15.   The _____ file customizes the computer's environment.

16.   _____ are pieces of software that allow hardware to operate.

17.   _____ is the text editor shipped with Microsoft DOS.

Appendix B: Introduction to Windows 95

OBJECTIVES

After completing this chapter you will
  1. Be able to perform basic functions within Windows 95 such as format a disk, copy files, start applications, delete files, shut down, install applications, configure DOS applications, and backup the registry.
  2. Be able to use Windows Explorer, the Find utility, and Help.
  3. Install Windows 95 and troubleshoot installation and startup problems.
  4. Understand the basic function of the registry.

KEY TERMS

BOOTLOG.TXT	REGEDIT
CFGBACK	registry
desktop	roaming profile
ERU	Safe Mode
HKEY_LOCAL_MACHINE	Start button
HKEY_USERS	step-by-step confirmation
HKEY_CURRENT_USER	SYSTEM.DAT
icon	taskbar
IO.SYS	USER.DAT
My Computer	Windows Explorer
Recycle Bin	

WINDOWS 95 OVERVIEW

Windows 95 is Microsoft's 32-bit operating system. Even though Microsoft has developed a more robust and powerful 32-bit operating system called Windows NT Workstation, many home computer users and businesses migrated to Windows 95. For people with Windows 3.x experience, there are some differences, but at least the Graphical User Interface (GUI) is familiar. Windows 95 has a more comprehensive GUI than Windows 3.x. A technician must be familiar with how to use the Windows 95 operating system, install it, install applications, and troubleshoot it. Below is a list of features in Windows 95:

1. Operating system - Windows 95 is a complete operating system, not an operating environment like Windows 3.x. An operating environment requires an operating system to run. For example, Windows 3.x requires DOS to run.
2. GUI - Windows 95 has a GUI similar to some features in Windows 3.x.
3. Software compatibility - Windows 95 runs DOS, Windows 3.x, and 32-bit applications designed for Windows 95.
4. Hardware compatibility - Windows 95 runs on an 80386DX 20MHz or higher microprocessor and recognizes existing floppy drives, hard drives, CD-ROM drives, monitors, and other hardware components.
5. Backward compatibility - Windows 95 supports the DOS file naming scheme as well as Windows 95's own file naming scheme that supports filenames up to 255 characters.
6. Hardware configuration - Window 95's hardware settings and configurations are in a central location called the Registry. Windows 95 supports the Plug and Play standard so adapters can be automatically configured.
7. Built-in networking - Windows 95 has built-in software for peer-to-peer networking.

USING WINDOWS 95: THE FIRST STEPS

Similar to Windows 3.x, when Windows 95 loads, the desktop is the first screen that appears. The **desktop** is where all work is accomplished just as in a real office environment. On the desktop are **icons** which are graphical representations of applications, file folders, and documents.

On the desktop are four standard items: the My Computer icon, Inbox icon, Recycle Bin icon, and the Set Up The Microsoft Network icon. The **My Computer** icon provides access to the computer's drives, files, and applications. The **Recycle Bin** is where deleted files, folder, or applications are placed. The Recycle Bin is similar to a trash can. The files or folders are not actually gone until the trash can (Recycle Bin) is emptied. At the bottom of the desktop is the taskbar. The **taskbar** allows you to switch between different applications. Launched applications and their associated buttons are on the taskbar to the right of the Start button. Also, any open folders appear on the taskbar. Switch between the applications or tasks by clicking on the taskbar buttons. Windows 95 Figure #1 illustrates the Windows 95 desktop.

WINDOWS 95 - FIGURE #1

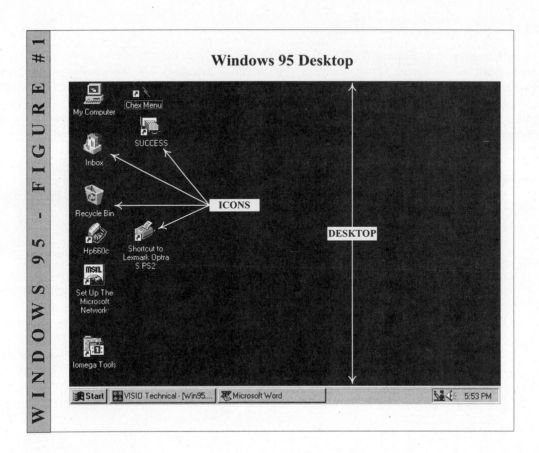

Windows 95 Desktop

START BUTTON

The Start button is on the taskbar. The **Start button** allows you to start applications, open the latest used documents, get help, shut down the computer, customize configuration settings, and find files, folders, or other computers in the network. The Start button also provides access to applications. Click once on the Start button to bring up the Start Menu. Windows 95 Figure #2 shows an example of the menu that appears after clicking the Start button.

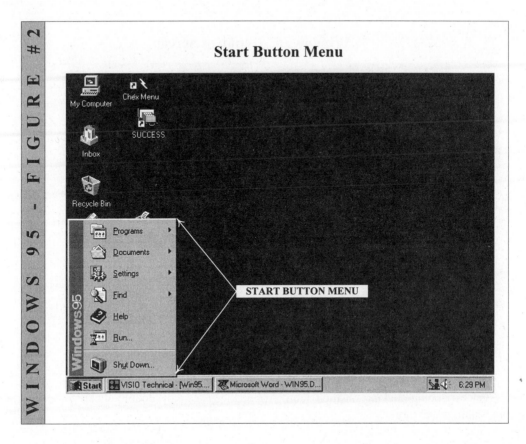

Start Button Menu

WINDOWS 95 - FIGURE #2

START BUTTON MENU

On the Start button menu, the choices of Programs, Documents, Settings, and Find have arrows to the right of them. When selecting one of the options, a separate sub-menu appears. For example, click once on Programs to display a list of all the main application groups. Start any application by clicking on the application's icon.

WINDOWS EXPLORER

The **Windows Explorer** program is on the list of applications started through the *Programs* Start menu option. The Explorer program is similar to the Windows 3.x File Manager. The Explorer window has two parts. The left side of the window lists the hard drive directories in a tree format. The right side lists the contents of the drive or folder selected on the left side. Reference Windows 95 Figure #3 for an example of the Windows Explorer window.

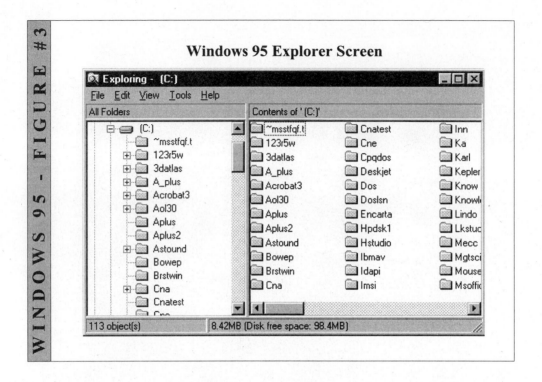

Folders open by double-clicking on their icon. Applications start by double-clicking the program's icon from within the Explorer.

Right-click the drive's icon within Explorer to bring up a menu that allows copying, labeling, and formatting as well as making a system disk or changing the current drive.

START BUTTON (CONT.)

The *Documents* item on the Start button menu, displays a list of the last 15 documents used. Click once on the Documents option. From within the list of documents, click once on any document. The document and the application that created it will open. Not all applications update the list in the Documents option. So, the latest document will not necessarily be there.

The Start menu *Settings* has a menu of its own with options of Control Panel, Printers, and Taskbar. Look at Windows 95 Figure #4 to see how the Settings menu item has a sub-menu that appears to the right.

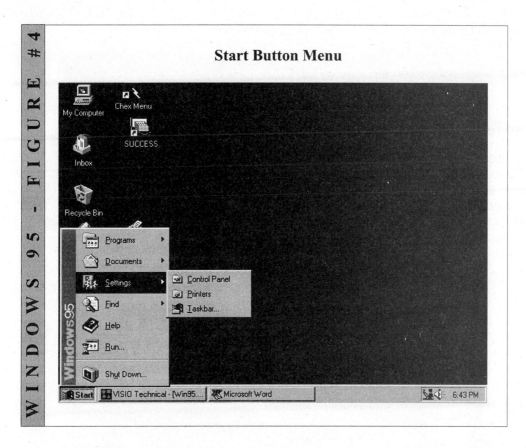

Start Button Menu

WINDOWS 95 - FIGURE #4

The *Control Panel* option is similar to Windows 3.x in that this is where to customize the Windows 95 interface and configure hardware items. The *Printers* option shows an icon for every printer installed and an icon for adding a printer. Double-click on a printer icon to change the printer's configuration and print jobs. The *Taskbar* option allows configuration of the taskbar. When choosing the taskbar option, two tabs appear in a window: Taskbar options and Start Menu Programs. *Taskbar options* determine how the taskbar appears on the desktop. The *Start Menu Programs* tab allows the addition or removal of program icons on the taskbar.

The exercises at the end of the chapter familiarize the technical student with the Windows 95 desktop and demonstrates the basics of using Windows 95.

DELETING FILES IN WINDOWS 95

As with all operations within the Windows 95 environment, deleting files and folders can be accomplished several ways. One method is to click once to select the file or folder icon. Then, choose the **File** option from the menu bar followed by the **Delete** menu option. Another way is to select the icon and press **DEL**. When a file is deleted, the file is sent to the Recycle Bin which is a special holding place for deleted files and folders. Another way to delete the file is to click once on the icon and drag it to the Recycle Bin icon. When a file or folder is in the Recycle Bin, the icon is not actually deleted from the hard drive. Not until the Recycle Bin is emptied is the file really gone.

Keep the Recycle Bin empty to conserve space on the hard drive.

START MENU — FIND OPTION

A technician sometimes needs to quickly find files, applications, or utilities within Windows 95. The Start menu Find option searches for files, folders, or other networked computers. When you click on the Find option, two menu options appear: Files or Folders and Computer. The Files or Folders option is the one most frequently used. The Files or Folders window contains three tabs: Name and Location, Date Modified, and Advanced. Each tab allows you to set different search conditions. Reference Windows 95 Figure #5 for an illustration of the Find window.

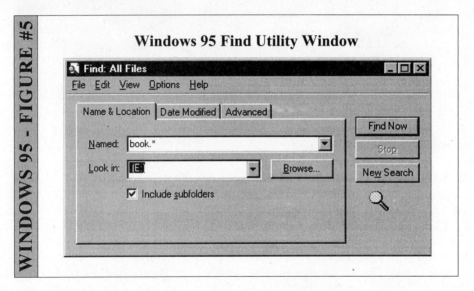

The Name and Location tab allows setting parameters on the name of the file or folder as well as where to look. Enter all or part of a filename into the Named: box. Wildcard characters such as *.DOC can be used. The Look in option is a drop-down list box to select the search drive. An Include subdirectories checkbox allows you to search further in the tree structure.

Use the Date Modified tab when you know the approximate file creation or modification date. The Advanced tab allows (1) the choice of a particular type of file (instead of the default of all files), (2) the choice of a text string to be found within a file, or (3) the choice of a file or folder size. To set the file or folder size, use the At least amount or the At most condition. Click on the Find Now button to execute the search. An application can be executed from the search result by double-clicking on the program in the list.

GETTING HELP IN WINDOWS 95

Online help is available in Windows 95 from the Start menu Help option. Help is also available through the Help option on My Computer or Windows Explorer menu bar. After choosing Help, three tabs appear: Contents, Index, and Find.

The Contents tab is used to look up information sorted by general topic. The topics are sorted into books that include Introducing Windows 95, Your Online User's Guide, How to, Tips and Tricks, and Troubleshooting. Technicians usually have an idea as to what they are looking for and will use the Index tab most often. The Index tab on the Help screen is similar to using a table of contents. After choosing the Index tab, an alphabetical list of topics appears with scroll bars that allow easy movement through the list. A quicker method of search is to type the first few letters of the word or topic being researched, and a list of topics will appear. Once the topic or word is found, double-click the entry to bring up the information in a window. Return to the Help window at any time by clicking on Help Topics button. Reference Windows 95 Figure #6 for an illustration of the Windows 95 Index tab in the Help window.

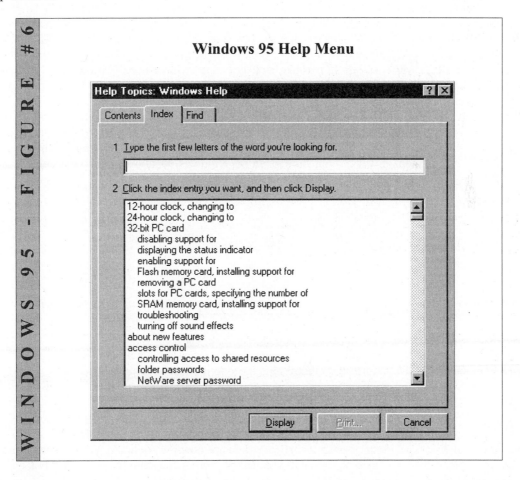

The third tab in the Help window is Find. Use the Find tab to look up a topic by a specific word or phrase. Use the Find tab as a last resort because the search extends to all Windows 95 help files.

SHUTTING DOWN WINDOWS 95

Just as Windows 3.x was never to be shut down while it was still running, Windows 95 requires the same proper shut down.

Never power the computer off without shutting down Windows 95 properly using the Shut Down option.

Shut Down is the last Start Button menu item. Shut down Windows 95 properly to save data and the Windows 95 environment settings without corruption. The Shut Down window shows three or four different options: Shut down the computer, Restart the computer, and Restart the computer in MS-DOS mode. The Close all programs and log on as a different user option is available if your computer is attached to a network.

The Shut down the computer option is used most frequently. This option brings Windows 95 to a safe stopping place while saving all settings and data. After you choose this option, Windows 95 places a message on the screen when it is safe to turn off the power to the computer. Do not shut the computer off until the message appears.

Use the Restart the computer option after installing a new piece of hardware or software. This option is not used very often once the operating system and hardware configurations are complete. The Restart the computer in MS-DOS mode option is available when DOS applications will not run in the Windows 95 environment. Even though the design of Windows 95 allows backward compatibility, some DOS applications have problems running in Windows 95.

Save all document files before going to the MS-DOS mode. Just as with Windows 3.x, return to the Windows 95 environment by typing **EXIT** then press **ENTER**.

MS-DOS APPLICATIONS IN WINDOWS 95 AND THE MS-DOS MODE

Running applications in MS-DOS mode should be a last resort. Windows 95 gives control to the MS-DOS mode and all the features of Windows 95 are lost. Also, when you finish working in the MS-DOS mode and control returns to Windows 95, the system must be restarted.

An MS-DOS Prompt option is available on the Start menu Programs list. The DOS commands execute inside a window that can be controlled by the Windows 95 environment more so than inside the MS-DOS mode of operation available on the Shut Down menu. Most DOS applications run fine within Windows 95 with the Windows 95 default settings for the application. However, MS-DOS applications can have specific properties assigned to enhance how the application runs under Windows 95. For example, right-click once on the DOS application icon or filename from within My Computer or Windows Explorer. Select the Properties option. The Properties option is similar to the PIF editor in

Windows 3.x. Within the Properties option, the Program Properties tab allows setting the path and command line, and the working directory.

The other tabs within the Properties option allow changing fonts, deciding whether the DOS program runs in a normal, maximized, or minimized window, what type of memory to use, and if the screen saver is active during the DOS program. Remember, do not change the DOS application settings chosen by Windows 95 unless absolutely necessary.

If the DOS application crashes, select the Memory tab's Protected checkbox. Also, if that does not work, try changing the expanded or extended memory setting to a reasonable and specific amount (instead of the Windows 95 Auto default). Always refer to the DOS application's manual and only set the type of memory the application uses. See the memory chapter as well.

Other DOS application troubleshooting tips are listed below. Try changing one thing at a time, then run the DOS application. Put the setting back the way it was and try a different recommendation. If the recommendations do not work individually, then try several at a time. Each setting is from within the application's Properties option.

1.   Disable the **Allow screen saver** setting from the Misc tab.
2.   If the DOS application uses text and graphics modes, disable the **Dynamic memory allocation** from the Screen tab.
3.   If the program does not type or place data on the screen correctly, try disabling **Fast ROM Emulation** from the Screen tab.
4.   Using the slider bar on the Misc tab, move the **Idle sensitivity** setting to Low.
5.   If the DOS application uses graphics, select the **Full-screen** option from the Screen tab.

If the DOS application will not operate with any above-mentioned recommendation, click on the Prevent MS-DOS-based programs from detecting Windows checkbox from the Program tab's Advanced button. If this does not work, undo all previous changes. From the Program tab's Advanced settings, click once in the MS-DOS mode checkbox. Then, if the DOS application needs specialized AUTOEXEC.BAT and CONFIG.SYS files, click once in the Specify a new MS-DOS configuration radio button and type the files into the windows provided. See the memory chapter for more on these settings.

As a final note, sometimes Windows 95 recommends running the DOS application in MS-DOS mode. If this is true, simply click the MS-DOS mode checkbox from within Program tab's Advanced button.

RUNNING APPLICATIONS IN WINDOWS 95

Several different methods allow you to start an application. Three ways already described are (1) using the Start menu's Programs option, (2) using the Find option then double-clicking on the program from the Find list, and (3) using the Start menu's Run option. After clicking on the Run option, simply type in the name of the program, folder, or file you want to open. If you are unsure about the location or path of the program, use the Browse button to locate the program.

The Run menu option is easier than using the Find utility only if you know the name and location of the program and the program is in the search path. If you do not know the name and location of the program, you can use the Browse button with the Run menu option. However, the Find utility is a quicker and easier way to run the application.

The **Browse** button is available with many Windows 95 utilities and is used to search through drives and folders similar to using Windows Explorer. The Run option can be used to install software applications. Choose the Run option and type in the drive letter and name of the installation program or use the Browse button. However, Windows 95 has an easier and more efficient utility wizard used to install software called Add/Remove Programs.

INSTALLING SOFTWARE

How an application is installed in Windows 95 depends on whether the application is a Windows 95 application, a Windows 3.x application, or a DOS application. The fastest and easiest way to install an application in Windows 95 is if the application is a Windows 95 application and on a CD. After inserting the CD into the drive, the Install New Program Wizard appears on the screen. This wizard allows you to select preferences regarding the software installation.

To install applications specifically written for Windows 95, use the *Add/Remove Programs* control panel. This utility looks for the proper installation file (INSTALL or SETUP), loads the appropriate software, and updates the Windows 95 Registry.

Use the Add/Remove Programs control panel for installing any Windows 95-based software applications for optimum performance. The Add/Remove Programs utility can remove old versions of DOS and Windows 3.x. Also, it can add or remove Windows 95 applets such as accessories, tutorials, networking options, and the Microsoft Network application. A startup disk (emergency boot floppy) can be created from the Add/Remove Programs control panel.

For a software manufacturer to place the Windows 95 logo on the application's package, the software must include an uninstall program accessed through the Add/Remove Programs utility. How well the uninstall utility performs the de-installation task is still based on the manufacturer who wrote the application.

When removing Windows 3.x applications from the hard drive, parts of the application are left in the INI files. Windows 95 still needs a third party uninstaller utility because so many people still use Windows 3.x-based applications within Windows 95. The Windows 95 Add/Remove Program utility cannot track the old Windows 3.x applications. Nevertheless, the Add/Remove Program utility installs Windows 3.x programs. However, with Windows 3.x applications, double-click the SETUP or INSTALL icon to perform the same function. The FIND utility or the RUN command discussed earlier may also be used to start the installation program. Windows 3.x applications run on top of Windows 95, but Windows 3.x applications are not designed to take advantage of the environment as true Windows 95 applications do.

INSTALLING DOS APPLICATIONS IN WINDOWS 95

DOS applications have many ways they can be installed in Windows 95, but even in the DOS environment this was also true. If the DOS application has an install program, double-click the icon representing the installation program or use the FIND or RUN options. If the DOS application needs to be copied from disks, create a folder for the application. Copy the files from each disk into the new folder.

CONFIGURING DOS APPLICATIONS

Even though DOS applications (and Windows 3.x applications) do not take advantage of the Windows 95 features, running a DOS application through Windows 95 is better than restarting the computer in MS-DOS mode. Configurations for how much memory and what kind of memory the DOS application uses, the font to use with the program, if the application runs in full screen or in a window, changing the program's icon, etc. are all set through the properties option of the DOS executable file's icon. Windows 95 Figure #7 shows the *Properties* window that appears when you right-click on the DOS application's executable icon.

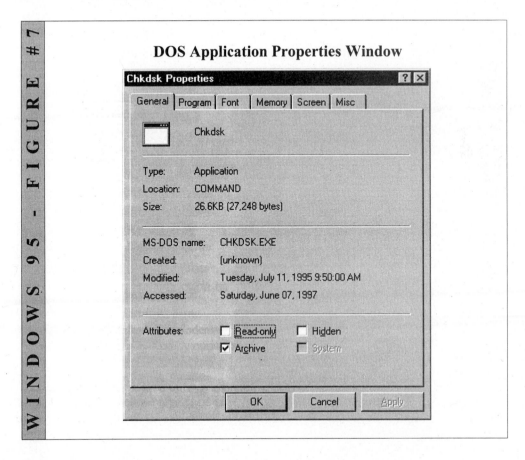

Refer to the chapter section on MS-DOS APPLICATIONS IN WINDOWS 95 AND THE MS-DOS MODE for more information.

The exercises at the end of the chapter allow you to practice with some of the concepts presented. Have fun!

INSTALLING WINDOWS 95

Before installing Windows 95, check over the following checklist. Any question answered with a yes will affect the Windows 95 installation.

1.   Is there another operating system already installed on the computer?
2.   Does the user want to keep the other operating system or environment?
3.   Is the computer a 80486 50MHz or higher microprocessor? (Microsoft recommends a 80386DX 20MHz or higher.)
4.   Does the computer have at least 4MB of RAM (8MB is preferable according to Microsoft)? According to Schmidt, 16MB is preferable.
5.   Does the computer have enough free hard disk space? See Windows 95 Table #1 for the hard drive space requirements.

Windows 95 Hard Disk Space Requirements

Type of Installation	Hard Drive Space
New Installation	40MB
Windows 3.1 Upgrade	30MB
Windows for Workgroups Upgrade	20MB

WINDOWS 95 - TABLE #1

6.   Is the installed computer hardware supported by Windows 95? The Windows 95 installation CD or disks have the README and SETUP.TXT files that contain information about hardware compatibility. When installing Windows 95, if any unsupported hardware is detected, Windows 95 installs a generic driver or uses a driver found on the hard drive.
7.   Has the hard drive been defragmented?
8.   Have all the .INI, .DAT, .PWL, .GRP files from an older Windows version been backed up?
9.   Have the CONFIG.SYS and AUTOEXEC.BAT files been backed up?
10.   Have the software drivers critical to the computer's operation been backed up?
11.   Has a virus check been completed?
12.   If this is an upgrade, has a backup of the hard drive been made?
13.   If upgrading from an older version of Windows, move or delete the Startup group icons.
14.   If upgrading from an older version of Windows, switch the video driver in Windows 3.x to a standard VGA or SVGA driver.

Once these issues are resolved, Windows 95 is ready to be installed. Windows 95 uses a SETUP program. The Windows 95 upgrade SETUP program can be started from the DOS prompt or from Windows 3.x. The preferred method of upgrade installation is through Windows 3.x. If the Windows 95 SETUP program starts from the DOS prompt, SETUP searches for old Windows 3.x files. If SETUP finds the Windows files, a message appears stating to run SETUP from within Windows. At the end of the chapter, an installation exercise demonstrates how to install Windows 95 and keep the DOS/Windows environment as well.

 TROUBLESHOOTING THE WINDOWS 95 INSTALLATION

Understanding the Windows 95 SETUP program steps help in troubleshooting SETUP problems. Below is a condensed version of the SETUP program steps:

1.   SETUP verifies the hardware (microprocessor, RAM, video, and available hard disk space) installed in the computer meets minimum requirements.
2.   SETUP looks for an extended memory manager such as HIMEM.SYS and a disk caching program such as SmartDrive. If either program is missing, Windows 95 loads its own version of SmartDrive.
3.   SETUP checks for incompatible TSRs.
4.   SETUP executes the SCANDISK program.
5.   SETUP switches to protected mode, makes extended memory available, and displays the "Welcome to Setup" message.
6.   SETUP gathers information such as user name, company name, and directory to place Windows 95.
7.   SETUP detects installed hardware devices such as CD-ROM drives, floppy drives, and sound cards.
8.   SETUP copies the Windows 95 files onto the hard disk.
9.   SETUP restarts the computer, configures the hardware, and converts old .GRP files to Windows 95. Some computers require a second restart to finalize hardware detections such as SCSI devices along a SCSI chain. (See the hard drive chapter for information on SCSI.)

Anywhere in the SETUP process, problems can occur. Clean booting into DOS or Windows, disabling all virus protection, removing unessential software drivers, and removing memory resident programs gives a better chance for a clean Windows 95 installation.

Viruses are a common source of Windows 95 installation problems. Boot the computer from a clean boot disk. Run a virus checker. After checking the computer for viruses, disable any anti-virus features through CMOS (if applicable). After installing Windows 95, do not forget to re-enable the virus features in CMOS (if applicable). If a virus infects a SETUP disk, the disk cannot be cleaned or used. The installation disks hold more information than common data disks and have a different type of format.

The SETUP program may hang because the SmartDrive double-buffering is not enabled. Some hard drives require double-buffering. Use the SETUP /C command to prevent SmartDrive from loading during the install process. Another possible problem occurs after SETUP is run from Windows 3.x and it causes the installation process to hang. Try disabling 32-bit disk access from the 386 enhanced control panel before starting the SETUP program again. If that does not solve the problem, run the SETUP program from the DOS prompt.

Problems with SETUP's first two steps sometimes occur due to insufficient hardware, a virus, or virus protection software. Even though the SETUP program actively scans for incompatible TSRs, they can cause problems anywhere in the installation process.

If ScanDisk is the suspect problem, restart the SETUP program using a switch to run ScanDisk in the foreground. Which switch to use depends on whether the SETUP program started from the DOS prompt or from Windows 3.x. Use SETUP /IQ when SETUP starts from DOS; use SETUP /IS when SETUP starts from Windows 3.x. Refer to the hard drive chapter for a thorough explanation of the ScanDisk program.

If Windows 95 hangs during the hardware detection phase, wait for at least *three* minutes to be certain SETUP is not working properly. Shut the computer off with the power button. Do NOT warm boot the computer. Turn the computer on and run the SETUP command again. Choose the **Safe Recovery** option. If SETUP still hangs during the hardware detection stage, perform the Safe Recovery SETUP option again. More than one hardware device may be causing the problem. During the SETUP process, the SETUP program skips a problem device. Each time SETUP hangs during the hardware detection phase, keep turning the computer off (after at least waiting three minutes), re-run SETUP, and choose the Safe Recovery option. Try this many times to see if each time SETUP gets further along in the installation process.

If SETUP will not get past the hardware detection phase in this manner, start the SETUP program. Choose the Full installation option and click on the **Custom Setup** button. When prompted if SETUP is to look for all hardware devices, click on the **No, I want to modify the hardware list** button. In the Hardware Types list, choose generic drivers for the floppy disk controller, hard disk controller, keyboard and mouse. For the display option, choose the **Standard Display Adapter (VGA)** option. Continue on with the installation. After Windows 95 is installed, the remaining hardware devices must be configured manually one-by-one. If SETUP still hangs during the hardware detection phase, continue to use the Custom SETUP option and select other hardware choices for the hardware types mentioned above.

If SETUP hangs after the computer reboots (the first time), the cause is most likely a video driver conflict. Restart the computer by powering off and back on. When the computer displays Starting Windows 95, press **F8**. From the Startup menu on the screen, choose the option for **Safe Mode**. When Windows 95 starts, click on the **Start** button. Select the **Settings** option from the Start menu. Select **Control Panel** from the sub-menu. Double-click on the **Display** icon. Click on the **Settings** tab. Click on the **Change display type** button. Click the Adapter Type section's **Change** button. Click the **Show All Devices** radio button. Click the **[Standard Display Types]** option. Double-click on the **Standard Display Adapter (VGA)** option. Click on the **Close** button. Close the Display window by clicking once in the close box located in the upper right corner. When a prompt appears, click on the **Restart** option.

The best starting place for Windows 95 SETUP problems is on the Internet using Microsoft's Knowledge Base. The Knowledge Base section on Windows 95 SETUP is at http://www.microsoft.com/support/tshoot/w95setup.htm. The starting point in the Knowledge Base for all Microsoft products is located on the Internet at http://www.microsoft.com/kb/default.asp. Microsoft also has access to support articles that may provide leads in the troubleshooting trail.

The following statements are SETUP switches used when troubleshooting the Windows 95 installation.

1. Use the SETUP /D command when a message states that the required Windows 3.x files are missing or damaged.
2. Use the SETUP /IH command if the computer hangs or displays an error during the ScanDisk program execution.
3. Use the SETUP /IQ command if you are using a disk compression program other than DoubleSpace or DriveSpace and the SETUP program was started from DOS.
4. Use the SETUP /IS command if you are using a disk compression program other than DoubleSpace or DriveSpace and the SETUP program was started from within Windows.

WINDOWS 95 CORE FILES

Three components comprise the Windows 95 core: KRNL386.EXE, USER.EXE, and GDI.EXE. The core files is what allows Windows 95 to operate at a minimum. Unlike the Windows 3.x core files which were confined to 64KB, the Windows 95 core files memory heap is unlimited. Therefore, no more out of memory errors occur due to the heaps being used (or heap space not being released by poorly written software). See the Memory chapter for more information on memory heaps. Even though checking the amount of free system resources is not as critical as it was in Windows 3.x, system resource usage is still available. *Right-click* on the **My Computer** icon. Select **Properties**. Click once on the **Performance** tab. The percentage of free system resources displays near the top of the window.

THE WINDOWS 95 REGISTRY

Instead of .INI files as Windows 3.x had, Windows 95 has a database of configuration information called the **registry** which tracks the system hardware, the software applications, the file's associated application, etc. Simply put, the Windows 95 registry is a database of hardware and software system information. The Windows 95 registry has six main branches. Two of the six branches are the most important to the technician: HKEY_LOCAL_MACHINE and HKEY_USERS. The other four branches of the registry are HKEY_CURRENT_USER, HKEY_CURRENT_CONFIG, HKEY_CLASSES_ROOT, and HKEY_DYN_DATA.

The **HKEY_LOCAL_MACHINE** branch holds global hardware configurations. Included in the branch is a list of hardware components installed in the computer, the software drivers that handle each component, and the settings for each device.

Windows 95 allows multiple users to use the same computer and have their own customized settings through the use of a login. The **HKEY_USERS** branch of the registry keeps track of individual users and their preferences. When a user logs into the computer, the settings previously set such as a desktop pattern, screen saver, network connections, etc. are still retained.

The **HKEY_CURRENT_USER** branch allows specific user configuration. It holds the software settings such as how the desktop appears for the current user. The HKEY_CURRENT_CONFIG branch holds hardware profiles for the hardware configurations.

Technicians sometimes set up different configurations for laptop users. One configuration is for a networked office configuration, whereas another configuration is for a remote computer. HKEY_CLASSES_ROOT provides backward compatibility with Windows 3.x. It also holds file associations and file linkings. HKEY_DYN_DATA holds hardware settings such as those used in a Plug and Play environment.

The registry database is actually contained in two files, SYSTEM.DAT and USER.DAT. **SYSTEM.DAT** is system-specific settings. **USER.DAT** is user-specific settings. Both are normally in the Windows 95 directory, but if the computer is connected to a network, Windows 95 allows the USER.DAT file to be on the user's home directory on the server. The settings are available from any Windows 95 machine the user logs into the server. This is a **roaming profile**. Windows 95 backs up the two files every time the computer starts. The backup copies are SYSTEM.DA0 and USER.DA0. Because the registry contains all the items necessary for operation, it should be backed up to a secure location at a different time (in addition to letting Windows 95 do it).

Within each main registry key are subkeys. A registry entry under a subkey has a value; the value has a name and associated binary or character data. The individual registry entry cannot be larger than 64KB, but the registry is limited in size only by the available hard drive space. To look at the registry, click on the **Run** option from the Start menu. Type **REGEDIT** and click on the **OK** button. The six main registry keys appear on the left side of the window. Click on the **plus sign** by the HKEY_CURRENT_USER key. Click on the **plus sign** by the Control Panel option. Click on the **plus sign** by the desktop option. Double-click on the **WindowMetrics** folder. The contents of the folder including the registry entries and values appear on the right side of the window. Binary values have small 1s and 0s on the icon beside the registry entry. Character values have a little *ab* on the icon beside the registry entry.

There are two ways to change the registry. One way is to make changes with an application and let the application modify the registry. All 32-bit applications *should* keep their settings in the registry. Also, any changes made through the control panels alter the registry. The second way to change the registry is to edit it directly using an editor such as REGEDIT.

The Windows 95 registry is sometimes edited by technicians like the Windows 3.x .INI files are. Make sure a backup of the registry is complete before editing. The Windows 95 **REGEDIT** program allows manual editing of the registry. REGEDIT can also be used to export a good working copy of the Registry to a safe location. Then, in case of failure, REGEDIT can be used to import the saved file allowing Windows 95 to work again.

Changing the registry directly requires knowledge of the exact subkey, the value to be edited, and the new value to be added. For example, if you want to change the registry so an unknown file type offers an *Open with Notepad* option when you right-click on the filename, the steps are as follows:

1.   Using the Start menu's **Run** option, type in **REGEDIT** or use the browse button to locate the program and open the registry editor.
2.   Open the **HKEY_CLASSES_ROOT\UNKNOWN\SHELL** subkey
3.   To add a new key, select **EDIT** from the menu bar.

4.   Select **New** and then **Key**.
5.   In the Name option, type **Open with Notepad**.
6.   To add a new key below Open With Notepad called Command, open your new key by choosing **Edit**, then **New**, and finally **Key**.
7.   Change the name to **Command**.
8.   *Right-click* on **Default** in the right panel and select **Modify**.
9.   Change the value for the command to match the path to Notepad and add the **%1** variable after the path. For example, type **C:\Windows\Notepad %1** or **D:\WIN95\Notepad %1** depending on where the Notepad program is located.
10.   To test the change, close the REGEDIT window.
11.   Create a new file using any editor and name the file **JESTER.XYZ**. The XYZ extension is one that Windows 95 does not normally recognize.
12.   Using Windows Explorer, find the JESTER.XYZ file.
13.   *Right-click* on the JESTER.XYZ file. A pop-up menu displays on the screen.
14.   Choose the **Open with Notepad** option and Notepad opens the file if you typed everything correctly while using REGEDIT.

Another registry edit makes the drop-down menus appear faster. The following steps describe the registry edit.

1.   Start the REGEDIT program.
2.   Click on the **plus sign** for HKEY_CURRENT_USER, Control Panel, and Desktop.
3.   *Right-click* on a blank area in the right window.
4.   Choose **New** and then **String Value**.
5.   Type **MenuShowDelay**.
6.   Double-click on the new entry.
7.   Type a **1** in the **Value data** field.
8.   Click on the **OK** button.
9.   Restart Windows 95 and see how much faster the menus appear. Use the start menu options as a test.

BACKING UP THE REGISTRY

Located on the Windows 95 CD in the OTHER\MISC subdirectory is the Microsoft Configuration Backup. This utility backs up the registry and also restores the registry in case of failure. To backup the registry, locate the **CFGBACK** application on the CD. Double-click on the application icon. After reading the three information screens and clicking on **Continue**, give the backup a name in the **Selected Backup Name:** textbox. Click on the **Backup** button. If a failure occurs, use the emergency boot disk. Then, execute the Microsoft Configuration Backup by locating the CFGBACK program on the CD. Double-click on the application icon and begin the restore process.

Another utility provided by Microsoft is the **ERU** (**Emergency Recovery Utility**) program located in the CD's OTHER\MISC subdirectory. It is used to back-up some INI files, and the CONFIG.SYS, AUTOEXEC.BAT, MSDOS.SYS, IO.SYS, COMMAND.COM, and USER.DAT files. Microsoft recommends that the ERU program be used to place the backup files on a disk. The SYSTEM.DAT file is too big to fit in with the other files and is not usually included with the backed up files.

Remove the system, hidden, and read-only attributes from the two .DAT files to manually back up the Registry to a disk. Boot up Windows 95 in SAFE MODE by pressing **F8** when the message "Starting Windows 95" appears on the screen. Select the **Safe Mode** option from the list. Once Windows 95 boots, go to the MS-DOS prompt by selecting this option from the Start Menu **Programs** list. Type in **ATTRIB -R -H -S** *driveletter:path***SYSTEM.DAT** and **ATTRIB -R -H -S** *driveletter:path***USER.DAT** where *driveletter* is the drive where Windows 95 is installed and *path* is the complete path to the directory containing Windows 95. Then at the command prompt, type **COPY** *driveletter:path****.DAT A:** to copy over the two registry files. Then, the file attributes must be reinstated by typing **ATTRIB +R +H +S** *driveletter:path***SYSTEM.DAT** and **ATTRIB +R +H +S** *driveletter:path***USER.DAT**.

To manually back up the registry using REGEDIT:
1. Make sure the REGEDIT command is on your computer.
2. Using the Start button, go to **Programs**, and then to **MS-DOS prompt**.
3. At the prompt, type **REGEDIT /E REGBACK.TXT**
4. Type **EDIT REGBACK.TXT**. The editor opens with the registry backup.
5. Close the editor and close the DOS prompt window.

WINDOWS 95 SYSTEM STARTUP FILES

The files Windows 95 uses to bring the operating system up are known as the startup files. The startup files include IO.SYS, MSDOS.SYS, CONFIG.SYS, AUTOEXEC.BAT, SYSTEM.INI, WIN.INI, and BOOTLOG.TXT. A technician must have a basic understanding of each file's purpose as well as the difference between these files and their predecessors of the same name.

The Windows 95 **IO.SYS** replaces the old DOS IO.SYS and MSDOS.SYS files. However, IO.SYS is still marked with the attribute of S for system, R for read-only, and H for hidden. Some of the old DOS CONFIG.SYS settings are automatically included as part of IO.SYS. To override the default IO.SYS values, a specific entry must be placed in the Windows 95 CONFIG.SYS file. Never add a path to an old Windows version in the IO.SYS file.

The Windows 95 CONFIG.SYS settings override the settings in IO.SYS. The FILES=, BUFFERS=, and STACKS= statements cannot be lowered through the Windows 95 CONFIG.SYS (lower than the values set in IO.SYS). Windows 95 Table #2 lists prior CONFIG.SYS settings now incorporated as a standard part of the Windows 95 IO.SYS.

Windows 95's IO.SYS Settings

WINDOWS 95 - TABLE # 2

Old CONFIG.SYS Setting	Windows 95 IO.SYS Setting
BUFFERS=	Set to 30. Not required by Windows 95.
DOS=HIGH	The UMB value is added if EMM386.EXE loads from the CONFIG.SYS file.
FCBS=	Set to 4.
FILES=	Set to 60. Not required by Windows 95.
HIMEM.SYS	Loads and executes Windows 95 DOS mode memory manager.
IFSHLP.SYS	IFSHLP (Installable File System Helper) loads device drivers. HIMEM.SYS, IFSHELP.SYS, SETVER.EXE, DBLSPACE.BIN or DRVSPACE.BIN loads by default. Until IFSHLP.SYS loads, the IO.SYS file system is used. After IFSHLP.SYS loads, the full file system is available.
LASTDRIVE=	Set to Z.
SETVER.EXE	Not required by Windows 95. Used for backward compatibility.
SHELL=COMMAND.COM	The /P switch included by default.
STACKS=	Value of 9,256 used.

The Windows 95 MSDOS.SYS file is not the same as the DOS MSDOS.SYS file. The Windows 95 MSDOS.SYS file holds the multiple operating system boot options as well as the paths to important Windows files such as the Registry. MSDOS.SYS has the attributes of system, hidden, and read-only. If a prior version of DOS boots instead of Windows 95, the IO.SYS file is renamed to WINBOOT.SYS. For MSDOS.SYS to be backward compatible with older DOS versions, the file has to be at least 1024KB. There is no limit to the maximum size, just the minimum. There are lines of Xs in the MSDOS.SYS file. Do not remove the Xs. The following lists the different sections and parameters possible for the MSDOS.SYS file.

[PATHS] section

    HostWinBootDrv=   Defines the root directory of the boot drive (normally C)

    WinBootDir= Specifies where the Windows 95 startup files are located (normally C:\WINDOWS). This is defined during SETUP.

[OPTIONS] section

    AutoScan=   Applies only to Windows 95 version B (OSR2). Tells Windows 95 whether or not to run ScanDisk after an improper shutdown. 1 is the default which notifies the user before running ScanDisk; 2 runs ScanDisk without notifying the user; 0 does not run ScanDisk.

    BootDelay=   Specifies the startup delay after the "Starting Windows 95" message displays, in x number of seconds. The default is 2. This delay allows the user time to press keys to get into the SETUP menu. BootKeys=0 disables this delay.

BootKeys=   The default of 1 enables the startup function keys. 0 disables the startup function keys so you can provide tighter system security by not allowing users to bypass the boot process.

BootSafe=   The default of 0 disables starting the system automatically in Safe Mode. 1 allows the system to automatically boot to Safe Mode.

BootGUI=   The default of 1 enables starting the system in the Windows 95 GUI. A 0 allows booting to a command prompt with all drivers and the registry loaded, but the GUI is not active. If 0 is placed here, a user can type WIN and get the GUI back.

BootMenu=   The default of 0 disables automatically displaying the Startup menu. If a 1 is placed here, the Startup menu automatically appears without having to press F8.

BootMenuDefault=   The default of 1 is a normal start, but the other options on the Startup menu, such as starting up Windows 95 in the Safe Mode, automatically display if no option is chosen.

BootMenuDelay=   The default of 30 seconds specifies how long to display the Startup menu before executing the default option.

BootMulti=   The default of 0 disables dual-booting capabilities. A 1 allows choosing between a prior version of DOS (by pressing F4) or choosing this option from the Startup menu or choosing Windows 95. This is only possible if the prior version of DOS was left on the machine.

BootWarn=   The default of 1 enables the prompt for starting up in Safe Mode after a problem has been detected with the boot process or if the registry is found to be corrupt.

BootWin=   The default of 1 enables Windows 95 as the default operating system on boot up. If 0 is chosen, an old version of DOS is the default.

DoubleBuffer= Default of 0 is disabled double-buffering; 1 allows double-buffering if the SCSI controller demands it; 2 forces double-buffering.

DrvSpace=   Default of 1 enables loading DRVSPACE.BIN. 0 does not load this file. DRVSPACE.BIN is the driver for the DriveSpace compression program.

LoadTop=   The default of 1 enables COMMAND.COM or DRVSPACE.BIN at the top of conventional memory space. If a software package that uses specific memory settings does not load properly, change this setting to 0.

Logo=   The default of 1 enables the animation shown during the startup process. Pressing ESC does the same thing when the logo shows. You may have to set this to 0 for certain memory managers.

Network=   The default is 1 on systems with network software installed which allows you to boot in Safe Mode with network drivers enabled. A 0 is the default for systems that does not detect any network software so that boot option just isn't there.

The Windows 95 CONFIG.SYS file is primarily used for backward compatibility with DOS applications. Most of the important files previously needed in CONFIG.SYS are now included as part of IO.SYS. By default, Windows 95 uses the drivers from IO.SYS and the registry rather than from CONFIG.SYS. However, CONFIG.SYS can contain application specific lines. If a CONFIG.SYS file exists, device settings in CONFIG.SYS take precedence over the Windows 95 hardware settings.

Do not use SmartDrive, a disk caching program commonly used with Windows 3.x, in the Windows 95 CONFIG.SYS. Windows 95 has built-in caching programs that are better than SmartDrive. Refer to the hard drive and CD-ROM chapters for more information on caching. Also, do not include the DEVICE=MOUSE.SYS line in the CONFIG.SYS file. Windows 95 has built-in mouse drivers.

Windows 95 does not require the AUTOEXEC.BAT file, but neither did DOS. However, if the AUTOEXEC.BAT file exists, it executes by default. Windows 95 has the following previously contained DOS-based AUTOEXEC.BAT settings included as a standard part of IO.SYS.

```
TMP=C:\WINDOWS\TEMP
TEMP=C:\WINDOWS\TEMP
PROMPT=$P$G
PATH=C:\WINDOWS;C:\WINDOWS\COMMAND
COMSPEC=C:\WINDOWS\COMMAND\COMMAND.COM
```

If the AUTOEXEC.BAT file connects the computer to a network, use a batch file instead. Run the batch file from the Startup folder rather than the AUTOEXEC.BAT file.

The Windows 95 SYSTEM.INI and WIN.INI files do not contain as much information because many of the entries are in the Registry. The files are only there for backward compatibility. Most often, changes to the SYSTEM.INI and WIN.INI files are done through the Control Panel folder.

The **BOOTLOG.TXT** file holds the startup record. When running Windows 95 SETUP for the first time, the SETUP program creates the BOOTLOG.TXT file. This file holds such things as what real mode (old DOS drivers) load, what Windows virtual device drivers load, and what internal commands load. It helps to have a printout of the BOOTLOG.TXT file once Windows 95 successfully loads to reference when Windows 95 has a problem. One of the startup options that appears after pressing F8 when the message "Starting Windows 95" displays on the screen is the *Create a boot log* option. The same can be done from the command line by typing WIN /B. Creating a BOOTLOG.TXT file after the machine fails allows you to compare the two lists to see what driver or component is causing the failure. The WIN /B command can be used in conjunction with the other WIN.COM switches to create the BOOTLOG.TXT file when booting from the command prompt. Use the BOOTLOG.TXT file when troubleshooting Windows 95 initialization problems.

TROUBLESHOOTING WINDOWS 95 BOOT PROCESS

Just as with other operating systems, ask yourself questions about why Windows 95 has a problem booting. For example, has any new software been installed or removed lately? Have any new hardware devices or adapters been recently installed or removed? Has a virus check been executed? If the answer is yes to the first two questions, check for a hardware or software conflict. If a virus scan has not been completed, run a virus check! Understanding the boot process is the best way to troubleshoot Windows 95 startup problems. Windows 95 boots in separate steps:

1.   The BIOS starts
2.   The Master Boot Record and boot sector processes
3.   The Windows 95 real-mode boots
4.   The real-mode configuration process executes
5.   The protected-mode boot process executes

BIOS Execution:
1.   POST executes
2.   If the computer has a Plug and Play BIOS, the devices are located, tested, and configured.
3.   Locates a bootable partition on the boot drive
4.   Loads the Master Boot Record and the partition table

Master Boot Record and Boot Sector Processing:
1.   Once the Master Boot Record finds the bootable partition, control is turned over to the boot sector in that partition.

If the program fails at this point, there is a chance of a boot virus or a problem with the Master Boot Record. Boot from the emergency boot disk and type FDISK /MBR to fix the boot record or get rid of the virus that affected the MBR.

2.   Locate the root directory
3.   IO.SYS executes

Real Mode Boot Process:
1.   Check MSDOS.SYS for boot configuration parameters. Incorrect settings in MSDOS.SYS can cause the system to not boot properly.
2.   The message, "Starting Windows 95", displays and the system waits two seconds for a function key to be pressed.
3.   If the file LOGO.SYS file is found, it displays. If not, IO.SYS has a copy of the Windows 95 image to display.
4.   If DBLSPACE.INI is present, DRVSPACE.BIN loads.
5.   Check the SYSTEM.DAT file. If the SYSTEM.DAT file is valid it loads. If not, the SYSTEM.DA0 backup file loads. After the machine boots, one file is loaded, the other is updated.
6.   If the system needs double-buffering, double-buffering loads.
7.   The hardware detection process detects if a hardware profile is chosen or prompts the user to choose one.
8.   If a CONFIG.SYS file exists, IO.SYS reads CONFIG.SYS and processes the commands.
9.   If an AUTOEXEC.BAT file exists, IO.SYS reads and executes the commands.

Real-Mode Configuration Process:
      If CONFIG.SYS does not exist, Windows 95 automatically loads its defaults. Refer back to Windows 95 Table #2 for the default commands.

Protected-Mode Boot Process:
1.   WIN.COM automatically executes.
2.   WIN.COM loads VMM32.VxD and any virtual device drivers referenced in the registry and SYSTEM.INI that are not already part of VMM32.VxD.
3.   The processor switches to protected mode. Virtual device drivers initialize.
4.   The core files (Kernel, GDI, and User libraries) load. Explorer loads. Network support, if installed, loads.
5.   Any programs located in the registry at Hkey_Local_Machine\Software\Microsoft\Windows\CurrentVersion\RunOnce will load.

If nothing recently has changed in the Windows 95 environment and Windows 95 has a problem booting, restart the computer and press the F8 key. Windows 95 displays a list of startup options including some for troubleshooting the Windows 95 boot process. Four options used frequently by technicians include the Safe Mode, Safe Mode Command Prompt Only, Step-by-Step Confirmation, and Command Prompt Only options.

The **Safe Mode** bypasses the startup files and uses only the minimum drivers needed to boot the system. To boot Windows 95 in the Safe Mode, press **F8** when the computer displays "Starting Windows 95" during the initialization process. From the startup menu on the screen, choose the option for Safe Mode. The same can be accomplished from the command prompt by typing **WIN /D:M**. The following are instances when the Safe Mode option might be used:
1.   After a long time (longer than three minutes), Windows 95 does not start, but the "Starting Windows 95" message does appear.
2.   The Windows 95 desktop appears incorrectly. Once the Windows 95 Safe Mode boots, change the video driver to begin troubleshooting.
3.   If Windows 95 constantly or intermittently locks, use the Safe Mode option to begin troubleshooting. Check for device conflicts. See the section in Chapter 3 on Windows 95 configuration for more information on device conflicts.

If Safe Mode works, the problem may be hardware settings, real-mode (old DOS or Windows) configurations or problems, or registry problems. Use the Step-by-Step Confirmation option to troubleshoot the Windows 95 boot problem. To single-step through Windows 95's CONFIG.SYS and AUTOEXEC.BAT files, press **F8** when the words "Starting Windows 95" appear. From the menu shown, chose the option that refers to Step-by-Step Confirmation. The **Step-by-Step Confirmation** option allows you to view and select the commands, drivers, and TSRs to execute while booting. This option is great for checking if any specific file, program, etc. is hindering the boot process. Also, this option allows you to view any Registry error messages. Answering *Yes* to each command prompt is the same result as if executing the command during the boot process. If you answer *No* to the Load All Windows Drivers? question, Windows 95 starts in the Safe Mode with the minimum hardware drivers needed to start the system. If this works, Windows 95 has a problem with one or more 32-bit drivers.

The quickest way to troubleshoot 32-bit driver problems, is to look at the BOOTLOG.PRV file located in the root directory. The BOOTLOG.PRV file lists the loading status of all drivers (16-bit real mode drivers and 32-bit protected mode drivers). Look at the last driver that loaded successfully in the BOOTLOG.PRV file using any text editor.

If that does not work, start Windows 95 in Safe Mode. Right-click on the **My Computer** icon. Select **Properties** on the menu. Click on the **Device Manager** tab and disable any display adapters, network adapters, hard disk controllers, ports, floppy disk controllers, sound, video, game controls, keyboard, mouse, PCMCIA sockets, and SCSI controllers. Write down any settings before disabling the devices. Once the disabling is complete, start re-enabling the devices in the following order: (1) COM ports, (2) hard disk controller, (3) floppy disk controller, and finish with any other devices installed. Be sure there are no conflicts shown. After completing the device re-enabling, restart Windows 95. If the problem is not resolved, disable devices one-by-one to find the troublesome device driver.

If answering *No* to the Load All Windows Drivers? question does not start Windows 95, look at Windows 95 Figure #8 for a troubleshooting flow chart used with the Step-by-Step Confirmation option.

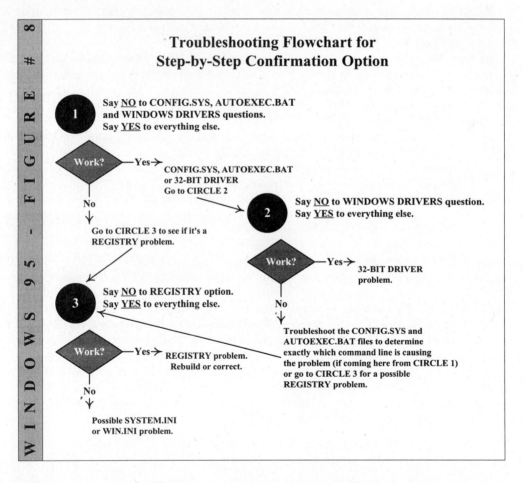

Troubleshooting AUTOEXEC.BAT and CONFIG.SYS problems is the same process in Windows 95 as it is in DOS. Load each line one by one until you discover the problem line. Determine if the cause is an incorrect path, corrupted file, etc.

The Windows 95 SYSTEM.INI and WIN.INI files are in the same directory as Windows 95. To determine if the SYSTEM.INI or WIN.INI files are the problem, boot to the command prompt. Make a copy of the SYSTEM.INI and WIN.INI files such as SYSTEM.CAS and WIN.CAS. Rename the WIN.INI file to WIN.AAA. Start Windows 95 by typing **WIN** at the command prompt. If this works, the problem is in the WIN.INI file. One problem might be if there are LOAD= or RUN= statements in the [Windows] section of WIN.INI. Remove any statements or place a semicolon at the beginning of the statement. Windows 95 does use these statements. Do not forget to rename the WIN.AAA file back to WIN.INI to restore the original problem for troubleshooting purposes.

To eliminate SYSTEM.INI as a possible problem, restart Windows 95 by selecting the Safe Mode Command Prompt Only option. After making a backup copy of SYSTEM.INI, copy the SYSTEM.CB file over to replace the SYSTEM.INI file. Edit the SYSTEM.INI and add the following lines to their appropriate section:

[386Enh]
mouse=*vmouse, msmouse.vxd
[boot]
drivers=mmsystem.dll
mouse.drv=mouse.drv

Start Windows 95 from the command prompt by typing **WIN**. If Windows 95 boots properly, the problem is in the SYSTEM.INI file (most likely in the [386Enh] or [boot] section). Copy the original SYSTEM.INI file back to troubleshoot the problem. Put a semicolon before each statement and start Windows 95 from the command prompt after each change to determine which line is causing the problem.

An option to use if Safe Mode does not work is the Safe Mode Command Prompt Only option. The Safe Mode Command Prompt Only option loads COMMAND.COM and the DoubleSpace or DriveSpace files (if applicable), but does not load Windows 95. Use this option if you want to use switches with the WIN command such as the WIN /D:X switch to troubleshoot memory conflicts. The memory chapter explains memory conflicts in more detail. Choose the **Safe Mode Command Prompt Only** option automatically by pressing the **SHIFT+F5** when the message "Starting Windows 95" appears.

If you start Windows 95 from the command prompt, type **WIN**. To bypass the applications that start automatically when Windows 95 starts, hold down **SHIFT** as Windows 95 is initializing. If a startup application is causing the problem, boot Windows 95 into the Safe Mode and remove the application from the Startup folder. Remove the application and reload it using the Add/Remove programs wizard or contact the application manufacturer for more details in troubleshooting the problem.

The *Command Prompt Only* option starts Windows 95 with just the startup files and the Registry loaded. Technicians use this option when Windows command line switches are needed. Reference Windows 95 Table #3 for a list of WIN.COM's available switches used when troubleshooting Windows 95.

Windows 95 WIN.COM Switches

WIN.COM Switch	Purpose
/D:F	Turns off 32-bit access. Use if Windows 95 stalls or has apparent hard disk problems.
/D:M	Starts Windows 95 in the Safe Mode.
/D:N	Starts Windows 95 in Safe Mode with Networking.
/D:S	Tells Windows 95 to not use the address space between F000:000 and 1MB for a breakpoint. Use if Windows 95 stalls during startup or during disk operations.
/D:V	Allows the ROM BIOS to handle hard disk controller interrupts instead of Windows 95. Use if Windows 95 stalls during startup or during disk operations.
/D:X	Tells Windows 95 to not use the Upper Memory Blocks normally used for adapters.
/W	Takes the CONFIG.WOS and AUTOEXEC.WOS files and restores them to CONFIG.SYS and AUTOEXEC.BAT. Used when rebooting a system back to Windows 95. Might need to use if the computer is shut off while running a DOS application in MS-DOS mode and want to return to Windows 95.
/WX	Takes the CONFIG.WOS and AUTOEXEC.WOS files and restores them to CONFIG.SYS and AUTOEXEC.BAT. Used when rebooting a system back to Windows 95. Might need to use if the computer is shut off while running a DOS application in MS-DOS mode and want to return to Windows 95.

WINDOWS 95 - TABLE #3

If Windows 95 does not boot properly using any of the switches or the Windows 95 Safe Mode, use the emergency boot disk and boot from the A: drive. Never forget to check for a virus. Also, one of the best resources available through the Internet is Microsoft's Knowledge Base for startup problems at http://www.microsoft.com/support/tshoot/w95startup.htm.

Name _____

Windows 95 Review Questions

1.   T/F   Windows 95 runs DOS applications.

2.   T/F   Windows 95 can be run on a 386SX computer.

3.   Where are the Windows 95 hardware settings kept?

4.   Match the following term with the appropriate definition.

_____ Desktop   A.   A graphic representation of something

_____ Icon   B.   Allows easy switching between applications

_____ Recycle Bin   C.   The place where the My Computer icon is located

_____ Taskbar   D.   A storage place for files and folders that have been
                                     deleted

5.   List three things that can be accomplished using Windows Explorer.

6.   Where would one go (what icon, folder, application, etc.) to change hardware settings such as for the monitor?

7.   Which Start menu option is chosen to change the taskbar or to add applications to the taskbar?

8.   Describe the recycle bin and how you delete files using Windows 95.

9.   For what is the FIND utility used?

10. How do you get help in Windows 95?

11. Describe two ways to start an application in Windows 95.

12. T/F   The Shut Down menu option must be used to properly exit Windows 95.

13. T/F   Old DOS programs perform better when executed in Windows 95's MS-DOS mode.

14. How do you install an old DOS game under Windows 95?

15. T/F   A virus check and defragment program should be run before installing Windows 95.

16. What is the minimum hard drive space required to install Windows 95 if the computer has Windows for Workgroups loaded?

17. T/F   During a Windows 95 installation, the hardware is detected before the "Welcome to Setup" screen displays.

18.   What are the most common causes of problems during the Windows 95 hardware detection, extended memory manager verification, and disk caching software search during the Windows 95 installation process?

19.   Describe what to do if Windows 95 hangs during the Windows 95 installation process.

20.   Describe how to manually backup the Registry in step-by-step detail.

21.   List the Windows 95 startup files.

22.   What two DOS files does the Windows 95 IO.SYS replace?

23.   T/F   Windows 95 requires the CONFIG.SYS file for proper operation.

24.   T/F   Windows 95 automatically places the DOS=HIGH, UMB line in the IO.SYS if the EMM386.EXE driver is in the CONFIG.SYS file.

25.   What is the Windows 95 minimum FILES= setting?

26.   What Windows 95 switch starts Windows 95 in Safe mode with network drivers loaded?

 Name _____

Windows 95 Fill-in-the-Blank

1. The Windows 95 main screen is known as the _____.

2. The _____ is a storage place for deleted files.

3. The _____ desktop icon provides access to main hardware components.

4. Click on the _____ to bring up the Start menu with Programs, Documents, Settings, Find, Help, Run, and Shut Down as menu options.

5. The _____ is the Windows 95 equivalent to the Windows 3.x File Manager.

6. The Windows 95 _____ control panel allows easy installation of 32-bit software.

7. The Windows 95 core files are _____, _____, and _____.

8. The Windows 95 _____ is a database of hardware and software settings.

9. The _____ Windows 95 registry branch holds plug and play settings.

10. The registry branch that tracks hardware components and their associated software drivers is the _____.

11. The user's screen saver settings are saved in the _____ registry branch.

12. The _____ allows a user's specific registry settings to be saved in a file on the network file server.

13. The two files that make up the registry are _____ and _____.

14. The _____ program allows editing the Windows 95 Registry.

15. The default directory for the registry files is _____.

16. The _____ Windows 95 startup file holds a record of everything that occurs during the startup process.

17. During the Windows 95 boot process the _____ file loads after the partition table and root directory have been located.

18. Once the Starting Windows 95 message displays, the system waits _____ seconds by default for a function key to be pressed.

19. The Windows 95 _____ startup option bypasses the startup files and minimally boots the system for troubleshooting purposes.

20. Holding the _____ key down during the startup process keeps applications from automatically loading.

Name _____

WINDOWS 95 BASIC USAGE EXERCISE

Objective: To correctly use the basic Windows 95 options

Parts: A computer with Windows 95 loaded
        A disk

Step 1:   Turn the computer on and start Windows 95. The desktop appears.
Step 2:   Double-click the **My Computer** icon in the top left corner. The My Computer window
            opens.
Step 3:   In the My Computer window are icons that represent resources in the computer. Individual
            icons represent the floppy drives, hard drives, and CD-ROM drives installed in the
            computer. Two folder icons commonly found in the My Computer window are Control
            Panel and Printers. Double-click on the icon for the first hard drive, the **C:** drive. Another
            window, the C: window, appears. On the title bar in the upper right corner of the C:
            window are three icons: the minimize button icon shown as a small line, the maximize
            button shown as a window box, and the close button that contains an X inside the icon.
            Reference Windows 95 Exercise Figure #1.

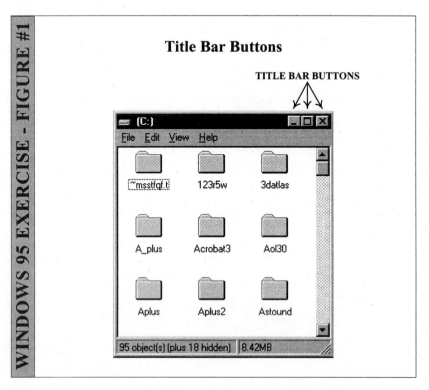

Question 1:   How many folder icons are in the My Computer window?

Question 2:   What is the purpose of the Control Panel folder icon?

Question 3:   What is the purpose of the Printers folder icon?

Step 4:   Click once on the **Close** button (the X icon in the upper right corner). The C: window closes and the My Computer window is on the desktop.
Step 5:   Close the My Computer window using its close box.

FORMATTING A DISK

Step 6:   Insert a blank floppy or a disk that does not contain useful information into the A: drive.
Step 7:   Open the **My Computer** window.
Step 8:   With the *right* mouse button, click once on the icon for the **A:** drive. A drop-down menu appears.
Step 9:   Click once on the **Format** command within the drop-down menu. The Format window appears.
Step 10:   Click on the **Capacity** down arrow to change the disk capacity to the type of disk installed in drive A:. By default, Windows 95 selects 1.44MB as the capacity.
Step 11:   Below the capacity setting is the Format Type setting. By default, Windows 95 selects Quick (erase) format. If the disk in drive A: has never been formatted or if unknown, click on the **Full** radio button. Otherwise, leave the selection of Quick Format.
Step 12:   Click once inside the **Label** edit box.
Step 13:   Type in **EXER1** as the disk label.
Step 14:   To make the disk bootable, click in the **Copy system file** checkbox.
Step 15:   Click once on the **Start** button.
Step 16:   When the format is complete, a Format results window appears. Click on the Close button.
Step 17:   Click once on the Close button to close the Format window.

COPYING A FILE

Step 18:   From the My Computer window, double-click on the **C:** drive icon. The C: window appears on the desktop.
Step 19:   Locate the Stock document icon. Use the scroll bars if necessary. Do *not* click on the icon.
Step 20:   Move the C: window so the My Computer's A: disk icon can be seen (in addition to the Stock icon in the C: window). Move the window by clicking once in the title bar and holding the mouse button down. Then, with the mouse button held down, move the window.
Step 21:   *Click and hold* the mouse button down on the **Stock** icon. While holding the mouse button down, move the Stock document over to the My Computer's **A:** icon. Release the mouse button when the A: drive icon highlights. A window appears showing the document transfer (copy).

Just like DOS and Windows 3.x, Windows 95 has many ways to do the same task. Below is another way to copy a file.

Step 22: Using the *right* mouse button, click once on the **HOME.STK** file icon. A menu appears.
Step 23: Click once on **Copy**.
Step 24: In the My Computer window, right-click once on the **A:** drive icon.
Step 25: Click once on **Paste**.
Step 26: Double-click the **A:** drive icon in the My Computer window.

Question 4: Is the HOME.STK file located on the floppy disk? If not, re-do Steps 22 through 26.

Step 27: Close the A: window.
Step 28: Close the My Computer window.
Step 29: Close the C: window.

ON YOUR OWN

1.   From within Windows 95 (without going to a DOS prompt), verify the Stock file is on the floppy disk, then close all windows on the desktop. Write the steps performed in the space below:

_____ Instructor's Initials

 Name_____

RUNNING AN APPLICATION, DELETING FILES, AND INSTALLING A WINDOWS 95 APPLICATION

Objective: To correctly run an application, delete files, and install an application using Windows 95

Parts: A computer with Windows 95 loaded
          A disk

Step 1:   Turn the computer on and verify that Windows 95 boots properly.
Step 2:   Double-click on the **My Computer** icon.
Step 3:   Double-click on the drive icon where Windows 95 is installed. Contact the instructor if you are unsure.
Step 4:   Double-click on the folder that holds Windows 95. The default is Windows. Contact the instructor if you are unsure.
Step 5:   Using the scroll bars if necessary, *locate* the **Notepad** icon.
Step 6:   Double-click on the **Notepad** icon.
Step 7:   From within the Notepad application, type in the following message:
           Change is inevitable, except from a vending machine.
Step 8:   Click on **File** from the menu bar.
Step 9:   Click on the **Save** option from the drop-down menu.
Step 10:   In the **File Name** text box, type in **FILE1**.
Step 11:   Click once on the **Save** button.
Step 12:   Click on **File** from the menu bar.
Step 13:   Click on the **New** option from the drop-down menu. A blank screen appears.
Step 14:   Type in the following message:
           When nobody is looking, "real" computer users pretend their mouse is a toy car and race it around the desk. They keep a large box of tissues by the computer to wipe the saliva off the screen after playing test drive. (Brrrrm! Brrrrm!)

ON YOUR OWN

1.   Save the file typed in Step 14 as **FILE2**.
2.   Use the steps outlined above to create three more files called **FILE3**, **FILE4**, and **FILE5**. Place any text desired into the documents. If you happen to be low on ideas for what to type, a few suggestions follow.

      "Real" computer users have problems with Windows 95 because when two or more applications are running, they only have room for one keyboard template at a time.

      A "real" computer user believes computer salesmen.

3.   Close (not minimize) the Notepad application. How did you close the application?

4.   Verify the five files are in the same folder as where the Notepad icon is. Write how the files
        were verified in the space below:

To make the five files appear in alphabetical order as all the other files, click once on **View** from the
menu bar. Click once on **Refresh**. Notice how FILE1, FILE2, FILE3, FILE4, and FILE5 are in
alphabetical order. If the files do not appear in alphabetical order, click once on the **View** menu option.
Click on **Arrange Icons** option, then select the **By name** option. The icons appear after using the
scroll bars to go to the "F" files.

COPYING FILES (WITH A FEW NEAT TRICKS)

Step 15:   Insert a disk into the **A:** drive.
Step 16:   *Click and hold* the mouse pointer on the **title bar** of the folder containing the five files.
           Move the window (and any other windows if necessary) so the **My Computer** window is
           visible.
Step 17:   Click once on the **My Computer** window to make it the active window on the screen. The
           My Computer's title bar is a different color than the other windows because it is the active
           window or the window where work is being done.

A shortcut to opening windows or applications while closing the old window is by holding the
CTRL key while double-clicking on the icon.

Step 18:   While holding **CTRL** down, double-click on the **A:** drive icon in the My Computer
           window. The My Computer window closes and the A: window is active.

A shortcut for copying files is to use the taskbar. Notice how the taskbar now contains a 3.5" floppy
[A:] option that is backlit. When the option is backlit, the A: window is the active window on the
screen. This taskbar option will be used momentarily.

Step 19:   Click once in the window that contains the five files you created.
Step 20:   Locate the **FILE1** icon in the window.
Step 21:   Click once and *hold* the mouse button down while pointing to the **FILE1** icon.
Step 22:   Continue to hold the mouse button down, and drag the **FILE1** icon to the 3 1/2" floppy [A:]
           taskbar option, *never letting the mouse button go!* The A: window becomes the active
           window on the screen.
Step 23:   With the mouse button still held down, drag the file icon into the **A:** window. Release the
           mouse button when the icon is inside the A: window.

ON YOUR OWN (cont.)

5.   Use any method you prefer and copy **FILE2**, **FILE3**, **FILE4**, and **FILE5** to the disk.

6.   Verify the five files are still in the hard disk folder *and* on the disk.

7.   Have a classmate verify the five files are in both places.

_____ Classmate's Initials

_____Classmate's Printed Name

8.   Close the **A:** window.

Step 24:   Make the window where the original five files are showing active by clicking somewhere within the window or on the folder name in the taskbar.

DELETING FILES

Step 25:   Click once on the **FILE1** icon to select it.

Step 26:   Press **DEL** on the keyboard. A confirmation message appears.

Step 27:   Click on the **Yes** button. The FILE1 document disappears from the window.

Step 28:   Double-click on the **Recycle Bin** icon. The Recycle Bin window appears with the FILE1 file appearing in the window.

Step 29:   One way to undelete the file is to *click and hold* the mouse pointer on the **FILE1** icon. Drag the **FILE1** icon over to the original window from which it came. The file is undeleted when it appears in the original folder's window again.

Step 30:   Drag the **FILE2** document to the **Recycle Bin** window.

Step 31:   Click once on the menu bar's **File** option.

Step 32:   Click once on the **Empty Recycle Bin** menu option. A confirmation message appears.

Step 33:   Click on the **Yes** button. FILE2 cannot be undeleted once the Recycle Bin is emptied.

Step 34:   Right-click on the **FILE3** icon. A menu appears.

Step 35:   Click once on the **Delete** option. A confirmation message appears.

Step 36:   Click on the **Yes** button. FILE3 appears in the Recycle Bin window.

ON YOUR OWN (cont.)

9.   Permanently delete **FILE1**, **FILE4**, and **FILE5** from the hard drive using any method.

Holding **SHIFT** down while dragging the icon to the Recycle Bin icon or window eliminates the "empty the Recycle Bin" step.

10.   Close all applications on the Desktop or in the taskbar.

Question 1:   What applications (if any) were open and had to be closed in Step 10?

INSTALLING A WINDOWS 95 OR A WINDOWS 3.X APPLICATION

Step 37:   Obtain a Windows 95 or Windows 3.x application from the instructor.
Step 38:   Double-click on the **My Computer** icon.
Step 39:   While *holding* down **CTRL**, double-click on the **Control Panel** folder icon.

Question 2:   What does holding CTRL down while double-clicking on an icon accomplish?

Step 40:   Double-click on the **Add/Remove Programs** icon.
Step 41:   Click on the **Install** button.
Step 42:   Insert a disk or CD into the appropriate drive.
Step 43:   Remove all other disks or CDs not being used for the installation.
Step 44:   Click on the **Next** button. If a SETUP or INSTALL executable file is found, the file name
           appears in the command line.

Always check the software documentation for the appropriate installation command. If the installation command is not correct on the command line, use the Browse button to locate it.

Step 45:   Click on the **Finish** button. The directions on the screen are different for each application.
           Refer to the application's documentation to answer any specific questions. Also, the
           Internet is a great place to research installation problems. The Appendix in the back of the
           book lists many software manufacturers. Always test the software installation by running
           the application.

ON YOUR OWN (cont.)

11.   Start the application installed in Steps 37 through 45 and verify the success of the installation.
      Does the application execute?

_____ Instructor's Initials

12.   Close the application.
13.   Using the Windows 95 HELP option, determine how to view the system hidden files when
      using either My Computer or the Windows 95 Explorer program. Write your discoveries in the
      space below.

Name _____

USING THE WINDOWS 95 FIND UTILITY
AND RUN MENU OPTION EXERCISE

Objective: To correctly use the Find and Run menu options within Windows 95

Parts: A computer with Windows 95 loaded
        A disk

USING THE FIND UTILITY

Step 1:   Turn the computer on and verify that Windows 95 boots properly.
Step 2:   Click on the **Start** button located in the bottom left corner of the screen.
Step 3:   Use the mouse pointer and point to the **Find** option.
Step 4:   Click on the **Files or Folders** option.
Step 5:   In the Named: text box, type **FONT**
Step 6:   Click on the **Find Now** button. A list of files and folders with the letters *FONT* in the file or folder name appears in a window.

Question 1:   How many files or folders contain the letters FONT?

Step 7:   Close the Find utility by clicking once in the close box.

USING THE RUN UTILITY

Step 8:   Click on the **Start** button located in the bottom left corner of the screen.
Step 9:   Insert the disk into the **A:** drive.
Step 10:   Click once on the **Run** menu option.
Step 11:   In the text box, type **EDIT A:\RAINA.TXT**
        A MS-DOS Editor screen appears.

The MS-DOS editor is a native Windows 95 external command. External commands execute from a command prompt in the MS-DOS mode, from within a batch file, from the Windows 95 Explorer program, and from the Windows 95 Run command. Internal Windows 95 commands, like DOS commands, execute from within batch files or from the command prompt.

Step 12:   From within the editor, type the following remembering to press **ENTER** at the end of each
           line.
           "There are three things which must guide all teachers:
           first, get into the subject; second, get that subject
           into you; third, try to lead your pupils to get the
           subject into them, not pouring into them, but leading
           them to see what you see, to know what you know,
           to feel what you feel." — Author unknown
Step 13:   From the MS-DOS Editor window's menu bar, click once on **File**.
Step 14:   Click once on **Save**.
Step 15:   Click on the close box in the upper right corner.

ON YOUR OWN

1.   Verify the RAINA.TXT file is on the disk. Write the steps below:

Name _____

UPGRADING TO WINDOWS 95 FOR A DUAL-BOOT OPTION
(WITH WINDOWS 3.X LOADED)

Objective: To install Windows 95 and keep the DOS/Windows environment and be able to boot
from either operating system

Parts: A computer with Windows 3.x and DOS 5 or higher loaded
A hard drive that has been defragmented
Windows 95 Upgrade CD or Disks

Step 1:   Turn the computer on and go to the DOS prompt.
Step 2:   Disable any TSRs (Terminate and Stay Resident programs) and time out features from the
SETUP, CONFIG.SYS, and AUTOEXEC.BAT files except any programs needed for hard
drive access, network drivers, video drivers needed for normal operation, and CD-ROM
drivers.

Question 1:   What TSRs or device drivers were REMed out in Step 2? List them below.

Step 3:   Restart the computer to make any changes in the AUTOEXEC.BAT and CONFIG.SYS
files take effect.
Step 4:   Start Windows 3.x and go into the Program Manager.
Step 5:   Insert the Windows 95 Upgrade CD into the CD-ROM drive or insert the first Windows 95
upgrade disk into the floppy drive.
Step 6:   Click on **File** from the menu bar.
Step 7:   Click on **Run** from the drop-down menu.
Step 8:   Click on the **Browse** button.
Step 9:   In the Drives selection box, click on the **down arrow**. A list of possible drives appears.
Step 10:   Select the drive that contains the Windows 95 CD or disk.
Step 11:   Click on the filename **SETUP.EXE** in the filename window.
Step 12:   Click once on the **OK** button. The Run Window's dialog box contains the SETUP.EXE
command in the Command Line text box. SETUP can be started using a variety of
switches. Windows 95 Exercise Table #1 lists the SETUP switches.

Windows 95 SETUP Switches

SETUP Switch	Purpose
/?	Shows all of the SETUP switches
/C	Does not load SmartDrive
/D	Does not use a prior version of Windows for the initial part of SETUP.
/filename	filename is the name of the script that has the settings information to automatically install Windows 95.
/ID	Ignore minimum hard disk requirement
/IH	SETUP displays the ScanDisk window
/IL	SETUP uses the driver for the Logitech series C mouse.
/IM	Ignore memory check
/IQ	Ignore the ScanDisk Quick check (when executing SETUP from the DOS prompt)
/IS	Ignore the ScanDisk Quick check (when executing SETUP from within Windows 3.x)
/IT	Does not check for incompatible TSRs
/IW	("IW" must be in caps) Bypasses the license agreement screen
/NOSTART	Copies the fewest Windows 3.x DLLs needed by SETUP and exits to the DOS prompt. Windows 95 is not installed.
/t:dir	dir is an existing directory for SETUP's temp files. Note: All files in the directory will be deleted through the installation process.

(Side label: WINDOWS 95 EXERCISE - TABLE # 1)

Step 13: Click on the **OK** button without adding any switches to the SETUP command (unless told otherwise by the instructor).

Step 14: Click on the **Continue** button from the Windows 95 SETUP window.

Step 15: The SETUP program does a system check. Then, the software license agreement appears. Click on the **Yes** button.

Step 16: Click on the **Next** button from the Windows 95 SETUP Wizard window.

Step 17: In the **Choose Directory** window, click in the **Other Directory** radio button. Click on the **Next** button.

Step 18: In the **Change Directory** window, type in a different directory name than where Windows 3.x is located. Otherwise, Windows 3.x will be replaced! For example, type in E:\WIN95. Then, click on the **Next** button. A message appears stating that all Windows 3.x applications will have to be installed individually in Windows 95. They will not automatically be available in Windows 95.

Step 19:   Click once on the **Yes** button and the SETUP Options window appears.

Step 20:   Click once on the radio button (Typical, Portable, Compact, or Custom) that applies most to the system onto which Windows 95 is being installed. Most machines will use the default of **Typical**. Then, click on the **Next** button.

Step 21:   In the User Info window, type in the name and company information. Click on the **Next** button.

Step 22:   Type in the registration number (10-digit CD key). Click on the **Next** button

Step 23:   If the computer has a network adapter, click in the **Network Adapter** checkbox. If the computer has a sound, MIDI, or video capture card, click in that checkbox. Contact the instructor if you are unsure. Click once on the **Next** button when finished. This step may take awhile. If there is no hard disk activity for a long period of time, turn off the computer and then turn it back on again. Run the SETUP program. Choose the Safe Recovery mode. Refer to the chapter's section on troubleshooting a Windows 95 installation.

Step 24:   Check with the instructor to see what option(s) to select in the **Get Connected** window. Click on the **Next** button when done.

Question 2:   What options were selected in the Get Connected window?

Step 25:   Selected in the Windows Components window is the Install the most common components radio button. Click on the **Next** button.

Step 26:   Selected in the Startup Disk window is the Yes, I want a startup disk option. Click on the **Next** button.

Step 27:   Click on the **Next** button in the Start Copying Files window.

Step 28:   A message appears on the screen prompting you to insert a disk into the A: drive and click on the **OK** button.

Step 29:   A message appears after awhile prompting you to remove the disk. Label the disk as a Windows 95 startup disk. Click on the **OK** button.

Step 30:   The SETUP program continues by copying files to the hard drive until the Finishing SETUP window appears. Click on the **Finish** button. Be sure to remove any disk from the floppy drive.

Step 31:   During the reboot process, Windows 95 prompts for a time zone. Click once in the area of the map where you are located or click once on the down arrow. Select the time zone from the list. When finished, click on the **Close** button.

Step 32:   When the Add Printer wizard appears, click once on the **Next** button.

Step 33:   Follow the directions on the screen for setting up the printer by clicking **Next** when needed. If the printer is not in the list, click on the **Cancel** button. A print driver can be loaded later.

Step 34:   When the configuration phase is over, Windows 95 restarts. Allow the process to complete until the Welcome Screen appears.

Step 35:   From the Welcome screen, click on the **Close** button.

Step 36:   To verify that the dual-boot option works, click once on the **Start button** located in the bottom left corner. The Start Menu appears.

Step 37:   Click on **Shut Down** from the Start menu.

Step 38:   Click on the **Restart the Computer** radio button from the Shut Down Windows screen. Do NOT select the Restart the computer in MS-DOS mode. Click on the **Yes** button.

Step 39:   When the computer displays the message, "Starting Windows 95", press **F8**. The Start menu appears.

Step 40:   Choose the number corresponding to a **Previous Version of MS-DOS**. Press **ENTER**. The configuration prior to the Windows 95 installation boots. If not, refer to the chapter's section on troubleshooting SETUP.

Reminder: Do not forget to go back into the AUTOEXEC.BAT and CONFIG.SYS files and remove all REM statements installed prior to the Windows 95 installation. Test the new configuration by performing Steps 39 and 40 again.

_____   Instructor's Initials

Name _____

CONFIGURING A DOS APPLICATION TO RUN IN
THE WINDOWS 95 MS-DOS MODE
(USING THE WINDOWS 95 DEFAULT SETTINGS)

Objective: To properly configure a DOS application to run using the MS-DOS mode

Parts: A computer with Windows 95 loaded

Step   1:   Power on the computer and start Microsoft Windows 95.
Step   2:   Double-click on the **My Computer** icon.
Step   3:   *Right*-click on the drive icon that contains the DOS application.
Step   4:   Click once on the **Explore** option.
Step   5:   Find the appropriate DOS application .EXE or .COM file that starts the application.
Step   6:   *Right*-click the DOS application's **.EXE** file.
Step   7:   Click on the **Properties** option
Step   8:   Click on the **Program** tab.
Step   9:   Click on the **Advanced** button.
Step 10:   In the Advanced Program Settings window, click on **MS-DOS** mode.

Question 1:   T/F   Microsoft Windows 3.x applications can be run in Windows 95's MS-DOS
          mode.

Question 2:   T/F   When MS-DOS mode is running, Windows 95 no longer has the control of
          providing virtual memory to the system.

Step 11:   Click on **OK**. The application's Properties window appears.
Step 12:   Click on the **OK** button to exit the Properties window.
Step 13:   Close the Exploring window.
Step 14:   Close the My Computer window.

_____ Instructor's Initials

Name_____

CREATING A CUSTOM STARTUP CONFIGURATION FOR DOS APPLICATIONS RUNNING IN THE WINDOWS 95 MS-DOS MODE

Objective: To configure a DOS application to run properly in the Windows 95 MS-DOS mode

Parts: A computer with Windows 95 loaded

Step 1:   Power on the computer and start Microsoft Windows 95.
Step 2:   Double-click on the **My Computer** icon.
Step 3:   *Right*-click on the drive icon containing the DOS application.
Step 4:   Click once on the **Explore** option.
Step 5:   Find the appropriate DOS application .EXE or .COM file which starts the application.
Step 6:   *Right*-click the DOS application's **.EXE** file.
Step 7:   Click on the **Properties** option.
Step 8:   Click on the **Program** tab.
Step 9:   Click on the **Advanced** button.
Step 10:   In the Advanced Program Settings window, click on **MS-DOS** mode.
Step 11:   Click on the **Specify a new MS-DOS Configuration**. The CONFIG.SYS for MS-DOS mode: and the AUTOEXEC.BAT for MS-DOS mode: windows are now made available for editing.
Step 12:   Modify or create the CONFIG.SYS and the AUTOEXEC.BAT according to what the DOS application needs to run as if the DOS application was running on a DOS-based computer.

Question 1:   T/F   All settings in the AUTOEXEC.BAT and CONFIG.SYS file override the Windows 95 IO.SYS file settings.

Step 13:   Click **OK** when finished editing the two files. The application's Properties window appears.
Step 14:   Click **OK** to exit the Properties window.
Step 15:   Close the Exploring window.

_____ Instructor's Initials

Name _____

CONFIGURING TWO COMPUTERS TO RUN
DIRECT CABLE CONNECTION

Objective: To properly configure two computers to communicate using the Direct Cable
      Connection

Parts: Two computer with either Windows 95 or Windows NT loaded
      Special cable that supports the Direct Cable Connection

Step   1:   Connect the special cable to both computers. One of the computers will be designated as
      the host. The **host** computer is the computer that has files to be shared by the other
      computer, the guest. The **guest** computer connects to the host computer and copies,
      executes, etc. files located on the host computer.

Question 1:   What port did you connect the special cable, the parallel or the serial port?

Step   2:   Go to one of the computers that will be designated as the host and create a document to be
      shared by clicking on the **Start** button.
Step   3:   Select **Accessories** and click once on the **Notepad** option.
Step   4:   Type **This is the shared file.** in the Notepad window.
Step   5:   Click once on the **File** menu option.
Step   6:   Click once on the **Save** option.
Step   7:   In the File Name: text box, type **SHARE**.
Step   8:   Double-click on the **My Computer** icon.
Step   9:   Double-click the drive where the folder containing the Windows 95 files exists. If unsure,
      check with the instructor.

Question 2:   What drive contains the Windows 95 folder?

Step 10:   Double-click on the Windows 95 folder.

Question 3:   What is the name of the folder that contains the Windows 95 files?

Step 11:   Click on the **Save** button.
Step 12:   Close the Notepad application by clicking on the close box.
Step 13:   On the same computer, the host, see if the Direct Cable Connect software is installed by
      clicking once on the **Start** button.

Step 14:   Select **Programs**, select **Accessories**, and look for the **Direct Cable Connection** option. If it is not there, install it by performing Steps 15-25. If it is available, proceed to Step 26.

Step 15:   Click on the **Start** button and select **Settings**.

Step 16:   Click on the **Control Panel** option.

Step 17:   Double-click on the **Add/Remove Programs** icon.

Step 18:   Click on the **Windows Setup** tab.

Step 19:   Click once on the **Communications** option.

Step 20:   Click on the **Details** button.

Step 21:   Select the **Direct Cable Connection** option. You are prompted that this option requires the Dial-up Networking option. Click on the **Yes** button to install both.

Step 22:   Click on the **OK** button to install the software. You are prompted, "You must provide computer and workgroup names to identify the computer to the network". Click on the **OK** button.

Step 23:   Type in the computer name and workgroup name and click once on the **Close** button when finished. You are prompted to restart the computer.

Step 24:   Click on the **Start** button and choose the **Restart the computer** option.

Step 25:   When the computer restarts, you are prompted for a Windows ID. Type in an ID, but do *not* type in a password. When prompted to verify the password, do *not* type anything; just click the **OK** button.

Step 26:   On the host computer, the one with the SHARE file on it, click on the **Start** button and select **Accessories**.

Step 27:   Click once on the **Direct Cable Connection** option. The Direct Cable Connection wizard begins.

Step 28:   When prompted for the type of computer, click once on the **host** radio button. Click once on the **Next** button.

Step 29:   When prompted for the type of port, select either parallel or serial depending on the type of cable you connected in Step 1. Refer to the answer to Question 1 if you are unsure.

Step 30:   Click on the **Next** button. You are prompted "To allow your guest computer to use a printer or copy files from this computer, click File and Print Sharing to display the Network Control Panel. Then click the File and Print Sharing button. NOTE: You may have to restart the computer and then restart Direct cable connection to enable these changes".

Step 31:   Click on the **File and Print Sharing** button. The Network Control Panel appears.

Step 32:   Click on the Network control panel's **File and Print Sharing** button.

Step 33:   Click on the **I want to be able to give others access to my files** checkbox and click on the **OK** button to close the Network control panel. Some computers will be prompted to restart the computer, If so, restart the computer and perform Steps 26-33 again.

Step 34:   You are prompted that no folders are marked as shared, so double-click on the **My Computer** desktop icon.

Step 35:   Double-click on the drive where Windows 95 is located. Refer to the answer to Question 2 if you are unsure.

Step 36:   Click once on the folder where the Windows 95 files are located. Refer to the answer to Question 3 if you are unsure.

Step 37:   Click on the **File** menu option followed by a single click on the **Properties** menu option.

Step 38:   Click on the **Sharing** tab. If the tab is not available, re-do steps 26-37.

Step 39:   Click on the **Shared As:** radio button and click on the **OK** button. A hand appears under the folder that contains the Windows 95 files.

Step 40:   Close the drive window by clicking on the close box.

Step 41:   Close the My Computer window by clicking on the close box.

Step 42:   Back in the Direct Cable Connection window, click on the **Next** button.

Step 43:   You are prompted that the host is set up. Click on the **Finish** button. A status window appears.

Step 44:   Go to the guest computer. Install the Direct Cable Connection software the same way. Refer to Steps 15-25 if necessary.

Step 45:   Click on the **Start** button and select **Accessories**.

Step 46:   Click once on the **Direct Cable Connection** option. The Direct Cable Connection wizard begins.

Step 47:   Click on the **guest** radio button option.

Step 48:   Select the port you want to use. Refer to the answer to Question 1 if you are unsure.

Step 49:   Click on the **Next** button.

Step 50:   Click on the **Finish** button. The folder that contains the Windows 95 files from the host computer appears in a window.

Step 51:   Double-click the folder and locate the **SHARE** file.

Step 52:   Double-click on the **Share** file icon. Notepad opens and you see the typed message.

_____ Instructor's Initials

Step 53:   Close Notepad by clicking in the close box.

Step 54:   Close the Windows 95 folder window by clicking in the close box.

Step 55:   Close the Direct Cable Connect window.

Step 56:   Click on the **Close** button in the Direct Cable Connect Dialog window.

Step 57:   On the host computer, click on the Direct Cable Connect window.

Step 58:   Continue working on the host computer by double-clicking the **My Computer** desktop icon.

Step 59:   Double-click on the hard drive icon that contains the folder with the Windows 95 files. Refer to the answer to Question 2 if you are unsure.

Step 60:   Click once on the folder that contains the Windows 95 files, the folder with a hand under it.

Step 61:   Click the **File** menu option.

Step 62:   Click once on the **Sharing** option.

Step 63:   Click once in the **Not Shared** radio button and click on the **OK** button. You are prompted that if you stop sharing the folder, you will be disconnected.

Step 64:   Click on the **Yes** button.

Step 65:   Close the drive window by clicking on the close box.

Step 66:   Close the My Computer window by clicking on the close box.

NOTES

Name _____

1. Which of the following COM ports are used with IR3? (Pick all that apply)
   A. COM1
   B. COM2
   C. COM3
   D. COM4

2. Which of the following ports allow information to be transferred between two devices, two computers, or a device and a computer? (Pick all that apply)
   A. Serial port
   B. IDE port
   C. Video port
   D. Parallel port
   E. Mouse port

3. Approximately how many bits per second does a 28.8 modem transmit?
   A. 270-290
   B. 2,700-2,900
   C. 28,000-29,000
   D. 280,000-290,000
   E. 2,800,000-2,900,000

4. The smallest video element on a monitor is a _____.
   A. dot pitch
   B. pixel
   C. aperture grille
   D. dot triad

5. What is the minimum amount of memory for a 1024x768 resolution with 256K colors?
   A. 512K
   B. 1MB
   C. 2MB
   D. 4MB

6. After installing a new video adapter, Windows 95 locks, what should you do?
   A. Buy a new video adapter
   B. Reinstall the old video adapter
   C. Restart Windows 95 in the MS-DOS mode
   D. Restart Windows 95 in the Safe mode

7.   Which of the following devices is affected most by EMI?
      A.   Printer
      B.   Mouse
      C.   Hard drive
      D.   Monitor
      E.   Floppy drive

8.   Which of the following devices should you avoid wearing an anti-static wrist strap when repairing?
      A.   Monitor
      B.   Ink jet printer
      C.   Hard drive
      D.   Laser printer

9.   Which of the following printers should you avoid connecting to a manual switch box?
      A.   Dot matrix
      B.   Ink jet
      C.   Laser
      D.   Thermal

10.   Which of the following are the most common pin configurations for dot matrix printers? (Pick all that apply)
      A.   9
      B.   18
      C.   24
      D.   27
      E.   32

11.   What is the *first* step when installing a printer?
      A.   Take the printer out of the box and inspect it for damage
      B.   Load the print driver
      C.   Connect the cable to the computer
      D.   Connect the cable to the printer

12.   What step of the laser printing process places the image on the drum?
      A.   Conditioning
      B.   Fusing
      C.   Transferring
      D.   Developing

13.   What step in the laser printing processes follows the transfer stage?
      A.   Charge
      B.   Fuse
      C.   Develop
      D.   Expose

14. What laser printer part allows the proper amount of toner to the drum surface?
   A. Toner roller
   B. Toner regulator
   C. Density control blade
   D. Drum sensor

15. Which of the following parts is least likely to cause a paper jam in a laser printer?
   A. Fuser rollers
   B. Erase lamp
   C. Drum
   D. Transfer rollers

16. The charge applied to the laser's drum during the conditioning stage applies a _____ voltage.
   A. Negative
   B. Positive
   C. Neutral

17. Paper should be printed on which side first? (Pick all that apply)
   A. Side with the arrow
   B. Felt side
   C. Wax side
   D. Wire side

18. T/F   TrueType fonts are scalable.

19. T/F   Soft fonts are faster than internal fonts.

20. Which of the following extensions are executable in DOS? (Pick all that apply)
   A. .TXT
   B. .BAT
   C. .INI
   D. .EXE
   E. .COM
   F. .SYS

21. Which of the following commands will keep users from accidentally erasing the AUTOEXEC.BAT file?
   A. REN +H C:\AUTOEXEC.BAT
   B. NONERASE C:\AUTOEXEC.BAT
   C. UNDELETE C:\AUTOEXEC.BAT
   D. ATTRIB +R C:\AUTOEXEC.BAT

22. Which of the following files make a DOS disk bootable? (Pick all that apply)
   A.   IO.SYS
   B.   AUTOEXEC.BAT
   C.   MSDOS.SYS
   D.   COMMAND.COM
   E.   CONFIG.SYS
   F.   WIN.COM

23. Which of the following files is a common device driver found in CONFIG.SYS?
   A.   MOUSE.EXE
   B.   PATH=C:\WINDOWS
   C.   MOUSE.SYS
   D.   DEVICE.SYS

24. Which of the following keystrokes bypasses the AUTOEXEC.BAT and CONFIG.SYS files in Windows 95?
   A.   F1 and pick the Bypass option
   B.   F3 and pick the Bypass option
   C.   F5 and pick the Safe Mode option
   D.   F8 and pick the Safe Mode option

25. If a customer has Windows 3.1 already and they want to upgrade to Windows 95, what is the minimum hard drive space required?
   A.   10MB
   B.   20MB
   C.   30MB
   D.   40MB

26. Which of the following files are considered part of the Windows 95 registry? (Pick all that apply.)
   A.   COMMAND.COM
   B.   AUTOEXEC.BAT
   C.   USER.DAT
   D.   SYSTEM.INI
   E.   CONFIG.SYS
   F.   SYSTEM.DAT

27. Which of the following would be done when Windows 95 displays "Starting Windows 95", but never boots?
   A.   Boot the computer into MS-DOS mode and reload Windows 95
   B.   Boot the computer into Safe Mode and check for a device conflict
   C.   Boot the computer from a bootable disk and reload the registry
   D.   Repartition the hard drive for a 32-bit File Allocation Table

Appendix C:
Internet Sites
For Technicians

DISCLAIMER

The following Internet sites are intended for technical support. Any material found at these sites not relating to computers is not meant to draw attention to. Also, Internet sites are constantly changing. Every effort has been made to make this appendix technician-oriented and as accurate as possible. The list is by no means inclusive and any company that has been omitted has my deepest regrets.

The ☺ symbol indicates one of my preferred sites.

Computer Help and Information

A:1 Computers: http://aloha-mall.com/a-1
ABIT: http://www.abit.com.tw/html/tech.htm
Apple Groups and Interests: http://www.apple.com/documents/groups.html
Apple Support: http://www.support.apple.com
Ask Dr. Tech!: http://www.drtech.com/index.html
Computer Abbreviations: http://www.access.digex.net/~ikind/babel.html
Computer-Related Frequently Asked Questions: http://www.sparco.com/archive/cfaq.html/
CNET Resources: http://www.cnet.com/Resources/Tech/PC.faqs/index.html
CyberMedia's Tech Support: http://www.cybermedia.com/support/helpsites.html
Data Communications Information: http://www.igc.org/support4/modems.html
Fringe Ryder's Corral (laptop information): http://www.fringeweb.com Here's How by PCWorld:
http://www.pcworld.com/resources/hereshow/index.hmtl
http://users.aol.com/balfer/help.htm
IEEE 1394 (Firewire): http://firewire.org
Kim Komando's Komputer Klinic: http://www.komando.com/
Links to computer companies: http://www.cmpcmm.com/cc/comp-comm.html
☺Microsoft's Knowledge Base: http://www.microsoft.com/kb
Networking Glossary: http://www.dayna.com/dayna/Solutions/glossary.html
☺PC Lube and Tune: http://pclt.cis.yale.edu/pclt/default.htm
PC Servicing 2: http://www.tafe.sa.edu.au/institutes/torrens-valley/programs/eit/pc2/pchdwre2.htm
☺People Helping One Another Know Stuff Resources: http://www.phoaks.com/comp/sys
Performance and Upgrade Tips: http://www.sysopt.com/sphelp.html
☺Sandy Bay's Software's PC Webopaedia: http://www.pcwebopaedia.com/
SupportHelp: http://www.supporthelp.com
TechWeb: http://www.techweb.com/
The Troubleshooting Flowchart: http://aloha-mall.com/a-1/START.HTM
Tom's Hardware Guide: http://sysdoc.pair.com/
Tools and Testers: http://www.cablesnmor.com/tools.html
USB: http://www.usb.org
USERNET FAQs: http://www.cis.ohio-state.edu/hypertext/faq/bngusenet/comp/sys
Vendors Online: http://www.slac.stanford.edu/comp/vendor/vendor.html
WWW Computer Architecture Home Page: http://www.cs.wisc.edu/~arch/www

Computer Companies

3COM Corp: http://www.3com.com
Abstract Technologies, Inc.: http://www.abstract.co.nz/
Acceleration Software International: http://www.accelerationsw.com
Acer: http://www.acer.com
Acma Computers: http://www.acma.com
Acorn Computer Group: http://www.acorn.co.uk
Activision: http://www.activision.com
Adaptec: http://www.adaptec.com

ADI Systems: http://www.adiusa.com
Adobe Systems Inc.: http://www.adobe.com
Advanced Gravis Technology: http://www.gravis.com
Advanced RISC Machines, Inc.: http://www.arm.com
Aerotek Data Services Group: http://www.aerotek.com/dataservices
Allaire Corp.: http://www.allaire.com
Alliance Semiconductor Corp.: http://www.alsc.com
ALPS Electric: http://www.alps.com
AMD (Advanced Micro Devices, Inc.): http://www.amd.com
Amdahl Corp.: http://www.amdahl.com
America On-line: http://www.aol.com
Amer. Power Conv.: http://www.apcc.com
(AMI) American Megatrends, Inc.: http://www.megatrends.com
AMS Tech: http://www.amsnote.com
Apex Software Corp.: http://www.apexsc.com
Apple Computer, Inc.: http://www.apple.com
Asante Technologies, Inc.: http://www.asante.com
AST: http://www.ast.com
Asymetrix: http://www.asymetrix.com
AT&T: http://www.att.com
ATI Technologies: http://www.atittech.ca
Authentex Software Corp.: http://www.authentex.com
Autodesk: http://www.autodesk.com
Award: http://www.award.com
Axis Communication: http://www.axisinc.com
Aztec Labs: http://www.aztechca.com
Banyan: http://www.banyan.com
Berkeley Software Design, Inc.: http://www.bsdi.com
Berkeley Systems, Inc.: http://www.berksys.com
Bitstream: http://www.bitstream.com
Borland: http://www.borland.com
Bristol Technology, Inc.: http://www.bristol.com
Broderbund Software: http://www.broderbund.com
Brother Int'l: http://www.brother.com
BTG Inc.: http://www.btg.com
BusLogic, Inc.: http://www.buslogic.com
Cabletron Systems: http://www.cabletron.com
Caere: http://www.caere.com
Calera Recognition Systems: http://www.calera.com
Canon: http://www.usa.canon.com
Carbon Based Software: http://www.carbonbased.com.au
Cardinal Technologies: http://www.cardtech.com
Centura Software Corp.: http://www.centurasoft.com
Cheyenne Software: http://www.cheyenne.com
Cirrus Logic: http://www.cirrus.com
Cisco Systems: http://www.cisco.com
Citizen: http://www.citizen-america.com

Claris Corp.: http://www.claris.com
Clear & Simple Inc.: http://www.clear-simple.com
CMD: http://www.cmd.com
Compaq: http://www.compaq.com
Compton's NewMedia, Inc.: http://www.comptons.com
CompuServe: http://www.compuserve.com
Computer Associates: http://www.cai.com
Connectix Corp.: http://www.connectix.com
ConnectSoft: http://www.connectsoft.com
Conner Peripherals: http://www.conner.com or http://www.seagate.com
Core Systems: http://www.corsys.com
Corel: http://www.corel.com
Cray Research: http://www.cray.com
Creative Labs: http://www.creaf.com
CyberMedia: http://www.cybermedia.com
Cybernet Systems, Inc.: http://www.cybernet.com/
Cyrix Corp.: http://www.cyrix.com
Datastorm: http://www.datastorm.com
Datavision Computer Video Inc.: http://www.datavis.com
Dataviz: http://www.dataviz.com
Day-Timer Technologies: http://www.daytimer.com
Dell Computer Corp.: http://www.dell.com
DeLorme Mapping: http://www.delorme.com
Delrina Corp.: http://www.delrina.com
Diamond Multimedia: http://www.diamondmm.com
Digi International: http://www.digibd.com
Digital Equipment Corp.: http://www.dec.com
DrSolomon Software: http://www.drsolomon.com
DTC: http:www.datatechnology.com
EarthLink Network: http://www.earthlink.net
Eastman Kodak: http://www.kodak.com
Electronic Arts: http://www.ea.com
ELSA: http://www.elsa.com
Encylopedia Britannica: http://www.eb.com
Epson: http://www.epson.com
Everex: http://www.everex.com
Evergreen Tech: http://www.evertech.com
Executive Software International Inc.: http://www.execsoft.com
Farallon: http://www.farallon.com
First Computer: http://www.fcsnet.com
Fractal Design Corporation: http://www.fractal.com
FTP Software: http://www.ftp.com
Fujitsu: http://www.fujitsu.com
Gateway: http://www.gateway2000.com
General Magic: http://www.genmagic.com
Genoa Systems Corp.: http://www.genoasys.com
Global Village Communication, Inc.: http://www.globalvillag.com

Goldmine Software: http://www.goldminesw.com
GRC: http://www.printgrc.om
Grolier Electronic Publishing: http://www.grolier.com
Hal Computer Systems: http://www.hal.com
Hayes: http://www.hayes.com
Hercules Computer Technology, Inc.: http://www.hercules.com
Hewlett-Packard Co.: http://www.hp.com
HiQ Computer: http://www.hiq.com
Hitachi: http://www.hitachi.com
Hughes Networking: http://www.hns.com
IBM Corporation: http://www.ibm.com
id Software, Inc.: http://www.idsoftware.com
Informix Software, Inc.: http://www.informix.com
Ingram Micro: http://www.ingram.com
Innoval Systems: http://www.innoval.com
Insight Enterprises: http://www.insight.com
Insight Software: http://www.wintools.com
Insignia Solutions, Inc.: http://www.insignia.com
Inso: http://www.inso.com
InstallShield Corp.: http://www.installshield.com
Intel Corp.: http://www.intel.com
Intergraph Corp.: http://www.intergraph.com
Interleaf: http://www.ileaf.com
Interplay Productions: http://www.interplay.com
Intuit Inc.: http://www.intuit.com
Iomega Corp.: http://www.iomega.com
Iona Technologies, Inc.: http://www.iona.ie
JVC: http://www.jvcinfo.com
Kingston Technology: http://www.kingston.com
Kodak: see Eastman Kodak)
Kyocera: http://www.kyocera.com
Labtec Enterprises: http://www.labtec.com
Lasermaster: http://www.lasermaster.com
LaserImpact: http://www/laserimpact.com
Legato Systems Inc.: http://www.legato.com
Lexis-Nexis: http://www.lexis-nexis.com
Lexmark: http://www.lexmark.com
Logitech: http://www.logitech.com
Lotus: http://www.lotus.com
LucasArts Entertainment: http://www.lucasarts.com
Macromedia: http://www.macromedia.com
MathSoft, Inc.: http://www.mathsoft.com
MathWorks, Inc.: http://www.mathworks.com
Matrox: http://www.matrox.com
Matsushita Electric: http://www.panasonic.com
Maxis: http://www.maxis.com
Maxtor: http://www.maxtor.com

McAfee Associates, Inc.: http://www.networkassociate.com
MECC: http://www.mecc.com
MegaHertz: http://www.megahertz.com
Meridian Data: http://www.meridian-data.com
Microcom: http://www.microcom.com
Micrografx: http://www.micrografx.com
MicroHelp: http://www.microhelp.com
Micro House International: http://www.microhouse.com
Micron Electronics: http://www.micron.com
MicroNet Technology: http://www.micronet.com
Micronics: http://www.micronics.com
Micropolis: http://www.micropolis.com
MicroProse Software: http://www.microprose.com
Microsoft Corp.: http://www.microsoft.com
Microsoft Network: http://www.msn.com
Microtek: http://www.mteklab.com
MidWest Micro: http://www.mwmicro.com
Mijenix Corp.: http://www.mijenix.com
MIPS Technologies, Inc.: http://www.mips.com
Mitsubishi Electronics: http://www.mela-itg.com
Mitsumi Electronics: http://www.mitsumi.com
Mosaix: http://www2.mosaix.com/
Motorola, Inc.: http://www.motorola.com
MRBIOS: http:www.mrbios.com
Multi-Tech Systems: http://www.multitech.com
Mylex Corp: http://www.mylex.com
National Center for Supercomputing Applications: See NCSA
NCR Microelectronics: http://www.ncr.com
NCSA: http://www.ncsa.uiuc.edu
NEC: http://www.nec.com
NETCOM On-Line: http://www.netcom.com
NETiS Technology: http://www.netistech.com
NetManage, Inc.: http://www.netmanage.com
Netscape Communications Corp.: http://www.netscape.com
Network Associates: http://networkassociate.com
Network Peripherals: http://www.npix.com
NeXt Computer, Inc.: http://www.next.com
Novell: http://www.novell.com
NTP Software: http://www.ntpsoftware.com
Number Nine Visual Technology Corp.: http://www.nine.com
NuReality: http://www.nureality.com
NVidia Corp.: http://www.nvidia.com
Okidata: http://www.okidata.com
Olivetti: http://www.olivetti.com
Olympus: http://www.olympusamerica.com
OnTrack: http://www.ontrack.com
Optima: http://www.optimatech.com

Optical Data Systems: http://www.ods.com
Oracle Corp.: http://www.oracle.com
Orchid Technology: http://www.orchid.com
Origin Systems: http://www.origin.ea.com
Packard Bell: http://www.packardbell.com
Panasonic Technologies, Inc.: http://www.panasonic.com
Parsons Technology: http://www.parsons.com
Peachtree Software: http://www.peach.com
Philips: http://www.philips.com
Phoenix Technologies: http://www.ptltd.com
PhotoDisk Inc.: http://www.photodisc.com
Pinnacle Micro: http://www.pinnaclemicro.com
Pinnacle Technology Inc.: http://www.pinnacletech.com
PKWare: http://www.pkware.com
Plasmon: http://www.plasmon.com
Plextor, Inc.: http://www.plextor.com
PNY Electronics: http://www.pny.com
Polywell Computers: http://www.polywell.com
Powerquest: http://www.powerquest.com
Practical Peripherals: http://www.practinet.com
Prodigy: http://www.prodigy.com
Promise: http://www.promise.com
QBS Software: http://www.qbss.com
Quadralay Corp.: http://www.quadralay.com
Qualcomm Inc.: http://www.qualcomm.com
Qualitas: http://www.qualitas.com
Quantex Microsystems: http://www.quantex.com
Quantum: http://www.quantum.com
Quark: http://www.quark.com
Quarterdeck Corp.: http://www.quarterdeck.com
Racal-Datacom: http://www.racal.com
Radius, Inc.: http://www.radius.com
Ricoh: http://www.ricoh.com
Rockwell Semiconductor Systems: http://www.nb.rockwell.com
S3 Inc.: http://www.s3.com
Samsung Semiconductor Corp.: http://www.samsung.com
SCO Open Systems Software: http://www.sco.com
Seagate: http://www.seagate.com
Sharp Electronics: http://www.sharp-usa.com
Shiva Corp.: http://www.shiva.com
Siemens-Nixdorf Information Systems: See SNI
Sierra On-Line: http://www.sierra.com
Sigma Designs: http://www.realmagic.com
Silicon Graphics: http://www.sgi.com or ftp://ftp.sgi.com/
Simple Tech.: http://www.simpletech.com
Site Technologies: http://www.sitetech.com/
Smart & Friendly: http://www.smartandfriendly.com/

SMC (Standard Microsystems Corp.): http://www.smc.com
SNI: http://www.sni.de
SofTouch Systems Inc.: http://www.softouch.com
SoftQuad, Inc.: http://www.sq.com
Software Publishers Association: http://www.spa.org
Sony Computer: http://www.sony.com
SPARC International, Inc.: http://www.sparc.com
SPRY, Inc.: http://www.spry.com
Spyglass, Inc.: http://www.spyglass.com
Stac Electronics: http://www.stac.com
Stardock Systems Inc: http://www.stardock.com
STB Systems, Inc.: http://www.stb.com
Storm Technology, Inc.: http://www.stormsoft.com
Sun Microsystems: http://www.sun.com
Supra Corp.: http://www.supra.com
Swan Tech.: http://www.swantech.com
Symantec Corp.: http://www.symantec.com
Syncronys Softcorp: http://www.syncronys.com
Synopsys, Inc.: http://www.synopsys.com
Syntegration: http://www.primenet.com/~syntegrn
SyQuest: http://www.syquest.com
Tadpole Technology: http://www.tadpole.com
Taligent, Inc.: http://www.taligent.com
Tandem Computers, Inc.: http://www.tandem.com
Tandy: http://www.tandy.com
Tatung Workstation R&D Group: http://www.www.tatung.com
Tekram: http://www.tekram.com
Tektronix: http://www.tek.com
Telebit Corp.: http://www.telebit.com
Texas Instruments: http://www.ti.com
The Learning Company: http://www.mecc.com
ThunderBYTE Corp.: http://www.thunderbyte.com
Toshiba: http://www.toshiba.com
Trusted Information Systems, Inc.: http://www.tis.com
Turtle Beach: http://www.tbeach.com
Tyan: http://www.tyan.com
U.S. Robotics: http://www.usrobotics.com
Ulead: http://www.ulead.com
Umax Tech.: http://www.umax.com
Unicore: http://www.unicore.com
UniPress Software Inc.: http://www.unipress.com
Unisys Corp.: http://www.unisys.com
VideoLogic: http://www.videologic.com
ViewSonic: http://www.viewsonic.com
Visio Corp.: http://www.visio.com
Visioneer: http://www.visioneer.com
VNP Software: http://www.vnp.com

VocalTec Inc.: http://www.vocaltec.com
Voyetra Technologies, Inc.: http://www.voyetra.com
Wall Data Inc.: http://www.walldata.com
Western Digital: http://www.wdc.com
White Pine Software: http://www.wpine.com
Wilson WindowWare, Inc: http://www.windowware.com
WordPerfect (Corel Corp.): http://www.wordperfect.com
Wyse Technology: http://www.wyse.com/wyse
Xerox: http://www.xerox.com
Xircom: http://www.xircom
Yamaha: http://www.yamahayst.com
Zenith Data Systems: http://www.zds.com
Zoom Telephonics Inc: http://www.zoomtel.com
ZyXel: http://www.zyxel.com

Windows 95

Bug Net Home Page: http://www.bugnet.com
Computer Clinic: http://www.compuclinic.com
Dylan Greene's Windows 95 Page: http://www.dylan95.com
Frank Condron's World of Windows: http://www.conitech.com/windows/drivers.html
http://www.microsoft.com/windows/software
☺http://www.process.com/win95
http://www.windows95.com
Mark's World-Windows 95 Drivers: http://www.cs.utk.edu/~kelly/drivers.html
The Windows 95 QAID: http://www.kingsoft.com/qaid/win40001.htm
Web Developers Journal: http://nctweb.com/webdev
WINSTUFF: http://www.winstuff.de
Windows 95.com: http://www.windows95.com
Windows 95 Annoyances: http://www.annoyances.org/win95
Windows Helpdesk: http://www.southwind.net/faq/help/win95/
Windows Weenie: http://www.nctweb.com/discuss/roar.htm
WWW.32bit.com: http://www.32bit.com

Hardware

CD Information Center: http://www.cd-info.com
Computer Buying and Upgrading: http://pw2.netcom.com/~rlw3/first.html
CPU Information Ctr: http://infopad.eecs.berkeley.edu/CIC
Dick Perron's PC Hardware Links:
http://emf.net/~mal/cdplus.html
http://scitexdv.com:8080/SCSI2
☺http://theref.c3d.rl.af.mil
☺http://thef-nym.sci.kun.nl/~pieterh
http://www.alt.comp.hardware

http://www.alt.periphs
http://www.alt.sys
☺http://www.cd-info.com
http://www.cis.ohio-state.edu/hypertext/faq/usenet/pc-hardware-faq
http://www.cis.ohio-state.edu/hypertext/faq/usenet/scsi-faq/
http://www.comp.multimedia
http://www.comp.os.ms-windows.*
http://www.comp.publish.cdrom.*
http://www.comp.sys.ibm.pc.hardware
http://www.lvr.com/parport.htm
http://www.randomc.com/~dperr/pc_hdwe.htm
http://www.scsita.com
http://www.tc.umn.edu/nlhome/g496/eric0139/Papers/paper.html
http://www.trio.com/noframes/techsup/troubleshoot.html
http://www.verinet.com/pc
☺Intel Newsgroup Forums: http://cs.intel.com
Intel Secrets: http://www.X86.org/
Mike Richter's collection of files and URLs related to CD-R: http://resource.simplenet.com
Monitor's Matter: http://www2.csf.org.uk/csf/campaigns/code/mmch03.htm
MPC: http://www.spa.org
☺Sci.Electronics.Repair FAQ Home Page: http://www.repairfaq.org

Diagnostics

AMIDiag: http://www.ami.com
Connectix: http://www.connectix.com
CyberMedia: http://www.cybermedia.com
Data Depot: http://www.datadepo.com
Dean Software Design: http://www.winutils.com
Quarterdeck Corp.: http://www.quarterdeck.com
Symantec: http://www.symantec.com
TouchStone: http://www.checkit.com
Watergate Software Inc.: http://www.ws.com

Viruses

Dr. Solomons: http://www.drsolomon.com
F-Prot Professional: http://www.datafellows.fi/f-prot.htm
IBM Antivirus: http://www.av.ibm.com
McAfee Associates: http://www.networkassociate.com
Virus bulletin: http://www.virusbtn.com
ViruSafe Web: http://www.eliashim.com/4home.html

Uninstallers

Alpha Software Publishing: http://www.alphasoftwaer.com
CyberMedia, Inc.: http://www.cybermedia.com
QBS Software: http://www.qbss.com
IMSI: http://www.imsisoft.com
MicroHelp Inc.: http://www.microhelp.com
Quarterdeck Corp.: http://www.quarterdeck.com
Remove-It: http://www.quarterdeck.com
Remover (Shareware by Chris Harris): http://homepages.enterprise.net/dodgy/remover2.shtml
Uninstaller: http://www.luckman.com/microhelp

Freeware and Shareware

Acrobat Reader: http://www.adobe.com
AJ's Desktop Themes: http://www.desktopthemes.com
Andy's Art Attach: http://www.andyart.com
Association of Shareware Professionals: http://www.asp-shareware.org
Astigmatic One Eye (Fonts): http://www.comptechdev.com/cavop/aoe
Autospell: http://www.spellchecker.com
Chankstore Fonts: http://www.bitstream.net/chankstore
Children's Software and more: http://www.gamesdomain.com/tigger/sw-kids.html
ClipMate 4 for Windows 95: http://www.thornsoft.com
Crypt-o-text: http://www.owt.com/users/rsavard/software.html
Decode Shell Extension for Windows 95: http://home.sprynet.com/sprynet/funduc
Desktop themes: http://www.impactsoft.com
Drag and View: http://www.canyonsw.com
DriversHQ: http://www.drivershq.com/
Dunce (Dial-Up Network Connection Enhancer) for Windows 95: http://www.vecdev.com
Father of Shareware: http://www.halcyon.com/knopf/jim.html
File-Ex: http://www.cottonwoodsw.com
FreeMinder: http://www.cvp.com/freemind
Freeware Favorites: http://www1.webdesigns1.com/freeware/
Gaming with ExecPc: http://galaxy.execpc.com/kali
Garbo FTP Archive at Waasa: http://garbo.uwasa.fi
Icon Libraries: http://www.di.unipi.it/iconbrowser/icons/icons1-6.html
Information Transfer Professional: http://www.sabasoft.com/info/xferpro.htm
Insanely Great Software: http://www.igsnet.com
Internet Goodies: http://www.ensta.fr/internet
Jackhammer: http://www.sausage.com/jackhammer.htm
Jumbo: http://www.jumbo.com
Let Me See for Windows 95: http://www.pcworld.com/resources/current_issue/files/aug96.html
LView Pro: http://www.lview.com
Microsoft Drivers: http://www.microsoft.com/msdownload/
Microangelo: http://www.impactsoft.com
Netmeeting: http://www.microsoft.com/netmeeting

NetMon: http://www.windows95.com/apps/dialup.html
OAK Software Repository/Oakland Univ.: http://www.acs.oakland.edu/oak
OS/2 stuff: http://www.ccsf.caltech.edu/~kasturi/os2.html
PassKeeper: http://www.isys.hu/staff/brad/passkeeper.html
PC Magazine: http://www.pcmag.com (choose download)
Pegasus Mail by David Harris: http://www.pegasus.usa.com
PKUnZip: http://www.pkware.com
Powermarks: http://www.kaylon.com/power.html
Quicktime: http://www.quicktime.apple.com/sw/
Realaudio Player: http://www.realaudio.com
Remind U-Mail: http://calendar.stwing.upenn.edu/
Remover by Chris Harris: http://homepages.enterprise.net/dodgy/remover2.shtml
Screensaver Heaven: http://www.galttech.com/ssheaven.shtml
Screen Savers for Windows: http://www.sirius.com/~ratloaf/
Shareware Author Network: http://www.bsoftware.com/snetwork.htm/
Shareware Distributors: http://www.halcyon.com/knopf/distrib.htm
Shareware Junkies: http://www.sharewarejunkies.com
Shareware.com: http://www.shareware.com
Shockwave: http://www.macromedia.com/shockwave/download/
SlipKnot Shareware Web Browser for Windows and OS/2:
http://plaza.interport.net/slipknot/slipknot.html
Softword Technology: http://users.aol.com/shareware/index/htm/
Surfinshield: http://www.finjan.com
TUCOWS: http://www.tucows.com
UnZip (doesn't truncate long filenames): http://www.cdrom.com/pub/infozip
VB Expressions' Home Page: http://members.aol.com/vbexpressn/index.htm
ViruSafe Web: http://www.eliashim.com/4home.html
Web Authoring Tools: http://www.uwsp.edu/help/toybox.html
Webferret: http://www.ferretsoft.com
Windows: http://www.winsite.com
Windows 95 32-bit shareware: http://windows95.com/apps
Winsock Software: http://www.tucows.com
WinZip: http://www.winzip.com
Xferpro32: http://www.sabasoft.com

Search Engines

http://galaxy.tradewave.com
http://www.infoseek.com
http://www.looksmart.com
http://www.mckinley.com
http://www.altavista.com
http://www.bigbook.com

http://www.excite.com
http://www.four11.com
http://www.lycos.com
http://www.search.com
http://www.whowhere.com
http://www.yahoo.com

Purchases

CompUSA: http://www.compusa.com/
Computer Suppliers Federation: http://www.techweb.com/
Egghead: http://www.egghead.com
http://www.all-internet.com/hardware.html
Internet Shopping Network (computer products): http:/www.isn.com
PC Buyer's Guide: http://www.intel.com/home/buyers/index.htm
The Guide to Where to Buy Computer Products: http://www.uvision.com

Training & Certification

CareerPro Training Inc.: http://www.netvis.com
CompTIA: http://www.comptia.org
Computer Prep: http://www.computerprep.com
DataTrain Institute: http://www.webcom.com/datatrn
Forefront Direct: http://www.ffg.com
Gartner: http://www.gartner.com/training
ICS Learning Systems: http://www.icslearn.com
Ingram Micro Tech: http://www.ingram.com
Institute for Certification of Computing Professionals: http://www.iccp.org
Marcraft International: http://www.owt.com/marcraft
Mastering Computers: http://www.masteringcomputers.com
MicroAge Meadowlands: http://microagemlc.com
MicroHouse International: http://www.microhouse.com
Microsoft: http://microsoft.com/train_cert
Mindworks: http://www.mindwork.com
Rob's Tech Site: http://www.concentric.net/~Redward/
Self Test Software: http://stsware.com
SHL Learning Technologies: http://www.shl-learn.co.uk
Tech Source: http://www.tech-source.com
Total Seminars, LLC: http://www.totalsem.com
Wave Technologies: http://www.wavetech.com
Xincom Technologies: http://www.computerny.com

Miscellaneous

Adobe Magazine: http://www.adobemag.com
Byte Magazine: http://www.byte.com
CD-ROM Magazine: http://www.widearea.co.uk/cdrom
Cobb Group: http://www.cobb.com/index.htm
Computer Shopper: http://www.zdnet.com/cshopper/
Datamation Magazine: http://www.datamation.com
FaulknerWeb: http://www.faulkner.com
Information Week Mag: http://techweb.cmp.com/iwk/current
InfoWorld Mag.: http://www.infoworld.com
Lan Times Mag: http://www.wcmh.com/lantimes
MacWorld Mag.: http://www.macworld.com
Microprocessors: http://www.intel.com/intel/educate
NetGuide Magazine: http://techweb.cmp.com/techweb/ng/current/
OS/2 (Best of OS/2): http://www.bestofos2
PC Computing: http://www.pccomp
PC Magazine: http://www.pcmag.com
PC Today: http://www.pctoday.com
PC Week: http://www.zdnet.com/~pcweek
PC World Magazine: http://www.pcworld.com
☺TechWeb: http://techweb.cmp.com
☺Top 100 Computer Magazines: http://www.internetvalley.com/top100mag.html
United Computer Exchange: http://www.uce.com/uce.html
Web Developer's Journal: http://nctweb.com/home.html
Windows Magazine: http://techweb.cmp.com/win/current
Windows Sources: http://www.winsources.com
Windows 95 Magazine: http://www.win95mag.com
Ziff Davis: http://www.zdnet.com

New Sites

New Sites (Cont.)

Appendix D: Glossary

1.2MB disk A 5.25" floppy disk without a hub ring commonly known as double-sided, double-density disk that only works in a 1.2MB floppy drive.

1.44MB disk A high density 3.5" floppy disk having both write-protect and high density windows that cannot be used in 720KB floppy drives.

32-bit disk access A feature of Windows 3.x that allows Windows to take over the ROM BIOS functions and allows DOS sessions to use virtual memory.

360KB disk A 5.25" floppy disk commonly known as double-sided, double-density. Normally has a reinforced center hub ring and works best in a 360KB floppy drive.

56Kbps modem A modem that produces higher transmission speeds by using digital phone lines.

720KB disk A 3.5" floppy disk commonly known as double-sided, double-density, and works best in a 720MB floppy drive.

<u>A</u>

a:drive The product name of a floptical drive developed using a patented laser servo technology. Also known as a LS-120 drive.

AC (Alternating Current) The type of electrical power from a wall outlet.

Access time Determines how fast data goes into and out of a memory chip. Measured in nanoseconds.

Active termination A type of end to a SCSI chain that allows for longer cable distance and provides correct voltage for SCSI signals.

Actuator arm Holds the read/write heads over hard disk platters.

Adapters Electronic circuit cards that connect into an expansion slot. Also called a controller, card, controller card, circuit card, circuit board, and adapter board.

AGP (Accelerated Graphics Port) An extension of the PCI bus that speeds up 3-D graphics in software applications.

Analog monitor A monitor that uses analog signals to obtain different color levels.

Anti-static wrist strap A strap connecting the technician to the computer which equalizes the voltage potential between the two to prevent ESD.

Aperture grille An alternative to the shadow mask used by Sony in their Trinitron monitors that uses wires instead of holes to direct the color beams to the front of the monitor.

Architecture A set of rules governing the physical structure of the computer. It regulates bit transfer rate, adapter SETUP configuration, and so forth. Three types of architectures used in PCs are ISA, EISA, and MCA.

ARCnet adapter A type of adapter for networks.

ASPI (Advanced SCSI Programming Interface) A type of software drive that supports SCSI devices.

Asynchronous Transmissions that do not require a clock signal, but instead use extra bits to rack the beginning and end of the data.

ATA standard The original IDE interface that supported two drives.

ATAPI (AT Attachment Packet Interface) The hardware side of the EIDE specification that supports devices like CD-ROM and tape drives.

ATX form factor A new type of computer chassis and motherboard design which allows easier cabling, full-length card installation, and cheaper cooling than the AT based design.

Average access time The time required for the drive to find and retrieve data on a disk.

Average seek time The time required for a drive to move randomly about the disk.

B

Bank A group of memory chips working together.

BIOS See ROM BIOS.

Berg connector A type of power connector that extends from the computer's power supply to various devices.

Bi-directional printing Printing that occurs from left to right and right to left to provide higher printing speeds.

Bit An electrically charged 1 or 0.

Blackout A total loss of AC power.

bps (bits per second) The number of bits transmitted per second.

breakout box A device that allows determination of serial connections.

Brownout A loss of AC power due to electrical circuits being overloaded.

Bus Electronic lines that allow 1s and 0s to move from one place to another.

Bus mastering A feature allowing an adapter to take over the external data bus from the microprocessor to execute operations with another bus-mastering adapter.

Bus mouse A mouse connected to a 9-pin DIN connector normally used when the computer does not have a built-in mouse port.

Byte Eight bits grouped together as a basic unit.

C

Cable modem A modem that connects to the cable TV network.

Cache memory A type of memory designed to increase microprocessor operations.

Caddy A holder for a compact disk that inserts into the CD-ROM drive.

CAM A type of software driver that supports SCSI devices.

Capacitive keyboard A reliable, but more expensive keyboard.

Card services The second software layer that allows PC Cards to operate.

CardBus An upgraded standard to PCMCIA that allows 32-bit transfers at up to 33MHz speeds.

Cascaded interrupts A bridged interrupt system using two interrupt controller chips in which priority requests travel from the second chip over the first chip and onto the microprocessor.

CD (Compact Disk) A CD-ROM disk that holds large amounts of data, up to (628MB), such as audio, video, and software applications.

CD-E (Compact Disk-Erasable) A CD drive that can write data multiple times to a particular disk.

CD-R (Compact Disk-Recordable) A CD drive that can create a compact disk by writing once to the disk. See also WORM.

CD-ROM (Compact Disk-Read Only Memory) A disk drive that uses compact disks.

CD-ROM Kit An upgrade to a computer system which includes the CD-ROM drive, sound card, cable, speakers, and drivers.

CD-RW (Compact Disk Re-Writable) A CD drive that can write data multiple times to a particular disk.

CDFS (CD-ROM File System) A Windows 95 file system driver with a dynamic cache which requires not specific configuration or allocation of memory by the user.

Chipsets Motherboard chips that work in conjunction with the microprocessor to allow certain computer features, such as motherboard memory and capacity.

CHS addressing (Cylinders Heads Sectors addressing) The method the BIOS uses to talk to the hard drive based on the number of cylinders, heads, and sectors of the drive.

Clamping speed The time elapsed from an over-voltage condition to when the surge protection begins.

Clamping voltage The voltage level at which the surge protector begins to protect the computer.

Cleaning pad The pad located above the laser printer's fuser roller that lightly coats it with silicon to prevent the paper sticking to the roller.

Clone A common name for an IBM-compatible computer.

Cluster The minimum amount of space that one saved file occupies.

CMOS (Complementary Metal Oxide Semiconductor) A special type of memory on the motherboard in which SETUP configuration is saved.

Cold boot Executes when the computer is turned on with the power switch. Executes POST.

Combinational mouse A mouse that allows connection to a PS/2 mouse port or a serial port.

Computer A unit that performs tasks using software applications. Also referred to as a microcomputer.

Conditioning roller Used in a laser printer to generate a large uniform negative voltage to be applied to the drum.

Conventional Memory The memory map area from 0 to 640KB of a microprocessor reserved for RAM chips in which DOS, DOS applications, and some of the Windows 95 operating system are mapped.

CPI (Characters Per Inch) A printing measurement that defines how many characters are printed within an inch. The larger the CPI, the smaller the font size.

CPS (Characters Per Second) The number of characters a printer prints in one second.

CRT (Cathode Ray Tube) The main part of a monitor, the picture tube.

Cylinder On a stack of hard drive platters, the same numbered concentric tracks of all platters.

D

D-shell connector A connector with more pins or holes on the top side than the bottom so that a cable inserts in only one direction. Examples include parallel, serial, and video ports.

Data bits A serial device setting for how many bits make up a data word.

Data compression A method of converting data into smaller sizes before transmission.

DC (Direct current) The type of power the computer needs to operate.

DCE (Data Circuit Terminating Equipment) A term used in mainframe days that refers to serial devices such as modems, mice, and digitizers.

DDC (Display Data Channel) A specification developed by VESA that Windows 95 supports.

Defragmentation A process of reordering and placing files in contiguous sectors.

Degausser A device that demagnetizes monitors. Also called a degaussing coil.

Density control blade A part inside the laser printer's toner cartridge that controls the amount of toner released to the drum.

Developing cylinder A component inside the laser printer's toner cartridge that applies a static charge to the toner so it will be attracted to the drum. Sometimes called a developing roller.

Device driver Special software that allows an operating system to access a piece of hardware.

Digital modem A modem that transmits directly on digital phone lines.

Digital monitor A monitor that uses digital signals to determine the amount of colors displayed. Digital monitors were used with the older computers.

Disk cache A set-aside portion of RAM in which hard drive data is stored and accessed to speed up the hard drive. A cache on a hard drive controller is also known as a data buffer.

DIMM (Dual In-line Memory Module) A style of 168-pin memory chip normally used for RAM chips on Pentium, Pentium Pro, or Pentium II motherboards.

DIN connector A round connector with small holes, normally keyed with a metal piece or notch so that cable only inserts one way. Examples include keyboard and mouse connectors.

DIP (Dual In-line Package) A style of memory chip that has a row of pins down each side and is normally used for ROM chips.

DIP switches Physical switches located on older computers' motherboards to manually set configuration. They normally come in slide-type or rocker-type switches.

DirectX A Microsoft DVD technology that integrates multimedia drivers, application code, and 3-D support for audio and video.

Disk The medium inserted into a floppy drive on which data is written. Also known as a floppy disk.

DMA channel (Direct Memory Access channel) A number assigned to an adapter which allows the adapter to bypass the microprocessor to communicate directly with the RAM chips.

Dot matrix printer Sometimes called an impact printer because of the printer's printwires physically impacting a ribbon which places an image on the paper.

Dot pitch The distance between like-colored phosphorous dots on adjacent dot triads.

Dot triad A grouping of three phosphorous color dots combined to make a single image on the monitor.

DPI (Dots per Inch) A printer measurement used with ink jet and laser printers that refers to how many dots are produced in an inch on the paper.

DPMS (Display Power Management Signaling) A standard that defines the signals used to inform the monitor to reduce it's power.

DRAM (Dynamic Random Access Memory) One of two types of RAM that is less expensive, but slower than SRAM. DRAM requires periodic refreshing of the electrical charges holding the 1s and 0s.

Drive select setting A number assigned to a drive that enables the controlling circuits to distinguish between two floppy drives.

Drive type A number that corresponds to a drive's geometry assigned during SETUP configuration.

DTE (Data Terminating Equipment) A term used in mainframe days that referred to computers and printers.

Dual-ported A type of video memory that allows data reads and writes simultaneously.

DVD-RAM See DVD Re-Writable.

DVD-ROM A recent technology that produces disks with superior audio and video performance and increased storage capacity.

DVD-WORM (DVD Write Once-Read Many) A developing technology that will hold audio and video data as well as normal data.

DVD Re-Writable A developing technology using re-writable media that could hold at least 2.6GB.

Dye polymer A technology for making CD-E or CD-RW disks by laser heating the disk surface to produce light reflecting bumps.

E

ECC (Error Correcting Code) An alternative method of checking data accuracy. ECC uses a mathematical algorithm to verify accuracy. ECC is more expensive than parity and the motherboard or memory controllers must also have additional circuitry to process ECC.

Echo mode setting Sometimes called the local echo setting. The setting that displays typed commands.

ECHS (Extended CHS) A method by which both the hard drive and the BIOS perform cylinders, heads, and sectors translation.

ECP (Enhanced Capabilities Port) A parallel communication standard that allows simultaneous bi-directional communication.

EDO (Extended Data Out) A technology to speed up DRAM access speed.

EIDE (Enhanced Integrated Drive Electronics) A specification set by Western Digital that supported two IDE connectors (four devices) and the ATAPI standard. EIDE is not the same as IDE interface standard.

EISA (Enhanced Industry Standard Architecture) Developed by a consortium of manufacturers in response to IBM's MCA standard. EISA utilizes a 32-bit 10MHz standard.

EMI (ElectroMagnetic Interference) Electronic noise generated by electrical devices. Also called ElectroMagnetic Radiation (EMR).

Enabler The third layer of software (sometimes call a super driver) that allows assignments of interrupts and I/O addresses for PC Cards.

Encoding The way in which binary 1s and 0s are placed on the hard drive.

EPP (Enhanced Parallel Port) A parallel port communication standard that allows bi-directional communication.

Erase lamp A component inside a laser printer that neutralizes any charges left on the drum so that the next printed page receives no residuals from the previous page.

Error correction A standard for the modem to check the data for errors rather than the microprocessor.

ESD (ElectroStatic Discharge) Occurs when stored up static electricity is discharged in an instantaneous surge of voltage. Cumulative effects of ESD weaken or destroy electronic components.

ESDI (Enhanced Small Devices Interface) The second generation of hard drive interfaces which increased hard drive capacities over the older ST506 drives.

Ethernet adapter A type of adapter for networks.

Expanded memory Also known as LIM memory standard or Expanded Memory Specification. A 64KB space in the memory map normally reserved for ROM chips that allows paging 32MB of memory, 64KB at a time. Also known as XMS.

Expansion slot Motherboard sockets into which adapters are connected.

Extended memory The area of the microprocessor's memory map above 1MB.

Extended partition A hard drive division.

External data bus The electronic lines which allow the microprocessor to communicate with external devices. Also known as external data path. See also Bus.

F

FAT (File Allocation Table) A method of organizing a computer's file system.

FAT32 The file system used by Windows 95 Service Release 2 patch that supports hard drives up to 2TB in size.

Fax modem A device hat functions as a modem and uses the printer and computer as a fax machine.

FDISK Software provided with DOS and Windows 95 that partitions the hard drive.

Felt side The side of the paper which should not be printed on. Also known as the wax side.

FIFO setting A serial device setting that enables or disables the UART's buffer.

Firmware Combines hardware and software attributes. An example is a ROM chip (tangible) which has instructions (software) written into it.

Flash BIOS A type of motherboard memory which allows updates by disk or downloading Internet files.

Flats An area that separates the pits on a CD-ROM.

Floppy drive A device which allows data storage to floppy disks.

Floptical drive Floppy drives that use optical technology to move the read/write heads over the disk surface.

Flow control A serial device setting that determines the communication method.

Flyback transformer A component inside the monitor that boosts the voltage to very high levels.

Font A group of printable characters of a particular style such as Times New Roman, Script, Arial, and Courier.

Font cartridge A printer add-on feature that allows different fonts to be loaded into the printer's memory.

Font size The point size of a particular font and is abbreviated pt. such as 10pt. or 12pt.

Font style A particular feature of a font such as bold or italic.

FPM (Fast Page Mode) A technology to speed up DRAM access speed.

Fragmentation Occurs over time as files are saved on the hard drive in clusters not adjacent to each other which slows hard disk access time.

Frequency response The number of samples taken by a sound card.

Frequency response range The range of sounds a speaker can reproduce.

Full duplex A serial device setting that allows the sending and receiving device to send data simultaneously.

Fusing roller A laser printer part responsible for heating the toner and melding it into the paper.

G

Game port An input port that connects a joystick to the computer.

Gigabyte Approximately one billion bytes of information (exactly 1,073,741,824 bytes).

Grayscale monitor A monitor that displays images in shades of gray instead of colors.

Green monitor A monitor that supports energy conservation.

Grounding problem Occurs when the motherboard or adapter is not installed properly and has a trace touching the computer's frame.

H

Half duplex A serial device setting that allows either the sending or the receiving device to send data, one device at a time.

Handshaking The method two serial devices negotiate communications.

Hard drive A sealed, data storage medium on which information is stored. Also called a hard disk.

Hardware A tangible item one can touch and feel like the keyboard or monitor.

Head crash Occurs when a read/write head touches a platter, causing damage to the heads or the platter.

Heaps Memory allocated to Windows 3.x and Windows 95 core files that records every Windows action, such as each mouse click, each re-sizing of a window, etc. In Windows 3.x, the GDI.EXE memory heap is limited to 64KB and the USER.EXE memory heap is divided into two 64KB sections. For Windows 95, the heaps are unlimited.

Hertz A measurement of electrical frequency equal to one cycle per second. Abbreviated Hz.

High-level format Process that sets up the file system for use by the computer. It is the third and last step in preparing a hard drive for use.

HMA (High Memory Area) The first 64KB above 1MB memory map that can be used as an extension of conventional memory.

Horizontal scanning frequency The rate in which a monitor's beam moves across the screen.

Hot Wire that brings AC current from the power supply to the PC's front panel.

HPFS (High Performance File System) The file system used by OS/2 to organize a computer's files.

HPPCL (Hewlett-Packard's Printer Control Language) A popular print software that translates between the printer and the computer.

Hub A device used with the Universal Serial Bus that allows multiple device connections to a single computer port.

I

I/O address (Input/Output address) A port address that allows an external device to communicate with the microprocessor. It is analogous to a mailbox number.

ICM (Intel Configuration Manager) A generic Plug and Play configuration driver developed by Intel.

ICU (ISA Configuration Utility) An Intel developed generic utility for Plug and Play cards in a DOS/Windows environment.

IDE (Integrated Drive Electronics) An improved hard drive interface that has controlling circuits built directly on the drive.

IEEE 1394 (FireWire) A standard that allows automatic installation and configuration of up to 63 devices on the same bus.

Ink jet printer A type of printer that squirts ink through tiny nozzles to produce print. Ink jet printers produce high quality, high resolution, color output.

INT 13 Interface Short for Interrupt 13, a standard that allows a system BIOS to locate data on the hard drive.

Intelligent I/O A new type of architecture under development to work with the PCI architecture to handle interrupts in a network server environment. Also known as I2O.

Interlacing A scanning method used with monitors in which only the odd numbered pixel rows are scanned followed by the even numbered pixel rows.

Interleaving The method of numbering platter sectors for the most efficient transfer of data between the hard drive and the controller.

Internal data bus The electronic lines inside a microprocessor. See also Bus.

Internal font A font stored inside a printer in its memory.

Interrupt See IRQ.

IRQ (Interrupt ReQuest) A microprocessor priority system which assigns a number to each expansion adapter or port to facilitate orderly communication.

ISA (Industry Standard Architecture) The oldest of the three types of architecture. Allows 16-bit transfers of data.

ISDN (Integrated Services Digital Network) A special phone line that has three separate channels, two B channels and an D channel. The B channel allows 64Kbps transmission speeds. The D channel allows 16Kbps transmissions.

J

Joule dissipation capacity A measure of a surge protector ability to absorb over-voltage power surges. The higher the capacity, the better protection.

Jumper A plastic cover for two metal pins on a jumper block.

K

K56flex A 56Kbps modem standard proposal from Lucent Technologies and Rockwell, International.

Keyboard Allows users to communicate with the computer.

Kilobyte Approximately 1,000 bytes of information (exactly 1,024 bytes).

L

L1 cache memory Cache memory located inside the microprocessor.

L2 cache memory Cache memory located inside the microprocessor on Pentium Pros and higher and located on the motherboard on lower microprocessor-based motherboards.

LADDR (Layered Device Driver Architecture) A type of software drive that supports SCSI devices.

LAPM (Link Access Procedure for Modems) Another name for Microcom's error correction levels.

Laser lens A component of the CD-ROM drive that reads the data from the compact disk. Also known as the objective lens and is susceptible to dust accumulation.

Laser printer A type of printer that produces output using a process similar to a copy machine. Laser printers are usually the most expensive type of printer.

Layered block device driver A Windows 95 software that manages hard drives by working with groups of bytes (blocks) instead of one byte at a time.

LBA (Logical Block Addressing) A method for the system BIOS to talk to the hard drive using sector intelligence translation.

Line Conditioner Device to protect the computer from over and under-voltage conditions as well as adverse noise conditions. Also known as a power conditioner.

Local bus A data channel that attaches to the microprocessor with a different expansion slot than ISA, EISA, and MCA.

Logical drives Dividing the extended partition into logical drives which appear as separate drives to the computer system.

Loopback plug A device used in troubleshooting that allows port checking.

Lost clusters Clusters that the file allocation table cannot associate with any file or directory.

Low-level format Creates and numbers all sectors on the hard drive as well as erases all existing data. It is the first step in preparing a hard drive for use.

M

Magneto-optical A technology for reading and writing multiple times to a compact disk.

Magneto-resistive heads A new hard drive technology which permits increased data capacities.

Marking subsystem Also called the marking engine. The part of the printer that places the image on the paper.

Math co-processor   A separate chip added to the motherboard to perform number-crunching functions.

MBR (Master Boot Record)   A program that reads the partition table to find the primary partition to boot the system.

MCA (MicroChannel Architecture)   A proprietary system developed by IBM, which is not compatible with ISA architecture.

MDRAM (Multi-bank Dynamic RAM)   Memory used with video adapters that acts like multiple independent 32-bit memory chips.

Mechanical keyboard   A keyboard cheaper in design than capacitive keyboards and more prone to failure.

Mechanical mouse   A mouse that uses a rubber ball to move the pointer.

Megabyte   Approximately one million bytes of data (exactly 1,048,576 bytes).

MegaHertz   The speed at which microprocessors and co-processors are measured. Equal to one million cycles per second, abbreviated MHz. See also Hertz.

Memory   The part of the computer that stores applications, user documents, and system operating information.

Memory map   A graphical representation the amount of a microprocessor's memory addresses.

Microcomputer   See Computer.

Microprocessor   The central electronic chip that determines the processing power of a computer.

MIDI (Musical Instrument Digital Interface)   An interface built into a sound card to create synthesized music.

MMX   Microprocessors that have 57 more multimedia instructions that speed up multimedia applications such as sound and video.

MNP (Microcom Network Protocol)   A set of standards error correction.

Modem (modulator/demodulator)   A device which connects a microcomputer to a phone line.

Modem isolator   See phone line isolator.

Molex connector   A type of power connector that extends from the computer's power supply to various devices.

Monitor Displays information from the computer to the user.

Motherboard The main circuit board of a microcomputer. Also known as the mainboard, planar, or systemboard.

Mouse A data input device that moves the cursor or select menus and options.

MOV (Metal Oxide Varistor) An electronic component built into some surge protectors to absorb over-voltage spikes or surges.

MPC (Multimedia Personal Computer) A specification that defines the standard for minimum multi-media operations.

MSCDEX.EXE Software program that assigns a drive letter to the CD-ROM drive.

Multi-scan monitor Sometimes called multi-synch monitor and it supports multiple horizontal and vertical scanning frequencies.

N

Nanosecond A billionth of a second.

nDRAM An improved DRAM memory chip designed to support data transfer speeds up to 1,600 MHz.

Non-cascaded interrupts An interrupt system in which two controller chips are not bridged together.

Null modem cable A cable that connects two computers together without the use of a modem.

O

Optical mouse A mouse that has optical sensors used to move the pointer.

Outline font Fonts computed from a mathematical formula and also known as vector fonts.

Over-voltage A condition when the AC voltage is over the rated amount of voltage.

Overdrive chip A chip that upgrades the performance of the microprocessor.

Ozone filter A part of the laser printer that filters out the ozone produced by the printer.

P

Paper transport The part of a printer that moves paper through the printer.

Parallel port A 25 pin, female D-shell connector used to connect a printer to a motherboard. Transfers eight bits of data at a time to parallel devices, such as printers, tape drives, Iomega's Zip drives and external hard drives.

Parity A method of checking data accuracy.

Parity chip A memory chip on a memory bank that checks for data accuracy.

Partition table Holds the information about the types and locations of partitions created. Occupies the outermost track on the platter (Cylinder 0, Head 0, Sector 1), and is part of the Master Boot Record.

Partitioning Dividing a hard drive so that the computer system sees more than one drive. Partitioning is the second step in preparing a hard drive for use.

Passive termination One type of end to a SCSI chain that is susceptible to noise interference over long cable distances.

PC (Personal Computer) A common name for a microcomputer, taken from the IBM PC brand.

PC Bus The original architecture for computers with the 8088 microprocessor which utilized 8-bit adapters.

PC Card A common local bus architecture used in laptops. Also known as PCMCIA.

PCI (Peripheral Component Interconnect) A common 64-bit, 66MHz local bus standard found in today's computers.

PCMCIA (Personal Computer Memory Card Industry Association) See PC Card.

PD (Phase-change Dual) A laser technology used to make CD-E or CD-RW disks.

PDL (Page Description Language) Software inside the printer that translates between the printer and the computer. Two examples are HPPCL and PostScript.

Phone line isolator A surge protector for the modem protecting against power fluctuations in a phone line. Also known as a modem isolator.

Picosecond A trillionth of a second.

Picture cell The smallest image shown on the front of a monitor made up of three color phosphorous dots.

Pin 1 A designated pin on every cable and connector which must be mated when attaching the two. Usually designated by a stenciled or etched number, a color stripe, etc.

Pipeline burst cache A type of cache memory that allows microprocessors and memory to process instructions faster.

Pipelines Separate internal data buses that operate simultaneously inside the microprocessor.

Pits Areas along the track of a compact disk.

Pixel Short for picture element. The smallest displayable unit on a monitor.

Platter A metal disk of a hard drive on which binary data is recorded.

Plug and Play (PnP) A bus specification that allows automatic configuration of an adapter.

Port A connector located on the motherboard or on a separate adapter.

POST (Power On Self Test) Startup software contained in the ROM BIOS chip that tests individual hardware components.

PostScript A type of printer software that translates between the printer and the computer.

Power rating A measurement expressed in watts-per-channel which represents how loud the speaker volume can go up without distorting the sound.

Power supply A device that converts AC voltage into DC voltage that the computer can use.

Primary corona A wire in the laser printer responsible for generating a large negative voltage to be applied uniformly to the laser's drum.

Primary partition The first detected drive on the hard drive.

Print cartridge Also known as an ink cartridge. The container that holds the ink and the nozzles for the ink jet printer.

Print driver A piece of software that coordinates between the operating system and the printer.

Print engine The part of a printer that translates commands from the computer and provides feedback when necessary. The print engine is the brains of the printer operation.

Print spooler Also known as a print manager. A software program that intercepts the request to print and sends the print information to the hard drive where it is sent to the printer whenever the microprocessor is not busy with other tasks and the printer is ready to accept data. A print spooler allows multiple print jobs to be queued inside the computer so other work can be performed.

Printer emulation A printer configuration allowing the printer to be configured to be a different type. Printers emulating other ones do not usually perform to their maximum.

Printhead The part of the dot matrix printer that holds the printwires and impacts the ribbon.

Printwire A component of the dot matrix printer's printhead that is a single wire that connects to a spring and impacts a ribbon to make a single dot on the paper.

PS/2 mouse A mouse that connects to a 6-pin DIN port.

R

RAM (Random Access Memory) A volatile type of memory that loses its data when power to the computer is shut off.

Raster A monitor's brightness pattern.

Raster font The most basic type of font normally used by dot matrix printers to create images.

RDRAM Memory chip developed by Rambus, Inc. that transfers data at rates up to 600MHz.

Read/Write heads The part of a floppy or hard drive that electronically writes binary data on disks.

Read-ahead caching A type of disk caching that attempts to guess what the next data requested will be and loads that data into RAM.

Ream 500 sheets of paper.

Reference disk Disk for older IBM PS/2 computers containing its SETUP program, advanced diagnostics, and special utilities for the hard drive.

Refresh rate The maximum time a monitor's screen is scanned in one second.

Registry A central database file produced by Windows 95 which holds hardware configuration information.

Reserved memory The area of a microprocessor from 640KB to 1MB of memory addresses. Used for ROM chips.

Resolution The number of pixels shown on a monitor or output on a printer.

RET (Resolution Enhancement Technology) A technology used with laser printers that allows higher resolutions by adjusting toner output.

Return Wires that return AC current from the PC's front panel to the power supply.

RFI (Radio Frequency Interference). A specific type of EMI noise that occurs in the radio frequency range. Often results from operation of nearby electrical appliances or devices.

ROM (Read-Only Memory) A non-volatile type of memory that keeps data in chips even when the computer is shut off.

ROM BIOS (ROM Basic Input/Output System) A read-only memory chip that contains computer start-up software, and important hardware configuration parameters.

RS232C A serial interface standard.

RTS/CTS (Request to Send/Clear to Send) A method of serial device handshaking that uses signals on specific pins of the connector to signal the other device when to stop or send data.

S

Sag A momentary under-voltage condition that occurs when the wall outlet AC voltage drops.

Scaleable font Fonts that can be created at any size. Outline fonts are an example of a scaleable font.

SCAM (SCSI Configured AutoMatically) A SCSI feature that automatically assigns priority numbers to each attached device.

SCANDISK A DOS 6 and Windows 95 software program to detect and repair lost clusters.

Screen saver A piece of software that constantly changes the image shown on the monitor to keep a particular image from burning into the screen.

SCSI (Small Computer System Interface) A hard drive interface standard that connects multiple small devices to the same adapter via a SCSI bus.

SCSI ID The priority number assigned to each device connected by a SCSI chain.

SDRAM (Synchronous DRAM) Provides very fast burst memory access (approximately 100MHz) by placing new memory addresses on the address bus before prior memory address retrieval and execution completes.

SDX (Storage Data Acceleration) A new technology developed by Western Digital that provides caching for existing removable media devices (such as CD-ROM), and can be interfaced with CD-R, CD-E, and DVD devices.

SEC cartridge (Single Edge Contact cartridge) Intel's cartridge design for its Pentium II and future microprocessors which mounts onto the motherboard.

Sector The smallest amount of storage space on a disk or platter which holds 512 bytes of data.

Serial mouse A mouse that connects to a 9 or 25-pin serial port.

Serial port Either a 9-pin, male D-shell connector, or a 25 pin, male D-shell connector. Transmits one bit at a time and used for input devices such as mice, modems, digitizers, trackballs, etc.

SETUP Software that tells the computer about itself and the hardware it supports such as how much RAM memory, type of hard drive installed, current date and time, etc.

SGRAM (Synchronous Graphics RAM) Memory chips used on video adapters and graphics accelerators to speed up graphics-intensive functions.

Shadow mask A screen used in monitors that direct the electron beams to the front of the monitor.

Shielding Cancels out and keeps magnetic interference from devices.

SIMM (Single In-line Memory Module) A style of 80-pin or 72-pin memory chip normally used for RAM.

Single-ported Memory that can be written to or read from, but not simultaneously.

SmartDrive A DOS and Windows 3.x software that creates a disk cache in extended memory for floppy, hard and CD-ROM drives.

Socket services The most basic software layer that allows PC Cards to operate.

Soft font Fonts loaded from the hard drive instead of being stored inside the printer. Soft fonts take longer to load than internal fonts.

Software An application consisting of a set of instructions that makes the hardware work.

Solder joint Solder connections on the back of motherboards and adapters.

Spike An over-voltage condition of short duration and intensity.

SPP (Standard Parallel Port) A name given before parallel standards were created to signify unidirectional data transfers from the computer to the parallel device.

SPS (Standby Power Supply) A device that provides power to the computer only after it first detects a AC voltage power out condition.

SRAM (Static Random Access Memory) SRAM is faster but more expensive than DRAM. SRAM is also known as cache memory, or L2 cache.

ST506 The oldest hard drive interface standard which transmits data serially.

Standoffs Plastic connectors on the bottom side of motherboards.

Start bit A bit used in asynchronous communications that signals the beginning of each data byte.

Stop bit A bit used in asynchronous communications that signals the end of each data byte.

Straight-through cable A cable without physically crossed (twisted) wires.

Surge An over-voltage condition like a spike but with a longer duration.

Surge protector A device to help protect power supplies from over-voltage conditions. Also known as surge strip or surge suppressor.

SVGA (Super VGA) A type of monitor that displays at least a 800x600 resolution and connects to a 15-pin D-shell connector.

Swap file A temporary file in hard disk space used by Windows 3.x and Windows 95 that varies in size depending on the amount of RAM installed and the amount of memory needed to run the application.

Switch bank A grouping of DIP switches to allow configuration setting.

Switch box A device that allows connection of two or more computers to a single printer or multiple printers to a single computer.

Synchronous Transmissions that require the use of a clock signal.

System resources The collective set of interrupt, I/O address, and DMA parameters. Also used in the Windows 3.x and Windows 95 environments defined as the amount of memory being used by specific applications.

T

Terabyte Approximately one trillion bytes of information.

Terminator Used to designate the end of a floppy drive cable. Also known as a terminating resistor.

Thread A unit of programming code that receives a slice of time from Windows 95 so it can run concurrently with other units of code or threads.

TokenRing adapter A type of adapter for networks.

Toner puddling A side effect sometimes experienced on laser printers that use Resolution Enhancement Technology. The toner dial must be adjusted to reduce the amount of toner released to the paper so that it does not appear to have too much toner in one area of the paper.

Track A concentric circle on a formatted floppy disk or a hard drive platter.

Trackball An input device that replaces a mouse.

Transfer corona A wire inside the laser printer that applies a positive charge on the back of the paper so the toner is attracted to the paper as it moves through the printer.

Transfer roller A roller inside the laser printer that replaces the transfer corona. The roller applies a positive charge on the back of the paper so the toner is attracted to the paper as it moves through the printer.

Translating BIOS A system BIOS that allows communication with hard drives larger than 504MB.

TrueType font A type of outline font that can be scaled and rotated.

TVS (Transient Voltage Suppressor) A measure of the surge protector's ability to guard against over-voltage conditions. The lower the TVS rating, the better.

Twisted cable A type of floppy or hard drive cable having crossed wires which physically moves the drive selection jumper position from the second to the first position.

U

UART (Universal Asynchronous Receiver/Transmitter) A chip that coordinates the serial port or device activity.

UDF (Universal Disk Format) A CD-R drive standard used by some manufacturers.

UMBs (Upper Memory Blocks) An area of the memory map between 640KB and 1MB that can be used for software.

Under-voltage A condition when AC power drops below 100 volts which may cause the computer's power supply to draw too much current and overheat.

UPS (Uninterruptable Power Supply) A device that provides power for a limited time to a computer or device during a power outage.

USB (Universal Serial Bus) A bus that allows 127 devices to be connected to a single computer port.

UVGA (Ultra VGA) A type of monitor that displays at least a 1024x768 resolution or greater and connects to a 15-pin D-shell connector.

V

VCACHE A dynamic disk caching program by Windows 95 that uses read-ahead and write-behind caching.

Vector font A font derived from a mathematical formula. Plotters frequently use vector fonts.

Vertical scan rate The rate the monitor's electron beam draws the entire screen.

VFAT (Virtual File Allocation Table) A file system used by Windows 95 to organize a computer's files.

VGA (Video Graphics Array) A type of monitor that displays at least a 640x480 resolution or greater and connects to a 15-pin D-shell connector.

Video processor Sometimes known as the video co-processor or video accelerator. The processor on the video adapter that coordinates communication between the adapter and the main microprocessor.

Virtual memory A method of simulating extra memory by using the hard disk space as if it were RAM.

VIS (Viewable Image Size) The actual area of the monitor seen by a user.

VL-bus (Video Electronics Association Video Local Bus) A type of local bus developed for transmitting large volume of video data. Also know as VESA.

Voice/fax modem A modem that combines the features of a voice mailbox system with a modem.

VRAM (Video RAM) Dual-ported memory found on video adapters.

W

Warm boot Restarting the computer by pressing CTRL-ALT-DEL. Puts less strain on the computer than a cold boot.

Watts An electrical measure in which computer power supplies are rated.

Wax side The side of the paper which should not be printed on. Also known as the felt side.

Wire side The side of the paper which should be printed on. The wire side is normally shown by an arrow on the end of a paper ream.

WORM (Write Once-Read Many) A CD-R technology that writes data once to a CD. Often used to make backups or to distribute software.

WRAM (Window RAM) Dual-ported memory found on video adapters.

Write-back cache memory A technique whereby the microprocessor stores 1s and 0s for later writing to regular memory when the microprocessor is not busy.

Write-behind caching A type of disk caching that stores data on the RAM and later records it to the disk.

Write-black laser printer A type of laser printer that produces a black dot every where the beam touches the drum. Write-black printers produce finer details than write-white laser printers.

Write-protect notch Located on the right side of a 5.25" disk, if covered, it prevents new data from being written on the disk.

Write-protect window An opening on a 3.5" floppy disk with a sliding tab. When the tab is closed, no new data may be written on the disk.

Write-through cache memory A technique whereby the microprocessor writes 1s and 0s into cache memory at the same time it writes data to regular memory.

Write-white laser printer A type of laser printer that produces a dot everywhere the beam does not touch the drum. Write-white printers produce darker shades of black than write-black printers.

X

x2 A proposed modem standard for 56Kbps data transfers.

XMS (Extended Memory Specification) See Extended Memory.

XON/XOFF A method of handshaking that uses special control characters to coordinate data transmissions.

Z

Zone bit recording A method of putting more sectors on the outer tracks of a hard drive platter than on the inner tracks.

ZV port (Zoomed Video Port) A new PC Card that allows data transfer from a PC Card to a VGA video adapter.

Index

A

I

I/O address: 71, 73-74, 78, 81-82, 93-94, 96, 103, 321-322, 325, 381, 387-388, 393, 395, 427-430, 432, 436-438, 449, 453, 669
I2O: See Intelligent I/O
IBM BIOS: 61, 158, 160-162
IBM-compatible: 25
icon: 591-592
ICM (Intel Configuration Manager): 82, 393-395, 669
ICU (ISA Configuration Utility): 82, 393-395, 669
IDE: 284-287, 295-297, 312, 321, 325, 378, 381, 386-387, 391, 399, 661, 669
IEEE 1284: 526-527
IEEE 1394 (FireWire): 451-452, 499-500, 669
IML (Initial Microcode Load): 66, 79, 98
impact printer: see dot matrix printer
Industry Standard Architecture: See ISA
ink cartridge: see print cartridge
ink jet printer: 515-518, 522-523, 533-534. 669
ink supply bladder: 517
Initial Microcode Load: See IML
Input/output address: See I/O address
Install New Modem wizard: 445
installing:
       CD-ROM drive: 386-393
       floppy drives: 266
       ISA adapters: 77-78
       memory: 194-199
       MicroChannel adapters: 79-80
       microprocessor: 35
       modem: 445-446
       printer: 527
       serial device: 436
       software (Windows 95): 600-602
       sound card: 393-396
       Windows 95: 602-603
INT13 interface: 309-310, 328, 670
Integrated Drive Electronics: see IDE
integrated motherboards: 14
Integrated Services Digital Network: see ISDN
Intel chipsets: 48
Intel Configuration Manager: See ICM
Intel microprocessors: 25-34
Intelligent I/O architecture: 45, 670
interface: 284
interlacing: 491, 670
interleaving: 282-283, 311, 670
Interlink: 329, 434-435
internal commands: 549, 552-556
internal data bus: 25, 670

light amplification stimulated by emission of radiation: see laser
LIM memory standard: see expanded memory
line conditioner: 139, 671
Link Access Procedure for Modems: see LAPM
lint-free cloths: 115
lint-free swabs: 115
lithium battery: 62-63, 65
local bus: 41-48, 77-86, 671, see also PCI, PC Card, and VL-bus
Logical Block Addressing: see LBA
logical drive: 314, 316-318, 671
logical troubleshooting: 157-165
loopback plug: 110, 437, 532, 671
lost cluster: 326, 671
low-level format: 310-312, 320, 671
LPT ports: 513
LS-120 drive: 260
Lucent Technologies: 448

M

Mace Utilities: 77, 323, 426
magneto-optical: 399, 671
magneto-resistive head: 330, 671
main corona: see primary corona
mainboard: See motherboard
male ports: 10-12
MANIFEST: 77
marking subsystem: 513, 671
mask pitch: see dot pitch
Master Boot Record: see MBR
master/slave setting: 295-297, 320, 378, 396
math co-processor: 29-30, 672
Matrox MGA: 498
MBR (Master Boot Record): 315-316, 323, 611-612, 672
MCA (MicroChannel): 39-43, 48-49, 77, 81-82, 86, 98, 177, 492, 672
MCI CD Audio driver: 394-396
MDA (Monochrome Display adapter): 486, see also monochrome adapter
MDRAM (Multi-bank Dynamic RAM): 493, 672
Mean Time Between Failure: see MTBF
mechanical keyboard: 454, 672
mechanical mouse: 453-454, 672
media: see floppy media
Media Player (Windows 3.x): 394
Megabyte (MB): 25, 672
MegaHertz: See MHz
MEMMAKER: 209, 221
memory: 8-9, 171-221, 672
memory bank: 180-189, 194, 661
memory map: 178-179, 201-209, 672

XGA adapter: 11
XMS: see extended memory
XON/XOFF: 431, 682
XT switch settings: 68-70
XT: See 8088, 8086, or PC

Y
Y power connector: 134-135
yellow book CD standard: 400

Z
ZBR: 381-282, 682
Zenith BIOS: 61
Zip Drive: 260
zone bit recording: see ZBR
Zoomed Video port: See ZV port
ZV port: 46, 682